Sustainability Analysis and Environmental Decision-Making Using Simulation, Optimization, and Computational Analytic

Sustainability Analysis and Environmental Decision-Making Using Simulation, Optimization, and Computational Analytic

Editors

Mariia Kozlova
Julian Scott Yeomans

MDPI • Basel • Beijing • Wuhan • Barcelona • Belgrade • Manchester • Tokyo • Cluj • Tianjin

Editors
Mariia Kozlova
School of Business and
Management
LUT University
Lappeenranta
Finland

Julian Scott Yeomans
Schulich School of Business
University of York
Toronto
Canada

Editorial Office
MDPI
St. Alban-Anlage 66
4052 Basel, Switzerland

This is a reprint of articles from the Special Issue published online in the open access journal *Sustainability* (ISSN 2071-1050) (available at: https://www.mdpi.com/journal/sustainability/special_issues/sustainability_analysis).

For citation purposes, cite each article independently as indicated on the article page online and as indicated below:

LastName, A.A.; LastName, B.B.; LastName, C.C. Article Title. *Journal Name* **Year**, *Volume Number*, Page Range.

ISBN 978-3-0365-3199-1 (Hbk)
ISBN 978-3-0365-3198-4 (PDF)

© 2022 by the authors. Articles in this book are Open Access and distributed under the Creative Commons Attribution (CC BY) license, which allows users to download, copy and build upon published articles, as long as the author and publisher are properly credited, which ensures maximum dissemination and a wider impact of our publications.

The book as a whole is distributed by MDPI under the terms and conditions of the Creative Commons license CC BY-NC-ND.

Contents

About the Editors vii

Preface to "Sustainability Analysis and Environmental Decision-Making Using Simulation, Optimization, and Computational Analytic" ix

Mariia Kozlova and Julian Scott Yeomans
Sustainability Analysis and Environmental Decision-Making Using Simulation, Optimization, and Computational Analytics
Reprinted from: *Sustainability* **2022**, *14*, 1655, doi:10.3390/su14031655 1

Huawei Li, Guohe Huang, Yongping Li, Jie Sun and Pangpang Gao
A C-Vine Copula-Based Quantile Regression Method for Streamflow Forecasting in Xiangxi River Basin, China
Reprinted from: *Sustainability* **2021**, *13*, 4627, doi:10.3390/su13094627 7

Jing Liu, Yongping Li, Gordon Huang, Yujin Yang and Xiaojie Wu
A Factorial Ecological-Extended Physical Input-Output Model for Identifying Optimal Urban Solid Waste Path in Fujian Province, China
Reprinted from: *Sustainability* **2021**, *13*, 8341, doi:10.3390/su13158341 29

Michael Binns
Analytical Models for Seawater and Boron Removal through Reverse Osmosis
Reprinted from: *Sustainability* **2021**, *13*, 8999, doi:10.3390/su13168999 47

Linda Navarro, Ahmed Mahmoud, Andrew Ernest, Abdoul Oubeidillah, Jessica Johnstone, Ivan Rene Santos Chavez and Christopher Fuller
Development of a Cyberinfrastructure for Assessment of the Lower Rio Grande Valley North and Central Watersheds Characteristics
Reprinted from: *Sustainability* **2021**, *13*, 11186, doi:10.3390/su132011186 69

Perry Sadorsky
Eco-Efficiency for the G18: Trends and Future Outlook
Reprinted from: *Sustainability* **2021**, *13*, 11196, doi:10.3390/su132011196 91

Michael Binns and Hafiz Muhammad Uzair Ayub
Model Reduction Applied to Empirical Models for Biomass Gasification in Downdraft Gasifiers
Reprinted from: *Sustainability* **2021**, *13*, 12191, doi:10.3390/su132112191 107

Christoph Lohrmann and Alena Lohrmann
Accuracy and Predictive Power of Sell-Side Target Prices for Global Clean Energy Companies
Reprinted from: *Sustainability* **2021**, *13*, 12746, doi:10.3390/su132212746 121

Mariia Kozlova and Alena Lohrmann
Steering Renewable Energy Investments in Favor of Energy System Reliability: A Call for a Hybrid Model
Reprinted from: *Sustainability* **2021**, *13*, 13510, doi:10.3390/su132413510 149

Maria-Kristiine Luts, Jyrki Savolainen and Mikael Collan
Profitability Determinants of Unlisted Renewable Energy Companies in Germany—A Longitudinal Analysis of Financial Accounts
Reprinted from: *Sustainability* **2021**, *13*, 13544, doi:10.3390/su132413544 167

Inka Ruponen, Mariia Kozlova and Mikael Collan
Ex-Ante Study of Biofuel Policies–Analyzing Policy-Induced Flexibility
Reprinted from: *Sustainability* **2022**, *14*, 147, doi:10.3390/su14010147 . . . . **185**

Yara Kayyali Elalem, Isik Bicer and Ralf W. Seifert
Why Do Companies Need Operational Flexibility to Reduce Waste at Source?
Reprinted from: *Sustainability* **2022**, *14*, 367, doi:10.3390/su14010367 . . . . **201**

Vishal Raul, Yen-Chen Liu, Leifur Leifsson and Amy Kaleita
Effects of Weather on Iowa Nitrogen Export Estimated by Simulation-Based Decomposition
Reprinted from: *Sustainability* **2022**, *14*, 1060, doi:10.3390/su14031060 . . . . **217**

Mariia Kozlova, Timo Nykänen and Julian Scott Yeomans
Technical Advances in Aviation Electrification: Enhancing Strategic R&D Investment Analysis through Simulation Decomposition
Reprinted from: *Sustainability* **2022**, *14*, 414, doi:10.3390/su14010414 . . . . **229**

Meiqin Suo, Feng Xia and Yurui Fan
A Fuzzy-Interval Dynamic Optimization Model for Regional Water Resources Allocation under Uncertainty
Reprinted from: *Sustainability* **2022**, *14*, 1096, doi:10.3390/su14031096 . . . . **241**

About the Editors

Mariia Kozlova is a passionate researcher with working experience in both academia and industry. She received her D.Sc. (Econ&BA) degree from LUT University, Lappeenranta, Finland, in 2017. Simulation, decision-making, and investment analysis are fields of her research focus. Graduations with distinction, numerous lead-authored publications in respectable journals, continuous external funding acquisition, and high feedback ratings from her students attest to the quality of her work.

Julian Scott Yeomans has been a Professor of Operations Management and Information Systems at the Schulich School of Business, York University since 1993. He is the Director for both the Master of Business Analytics (MBAN) program and the Master of Artificial Intelligence (MMAI) program at Schulich. He holds degrees in management science/information systems, environmental engineering, and statistics. He generally teaches courses on VBA programming and spreadsheet-based decision support systems. He has published six books and over 125 peer-reviewed, academic journal articles on a wide range of topics. His current research focuses upon simulation-decomposition, simulation-optimization, machine learning, visual analytics, population-based metaheuristics, and modelling-to-generate-alternatives. Recent application areas have included environmental informatics, solid/hazardous waste management, empirical finance, and the optimal osmotic dehydration of fruits, vegetables, and fungi.

Preface to "Sustainability Analysis and Environmental Decision-Making Using Simulation, Optimization, and Computational Analytic"

In practice, environmental analytics incorporates an amalgamation of science, methods, and techniques that combines computational intelligence, information technology, mathematical modelling, system science, and computer technology to address "real-world"environmental and sustainability problems. Effective environmental decision-making is often challenging and complex, where final solutions frequently possess inherently subjective political and socio-economic components. In addition, while certain environmental and sustainability decision-making aspects might appear self-evident, more typical problems possess elements that cannot be directly included in the underlying decision process without additional manipulation. Such decision-making can be further complicated by accompanying stochastic uncertainties. Consequently, complex sustainability applications in the "real world"frequently employ computational decision-making approaches to construct solutions to problems containing numerous quantitative dimensions and considerable sources of uncertainty.

This volume includes a number of such applied computational analytics papers that either create new decision-making methods or provide innovative implementations of existing methods for addressing a wide spectrum of sustainability applications, broadly defined. The rich diversity of applications within the papers exemplifies the considerable range of both methodological relevance and practical contributions to research in environmental analysis. The disparate contributions all emphasize novel approaches of computational analytics as applied to environmental decision-making and sustainability analysis –be this on the side of optimization, simulation, modelling, computational solution procedures, visual analytics, and/or information technologies.

Mariia Kozlova, Julian Scott Yeomans
Editors

Editorial

Sustainability Analysis and Environmental Decision-Making Using Simulation, Optimization, and Computational Analytics

Mariia Kozlova [1,*] and Julian Scott Yeomans [2]

[1] School of Business and Management, LUT University, FI-53851 Lappeenranta, Finland
[2] Operations Management and Information Systems Area, Schulich School of Business, York University, Toronto, ON M3J 1P3, Canada; syeomans@schulich.yorku.ca
* Correspondence: mariia.kozlova@lut.fi

Citation: Kozlova, M.; Yeomans, J.S. Sustainability Analysis and Environmental Decision-Making Using Simulation, Optimization, and Computational Analytics. *Sustainability* **2022**, *14*, 1655. https://doi.org/10.3390/su14031655

Received: 20 January 2022
Accepted: 25 January 2022
Published: 31 January 2022

Publisher's Note: MDPI stays neutral with regard to jurisdictional claims in published maps and institutional affiliations.

Copyright: © 2022 by the authors. Licensee MDPI, Basel, Switzerland. This article is an open access article distributed under the terms and conditions of the Creative Commons Attribution (CC BY) license (https://creativecommons.org/licenses/by/4.0/).

In practice, environmental analytics involves an integration of science, methods, and techniques involving a combination of computers, computational intelligence, information technology, mathematical modelling, and system science to address "real-world" environmental and sustainability problems. Effective environmental decision-making is often challenging and complex where final results often involve inherently subjective political and socio-economic facets. Furthermore, while certain environmental and sustainability decision-making specifications may be self-evident (post hoc analysis always tends to be incredibly accurate), more typical problems possess components that cannot be directly included in the underlying decision process without additional manipulation. Such decision-making is frequently further compounded by additional stochastic uncertainties. Consequently, complex "real world" sustainability problems frequently employ computational decision-making approaches to construct solutions to applications containing numerous quantitative dimensions and considerable sources of uncertainty.

This Special Issue includes a number of applied computational analytics papers that either create new decision-making methods or provide innovative implementations of existing methods for assisting with a wide spectrum of sustainability applications, broadly defined. In line with the aims and scope of this issue, the rich diversity of applications within the papers exemplifies the considerable range of both methodological relevance and practical contributions to research in environmental analysis. The disparate contributions included in the Special Issue all emphasize novel approaches of computational analytics as applied to environmental decision-making and sustainability analysis—be this on the side of optimization, simulation, modelling, computational solution procedures, visual analytics, and/or information technologies.

In the first paper, *A C-Vine Copula-Based Quantile Regression Method for Streamflow Forecasting in Xiangxi River Basin, China*, Li, Huang, Li, Sun, and Gao introduce a C-vine copula-based quantile regression (CVQR) model for forecasting streamflow. The CVQR model integrates techniques for vine copulas and quantile regression into a framework that can effectively establish relationships between the multidimensional response-independent variables with asymmetrical extreme values and apply the model to the Xiangxi River Basin. Multiple linear regression and artificial neural network are also compared to illustrate the applicability of CVQR. Their findings can be directly applied to hydrological process identification and water resource management practices.

In the second paper, *A Factorial Ecological-Extended Physical Input-Output Model for Identifying Optimal Urban Solid Waste Path in Fujian Province, China*, Liu, Li, Huang, Yang, and Wu develop a factorial ecological-extended physical input–output model to identify an optimal urban solid waste path in an urban solid waste system. Such a model is crucial for balancing the tradeoff between economic development and environmental protection. Their model integrates a physical input–output model, ecological network analysis, and fractional factorial analysis into a general framework that is applied to managing the urban waste system of Fujian Province, China.

In *Analytical Models for Seawater and Boron Removal through Reverse Osmosis*, Binns simultaneously examines the total salt and boron concentrations in the purification process of seawater into safe drinking water. Reverse osmosis modules are designed by computer models to establish energy efficient configurations and operating conditions. A new analytical model is applied to two case studies and, in both cases, the new analytical approach predicts the performance with similar accuracy to existing finite-difference numerical models from the literature.

In *Development of a Cyberinfrastructure for Assessment of the Lower Rio Grande Valley North and Central Watersheds Characteristics*, Navarro, Mahmoud, Ernest, Oubeidillah, Johnstone, Santos Chavez, and Fuller construct a watershed characterization to determine potential pollution sources by developing a cyberinfrastructure to collect a wide inventory of data to identify which waterways contribute the highest concentrations of bacteria and lowest levels of dissolved oxygen. The cyberinfrastructure development employs a Geographic Information System database in which geospatial and non-geospatial data are incorporated from numerous point and nonpoint pollution sources. Their results identify the potential major sources of water quality impairments such as cultivated crops, urbanized areas, on-site sewage facilities, colonias, and wastewater effluents.

In *Eco-Efficiency for the G18: Trends and Future Outlook*, Sadorsky explores eco-efficiency as an important ecological indicator for tracking the progress of how countries' environmental-adjusted economic activity change over time and calculates country-level eco-efficiency for 18 major countries (G18) that are part of the G20. Eco-efficiency leaders include Australia, Brazil, France, Germany, Great Britain, Italy, Japan, Russia, and the United States, while the laggards include Canada, China, India, and Indonesia. The laggard countries recorded negative growth rates in eco-efficiency over the period 1997 to 2019 and 2019 to 2040, where negative growth points to a worsening of environmental sustainability. Large variations in eco-efficiency between countries make it more difficult to negotiate major international environmental/sustainability agreements and it is imperative that the G18 demonstrate leadership by increasing their eco-efficiency.

In the paper *Model Reduction Applied to Empirical Models for Biomass Gasification in Downdraft Gasifiers*, Binns and Ayub use various modeling approaches for the modeling and simulation of gasification processes to predict gasifier performance at different condition levels and use different feedstocks to optimally design efficient gasifiers. Complex models require significant time and effort to develop, and are only be accurate for use with a specific catalyst. Based on linear regression, Binns and Ayub develop linear and quadratic expressions of the gasifier input value parameters. A shrinkage method is applied to identify significant parameters and reduce the complexity of these expressions, thereby revealing significant parameters from which simple models with reasonable accuracy are obtained.

In the paper *Accuracy and Predictive Power of Sell-Side Target Prices for Global Clean Energy Companies*, Lohrmann and Lohrmann focus on mean target prices for stocks on the Standard and Poor's Global Clean Energy Index during the time period from 2009 to 2020. Their analysis shows that for all models, the mean target price is the most relevant variable, whereas the number of target prices appears to be highly relevant as well. Moreover, their results indicate that following the rare positive predictions of a random forest for the highest target return groups may potentially represent attractive investment opportunities.

In *Steering Renewable Energy Investments in Favor of Energy System Reliability: A Call for a Hybrid Model*, Kozlova and Lohrmann examine the volatility of electricity system reliability and the role played by renewable energy sources within these systems. While renewable energy is a key element in debates on future global energy systems, more extensive use of renewable energy sources within these systems implies a higher dependence on intermittent power, which places the reliability of the entire electricity system at risk. However, renewable energy use has often been designed without accounting for system reliability. This paper provides a hybrid model that guides renewable energy investments toward energy system reliability by incorporating reliability-based support for renewable energy sources. It is shown that this reliability-based support can substantially reduce backup capacity, cut the overall costs, and reduce its environmental footprint.

In *Profitability Determinants of Unlisted Renewable Energy Companies in Germany—A Longitudinal Analysis of Financial Accounts*, Luts, Savolainen, and Collan, identify key profitability determinants of several unlisted, German, electricity-producing, renewable-energy companies. A multi-year analysis based on 783 companies for the years 2010–2018 is used. The results show that both company- and industry-specific profitability determinants are statistically significant, but that company-specific determinants seem to be a more important factor. The results shed new light on what drives the profitability of private German renewable-energy companies. The implications of the study hold wider environmental and economic importance as the performance of the renewable-energy companies is critical for achieving the emission targets of the energy industry and for ensuring more sustainable energy production for the future.

In *Ex-Ante Study of Biofuel Policies—Analyzing Policy-Induced Flexibility*, Ruponen, Kozlova, and Collan examine the appropriate policy selection process to enable various business sectors to optimize their transition toward a low-carbon economy. To accomplish this task efficiently, it is essential to recognize how different mechanisms incentivize the investments in terms profitability, flexibility, and inherent uncertainty. This paper focuses on financial incentive policies for the bio-component of fuel, in combination with penalties and tax-relief, on transportation-biofuel policies. Using the pay-off method and simulation-decomposition, their study shows that a combination of penalties and tax-relief can be employed to efficiently lead fuel-production towards sustainability. Their approach provides important insights to the decision-making process beyond more commonly-used profitability analysis methods.

In *Why Do Companies Need Operational Flexibility to Reduce Waste at Source?*, Elalem, Bicer, and Seifert analyze the environmental benefits of operational flexibility that emerge in the form of less product waste during the sourcing process by reducing overproduction. They employ a multiplicative demand process to model the evolutionary dynamics of demand uncertainty and quantify the impact of key modeling parameters for each operational-flexibility strategy on the waste ratio. Their results indicate that operational-flexibility strategies that rely on the localization of production are key to reducing waste and improving environmental sustainability at source.

In *Technical Advances in Aviation Electrification: Enhancing Strategic R&D Investment Analysis Through Simulation Decomposition*, Kozlova, Nykänen, and Yeomans examine the climate impacts arising from the electrification of aviation using the newly created analytical technique, Simulation-Decomposition (SimDec). It has been estimated that the carbon contributions from aviation contribute between 2–5% of all global emissions, annually. Consequently, decreasing carbon emissions from the aviation industry has become one of the primary initiatives within current global climate policy formulation and represents a significant component of the overall strategy for achieving climate neutrality by 2050. This paper examines the sustainability of aviation electrification by concurrently integrating environmental impacts from the ongoing technological developments of electric motors into the R&D investment analysis. A Monte Carlo model in combination with SimDec is used to model the flying range of an all-electric aircraft based upon improvements to its batteries together with the specific power of its motors. At the strategic level, SimDec enables a visual analytic display of the simultaneous interaction between multiple different factors that affect the flying range of electrical aircraft, thereby more fully portraying the financial and environmental benefits of aviation electrification to the decision-makers. Since SimDec can be run concurrently with any Monte Carlo model with only negligible additional overhead, it can easily be extended into the analysis of any environmental application that employs simulation. This generalizability in conjunction with its straightforward visualizations of complex stochastic uncertainties makes the practical contributions of SimDec very powerful in sustainability analysis and environmental decision-making.

In *Effects of Weather on Iowa Nitrogen Export Estimated by Simulation-Based Decomposition*, Raul, Liu, Leifsson, and Kaleita examine the impacts of weather variability on the State of Iowa's food–energy–water system and the resulting agricultural nitrogen that is exported from Iowa. The delivery of nutrients, especially nitrogen, from the upper Mississippi River Basin, is a function not only of agricultural activity but also of hydrology and the hypoxic zone in the Gulf of Mexico is a direct consequence of the nutrient-rich water it receives from the Mississippi River. Extreme weather conditions, such as drought and flooding, not only have a significant impact on the agriculture system, but also directly affect the nitrogen loading that enters the Mississippi River. A SimDec approach is implemented using a combined IFEW/crop-weather simulation model to better understand the impacts of weather on the nitrogen exported from the agricultural industry in Iowa. The SimDec analysis of the IFEW simulation model provides an enhanced understanding of weather variability on the environmental impacts from the soil nitrogen surplus.

In *A Fuzzy-Interval Dynamic Optimization Model for Regional Water Resources Allocation under Uncertainty*, Suo, Xia, and Fan propose a fuzzy-interval dynamic programming model for regional water management under uncertainty by combining fuzzy-interval linear programming with dynamic programming. Their model treats inherent uncertainties expressed as intervals while simultaneously considering the dynamic characteristics in the optimal allocation of water resources. The benefits of this modelling approach are demonstrated on the case study of optimal allocation of water resources under uncertainty in Handan, Hebei Province, China.

We trust that the number and quality of the papers will prove to be of significant value to the many different researchers and practitioners who actively engage in applying disparate computational methodologies to sustainability analysis and environmental decision-making using simulation, optimization, and analytics. It is our sincere hope that this issue will not only enlighten readers on the current state-of-the-art applications in computational sustainability, but will also serve to inspire further collaboration and cooperation on extensions to these topics. Continuing advancement on these topics is always necessary as "It is difficult to predict, especially the future" (Danish proverb often attributed to Niels Bohr) but, more to the point and borrowing from the deeply philosophical characters in the cartoon Calvin and Hobbes, "The trouble with the future is that it keeps turning into the present".

List of Contributions

1. Li, H.; Huang, G.; Li, Y.; Sun, J.; Gao, P. A C-Vine Copula-Based Quantile Regression Method for Streamflow Forecasting in Xiangxi River Basin.
2. Liu, J.; Li, Y.; Huang, G.; Yang, Y.; Wu, X. A Factorial Ecological-Extended Physical Input-Output Model for Identifying Optimal Urban Solid Waste Path in Fujian Province, China.
3. Binns, M. Analytical Models for Seawater and Boron Removal through Reverse Osmosis.
4. Navarro, L.; Mahmoud, A.; Ernest, A.; Oubeidillah, A.; Johnstone, J.; Chavez, I.R.S.; Fuller, C. Development of a Cyberinfrastructure for Assessment of the Lower Rio Grande Valley North and Central Watersheds Characteristics Osmosis.
5. Sadorsky, P. Eco-Efficiency for the G18: Trends and Future Outlook.
6. Binns, M.; Ayub, H.M.U. Model Reduction Applied to Empirical Models for Biomass Gasification in Downdraft Gasifiers.
7. Lohrmann, C.; Lohrmann, A. Accuracy and Predictive Power of Sell-Side Target Prices for Global Clean Energy Companies.
8. Kozlova, M.; Lohrmann, A. Steering Renewable Energy Investments in Favor of Energy System Reliability: A Call for a Hybrid Model.
9. Luts, M-K.; Savolainen, J.; Collan, M. Profitability Determinants of Unlisted Renewable Energy Companies in Germany—A Longitudinal Analysis of Financial Accounts.
10. Ruponen, I.; Savolainen, J.; Collan, M. Ex-Ante Study of Biofuel Policies—Analyzing Policy-Induced Flexibility.

11. Elalem, Y.K.; Bicer, I.; Seifert, R. Why Do Companies Need Operational Flexibility to Reduce Waste at Source?
12. Kozlova, M.; Nykänen, T.; Yeomans, J.S. Advances in Aviation Electrification: Enhancing Strategic R&D Investment Analysis Through Simulation Decomposition.
13. Raul, V.; Liu, Y-C.; Leifsson, L.; Kaleita, A. Effects of Weather on Iowa Nitrogen Export Estimated by Simulation-Based Decomposition.
14. Suo, M.; Xia, F.; Fan, Y. A Fuzzy-Interval Dynamic Optimization Model for Regional Water Resources Allocation under Uncertainty.

Funding: This research was supported in part by grant OGP0155871 from the Natural Sciences and Engineering Research Council and by funding from Finnish Foundation for Economic Foundation, grant number #200153.

Acknowledgments: As Guest Editors, we wish to convey our gratitude to all of the authors and reviewers for their stellar contributions. We greatly appreciate having had the opportunity to participate in all facets of the workings of this Special Issue and would also like to thank the editorial team affiliated with *Sustainability* for their ongoing support throughout this endeavor—especially to Szilvia Duduj, the Section Managing Editor at MDPI for this issue for her ongoing, indefatigable encouragement.

Conflicts of Interest: The authors declare no conflict of interest.

Article

A C-Vine Copula-Based Quantile Regression Method for Streamflow Forecasting in Xiangxi River Basin, China

Huawei Li [1,2], Guohe Huang [3], Yongping Li [2,3,*], Jie Sun [4] and Pangpang Gao [1]

[1] Sino-Canada Energy and Environmental Research Center, North China Electric Power University, Beijing 102206, China; hwlee121@163.com (H.L.); 17755837728@163.com (P.G.)
[2] State Key Joint Laboratory of Environmental Simulation and Pollution Control, School of Environment, Beijing Normal University, Beijing 100875, China
[3] Institute for Energy, Environment and Sustainable Communities, University of Regina, Regina, SK S4S 7H9, Canada; huang@iseis.org
[4] School of Environmental Science and Engineering, Xiamen University of Technology, Xiamen 361024, China; sunj@xmut.edu.cn
* Correspondence: yongping.li@iseis.org

Abstract: In this study, a C-vine copula-based quantile regression (CVQR) model is proposed for forecasting monthly streamflow. The CVQR model integrates techniques for vine copulas and quantile regression into a framework that can effectively establish relationships between the multidimensional response-independent variables as well as capture the upper tail or asymmetric dependence (i.e., upper extreme values). The CVQR model is applied to the Xiangxi River basin that is located in the Three Gorges Reservoir area in China for monthly streamflow forecasting. Multiple linear regression (MLR) and artificial neural network (ANN) are also compared to illustrate the applicability of CVQR. The results show that the CVQR model performs best in the calibration period for monthly streamflow prediction. The results also indicate that MLR has the worst effects in extreme quantile (flood events) and confidence interval predictions. Moreover, the performance of ANN tends to be overestimated in the process of peak prediction. Notably, CVQR is the most effective at capturing upper tail dependences among the hydrometeorological variables (i.e., floods). These findings are very helpful to decision-makers in hydrological process identification and water resource management practices.

Keywords: streamflow forecasting; C-vine copula; quantile regression; joint dependencies; water resource management

Highlights

- A C-vine copula-based quantile regression (CVQR) model is developed.
- The CVQR model is applied to monthly streamflow forecasting in the Xiangxi River basin.
- It can establish relationships between multidimensional response and independent variables.
- It can also capture tail or asymmetric dependences such as extremes values.
- The results are helpful to decision-makers in water resource management practices.

1. Introduction

With continuously growing populations, water resources are becoming more and more important for urbanization and agricultural intensification, especially for developing countries [1–3]. In the process of water resource planning, streamflow forecasting plays a key role in hydrological risk assessment, reservoir operations, drought/flood prevention, and water resource allocation [4–6]. More importantly, the management efficiency of water resource systems mainly depends on the reliability and accuracy of hydrological prediction. Consequently, it is desirable to employ streamflow forecasting models for effective water resources planning and management.

Over the last few decades, great efforts have been made towards developing advanced forecasting techniques to improve hydrological prediction, including process-driven and data-driven statistical approaches [7–9]. Process-based modeling methods are based on the principle of water cycle balance coupling various physical processes, such as precipitation, evaporation, infiltration, and other processes [10,11]. These models use large amounts of data (e.g., hydrometeorology, topography, and land use/cover) and robust calibration techniques, while data-driven models can be easily built in practice without considering physical process information from hydrological models and have been extensively used [12–14]. Therefore, data-driven technology is very useful and valuable as an option for streamflow forecasting.

Previously, a variety of data-driven modeling techniques were proposed and promoted for streamflow forecasting, including autoregressive moving average, multiple linear regression (MLR), stepwise cluster analysis, artificial neural networks (ANN), genetic programming, and support vector regression (SVR) [15–17]. For example, Besaw et al. [18] employed the ANN method for streamflow forecasting in ungauged basins. The results showed that local climate measurements with time delays as the input to the model are key to improving hydrological forecasting. Guo et al. [19] coupled an SVR model with adaptive insensitive factors to predict monthly streamflow, which was proven to be effective and to have high accuracy in streamflow prediction. Terzi and Ergin [20] used autoregressive (AR) modeling, gene expression programming (GEP), and adaptive neuro-fuzzy inference system (ANFIS) to predict the monthly mean flow of a watershed in Turkey. The results indicated that the developed models had good performance. Fan et al. [21] established a stepwise cluster forecasting (SCF) model for monthly streamflow forecasting, which effectively reflected the nonlinear and discrete relationships between climatic factors and streamflow. In general, these data-driven techniques can effectively simulate hydrological elements by capturing the complex interrelationships among the multiple hydrometeorological inputs. However, these models can often be flawed when predicting outliers (such as flood events), leading to illusory relationships between the response and independent variables [22].

To overcome these limitations, in this study, the copula method is proposed to flexibly construct the joint distribution to describe the complicated dependence structure between stochastic variables. Copula functions have been extensively applied to construct multivariate models and forecasting in several areas such as flood frequency and drought analysis, rainfall and climate predictions, financial risks, and energy [23–26]. However, it is difficult to derive multivariate copulas directly. Fortunately, vines known as pair copula constructions (PCCs) can describe the correlation structures between high-dimensional response-independent variables, providing an efficient and flexible tool to analyze the dependency structures between complex coupled correlated variables [27]. Moreover, the vine copulas coupling the quantile regression provide a more complete statistical analysis of random relationships between stochastic variables, such as tail or asymmetric dependence. Specially, quantile regression (QR) was introduced by Koenker and Bassett to estimate the conditional quantiles [28]. Given the distribution of the variables, the QR method can capture the total variation, heavy tail, skewness, and kurtosis of variables and can support the calculation of confidence intervals. Moreover, the method can estimate the levels of risk in extreme cases [29,30]. Quantile regression has been successfully applied in various scientific fields, such as economics, finance, and medicine [31–33]. Therefore, this study integrates the copula and quantile regression methods to explore the complex dependence among variables. Notably, the data-driven model is often influenced by the division of training and validation data sets. In many cases, the simulation and validation effects of the model are often affected by the data inputs, especially in a changing climate environment. Therefore, in order to overcome the possible influence of different data inputs on the model and randomness errors in the simulation process, the calibration and verification data sets are divided at certain points with the five-fold cross-validation method. In this study, the predictions are repeated five times using different training and test data sets.

Therefore, this study aims to develop a C-vine copula-based quantile regression (CVQR) model for streamflow forecasting. The proposed CVQR model can construct a conditional copula prediction model to capture the relationship between streamflow and hydrometeorology variables. The developed method has advantages in (i) modelling the dependence among the multidimensional response-independent variables, (ii) revealing the complicated interrelationships among hydrometeorological factors, and (iii) outperforming MLR and ANN on issues related to upper tail dependence (i.e., flood events). These findings are very helpful to decision-makers in hydrological process identification and water resource management practices.

In this study, the CVQR model is applied to the Xiangxi River basin to illustrate its applicability in streamflow prediction with multiple hydrometeorological factors. Specially, the structure of this article is as follows. Firstly, the MLR, ANN, and CVQR models are introduced in Section 2. Next, the study area and database, and the method of evaluation for the various functions are depicted in Section 3. In Sections 4 and 5, relevant results from the proposed model applied in our research area, and a comparison with and discussion about the results of different models are described.

2. Model Development

In this study, multiple linear regression (MLR), artificial neural network (ANN), and the proposed C-vine copula-based quantile regression (CVQR) models are used for streamflow forecasting. In the model development section, the MLR, ANN, and CVQR models are described, which together constitute the main modules of the proposed framework shown in Figure 1. Generally, the framework of this study entails the next four steps: (1–2) fitting and standardizing the predictors (i.e., $x_1, \ldots x_{n-1}$) and predicted variable (x_n); (3) simulating the monthly streamflow for the calibration process using the MLR, ANN, and proposed CVQR models; and (4) performing monthly streamflow prediction during the calibration and verification periods based on the results of step 3 and comparing the results of R^2, RMSE, and NSE for each model.

2.1. Multiple Linear Regression (MLR)

The purpose of multiple linear regression (MLR) is to investigate the relationship between the independent variables and a dependent variable. Assuming that the dependent variable y is a function of n independent variables $x_1, x_2, x_3, \ldots, x_n$, then the MLR can be expressed as follows:

$$y = a + b_1 x_1 + \ldots + b_n x_n + e \tag{1}$$

where a indicates the intercept; $b_1, \ldots, b_n$ are the slope coefficients of the corresponding independent variables; e is the random error; and y represents the independent variable. For more details, please refer to Yan and Su [34]. In this study, a generalized linear regression model is used to fit the relationship between the response variable y (monthly streamflow data) and the explanatory variables x (other hydrometeorological factors), and then, the model is used to predict the streamflow (y) with the new observations (x).

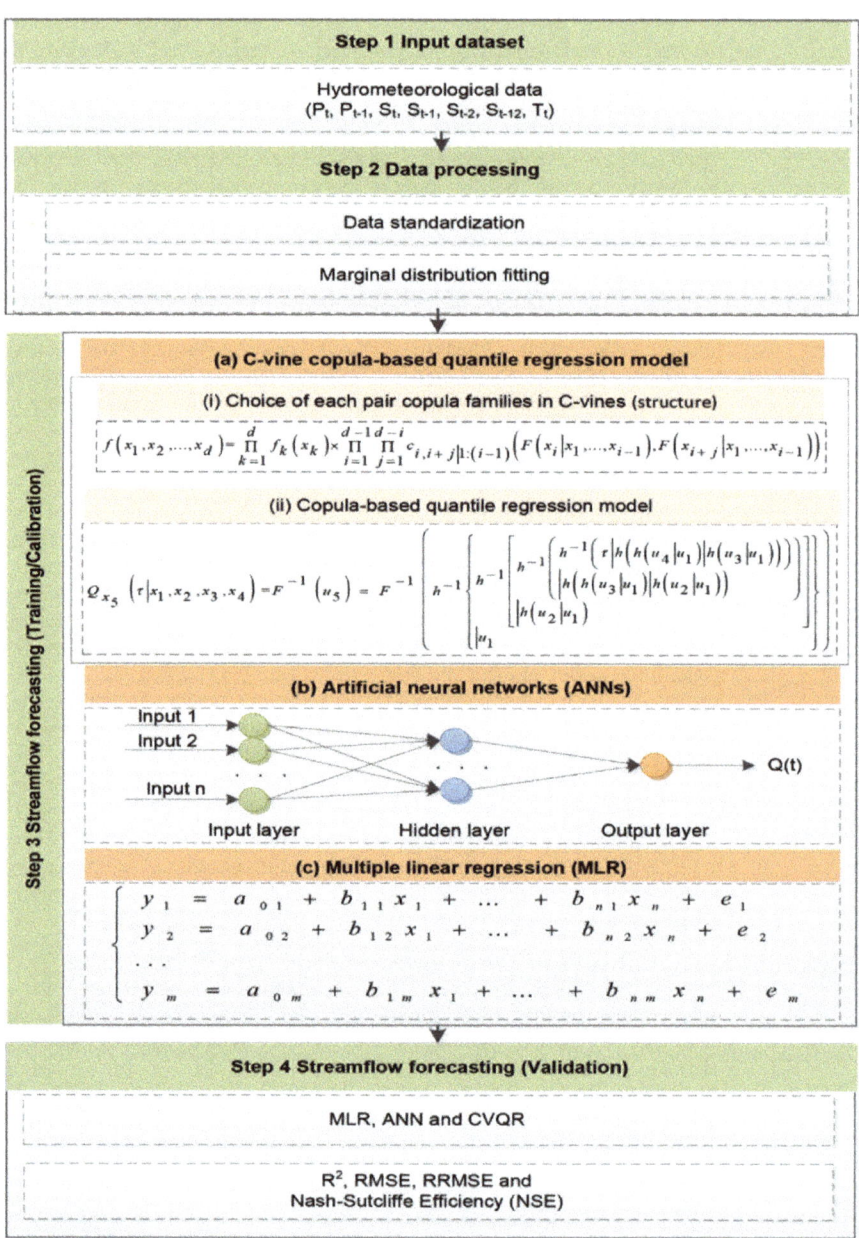

Figure 1. Framework of this study.

2.2. Artificial Neural Networks (ANNs)

An artificial neural network is an information processing system inspired by biological neural networks (such as the brain). Artificial neural networks can model the complex relationships between the input and output by simulating human learning [35]. Neural networks can be described as simple processing nodes or neurons, which generally include inputs, weights, a sum function, an activation function, and outputs and perform the corresponding numerical operations in a specific order [36]. An ANN model is usually made up of three parts: the input layer, the hidden layer, and the output layer, each of which do not have a unique number of layers. Multilayer feedforward ANNs, also known as multilayer perceptron, are commonly used in drought and water resource management and contain one input layer, one or more hidden compute node layers, and one output layer [37]. The three-layered ANNs can be expressed as follows:

$$\begin{cases} \underbrace{x_j}_{\text{the input layer } I} \Rightarrow \\ \underbrace{H_i^{in} = \sum_{j=1}^{m} w_{ij} x_j + b_{hi}}_{\text{iutput ith node for the hidden layer } H} \Rightarrow \underbrace{H_i^{out} = \varphi\left(\sum_{j=1}^{m} w_{ij} x_j + b_{hi}\right)}_{\text{output ith node for the hidden layer } H} \Rightarrow \\ \underbrace{O_k^{in} = \sum_{i=1}^{p} w_{ki} \left(H_i^{out}\right) + b_{ok}}_{\text{input kth node for the output layer } O} \Rightarrow \underbrace{y_k = \psi\left(\sum_{i=1}^{p} w_{ki} \left(\varphi\left(\sum_{j=1}^{m} w_{ij} x_j + b_{hi}\right)\right) + b_{ok}\right)}_{\text{output kth node for the output layer } O} \end{cases} \quad (2)$$

where w_{ij} is the weight between node i of the hidden layer and node j of the input layer; w_{ki} is the weight between the ith hidden layer node and the kth output layer node; b_{hi} and b_{ok} are the bias weights of ith node for the hidden layer and of the kth node for the output layer; and $\varphi()$ and $\psi()$ indicate the activation functions of the hidden and output layers, respectively. In this study, the multilayer feedforward ANNs with the back-propagation algorithm are used for monthly streamflow forecasting, and the number of hidden nodes is determined as five by the trial and error method. For more details, refer to Tan et al. [38].

2.3. Development of C-Vine Copula-Based Quantile Regression (CVQR) Model

In general, vine copulas are represented using a graph called R-vine, which consists of a series of trees (undirected acyclic graphs) [39]. Specially, the hierarchical structure, called a regular vine (R-vine), contains a series of connected trees $T := (T_1, T_2, \ldots, T_d)$ along with the series of edges $E(T) := E_1 \cup E_2 \cup \ldots \cup E_{d-1}$ and the series of nodes $N(T) := N_1 \cup N_2 \cup \ldots \cup N_{d-1}$. However, regular vines in terms of pair-copulas are still very general and do not have unique decomposition. Thus, the canonical vine (C-vine) and the D-vine are two most common structures of regular vines [40]. C-vine has a stellar structure in their tree sequence, while D-vine has a path structure. In hydrological field in this study, the monthly streamflow is affected by various climatic and hydrological factors. Therefore, the runoff factor that has a strong dependence on all other variables is selected as the first root for C-vine construction instead of D-vines. Here, two five-dimensional examples of possible tree sequences are shown in Figure 2.

2.3.1. Copula Function

The general expression of bivariate copulas can be written as follows:

$$H(x,y) = C(u_x, u_y; \theta) \quad (3)$$

where (x, y) are correlated random variables. θ can often be derived from Kendall's τ as a preliminary estimation, and (u_x, u_y) are the marginal cumulative distribution functions of x and y, respectively. Kendall's τ is the rank correlation coefficient proposed by Kendall [41]. Let $(x_1, y_1), (x_2, y_2), \ldots, (x_n, y_n)$ be a set of observations of the joint random variables X and Y, respectively, and empirical Kendall's τ can be defined as $\tau = 2(C_n - D_n)/n(n-1)$, where C_n and D_n indicate the number of concordant and discordant pairs, respectively.

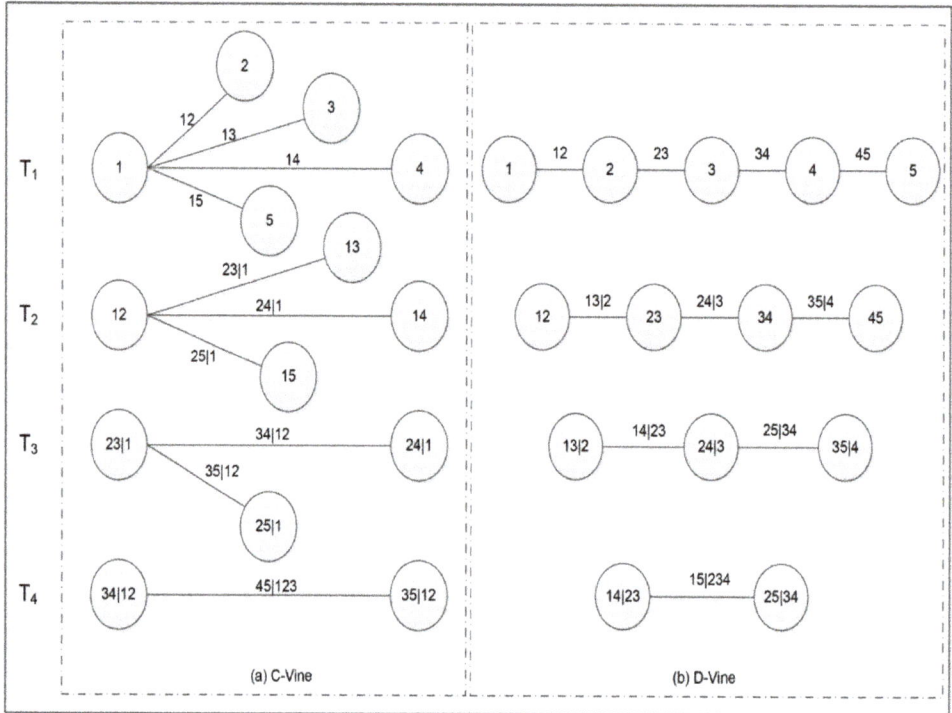

Figure 2. Examples of 5-dimensional C-vine (**a**) and D-vine (**b**).

A d-dimensional copula C: [0, 1] d → [0, 1] with uniformly distributed marginals U (0, 1) on the interval [0, 1] was introduced by Sklar [42]. According to Sklar's theorem, every joint cumulative distribution function (CDF) F on R^d with marginals $F_1(x_1), F_2(x_2), \ldots, F_d(x_d)$ can be written as follows:

$$F(x_1, x_2, \ldots, x_d) = C(F_1(x_1), F_2(x_2), \ldots, F_d(x_d)), \forall x = (x_1, x_2, \ldots, x_n) \in R^d \quad (4)$$

Similarly, the multivariate density $f(x_1, x_2, \ldots, x_d)$ with marginal densities $f_1(x_1), f_2(x_2), \ldots, f_d(x_d)$ and join probability density of copula c $(u_1, u_2, \ldots, u_d)$ can be written as follows:

$$f(x_1, x_2, \ldots, x_d) = \left[\prod_{i=1}^{d} f_i(x_i)\right] c(u_1, u_2, \ldots, u_d), \forall x = (x_1, x_2, \ldots, x_n) \in R^d \quad (5)$$

and vice versa:

$$C(u_1, u_2, \ldots, u_d) = F\left(F_1^{-1}(u_1), F_2^{-1}(u_2), \ldots, F_d^{-1}(u_d)\right), \forall u = (u_1, u_2, \ldots, u_d) \in (0, 1) \quad (6)$$

where $u_i = F_i(x_i)$, $(i = 1, 2, \ldots, d)$, and $F_1^{-1}(u_1), F_2^{-1}(u_2), \ldots, F_d^{-1}(u_d)$ are the inverse distribution functions of the marginals.

2.3.2. Vine Copulas

For actual statistical inference, a d-dimensional copula density c can be decomposed into a product of d (d−1)/2 so-called pair-copula constructions (PCCs) based on bivariate (conditional) copulas [43]. The PCCs involve marginal conditional distributions of the form $F(x|\omega)$. Joe [44] showed that, for every j,

$$h(x|\omega) := F(x|\omega) = \frac{\partial C_{x,\omega_j|\omega_{-j}}(F(x|\omega_{-j}), F(\omega_j|\omega_{-j}))}{\partial F(\omega_j|\omega_{-j})} \quad (7)$$

where $\omega = (\omega_1, \ldots, \omega_j, \ldots, \omega_n)$ is a n-dimensional vector, ω_j is an arbitrarily selected component of the vector ω, and ω_{-j} is a vector of ω without the jth component; $h(x|\omega)$ is the conditional distribution function given the k-dimensional vector ω (i.e., h-function) [43].

Then, the C-vines with one node connected to all others is the focus of this study (as shown in a). The density of the d-dimensional C-vine can be factorized as follows [45]:

$$f(x_1, x_2, \ldots, x_d) = \prod_{k=1}^{d} f_k(x_k) \times \prod_{i=1}^{d-1} \prod_{j=1}^{d-i} c_{i,i+j|1:(i-1)}\left(F(x_i|x_1, \ldots, x_{i-1}), F(x_{i+j}|x_1, \ldots, x_{i-1})\right) \quad (8)$$

where $c_{i,i+j|1:(i-1)}$ are the bivariate (conditional) copula densities, index j indicates the trees, while i runs over the edges in each tree.

In order to understand the decomposition of C-vine structures, only 5-dimensional C-vine structure is taken as an example to show the pair-copulas of vine structure decomposition in Figure 2a, that is, the joint density of C-vine copula can be decomposed into the following:

$$\begin{aligned}
f_{12345}(x_1, x_2, x_3, x_4, x_5) &= f_1(x_1) \cdot f_2(x_2) \cdot f_3(x_3) \cdot f_4(x_4) \cdot f_5(x_5) \\
&\cdot c_{12}(F_1(x_1), F_2(x_2)) \cdot c_{13}(F_1(x_1), F_3(x_3)) \cdot c_{14}(F_1(x_1), F_4(x_4)) \cdot c_{15}(F_1(x_1), F_5(x_5)) \\
&\cdot c_{23|1}\left(F_{2|1}(x_2|x_1), F_{3|1}(x_3|x_1)\right) \cdot c_{24|1}\left(F_{2|1}(x_2|x_1), F_{4|1}(x_4|x_1)\right) \cdot c_{25|1}\left(F_{2|1}(x_2|x_1), F_{5|1}(x_5|x_1)\right) \\
&\cdot c_{34|12}\left(F_{3|12}(x_3|x_1, x_2), F_{4|12}(x_4|x_1, x_2)\right) \cdot c_{35|12}\left(F_{3|12}(x_3|x_1, x_2), F_{5|12}(x_5|x_1, x_2)\right) \\
&\cdot c_{45|123}\left(F_{4|123}(x_4|x_1, x_2, x_3), F_{5|123}(x_5|x_1, x_2, x_3)\right)
\end{aligned} \quad (9)$$

where $c_{12}(F_1(x_1), F_2(x_2))$, denoted as c_{12}, represents the density function of pair-copula with marginal distributions $F_1(x_1)$ and $F_2(x_2)$.

According to the joint density of a C-vine copula presented in Equation (9), a C-vine copula with a certain order for given data can be fitted using all of the pair-copulas (conditional bivariate copulas). Then, the conditional distribution function $C_{34|12}$ and $C_{35|12}$ from tree 3, with edges $F_{3|12}(x_3|x_1, x_2)$, $F_{4|12}(x_4|x_1, x_2)$, and $F_{5|12}(x_5|x_1, x_2)$, can be obtained using Equation (7) along with $C_{3|12}$, $C_{4|12}$, $C_{5|12}$ and C_{12}, C_{13}, C_{14}, C_{15} from the first two trees. In general, the whole inferences for the conditional distribution function of predicted variable x_5 given x_1, x_2, x_3, and x_4 can be decomposed recursively from the bivariate copulas as follows:

$$\begin{cases}
F_{2|1}(x_2|x_1) = h_{2|1}(F_2(x_2)|F_1(x_1)) \\
F_{3|1}(x_3|x_1) = h_{3|1}(F_3(x_3)|F_1(x_1)) \\
F_{4|1}(x_4|x_1) = h_{4|1}(F_4(x_4)|F_1(x_1)) \\
F_{5|1}(x_5|x_1) = h_{5|1}(F_5(x_5)|F_1(x_1))
\end{cases} \text{For Tree 2} \\
\begin{cases}
F_{3|12}(x_3|x_1, x_2) = h_{3|12}\left(F_{3|1}(x_3|x_1) \middle| F_{2|1}(x_2|x_1)\right) = h_{3|12}\left(h_{3|1}(F_3(x_3)|F_1(x_1)) \middle| h_{2|1}(F_2(x_2)|F_1(x_1))\right) \\
F_{4|12}(x_4|x_1, x_2) = h_{4|12}\left(F_{4|1}(x_4|x_1) \middle| F_{2|1}(x_2|x_1)\right) = h_{4|12}\left(h_{4|1}(F_4(x_4)|F_1(x_1)) \middle| h_{2|1}(F_2(x_2)|F_1(x_1))\right) \\
F_{5|12}(x_5|x_1, x_2) = h_{5|12}\left(F_{5|1}(x_5|x_1) \middle| F_{2|1}(x_2|x_1)\right) = h_{5|12}\left(h_{5|1}(F_5(x_5)|F_1(x_1)) \middle| h_{2|1}(F_2(x_2)|F_1(x_1))\right)
\end{cases} \text{For Tree 3} \\
\cdots \\
\Rightarrow F(x_5|x_1, x_2, x_3, x_4) = h(h(T_{25,1}|T_{23,1})|h(T_{24,1}|T_{23,1}))
\quad (10)$$

where $T_{ij,1} = h(h(u_j|u_1)|h(u_i|u_1))$, $2 \leq i < j \leq 5$.

2.3.3. CVQR Model

Generally, taking the bivariate copula as an example, the condition distribution function of Y under the condition of X = x, i.e., $F_{Y|X}(y|x)$ can be expressed as follows:

$$F_{Y|X}(y|x) = C_1(F_X(x), F_Y(y)) = \partial C(u,v)/\partial u \tag{11}$$

where $u = F_X(x)$, $v = F_Y(y)$ are the cumulative distribution function of y and x, respectively.

For any probabilities $\tau \in (0,1)$ (e.g., τ = 0.05, 0.1, ..., 0.95), the τth quantile function of Y given X = x from $C_1(F_X(x), F_Y(y))$ can be derived from the h-function:

$$\tau = F_{Y|X}(y|x) \equiv C_1(F_X(x), F_Y(y)) \tag{12}$$

$$Q_Y(\tau|X=x) = F_Y^{-1}\left(h^{-1}(\tau|u)\right) \tag{13}$$

where $h^{-1}()$ indicates the inverse conditional distribution function (inverse h-function) of a given parametric bivariate copula.

In this study, the main purpose of the C-vine copula-based quantile regression (CVQR) model is to predict the quantile of a response variable Y given the outcome of some predictor variables. For the five-dimensional case, according to Equations (10)–(13), the τth conditional quantile function of x_5, $Q_{x_5}(\tau|x_1, x_2, x_3, x_4)$, can be derived from the recursive formulation:

$$\begin{aligned}Q_{x_5}(\tau|x_1,x_2,x_3,x_4) &= F^{-1}(u_5) = \\ F^{-1}\big(h^{-1}\big\{h^{-1}\big[h^{-1}\big(h^{-1}&(\tau|h(h(u_4|u_1)|h(u_3|u_1)))|h(h(u_3|u_1)|h(u_2|u_1)))|h(u_2|u_1)\big]|u_1\big\}\big)\end{aligned} \tag{14}$$

A C-vine copula-based quantile regression (CVQR) model is developed for monthly streamflow forecasting coupling a C-vine copula model and a quantile regression method within a general optimization framework. Specially, the CVQR model is constructed by modelling the distributions of predictors (i.e., $x_1, \ldots x_{n-1}$) and predicted variable (x_n) with the selected n-d C-vine (structure), i.e., unconditioned and conditioned pairs (e.g., Equation (9)); then, the predicted variable of x_n is derived from the conditional distribution function (Equations (10)–(14)). In detail, the predicted variable x_5 can be obtained from the given predictor variables x_1, x_2, x_3, and x_4. Firstly, the Monte Carlo simulation is used to generate a sample of 5000 uniformly distributed random numbers spaced [0, 1] as the quantiles τ. Secondly, the 5000 implementations of x_5 can be generated using Equation (14), with one random number generated for each quantile τ. Then, the average of these realizations is considered the general prediction.

A recommended tool for statistical inference of vine copulas is statistical software R with the VineCopula package (http://CRAN.R-project.org/, accessed on 20 January 2021). In this study, the Archimedean copula family (Frank, Clayton, and Gumbel copulas [46,47]) and Normal and Student's t copulas are employed to build the C-vine structures. The optimal bivariate copula families associated with parameter estimation are selected and calculated depending on the AIC and BIC using the maximum likelihood estimation (MLE) for the first C-vine tree. Then, based on these pair-copula families and the corresponding estimated parameters, the h-function can be used to calculate and specify the pair-copula input for the second C-vine tree. The process is iterated tree by tree until the last pair-copula is evaluated. The building steps were detailed in Brechmann and Schepsmeier [48]. Meanwhile, the goodness-of-fit test includes the λ-function and Kolmogorov–Smirnov (KS) test with p-values and statistics (Sn) to check whether the selected copula is suitable for describing the observed dependencies, where the λ function is defined as follows:

$$\lambda(v, \theta) = v - K(v, \theta) \tag{15}$$

where $K(v, \theta) = P(C(u_1, u_2|\theta) \leq v)$ is the Kendall distribution function of copula C with parameter θ, and $v \in [0,1]$, and (u_1, u_2) are the marginal cumulative distribution functions of copula C. The λ-function can be obtained by the 'BiCopLambda' function in the VineCopula package. For more descriptions, please refer to Genest and Favre [49], and Genest and Rivest [50].

In general, the main procedures of the proposed CVQR model for monthly streamflow predictions can be expresses as follows:

Step 1: Fit optimal marginal distributions, denoted as $u_i = F_i(x_i)$, $(i = 1, 2, \ldots, d)$;

Step 2: Model the joint probability distributions $C(u_1, u_2)$, ..., $C(u_1, u_d)$, and then, the C-vine copula is iterated tree by tree until the last pair-copula is evaluated $F(x_1, x_2, \ldots, x_d) = C(u_1, u_2, \ldots, u_d)$;

Step 3: Calculate the conditional distribution of the predictive variable (monthly streamflow) u_d, $F(x_d|x_1, x_2, \ldots, x_{d-1})$;

Step 4: Generate uniformly distributed random numbers τ, and then, predictive variable is derived from the inverse function of the conditional distribution in Step 3, that is, $x_d = F^{-1}(\tau|x_1, x_2, \ldots, x_{d-1})$.

3. Application

3.1. Study Area and Datasets

Application of the proposed approach is proven to forecast monthly streamflow in the Xiangxi River basin, which is located in the western Hubei province and is part of the Three Gorges Reservoir region with a basin area of about 3100 km² (between 30°57′–31°34′ N and 110°25′–111°06′ E, shown in Figure 3) in China. The Xiangxi River, originating in the Shennongjia Mountain area, is a tributary of the Yangtze River with a main stream length of 94 km [51,52]. Due to the influence of typical subtropical continental monsoon climate characteristics, the annual precipitation in this basin is between 670 and 1700 mm [53]. The annual average temperature of this region is 15.6 °C and ranges between 12 °C and 20 °C.

The amount of streamflow is affected by many factors, a large part of which involve geographical and climatic conditions. Specifically, the climatic conditions consist of a collection of meteorological variables such as the air temperature (°C) and the precipitation (mm). Previous studies have proven that precipitation has a significant effect on both short- and long-term streamflow [54,55]. Therefore, the total monthly precipitation is used as a predictor in this study. Most importantly, the initial catchment conditions are nonnegligible factors affecting the streamflow generation and confluence. Moreover, the monthly average temperature is also applied as a predictor for streamflow forecasting [56]. It is noted that observations of hydrological processes tend to vary with time [57]. The occurrence of rainfall events is closely related to the fluctuation in streamflow, especially the distribution of a rainfall event is crucial to the influence of peak discharge (i.e., flood events). In addition, considering the climatic characteristics of the watershed, the snowmelt runoff (mainly in winter) is relatively little, so the influence of snowmelt runoff is ignored. The available hydrological (streamflow, unit: m3/s) and meteorological data (temperature and precipitation) from 1962 to 2009 were obtained from the Xingshan Hydrometric Station (located at 110°45′0″ E, 31°13′0″ N, as shown in Figure 3), which was provided by the Hydrological Bureau of Xingshan County. Considering that Xingshan Hydrometric Station is the largest hydrological control station in Xiangxi watershed (the representative station of the Three Gorges Hydrological Zone between 1000–3000 km²), the hydrometeorological data of Xingshan Station was used for the streamflow forecasting. Moreover, as a lumped hydrological model, good results have also been achieved in the process of streamflow simulation in the earlier study of Kong [51].

In this study, considering that the current streamflow at month t and the streamflow (and precipitation) of the previous month has a certain correlation, the monthly streamflow (St) and precipitation (Pt) data sets were separated into multiple lead time factors such as Pt-1 and St-1, St-2, and St-12, where St-1, St-2, and St-12 represent streamflow at 1, 2, and 12 months ahead of forecast month t, respectively [58,59]. These factors together with the monthly average temperature (Tt) are potential prediction factors (inputs) to predict the monthly streamflow St (response variable). In the out-of-sample test of this study, the data set at a specific time point was divided into a training data set (38 years) for model calibration and a test data set (10 years) for validation of the model performance. Then, the predictions were repeated five times using different training and test data sets. The specific data set division method, namely 5-fold cross-validation models, is jointly shown in Table 1 and Figure 4.

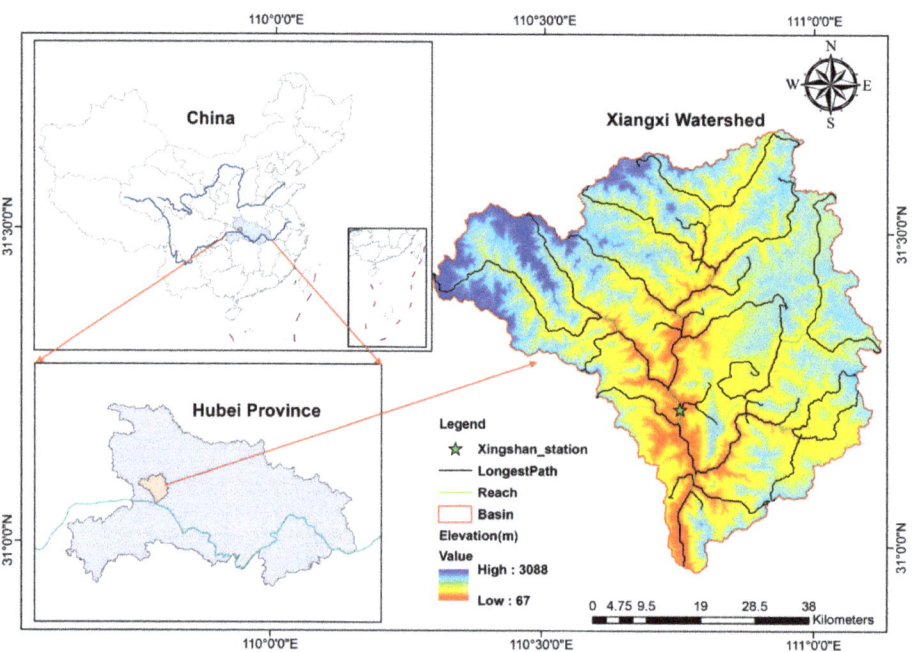

Figure 3. The study area.

Table 1. Cross-validation models with different sets of calibration and validation data.

Cross-Validation Models	Calibration Data	Validation Data
K1	1962–1971 and 1982–2009	1972–1981
K2	1962–1980 and 1991–2009	1981–1990
K3	1962–1989 and 2000–2009	1990–1999
K4	1962–1999	2000–2009
K5	1972–2009	1962–1971

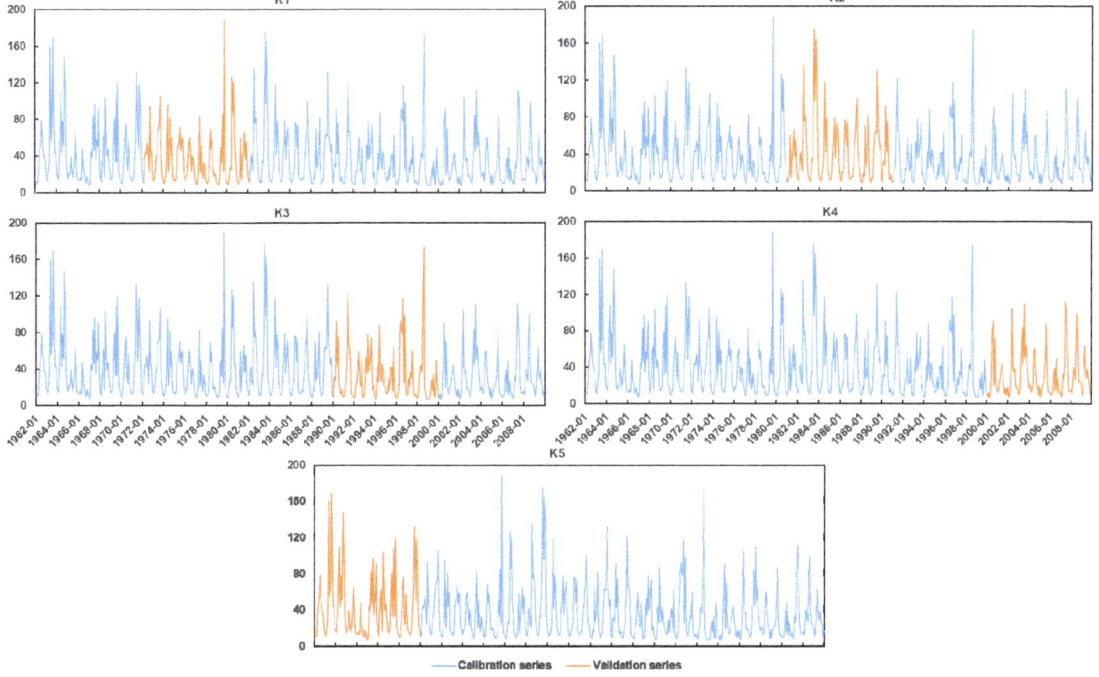

Figure 4. Selection of calibration and validation dataset with the 5-fold cross-validation method.

3.2. Evaluation Measures

In order to evaluate the performance of the developed models, in this study, four commonly used statistical evaluation methods are selected for model evaluation, including the coefficient of determination (R^2), the root mean square error (RMSE), and the Nash–Sutcliffe efficiency coefficient (NSE) and Mean Absolute Error (MAE). Then, the formulae for R^2, RMSE, NSE, and MAE can be written as follows:

$$R^2 = \frac{1}{K}\sum_{j=1}^{K}\left[\left(\frac{\sum_{i=1}^{n}(Q_i - Q_{avg})(P_i - P_{avg})}{\sqrt{\sum_{i=1}^{n}(Q_i - Q_{avg})^2}\sqrt{\sum_{i=1}^{n}(P_i - P_{avg})^2}}\right)^2\right] \quad (16)$$

$$RMSE = \frac{1}{K}\sum_{j=1}^{K}\left[\sqrt{\frac{1}{n}\sum_{i=1}^{n}(Q_i - P_i)^2}\right] \quad (17)$$

$$MAE = \frac{1}{K}\sum_{j=1}^{K}\left[\frac{1}{N}\sum_{i=1}^{N}|(P_i - Q_i)|\right] \quad (18)$$

$$NSE = \frac{1}{K}\sum_{j=1}^{K}\left[1 - \frac{\sum_{i=1}^{n}(Q_i - P_i)^2}{\sum_{i=1}^{n}(Q_i - Q_{avg})^2}\right] \quad (19)$$

where n indicates the total number of observations (or predictions), K is the number of repeated forecasting periods (K = 5), Q_i and P_i are the observed and simulated values; Q_{avg} and P_{avg} are the averages of all of the observed and simulated values, respectively.

The 90% confidential interval containing ratio (CR90) and its dispersion index (DI) are also used to evaluated the reliability and sharpness of the probabilistic predictions, respectively. CR90 is the ratio of observations covered by the 90% prediction interval. The range is between 0 and 1, and the best effect is 0.90. DI is the ratio of the average width of the 90% prediction interval to the observed value, with the lower the value, the better the prediction [60].

$$\begin{cases} CR90 = \frac{\sum_{i=1}^{N} k_i}{N}, k = \begin{cases} 1, s_l(i) \leq o_i \leq s_u(i) \\ 0, o_i < s_l(i) \text{ or } o_i > s_u(i) \end{cases} \\ DI = \frac{1}{N} \sum_{i=1}^{N} \frac{s_u(i) - s_l(i)}{o_i} \end{cases} \quad (20)$$

where k_i indicates the ith observation o_i in the 90% confidence interval with the bound $[s_l(i), s_u(i)]$ and N is the number of observations. Notably, from the perspective of flood forecasting, A high CR90 is still insufficient to illustrate a good prediction, and a high corresponding DI indicates an overestimation of uncertain boundaries.

To further illustrate the applicability of the CVQR model in streamflow forecasting, the relative estimated root mean square error (RRMSE) and relative mean absolute error (RMAE) are used to evaluate the comparison between the CVQR, ANN, and MLR models at different quantiles [61]:

$$\begin{cases} RRMSE = \frac{RMSE^{model}}{RMSE^{CVQR}} \\ RMAE = \frac{MAE^{model}}{MAE^{CVQR}} \end{cases} \quad (21)$$

in which the RMSE and MAE of the three models are acquired from Equations (17) and (18); RMAE and RRMSE stand for the relative performances of the proposed model (CVQR), for which values greater than one suggest a worse relative performance compared to the proposed model.

4. Result and Discussion

4.1. Marginal Probability Distribution Functions of C-Vine Model Variables

A two-step approach that separately evaluates the dependence function and the marginals is of great advantage in stochastic modeling of multivariate data, since many manageable distribution models are available for simulating the marginal distributions. In this study, in order to build the CVQR model, firstly, after standardization, the data are fitted with some parametric distribution functions, including the gamma, lognormal, general extreme value (GEV), and Pearson type-III (P-III) distributions, which are commonly used parameter distributions to quantify the probability distribution characteristics of hydrometeorological variables in the hydrological process [62–64]. The expressions for the gamma, GEV, lognormal, P-III, and the associated parameter values for probability functions (PDFs) are shown in Table 2. The parameters of the above distributions were obtained through the Maximum Likelihood Estimation (MLE) method.

Table 2. Parameters of optimal marginal distribution functions.

Name	Probability Density Function		S_{t-1}	P_{t-1}	S_{t-2}	S_{t-12}	T_t	P_t	S_t
P-III	$f(x) = \frac{\beta^{\alpha}(x-a_0)^{\alpha-1}e^{-\beta(x-a_0)}}{\Gamma(\alpha)}$ ***	a_0	1.88	32.12 *	1.86	2.35	Nan	32.34 *	1.83
		α	1.33	2.70	1.33	1.32	Nan	2.71	1.33
		β	0.04	0.02	0.04	0.04	Nan	0.02	0.04
Lognormal	$f(x) = \frac{1}{x\sigma\sqrt{2\pi}}e^{-(\ln x - \mu)^2/2\sigma^2}$	μ	3.37	3.92	3.37	3.38	2.70	3.91	3.37
		σ	0.77	1.23	0.77	0.76	0.56	1.23	0.77
GEV	$f(x) = \frac{1}{\sigma}(m)^{1+\xi}\exp(-m)$ **	ξ	0.65	0.30	0.65	0.64	-0.53	0.30	0.66
		μ	20.06	44.54	20.08	20.45	15.30	44.48	20.00
		σ	13.34	41.81	13.37	13.52	8.60	41.85	13.31
Gamma	$f(x) = \frac{\beta^{\alpha}}{\Gamma(\alpha)}x^{\alpha-1}e^{-\beta x}$ ***	α	1.84	1.14	1.84	1.87	3.84	1.14	1.84
		β	0.05	0.01	0.05	0.05	0.22	0.01	0.05

Note: 32.12 *, 32.34 * indicate for −32.12 and −32.34, respectively; ** $m = \left(1 + \xi\left(\frac{x-\mu}{\sigma}\right)\right)^{-1/\xi}$; *** $\Gamma(\alpha) = \int_0^{\infty} u^{\alpha-1}e^{-u}du$.

The goodness-of-fit (GOF) of each distribution was computed by using RMSE and AIC values to select the most appropriate distribution for fitting each individual variable. The results of GOF are presented in Table 3. The results demonstrate that all of the proposed four distribution models can be applied for processing the distributions of the variables (i.e., St-1, Pt-1, St-2, St-12, Tt, Pt, and St), except that the P-III distribution is not suitable for the average temperature (Tt). Specially, the P-III distribution are most suitable for the streamflow data series (i.e., St-1, St-2, St-12, and St), the Gamma distribution would perform best when fitting the distributions of precipitation data (Pt-1 and Pt), and the GEV method has advantages in quantifying the distributions of the average temperature (Tt).

Table 3. Comparison of RMSE and AIC values for marginal distribution estimation.

Name	RMSE							AIC						
	S_{t-1}	P_{t-1}	S_{t-2}	S_{t-12}	T_t	P_t	S_t	S_{t-1}	P_{t-1}	S_{t-2}	S_{t-12}	T_t	P_t	S_t
P-III	**0.0340**	0.0280	**0.0340**	**0.0315**	NaN	0.028	**0.0343**	**−3076.67**	−3249.25	**−3076.47**	**−3146.55**	NaN	−3259.76	**−3068.64**
Gamma	0.0486	**0.0214**	0.0485	0.0466	0.060	**0.021**	0.0488	−2754.30	**−3494.98**	−2756.02	−2792.48	−2555.94	**−3498.64**	−2751.05
Lognormal	0.0382	0.0550	0.0385	0.0368	0.069	0.055	0.0386	−2972.55	−2632.66	−2966.17	−3007.10	−2434.36	−2636.50	−2963.20
GEV	0.0409	0.0359	0.0414	0.0415	**0.050**	0.036	0.0415	−2908.32	−3016.77	−2898.84	−2896.32	**−2719.98**	−3029.44	−2897.00

Note: The RMSE and AIC values of the optimal fitting distribution are shown in bold.

4.2. Selection and Estimation of C-Vine Copula

In this section, we introduce how to define the C-vine structures according to the learning data obtained from Section 4.1. Figure 5 shows the pair plots of the learning data set. The histograms along on the diagonal represent the marginal distributions discussed in Section 4.1. Additionally, Figure 5 (above the diagonal) indicates the values of Kendall's τ between two pairs of the variables, and the results show that the correlation between the variable St-1 and other variables is approximately stronger than that other pair variables (i.e., Kendall's τ = 0.65, 0.46, 0.33, 0.40, 0.32, and 0.46). Therefore, we define the variable St-1 as the central variate 1 (e.g., in Figure 1) in the first tree. In detail, considering that the monthly streamflow (S) is affected by various climatic and hydrological factors, such as temperature and precipitation, the monthly streamflow at last month (St-1) is selected as the first root in the first tree. Moreover, the predicted variable (St) is placed last because it is the more convenient option to evaluate the probability of St and to predict the St. The rest of the tree structures follow this principle and so forth (e.g., as shown in Figure 1). In general, the order of these variables is 1-St-1, 2-Pt-1, 3-St-2, 4-St-12, 5-Tt, 6-Pt, and 7-St. Figure 5 (below the diagonal) shows scatter plots for each pair of learning data and provides a basis for revealing the dependence structures between the variables. For example, we may find that there exists a lower tail correlation between St-1 and St-2. Obviously, the Clayton copula can be used to fit the relationship between variables St-1 and St-2.

According to the process of construction of the bivariate copula, the vine copula is constructed by a series of pair-copulas iterated tree by tree. Table 4 presents the C-vine structures consisting of 6 trees, 21 nodes, and the corresponding bivariate copulas with the parameters for every edge and KS test statistics. As mentioned above, the variables from 1 to 7 correspond to St-1, Pt-1, St-2, St-12, Tt, Pt, and St, respectively. In fact, due to the flexibility of the vines' structure, this order of the variables above is only such structure. It is the best arrangement made by considering the dependence of the variables in practical applications in this study. Meanwhile, in the process of constructing the paired copula, the vine copulas are simplified by ignoring the conditional variables.

λ-function is used to test the goodness of fit for the estimation of bivariate copula in each C-vine structure. Figure 6 illustrates the dependence of St-1 and other variables with the main node in tree 1 using λ-function. The results indicate that the selected and empirical copula are consistent with each other in all edges of tree 1. As shown in Figure 6a, the empirical λ-function (black) of the observations and the theoretical λ-function (grey) of the fitted copula coincide with each other, which means that the fitted copula is consistent with the empirical values. Combined with the KS test results in Table 4, all other selected pair-copulas obtained the optimal fitting results with $p > 0.05$ for the KS test.

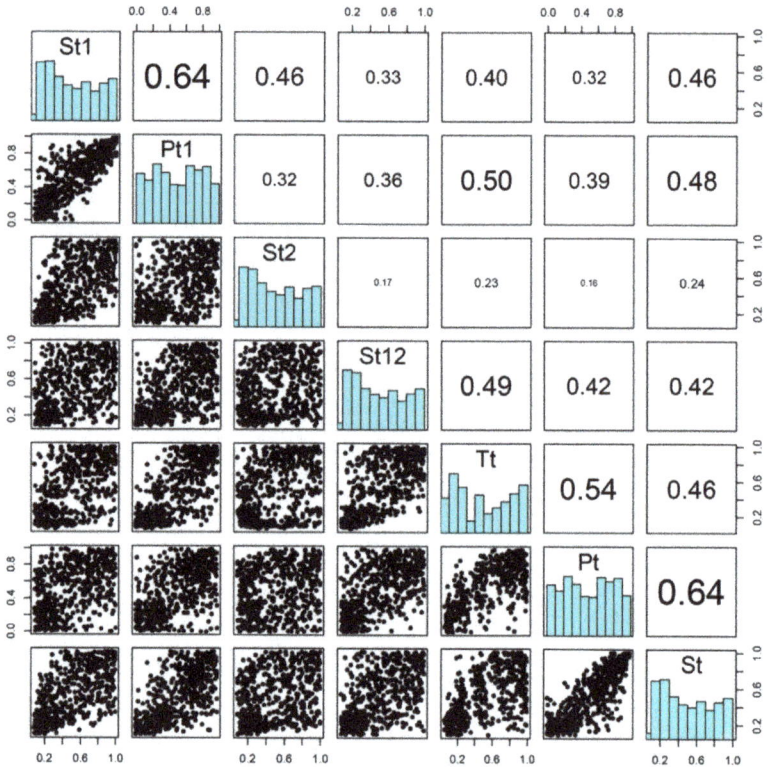

Figure 5. Pair plots of the learning data set with scatter plots below and Kendall's τ above the diagonal and histograms on the diagonal.

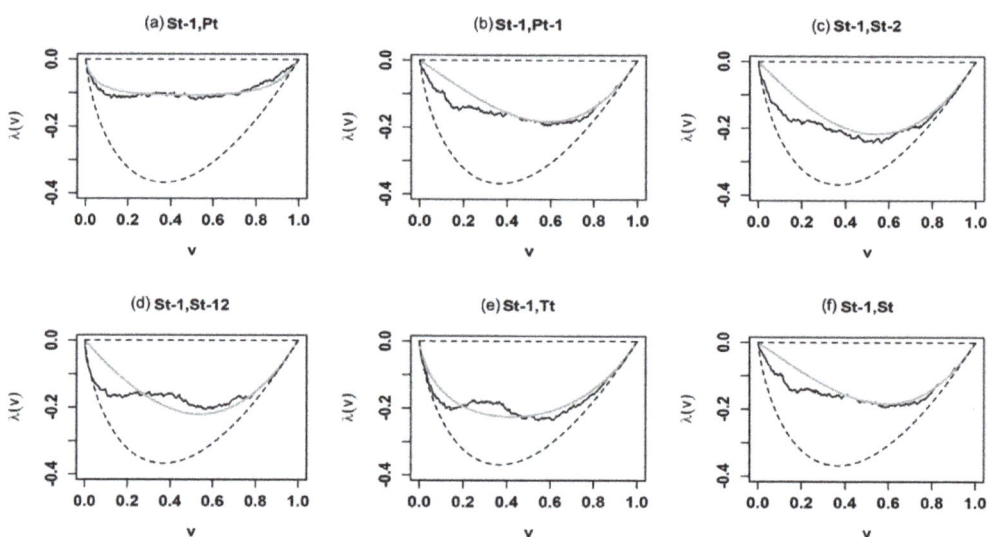

Figure 6. Correlation diagram of S_{t-1} with other variables of the λ-function with the main node in tree 1 (empirical function (black line), theoretical function of a fitted copula with parameters (grey line), as well as independence and comonotonicity limits (dashed lines)).

Table 4. Estimation of the 7-d C-vine model with bivariate copula-corresponding parameters of every node and the KS test.

Trees	C-Vine			KS Test	
	Nodes	Copulas	Parameters	p	Sn
Tree 1	12	F	9.50	0.94	0.01
	13	C	2.22	0.63	0.27
	14	C	1.52	0.68	0.19
	15	C	1.45	0.55	0.39
	16	F	3.12	0.74	0.12
	17	C	2.22	0.65	0.17
Tree 2	23|1	N	−0.21	0.53	0.05
	24|1	N	0.25	0.59	0.04
	25|1	N	0.39	0.68	0.05
	26|1	F	2.11	0.98	0.00
	27|1	F	1.95	0.58	0.07
Tree 3	34|12	F	−0.74	0.68	0.03
	35|12	F	−0.51	0.54	0.00
	36|12	F	−0.62	0.53	0.01
	37|12	F	−0.69	0.55	0.13
Tree 4	45|123	T	0.46, 13.95	0.98	0.07
	46|123	T	0.41, 8.72	0.61	0.28
	47|123	T	0.39, 5.40	0.65	0.17
Tree 5	56|1234	F	2.81	0.75	0.11
	57|1234	F	1.26	0.73	0.12
Tree 6	67|12345	G	1.94	0.68	0.28

Notes: 1–7 represent St-1, Pt-1, St-2, St-12, Tt, Pt, and St, respectively; F—Frank, C—Clayton, G—Gumbel, N—Normal, and T—t-copula.

4.3. Predicted Monthly Streamflow of MLR, ANN, and C-Vine Models

Figure 7 shows a comparison of the predicted and observed streamflow acquired by the MLR, ANN, and CVQR models. For the MLR model, the results indicate that the values of R^2, NSE, and RMSE are 0.73, 0.72, and 16.16 in the calibration period and 0.73, 0.66, and 16.72 in the validation period. For the MLR model (Figure 7a), the predicted value is slightly underestimated in the case of high flow observation values (1980–1986), and vice versa, the predicted value is slightly overestimated during 2004–2009. Due to the inherent characteristics of the algorithm, the predicted values even become negative at some low-flow records (e.g., 1999 and 2000).

The ANN model performs better than the MLR model in the calibration period (Figure 7b). The ANN model obtains an R^2 of 0.75, an NSE of 0.73, and an RMSE of 15.57 in the calibration period. Similar to the results of the MLR model, the ANN model, with values of R^2 at 0.72, NSE at 0.69, and RMSE at 16.53, performs worse in the validation period than that in the calibration period. Moreover, as presented in Figure 7b, the ANN model also underestimates some streamflow during the high flow periods (e.g., 1963–1964) but overestimates more records during 2004–2009.

As presented in Figure 7c, the predicted monthly streamflow using the CVQR model could satisfy the observed values well. In the calibration period, the values of R^2, NSE, and RMSE obtained by the CVQR model are 0.73, 0.70, and 16.75, respectively. In the validation period, the values are 0.74, 0.71, and 16.13, which shows that the performance of CVQR model in the validation period is similar to that in the calibration period. The CVQR model underestimates some high flow values (e.g., during 1980–1986). Generally, compared with MLR and ANN models, the CVQR model performs best in the calibration period for monthly streamflow prediction. The CVQR model can effectively capture both linear and nonlinear dependence of these input variables (e.g., temperature, precipitation, and streamflow). Additionally, the CVQR model based on the multivariate copula functions could effectively reveal the correlation structures between predictor–response variables, which provides a potent and adaptable tool to model the dependence of such complex and jointly correlated variables.

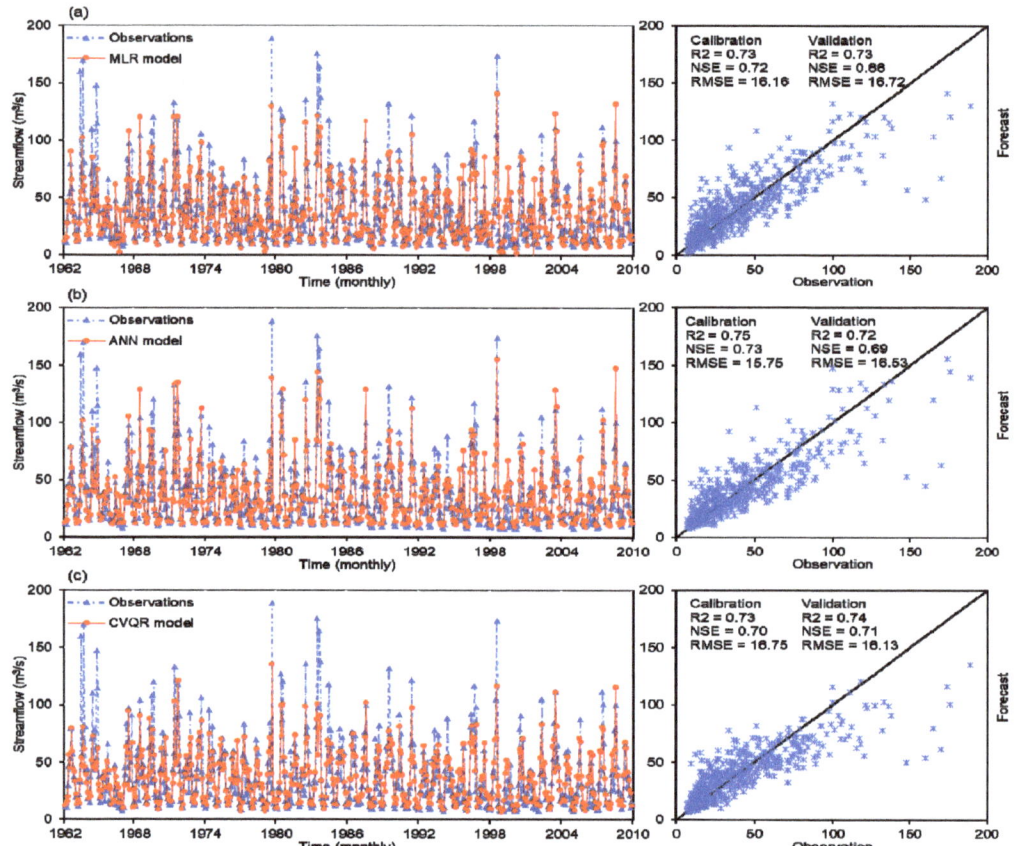

Figure 7. Comparison of predicted and observed monthly streamflow using the MLR (**a**), ANN (**b**), and CVQR (**c**) models.

Table 5 illustrates the general resulting statistics from the ANN, MLR, and CVQR models for forecasting during the calibration and validation periods. For the results of R^2, NSE, and RMSE, these results indicate that the ANN model performs best in the calibration period compared to the MLR and CVQR models while the proposed CVQR achieves the best results among the validation period compared to other models. However, the results show that ANN and CVQR performed best in terms of 90% confidence interval prediction (CR90 and DI) while MLR performed worst. The result, on the other hand, shows that MLR is not effective in quantifying nonlinear relationships among hydrological variables. In general, the results show that CVQR performs best in the calibration period for monthly streamflow prediction compared to ANN and MLR models. Moreover, the CVQR and ANN models can reflect the complex nonlinear relationships between the hydrological and meteorological factors. Therefore, in order to understand the prediction performance of CVQR in the tail correlations, the comparison of regression predictions between the CVQR and ANN models at different quantiles are explored in the next section.

Table 5. Summary statistics of streamflow forecasting during the validation period through different models.

Models	Calibration				Validation			
	R^2	NSE	RMSE	CR90/DI	R^2	NSE	RMSE	CR90/DI
MLR	0.73	0.72	16.16	0.43/0.46	0.73	0.66	16.72	0.47/0.48
ANN	0.75	0.73	15.57	0.89/1.14	0.72	0.69	16.53	0.81/1.32
CVQR	0.73	0.70	16.75	0.88/1.18	0.74	0.71	16.13	0.83/1.27

4.4. Probabilistic and Interval Predictions Obtained by the CVQR Model

As mentioned in Section 2.3, according to the C-vine copula-based quantile regression (CVQR) model, for any quantile $\tau \in (0,1)$, the τth conditional quantile function of the predicted variable can be obtained. In this section, the relationships between the streamflow (St) abnormalities and other hydrometeorological indices at different levels of quantiles τ (i.e., τ = 0.05, 0.25, 0.50, 0.75, and 0.95) are explored.

The median prediction (i.e., α = 0.5) provides a general level about the monthly streamflow, while extreme values (e.g., flood, drought) in the upper tail ($\tau \geq 0.75$) or lower tail ($\tau \leq 0.25$) indicate the worst forecast scenarios. Table 6 describes the relative performance of the ANN model with respect to the CVQR model at different quantiles. It can be seen that the proposed CVQR model outperforms the ANN model at quantiles τ = 0.75 and 0.95 and that the ANN model performs better than the CVQR model at quantiles τ = 0.25 and 0.50, which indicate that the proposed CVQR model could perform better at upper extreme events (i.e., τ = 0.75 and 0.95 quantile levels) and that the ANN model provides good results in some cases of the mean and lower quantile values.

Table 6. The performance RRMSE and RMAE of the ANN model with respect to the CVQR model at different quantiles.

τ	All		Calibration		Validation	
	RMAE	RRMSE	RMAE	RRMSE	RMAE	RRMSE
0.05	0.93	0.97	0.92	0.95	0.97	0.95
0.25	0.95	0.92	0.93	0.92	1.00	0.96
0.50	0.96	0.95	0.93	0.93	1.06	1.02
0.75	1.01	1.05	1.01	1.03	1.05	1.11
0.95	1.03	1.02	1.02	1.00	0.99	1.07

A scatter diagram of the simulated streamflow at different quantiles (τ = 0.05, 0.25, 0.5, 0.75, and 0.95) by the ANN and CVQR models with five-fold K cross-validations is depicted in Figure 8. The results also show that the proposed CVQR model performs a better fit in most cases, especially in the process of upper tail predictions, which are consistent with the earlier study of Kong in Xiangxi River basin [51]. While the ANN tends to overfit overestimated in the aspect of upper tail prediction. In general, the CVQR model shows a higher accuracy at upper tail levels while the ANN model provides overestimation predictions. The results indicate that the CVQR model can effectively capture upper tail dependences and has a relatively accurate assessment of the impact of upper extreme conditions (i.e., flood) in Xiangxi watershed.

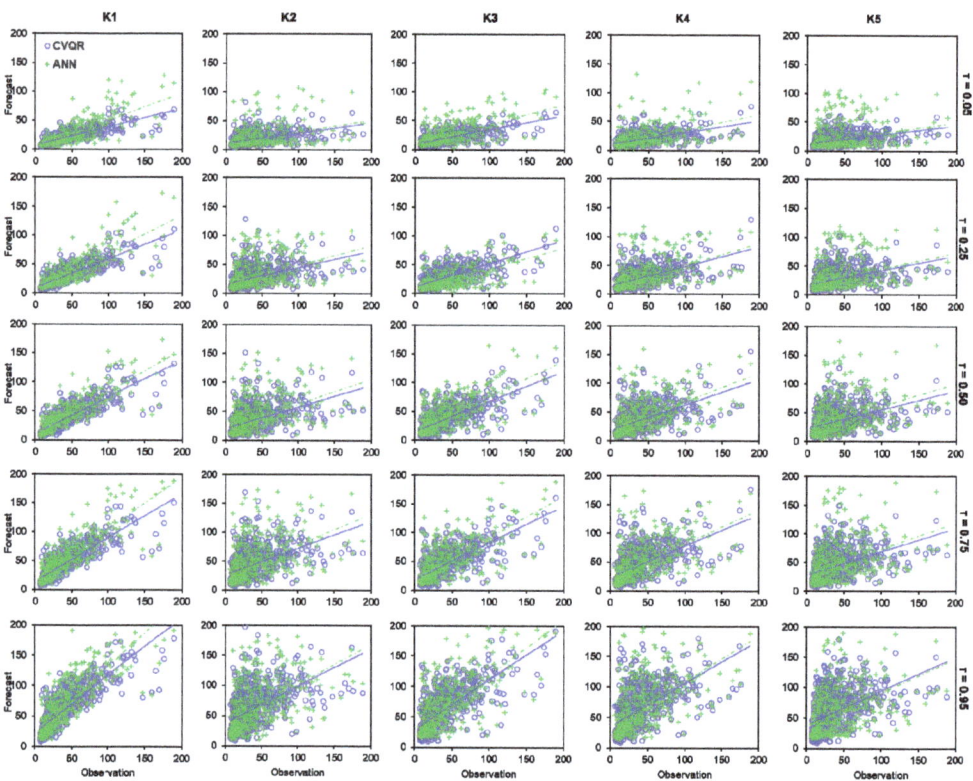

Figure 8. Scatter diagram of predicted and observed monthly streamflow using the CVQR and ANN models and their corresponding fitting lines at different quantiles (τ = 0.05, 0.25, 0.5, 0.75, and 0.95) with the five-fold K cross-validation models.

Figure 9 depicts the simulated streamflow with quantiles of 5% and 95% (90% uncertainty prediction intervals) using the ANN and CVQR models. The results indicate that the quantiles τ = 5% and 95% values of the predicted variable cover most of the observations and effectively reflect the fluctuation of the actual streamflow for the two models. Usually, hydrological forecasting in extreme cases can help policy makers make timely policy responses within the maximum risk range. The predicted 90% CI can reflect the fluctuation trend and abnormal value of the records well, whereas compared with the CVQR model, the ANN model often overestimates peaks in the prediction of flood events. Therefore, the CVQR model can effectively capture the complex nonlinear dependences among hydrological meteorological factors. This is of great significance to the practice of water resource management, for example, in rainy and dry seasons, managers can well prevent and control the occurrence of flood and make timely corresponding countermeasures.

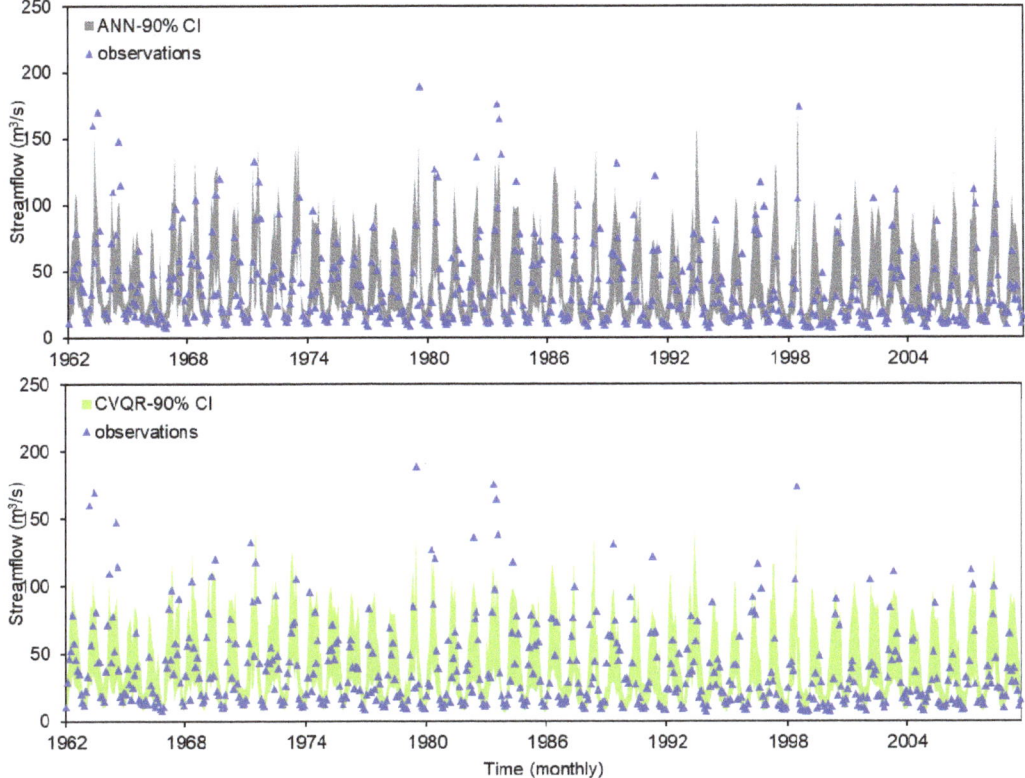

Figure 9. Comparison of the predicted and observed monthly streamflow using the CVQR and ANN models with $\tau = 5\%$ and 95% (90% uncertainty prediction intervals).

5. Conclusions

In this study, a C-vine copula-based quantile regression (CVQR) model was developed to model the relationship between streamflow and other hydrometeorological variables, such as temperature and precipitation. The proposed CVQR model couples vine copulas (known as pair copula constructions) with a quantile regression method, which was applied to monthly streamflow forecasting in the Xiangxi River basin.

Specifically, the CVQR model could process multidimensional data problems while satisfying the wide range of dependence. Meanwhile, the CVQR model can effectively capture the upper correlations between independent and dependent variables (i.e., flood events). In this paper, comparisons between the proposed CVQR model and the MLR and ANN models for monthly streamflow prediction are explored. The results indicate that the performance of the CVQR model is most effective for monthly streamflow forecasting in the calibration period. The performance of the MLR model in extreme quantile (flood events) and confidence intervals is the worst and is mainly determined by the inherent characteristics of the algorithm. Compared with the MLR model, the ANN model has good advantages in this aspect of flood events and confidence intervals, but it tends to be over-fit in the process of peaks prediction. Undeniably, the CVQR model can effectively capture both the linear and nonlinear dependence of these input variables and to perform best when dealing with upper tail correlation issues (i.e., flood events) in this study.

In summary, this proposed method can effectually depict the complicated dependencies between the hydrometeorological variables. However, there still remain some flaws in the process of model building. Pair-copula is joined by marginal distributions irrespective of the conditional variables, which simplifies the construction of vine copulas [65]. The structure of PCCs is often not unique due to the flexibility of vine copulas [66]. Moreover, the proposed model can be used to explore temporal and spatial dependencies among hydrological series while spatial dependence is not considered in this study [67]. Consequently, the model will be explored further in the application process of future extensions.

Author Contributions: Conceptualization, H.L.; methodology, H.L.; software, H.L.; validation, P.G. and J.S.; formal analysis, H.L.; investigation, P.G.; resources, G.H. and Y.L.; data curation, J.S.; writing—original draft preparation, H.L.; writing—review and editing, J.S. and Y.L.; visualization, H.L.; supervision, G.H. and Y.L.; project administration, G.H. and Y.L.; funding acquisition, G.H. and Y.L. All authors have read and agreed to the published version of the manuscript.

Funding: This research was supported by the Strategic Priority Research Program of Chinese Academy of Sciences (Grant Number: XDA20060302).

Data Availability Statement: Publicly available datasets were analyzed in this study. The data presented in this study are available at http://data.cma.cn/, accessed on 20 January 2021.

Acknowledgments: The authors gratefully acknowledge all the reviewers and editors for their insightful comments.

Conflicts of Interest: The authors declare no conflict of interest.

References

1. Li, Y.P.; Huang, G.H.; Nie, S.L.; Liu, L. Inexact multistage stochastic integer programming for water resources management under uncertainty. *J. Environ. Manag.* **2008**, *88*, 93–107. [CrossRef]
2. Gu, H.; Yu, Z.; Wang, G.; Wang, J.; Ju, Q.; Yang, C.; Fan, C. Impact of climate change on hydrological extremes in the Yangtze River Basin, China. *Stoch. Environ. Res. Risk Assess.* **2015**, *29*, 693–707. [CrossRef]
3. Zhu, F.L.; Zhong, P.A.; Sun, Y.; Yeh, W.-G. Real-Time Optimal Flood Control Decision Making and Risk Propagation Under Multiple Uncertainties. *Water Resour. Res.* **2017**, *53*, 10635–10654. [CrossRef]
4. Brooks, K.N.; Ffolliott, P.F.; Magner, J.A. *Hydrology and The Management of Watersheds*, 4th ed.; John Wiley & Sons: Hoboken, NJ, USA, 2012.
5. Fu, Z.H.; Zhao, H.J.; Wang, H.; Lu, W.T.; Wang, J.; Guo, H.C. Integrated planning for regional development planning and water resources management under uncertainty: A case study of Xining, China. *J. Hydrol.* **2017**, *554*, 623–634. [CrossRef]
6. Chen, J.; Zhong, P.-A.; An, R.; Zhu, F.; Xu, B. Risk analysis for real-time flood control operation of a multi-reservoir system using a dynamic Bayesian network. *Environ. Model. Softw.* **2019**, *111*, 409–420. [CrossRef]
7. Craig, J.R.; Brown, G.; Chlumsky, R.; Jenkinson, R.W.; Jost, G.; Lee, K.; Mai, J.; Serrer, M.; Sgro, N.; Shafii, M.; et al. Flexible watershed simulation with the Raven hydrological modelling framework. *Environ. Model. Softw.* **2020**, *129*, 104728. [CrossRef]
8. Ghobadi, Y.; Pradhan, B.; Sayyad, G.A.; Kabiri, K.; Falamarzi, Y. Simulation of hydrological processes and effects of engineering projects on the Karkheh River Basin and its wetland using SWAT2009. *Quat. Int.* **2015**, *374*, 144–153. [CrossRef]
9. Zhang, D.; Lin, J.; Peng, Q.; Wang, D.; Yang, T.; Sorooshian, S.; Liu, X.; Zhuang, J. Modeling and simulating of reservoir operation using the artificial neural network, support vector regression, deep learning algorithm. *J. Hydrol.* **2018**, *565*, 720–736. [CrossRef]
10. Hrachowitz, M.; Clark, M.P. HESS Opinions: The complementary merits of competing modelling philosophies in hydrology. *Hydrol. Earth Syst. Sci.* **2017**, *21*, 3953–3973. [CrossRef]
11. Baroni, G.; Schalge, B.; Rakovec, O.; Kumar, R.; Schüler, L.; Samaniego, L.; Simmer, C.; Attinger, S. A Comprehensive Distributed Hydrological Modeling Intercomparison to Support Process Representation and Data Collection Strategies. *Water Resour. Res.* **2019**, *55*, 990–1010. [CrossRef]
12. Yifru, B.A.; Chung, I.-M.; Kim, M.-G.; Chang, S.W. Assessment of Groundwater Recharge in Agro-Urban Watersheds Using Integrated SWAT-MODFLOW Model. *Sustainability* **2020**, *12*, 6593. [CrossRef]
13. Yang, S.; Yang, D.; Chen, J.; Santisirisomboon, J.; Zhao, B.A. Physical process and machine learning combined hydrological model for daily streamflow simulations of large watersheds with limited observation data. *J. Hydrol.* **2020**, *590*, 125206. [CrossRef]
14. Sharma, S.; Siddique, R.; Reed, S.; Ahnert, P.; Mejia, A. Hydrological model diversity enhances streamflow forecast skill at short- to medium-range timescales. *Water Resour. Res.* **2019**, *55*, 1510–1530. [CrossRef]
15. Zounemat-Kermani, M.; Mahdavi-Meymand, A.; Alizamir, M.; Adarsh, S.; Yaseen, Z.M. On the complexities of sediment load modeling using integrative machine learning: Application of the great river of Loíza in Puerto Rico. *J. Hydrol.* **2020**, *585*, 124759. [CrossRef]
16. Amaranto, A.; Munoz-Arriola, F.; Solomatine, D.P.; Corzo, G. A Spatially Enhanced Data-Driven Multimodel to Improve Semiseasonal Groundwater Forecasts in the High Plains Aquifer, USA. *Water Resour. Res.* **2019**, *55*, 5941–5961. [CrossRef]
17. Luo, X.G.; Yuan, X.H.; Zhu, S.; Xu, Z.Y.; Meng, L.S.; Peng, J. A hybrid support vector regression framework for streamflow forecast. *J. Hydrol.* **2019**, *568*, 184–193. [CrossRef]

18. Besaw, L.E.; Rizzo, D.M.; Bierman, P.R.; Hackett, W.R. Advances in ungauged streamflow prediction using artificial neural networks. *J. Hydrol.* **2010**, *386*, 27–37. [CrossRef]
19. Guo, J.; Zhou, J.; Qin, H.; Zou, Q.; Li, Q. Monthly streamflow forecasting based on improved support vector machine model. *Expert Syst. Appl.* **2011**, *38*, 13073–13081. [CrossRef]
20. Terzi, Ö.; Ergin, G. Forecasting of monthly river flow with autoregressive modeling and data-driven techniques. *Neural Comput. Appl.* **2014**, *25*, 179–188. [CrossRef]
21. Fan, Y.R.; Huang, G.H.; Li, Y.P.; Wang, X.Q.; Li, Z. Probabilistic prediction for monthly streamflow through coupling stepwise cluster analysis and quantile regression methods. *Water Resour. Manag.* **2016**, *30*, 5313–5331. [CrossRef]
22. Hassani, B.K. *Dependencies and Relationships between Variables. Scenario Analysis in Risk Management*; Springer: Berlin/Heidelberg, Germany, 2016.
23. Ayantobo, O.O.; Li, Y.; Song, S.; Javed, T.; Yao, N. Probabilistic modelling of drought events in china via 2-dimensional joint copula. *J. Hydrol.* **2018**, *559*, 373–391. [CrossRef]
24. Chen, L.; Singh, V.P.; Guo, S.; Zhou, J.; Zhang, J. Copula-based method for multisite monthly and daily streamflow simulation. *J. Hydrol.* **2015**, *528*, 369–384. [CrossRef]
25. Grimaldi, S.; Serinaldi, F. Asymmetric copula in multivariate flood frequency analysis. *Adv. Water Resour.* **2006**, *29*, 1155–1167. [CrossRef]
26. Bessa, R.J.; Miranda, V.; Botterud, A.; Zhou, Z.; Wang, J. Time-adaptive quantile-copula for wind power probabilistic forecasting. *Renew. Energy* **2012**, *40*, 29–39. [CrossRef]
27. Schepsmeier, U. Efficient information based goodness-of-fit tests for vine copula models with fixed margins: A comprehensive review. *J. Multivar. Anal.* **2015**, *138*, 34–52. [CrossRef]
28. Koenker, R.; Bassett, G. Regression quantiles. *Econometrica* **1978**, *46*, 33–50. [CrossRef]
29. Volpi, E.; Fiori, A. Design event selection in bivariate hydrological frequency analysis. *Hydrol. Sci. J.* **2012**, *57*, 1506–1515. [CrossRef]
30. Ye, W.; Luo, K.; Liu, X. Time-varying quantile association regression model with applications to financial contagion and var. *Eur. J. Oper. Res.* **2017**, *256*, 1015–1028. [CrossRef]
31. Machado, J.A.F.; Mata, J. Counterfactual decomposition of changes in wage distributions using quantile regression. *J. Appl. Econom.* **2005**, *20*, 445–465. [CrossRef]
32. Baur, D.; Schulze, N. Coexceedances in financial markets—A quantile regression analysis of contagion. *Emerg. Mark. Rev.* **2005**, *6*, 21–43. [CrossRef]
33. Boucai, L.; Hollowell, J.G.; Surks, M.I. An approach for development of age-, gender-, and ethnicity-specific thyrotropin reference limits. *Thyroid* **2011**, *21*, 5–11. [CrossRef]
34. Yan, X.; Su, X. *Linear Regression Analysis: Theory and Computing*; World Scientific: Singapore, 2009.
35. Adamowski, J.; Chan, H.F.; Prasher, S.O.; Bogdan, O.Z.; Sliusarieva, A. Comparison of multiple linear and nonlinear regression, autoregressive integrated moving average, artificial neural network, and wavelet artificial neural network methods for urban water demand forecasting in Montreal, Canada. *Water Resour. Res.* **2012**, *48*, 273–279. [CrossRef]
36. Sharifi, E.; Saghafian, B.; Steinacker, R. Downscaling satellite precipitation estimates with multiple linear regression, artificial neural networks, and spline interpolation techniques. *J. Geophys. Res. Atmos.* **2019**, *124*, 789–805. [CrossRef]
37. Mouatadid, S.; Raj, N.; Deo, R.C.; Adamowski, J.F. Input selection and data-driven model performance optimization to predict the Standardized Precipitation and Evaporation Index in a drought-prone region. *Atmos. Res.* **2018**, *212*, 130–149. [CrossRef]
38. Tan, Q.-F.; Lei, X.-H.; Wang, X.; Wang, H.; Wen, X.; Ji, Y.; Kang, A.-Q. An adaptive middle and long-term runoff forecast model using EEMD-ANN hybrid approach. *J. Hydrol.* **2018**, *567*, 767–780. [CrossRef]
39. Bedford, T.; Cooke, R.M. Vines—A new graphical model for dependent random variables. *Ann. Stat.* **2002**, *30*, 1031–1068. [CrossRef]
40. Kurowicka, D.; Cooke, R.M. Distribution-free continuous bayesian belief nets. In *Modern Statistical and Mathematical Methods in Reliability*; World Scientific: London, UK, 2005; pp. 309–322.
41. Kendall, M.G. A new measure of rank correlation. *Biometrika* **1938**, *30*, 81–93. [CrossRef]
42. Sklar, A. Fonctions de Repartition a n Dimensions et Leurs Marges. *Publ. Inst. Stat. Univ. Paris* **1959**, *8*, 229–231.
43. Aas, K.; Czado, C.; Frigessi, A.; Bakken, H. Pair-copula constructions of multiple dependence. *Insur. Math. Econ.* **2009**, *44*, 182–198. [CrossRef]
44. Joe, H. Distributions with fixed marginals and related topics || families of m-variate distributions with given margins and m(m-1)/2 bivariate dependence parameters. *Lect. Notes Monogr. Ser.* **1996**, *28*, 120–141.
45. Bedford, T.; Cooke, R.M. Probability Density Decomposition for Conditionally Dependent Random Variables Modeled by Vines. *Ann. Math. Artif. Intell.* **2001**, *32*, 245–268. [CrossRef]
46. Serinaldi, F.; Grimaldi, S. Fully nested 3-copula: Procedure and application on hydrological data. *J. Hydrol. Eng.* **2007**, *12*, 420–430. [CrossRef]
47. Trivedi, P.K.; Zimmer, D.M. Copula Modeling: An Introduction for Practitioners. *Found. Trends Econom.* **2006**, *1*, 1–111. [CrossRef]
48. Brechmann, E.; Schepsmeier, U. Modeling Dependence with C- and D-Vine Copulas: The R Package CDVine. *J. Stat. Softw.* **2013**, *52*, 1–27. [CrossRef]

49. Genest, C.; Favre, A.-C. Everything You Always Wanted to Know about Copula Modeling but Were Afraid to Ask. *J. Hydrol. Eng.* **2007**, *12*, 347–368. [CrossRef]
50. Genest, C.; Rivest, L.-P. Statistical Inference Procedures for Bivariate Archimedean Copulas. *J. Am. Stat. Assoc.* **1993**, *88*, 1034–1043. [CrossRef]
51. Kong, X.M.; Huang, G.H.; Fan, Y.R.; Li, Y.P. Maximum Entropy-Gumbel-Hougaard copula method for simulation of monthly streamflow in Xiangxi river, China. *Stoch. Environ. Res. Risk Assess.* **2015**, *29*, 833–846. [CrossRef]
52. Zhang, J.L.; Li, Y.P.; Huang, G.H.; Baetz, B.W.; Liu, J. Uncertainty analysis for effluent trading planning using a bayesian estimation-based simulation-optimization modeling approach. *Water Res.* **2017**, *116*, 159–181. [CrossRef] [PubMed]
53. Xu, H.; Taylor, R.G.; Kingston, D.G.; Jiang, T.; Thompson, J.R.; Todd, M.C. Hydrological modeling of river Xiangxi using SWAT2005: A comparison of model parameterizations using station and gridded meteorological observations. *Quat. Int.* **2010**, *226*, 54–59. [CrossRef]
54. Rosenberg, E.A.; Wood, A.W.; Steinemann, A.C. Statistical applications of physically based hydrologic models to seasonal streamflow forecasts. *Water Resour. Res.* **2011**, *47*, 1995–2021. [CrossRef]
55. Robertson, D.E.; Pokhrel, P.; Wang, Q.J. Improving statistical forecasts of seasonal streamflows using hydrological model output. *Hydrol. Earth Syst. Sci.* **2013**, *17*, 579–593. [CrossRef]
56. Gómez, M.; Concepción Ausín, M.; Carmen Domínguez, M. Seasonal copula models for the analysis of glacier discharge at King George Island, Antarctica. *Stoch. Environ. Res. Risk Assess.* **2017**, *31*, 1107–1121. [CrossRef]
57. Shao, Q.; Wong, H.; Li, M.; Ip, W.C. Streamflow forecasting using functional-coefficient time series model with periodic variation. *J. Hydrol* **2009**, *368*, 88–95. [CrossRef]
58. Fan, Y.R.; Huang, G.H.; Li, Y.P.; Wang, X.Q.; Li, Z.; Jin, L. Development of PCA-based cluster quantile regression (PCA-CQR) framework for streamflow prediction: Application to the Xiangxi river watershed, China. *Appl. Soft Comput.* **2016**, *51*, 280–293. [CrossRef]
59. Liu, Z.; Zhou, P.; Chen, X.; Guan, Y. A multivariate conditional model for streamflow prediction and spatial precipitation refinement. *J. Geophys. Res. Atmos.* **2015**, *120*, 10116–10129. [CrossRef]
60. Darbandsari, P.; Coulibaly, P. Introducing entropy-based Bayesian model averaging for streamflow forecast. *J. Hydrol.* **2020**, *591*, 125577. [CrossRef]
61. Kraus, D.; Czado, C. D-vine copula based quantile regression. *Comput. Stat. Data Anal.* **2017**, *110*, 1–18. [CrossRef]
62. Adamowski, K. A Monte Carlo comparison of parametric and nonparametric estimation of flood frequencies. *J. Hydrol.* **1989**, *108*, 295–308. [CrossRef]
63. Shiau, J.T. Fitting Drought Duration and Severity with Two-Dimensional Copulas. *Water Resour. Manag.* **2006**, *20*, 795–815. [CrossRef]
64. Šraj, M.; Bezak, N.; Brilly, M. Bivariate flood frequency analysis using the copula function: A case study of the Litija station on the Sava River. *Hydrol. Process.* **2015**, *29*, 225–238. [CrossRef]
65. Acar, E.F.; Genest, C.; Neslehova, J. Beyond simplified pair-copula constructions. *J. Multivar. Anal.* **2012**, *110*, 74–90. [CrossRef]
66. Geidosch, M.; Fischer, M. Application of vine copulas to credit portfolio risk modeling. *J. Risk Financ. Manag.* **2016**, *9*, 4. [CrossRef]
67. Armando, D.; Veiga, A. Periodic copula autoregressive model designed to multivariate streamflow time series modelling. *Water Resour. Manag.* **2019**, *33*, 3417–3431.

Article

A Factorial Ecological-Extended Physical Input-Output Model for Identifying Optimal Urban Solid Waste Path in Fujian Province, China

Jing Liu [1,2], Yongping Li [1,2,3,*], Gordon Huang [3], Yujin Yang [1] and Xiaojie Wu [1]

1 School of Environmental Science and Engineering, Xiamen University of Technology, Xiamen 361024, China; zyljing@126.com (J.L.); ctulip@163.com (Y.Y.); wuxiaojie19966@163.com (X.W.)
2 Fujian Engineering and Research Center of Rural Sewage Treatment and Water Safety, Xiamen University of Technology, Xiamen 361024, China
3 Institute for Energy, Environment and Sustainable Communities, University of Regina, Regina, SK S4S 0A2, Canada; huang@uregina.ca
* Correspondence: yongping.li@iseis.org

Abstract: Effective management of an urban solid waste system (USWS) is crucial for balancing the tradeoff between economic development and environment protection. A factorial ecological-extended physical input-output model (FE-PIOM) was developed for identifying an optimal urban solid waste path in an USWS. The FE-PIOM integrates physical input-output model (PIOM), ecological network analysis (ENA), and fractional factorial analysis (FFA) into a general framework. The FE-PIOM can analyze waste production flows and ecological relationships among sectors, quantify key factor interactions on USWS performance, and finally provide a sound waste production control path. The FE-PIOM is applied to managing the USWS of Fujian Province in China. The major findings are: (i) waste is mainly generated from primary manufacturing (PM) and advanced manufacturing (AM), accounting for 30% and 38% of the total amount; (ii) AM is the biggest sector that controls the productions of other sectors (weight is from 35% to 50%); (iii) the USWS is mutualistic, where direct consumption coefficients of AM and PM are key factors that have negative effects on solid waste production intensity; (iv) the commodity consumption of AM and PM from other sectors, as well as economic activities of CON, TRA and OTH, should both decrease by 20%, which would be beneficial to the sustainability of the USWS.

Keywords: ecological relationship; factorial analysis; input-output analysis; optimal path; reduction; urban solid waste system

1. Introduction

1.1. Importance and Motivation

With rapid urbanization and industrialization, humans consume increasing goods and services which cause the growth of direct and indirect urban solid waste generation [1]. Urban solid waste often has harmful impacts on human health and the ecological environment. Urban solid waste management, regarding the treatment of solid, liquid and/or atmospheric wastes before they are released into the environment is an issue of growing global concern [2]. In China, solid waste generation shows a trend of growth, and the corresponding utilization-disposal rate is trending downward. In 2011, the amounts of industrial solid waste and household garbage reached 3.62 billion and 0.16 billion Mg, respectively. The disposal rate and utilization rate were about 25.88% and 54.24%, respectively. In 2019, the amounts of industrial solid waste and household garbage increased to 3.86 billion and 0.24 billion Mg, respectively, whereas the disposal rate and utilization rate were about 24.31% and 53.33%, respectively. Investment in environmental protection occupied about 1.21% of GDP, while investment in solid waste production was much less [3]. Strategies that can help reduce the negative impacts of large amount of urban solid waste are desired [4].

The formulation of sound strategies requires the cooperation of numerous economic sectors [5]. When considering the city as a complex system, various economic sectors have direct or indirect relationships. The urban system can be treated as a network in which sectors are comparable to nodes and intersectoral transactions correspond to edges [6]. There are often sectors that are essential to reduce solid waste production as transfer centers [7]. These sectors are located in the middle of the supply chain path and simultaneously multiple supply chains of different path lengths [8]. The intermediate inputs of these sectors indirectly promote upstream production, while the intermediate outputs of these sectors are broadly used by downstream sectors resulting in more generation of direct solid waste production. Therefore, it is crucial to analyze urban solid waste generation from a systematic perspective aimed at recognizing the direct/indirect relationships among economic sectors, as well as assessing the direct solid waste (i.e., waste generated in the process of production), and indirect solid waste (i.e., when sector i receives products from other sectors, direct solid waste in the process of products production is the indirect solid waste of sector i) embodied in goods flowing within the regional and national scale economic system. This is helpful for global cities to achieve sustainable development target.

1.2. Literature Review

The physical input-output model (PIOM) proposed by Leontief [9] is effective for assessing the direct/indirect solid waste embodied in the flow of goods [10]. In the PIOM, a conventional economic system is transformed into an urban solid waste system (USWS). It can facilitate managers to account the solid waste flows in a USWS based on the material balance principle. Liang and Zhang [11] employed a PIOM to investigate the impacts of four categories of solid waste recycling on urban solid waste metabolism to support sustainable development. Wang et al. [12] used the PIOM for estimating the whole regional energy and environmental benefits of solid waste utilization for energy recovery, where power generation from energy recovery (e.g., waste incineration) and total mitigation potentials for air pollutant emissions were predicted. Meyer et al. [13] utilized the PIOM to model three streams of solid waste generated from commercial economic sectors in the United States; the model ranked all economic sectors based on solid waste production and pointed out potential areas to continue to pursue innovations in material use. Huang et al. [14] employed a PIOM to quantify different types of solid waste production recycling over the period 2005–2017 in China. The results revealed that China experienced an increment in the recycling of five types of solid waste.

The USWS contains various sectors, diversified flows, and compounded interactions [14]. Diagnosing the metabolism of the USWS by analyzing sector metabolic relationships and figuring out hierarchical structure is helpful [15]. The PIOM can be extended to handle these problems through introducing ecological network analysis (ENA). Zhang et al. [16] integrated a PIOM with ENA to analyze the directions, locations and drivers of carbon flows resulting from global trade, where large CO_2 transfers were recognized and adjustments of the national mitigation targets were proposed. Wang et al. [17] coupled a PIOM with ENA to evaluate water-related impacts of energy-related decisions, where sectoral embodied consumption of water and energy, and their intersector flows, were mapped. Wang [18] incorporated a PIOM with ENA to comprehensively estimate the metabolic status of an energy system in China, in which the system properties, indicators of sectors (e.g., the out-degree, betweenness, and closeness centrality degree), and betweenness-based energy consumption were calculated. Zheng et al. [19] combined ENA with a PIOM to investigate integral carbon emissions at the city scale; the complex structures and relationships of carbon emission flows in 2010 due to inter-sector trade were assessed.

In fact, a USWS has complexities related to different production technologies, industry scales, and pollution intensities. Valuable information is often hidden under the interrelationships between these factors and the consequent effects [20,21]. For example, variations in metal productive capability can affect the amount of solid waste delivered to the electrical equipment manufacture sector, as well as the amount of solid waste received from the metal ore mining sector. Finding crucial impact factors is beneficial to develop more specific solid waste reduction strategies. Factorial analysis (FA) has the ability to quantify the sensitivity of model response to significant factors and their interactions [22]. One concern is that traditional full factorial analysis may be unfeasible when many factors are taken into account (due to a large number of calculations). Fractional factorial analysis (FFA) is effective for quantifying the significance of factors by carrying out a small number of computed cases, which decreases the calculation cost and ensures result accuracy [23]. FFA has been successfully used in experimental designs for detecting response sensitivity [24–26].

Previous studies proved the feasibility and practicability of PIOM, ENA, and FFA (a summary of previous literature is presented in Table A1); however, there are some research gaps to be filled. First, a PIOM can assess physical direct and indirect solid waste production flows of USWS but has difficulty in analyzing ecological relationships between various sectors. Secondly, ENA can effectively reveal the metabolic condition including ecological control and utility relationships but cannot screen the key factors and evaluate their interactions. Third, FFA can help decision-makers accurately adjust key factors to improve system performance, with few studies applied FFA to USWS. Fourth, no previous study has been reported on the integration of PIOM, ENA and FFA for urban solid waste reduction in USWS.

1.3. Contribution and Novelty

The objective of this study was to develop a factorial ecological-extended physical input-output model (abbreviated as FE-PIOM) and apply it to a real USWS of Fujian Province (in China). The innovations and contributions are: (i) a novel integrated model (FE-PIOM) developed through incorporating a physical input-output model (PIOM), ecological network analysis (ENA), and fractional factorial analysis (FFA) within a general framework; (ii) FE-PIOM can analyze urban solid waste production flows and associated ecological relationships among economic sectors; (iii) FE-PIOM can recognize key factors in complex USWS, quantify their single and joint effects on USWS performance and provide sound urban solid waste production control path; (iv) this is the first attempt to apply such an integrated model (FE-PIOM) to a real case of USWS, and results can help managers to generate desired strategies for urban solid waste reduction.

2. Materials and Methods

2.1. Physical Input-Output Model

The PIOM originates from the monetary IOM proposed by Leontief, and can reflect urban solid waste flows among sectors and investigate the multiple sectoral linkages [5,23]. The basic form of IOM can be presented as [27]:

$$x_i = \sum_{j=1}^{n} z_{ij} + fd_i \text{ for } i = 1 \text{ to } n \qquad (1)$$

where x_i is the total output of sector i, z_{ij} is the amount of goods i that sector j consumes, and fd_i is the final demand of sector i. Solid waste intensity is then introduced to transform the monetary IOM into PIOM as follows [28,29]:

$$\mathbf{E} + \varepsilon \mathbf{Z} = \varepsilon \mathbf{X} \qquad (2)$$

$$\varepsilon = \mathbf{E}(\mathbf{X} - \mathbf{Z})^{-1} \qquad (3)$$

$$\mathbf{F} = diag(\varepsilon) * \mathbf{Z} \qquad (4)$$

where $\mathbf{E} = [e_i]_{1 \times n}$ is the amount of sectoral solid waste; $\varepsilon = [\varepsilon_i]_{1 \times n}$ is the solid waste intensity vector, ε_i is the embodied solid waste per unit of monetary value of sector i; $\mathbf{Z} = [z_{ij}]_{n \times n}$, z_{ij} is the amount of goods i that sector j consumes; $\mathbf{X} = [x_j]_{1 \times n}$ is the total economic output and $\mathbf{F} = [f_{ij}]_{n \times n}$ is the solid waste flows among various sectors. By physical units, it is referred to mass units for presenting waste flows (e.g., Mg). Direct solid waste production equals the initial input of the monetary-physical input-output table, and the indirect solid waste production of each sector equals the sum of its column elements in the physical input-output table. For instance, sector i produces 1 Mg solid waste per unit product production, meaning 1 Mg is the amount of direct solid waste in sector i. Sector i sells product to sector j, implying that the 1 Mg solid waste is indirectly transferred to sector j (i.e., the amount of indirect solid waste in sector j is 1 Mg).

Then, the amount of sectoral indirect solid waste and sectoral total flows can be calculated based on Equations (5) and (6) [30]:

$$IF_j = \sum_{i=1}^{n} f_{ij} \tag{5}$$

$$T_i = \sum_{j=1}^{n} f_{ij} + e_i \tag{6}$$

where f_{ij} is the direct solid waste flowing from sector i to sector j; e_i is the amount of direct solid waste; IF_j is the amount of indirect sectoral solid waste and T_i is the total amount of waste. Taking all pathway flows with different lengths between two sectors into account, the dimensionless integral solid waste flow intensity matrix (**N**) can be obtained through:

$$g_{ij} = f_{ij}/T_i \tag{7}$$

$$\mathbf{N} = (\mathbf{G})^0 + (\mathbf{G})^1 + (\mathbf{G})^2 + \ldots (\mathbf{G})^\infty = (\mathbf{I} - \mathbf{G})^{-1} \tag{8}$$

where g_{ij} is the dimensionless input-oriented intercomponent flow from sector i to sector j; $\mathbf{G}^n$ is the dimensionless integral flow intensity matrix with n path length and $\mathbf{I}(n \times n)$ is the identity matrix.

2.2. Ecological Network Analysis

The dependence and control degrees of one sector to other sectors can present the system's ecological hierarchy structure. The dependence degree means the ability of one sector receives urban solid waste from other sectors, while the control degree denotes the ability of one sector delivers urban solid waste to other sectors. The sum of all sectors' dependence (or control) degrees is equal to 1. To reflect how the variations in solid waste flow of a sector influence the USWS's ecological hierarchy structure, indexes (i.e., pulling force weight and driving force weight) in the ecological control analysis method are used to detect the sectoral dependence and control degrees as follows [31]:

$$\mathbf{Y} = diag(\mathbf{T}) * \mathbf{N} \tag{9}$$

$$\mathbf{ID} = \mathbf{Y} - \mathbf{D} = y_{ij} - f_{ij} \tag{10}$$

$$w_i = \sum_{j=1}^{n} y_{ij} / \sum_{i=1}^{n}\sum_{j=1}^{n} y_{ij} \tag{11}$$

$$w_j = \sum_{i=1}^{n} y_{ij} / \sum_{i=1}^{n}\sum_{j=1}^{n} y_{ij} \tag{12}$$

where **Y** is the sectoral contribution weight, y_{ij} is the integral flow from sector i to j, **ID** is the indirect flows of solid waste of sectors, w_j is the pulling force weight (PFW) of sector j, indicating the ability of sectors j receives solid waste from other sectors and w_i is the driving force weight (DFW) of sector i, meaning the ability of sector i delivers solid waste to other sectors. The difference between PFW and DFW indicates the role one sector plays in the waste flow chain.

Ecological utility analysis can be utilized to reveal the interconnection among various sectors in the USWS. The dimensionless direct utility matrix **D** examines the mutual benefit, and the integral utility intensity matrix **U** contains all solid waste interflows pathway. **D** and **U** can be calculated based on Equations (13) and (14) [32,33]:

$$\mathbf{D} = [d_{ij}] = (f_{ij} - f_{ji})/T_i \tag{13}$$

$$\mathbf{U} = (\mathbf{D})^0 + (\mathbf{D})^1 + (\mathbf{D})^2 + \ldots (\mathbf{D})^\infty = (\mathbf{I} - \mathbf{D})^{-1} \tag{14}$$

Transforming $\mathbf{U}$ to $\text{sign}(\mathbf{U})$ (including $\text{sign}U(+)$ and $\text{sign}U(-)$) judges the integral ecological relationships between pairwise sectors. Relationships include: (i) exploitation $(+, -)$ means sector i exploits j, indicating sector i receive wastes from j (the same applies to $(-, +)$); (ii) competition $(-, -)$ means the relationship is harmful to both sectors; (iii) mutualism $(+, +)$ means the relationship is beneficial to both sectors; (iv) neutralized $(0, 0)$ means there is no impact on each other. Three indexes are employed to assess the comprehensive properties of the USWS:

$$SI = \sum_{i=1}^{n}\sum_{j=1}^{n} u_{ij} \tag{15}$$

$$MI = \text{sign}U(+)/\text{sign}U(-) \tag{16}$$

$$R = \frac{N(+,+) + N(-,-)}{N} \tag{17}$$

where $\text{sign}U(+)$ and $\text{sign}U(-)$ are the number of positive and negative signs in $\mathbf{U}$; $N(+, +)$ and $N(-, -)$ are the amounts of mutualism and competition relationships and N is the total number of all relationships. Synergism index (SI) and mutualism index (MI) assess fitness and symbiosis of the USWS [34]. When $MI > 1$ and $SI > 0$, the USWS is mutualistic. Otherwise, the USWS requires to be modified.

2.3. Fractional Factorial Analysis

The USWS involves a number of economic sectors. These sectors' solid waste production may be interrelated to each other, increasing the complexity of the decision-making process. Fractional factorial analysis (FFA) can be employed to recognize the main factors and detect their interactions on the response variables of the USWS. Sectoral solid waste production (e_i in $\mathbf{E}$) and sectoral direct consumption coefficient ($a_{ij} = z_{ij}/x_j$) can be chosen as factors, which are divided into multiple levels. Solid waste production intensity (abbreviated as SPI) can be selected as the response when SPI = direct solid waste production (Mg)/gross domestic product (10^4 RMB¥ = 1542 USD). Using a fractional factorial analysis can screen main e_i and a_{ij} as well as quantify their interactions with reduced experimental cost. Researchers select an appropriate experimental matrix based on the number of e_i and a_{ij} [35]. A set of SPI values are gained by running the EIOM based on the matrix. Fractional factorial analysis quantifies the sensitivity of SPI to important factors and their combinations through addressing the curve traits of SPI when factors change at various levels. The quadratic sum for single factor and two-factor combinations are presented as follows [36,37]:

$$SS_A = \sum_{i=1}^{I}\left(\sum_{j=1}^{J}\sum_{k=1}^{K} Y_{ijk}\right)^2 /JK - \left(\sum_{i=1}^{I}\sum_{j=1}^{J}\sum_{k=1}^{K} Y_{ijk}\right)^2 /IJK \tag{18}$$

$$SS_B = \sum_{j=1}^{J}\left(\sum_{i=1}^{I}\sum_{k=1}^{K} Y_{ijk}\right)^2 /IK - \left(\sum_{i=1}^{I}\sum_{j=1}^{J}\sum_{k=1}^{K} Y_{ijk}\right)^2 /IJK \tag{19}$$

$$SS_{A\times B} = \sum_{i=1}^{I}\sum_{j=1}^{J}\left(\sum_{k=1}^{K} Y_{ijk}\right)^2 /K - \left(\sum_{i=1}^{I}\sum_{j=1}^{J}\sum_{k=1}^{K} Y_{ijk}\right)^2 /IJK - SS_A - SS_B \tag{20}$$

$$SS_T = \sum_{i=1}^{I}\sum_{j=1}^{J}\sum_{k=1}^{K} Y^2_{ijk} - \left(\sum_{i=1}^{I}\sum_{j=1}^{J}\sum_{k=1}^{K} Y_{ijk}\right)^2 /IJK \tag{21}$$

where I and J are the designed levels of factors A and B, respectively; y_{ijk} is the observed value in the K_{th} replication when A and B are at level I_{th} and J_{th}; SS_A, SS_B, and $SS_{A\times B}$ denote the square sum of A, B, and their combinations and SS_T is the total of squares. The contribution of each factor is calculated as the sum of its squares to the sum of the total squares.

3. Case Study

3.1. Study Area

Fujian Province lies between latitudes 23°33′ and 28°20′ N, and longitudes 115°50′ and 120°40′ E. It is an important economic development province with a land area of 121,400 km^2 located in the southeast coast of China. The total population of Fujian reached 41.54 million in 2020. It had a gross domestic product (GDP) of 0.677 trillion USD in 2020, occupying 4.3% of the whole country (the eighth place of all provinces in China). Over the past 40 years, the economic output of primary industry significantly decreased and the economic output of tertiary industry greatly increased. In 2017, the primary, secondary, and tertiary industries accounted for 6.9%, 47.7%, and 45.4% of the total GDP. The amount of direct urban solid waste reached 73.7 × 10^6 Mg in 2017, while the corresponding comprehensive disposal-utilization rate was 66.9%. Compared with 2012, the amount of direct solid waste decreased 23.3% and disposal-utilization rate also decreased 22.7%. The decrease in direct waste production indicated that Fujian made some achievements in urban solid waste production reduction; however, the problem still concerns local managers.

3.2. Data Collection and Analysis

The 42-sector IOT of Fujian Province in 2012 and 2017 were extracted from Fujian Statistics Bureau. The 42 sectors were merged into nine sectors based on the Industrial Classification for Nation Economic Activities (GB/T 4754-2017), as described in Table 1. Table 2 lists the merged economic input-output tables in 2012 and 2017. The data of urban solid waste was obtained from Fujian Statistical Yearbook, related official website and literature [38,39]. A two-level fractional factorial analysis was adopted for designing a set of scenarios. Five sectoral solid waste production (e_i) and five sectoral direct consumption coefficients (a_{ij}) were selected as deigned factors, with each divided into low (L) and high (H) levels. According to the number of factors, a $2^{(10-5)}$ orthogonal array was chosen to present the experimental scenarios. Thirty-two SPI values were obtained through repeatedly running the model. The square sum of individual factor and factor combinations was calculated.

Table 1. Abbreviations of 9 sectors.

No.	Abbreviation	Sector
1	AGR	Agriculture, Forestry, Animal Husbandry and Fishery
2	MIN	Mining Industry
3	PM	Food, Wine, Drink, Tea Manufacturing and Tobacco Processing
		Textile Garments Products
		Timber Processing
		Paper Products
4	AM	Petroleum Processing, Coking and Nuclear Fuel Processing
		Chemical Products
		Nonmetal Minerals Products
		Smelting and Pressing of Metals
		Metal Products
		General and Special Equipment
		Transportation Equipment
		Electric Equipment and Machinery
		Computer, Communication and Other Electronic Equipment
		Instruments and Meters Machinery
		Others Manufacturing
5	ELE	Production and Supply of Electricity, Gas and Water
6	CON	Construction
7	TRA	Transportation, Storage and Postal Services
8	WHO	Wholesale, Retail and Accommodation
9	OTH	Other Social Services

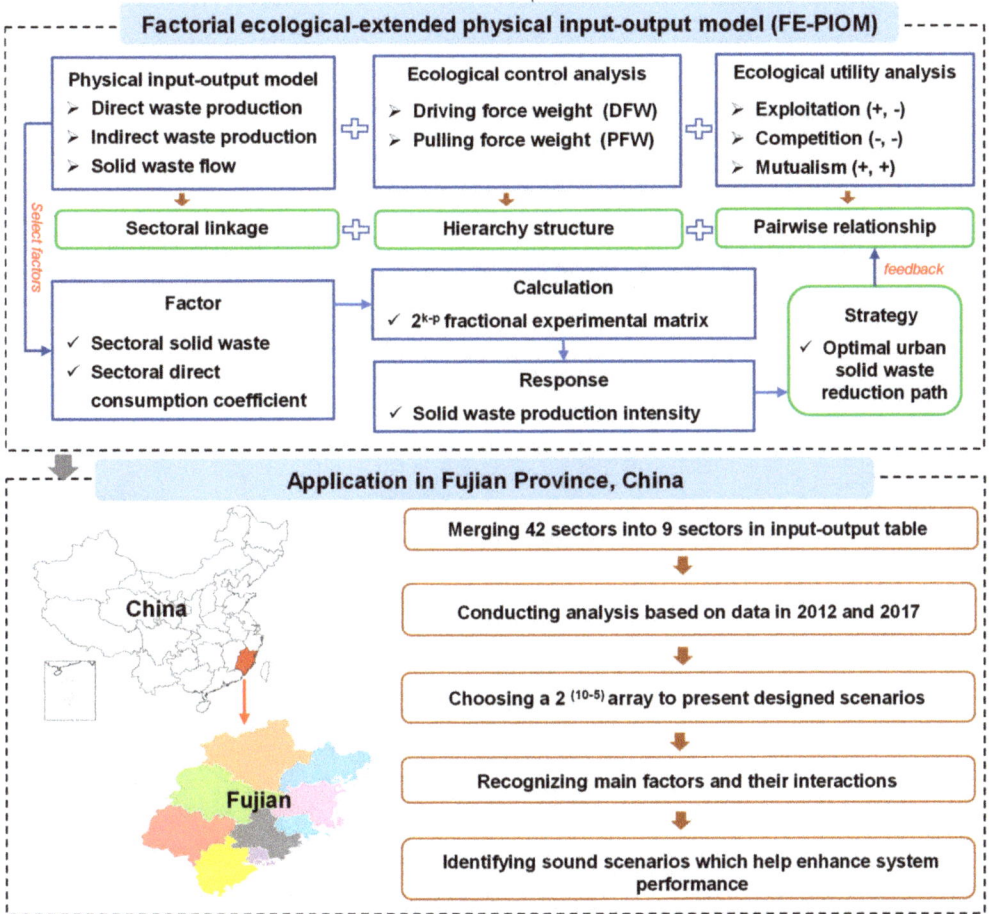

Figure 1. The formulation and application of the FE-PIOM model.

Figure 1 summarizes the formulation and application of the FE-PIOM model. The first step is to merge a large number of sectors into a small number of sectors in input-output table and transform the monetary input-output model into physical input-output model to describe sectoral linkages; calculate the driving force weight and pulling force weight to detect ecological hierarchy structure and then figure out the exploitation, competition, and mutualism to calculate ecological pairwise relationships. The second step is to select a set of proper factors, choose fractional experimental matrix, repeat the first step according to the matrix, recognize main factors and their interactions and identify a sound strategy.

Table 2. Merged economic input-output tables in 2012 and 2017 (10^6 USD).

Output \ Input		AGR	MIN	PM	AM	ELE	CON	TRA	WHO	OTH	Final Demand	Import	Import from Other Provinces	Total Output
							In 2012							
Intermediate input	AGR	3731	9	21,560	1276	1	770	83	3232	325	18,403	244	2590	46,555
	MIN	56	2253	772	19,410	4658	630	18	0	2	1311	4501	12,849	11,758
	PM	5793	189	80,049	7430	125	1237	486	3952	6523	110,528	12,345	4611	199,356
	AM	5387	2055	19,024	135,624	1677	42,888	8856	1359	7270	119,423	36,241	36,670	270,652
	ELE	570	653	4219	10,304	6444	692	1520	590	1844	3267	678	0	29,425
	CON	447	22	227	303	109	1237	615	14	467	117,306	36,221	0	84,652
	TRA	580	1040	5814	14,375	4348	6273	580	566	2232	12,003	8528	0	39,283
	WHO	717	324	6373	8237	1951	2413	1144	1647	7987	24,287	2348	0	52,733
	OTH	1770	817	5344	9181	2765	3031	9106	10,170	20,175	74,040	17,740	17	118,642
Added value		177,671	27,503	4397	55,975	64,512	7346	25,480	16,874	31,080	71,817	0	0	0
							In 2017							
Intermediate input	AGR	5635	6	34,154	1820	0	160	4866	692	786	27,473	9784	4707	61,102
	MIN	54	6112	13,257	24,993	3807	4367	7	0	152	141	24,102	16,587	12,201
	PM	7094	317	174,240	17,362	144	20,976	9144	8746	10,322	189,337	18,374	8410	410,896
	AM	7768	534	43,473	207,395	2215	30,917	13,514	732	7617	157,184	78,588	31,481	361,282
	ELE	571	439	4899	3574	18,867	680	4220	460	5870	1961	0	426	41,113
	CON	627	25	1182	982	723	1331	1345	153	974	145,435	0	352	152,426
	TRA	1183	454	11,048	7535	954	44,847	8090	2085	7611	24,938	0	4428	104,318
	WHO	798	198	14,900	7825	2587	2726	5977	1422	8144	47,164	0	3858	87,883
	OTH	1853	354	10,851	8040	2559	4505	14,481	23,786	56,404	118,745	32	11,611	229,935
Added value		229,443	35,518	3762	102,892	81,757	9257	41,917	42,675	49,807	132,055	0	0	0

4. Results and Discussion

4.1. Status in 2012 and 2017

Table 3 lists sectoral solid waste production, solid waste production coefficients, and export/import of solid waste in Fujian. The total waste production approached 275.66×10^6 t in 2012, where the direct and indirect productions accounted for 34.82% and 65.18%, respectively. Total waste production decreased to 236.05×10^6 t in 2017, with direct and indirect productions decreasing by 23.23% and 9.63%, respectively. The amount of indirect waste production was more than that of direct waste production, implying the significance of the indirect production flow calculation. In 2012, PM, AM, and CON were the dominant contributors, occupying 27.73, 42.75 and 12.59% of the total solid waste production. In 2017, the proportions of the three sectors' production were 34.17, 34.50, and 11.59%, respectively. These results revealed that solid waste was mainly produced by primary manufacturing (PM) and advanced manufacturing (AM). In addition, PM was the biggest solid waste net exporter (23.982×10^6 t in 2012 and 22.019×10^6 t in 2017) and CON was the largest importer (13.627×10^6 t in 2012 and 10.229×10^6 t in 2017). Fujian highly relied on clothing, lithium cells, auto parts manufacturing and food processing, and large amounts of construction materials were purchased from other provinces. Therefore, a future reduction strategy should focus on cutting down waste from these sectors.

Table 3. Results gained from physical input-output table in Fujian in 2012 and 2017.

Sector	Sectoral Direct Solid Waste Production (10^6 Mg)	Sectoral Indirect Solid Waste Production (10^6 Mg)	Total Solid Waste Production Coefficient (10^{-6} Mg/USD)	Final Demand Production (10^6 Mg)	Export (10^6 Mg)	Import (10^6 Mg)	Net Import (10^6 Mg)
In 2012							
AGR	1.091	5.899	3.598	2.115	0.649	0.426	−0.223
MIN	1.776	2.295	8.296	0.125	0.329	6.007	5.678
PM	30.105	46.337	9.188	11.898	30.484	6.502	−23.982
AM	40.871	76.985	10.435	20.202	31.802	31.750	−0.052
ELE	4.444	5.991	8.498	1.109	0.050	0.240	0.191
CON	12.783	21.925	9.825	46.873	1.224	14.851	13.627
TRA	0.921	6.051	4.253	1.224	0.906	1.514	0.607
WHO	1.236	4.220	2.479	1.346	1.167	0.243	−0.924
OTH	2.781	9.950	2.571	7.277	0.668	1.905	1.237
In 2017							
AGR	1.138	4.164	2.080	2.331	0.054	1.257	1.204
MIN	0.807	1.526	4.582	0.009	0.018	7.780	7.762
PM	27.185	53.466	4.703	9.887	27.277	5.257	−22.019
AM	23.903	58.004	5.433	20.911	14.725	24.954	10.229
ELE	2.720	5.639	4.872	0.387	0.012	0.087	0.075
CON	10.085	17.274	4.301	26.090	0.013	0.063	0.050
TRA	1.943	8.459	2.389	2.038	0.449	0.442	−0.007
WHO	1.637	3.836	1.492	2.438	0.499	0.240	−0.259
OTH	4.283	9.985	1.487	7.149	0.220	0.722	0.503

Figure 2 describes the direct and indirect solid waste flows among sectors in 2012 and 2017. Each sector has a specific color and the line between sectors indicates the direction of waste flows. The width of the line in each sector represents the amount of waste inflow and outflow. All direct waste flows are positive, while indirect waste flows have positive and negative values. A positive value means one sector receives waste from the other sector, whereas a negative value denotes one sector delivers waste to the other sector. It can be seen that direct waste mainly flowed to CON, while indirect waste flowed to all sectors. In Figure 2a,b, the largest contributor of direct waste flow was AM, which contributed 54.23% and 44.18 % of the total amount in 2012 and 2017, respectively. It contributed a large part of its direct waste flow to CON and PM (occupying 27.62% in 2012 and 23.67% in 2017) and itself (accounting for 60.50% in 2012 and 66.01% in 2017). In Figure 2c,d, AM was still the largest contributor of indirect waste flow, which contributed 73.29% and 57.62 % of the total amount in 2012 and 2017, respectively. The indirect waste of AM flowing to all other sectors was almost the same (occupying 20% to 30%). These results show the relationship of indirect waste flows is more complicate than that of direct flows.

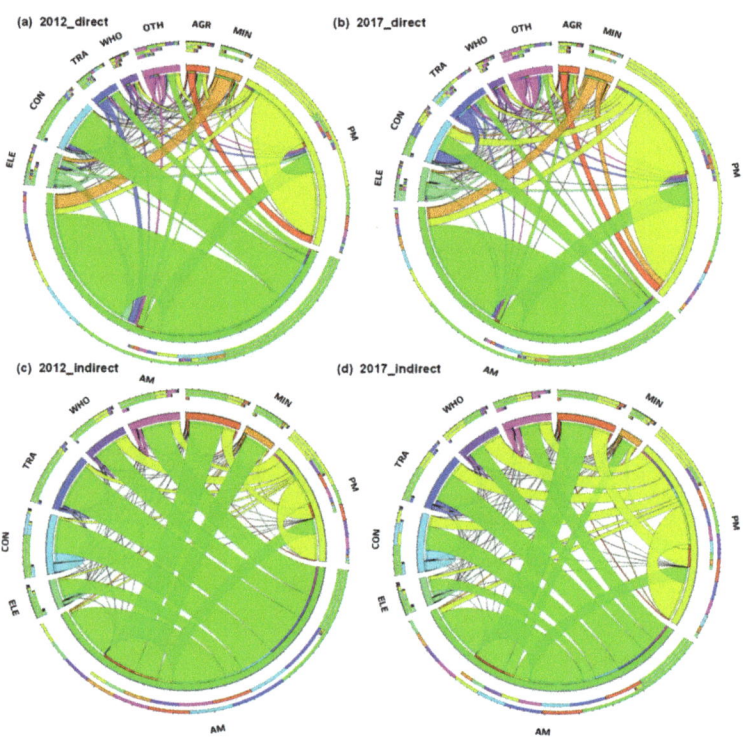

Figure 2. Direct and indirect solid waste flows among sectors. (**a**) 2012_direct; (**b**) 2017_direct; (**c**) 2012_indirect; (**d**) 2017_indirect.

Figure 3a displays the sectoral DFW (driving force weight) and PFW (pulling force weight) in 2012 and 2017, representing the control and dependent degrees of a sector on the USWS. AM's DFW and PFW were the highest; the values of DFW were 71.34% in 2012 and 55.43% in 2017; the values of PFW were 16.90% in 2012 and 17.89 % in 2017. These results indicate that AM was the biggest control sector and dependent sector that affected upstream sectors (basic industries that provide raw materials and primary products) and downstream sectors (advanced industry that consumes products from upstream). The sectoral total weight equals the difference between sectoral DFW and sectoral PFW. The sector was a controller in the system when DFW was greater than PFW, whereas the sector was a dependent sector in the system when DFW was smaller than PFW. Thus, AM finally acted as a controller, since its DFW was greater than PFW (Sectoral total weight = DFW−PFW > 0). It was obvious that AM and PM were dominant sectors that controlled the other producers, while the seven sectors (i.e., AGR, MIN, ELE, CON, TRA, WHO, and OTH) depended on the other sectors' product supply. In 2017, the total weight of AM and PM decreased by 7.34% compared with 2012 due to reduced economic production scales. Generally, the ecological hierarchy structure was not healthy due to the high sectoral total weight value of AM. Carrying out reduction measures from the production side (especially from AM) could be helpful for adjusting hierarchy structure of the USWS.

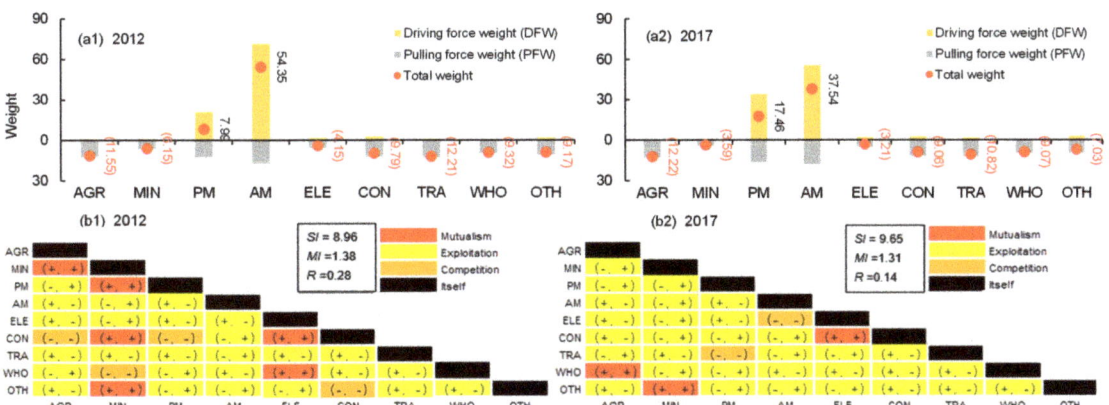

Figure 3. Ecological network analysis. (**a1**) sectoral DFW and PFW in 2012; (**a2**) sectoral DFW and PFW in 2017; (**b1**) sectoral pairwise relationships in 2012; (**b2**) sectoral pairwise relationships in 2017.

Figure 3b shows the sectoral pairwise relationships related to solid waste production in 2012 and 2017, with a total of 45 pairs of relationships in each year. Exploitation relationships contributed 54.77% and 68.89% to all pairs of relationships in 2012 and 2017. The proportions of mutualism relationships were 13.33% in 2012 and 6.67% in 2017. High value of SI (i.e., $SI = 8.96 > 0$ in 2012, $SI = 9.65 > 0$ in 2017) indicated the synergistic effect of the USWS. A high value of MI (i.e., $MI = 1.38 > 1$ in 2012, $MI = 1.31 > 1$ in 2017) showed that the USWS was mutualistic. Results of sectoral pairwise relationships were acceptable for decision makers. However, the number of mutualism relationships in 2017 was less than that in 2012. In order to make the USWS more beneficial, exploitation relationships needed to be transformed to mutualism relationships, as much as possible, through adjusting strategies. It was also found that the production structure of Fujian had little changes.

4.2. Identification of Key Factors

Based on the former status analysis, the effects of different sectoral solid waste production coefficients and sectoral direct consumption coefficients on USWS performance can be quantified. The designed factors, and corresponding experimental scenarios, are presented in Table A2. Figure 4 presents half-normal plots of the standardized effects. The further a factor lies away from the red line, the corresponding effect is more obvious. The significant factors that affected the SPI were AM_a, PM_a, AM_e and PM_e. The most important factor causing solid waste pollution in Fujian Province was AM_a, which contributed 64.71% in 2012 and 51.14% in 2017, followed by PM_a accounting for 22.01% and 37.04%. SPI was sensitive to the changes in sectoral direct consumption coefficients of AM and PM. These results implied that unit GDP solid waste production of AM and PM were higher than in other sectors. The contributions of AM_a decreased and PM_a increased in 2017, indicating that the Fujian Province gradually focused on the economic development of PM.

Figure 5 shows the effect plots of significant factors, which described the single and joint effects of the imperative factors on SPI. In Figure 5(a1,b1), results indicate that PM_a, AM_a, ELE_a and OTH_a had negative effects on SPIm, while other factors had positive effects on SPI. For example, in 2012, the average value of SPI was 0.632 under L level of PM_a and 0.533 under H level of PM_a. To reduce the SPI of USWS, the increment of factors that had negative effects, and the decrement of factors that had positive effects, might be helpful. In terms of joint effects presented in Figure 5(a2,b2), the most significant interactions between two sectors were CON_e*OTH_e in 2012 (contributed 1.53%) and TRA_e*OTH_e in 2017 (contributed 2.53%). The two crossed lines denote that the effect of another factor changes when one factor is at different levels. These demonstrated that control of the economic products of social service sectors (e.g., public infrastructure management sub-sector, culture, sports and entertainment sub-sector) can help reduce the SPI, even if the amounts of solid waste production of CON and TRA increased.

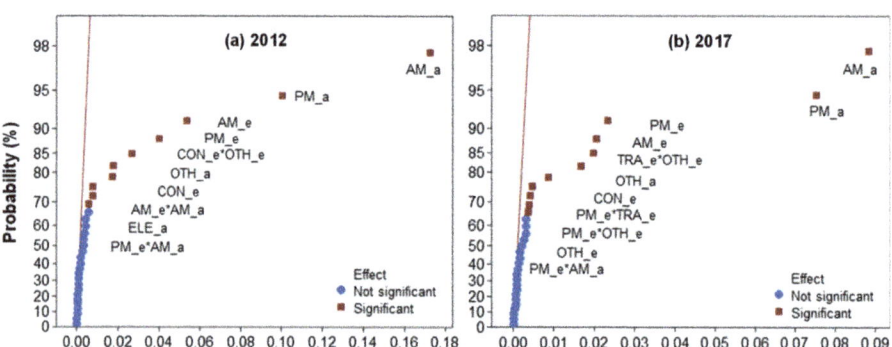

Figure 4. Half-normal plots of the standardized effects: (a) 2012; (b) 2017.

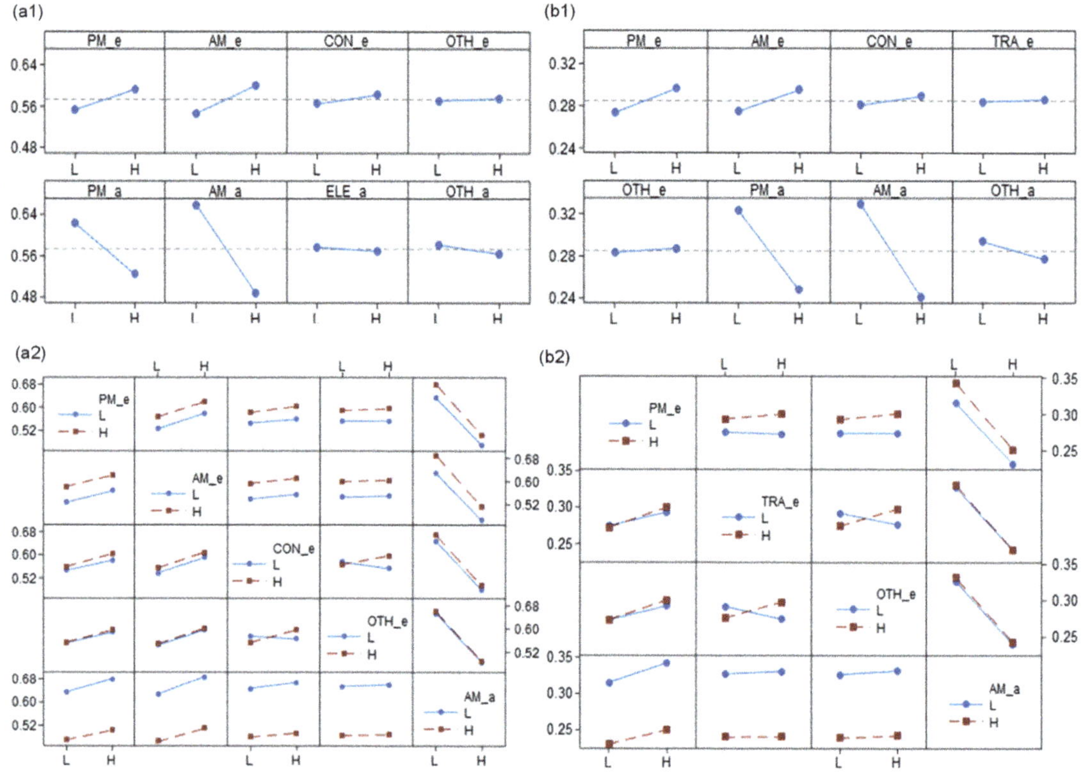

Figure 5. Effect plots of significant factors. (a1) main effect in 2012; (a2) joint effect in 2012; (b1) main effect in 2017; (b2) joint effect in 2017.

4.3. Adjustment of USWS

Figure 6 presents the values of solid waste production intensity (SPI) under 32 scenarios, showing the value of SPI was volatile. The SPI approached 0.487 (under S32) in 2012 and reached 0.228 (under S32) in 2017. The SPI decreased by 1.43% (under S4) to

18.89% (under S1) in 2012, and the SPI declined by 3.51% (under S6) to 17.98% (under S1) in 2017. Under S1, the strictest direct solid waste reduction policy was implemented in all sectors, while the sectoral direct consumption coefficients were maintained at high levels. Under S4 and S6, the loose direct solid waste reduction policy was implemented to PM, while the sectoral direct consumption coefficients of PM and AM were maintained at high levels. This implies that conducting strict environmental policy on AM and PM, as well as reducing the commodity consumption of CON, TRA, and OTH from other sectors (e.g., improve material usage efficiency and develop advanced material) would be useful for reducing SPI of the USWS.

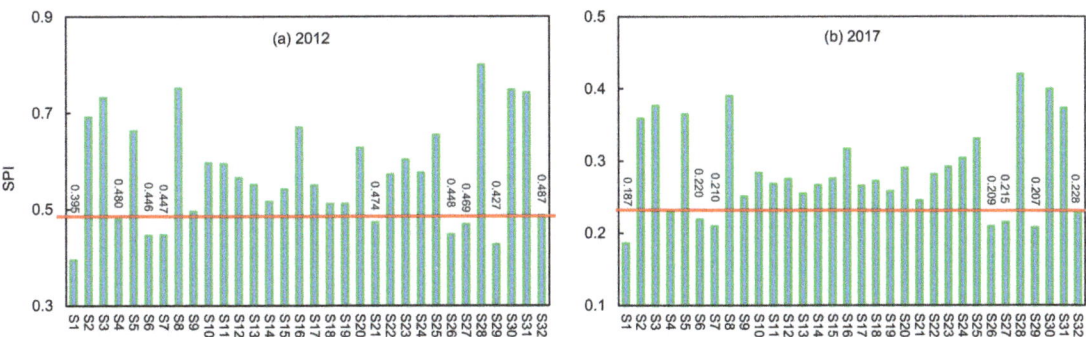

Figure 6. The values of solid waste production intensity (SPI) under 32 scenarios: (**a**) 2012; (**b**) 2017. ("S" means "Scenario).

Figures 7–9 describe results of sectoral solid waste production and ecological network analysis under six scenarios in 2012 and 2017. Corresponding SPI values were lower than the actual values. In Figure 7, results showed that the amounts of solid waste production decreased by 3.82% (under S27) to 17.95% (under S1) in 2012 and decreased by 3.39% (under S27) to 16.30% (under S1) in 2017. The reduction of AM solid waste production was the highest among all sectors. In 2012, the amount decreased 34.438 × 10^6 t (under S27) to 49.834 × 10^6 t (under S1); in 2017, the amount reduced 1.511 × 10^6 t (under S27) to 13.885 × 10^6 t (under S1). These results reveal that the selected scenarios can effectively reduce solid waste production. In Figure 8, results indicate that the total weights of all sectors changed with the varied scenarios, implying that the system hierarchy structure was sensitive to the variations in factors. In 2012, the total weight of PM and AM were in the range of 61.47% (under S1) and 63.71% (under S4), an increase of −0.87% to 1.37% compared with that under S32. In 2017, the total weight of PM and AM was in the range of 53.53% (under S1) and 54.24% (under S6), a decrease by 0.75% to 1.46% compared with that under S32. According to former descriptions in status analysis, it was desired that the total weight of PM and AM should decrease. These results indicate that the selected designed scenarios could help adjust the hierarchical structure of USWS. In Figure 9, results show that the number of mutualistic, competitive, and exploitation relationships had no obvious changes; other measurements needed to be detected.

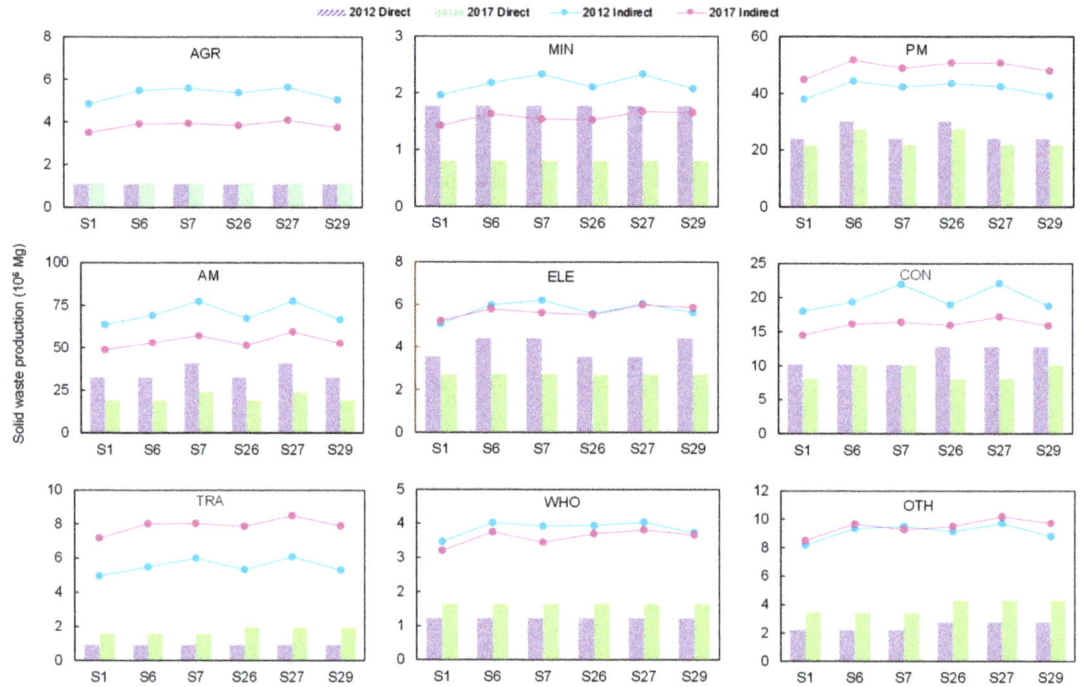

Figure 7. Sectoral urban solid waste production under different scenarios.

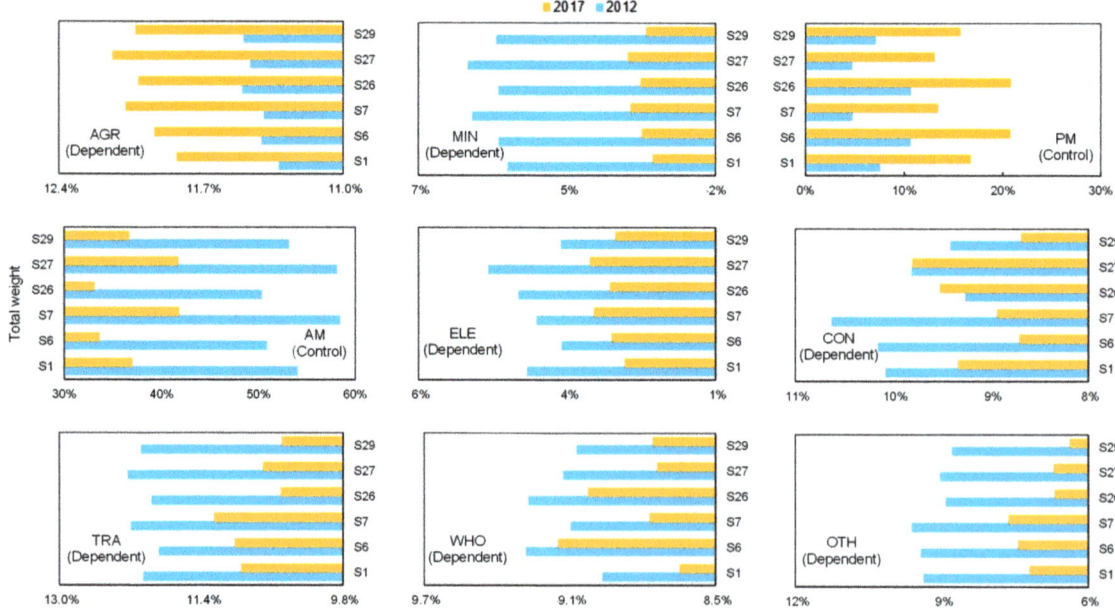

Figure 8. Sectoral total weight under different scenarios.

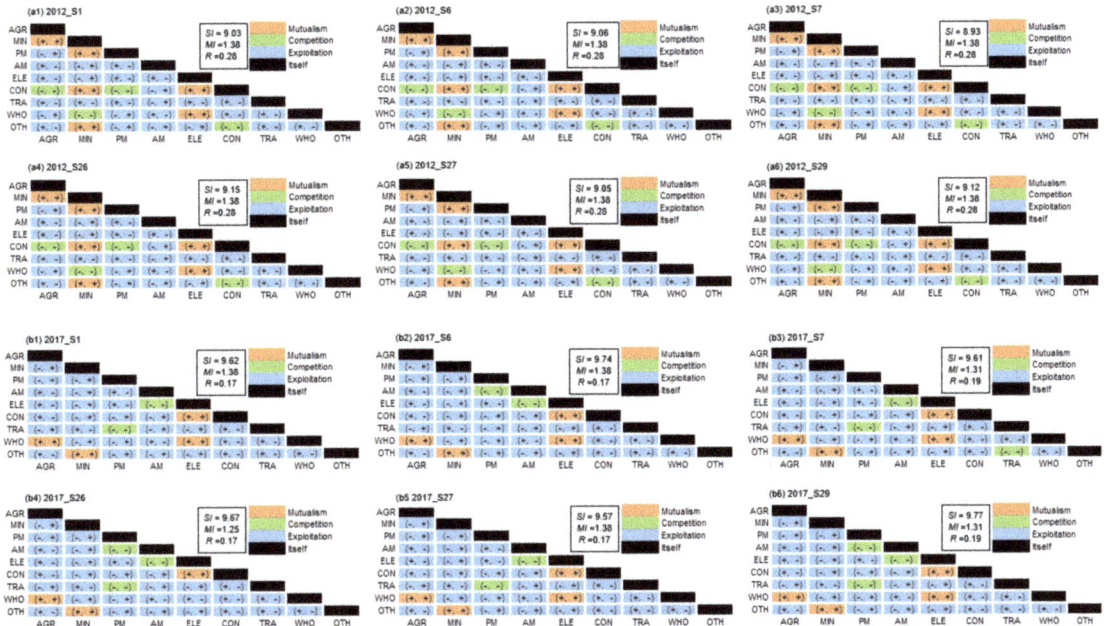

Figure 9. Pairwise sectoral relationships under different scenarios. (**a1**) 2012_S1; (**a2**) 2012_S6; (**a3**) 2012_S7; (**a4**) 2012_S26; (**a5**) 2012_S27; (**a6**) 2012_S29; (**b1**) 2017_S1; (**b2**) 2017_S6; (**b3**) 2017_S7; (**b4**) 2017_S26; (**b5**) 2017_S27; (**b6**) 2017_S29.

5. Conclusions

A factorial ecological-extended physical input-output model (FE-PIOM) was developed for enhancing urban solid waste system (USWS) performance, which integrated techniques of physical input-output model (PIOM), ecological network analysis (ENA), and fractional factorial analysis (FFA). The FE-PIOM could effectively assess urban solid waste productions and embodied flow path, quantify single and joint effects of multiple factors, as well as provide sound urban solid waste reduction path. The developed FE-PIOM was employed to a real case study of Fujian, an important economic development province in China, for supporting the tradeoff between economic development and environmental protection.

The main findings are summarized as: (i) the amount of indirect waste production was higher than the direct waste production, with the indirect production occupying more than 60 to 70% of the total production (i.e., the sum of direct and indirect productions); (ii) the indirect waste flows were more complicated than those of direct flows; (iii) solid waste mainly was produced by primary manufacturing (PM) and advanced manufacturing (AM), accounting for 30% and 38% of the total production, respectively; (iv) AM was the biggest sector which controlled the other producers, while its control weight was too high (35 to 50% of the total weight); (v) the USWS was mutualistic due to $SI > 0$ and $MI > 1$; (vi) AM_a (i.e., direct consumption coefficient of AM) and PM_a (i.e., direct consumption coefficient of PM) were the most important factors which had negative effects on USWS solid waste production intensity (SPI), contributing 50–60% and 22–37% to standard effects; (vii) the interactions between CON_e*OTH_e (i.e., solid waste production of CON*solid waste production of OTH) and TRA_e*OTH_e were obvious; (viii) for enhancing USWS performance, reducing the commodity consumption of AM and PM from other sectors by 20% (e.g., improve material usage efficiency and develop advanced material), as well as decreasing economic activities of CON, TRA, and OTH by 20%, would be useful.

This is the first attempt to apply the FE-PIOM to a real-world case, and results can support decision makers to adjust related economic activity strategies for reducing urban solid waste production, improving ecological hierarchy structure and promoting ecological pairwise relationships. More efforts can be made in future work. This research used the input-output tables of 2012 and 2017 due to data limitation; meanwhile, the production structure of Fujian had little changes in previous years. Predicting future input-output tables (e.g., for the periods of 2021–2025, 2026–2030, and 2031–2035) using the RAS method could help plan an optimal urban solid waste reduction path. It is essential to integrate fuzzy/stochastic analysis methods into the FE-PIOM to cope with the inherent uncertainties existing in economic growth, industrial structure transition and solid waste reduction.

Author Contributions: Conceptualization, methodology, writing—original draft, writing-review & editing, J.L.; conceptualization, funding acquisition, supervision, writing—review & editing, Y.L.; conceptualization, resources, G.H.; software, data duration, Y.Y.; methodology, X.W. All authors have read and agreed to the published version of the manuscript.

Funding: This research was funded by the National Key Research & Development Program of China (2016YFC0502803) and the Education Department of Fujian Province (JT180453).

Institutional Review Board Statement: Not applicable.

Informed Consent Statement: Not applicable.

Acknowledgments: This research was supported by the National Key Research and Development Program of China (2016YFC0502803) and the Education Department of Fujian Province (JT180453). The authors are grateful to the editors and the anonymous reviewers for their insightful comments and suggestions.

Conflicts of Interest: The authors declare that they have no known competing financial interests or personal relationships that could have appeared to influence the work reported in this paper.

Appendix A

Table A1. Summarization of Previous Literature.

Category	Description	References
Physical input-output model	Investigate the impacts of four categories of solid waste recycling on urban solid waste metabolism to support sustainable development.	Liang and Zhang
	Estimate the regional energy and environmental benefits of solid waste utili-zation for energy recovery.	Wang et al.
	Rank economic sectors based on solid waste productions and pointed out potential areas to pursue innovations in material use.	Meyer et al.
	Quantify different types of solid waste production recycling over the period 2005–2017 in China.	Huang et al.
Ecological network analysis	Analyze the directions, locations, and drivers of carbon flows resulting from global trade.	Zhang et al.
	Evaluate water-related impacts of energy-related decisions.	Wang et al.
	Estimate the metabolic status of energy system in China.	Wang
	Investigate integral carbon emissions at city scale.	Zhang et al.
Fractional factorial analysis	Experimental designs for detecting response sensitivity in environmental fields.	Jiang et al. Gerrewey et al. Li et al.

Appendix B

Table A2. Designed Scenarios.

Scenario	PM_e	AM_e	ELE_e (in 2012) / CON_e (in 2017)	CON_e (in 2012) / TRA_e (in 2017)	OTH_e	PM_a	AM_a	ELE_a (in 2012) / CON_a (in 2017)	CON_a (in 2012) / TRA_a (in 2017)	OTH_a
1	L	L	L	L	L	H	H	H	H	H
2	H	L	L	L	L	L	L	L	L	H
3	L	H	L	L	L	L	L	L	H	L
4	H	H	L	L	L	H	H	H	L	L
5	L	L	H	L	L	L	L	H	L	L
6	H	L	H	L	L	H	H	L	H	L
7	L	H	H	L	L	H	H	L	L	H
8	H	H	H	L	L	L	L	H	H	H
9	L	L	L	H	L	L	H	L	L	L
10	H	L	L	H	L	H	L	H	H	L
11	L	H	L	H	L	H	L	H	L	H
12	H	H	L	H	L	L	H	L	H	H
13	L	L	H	H	L	H	L	L	H	H
14	H	L	H	H	L	L	H	H	L	H
15	L	H	H	H	L	L	H	H	H	L
16	H	H	H	H	L	H	L	L	L	L
17	L	L	L	L	H	H	L	L	L	L
18	H	L	L	L	H	L	H	H	H	L
19	L	H	L	L	H	L	H	H	L	H
20	H	H	L	L	H	H	L	L	H	H
21	L	L	H	L	H	L	H	L	H	H
22	H	L	H	L	H	H	L	H	L	H
23	L	H	H	L	H	H	L	H	H	L
24	H	H	H	L	H	L	H	L	L	L
25	L	L	L	H	H	L	L	H	H	H
26	H	L	L	H	H	H	H	L	L	H
27	L	H	L	H	H	H	H	L	H	L
28	H	H	L	H	H	L	L	H	L	L
29	L	L	H	H	H	H	H	H	L	L
30	H	L	H	H	H	L	L	L	H	L
31	L	H	H	H	H	L	L	L	L	H
32	H	H	H	H	H	H	H	H	H	H

References

1. Batista, M.; Caiado, R.G.G.; Quelhas, O.L.G.; Lima, G.B.A.; Filho, W.L.; Yparraguirre, I.T.R. A framework for sustainable and integrated municipal solid waste management: Barriers and critical factors to developing countries. *J. Clean. Prod.* **2021**, *312*, 127516. [CrossRef]
2. Karagoz, S.; Deveci, M.; Simic, A.; Aydin, N.; Bolukbas, U. A novel intuitionistic fuzzy MCDM-based CODAS approach for locating an authorized dismantling center: A case study of Istanbul. *Waste Manag. Res.* **2020**, 1–13. [CrossRef]
3. *China Statistical Yearbook*; National Bureau of Statistics Press: Beijing, China, 2020. (In Chinese)
4. Simic, V.; Karagoz, S.; Deveci, M.; Aydin, N. Picture fuzzy extension of the CODAS method for multi-criteria vehicle shredding facility location. *Expert Syst. Appl.* **2021**, *175*, 114644. [CrossRef]
5. Danilina, V.; Grigoriev, A. Information provision in environmental policy design. *J. Environ. Inform.* **2020**, *36*, 1–10. [CrossRef]
6. Xu, X.; Huang, G.; Liu, L.; He, C. A factorial environment-oriented input-output model for diagnosing urban air pollution. *J. Clean. Prod.* **2019**, *237*, 117731. [CrossRef]
7. Xing, L.; Dong, X.; Guan, J.; Qiao, X. Betweenness centrality for similarity weight network and its application to measuring industrial sectors' pivotability on the global value chain. *Phys. A Stat. Mech. Appl.* **2018**, *516*, 19–36. [CrossRef]
8. Liang, S.; Qu, S.; Xu, M. Betweenness-based method to identify critical transmission sectors for supply chain environmental pressure mitigation. *Environ. Sci. Technol.* **2016**, *50*, 1330–1337. [CrossRef]
9. Leontief, W. *Input-Output Economics*; Oxford University Press: Oxford, UK, 1986.
10. Towa, E.; Zeller, V.; Achten, W.M.J. Input-output models and waste management analysis: A critical review. *J. Clean. Prod.* **2020**, *249*, 119359. [CrossRef]

11. Liang, S.; Zhang, T.Z. Comparing urban solid waste recycling from the viewpoint of urban metabolism based on physical input–output model: A case of Suzhou in China. *Waste Manag.* **2012**, *32*, 220–225. [CrossRef]
12. Wang, H.N.; Wang, X.E.; Song, J.N.; Wang, S.; Liu, X.Y. Uncovering regional energy and environmental benefits of urban waste utilization: A physical input-output analysis for a city case. *J. Clean. Prod.* **2018**, *189*, 922–932. [CrossRef]
13. Meyera, D.E.; Li, M.; Ingwersen, W.W. Analyzing economy-scale solid waste generation using the United States environmentally-extended input-output model. *Resour. Conserv. Recycl.* **2020**, *157*, 104795. [CrossRef]
14. Huang, Q.; Chen, G.W.; Wang, Y.F.; Xu, L.X.; Chen, W.Q. Identifying the socioeconomic drivers of solid waste recycling in China for the period 2005–2017. *Sci. Total Environ.* **2020**, *725*, 138137. [CrossRef]
15. Balogun, A.; Quan, S.; Pradhan, B.; Dano, U.; Yekeen, S. An improved flood susceptibility model for assessing the correlation of flood hazard and property prices using geospatial technology and fuzzy-ANP. *J. Environ. Inform.* **2021**, *37*, 1–10. [CrossRef]
16. Zhang, Y.; Li, Y.G.; Hubacek, K.; Tian, X.; Lu, Z.M. Analysis of CO_2 transfer processes involved in global trade based on ecological network analysis. *Appl. Energy* **2019**, *233–234*, 576–583. [CrossRef]
17. Wang, S.; Fath, B.; Chen, B. Energy-water nexus under energy mix scenarios using input-output and ecological network analyses. *Appl. Energy* **2019**, *232–234*, 827–839. [CrossRef]
18. Wang, R. Ecological network analysis of China's energy-related input from the supply side. *J. Clean. Prod.* **2020**, *272*, 122796. [CrossRef]
19. Zheng, H.M.; Li, A.M.; Meng, F.X.; Liu, G.Y.; Hu, Y.C.; Zhang, Y.; Casazza, M. Ecological network analysis of carbon emissions from four Chinese metropoles in multiscale economies. *J. Clean. Prod.* **2021**, *279*, 123226. [CrossRef]
20. Montoya, A.C.V.; Mazareli, R.C.S.; Delforno, T.P.; Centurion, V.B.; Oliveira, V.M.; Silva, E.L.; Varesche, M.B.A. Optimization of key factors affecting hydrogen production from coffee waste using factorial design and metagenomic analysis of the microbial community. *Int. J. Hydrog. Energy* **2020**, *45*, 4205–4222. [CrossRef]
21. Yang, Y.; Huang, T.T.; Shi, Y.Z.; Wendroth, O.; Liu, B.Y. Comparing the performance of an autoregressive state-space approach to the linear regression and artificial neural network for streamflow estimation. *J. Environ. Inform.* **2021**, *37*, 1–10. [CrossRef]
22. Liu, J.; Li, Y.P.; Huang, G.H.; Fu, H.Y.; Zhang, J.L.; Cheng, G.H. Identification of water quality management policy of watershed system with multiple uncertain interactions using a multi-level-factorial risk-inference-based possibilistic-probabilistic programming approach. *Environ. Sci. Pollut. Res.* **2017**, *24*, 14980–15000. [CrossRef]
23. Lagrandeur, J.; Croquer, S.; Poncet, S.; Sorin, M. A 2D numerical benchmark of an air Ranque-Hilsch vortex tube based on a fractional factorial design. *Int. Commun. Heat Mass Transf.* **2021**, *125*, 105310. [CrossRef]
24. Jiang, Y.; Zhang, Y.; Banks, C.; Heaven, S.; Longhurst, P. Investigation of the impact of trace elements on anaerobic volatile fatty acid degradation using a fractional factorial experimental design. *Water Res.* **2017**, *125*, 458–465. [CrossRef]
25. Gerrewey, T.V.; Ameloot, N.; Navarrete, O.; Vandecruys, M.; Perneel, M.; Boon, N.; Geelen, D. Microbial activity in peat-reduced plant growing media: Identifying influential growing medium constituents and physicochemical properties using fractional factorial design of experiments. *J. Clean. Prod.* **2020**, *256*, 120303. [CrossRef]
26. Li, S.; Zhao, T.Y.; Chu, C.Q.; Wang, J.Q.; Alam, M.S.; Tong, T. Lateral cyclic response sensitivity of rectangular bridge piers confined with UHPFRC tube using fractional factorial design. *Eng. Struct.* **2021**, *235*, 111883. [CrossRef]
27. Almazán-Gómez, M.A.; Duarte, R.; Langarita, R.; Sánchez-Chóliz, J. Effects of water re-allocation in the Ebro river basin: A multiregional input-output and geographical analysis. *J. Environ. Manag.* **2019**, *241*, 645–657. [CrossRef]
28. Shafiei, M.; Moosavirad, S.H.; Azimifard, A.; Biglari, S. Water consumption assessment in Asian chemical industries supply chains based on input-output analysis and one-way analysis of variance. *Environ. Sci. Pollut. Res.* **2020**, *27*, 12242–12255. [CrossRef]
29. Chen, B.; Yang, Q.; Zhou, S.L.; Li, J.S.; Chen, G.Q. Urban Economy's Carbon flow through external trade: Spatial-temporal evolution for macao. *Energy Policy* **2017**, *110*, 69–78. [CrossRef]
30. He, C.Y.; Huang, G.H.; Liu, L.R.; Xu, X.L.; Li, Y.P. Evolution of virtual water metabolic network in developing regions: A case study of Guangdong province. *Ecol. Indic.* **2020**, *108*, 105750. [CrossRef]
31. Zhai, M.Y.; Huang, G.H.; Liu, L.R.; Su, S. Dynamic input-output analysis for energy metabolism system in the Province of Guangdong, China. *J. Clean. Prod.* **2018**, *196*, 747–762. [CrossRef]
32. Owen, A.; Scott, K.; Barrett, J. Identifying critical supply chains and final products: An input-output approach to exploring the energy-water-food nexus. *Appl. Energy* **2018**, *210*, 632–642. [CrossRef]
33. Fath, B.D.; Patten, B.C. Review of the foundations of network environ analysis. *Ecosystems* **1999**, *2*, 167–179. [CrossRef]
34. Xia, C.Y.; Chen, B. Urban land-carbon nexus based on ecological network analysis. *Appl. Energy* **2020**, *276*, 115465. [CrossRef]
35. Fang, D.L.; Chen, B. Ecological network analysis for a virtual water network. *Environ. Sci. Technol.* **2015**, *49*, 6722–6730. [CrossRef] [PubMed]
36. Norouzi-Ghazbi, S.; Akbarzadeh, A.; Akbarzadeh-T, M.R. Application of Taguchi design in system identification: A simple, generally applicable and powerful method. *Measurement* **2020**, *151*, 106879. [CrossRef]
37. Montgomery, D.C. *Design and Analysis of Experiments*; John Wiley & Sons: Hoboken, NJ, USA, 1976.
38. *Statistical Yearbook of Fujian Province*; Fujian Provincial Bureau of Statistics: Fuzhou, China, 2013. (In Chinese). Available online: https://www.chinayearbooks.com/fujian-statistical-yearbook.html (accessed on 2 June 2021).
39. *Statistical Yearbook of Fujian Province*; Fujian Provincial Bureau of Statistics: Fuzhou, China, 2018. (In Chinese). Available online: https://www.chinayearbooks.com/fujian-statistical-yearbook-2018.html (accessed on 2 June 2021).

Article

Analytical Models for Seawater and Boron Removal through Reverse Osmosis

Michael Binns

Department of Chemical and Biochemical Engineering, Dongguk University, 30 Pildong-ro 1-gil, Jung-gu, Seoul 04620, Korea; mbinns@dongguk.edu

Abstract: Regarding the purification of seawater, it is necessary to reduce both the total concentration of salt and also the concentration of boron to meet purity requirements for safe drinking water. For this purpose reverse osmosis membrane modules can be designed based on experimental data supported by computer models to determine energy efficient configurations and operating conditions. In previous studies numerical models have been suggested to predict the performance of the removal with respect to difference pressures, pH values, and temperatures. Here, an analytical model is suggested which allows for both the simplified fitting of the parameters required for predicting boron transport coefficients and also the simple equations that can be used for the design of combined seawater and boron removal systems. This modelling methodology is demonstrated through two case studies including FilmTec and Saehan membrane modules. For both cases the model is shown to be able to predict the performance with similar accuracy compared with existing finite-difference type numerical models from the literature.

Keywords: desalination; reverse osmosis; modelling; simulation; parameter estimation; seawater; boron

Citation: Binns, M. Analytical Models for Seawater and Boron Removal through Reverse Osmosis. *Sustainability* **2021**, *13*, 8999. https://doi.org/10.3390/su13168999

Academic Editors: Julian Scott Yeomans and Mariia Kozlova

Received: 14 July 2021
Accepted: 10 August 2021
Published: 11 August 2021

Publisher's Note: MDPI stays neutral with regard to jurisdictional claims in published maps and institutional affiliations.

Copyright: © 2021 by the author. Licensee MDPI, Basel, Switzerland. This article is an open access article distributed under the terms and conditions of the Creative Commons Attribution (CC BY) license (https://creativecommons.org/licenses/by/4.0/).

1. Introduction

Due to global population growth and the spread of pollution it is becoming more challenging to provide clean drinking. A sustainable method for obtaining clean water is through seawater desalination by reverse osmosis. A reverse osmosis membrane system is composed of high-pressure pumps, one or more reverse osmosis membranes, and energy recovery devices which are designed to meet purity requirements while also minimizing energy consumption. The pressure of the seawater supplied by the high-pressure pump varies depending on the salt concentration of the seawater. The standard criteria in the seawater desalination process is the concentration of TDS (total dissolved solids) and boron in fresh water. The WHO (World Health Organization) states that the palatability of water with TDS lower than 600 mg/L is considered good and they specify guidelines for 2.4 mg/L of boron [1], although lower values are generally preferred. These WHO criteria have an impact on the design of the seawater reverse osmosis (SWRO) processes such that both salt rejection and boron rejection must be considered.

The removal of boron through reverse osmosis is complicated by the fact that boron exists in seawater mainly as boric acid and borate ions (with negligible concentrations of other boron compounds) [2]. This is a problem because reverse osmosis membranes are known to easily permeate only the negatively charged borate ions while having more difficulty removing the neutrally charged boric acid [3]. For this reason the pH should typically be increased to give higher fractions of borate ions [2]. This has been demonstrated using FilmTec membranes which are shown to give very high boron rejection at high pH values [4]. Additionally, Koseoglu et al. tested FilmTec and Toray membranes and found that around 85–90% rejection is possible at pH 8.2 while pH 11 allows for 98% or higher rejection using both membranes [5]. More recently Ali et al. have developed a membrane material which is able to achieve 99% boron rejection at pH 10 [6]. At a lower pH of 8 Li et al.

have developed a membrane modification process which embeds 4-nitrobenzenesulfonyl chloride into an existing membrane and is able to increase the boron rejection from 82.12% up to 93.1% [7]. In addition to the development of new materials, the design of feed spacers inside the membrane modules is also important. A review of the impact of feed spacer design by Haidari et al. discusses their effects on pressure drop, flux through the membrane, and fouling [8]. Additionally, it is suggested by Ruiz-Garcia and Nuez based on experimental and modelling results that feed spacers should be chosen based on the designed operating conditions to reduce energy consumption and enhance the quality of the permeate [9].

In order to meet boron drinking water criteria, a multistage design of reverse osmosis modules is typically required [2]. For example, Tu et al. state that in practice a first stage with natural pH might be used to reduce TDS and a second stage with elevated pH might be used to remove boron [10]. In addition to reverse osmosis, Najid et al. consider and discuss alternative technologies for boron removal including electrocoagulation, adsorption, ion exchange, and various other membrane processes such as forward osmosis and membrane distillation [2]. Their comparison showed that reverse osmosis has the potential to remove boron but can be uneconomical due to high energy requirements and the requirement to alter pH, and hence they suggest that a hybrid process combining different technologies could be the best solution [2]. To reduce the costs of two-stage processes Ban et al. also consider a hybrid process with one stage of forward osmosis followed by a second stage with reverse osmosis [11]. They compare this against a two-stage reverse osmosis design and show that the costs associated with chemically altering the pH can be eliminated by using the hybrid forward osmosis plus reverse osmosis process, but this comes at the expense of higher capital costs [11]. Instead of chemical modification Jung et al. have suggested electrochemical modification using a layer of carbon nanotubes on the membrane surface as a cathode to increase the pH. While this does increase boron rejection over 90% it also causes some scaling [12]. In another recent study a hybrid system is suggested combining electro dialysis as a pretreatment with a nanofiltration reverse osmosis to enhance the overall boron removal [13].

Despite this progress in membrane materials and potential hybrid systems there is still the need for modelling and optimization of such systems. This would allow, for example, the prediction of salt and boron rejection for wide ranges of possible conditions to identify low energy and low cost designs. For example, Ruiz-Garcia et al. use modelling to compare the performance of two different Toray membranes (TM820L-440 and TM820S-400) for the purpose of boron removal over a range of conditions and show that the TM820L-440 generally gives lower boron concentrations of under 1ppm [14].

Modelling can also be used to simulate and compare different configurations of separators to further enhance energy efficiency. For example, Al-Obaidi et al. evaluated the performance of a multistage reverse osmosis system with varying operating parameters through a modelling approach [15]. In other work Al-Obaidi et al. also utilized modelling to compare a number of different recycling options in a multistage reverse osmosis membrane process [16]. More recently Alsarayreh et al. also used a modelling approach to investigate different retentate recycle ratios [17].

The review of Alsarayreh et al. shows that a larger number of models have been developed for the prediction of performance for spiral wound reverse osmosis membrane modules [18]. These models can be divided into two categories: numerical models which discretize the length of the module and formulate model equations using finite difference type methods, and analytical models which use integration of model equations to obtain expressions for directly calculating the outlet conditions. While the majority of models developed have been for steady state solutions, model equations can also be solved dynamically as shown by Joseph and Damodaran [19]. Regarding steady state modelling, Ben Boudinar et al. have developed a numerical model solved through finite differences and they show that their model fits well for desalination of brackish water but is less accurate for seawater desalination [20]. They suggest that this is due to an inaccuracy in the mass transfer coefficient [20]. This has been addressed by Senthilmurugan et al. who also fitted parameters for mass transfer correlations as well as solving the model equations using finite differences [21]. In other studies, such as the work of Geraldes et al., mass transfer correlations for "typical spiral wound modules" are assumed to be valid [22]. While Geraldes et al. do not provide validation for their model they have fitted water and salt transport coefficients which are then used to optimize the configuration and operating conditions of a two-stage desalination system [22].

Following these works numerical models have also been developed to predict the removal of boron. For example, the study of Mane et al. developed a finite elements model to predict the removal of boron [23]. In that study the parameters and correlations for boron transport coefficients developed by Hyung and Kim based on experimental results are used to account for the effects of pH and temperature [24]. Another study of Ruiz-Garcia et al. proposed a function for boron permeability in terms of feed pressure, temperature, and operating time based on plant data which might also be used in modelling studies [25]. Alternatively the model developed by Sassi et al. [26] used a finite-difference type numerical model which accounts for boron permeation using data and correlations from the experimental study of Taniguchi et al. [27]. More recently the study of Du et al. [28] also considered boron removal through numerical models based on a combination of the equations from the studies of Geraldes et al. [22] and Hyung and Kim [24] which they use to optimize a superstructure of different configurations.

A number of studies have also developed analytical models where the model equations are integrated to give analytical expressions. For example, Avlonitis et al. developed equations for calculating the variation of concentration, pressure, and flow rates along the length of the module, although they assume that the mass transfer coefficient is constant along the length [29]. More recently Sundaramoorthy et al. suggested an analytical model which includes the variation of the mass transfer coefficient across the length [30]. They have demonstrated the validity of their approach through the removal of chlorophenol [31] and dimethylphenol [32] from waste water where they show how model parameters and parameters for mass transfer coefficients can be estimated through linear fitting of experimentally measured values. Following these earlier studies an analytical model was developed by Fraidenraich et al. for the desalination of brackish water which they showed to be accurate for the conditions tested [33]. Additionally, Al-Obaidi et al. have published numerous models including the development of analytical expressions from integration [34] and using average pressure and salt concentrations to simplify calculations which can be used to evaluate and test different configurations of modules [35].

While great progress has been made simulating desalination membrane modules using finite-difference type numerical models, these models generally involve large numbers of equations (due to the discretization) which can be solved simultaneously or possibly sequentially using numerical algorithms. Meanwhile, analytical models will have a relatively small number of equations which can be solved using less computational time and simpler algorithms; for example, in a spreadsheet program. Hence, analytical models should be more suitable for the design and optimization of multistage configurations which require the simulation of individual module performance a large number of times, provided they are shown to give reasonable accuracy.

However, to the best of our knowledge, there has not been any analytical model (based on integration of model equations) which has been developed to predict the removal of both salt and boron simultaneously. Therefore, for this reason, a combined salt and boron removal analytical model is developed here. Additionally, in many cases the fitting of parameters for spiral wound reverse osmosis models are often proposed based on nonlinear optimization using least-squares methods. In this study the methods of Sundaramoorthy et al. [30] and Avlonitis et al. [29] are extended such that all the model parameters can be estimated though simpler linear optimization in a new sequential parameter estimation procedure.

2. Development of a New Analytical Model for Predicting Salt and Boron Removal

The modelling equations given here are based on the method suggested by Sundaramoorthy et al. [30,31], who developed a model for the removal of organic solutes using spiral wound reverse osmosis membranes. Here, this model is modified in the following ways:

- Modified to use for seawater purification;
- Estimation of pressure drop coefficients for cases where outlet pressure is not measured;
- Including temperature dependence of water and salt transport coefficients;
- Including equations for boron transport.

2.1. Modelling Equations

The transport of water and salts through a membrane are typically described according to the solution–diffusion model which can be used to calculate the flux of water (J_W) and salt (J_S):

$$J_W = A_W(\Delta P - \Delta \pi) \qquad (1)$$

$$J_S = B_S(C_b - C_p) \qquad (2)$$

where ΔP and $\Delta \pi$ are the transmembrane pressure and osmotic pressure, and C_b and C_p are the brine-side and permeate-side concentrations of salt. A_W and B_S are the water and salt transport coefficients.

Accounting for the effect of concentration polarization which causes the concentration of salt to increase at the membrane surface, these equations should be modified to use the concentration of salt at the membrane wall (C_w). The concentration at the membrane wall can be calculated based on the following relation [30]:

$$\frac{C_w - C_p}{C_b - C_p} = exp\left(\frac{J_W}{k}\right) \qquad (3)$$

where k is the mass transfer coefficient and so that Equation (2) is modified:

$$J_S = B_S(C_w - C_p) \qquad (4)$$

The pressure drop can be estimated based on Darcy's law which might be written as [30]:

$$\frac{dP}{dx} = bF(x) \qquad (5)$$

which gives the pressure drop as a function of volume flow rate multiplied by a fixed parameter b. Alternatively, if knowledge about feed spacer geometry is available, pressure drop can also be estimated using more complex equations suggested by Koutsou et al. [36].

The osmotic pressure is a function of salt concentration and temperature. For low concentrations, such as those used in seawater, it may be approximated by the van't Hoff relation in Equation (6). Thus the transmembrane osmotic pressure can be calculated using Equation (7):

$$\pi = i\gamma TC \qquad (6)$$

$$\Delta \pi = i\gamma T(C_w - C_p) \qquad (7)$$

where γ is the gas law constant, T is temperature, and i is the number of ionic species formed. For the organic solutes considered by Sundaramoorthy, i is equal to 1 [31,32] but for NaCl the value of i is 2.

Combining and rearranging the above equations, the flux of water and the permeate salt concentration can be calculated as follows:

$$J_W = \frac{A_W \Delta P}{1 + \left(\frac{A_W i \gamma}{B_S}\right) TC_p} \qquad (8)$$

$$C_p = \frac{C_b}{\left[1 + \frac{(J_W/B_s)}{exp(J_W/k)}\right]} \quad (9)$$

The above equations can also be modified using a reflection coefficient, but for simplicity this will be assumed to be equal to 1.

To estimate the transport flux of boron an expression similar to Equation (4) can be used:

$$J_B = B_B(C_{Bw} - C_{Bp}) \quad (10)$$

where B_B is the boron transport coefficient and $C_{Bw} - C_{Bp}$ is the difference in boron concentrations. The wall concentration of boron can also be estimated with an equation similar to Equation (3) which also requires a mass transfer coefficient k_B:

$$\frac{C_{Bw} - C_{Bp}}{C_{Bb} - C_{Bp}} = exp\left(\frac{J_W}{k_B}\right) \quad (11)$$

$$C_{Bp} = \frac{C_{Bb}}{\left[1 + \frac{(J_W/B_B)}{exp(J_W/k_B)}\right]} \quad (12)$$

$$B_B = \frac{\{H^+\}}{\{H^+\} + K_{a1}} B_{(H_3BO_3)0} e^{(0.067(T-T_0))} + \frac{K_{a1}}{\{H^+\} + K_{a1}} B_{(H_2BO_3^-)0} e^{(0.049(T-T_0))} \quad (13)$$

To estimate the boron transport coefficients Hyung and Kim [24] proposed Equation (13) where they found the temperature dependence follows the same trend for all the membranes they tested. The effect of pH is included through the calculation of the fraction of boric acid (H_3BO_3) and borate ion ($H_2BO_3^-$) which have different transport coefficients: $B_{(H_3BO_3)0}$ and $B_{(H_2BO_3^-)0}$ (the values at $T = T_0$).

Various correlations have been proposed in the literature for estimating the mass transfer coefficient, although in most cases these correlations predict the Sherwood number (sh) as a function of the feed-side Reynolds number (Re_f) and Schmidt number (Sc) and also sometimes consider the permeate-side Reynolds number (Re_p) [31]. In this study the following general expression is considered:

$$sh = e^A \left(Re_f^B\right)\left(Re_p^C\right)\left(Sc^D\right) \quad (14)$$

To model the performance of a spiral wound reverse osmosis membrane for purification of seawater and boron, we made the following assumptions:

- Pressure drop is neglected in the permeate side;
- Darcy's law applies for pressure drop in the feed side;
- Validity of the solution–diffusion equations;
- Feed-side: velocity in the y and z directions is neglected;
- Permeate-side: velocity in the x and z directions is neglected;
- The unwound spiral can be represented by the diagram in Figure 1;
- The boron mass transfer coefficient is the same as that used for salt.

Based on these assumptions, Sundarmoorthy et al. showed that analytical solutions can be obtained for the pressure P, volume flow rate F, and water flux J_W [30,31]. The permeate-side fluid velocities are much lower than those on the retentate side and thus the permeate-side pressure drop should be significantly lower, which is why it is often neglected, allowing for the development of Equations (15)–(19) [30]. Additionally, it has been shown by Taniguchi et al. that the mass transfer coefficient for salt is very close to that of boron and so for simplicity they are considered equal in this study [27]. The equations for pressure and volume flow can be used to calculate the outlet pressure and outlet volume flow rate as given below:

$$F_o = F_i \cosh\phi - \frac{\phi \sinh\phi}{bL}\Delta P_i \quad (15)$$

$$P_o = P_i - \frac{bL}{\phi \sinh\phi}[(F_i + F_o)(\cosh(\phi) - 1)] \tag{16}$$

$$C_o = C_p + \frac{F_i(C_i - C_p)}{F_o}\cosh\phi - \frac{\phi \sinh\phi}{bL}\Delta P_i \tag{17}$$

where $\Delta P_i = P_i - P_p$ is the transmembrane pressure at the inlet and the ϕ is given by the following equation:

$$\phi = L\sqrt{\frac{WbA_w}{\left(1 + A_w\left(\frac{i\gamma}{B_S}\right)TC_p\right)}} \tag{18}$$

This parameter ϕ is a dimensionless number which is defined by Sundaramoorthy et al. in the following equation relating the second order derivative of the feed channel volume flow rate with respect to distance along the module [30]:

$$\frac{d^2 F(x)}{dx} = \frac{\phi^2}{L^2}F(x) \tag{19}$$

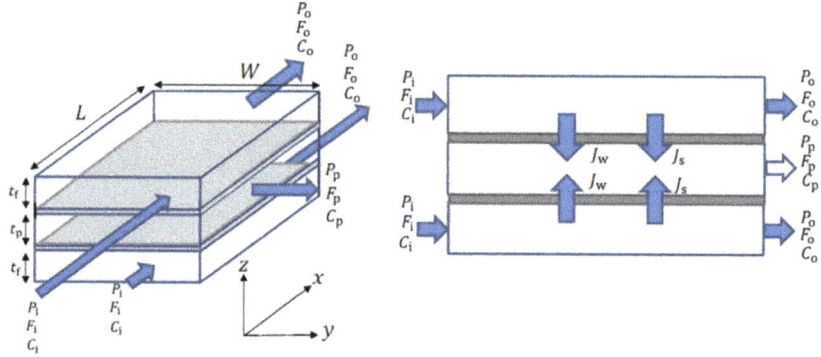

Figure 1. Spiral wound membrane geometry (unwound diagram).

2.2. Parameter Estimation

Based on the above equations a number of parameters need to be fit in order to model the performance of the spiral wound reverse osmosis membrane for the prediction of salt and boron removal. Hence, in this study we suggest the sequential procedure of parameter fitting steps as given in Figure 2. Sundaramoorthy et al. [30,31] suggested procedures for steps 1, 2, and 4 where they suggest linear fitting for steps 1 and 2 and a least-squares (presumably nonlinear) fitting for step 4. Additionally, in step 2 they assumed that A_w and B_S are fixed and do not change with temperature.

In the procedure shown in Figure 2, the first step should be to estimate pressure drop. Subsequently the water and salt transport coefficients A_w and B_S should be estimated for each inlet temperature such that the temperature dependence can be predicted. Steps 3 and 4 are independent of each other but both rely on parameters fitted in steps 1 and 2. All of these steps can be realized through linear fitting using experimentally measured values.

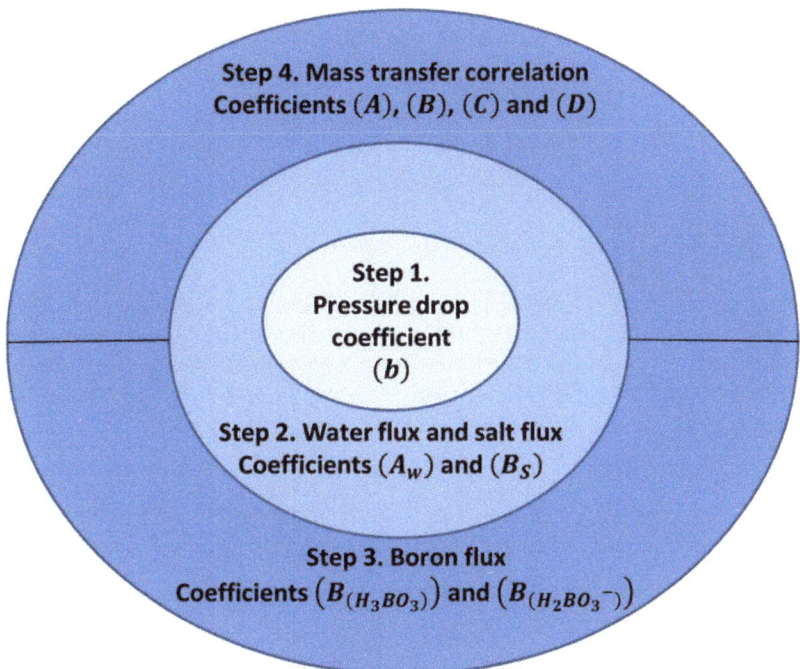

Figure 2. Parameter estimation steps for a spiral wound reverse osmosis desalination membrane.

2.2.1. Step 1. Pressure Drop Parameter Estimation

As mentioned above the pressure drop on the feed/brine side can be estimated through Darcy's law as given by Equation (5) which is written in terms of the volume flow. However, this can also be written as [21]:

$$\frac{dP}{dx} = k_{fb}\, \mu\, v_f^{n_f} \qquad (20)$$

where v_f is the feed-side fluid velocity, μ is the fluid viscosity, k_{fb} is a friction parameter, and n_f is a constant which is commonly assumed to be 1, although some studies have considered other values. For example, Sentilmurugan at al. also considered $n_f = 1.5$ and found that changing this value only had a small effect on results [21]. In this study it is assumed $n_f = 1$ and hence Equation (20) is equivalent to Equation (5).

The estimation of b is possible through plotting $P_o - P_i$ against $\frac{L}{\phi \sinh \phi}[(F_i + F_o)(\cosh(\phi) - 1)]$ (from Equation (16)) and fitting a linear expression should give b as the gradient, as suggested by Sundaramoorthy et al. [30,31].

However, this requires knowledge of the feed/brine side outlet pressure which may not be provided or possibly not measured as part of experimental studies looking at reverse osmosis desalination. In these cases the pressure drop might be estimated based on the maximum pressure drop specified by the manufacturer. For example, we might estimate that the highest flow rate tested experimentally gives a pressure drop which is 100% of the maximum:

$$b = \frac{P_{\text{dropmax}}}{L\, F_{i,\max}} \qquad (21)$$

Alternatively, if a friction factor is available the value of b can be readily found:

$$b = \frac{k_{fb}\, \mu}{A_f} \qquad (22)$$

where A_f is the cross sectional area of the feed channel and the viscosity is calculated for a single typical experimental inlet value.

2.2.2. Step 2. Water and Salt Transport Parameter Estimation

The values of coefficients A_w and B_S can be estimated based on the equations given by Sundaramoorthy et al. which are as follows [30,31]:

$$\phi = \cosh^{-1}\left[\frac{(F_i + F_o) - \beta \, F_o}{(F_i + F_o) - \beta F_i}\right] \tag{23}$$

$$\beta = \frac{P_i - P_o}{P_i - P_p} \tag{24}$$

The value of ϕ can be calculated directly from inlet and outlet volumetric flow rates and pressures. Hence, a plot of $1/\phi^2$ against TC_p should give a linear fitting which can be used to calculate the values of A_w and B_S:

$$\frac{1}{\phi^2} = \left(\frac{i\gamma}{L^2 WbB_S}\right)TC_p + \left(\frac{1}{L^2 WbA_w}\right) \tag{25}$$

This is the same as the equation given by Sundaramoorthy et al. [30,31] except with the addition of i to account for the presence of NaCl.

If the outlet pressures P_o are not measured then this can be estimated using the fitted b value and the following approximate expression:

$$P_i - P_o = L\,b\,\frac{(F_i + F_o)}{2} \tag{26}$$

It is also worth noting that the above fitting should utilize the inlet and outlet conditions for a single feed channel, accounting for the number of leaves and the number of feed channels per leaf. Additionally, while Sundaramoorthy et al. [30,31] assume the fitted constants are independent of temperature, this fitting can also be performed separately for each set of data at each temperature which can then be used to fit a temperature dependent term. For example, Arrhenius-type equations can be used [23,37]:

$$A_w = A_{w0}\,exp\left[\frac{-E_A}{R}\left(\frac{1}{T} - \frac{1}{T_0}\right)\right] \tag{27}$$

$$B_S = B_{S0}\,exp\left[\frac{-E_B}{R}\left(\frac{1}{T} - \frac{1}{T_0}\right)\right] \tag{28}$$

where E_A and E_B are apparent activation energies, R is the gas constant, and A_{w0} and B_{S0} are the values of water and salt transport coefficients at temperature T_0. The above equations can be used to evaluate the values at other temperatures. Although Arrhenius equations are more commonly associated with chemical reactions, Mehdizadeh et al. have shown that this type of relation also works well for predicting fluxes through membranes at different temperatures as they argue it is a similar phenomenological process [37].

2.2.3. Step 3. Boron Transport Parameter Estimation

The transport coefficients of boron can be estimated based on the following equation suggested by Hyung and Kim which accounts for the transport of boric acid (H_3BO_3) and borate ion ($H_2BO_3^-$) [24]:

$$B_B = \alpha_0 B_{(H_3BO_3)} + \alpha_1 B_{(H_2BO_3^-)} \tag{29}$$

In this equation, α_0 and α_1 represent the fractions of boric acid and borate ion which can be estimated using the apparent dissociation constant K_{a1} and the H^+ ion concentration [24]:

$$\alpha_0 = \frac{\{H^+\}}{\{H^+\} + K_{a1}} \tag{30}$$

$$\alpha_1 = \frac{K_{a1}}{\{H^+\} + K_{a1}} \tag{31}$$

The value of K_{a1} can be determined by a correlation in terms of salt concentration and temperature as given by the correlation of Edmond and Gieskes as presented by Nir and Lahav [38]:

$$\log_{10} K_{a1} = \frac{2291.90}{T} + 0.01756\,T - 3.3850 - 0.32051 \left(\frac{S}{1.80655}\right)^{1/3} \tag{32}$$

where T is the temperature in kelvin, and S is the concentration of salt in g/L. It was also noted by Nir and Lahav [38] that a number of authors have missed the temperature dependence from the $0.01756\,T$ term when writing this correlation.

Although in principle the temperature dependent factors can also be estimated here through fitting expressions similar to Equation (27), the temperature-dependent expressions determined by Hyung and Kim can also be used since they show that their fitted parameters fit well for a number of different membranes tested [24]. The work of Hyung and Kim also gives values for the boric acid and borate ion transport coefficients for those types of membranes, and these values are used by Mane et al. as part of their numerical simulation model [23]. However, the simulation results of Mane et al. underpredict the rejection of boron for higher pH values (8.5 and 9.5) compared with their experimental results [23]. This difference could be due to the fact that the transport coefficient values determined by Hyung and Kim were based on a flat sheet membrane [24] while Mane et al. utilized a spiral wound module with the same material [23]. To account for this, it is suggested here that the values of $B_{(H_3BO_3)0}$ and $B_{(H_2BO_3^-)0}$ should be fitted for each membrane material and for each design of membrane module.

The values of B_B can be determined from experimental measurements and calculation with Equation (12) rearranged as (assuming that $k_B = k$):

$$B_B = \frac{C_{Bp}\,J_W}{(C_{Bb} - C_{Bp})\,e^{(Jw/k)}} \tag{33}$$

Since $\alpha_0 + \alpha_1 = 1$ then for each temperature measured the values of B_B can be plotted against α_0 which should give a linear fit with intercept $B_{(H_2BO_3^-)}$ and gradient equal to $\left(B_{(H_3BO_3)} - B_{(H_2BO_3^-)}\right)$ so that the transport coefficients of boric acid and borate ion can be determined. If values are fitted at each temperature the temperature dependence can also be included.

2.2.4. Step 4. Mass Transfer Parameter Estimation

If the mass transfer correlation is given by Equation (14), the fitting of parameters A, B, C, and D can be realized through writing this as a linear equation in terms of these parameters:

$$\ln(sh) = A + B\ln(Re_f) + C\ln(Re_p) + D\ln(Sc) \tag{34}$$

This is similar to the approach taken by Avlonitis et al. who sequentially determined the parameters by plotting $\ln(sh)$ against the log of different dimensionless numbers [29]. However, depending on the membrane being used, some of these values could be statistically insignificant in which case some terms may be eliminated to give a simpler expression. In principle all the parameters can be fitted simultaneously using multivariable linear fitting.

2.3. Model Prediction Algorithm

The analytical equations from Sections 2.1 and 2.2 can be solved to predict the performance of a desalination membrane given the input conditions and fitted parameters. This is the same procedure suggested by Sundaramoorthy et al. [31] but with some changes including the addition of boron transport equations, accounting for a different module design (two feed channels and a single permeate channel) and including the effect of temperature on water and salt transport coefficients.

2.3.1. Input Membrane Geometry

- Width W;
- Length L;
- Feed channel height t_f;
- Number of membrane leaves n;
- Input conditions;
- Inlet salt concentration C_i;
- Total feed flow rate Q_f;
- Inlet flow rate (calculated for a single feed channel) $F_i = \frac{Q_f}{2n}$;
- Inlet pressure P_i;
- Permeate pressure P_p;
- Temperature T;
- Potential hydrogen pH;
- Fitted parameters;
- Pressure drop coefficient b;
- Water and salt transport coefficients A_{w0} and B_{S0} at temperature T_0;
- Apparent activation energies E_A and E_B;
- Boric acid and borate ion transport coefficients $B_{(H_3BO_3)0}$ and $B_{(H_2BO_3^-)0}$ at temperature T_0;
- Boron apparent activation energies E_{B3} and E_{B2};
- Mass transfer coefficients A, B, C, and D.

In cases where temperature dependent parameters (apparent activation energies) are unavailable, fixed values for A_w, B_S, $B_{(H_3BO_3)}$, and $B_{(H_2BO_3^-)}$ might be used.

2.3.2. Solution Procedure Using Model Equations

Step 1: Assume $C_p = C_{pA}$ (*initial guess* $C_{pA} = 0$)
Step 2: Calculate $\{H^+\} = 10^{-pH}$
Step 3: Calculate $\Delta P_i = P_i - P_p$
Step 4: Calculate A_w and B_S (Equations (27) and (28))
Step 5: Calculate ϕ (Equation (18))
Step 6: Calculate F_o (Equation (15))
Step 7: Calculate P_o (Equation (16))
Step 8: Calculate $\Delta P_o = P_o - P_p$
Step 9: Calculate $J_{wi} = \frac{2 \cdot A_w \Delta P_i}{1 + \left(\frac{A_w t_\gamma}{B_S}\right) TC_p}$ and $J_{wo} = \frac{2 \cdot A_w \Delta P_o}{1 + \left(\frac{A_w t_\gamma}{B_S}\right) TC_p}$
Step 10: Calculate $v_i = \frac{F_i}{A_f}$ and $v_o = \frac{F_o}{A_f}$
Step 11: Calculate $C_o = C_p + \frac{F_i(C_i - C_p)}{F_o}$
Step 12: Calculate $Re_{f,i}$, $Re_{p,i}$, Sc_i and $Re_{f,o}$, $Re_{p,o}$, Sc_o
Step 13: Calculate Sh_i and Sh_o (Equation (14))
Step 14: Calculate $k_i = \frac{Sh_i \cdot D_i}{d_e}$ and $k_o = \frac{Sh_o \cdot D_o}{d_e}$
Step 15: Calculate $C_{pi} = \frac{C_i}{\left[1 + \frac{(J_w/B_s)}{exp(J_w/k_i)}\right]}$ and $C_{po} = \frac{C_o}{\left[1 + \frac{(J_{wo}/B_s)}{exp(J_{wo}/k_o)}\right]}$
Step 16: Calculate $C_{pA} = \frac{C_{pi} + C_{po}}{2}$

Step 17: Calculate $C_{iw} = C_{pA} + \frac{J_{wi} \cdot C_{pA}}{B_S}$
Step 18: Calculate K_{a1} (Equation (32)), where $S = C_{iw} \cdot MW_{NaCl}$)
Step 19: Calculate B_B (Equations (29)–(31))
Step 20: Calculate $C_{Bp} = \frac{C_{Bi}}{\left[1 + \frac{(J_w/B_B)}{exp(J_w/k_i)}\right]}$
Step 21: If $|C_p - C_{pA}| >$ tolerance $\rightarrow$ Go to step 5, otherwise stop

In step 21 a tolerance of 1×10^{-6} was implemented to give a reasonable convergence of the calculated concentration. Additionally, the dimensionless numbers were calculated using the following correlations [22,31]:

$$Re_f = \frac{\rho \, d_e \, v}{\mu} \qquad (35)$$

$$Re_p = \frac{\rho \, d_e \, J_w}{\mu} \qquad (36)$$

$$Sc = \frac{\mu}{\rho \, D} \qquad (37)$$

where $d_e = t_f/2$ is the equivalent diameter [31]. In addition, the density and viscosity can be estimated through the following correlations of Koroneos et al. [39]:

$$\rho = 498.4m + \sqrt{248400m^2 + 752.4 \, m \, S} \qquad (38)$$

$$m = 1.0069 - 2.757 \times 10^{-4} \cdot (T - 273.15) \qquad (39)$$

$$\mu = 1.234 \times 10^{-6} \cdot exp\left[0.0212 \cdot S + \frac{1965}{T}\right] \qquad (40)$$

$$D = 6.725 \times 10^{-6} \times exp\left[0.1546 \times 10^{-3} S - \frac{2513}{T}\right] \qquad (41)$$

3. Case Studies

To demonstrate the parameter fitting methods and to evaluate the accuracy of the model predictions the methodology from Section 2 is applied to two case studies including FilmTec 2.5 inch FT30 and Saehan Industries RE4040-SR spiral wound membrane modules.

For the purpose of fitting parameters, experimental data values from the literature have been used. This includes 32 data points using the FilmTec module with varying salt concentrations (25–40 g/L), feed pressures (50–80 bar), and temperatures (20–35 °C) and associated varying feed and permeate volume flow rates as given in Table 1 of the study of Avlonitis et al. [29]. Unfortunately this data set does not include brine outlet pressure or boron concentrations so steps 1 and 3 from Figure 1 are not possible based on this data.

Table 1. Spiral wound membrane module details using literature values for FilmTec [29] and Saehan [23] modules.

Spiral Wound Module	FilmTec FT30	Saehan RE4040-SR
Length (m)	0.8665	0.88
Width (m)	1.17	0.8
Number of leaves	1	5
Feed channel height (m)	7.7×10^{-4}	9.4×10^{-4}
Permeate channel height (m)	4.3×10^{-4}	4.0×10^{-4}

For the Saehan module a set of 15 data points can be found in the study of Mane et al. [23] with varying pressures (600–800 psi or approximately 4,137,000–5,516,000 Pa) and pH (7.5, 8.5 and 9.5) and with varying permeate flow rates (maintaining feed to permeate flow ratio at a constant). In this study, 10 of these data points were used for fitting parameters (pH at 7.5 and 9.5) and the remaining 5 data points were used for validation. These data are measured only at 25 °C and, as with the other case study, pressure drop data are also not given in the literature. Hence, in this case, steps 2, 3, and 4 are possible in the fitting procedure from Figure 1.

3.1. Determination of Pressure Coefficient b

Since the brine outlet pressures are not provided the above references, alternative methods must be used to estimate b.

Although the study of Avlonitis et al. [29] does not give a value of the friction coefficient k_{fb}, the value for this coefficient is given by the study of Senthilmurugan et al. as 2.5008×10^8 m^{-2} [21]. This value is used together with the temperature and feed concentration from a selected feed condition from the 32 data points of Avlonitis et al., in this case 20 °C and 35 g/L are used together with Equations (35) and (19) to give the value of coefficient b.

For the Saehan module, the study of Mane et al. provides a value of the friction coefficient $k_{fb} = 5.18 \times 10^{10}$ m^{-2} [23]. However, using this value leads to a calculated pressure drop which is much greater than the maximum pressure drop specified by the manufacturer for similar modules [40]. For this reason, the b value is estimated for this case using the maximum pressure drop and the highest tested flow rate in Equation (20).

The estimated values of b are in this way given in Table 2.

3.2. Determination of Water and Salt Transport Coefficients

As mentioned in Section 2.2 the values of water and salt transport coefficients can be determined by plotting $1/\phi^2$ against TC_p. In the study of Sundaramoorthy et al. a single value of these parameters (A_W and B_S) is found to be sufficient for all the temperatures used when considering the removal of chlorophenol [30,31]. However, for the desalination of seawater, it is shown in Figure 3 that a separate linear fitting is required for each temperature, each giving different values of A_W and B_S.

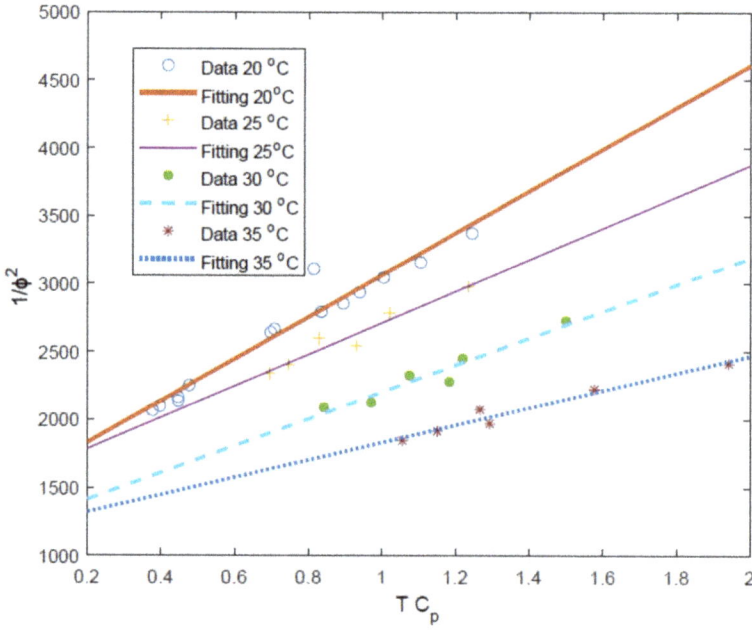

Figure 3. Plot of the $1/\phi^2$ against TC_p with linear fitting against the data of Avlonitis et al. [29] using the calculated value of b from Table 2.

The data of Mane et al. is used for the fitting of A_w and B_S for the Saehan module (see Figure 4) although this is only a relatively small sample size using 10 out of the 15 data points available. Furthermore, this data set is also measured in a relatively narrow range of conditions including feed flow rates of 2.27 to 4 m^3 day^{-1} and salt rejection in the very narrow range of 99.6 to 99.7 % [23]. This is perhaps due to the study of Mane et al. focusing on boron recovery at different conditions [23]. Despite these limited data, it is still possible to estimate the values of water and salt coefficients with fitted values given in Table 2.

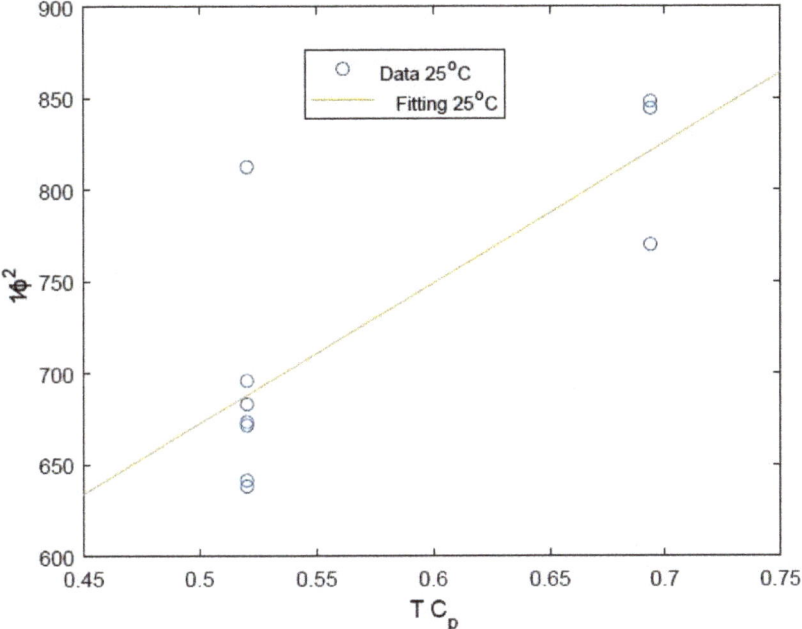

Figure 4. Plot of the $1/\phi^2$ against TC_p with linear fitting against the data of Mane et al. [23] using the calculated value of b from Table 2.

3.3. Determination of Boron Transport Coefficients

Since the data regarding boron are not available in the data of Avlonitis et al. [29] for the FilmTec module, parameters are fitted here only for the Saehan module based on the data of Mane et al. [23].

This is possible through plotting B_B (calculated using Equation (33)) against α_0 (calculated using Equation (30)) giving the plot and linear fit shown in Figure 5. The gradient and intercept of this linear fit are used to calculate $B_{(H_3BO_3)0}$ and $B_{(H_2BO_3^-)0}$ as given in Table 2.

3.4. Determination of Mass Transfer Correlation Coefficients

The value of the Sherwood number can be calculated for each experimental point. If both brine inlet and outlet data are available then the mass transfer coefficient and Sherwood number can be calculated for both points. However, in this case since the outlet pressures are not given in the case study references, only the inlet conditions are used to estimate mass transfer correlations:

$$k_i = \frac{J_{Wi}}{\ln\left[\left(\frac{J_{Wi}}{B_S}\right)\left(\frac{C_p}{C_i - C_p}\right)\right]} \tag{42}$$

$$sh_i = \frac{k_i D_i}{d_e} \tag{43}$$

Table 2. Estimated and fitted parameters for case study of spiral wound membrane modules.

Spiral Wound Module	FilmTec FT30	Saehan RE4040-SR
b (atm m^{-4} s^{-1})	2.9760×10^3	1.0126×10^3
T_0 (K)	293.15	298.15
A_{w0} (m atm^{-1}s^{-1})	2.5258×10^{-7}	2.7550×10^{-7}
B_{S0} (m s^{-1})	4.0699×10^{-8}	1.7062×10^{-8}
E_A (J mol^{-1})	1.4192×10^4	
E_B (J mol^{-1})	4.2116×10^4	
$B_{(H_3BO_3)0}$ (m s^{-1})		5.4306×10^{-7}
$B_{(H_2BO_3^-)0}$ (m s^{-1})		5.3760×10^{-8}
A	-1.2604	5.619
B	0.35923	
C	0.65885	0.5641
D	0.86483	

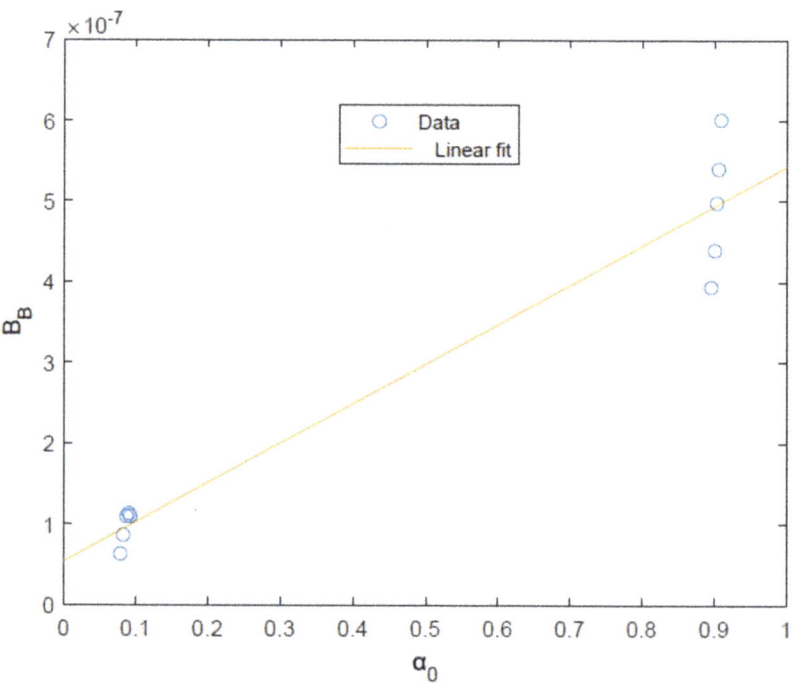

Figure 5. Plot of B_B (calculated using experimental data [23] and fitted parameters b, A_w, and B_s) against α_0 together with linear fit.

These values can be calculated for the two case studies considered here which can be used to fit values of A, B, C, and D in Equation (34). In principle, all four of these parameters can be fitted simultaneously using linear fitting, but some of these may be statistically insignificant, in particular for the Saehan membrane data which are based on 10 data points [23] all with very similar salt rejection and with the same value of Sc at the inlet. For this reason initially A, B, and C were fitted simultaneously. However, when used in the prediction code, this sometimes led to erroneous calculations of $C_p = C_i$; perhaps because the correlation is overfitted to a narrow range of conditions. Hence, a simpler expression is tested using either A and B or A and C. In other words, trying to fit a linear relation between either $\ln(sh)$ and $\ln(Re_f)$ or $\ln(sh)$ and $\ln(Re_p)$ and in this case $\ln(Re_p)$ was found to more statistically significant; the values of A and C are given in Table 2.

For the FilmTec membrane module a larger set of data with 32 data points [29] was used to fit all four parameters as given in Table 2.

4. Model Validation

To show the prediction accuracy of the analytical model proposed here the model was tested both with the training set data and also data and conditions other than the training data.

For the FilmTec module the data from Table 2 is used in the model to predict the performance for the 32 data points used for training. The model is shown to predict reasonably well the permeate flow rate (Figure 6) and permeate salt concentration (Figure 7).

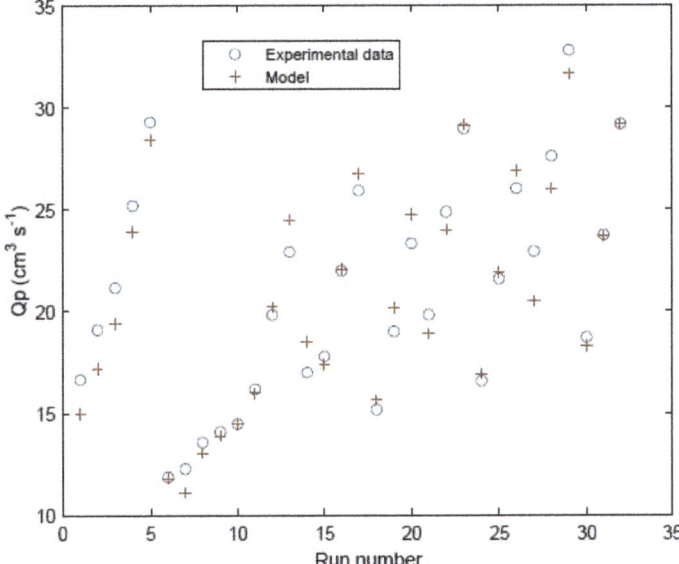

Figure 6. Permeate flow rate of FilmTec module comparison of experimental values [29] against model predictions for the 32 data points used to train the model.

Furthermore this model is then validated against two sets of experimental data and associated models from the literature (11 data points and analytical model results from Table 2 in the study of Avlonitis et al. [29] and 13 data points and numerical model results from Table 9 in the study of Senthilmurugan et al. [21]) which are labelled as run numbers 1–11 and run numbers 12–24 in Figures 8 and 9. This validation shows that the proposed model is reasonably accurate for all of the data points. The only exception is the permeate concentrations for run numbers 1–11 which are overpredicted by the model. The model of Avlonitis et al. is shown to predict these values slightly more accurately [29]. This is presumably because the model of Avlonitis et al. has been trained/fitted using a wider range of data which are not covered inside the training set of 32 data points [29]. The proposed model is shown to give similar accuracy compared to the numerical model of

Senthilmurugan et al. [21] in most of the run numbers 12–24. The overall accuracy of the proposed model is 6.3% for water permeation and 24.7% for permeate concentration. However, the accuracy of the model for runs 12–24 is 7.2% for water permeation and 8.9% for permeate concentration. If the model was retrained using data from run numbers 1–11 these errors in the permeate concentration could potentially be reduced. The more complex numerical model of Senthilmurugan et al. gives an accuracy for runs 12–24 of 8.8% for water permeation and 4.5% for permeate concentration.

Run numbers 1–11 show the experimental and model results from Avlonitis et al. [29] and run numbers 12–24 show the experimental and model results from Senthilmurugan et al. [21].

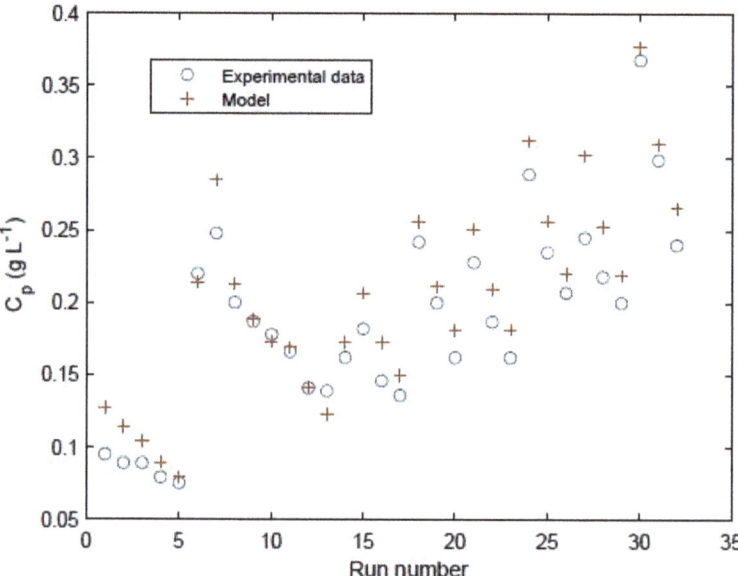

Figure 7. Permeate salt concentration of FilmTec module comparison of experimental values [29] against model predictions for the 32 data points used to train the model.

For the Saehan module the data from Table 2 is used in the model to predict the performance for the 5 data points used for testing/validation. The model is shown to predict reasonably well the permeate flow rate (Figure 10).

Furthermore, the boron rejection predicted by this model is compared against the experimental and model predictions of Mane et al. [23], as shown in Figure 11. In this Figure, the 10 data points denoted by empty circles/rings are those which were used for training and the squares are the data points which were used for testing. In this Figure, the literature model results are those given in the study of Mane et al. which were generated using a complex finite elements numerical model [23]. That model uses the boric acid (H_3BO_3) and borate ion ($H_2BO_3^-$) transport coefficients given by Hyung and Kim [24], while the proposed model uses coefficients which are fitted to the experimental data of Mane et al. [23]. It can be seen that the model of Mane et al. fits well to the values at lower rejection data points (these values are for pH 7.5) but underpredicts the values at higher rejection (with pH at 8.5 and 9.5). Meanwhile, the proposed model gives a reasonably accurate prediction for all data points, except for some slight over- and underprediction at the lower pH values. For the testing data in Figure 11, the proposed model gives an absolute average error of 0.82% while the model of Mane et al. gives an absolute average error of 1.44%.

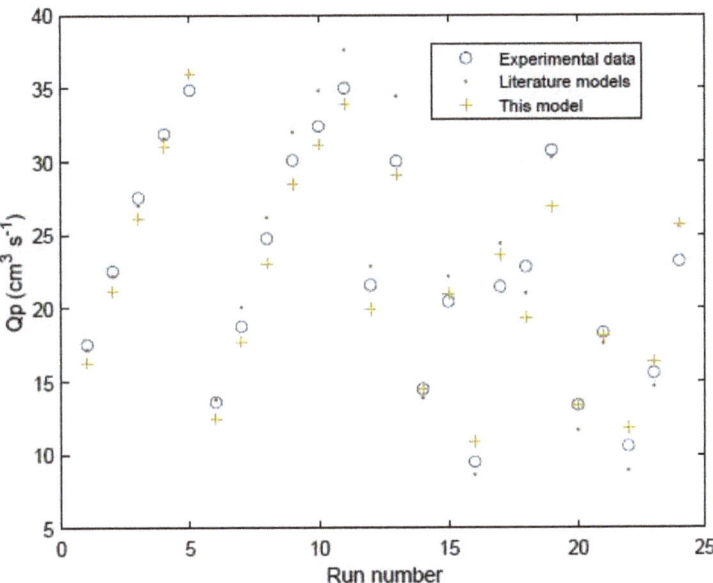

Figure 8. Permeate flow rate of FilmTec module comparison of experimental values [4,11] against model predictions for 24 different data points for testing/validation.

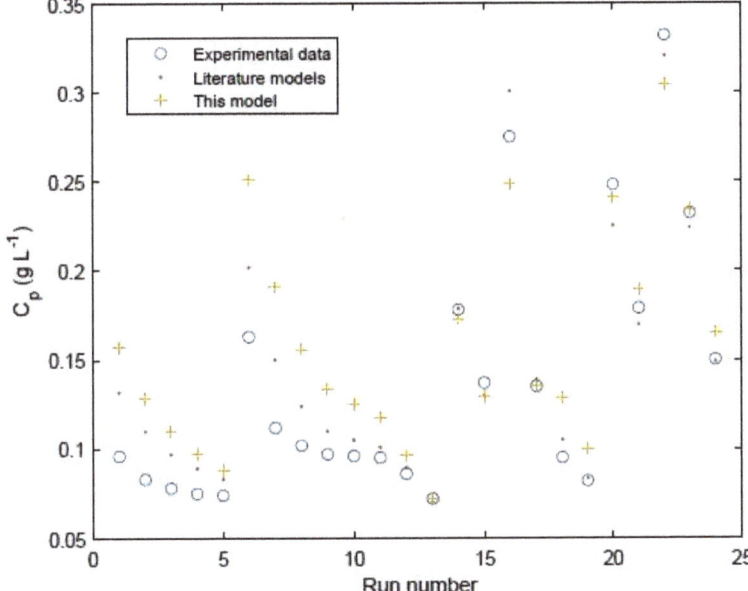

Figure 9. Permeate salt concentration of FilmTec module comparison of experimental values [4,11] against model predictions for 24 different data points for testing/validation. Run numbers 1–11 show the experimental and model results from Avlonitis et al. [29] and run numbers 12–24 show the experimental and model results from Senthilmurugan et al. [21].

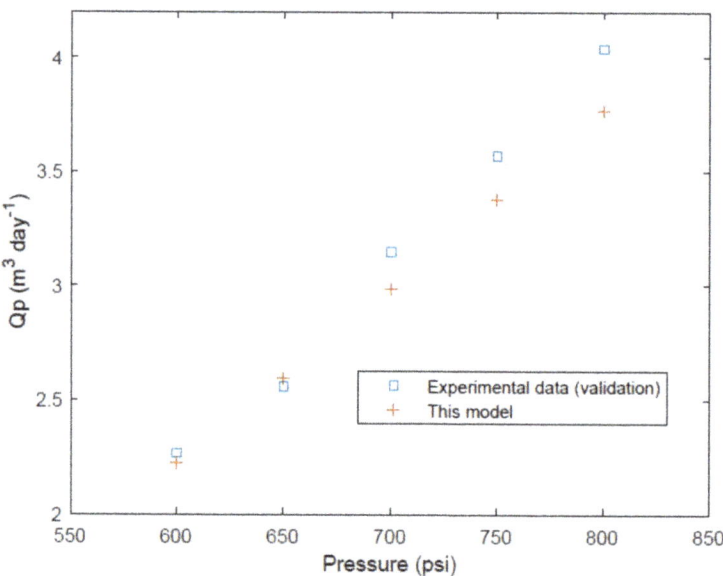

Figure 10. Permeate volume flow rate. A comparison of experimental data [23] and model predictions.

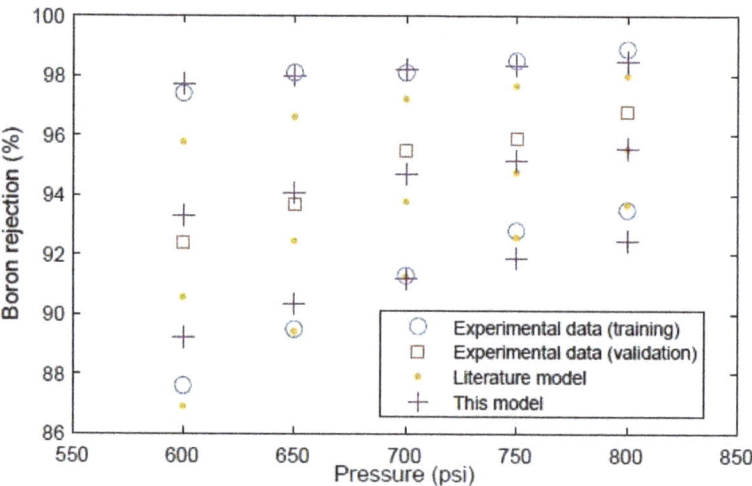

Figure 11. Boron rejection for the Saehan module. A comparison of experimental data [23] and model predictions.

5. Conclusions

An analytical model is proposed in this study for simultaneously predicting the removal of both salt and boron from seawater through reverse osmosis using spiral wound desalination membrane modules. This model and the fitting procedure is an extension of the methods proposed by Sundaramoorthy et al. for the removal of organic solutes [30,31] which is modified and extended to predict the removal of both salt and boron from seawater.

The fitting procedure proposed here is sequential, starting with the prediction of a pressure drop coefficient, followed by the fitting of water and salt transport coefficients. Subsequently the boron transport coefficients and the mass transfer correlation coefficients can be fitted independently of each other. In all of these steps it is shown that the parameters can be obtained through linear fitting using experimental values and calculated parameters from previous steps. Hence, this approach offers a very simple method for obtaining all the parameters needed to build the predictive model.

The analytical model equations can be solved by following the steps given in Section 2.3 which offers a much simpler method for simulation of separation performance compared with the more complex numerical finite-difference type models which require solving much larger numbers of equations and more computational effort. A basic comparison of the CPU time required to simulate three modules 1000 times (optimization will typically require simulation of configurations at least 1000 times, in some cases much more) shows that the proposed analytical model required 7.3 s while a numerical model with 100 discrete points required 4 min 21.2 s using an i7 3.30 GHz intel computer.

Although the proposed model is simpler than numerical finite-difference type models it is shown to give similar accuracy when comparing the predicted outlet permeate flow rate, salt, and boron rejection. This type of model should be appropriate for the design and optimization of multistage desalination systems due to its simplicity and low computational requirements.

Supplementary Materials: The following are available online at https://www.mdpi.com/article/10.3390/su13168999/s1.

Funding: This research received no external funding.

Institutional Review Board Statement: Not applicable.

Informed Consent Statement: Not applicable.

Data Availability Statement: Data is contained within the article, in a supplementary file and in references. Experimental data used for fitting parameters and validation can be found in references [21,23,29]. Parameters fitted in this study can be found in Table 2 in this article. Model predictions from Figures 6–11 using the developed model can be found in the supplementary spreadsheet file.

Conflicts of Interest: The authors declare no conflict of interest.

Nomenclature

A	dimensionless parameter used in Equation (14)
A_f	cross sectional area of feed channel (m^2)
A_W	water transport coefficient (m atm^{-1} s^{-1})
B	dimensionless parameter used in Equation (14)
B_S	salt transport coefficient (m s^{-1})
b	pressure drop parameter defined by Equation (5) (atm s m^{-4})
C	concentration (kmole m^{-3}) or dimensionless parameter used in Equation (14)
D	dimensionless parameter used in Equation (14)
D	diffusivity (m^2 s^{-1})
F	volume flow rate (m^3 s^{-1})
i	number of ionic species generated when molecule is dissolved in water
J_W	water flux (m s^{-1})
J_S	salt flux (kmol m^{-2} s^{-1})
J_B	boron flux (kmol m^{-2} s^{-1})
k	mass transfer coefficient (m s^{-1})
k_{fB}	friction parameter used in Equations (20) and (22) (m^{-2})
L	membrane effective length (as in Figure 1) (m)
P	pressure (atm)
Re	Reynolds number

Sc	Schmidt number
Sh	Sherwood number
T	temperature (K)
W	membrane effective width (un-wound as in Figure 1) (m)
x	distance in x direction (see Figure 1) (m)

Greek letters

β	Ratio of pressures defined by Equation (24)
π	osmotic pressure (atm)
μ	fluid viscosity (kg m^{-1} s^{-1})
ρ	fluid density (kg m^{-3})
γ	gas law constant (atm m^3 K^{-1} kmole^{-1})
ϕ	dimensionless parameter defined by Equation (18)

Subscripts

b or f	brine side/feed side
B	boron
p	permeate side
S	Salt
W	"Water" when referring to water flux or "Wall" when referring to wall concentration
0	at a reference temperature
i	feed side inlet
o	feed side outlet

References

1. WHO. *Guidelines for Drinking-Water Quality: Fourth Edition Incorporating the First Addendum*; World Health Organization: Geneva, Switzerland, 2017; Licence: CC BY-NC-SA 3.0 IGO.
2. Najid, N.; Kouzbour, S.; Ruiz-Garcia, A.; Fellaou, S.; Gourich, B.; Stiriba, Y. Comparison analysis of different technologies for the removal of boron from seawater: A review. *J. Environ. Chem. Eng.* 2021, *9*, 105133. [CrossRef]
3. Hilal, N.; Kim, G.J.; Somerfield, C. Boron removal from saline water: A comprehensive review. *Desalination* 2011, *273*, 23–35. [CrossRef]
4. Redondo, J.; Busch, M.; De Witte, J.-P. Boron removal from seawater using filmtech high rejection SWRO membranes. *Desalination* 2003, *156*, 229–238. [CrossRef]
5. Koseoglu, H.; Kabay, N.; Yuksel, M.; Sarp, S.; Arar, O.; Kitis, M. Boron removal from seawater using high rejection SWRO membranes—Impact of pH, feed concentration, pressure, and cross-flow velocity. *Desalination* 2008, *227*, 253–263. [CrossRef]
6. Ali, Z.; Sunbul, Y.A.; Pacheco, F.; Ogieglo, W.; Wang, Y.; Genduso, G.; Pinnau, I. Defect-free highly selective polyamide thin-film composite membranes for desalination and boron removal. *J. Membr. Sci.* 2019, *578*, 85–94. [CrossRef]
7. Li, Y.; Wang, S.; Song, X.; Zhou, Y.; Shen, H.; Cao, X.; Zhang, P.; Gao, C. High boron removal polyamide reverse osmosis membranes by swelling induced embedding of a sulfonyl molecular plug. *J. Membr. Sci.* 2020, *597*, 117716. [CrossRef]
8. Haidari, A.H.; Heijman, S.G.J.; van der Meer, W.G.J. Optimal design of spacers in reverse osmosis. *Sep. Purif. Technol.* 2018, *192*, 441–456. [CrossRef]
9. Ruiz-Garcia, A.; Nuez, I. Performance assessment of SWRO spiral-wound membrane modules with different feed spacer dimensions. *Processes* 2020, *8*, 692. [CrossRef]
10. Tu, K.L.; Nghiem, L.D.; Chivas, A.R. Boron removal by reverse osmosis membranes in seawater desalination applications. *Sep. Purif. Technol.* 2010, *75*, 87–101. [CrossRef]
11. Ban, S.-H.; Im, S.-J.; Cho, J.; Jang, A. Comparative performance of FO-RO hybrid and two-pass SWRO desalination processes: Boron removal. *Desalination* 2019, *471*, 114114. [CrossRef]
12. Jung, B.; Kim, C.Y.; Jiao, S.; Rao, U.; Dudchenko, V.; Tester, J.; Jassby, D. Enhancing boron rejection on electrically conducting reverse osmosis membranes through local electrochemical pH modification. *Desalination* 2020, *476*, 114212. [CrossRef]
13. Landsman, M.R.; Lawler, D.F.; Katz, L.E. Application of electrodialysis pretreatment to enhance boron removal and reduce fouling during desalination by nanofiltration/reverse osmosis. *Desalination* 2020, *491*, 114563. [CrossRef]
14. Ruiz-Garcia, A.; Nuez, I. Performance evaluation and boron rejection in a SWRO system under variable operating conditions. *Comput. Chem. Eng.* 2021, *153*, 107441. [CrossRef]
15. Al-Obaidi, M.A. Evaluation of chlorophenol removal from wastewater using multi-stage spiral-wound reverse osmosis process via simulation. *Comput. Chem. Eng.* 2019, *130*, 106522. [CrossRef]
16. Al-Obaidi, M.A.; Kara-Zaitri, C.; Mujtaba, I.M. Performance evaluation of multi-stage reverse osmosis process with permeate and retentate recycling strategy for the removal of chlorophenol from wastewater. *Comput. Chem. Eng.* 2019, *121*, 12–26. [CrossRef]
17. Alsarayreh, A.A.; Al-Obaidi, M.A.; Al-Hroub, A.M.; Patel, R.; Mujtaba, I.M. Performance evaluation of reverse osmosis brackish water desalination plant with different recycled ratios of retentate. *Comput. Chem. Eng.* 2020, *135*, 106729. [CrossRef]
18. Alsarayreh, A.A.; Al-Obaidi, M.A.; Patel, R.; Mujtaba, I.M. Scope and limitations of modelling, simulation, and optimisation of a spiral wound reverse osmosis process-based water desalination. *Processes* 2020, *8*, 573. [CrossRef]

19. Joseph, A.; Damodaran, V. Dynamic simulation of the reverse osmosis process for seawater using labview and an analysis of the process performance. *Comput. Chem. Eng.* **2019**, *121*, 294–305. [CrossRef]
20. Ben Boudinar, M.; Hanbury, W.T.; Avlonitis, S. Numerical simulation and optimisation of spiral-wound modules. *Desalination* **1992**, *86*, 273–290. [CrossRef]
21. Senthilmurugan, S.; Ahluwalia, A.; Gupta, S.K. Modeling of a spiral-wound module and estimation of model parameters using numerical techniques. *Desalination* **2005**, *173*, 269–286. [CrossRef]
22. Geraldes, V.; Periera, N.E.; de Pinho, M.N. Simulation and optimization of medium-sized seawater reverse osmosis processes with spiral-wound modules. *Ind. Eng. Chem. Res.* **2005**, *44*, 1897–1905. [CrossRef]
23. Mane, P.P.; Park, P.K.; Hyung, H.; Brown, J.C.; Kim, J.H. Modeling boron rejection in pilot- and full-scale reverse osmosis desalination processes. *J. Membr. Sci.* **2009**, *338*, 119–127. [CrossRef]
24. Hyung, H.; Kim, J.H. A mechanistic study on boron rejection by sea water reverse osmosis membranes. *J. Membr. Sci.* **2006**, *286*, 269–278. [CrossRef]
25. Ruiz-Garcia, A.; Leon, F.A.; Ramos-Martin, A. Different boron rejection behavior in two RO membranes installed in the same full-scale SWRO desalination plant. *Desalination* **2019**, *449*, 131–138. [CrossRef]
26. Sassi, S.M.; Mujtaba, I.M. MINLP based superstructure optimization for boron removal during desalination by reverse osmosis. *J. Membr. Sci.* **2013**, *440*, 269–278. [CrossRef]
27. Taniguchi, M.; Kurihara, M.; Kimura, S. Boron reduction performance of reverse osmosis seawater desalination process. *J. Membr. Sci.* **2001**, *183*, 259–267. [CrossRef]
28. Du, Y.; Liu, Y.; Zhang, S.; Xu, Y. Optimization of seawater reverse osmosis desalination networks with permeate split design considering boron removal. *Ind. Eng. Chem. Res.* **2016**, *55*, 12860–12879. [CrossRef]
29. Avlonitis, S.; Hanbury, W.T.; Ben Boudinar, M. Spiral wound modules performance an analytical solution: Part II. *Desalination* **1993**, *89*, 227–246. [CrossRef]
30. Sundaramoorthy, S.; Srinivasan, G.; Murthy, D.V.R. An analytical model for spiral wound reverse osmosis membrane modules: Part I—Model development and parameter estimation. *Desalination* **2011**, *280*, 403–411. [CrossRef]
31. Sundaramoorthy, S.; Srinivasan, G.; Murthy, D.V.R. An analytical model for spiral wound reverse osmosis membrane modules: Part II—Experimental validation. *Desalination* **2011**, *277*, 257–264. [CrossRef]
32. Srinivasan, G.; Sundaramoorthy, S.; Murthy, D.V.R. Validation of an analytical model for spiral wound reverse osmosis membrane module using experimental data on the removal of dimethylphenol. *Desalination* **2011**, *281*, 199–208. [CrossRef]
33. Fraidenraich, N.; de Castro Vilela, O.; dos Santos Viana, M.; Gordon, J.M. Improved analytic modeling and experimental validation for brackish-water reverse-osmosis desalination. *Desalination* **2016**, *380*, 60–65. [CrossRef]
34. Al-Obaidi, M.A.; Kara-Zaitri, C.; Mujtaba, I.M. Removal of phenol from wastewater using spiral-wound reverse osmosis process: Model development based on experiment and simulation. *J. Water Process Eng.* **2017**, *18*, 20–28. [CrossRef]
35. Al-Obaidi, M.A.; Li, J.-P.; Alsadaie, S.; Kara-Zaitri, C.; Mujtaba, I.M. Modelling and optimisation of a multistage reverse osmosis processes with permeate reprocessing and recycling for the removal of N-nitrosodimethylamine from wastewater using species conserving genetic algorithms. *Chem. Eng. J.* **2018**, *35*, 824–834. [CrossRef]
36. Koutsou, C.P.; Yiantsios, S.G.; Karabelas, A.J. Direct numerical simulation of flow in spacer-filled channels: Effect of spacer geometrical characteristics. *J. Membr. Sci.* **2007**, *291*, 53–69. [CrossRef]
37. Mehdizadeh, H.; Dickson, J.M.; Eriksson, P.K. Temperature effects on the performance of thin-film composite, aromatic polyamide membranes. *Ind. Eng. Chem. Res.* **1989**, *28*, 814–824. [CrossRef]
38. Nir, O.; Lahav, O. Coupling mass transport and chemical equilibrium models for improving the prediction of SWRO permeate boron concentrations. *Desalination* **2013**, *310*, 87–92. [CrossRef]
39. Koroneos, C.; Dompros, A.; Roumbas, G. Renewable energy driven desalination systems modelling. *J. Clean. Prod.* **2007**, *15*, 449–464. [CrossRef]
40. Saehan Technical Manual. Available online: http://www.csmfilter.co.kr/searchfile/file/Tech_manual.pdf (accessed on 11 May 2021).

Article

Development of a Cyberinfrastructure for Assessment of the Lower Rio Grande Valley North and Central Watersheds Characteristics

Linda Navarro [1], Ahmed Mahmoud [2,*], Andrew Ernest [1], Abdoul Oubeidillah [1], Jessica Johnstone [3], Ivan Rene Santos Chavez [1] and Christopher Fuller [4]

1. Department of Civil Engineering, University of Texas Rio Grande Valley, Edinburg, TX 78539, USA; lnavarro@office.ratesresearch.org (L.N.); andrew.ernest@utrgv.edu (A.E.); abdoul.oubeidillah@utrgv.edu (A.O.); ivan.santoschavez01@utrgv.edu (I.R.S.C.)
2. Department of Biological and Agricultural Engineering, University of Arkansas, Fayetteville, AR 72704, USA
3. Nonpoint Source Program, Texas Commission on Environmental Quality, Austin, TX 78753, USA; jessica.johnstone@tceq.texas.gov
4. Research, Applied, Technology, Education and Service, Inc., Rio Grande Valley, Edinburg, TX 78540, USA; cfuller@office.ratesresearch.org
* Correspondence: ahmedm@uark.edu

Abstract: Lower Laguna Madre (LLM) is designated as an impaired waterway for high concentrations of bacteria and low dissolved oxygen. The main freshwater sources to the LLM flow from the North and Central waterways which are composed of three main waterways: Hidalgo/Willacy Main Drain (HWMD), Raymondville Drain (RVD), and International Boundary & Water Commission North Floodway (IBWCNF) that are not fully characterized. The objective of this study is to perform a watershed characterization to determine the potential pollution sources of each watershed. The watershed characterization was achieved by developing a cyberinfrastructure, and it collects a wide inventory of data to identify which one of the three waterways has a major contribution to the LLM. Cyberinfrastructure development using the Geographic Information System (GIS) database helped to comprehend the major characteristics of each area contributing to the watershed supported by the analysis of the data collected. The watershed characterization process started with delineating the boundaries of each watershed. Then, geospatial and non-geospatial data were added to the cyberinfrastructure from numerous sources including point and nonpoint sources of pollution. Results showed that HWMD and IBWCNF watersheds were found to have a higher contribution to the water impairments to the LLM. HWMD and IBWCNF comprise the potential major sources of water quality impairments such as cultivated crops, urbanized areas, on-site sewage facilities, colonias, and wastewater effluents.

Keywords: watershed management; nonpoint source pollution; point source pollution; water quality; pollutant loadings; South Texas

1. Introduction

The Lower Rio Grande Valley (LRGV) region has undergone sudden hydrologic change due to urbanization. This abrupt change has produced a decline in water quality in the primary waterways of the region. The Laguna Madre is an estuarine wetland system along the Gulf of Mexico that receives freshwater from the LRGV [1]. This watershed is known for its recreational activities and is currently threatened by the inflows of main drainage pathways that carry significant levels of contaminants. According to the Texas Commission on Environmental Quality (TCEQ) 2020 Integrated Report [2], two water segments from the Lower Laguna Madre are considered impaired due to high levels of bacteria and low dissolved oxygen. The watershed is comprised of three waterways, Hidalgo/Willacy Main Drain (HWMD), Raymondville Drain (RVD), and International

Boundary & Water Commission North Floodway (IBWCNF), that provide freshwater inflows to the Lower Laguna Madre. Prior to this study, these waterways had not been characterized. Watershed characterization can enable proper identification of potential sources of pollution to help reduce water impairments to the Laguna Madre and preserve the ecosystem.

One of the emerging tools for watershed characterization is cyberinfrastructure that can assist in both data collection and decision-making processes within the watershed. Cyberinfrastructure supports the process of accessing data via an extensive network and provides updated water quality data for further research. The introduction of a cyberinfrastructure can provide an efficient data collection to well demonstrate the watershed characteristics. In one study, cyberinfrastructure not only utilized widespread data but also allowed researchers to analyze large amounts of data over time at different locations [3–5]. This platform offers a rapid generation of new relationships between wide inventories of data. Cyberinfrastructure secures data and delivers interpreted information via a sequence of web services and portals in forms that are universally coherent by distinct stakeholders [6]. Further, it serves as the center for a variety of data from distinct sources, such as non-point and point source and watershed delineation characteristics. Cyberinfrastructure and the watershed delineation are crucial for the watershed characterization since together they will help identify sources of pollution data within the drainage area.

An ample watershed delineation is key for a successful watershed characterization. A watershed delineation is developed by using elevation data and computing several elevation-based files that represent the overall drainage area as well as the hydrological characteristics of a watershed [7]. Each watershed can be divided into sub-watersheds to produce a more detailed drainage structure. The Geographical Information systems (GIS) platform has facilitated the development of hydrological analysis, such as drainage areas based on elevation data. In 2010, a watershed GIS-based applications study performed a hydrological analysis which showed positive outcomes regarding GIS-applications for watershed management and water quality by providing a full overview of watershed characteristics, such as land cover [8]. Hydraulic and hydrological modelling as well as water resource management commonly require investigation of landscape and hydrological features, such as terrain slope, drainage networks, drainage divides, and catchment boundaries [9]. Additionally, high resolution in data resources is important to obtain accurate results in watershed drainage areas [10]. When the land slope is very flat and has few contours, it is challenging for the acquisition of topographic maps. Light Detection and Ranging (LIDAR) is a high-resolution digital elevation model (DEM) that is an ideal source for the type of topography characterized in low elevation areas [11]. Although the terrain in the LRGV is flat, the complex hydrologic features make the process difficult and challenging with even high-resolution DEM. Hence, a previous study focused on enhancing streamlines and watershed boundaries derived from a high-resolution DEM for future hydrologic modeling and flood forecasting [12]. To determine accurate stream networks, an effective method of eliminating pits or depressions is the stream burning algorithm. This algorithm often identifies river channels or lakes that are not recorded in the DEM, avoiding serious errors in the streaming [3,4]. A stream-burning algorithm can enhance the replication of streams' positions by using raster representation of a vector stream network to trench known hydrological features into a DEM, resulting in a comprehensive watershed delineation [4,13,14]. In addition, delineation of watersheds will not only serve to determine drainage boundaries but to distinguish existing sources of nonpoint sources (NPS) and point sources (PS) pollution.

Part of watershed characterization is to identify potential sources of pollution within the watershed. Pollutant sources have been divided into two different classifications: NPS and PS; with this distinction, it becomes easier to study, analyze, understand, and propose actions to mitigate the pollutant load. NPS pollutants are difficult to identify because they cannot be tracked and usually come from several land uses. The major contributor of NPS pollution is stormwater runoff originated by rainfall [15] and other forms of water flow through several different land uses. They ultimately discharge to lakes, canals, and coastal waters. This runoff carries significant levels of pollution caused by fertilizers, oil, grease, sediments, bacteria, and nutrients [16]. NPS pollutants contained a significant amount of nutrients, such as nitrogen and phosphorus [17]. There has been increasing emphasis on tackling NPS pollution from agricultural land for the presence of high nutrient contamination [18]. Currently, urbanization has led to increased water transfers from agriculture to urban uses [1,19]. These changes are altering the nature, location, and scope of wastewater loadings into the river. Urban runoff has caused negative results on water quality due to high bacteria and low dissolved oxygen (DO) levels [15]. Recent reports indicated that more than 40% of all impaired waters were affected solely by NPS pollutants, while only 10% of impairments were caused by PS pollutant discharges alone [20].

Unlike NPS pollutants, PS pollutants can be identified because they come from only one source. However, they still present a problem when addressing the pollution issues in primary waterways. To establish the proper actions to reduce or stop the pollutant load into waterbodies, it is necessary to identify the source of the pollutant. PS pollution identification is a challenging task because of the uncertainties and nonlinearity in the transport process of pollutants [21]. The typical way to identify PS pollution requires obtaining prior information of the pollution source, gaining complex information about pollution such as incidents regarding flow simulation dimensions, tabulating the number of PS pollutants involved, and evaluating the pollutant release process [22]. Determining potential sources is the first step in acting toward reducing the effects of water quality problems. Unlike NPS, PSs can be identified because they come from only one source. However, they still present a problem when addressing the pollution issues in primary waterways. To establish the proper actions to reduce or stop the pollutant load into waterbodies, it is necessary to identify the source of the pollutant. PS identification is a challenging task because of the uncertainties and nonlinearity in the transport process of pollutants [21]. The typical way to identify a PS requires obtaining prior information of the pollution source, gaining complex information about pollution such as incidents regarding flow simulation dimensions, tabulating the number of PS involved, and evaluating the pollutant release process [22]. Determining potential sources is the first step in acting toward reducing the effects of water quality problems.

Almost 70% of all rivers and streams in the United States are unassessed. In the State of Texas, 88% of all rivers and streams are unassessed. In the United States, 53% of the assessed water bodies were considered impaired due to high levels of *E. coli* and fecal coliform [23]. In addition, fecal coliform bacteria and other pathogens present in stormwater discharges threaten public health and have been responsible for numerous beach closings in the region [24]. Some studies have found that both livestock and manure management can potentially be agricultural sources of fecal indicator bacteria in watersheds [25]. Moreover, estuaries have faced eutrophication because of increased inputs of nutrients, such as nitrogen and phosphorus. This phenomenon is now considered to be a worldwide issue [26–28]. Ammonia can enter the aquatic environment via direct means of municipal effluent discharge and excretion of nitrogenous wastes from animals. It may also contaminate certain areas through indirect means such as nitrogen fixation, air deposition, and runoff from agricultural lands [29]. Improper wastewater management practices in this under-served region have caused severe water quality problems, and sections of the river have experienced poor water quality with regard to dissolved oxygen, bacteria, and algae [30].

The Laguna Madre is identified as an impaired waterbody due to the presence of high concentrations of bacteria and low dissolved oxygen [2]. The Lower Laguna Madre receives freshwater inflows from three waterways located in the north and central part of the LRGV. The three waterways are HWMD, RVD and IBWCNF, which are not fully characterized due to insufficient data. The aim of this paper is to provide a comprehensive characterization of the north and central watersheds to analyze pollution sources. A cyberinfrastructure database was developed to facilitate navigating through distinct information to obtain potential sources of pollution. Watershed delineation was developed using as GIS platform to determine the watersheds' drainage areas. Quantifying this information will support the identification of which of the three watersheds contribute the most to water impairments in the Lower Laguna Madre by assessing each watershed independently. The watershed characterization has been shown to support stakeholders in the region for optimal watershed management and enhance their decision-making process.

2. Study Area

The Laguna Madre is composed of two sections: The Upper Laguna Madre and the Lower Laguna Madre (LLM). The Laguna Madre is also unusual for being one of only five hypersaline coastal ecosystems in the world [31,32]. This estuary encompasses 20% of Texas's protected coastal waters while contributing 40–51% of the state's commercial fish catch historically as well as providing a common ground for migratory birds [1,32,33]. The LLM is the area of interest in this study since the north and central watersheds inflow to two of the three segments that are currently considered impaired. The north and central watersheds encompass an area of 3116 km^2 located in South Texas in the northern and central area of the LRGV region. The LRGV is a semiarid region in South Texas bordered by Mexico to the south and the Gulf of Mexico to the east [16]. This watershed is comprised of three main waterways: HWMD in the southwest extending to the east, RVD in the north, and IBWCNF in the southeast (Figure 1). The study area takes up a large plain of South Laguna Madre Watershed Hydrologic Unit Code 12110208 (8-digit HUC). North and central watersheds encompass 37% of the area in the LLM watershed. The study area has significant hydrology challenges due to flat terrain, where previous studies will be considered when processing the data. Its elevation gradually slopes from 102 to 0 m with a high range of precipitation between 50–70 cm/year. The Arroyo Colorado is located south of the IBWCNF waterway. Although relatively close to one another, they are not considered intersecting. In general, soils in the LRGV region consist of calcareous to neutral clays, clay loams, and sandy loams [20]. Therefore, the low permeability of the soils influences the drainage characteristics.

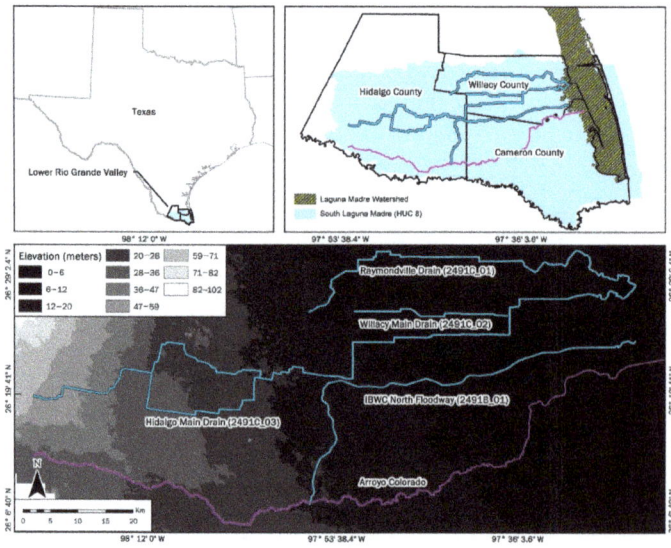

Figure 1. Location and elevation map of Study area is the North and Central watersheds located in the Lower Rio Grande Valley, of South Texas, Hidalgo/Willacy Main Drain (HWMD), Raymondville Drain (RVD), and International Boundary & Water Commission North Floodway (IBWCNF).

3. Methodology

The methodology to collect and analyze data for the characterization of the three watersheds was the acquisition of geospatial data and non-geospatial data. Geospatial data were obtained to develop a GIS database through a cyberinfrastructure to recognize the dominated attributes contributing to the watersheds. Therefore, the elaboration of watershed maps facilitated the identification of these attributes. Due to the wide inventory of data, a cyberinfrastructure was used to make data collection more efficient. Then, the elevation data were reconditioned to better represent the drainage areas of the watershed with respect to the terrain of the study area. In addition, NPS and PS pollution data were obtained to fully characterize the watersheds and to determine relative sources of pollution. Non-geospatial data were divided into two sections: water quality and flow data. Water quality was incorporated to determine the relationships between potential sources of pollution with the parameters found in each watershed. Available flow data were used to determine the load concentrations for each water quality parameter.

3.1. Cyberinfrastructure Development

In this study, cyberinfrastructure was established by developing the River and Estuary Observatory Network (REON) (http://dev.reon.cc:8607/ accessed on 17 August 2021). REON provides an extensive overview of all the available data from national, state, and local sources on this site. This platform helped in obtaining quality data for an overview of the north and central watersheds' characteristics, where stakeholders from the study area could support the characterization. The website now serves as a cyber-collaboratory platform for engaging stakeholders with an interest in data and information for a certain location [6]. Due to the wide inventory of data, the cyberinfrastructure also supported the acquisition of geospatial data, making the process more efficient which consisted of having all the geospatial data in only one source, REON. The value of the REON website in this study is that it portrays special features such as metadata, properties of the layers, and layer attributes to enhance watershed characteristics. The REON website was used to incorporate geospatial data and layers to show relative characteristics of the watersheds based on the watershed boundaries. To fully demonstrate watershed characteristics, the delineation of watershed boundaries was crucial for the assessment. Watershed delineation played an important role in this study, especially for the REON website to understand the extent of the study area.

3.2. Development of Watershed Delineation

The watershed delineation process is fundamental for the overall characterization to define the watershed boundaries and subwatersheds within each watershed. Generally, the watershed slopes from west to east through the heart of the LRGV, with an average slope of fewer than 0.3 m per kilometer [34]. Overall, its flat terrain varies from 0 m to 100 m. The resolution of the elevation raster-files was changed from 1 m to 60 m, which contributed to the reduction of file size and thus provided an efficient analysis. Since watershed delineation is key for this study, an ample watershed delineation was implemented to better assess the drainage areas of the watersheds. Previous studies have shown positive results for DEM reconditioning in watershed delineations in flat terrains [14]. Moreover, the assessment of satellite data and National Hydrography Dataset (NHD) was considered when evaluating the waterways and other laterals for the process. The satellite data were used to determine the accuracy of the location of the North and Central waterways. The NHD flowlines were used to determine the addition of laterals that could potentially drain into the waterways. LIDAR elevation data were reconditioned by developing several raster-elevation files to incorporate waterways into the data. This processing refers to burning waterways because the elevation data are not able to detect the waterways (Figure 2). Burning waterways consist of a rasterized version of the digital vector file to decrease the relative elevations of stream pixels by a uniform depth. Therefore, burning new channels into the DEM is an attempt to force alignment between topographically derived flowlines and independently mapped hydrography [35].

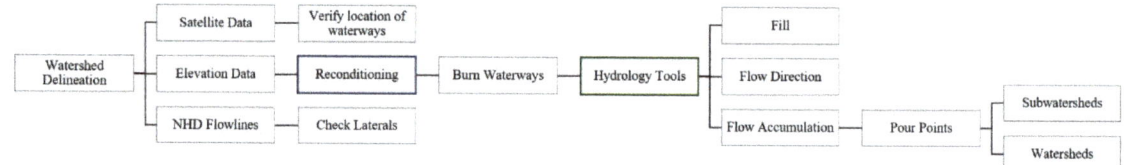

Figure 2. Watershed delineation methodology.

Once processing the LIDAR elevation data, the hydrology tools were used to develop elevation raster files such as fill, flow direction, and flow accumulation. Only three pour points were added manually to each corresponding waterway and then automated sub-watersheds were developed. With the subwatersheds delineated, the overall watershed boundaries for the three watersheds were determined based on the flow accumulation lines. The flow accumulation lines correspond to the flow path for each watershed based on elevation data. The flow accumulation lines embody the actual waterways in mostly all the watersheds. The watershed boundaries correspond to the flowlines and follow an enhanced methodology for the type of terrain in the region.

3.3. Data Collection

The study was developed based on the guidelines of the United States Environmental Protection Agency (USEPA) Handbook for Developing Watershed Plans to Restore Our Waters [36]. A summary of the data used in the study can be found in Table 1. NPS pollutant loads through sediment and runoff courses are highly related not only to land use/cover characteristics but also to topography [37–39]. This study integrates land cover data from the 2016 National Land Cover Database (NLCD) [40] with a spatial resolution of 30 m to determine relative contributions of NPS pollution in the north and central watersheds. The land cover type data identified as NPS pollution encompass urban and agricultural areas only. Each watershed was treated individually to characterize the type of land cover in the area. The NPS pollutants identified within the watersheds were cultivated crops areas and urbanized areas and South Texas large ranches (STLR), species, wildlife management areas (WMA), Onsite Sewage Facility (OSSF), and colonias.

Table 1. Data sources used for characterization the IBWCNF, HWMD and RVD.

Data	Source	Year	Usage
LIDAR Data	USGS, TNRIS	2018	Watershed Delineation
Hydrograph (NHD)	USGS	2012–2019	Watershed Delineation
Land Cover	NLCD	2016	NPS
STLR	TCEQ	2018	NPS
TLAP	TCEQ	N/A	PS
WWO	TCEQ	N/A	PS
MSW	TCEQ	N/A	PS
OSSF	Colonias	2021	NPS
MS4s	TCEQ	N/A	PS
Colonias	TCEQ	2015	NPS; OSSF points
Desalination Plants	TWDB	2021	PS
Address Points	TNRIS	2018	OSSF points
IBWC Gage Stations	IBWC	2012–2020	Flow data (IBWCNF)
SWQM Station	TCEQ	2011–2019	Flow and water quality (IBWCNF)
SWQM Stations	TCEQ	2017–2019	Flow and Water quality (HWMD and RVD)

Cultivated crops and urban areas are two types of land cover that can be contributing to NPS pollution. Agricultural and stormwater runoff generated from cultivated crops and urban areas; respectively. Runoff carries various pollutants such as nutrients, sediments, heavy metals, and bacteria which have a negative impact on the receiving waterbodies [41]. In peri-urban areas, agricultural/rural NPS pollution and urban NPS pollution are two types of sources that have gained considerable concern because urban expansion and agriculture intensification may act as a source or sink for contaminants to move toward surface water bodies [42]. Agricultural and urban areas in a watershed have shown in previous studies to be the main contributors to NPS pollution. Another type of NPS pollutants source is the STLR. The main concern with this type of NPS pollutants is the exposure to several hazardous contaminants from the practice of livestock. The improper management of livestock wastes (manure) can cause surface and groundwater pollution [43]. Water pollution from animal production systems can be by direct discharge, runoff, and/or seepage of pollutants to surface or groundwater [44].

OSSFs are designed to treat domestic wastewater using a septic tank for screening and pretreatment and a drain field where pretreated septic effluent is distributed for soil infiltration and final treatment by naturally existing microorganisms [45]. Species with WMA were found close to the coast of each watershed. These NPS pollutants contribute to high bacteria loadings to waterbodies from wildlife in the region. Grazing animals and wildlife can also negatively affect the water quality of runoff and waterbodies with bacterial contamination [46]. In Texas, non-avian wildlife, such as deer or feral hogs, are commonly found to be significant contributors of bacteria to natural streams [43,46]. In addition, colonias are considered the most distressed areas in the United States. They are usually found along the U.S.–Mexico border, which often lacks necessities such as sewer systems, drinkable water, and overall sanitary housing. Many homes within colonias cannot meet county building codes because they lack indoor bathrooms and plumbing, a prerequisite for connection to local water lines and sewage systems [17]. Consequently, colonias can be a potential contributor of NPS pollutants since they lack adequate solid waste disposal and wastewater systems. TCEQ created a classification system to identify the colonias with adequate utilities and the ones that lack basic utilities. The red and yellow classification was the one selected for colonias that potentially carry NPS pollution. Based on the priority classification by the Rural Community Assistance Partnership, OSSFs located in the colonias having a health hazard (red colonias) were assumed to have a greater failure rate of 70%. Conversely, a 30% failure rate (determined based on local expert knowledge) was assigned to areas having the lower priority ratings (yellow colonias) [47]. The term "colonia" refers to a settlement or neighborhood that is an unincorporated rural and peri-urban subdivision along Texas' border with Mexico [48].

STLR and colonias were extracted from TCEQ NPS Pollution database. There are currently limited studies in quantifying NPS pollution in semi-urban areas such as LRGV, where the topography is relatively flat. Furthermore, species and wildlife management areas WMA were considered as well as part of the NPS pollution for the effort in assessing their contaminants to the waterbodies. These were extracted from Texas Parks and Wildlife Department (TPWD). In addition, OSSF locations were mainly extracted from the colonias layer that identified OSSF as their wastewater collection facility. In Jeong's study [47], they utilized a methodology to extract OSSFs from merging address points with colonias. To estimate the number of OSSFs within the watershed, 911 address data for Cameron, Willacy, and Hidalgo counties were obtained. The address points represent the number of homes within a specific area. Combing this layer with the colonias areas, the acquisition of OSSFs was achieved. The colonias layer provided information about this classification and identified the type of colonias with limited wastewater disposal as well as adequate solid waste disposal. OSSFs were extracted from the red and yellow classification from colonias as well as the wastewater community section for onsite systems.

With the collaboration of local stakeholders and state-wide resources, the compilation of PS pollutants was obtained. The PS of pollutants identified in the north and central watersheds include permitted wastewater outfalls (WWO), Texas Land Application Permit (TLAP), Municipal Solid Waste (MSW), Municipal Separate Storm Sewer System (MS4), and desalination plants [48].

There is a substantial contribution of bacteria from wastewater outfalls, which potentially discharges to the waterways. Fecal contamination of water normally results from direct entry of wastewater from a municipal treatment plant into a water body [46,47]. There were two types of WWOs identified in these watersheds: domestic and industrial wastewater discharge. Domestic WWOs discharge less than 1 million gallons per day (MGD) while the ones with a discharge greater than 1 MGD may be either domestic sources or industrial wastewater treatment plant effluent. According to TCEQ, TLAP refers to the spreading of sewage from several applications, such as surface irrigation, evaporation, drain fields, or subsurface land application [49]. MSW facilities not only affect the surface water within the watershed but also groundwater. Closed landfills are commonly unlined and poorly capped and may be sources of a large number of organic compounds to surrounding groundwater and surface water [50]. Polluted stormwater runoff is commonly transported through MS4s and then often discharged, untreated, into local water bodies [51]. MS4s are identified to discharge significant levels of contaminants to waterbodies in the United States and are now one of the major sources of water pollution in the nation [24]. Information about desalination plants was obtained from the Texas Water Development Board (TWDB) to support the PS pollution contribution to the watersheds. Disposing the concentrate from the desalination plant in the surface water is the most common method of concentrate disposal which is considered a point source [52]. These sources can be potential contributors to water quality impairments to the North and Central waterways.

Water quality data were obtained for the three watersheds from the Surface Water Quality Monitoring Information System (SWQMIS) database. The TCEQ maintains SWQMIS database to serve as a repository for surface water data throughout Texas. All the data available in the SWQMIS database have to be collected according to TCEQ surface water quality monitoring standards. Moreover, data must be verified and validated prior to its loading into SWQMIS. HWMD has a TCEQ monitoring station (ID 22003) located at FM 1420 1.65 KM south of the intersection with FM 490 east of Raymondville (Figure 3). In addition, RVD has a TCEQ monitoring station (ID 22004) located at Willacy County Road 445 800 m north of the intersection with FM 3142. Both HWMD and RVD monitoring stations have 8 water quality samples available on the SWQMIS database. Data from both sites were collected by Clean River Programs (CRP) from 2017 to 2019 [53]. For IBWCNF, one TCEQ monitoring station was installed to collect water quality data since 2012. IBWCNF station ID is 20930 and is located at US 77 2.5 KM south of the intersection of US 77 and FM 2629 in the city of Sebastian. There were 25 water quality samples for the IBWCNF watershed available from SWQMIS from 2012 to 2019 [54,55]. The water quality parameters assessed in this study include the following: bacteria, ammonia, total Kjeldahl nitrogen (TKN), total phosphorus (TP), chlorophyll-a, nitrite, and nitrate. On the other hand, there is currently limited flow data for HWMD and RVD waterways since the monitoring in both stations started in 2017. The data were quantified on a quarterly basis for the period of two years. However, IBWCNF has a flow monitoring station (ID 08470200) installed by USIBWC at the same location of the SWQM near Sebastian that collected data from 2012 to 2020.

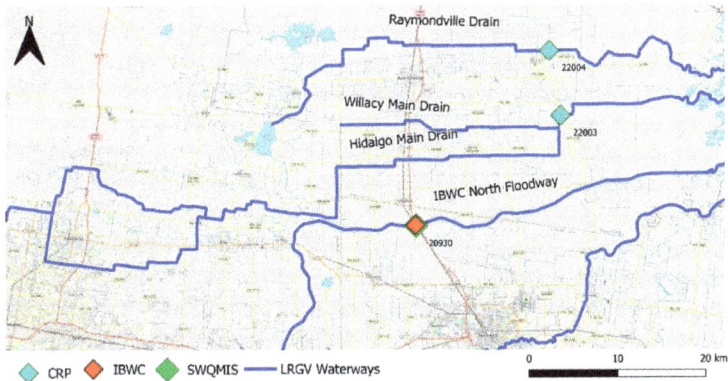

Figure 3. Location of water quality and flow data monitoring stations.

4. Results

4.1. REON Cyberinfrastructure

With the collaboration of REON, a cyberinfrastructure website, both data collection and the development of maps were accomplished. This platform provided an efficient watershed characterization by exposing significant guidelines from the EPA watershed characterization manual. This manual provides the basis to meet water quality and watershed management goals. Physical and natural features, land use, waterbody conditions, pollutant sources, and waterbody monitoring information are the data needed to characterize a watershed [56]. The first step for the watershed characterization was to develop the watershed delineation for the three watersheds. The results were then uploaded to the REON website to show watershed boundaries. Additionally, NPS and PS pollution layers were included in each watershed to facilitate the characterization process based on EPA watershed characterization. The cyberinfrastructure gathers existing watershed boundaries, hydrology, land use, NPS pollution, PS pollution, water quality stations, and flow stations to support the overview of the watershed characteristics. Three maps were created: Watershed delineation results, NPS pollution, and PS pollution maps. The maps created facilitated the watershed characterization by integrating geospatial data for NPS and PS pollutants for each watershed individually. The development of maps portrayed in the cyberinfrastructure helped stakeholders collaborate in the characterization by providing inputs for each potential source that could contaminate the area. The web user interface at the regional level is available for every stakeholder regardless of time or location.

4.2. Watershed Delineation

This section introduces the watershed delineation results for the study area (Figure 4) (Table 2). The watershed delineation encompassed a comprehensive LIDAR elevation data reconditioning to well display the North and Central Watersheds' characteristics. Elevation reconditioning has revealed improved results in areas with very flat terrain. Previous studies had positive results with respect to their watershed delineation by performing this methodology [13]. Burning the waterways to the elevation data has enhanced the terrain to better support the current conditions of the elevation changes in the waterways. Generally, all the waterways within the area are man-made, which makes it challenging for the elevation data to capture the waterways. The north and central watersheds presented a total area of 3116 km^2 of which HWMD watershed presented an area of 1357 km^2, RVD watershed is 1021 km^2, and IBWCNF watershed is 737 km^2 (Table 2). HWMD watershed covers 68% of its area in Hidalgo County, 31% in Willacy County, and 1% in Cameron County. This watershed covers a wide central area of the LRGV region. It extends across nine cities in the region. Moreover, it covers the McAllen-Edinburg-Mission Metropolitan Statistical Area (MSA) of the LRGV region, which is ranked the 5th largest in the state of

Texas. The RVD watershed, located in the north area of the LRGV region, covers 30.7% in Hidalgo County, 68.9% in Willacy County, and 0.4% in Kennedy County. The city of Raymondville, San Perlita, and a northeast portion of the city of Edinburg are the only cities within the watershed.

Figure 4. North and Central subwatersheds within each of the watersheds; top: Raymondville Drain (RVD); middle: Hidalgo/Willacy Main Drain (HWMD); bottom: International Boundary & Water Commission North Floodway (IBWCNF).

Table 2. Watershed delineation results for the three waterways.

	HWMD	RVD	IBWCNF
Watershed Area (km^2)	1357	1021	737
Number of Sub-watersheds	91	72	73
Hidalgo County	68%	31%	52%
Willacy County	31%	69%	24%
Cameron County	1%	0%	24%

IBWCNF watershed is located 53% in Hidalgo County, 24% in Willacy County, and 24% in Cameron County. This watershed is within the southern area of the North and Central Watersheds and intersects with the Arroyo Colorado Watershed. Eight cities are included in the IBWCNF watershed. The IBWCNF branches off of the Main Floodway at the Llano Grande, a shallow lake located southwest of the city of Mercedes [57]. The IBWCNF Waterway is considered a man-made waterway approximately 77 km long and is used to divert the Arroyo Colorado's flow. The city of Mercedes is upstream of IBWCNF flow and downstream of the Arroyo Colorado Waterway when the flow is exceeding its capacity. During flood conditions, which the IBWC defines as flow exceeding 40 cubic meters per second, approximately 80% of the flow in the Arroyo Colorado is diverted to the IBWCNF [58].

4.3. Nonpoint Sources

In this section, the watershed sources that potentially contribute the most to NPS pollutants were identified. Table 3 shows the results of the ratio of PS and NPS pollution sources to the area of each watershed. The predominant land cover for the North and Central Watersheds is cultivated crops representing 53% of the total area located mostly in the northeast sector of the watersheds. This type of land use is within the downstream tributary areas of the watersheds. Urbanization areas within the North and Central Watersheds cover 13% of the total area. STLR were found near the coast of the three watersheds.

Table 3. Ratio of NPS and PS pollution sources with respect to the area of each watershed.

	Sources	HWMD	RVD	IBWNF
Nonpoint Source Pollution	Urbanized Areas	0.20	0.05	0.24
	Cultivated Crops	0.47	0.52	0.59
	STLR	0.06	0.20	0.04
	Species *	0.03	0.10	0.20
	OSSFs	3.38	0.05	6.13
	Colonias	0.25	0.01	0.29
Point Source Pollution	Texas Land Application Permit	0.006	0.004	0.004
	Wastewater Outfalls	0.008	0.005	0.012
	Municipal Solid Waste	0.013	0.004	0.004
	MS4 Permit	0.006	0.001	0.016
	Desalination Plants	0.001	0.001	0.003

* Quantified data.

About 73% of the HWMD watershed area is covered with NPS pollutants sources. The watershed's cultivated crops correspond to approximately 47%, and 20% of urbanized areas. Urban growth in the watershed will primarily occur in areas that are currently cultivated and will influence the region's water quality [34]. Therefore, the HWMD watershed was identified with the highest ratio of urban areas among the other watersheds, with respect to their watershed area. The watershed encompasses 6.4% of STLR areas. Only El Suaz ranch pertains to the watershed. These STLR areas have grazing livestock activities that ultimately carry significant levels of bacteria. There were 46 species identified in this watershed along with two WMA units. La Palomas units, Longoria, and Fredrick, were found to possess hunting activities for their diversity of species. A total of 4591 OSSFs were found in the HWMD watershed from a total of 9170 in the north and central watersheds. All OSSFs have a potential for adverse environmental impact if they are improperly functioning, but those closer to streams present an elevated risk [34]. The watershed has 336 colonias, where 80 are classified with limited solid waste disposal, and 33 lack adequate solid waste and wastewater disposal. The total area of the colonias in the watershed is 26.8 km^2.

NPS pollutants sources cover almost 86% of the total area of the RVD watershed. The watershed has 51% of cultivated crops and only 2% of urban areas. The RVD watershed encompasses 19% of STLR areas. King Ranch, East Foundation, and El Suaz are the ranches that cover the watershed. Not only agriculture activities take place within the STLR areas. Livestock also grazes in this area, which can increase the relative contribution of bacteria. Fecal pollution brought to the rivers through surface runoff and soil leaching represents the NPS pollution; its origin can be the wild animals and grazing livestock feces and cattle manure spread on cultivated areas [50–52]. A total of 56 OSSFs were identified in the watershed. The RVD watershed has only 13 colonias recorded from which 1 is limited to solid waste disposal and 3 lack of basic utilities. Colonias within the watershed cover an area of 21.6 km^2.

The IBWCNF watershed corresponds to 73% of cultivated crops and 13% of urban areas. This watershed has the highest ratio of agricultural lands that can be a possible source of ammonia and nitrogen in the surface water. According to the EPA, watersheds could be affected by the level of decomposition of organic matters and some fertilizers used in agriculture. This watershed covers a portion of El Suaz ranch with 5% of STLR areas. There were 4523 OSSFs identified in this watershed, corresponding to a 6.33 ratio between the total OSSFs and the total area of the watersheds. The colonias cover an area of 23.4 km^2 within the IBWCNF watershed. This watershed has 216 colonias from which 65 lack proper solid waste disposal, and 51 lack both solid waste and wastewater disposal.

In summary, the HWMD watershed was identified with the highest ratio of urban areas among the other watersheds with respect to their watershed area. The identification of McAllen-Edinburg-Mission MSA in this watershed demonstrates the high presence of urban areas. The HWMD had 20.3% of urban areas and 8.8% from the three watersheds.

In contrast, the IBWCNF presented a higher percentage of 24.3% in urban areas, but it only had 5.8% with respect to the overall area of the North and Central Watersheds. The RVD and IBWCNF watersheds were the ones to have greater NPS pollution derived from cultivated crops [46]. The RVD watershed was the highest with STLR areas.

4.4. Point Source

The HWMD watershed has a total of 11 WWOs from which 5 were found to discharge less than 1 MGD, and the rest discharged more than 1 MGD. Major PS pollutants identified in this watershed were TLAP and MSW. The TLAP corresponds to the presence of high levels of nitrogen in the watershed, and the MSW corresponds to the presence of high total phosphorus levels. There were 8 TLAPs found upstream of the watershed. Currently, there are 2 active MSW facilities in the HWMD watershed. This watershed has a total of 17 MSW facilities recorded from which 4 are considered closed facilities, 4 are inactive, 2 posted closed, and the rest are not constructed. HWMD watershed covers 13% of MS4s. There are currently 7 MS4s permitted areas within the HWMD watershed. The HWMD watershed has the highest MS4s areas among the other watersheds. Therefore, the HWMD watershed shows severe impact by the PS pollution compared to the other watersheds

Although the RVD watershed has a greater area compared to the IBWCNF watershed, it is limited with PS pollution (Figure 5). Five WWOs were identified within the watershed boundaries from which 3 are considered industrial wastewater effluent and 2 domestic. Only 4 TLAPs were found in the RVD watershed. Currently, the City of Edinburg Landfill is an active MSW in the RVD watershed. A total of 4 MSWs were identified in the RVD watershed: 2 not constructed, 1 closed, and 1 post closed MSWs. RVD watershed is considered to contribute to 0% of MS4s, with only 0.3% of the city of Edinburg's MS4 found. This watershed covers almost the entire Willacy County, which is identified as limited in MS4s. The IBWCNF watershed presents 9 WWOs from which 4 are domestic and 5 are industrial wastewater effluent. For instance, only 3 TLAP were found, and 3 active MSWs were identified. These PS pollutants are mainly located upstream of the watershed. As a result, it is important to identify the potential PS pollutants of the downstream area of the Arroyo Colorado Watershed that diverts to the IBWCNF watershed. The IBWCNF watershed has 7% of MS4s permitted areas. The MS4s permitted areas include 11 cities. Consequently, it is important to improve stormwater management within these areas to mitigate PS pollutants. Unlike sanitary sewer systems, MS4 systems do not treat the stormwater collected; instead MS4s are required to develop and implement stormwater management programs (SWMP) that reduce the amount of contaminants that enter the system and prohibit illicit discharges [24].

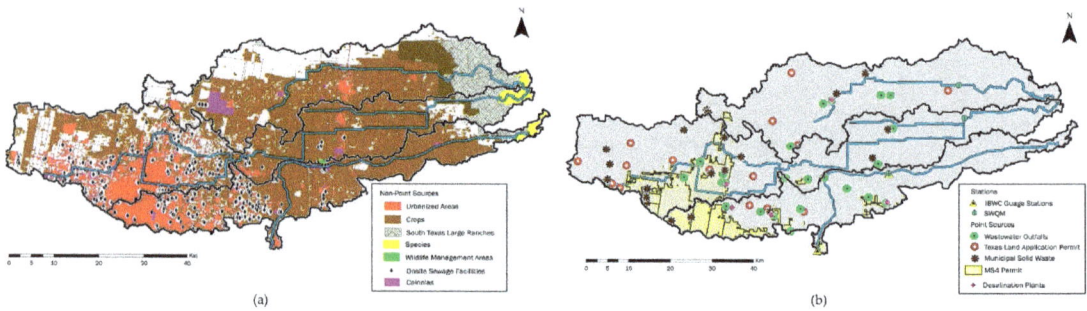

Figure 5. Location of potential sources of pollution in the North and Central Watersheds: (**a**) non-point sources and (**b**) point sources of pollution identified in each watershed.

4.5. Water Quality Parameters

The water quality parameters samples for the north and central watersheds are shown in Figure 6, where the red line represents the screening level according to TCEQ water quality standards. HWMD watershed has *E. coli* levels higher than the screening level of 126 MPN/100 mL from 2017 and 2019 [2]. In 2019, the *E. coli* levels were above 2000 MPN/100 mL. The existence of high levels of bacteria is caused by a variety of NPS and PS pollution sources such as urban runoff, agricultural lands, ranches, WWO, OSSF, MS4s, and colonias. Ammonia levels in this watershed were below the screening level with 2.7 mg/L as N, which is considered the highest record. In 2018, the TKN levels were the highest compared to the other years with more than 3.0 MGL as N. The presence of TKN in the HWMD watershed, according to the EPA, can be traced to failing septic systems, croplands, and industrial discharges [59]. TP levels barely exceed the screening level of 0.7 mg/L with the maximum value of 0.8 mg/L in 2017. Moreover, the nitrite and nitrate levels found in the watershed are higher than the screening level of 1.95 mg/L [2,60]. Chlorophyll-a levels identified surpassed the screening level of 14 µg/L for the three years [2]. In 2018, chlorophyll-a had the highest level of 98 µg/L.

The RVD watershed had higher levels of *E. coli* compared to the other watersheds, which suggests that there could be several sources of NPS and PS such as septic tanks that can be leaking. Further, sewage may overflow from poorly structured sewage systems and create polluted stormwater runoff [61]. However, ammonia levels for the RVD watershed are acceptable since they are below the screening level of 0.33 mg/L with a maximum value of 0.2 mg/L in 2018 and 2019 [60]. The TKN levels mainly surpassed the screening level of 1.0 mg/L in 2018 and 2019. TP levels were lower in all the years recorded, with a maximum value of 0.4 mg/L in 2019. According to the USGS report, bank erosion is the main source of total phosphorus during flooding events that can be the potential source in these watersheds [62]. Nitrite and nitrate levels surpassed only in 2017, but the highest level identified was almost 6 mg/L as N in 2019. For Chlorophyll-a levels, the RVD watershed showed its highest level of 70 µg/L in 2019.

In the IBWCNF watershed, the levels of bacteria were identified to be higher in 2013, 2014, 2015, and 2019. The highest level was around 8000 MPN/100 mL in 2013. The bacteria levels from 2016 through 2018 were determined to be slightly below the screening level of 126 MPN/100 mL. The results showed, according to Olmstead [46], that the watershed is affected by wildlife with small contributions of domestic animals and point sources. The ammonia levels were identified to be less than the screening level during all the years. This finding indicates that the watershed is limited to carrying significant levels of ammonia from agricultural runoff. TKN levels have shown to be relatively higher than the screening level with the highest of 2 mg/L as N in 2018. High levels of total nitrogen are caused by the decomposition of detritus and any anthropogenic loadings [63]. High levels of total nitrogen are caused by the decomposition of detritus and any anthropogenic loadings [63]. TP levels were lower than the screening level of 0.7. The IBWNF watershed is limited to algae growth since TP levels are low. Nitrite and nitrate levels are higher than the screening levels; 7 mg/L was the highest level recorded in 2015. Chlorophyll-a levels were determined to be higher than the screening levels for nearly all the years. This finding indicates the presence of excess quantities of algae [64].

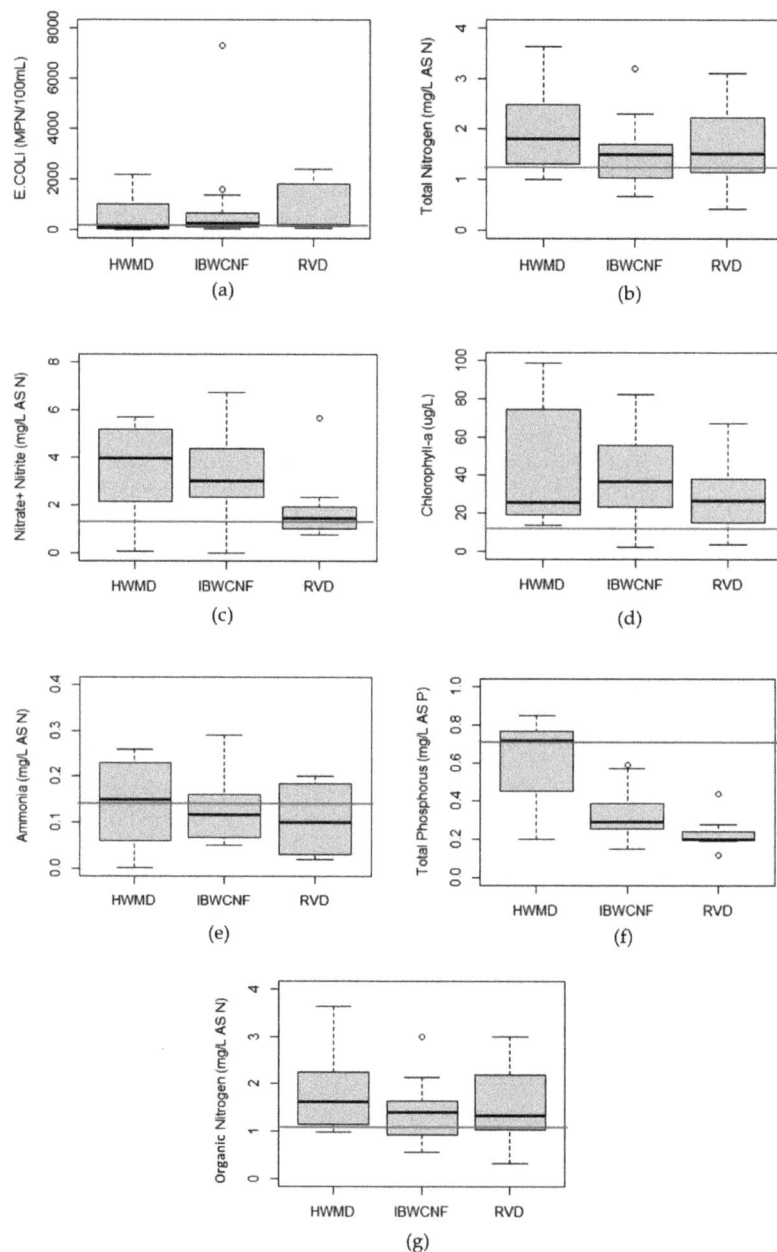

Figure 6. Comparison between water quality concentration levels for Hidalgo/Willacy Main Drain (HWMD), Raymondville Drain (RVD), and International Boundary & Water Commission North Floodway (IBWCNF)): (**a**) *E.coli*, (**b**) total nitrogen, (**c**) nitrate + nitrite, (**d**) chlorophyll-a, (**e**) ammonia, (**f**) total phosphorus, and (**g**) organic nitrogen. Redline represents the TCEQ screening level for each parameter (data source: SWQMIS).

4.6. Flow Data

Waterbody monitoring data are used to portray historical data that would represent most conditions of the study area. Flow data encompassed the volumetric flow rate for each waterway recorded from each station available. HWMD waterway flow data reflect high flow values in 2019 with a mean value of 12 CMS, and in 2018 the mean value was below 10 CMS. These levels reflect a high correlation with flooding patterns with respect to sudden storm events from those years. Moreover, the RVD flow data showed high flow values in 2018 of almost 10 CMS (Figure A1 in Appendix A). Both HWMD and RVD flow data correspond to past abnormal flooding events in the LRGV region. The region has experienced high storm events since 2018 with over 38.1 cm to 50.8 cm of rainfall causing severe flooding damage [65]. Such flooding's caused a halt to everyday functions for weeks and months because of minor to destructive varying degrees of flood damage in city roads, frontage roads, residences and businesses, and infrastructure in the LRGV region. Hidalgo, Cameron, and Willacy counties have received the Presidential Disaster Declaration in which have been determined to be the most impacted areas [66]. There are limited data for this watershed since they are only available for three years with limited monitoring campaigns. Therefore, among the three watersheds, it has been determined that the HWMD waterway has the highest flow values that affect the loadings even if the water quality concentrations are low.

The IBWCNF watershed has two stations: Mercedes and Sebastian. However, only the flow values utilized for further analysis were the ones from Sebastian since the water quality samples were obtained near that station. This finding would represent a better overview of the IBWCNF watershed behavior with respect to load concentrations. In 2017 and 2018, flow data measured were more than 10 CMS. The flow values throughout 2012 to 2020 seem to have mean values below 5 CMS, which suggests a constant uniform flow for this watershed.

4.7. Pollutant Loadings

Pollutant loading calculations were obtained from quantifying flow and water quality data. To well represent the loadings with each respected watershed, the pollutant loadings were based on the watershed area for the three watersheds. Table 4 shows the results for the unit area loading rates for each watershed reflecting which of the three watersheds has the highest loading. The HWMD watershed shows higher results with respect to the flow, water quality parameters, and the overall watershed area, where both NPS and PS pollution are potential attributes of these elevated results. These data are not representative of the whole profile of the watersheds. More data should be quantified to better distinguish which watershed contributes the most to water impairments to the LLM.

Table 4. Summary of the pollutant loading (kg/km^2/year) for the three watersheds.

Water Quality Parameters	HWMD	RVD	IBWCNF
Bacteria (Log *E.coli*) [1]	12.8	12.3	12.4
Ammonia	121	31	48
TKN	1586	670	477
Organic Nitrogen	1466	639	429.4
TP	519	63.3	122.6
Nitrite + Nitrate	2950	581.46	1512.10
Chlorophyll-a	32.6	9.9	13.2

[1] Bacteria loading unit is in MPN/km^2/year. Source: SWQMIS.

The pollutant loadings per unit area distribution for each water quality parameter were provided with respect to each watershed area (Figure 7). Methods for calculating the loadings for each pollutant can be found in the USEPA Handbook for Developing Watershed Plans to Restore Our Waters [36]. These loadings were generated automatically through ArcGIS properties to show the difference among pollutant loadings. Bacteria loadings per unit area were determined to be slightly higher for the IBWCNF watershed than RVD. However, IBWCNF has more potential NPS and PS sources for bacteria than RVD. The mean value for the bacteria loadings in IBWCNF and RVD was 12.4 (kg/km^2/year) and 12.3 (kg/km^2/year); respectively. This can be explained by the fact that the main bacterial sources in both watersheds come from agricultural activities. The ratio in cultivated crops in IBWCNF was slightly higher than RVD. IBWCNF covered 59% of cultivated crops, while RVD covered 52%. Additionally, the flow volume in RVD was higher than IBWCNF. The average flow rate in RVD was 2.57 CMS, while in IBWCNF it was 2.38 CMS. This could be the reason why the bacteria loadings in both watersheds have a minor difference. TKN results proved to be higher for the HWMD, which support the relative contribution of the TLAP to this watershed. Nitrate and nitrite and chlorophyll-a concentrations were high in the HWMD, corresponding to the significant presence of urban areas in the watershed. Ammonia results showed to be higher in the IBWCNF watershed, supporting the identification of a substantial percentage of agricultural lands. The HWMD had the highest loadings for TP and organic nitrogen, supporting the presence of MSWs. Figure 6a–g reflects the loading with respect to the subwatersheds of the three North and Central Watersheds. The HWMD watershed was identified to be higher in all the water quality parameters due to the high flow recordings in this watershed.

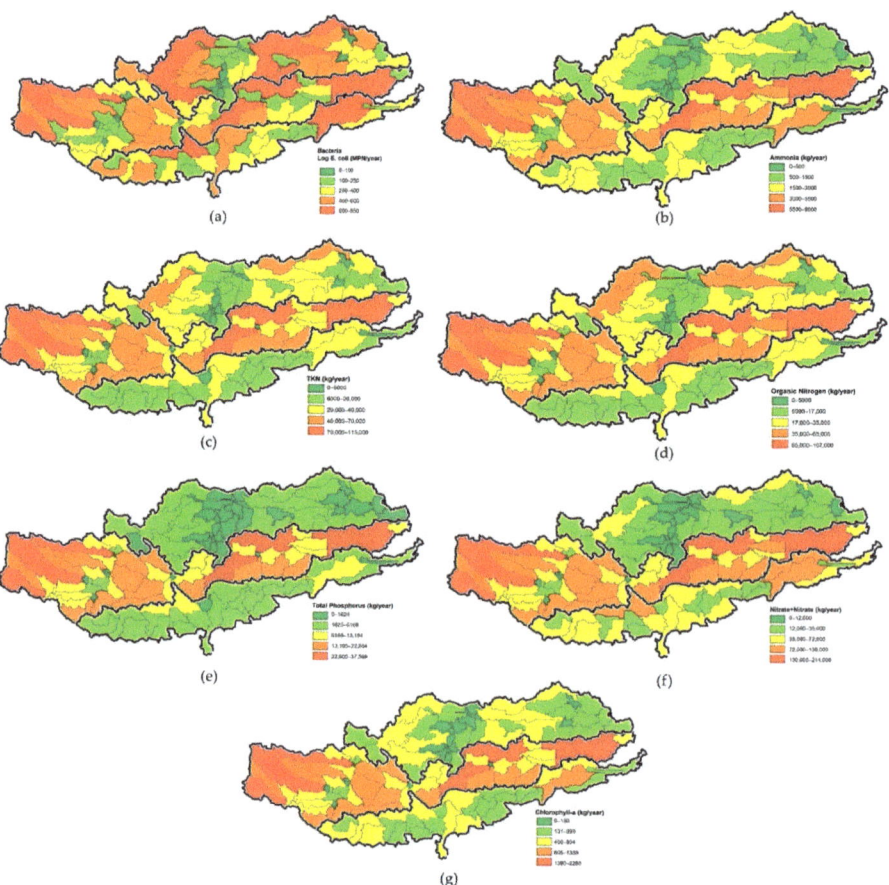

Figure 7. Spatial distribution of the pollutant loading for different parameters in the North and Central Watersheds: (**a**) bacteria, (**b**) ammonia, (**c**) total nitrogen, (**d**) organic nitrogen, (**e**) total phosphorus, (**f**) nitrite + nitrate, and (**g**) chlorophyll-a.

5. Discussion and Conclusions

The cyberinfrastructure and REON website contributed significantly to this study in portraying relevant characteristics of each of the North and Central Watersheds. The REON website not only collects distinct information into one single source but also allows the stakeholders within each watershed to assess the watershed characteristics. Therefore, this platform is an innovative tool that supports effective watershed characterization. ArcGIS automated hydrology tools have shown to have satisfactory results in delineating watersheds. Overall, the study showed that the watershed delineation process used provided acceptable results to characterize the North and Central Watersheds.

Although the HWMD watershed was not the highest regarding the urban areas, it is considered higher in NPS pollution with respect to the entire area of the North and Central Watersheds. Urban areas have more impact on the HWMD in comparison to the other watersheds regarding the overall watershed areas. This finding suggests that urban areas in this watershed are linked to the presence of bacteria and chlorophyll-a. Based on the water quality data obtained, only chlorophyll-a levels were higher than the other watershed levels. The high levels of chlorophyll-a relate to the HWMD watershed in extensive urban areas. Based on the total PS pollution found in the North and Central Watersheds, HWMD is the watershed to contribute a 3.66 ratio with respect to the watershed area. While this watershed has greater PS pollution than the other two watersheds, it is not particularly the most affected watershed with respect to the drainage area. The NPS and PS results for HWMD were consistent with the elevated levels of the water quality data analyzed from the SWQMIS database. Bacteria, total nitrogen, nitrate and nitrite, chlorophyll-a, ammonia, total phosphorus, and organic nitrogen in HWMD had significant values in this watershed compared to the other watersheds. In addition, the high pollutant loadings in this watershed correspond to the high flow values recorded. Therefore, more flow data are needed in the future to further support this characterization and make the proper connections between sources of pollution and pollutant loads.

The RVD watershed had a higher percent of 20.3% for ranches and was identified to be higher regarding the total area of the North and Central Watersheds as well. The water quality parameters associated with the presence of ranches are bacteria, ammonia, TP, nitrite, and nitrate. The results showed that the RVD watershed has greater bacteria levels in comparison to the other watersheds, which suggests ranches and the activities within these areas are causing high levels of bacteria. The RVD watershed pollutant loadings were generally low, but bacteria loadings were significant because of the high presence of NPS pollutants. Bacteria loading mean value corresponds to almost 12.3 MPN/km^2/year.

The IBWCNF watershed was identified to have higher crop areas with 58.5% regarding the area as well as the overall area of the three watersheds, which suggests the presence of significant agricultural activities. Therefore, it was determined that agricultural runoff is prone to release higher levels of ammonia where this watershed was limited to carry high ammonia levels. This finding indicates a possible change in land cover from 2016 to 2020. In addition to ammonia, bacteria, TKN, TP, nitrite and nitrate, and chlorophyll-a are present in agricultural areas. The IBWCNF watershed has a greater presence of nutrient water impairments because of the high agricultural area. This finding suggests the high levels of nitrite and nitrate in this watershed correspond to agricultural lands. This watershed had the higher contribution of PS pollutants such as WWO, OSSFs, MS4s, and colonias among the watersheds. The sources contributing to the high levels of water quality concentrations were identified. Ammonia, nitrate, and nitrite primary sources can be related to WWO, MS4s, and colonias. The load concentration results showed the IBWCNF to have high bacteria and ammonia loads. This finding suggests that the presence of a significant contribution of OSSFs is linked to bacteria loadings.

To uncover which North and Central watersheds contributed the most to the LLM watershed impairment, a cyberinfrastructure was established along with an ample watershed delineation. Then NPS pollution, PS pollution, water quality concentrations, flow data, and pollutant loadings were enhanced to identify unique characteristics of the watershed.

HWMD and IBWCNF were the watersheds to contribute the most in water impairments to the LLM watershed. They were found to have significant loadings of water quality parameters as well as NPS and PS pollutant contributions. Urban areas, TLAP, and MSW were related to the high contribution of chlorophyll-a, TKN, and TP. OSSFs and colonias were linked to the major influence of bacteria concentrations and loadings of which the IBWCNF watershed possesses the most. These results along with the user-friendly cyberinfrastructure may assist stakeholders from the region in identifying the characteristics of watersheds and mitigate the sources of pollution. This study is essential in bringing awareness to the local communities that reside within these watersheds, especially the people who visit the LLM watershed. One of the limitations of this study was the acquisition of available data for such an extensive study area of more than 3000 km^2. Additional flow data and water quality data could enhance the characterization as it was limited to only 8 samples for the HWMD and the RVD watersheds. Flow data are essential for determining the load concentrations and provide a better overview of the north and central watersheds' potential sources of pollution.

Author Contributions: Conceptualization, A.E. and A.M.; methodology, A.M., A.O. and A.E.; software, A.E. and C.F.; formal analysis, A.O. and L.N.; writing—original draft preparation, L.N., J.J., I.R.S.C. and A.M.; visualization, I.R.S.C.; supervision, A.M. and A.E.; project administration, J.J. All authors have read and agreed to the published version of the manuscript.

Funding: Funding for this research was provided by the Texas Commission on Environmental Quality (Project Contract# 582-19-90196) and financed through grants from the U.S. Environmental Protection Agency (Federal ID# 99614623).

Institutional Review Board Statement: Not applicable.

Informed Consent Statement: Not applicable.

Data Availability Statement: The data presented in this study are available on request from the corresponding author.

Acknowledgments: The authors would like to thank Tim Cawthon (Texas Commission on Environmental Quality) for his support and contribution in data for the study. The authors also would like to thank Javier Guerrero and the Lower Rio Grande Valley Stormwater Taskforce members for their collaboration in the study.

Conflicts of Interest: The authors declare no conflict of interest.

Appendix A

Table A1. Hidalgo Willacy Main Drain Water Quality.

Date	Bacteria	Ammonia	TKN	TP	Nitrite	Nitrate	Chlorophyll-a
10/4/2017	610	0.02	1	0.733	3.02	0	57
12/3/2017	10	0.26	2.85	0.847	3.87	0	13.5
5/1/2018	120	0.002	3.63	0.755	4.71	0	91.5
7/18/2018	20	0.2	2.1	0.2	1.2	0.099	98.5
10/31/2018	80	0.1	1.5	0.67	5.6	0.09	23.9
1/29/2019	31	0.1	1.21	0.7	5.6	0.06	19.3
4/2/2019	1400	0.2	1.4	0.78	4.02	0.06	27
7/16/2019	2200	0.26	2.1	0.23	0.03	0.02	19.3

Table A2. Raymondville Drain Water Quality.

Date	Bacteria	Ammonia	TKN	TP	Nitrite	Nitrate	Chlorophyll-a
10/4/2017	1940	0.02	1	0.28	1.17	0	36.3
12/3/2017	150	0.1	0.42	0.2	1.52	0	18
5/1/2018	220	0.02	2.75	0.12	2.34	0	33.3
7/18/2018	150	0.1	3.1	0.2	0.8	0.05	39.8
10/31/2018	1700	0.2	1.3	0.2	1.5	0.05	11.7
1/29/2019	74	0.17	1.43	0.2	5.6	0.06	3.8
4/2/2019	2400	0.04	1.7	0.44	1.34	0.08	67
7/16/2019	130	0.2	1.6	0.19	0.64	0.11	19.8

Table A3. IBWC North Floodway Water Quality.

Date	Bacteria	Ammonia	TKN	TP	Nitrate + Nitrite	Chlorophyll-a
11/3/2011	0	0.16	2.03	0.00	2.42	29.70
2/23/2012	0	0.09	0.95	0.21	5.28	35.00
5/3/2012	0	0.13	1.49	0.29	4.47	40.20
8/23/2012	0	0.12	1.04	0.23	2.26	55.70
11/19/2012	0	0.06	1.50	0.59	2.75	42.60
3/12/2013	110	0.16	1.08	0.00	2.68	40.50
8/21/2013	640	0.23	0.89	0.23	2.01	51.40
11/25/2013	7300	0.12	0.68	0.41	3.96	9.50
8/14/2014	0	0.06	1.70	0.00	2.03	82.30
11/24/2014	1100	0.11	1.36	0.34	3.82	44.40
2/25/2015	110	0.13	1.57	0.27	3.08	35.40
3/26/2015	0	0.25	1.66	0.35	6.71	26.00
8/26/2015	1400	0.12	1.84	0.32	3.10	60.20
8/27/2015	0	0.07	1.53	0.26	3.02	76.20
11/30/2015	610	0.19	3.19	0.25	4.98	23.40
5/4/2016	360	0.21	2.01	0.31	4.37	68.30
8/4/2016	0	0.00	0.00	0.27	2.08	20.10
11/2/2016	95	0.05	0.74	0.42	2.98	52.80
2/8/2017	0	0.08	1.72	0.39	4.29	11.00
5/3/2017	75	0.08	1.55	0.27	4.37	2.31
7/25/2017	120	0.05	0.00	0.25	1.07	19.60
11/29/2017	160	0.00	0.00	0.00	0.00	9.94
1/30/2018	20	0.16	0.00	0.29	3.80	6.91
4/18/2018	340	0.05	1.29	0.50	4.43	66.90
7/18/2018	96	0.05	2.30	0.39	2.36	78.10
10/16/2018	300	0.29	1.51	0.57	1.79	72.30
1/23/2019	200	0.10	1.03	0.35	4.67	28.60
4/16/2019	1600	0.05	1.03	0.24	2.65	36.30
11/7/2019	0	0.21	1.20	0.15	2.35	32.60

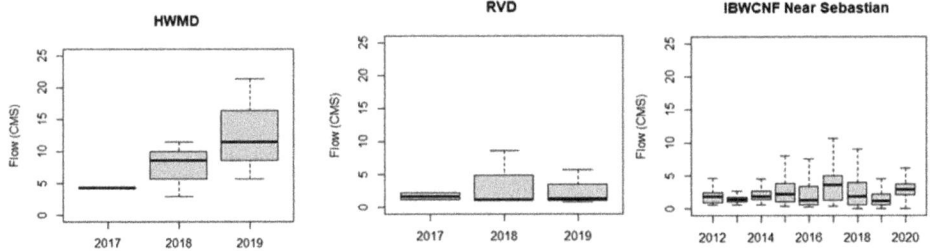

Figure A1. North and Central Watersheds Flow Data.

References

1. Hernandez, E.A.; Uddameri, V. An assessment of optimal waste load allocation and assimilation characteristics in the Arroyo Colorado River watershed, TX along the US–Mexico border. *Clean Technol. Environ. Policy* **2013**, *15*, 617–631. [CrossRef]
2. TCEQ. 2020 Texas Integrated Report—Texas 303(d) List (Category 5). 2020. Available online: https://www.tceq.texas.gov/assets/public/waterquality/swqm/assess/20txir/2020_303d.pdf (accessed on 8 March 2021).
3. Li, L.; Yang, J.; Wu, J. A Method of Watershed Delineation for Flat Terrain Using Sentinel-2A Imagery and DEM: A Case Study of the Taihu Basin. *ISPRS Int. J. Geo-Inf.* **2019**, *8*, 528. [CrossRef]
4. Chen, Y.; Wilson, J.P.; Zhu, Q.; Zhou, Q. Comparison of drainage-constrained methods for DEM generalization. *Comput. Geosci.* **2012**, *48*, 41–49. [CrossRef]
5. Yu, Y.; Ibarra, J.E.; Kumar, K.; Chergarova, V. Coevolution of cyberinfrastructure development and scientific progress. *Technovation* **2021**, *100*, 102180. [CrossRef]
6. Gutenson, J.L.; Ernest, A.N.S.; Bearden, B.L.; Fuller, C.; Guerrero, J. Integrating Societal and Scientific Elements into Sustainable and Effective Water Resource Policy Development. *J. Environ. Inform. Lett.* **2020**. [CrossRef]
7. Terra, A. *Lecture 3 Watershed Delineation EPA*; EPA: Washington, DC, USA, 2015.
8. Strager, M.P.; Fletcher, J.J.; Strager, J.M.; Yuill, C.B.; Eli, R.N.; Petty, J.T.; Lamont, S.J. Watershed analysis with GIS: The watershed characterization and modeling system software application. *Comput. Geosci.* **2010**, *36*, 970–976. [CrossRef]
9. Vaze, J.; Teng, J.; Spencer, G. Impact of DEM accuracy and resolution on topographic indices. *Environ. Model. Softw.* **2010**, *25*, 1086–1098. [CrossRef]
10. Amatya, D.; Trettin, C.; Panda, S.; Ssegane, H. Application of LiDAR Data for Hydrologic Assessments of Low-Gradient Coastal Watershed Drainage Characteristics. *J. Geogr. Inf. Syst.* **2013**, *5*, 175–191. [CrossRef]
11. Whitko, A.N. *Advanced Floodplain Mapping of a Rio Grande Valley Resaca Using LIDAR and Distributed Hydrologic Model*. 2005. Available online: https://scholarship.rice.edu/handle/1911/17839 (accessed on 1 March 2021).
12. Maidment, D.R.; Rajib, A.; Lin, P.; Clark, E.P. National Water Center Innovators Program Summer Institute Report 2016. Available online: https://www.cuahsi.org/uploads/library/cuahsi_tr13_8.20.16.pdf (accessed on 1 March 2021).
13. Callow, J.N.; Van Niel, K.P.; Boggs, G.S. How does modifying a DEM to reflect known hydrology affect subsequent terrain analysis? *J. Hydrol.* **2007**, *332*, 30–39. [CrossRef]
14. Sanders, W. Preparation of DEMs for Use in Environmental Modeling Analysis. 1999. Available online: https://proceedings.esri.com/library/userconf/proc99/proceed/papers/pap802/p802.htm (accessed on 1 March 2021).
15. Mahmoud, A.; Alam, T.; Sanchez, A.; Guerrero, J.; Oraby, T.; Ibrahim, E.; Jones, K.D. Stormwater Runoff Quality and Quantity from Permeable and Traditional Pavements in Semiarid South Texas. *J. Environ. Eng.* **2020**, *146*, 05020001. [CrossRef]
16. TCEQ. *Managing Nonpoint Source Pollution in Texas 2007 Annual Report*; Texas State Soil and Water Conservation Board: Temple, TX, USA, 2007.
17. Shin, M.; Jang, J.; Lee, S.; Park, Y.; Lee, Y.; Shin, Y.; Won, C. Application of surface cover materials for reduction of NPS pollution on field-scale experimental plots: Effects of surface cover materials for reduction of NPS pollution. *Irrig. Drain.* **2016**, *65*, 159–167. [CrossRef]
18. Burt, T.P.; Howden, N.J.K.; Worrall, F.; Whelan, M.J.; Bieroza, M. Nitrate in United Kingdom Rivers: Policy and Its Outcomes Since 1970 †. *Environ. Sci. Technol.* **2011**, *45*, 175–181. [CrossRef] [PubMed]
19. Black&Veatch. Rio Grande Regional Water Plan. 2016. Available online: https://www.twdb.texas.gov/waterplanning/rwp/plans/2016/M/Region_M_2016_RWPV1.pdf (accessed on 1 March 2021).
20. EPA. Section 319: Nonpoint Source Program. Available online: https://cfpub.epa.gov/watertrain/moduleFrame.cfm?parent_object_id=2165 (accessed on 4 February 2021).
21. Boano, F.; Revelli, R.; Ridolfi, L. Source identification in river pollution problems: A geostatistical approach. *Water Resour. Res.* **2005**, *41*. [CrossRef]
22. Guozhen, W.; Zhang, C.; Li, Y.; Haixing, L.; Zhou, H. Source identification of sudden contamination based on the parameter uncertainty analysis. *J. Hydroinform.* **2016**, *18*, 919–927. [CrossRef]
23. EPA. National Summary of State Information. 2017. Available online: https://ofmpub.epa.gov/waters10/attains_nation_cy.control#total_assessed_waters (accessed on 3 March 2021).
24. Abrams, R. Municipal Separate Storm Sewer Systems (MS4)-Assigning Responsibility for Pollutants That Reach the Nation's Waters. *Preview US Supreme Court Cases Chic.* **2012**, *40*, 129.
25. UWRRC. Pathogens, Lewis Publishers, Boca Raton, Fla. 2014. Available online: https://www.asce-pgh.org/Resources/EWRI/Pathogens%20Paper%20August%202014.pdf (accessed on 3 March 2021).
26. Nixon, S.W. Coastal marine eutrophication: A definition, social causes, and future concerns. *Ophelia* **1995**, *41*, 199–219. [CrossRef]
27. Smith, V.H.; Tilman, G.D.; Nekola, J.C. Eutrophication: Impacts of excess nutrient inputs on freshwater, marine, and terrestrial ecosystems. *Environ. Pollut.* **1999**, *100*, 179–196. [CrossRef]
28. Percuoco, V.P.; Kalnejais, L.H.; Officer, L.V. Nutrient release from the sediments of the Great Bay Estuary, N.H. USA. *Estuar. Coast. Shelf Sci.* **2015**, *161*, 76–87. [CrossRef]
29. USEPA. Aquatic Life Ambient Water Quality Criteria for Ammonia—Freshwater. 2013. Available online: https://www.regulations.gov/document/EPA-HQ-OW-2009-0921-0068 (accessed on 5 February 2021).

30. TCEQ. Pollutant Reduction Plan for the Arroyo Colorado: Segments 2201 and 2202, Hidalgo, Cameron, and Willacy Counties. Texas Commission on Environmental Quality. 2006. Available online: https://arroyocolorado.org/media/zs1fkpzw/pollutantreductionplanseg2201-2202.pdf (accessed on 1 March 2021).
31. Javor, B. Hypersaline Environments. 1989. Available online: https://link.springer.com/book/10.1007%2F978-3-642-74370-2 (accessed on 4 March 2021).
32. Onuf, C.P. Laguna Madre. 2002. Available online: https://www.arlis.org/docs/vol1/234196545/lagunamadre.pdf (accessed on 1 March 2021).
33. Hedgpeth, J.W. *The Laguna Madre of Texas: North American Wildlife Conference*. 1947, Volume 12. Available online: https://wildlifemanagement.institute/store/product/11 (accessed on 4 March 2021).
34. Flores, J.; Wagner, K.; Gregory, L.; Benavides, J.; Cawthon, T. Update to the Arroyo Colorado Watershed Protection Plan. Texas Water Resources Institute Technical Report. 2017. Available online: https://www.lrgvdc.org/downloads/water/arroyo-colorado-wppfinaloptimized%202017.pdf (accessed on 25 September 2021).
35. Baker, M.E.; Weller, D.E.; Jordan, T.E. Comparison of Automated Watershed Delineations. *Photogramm. Eng. Remote Sens.* **2006**, *72*, 159–168. [CrossRef]
36. USEPA. *Handbook for Developing Watershed Plans to Restore and Protect Our Waters*; 2008. Available online: https://www.epa.gov/sites/default/files/2015-09/documents/2008_04_18_nps_watershed_handbook_handbook-2.pdf (accessed on 19 July 2021).
37. Chen, L.; Fu, B.; Xu, J.; Gong, J. Location-weighted landscape contrast index: A scale independent approach for landscape pattern evaluation based on 'Source-Sink' ecological processes. *Acta Ecol. Sin.* **2003**, *23*, 2406–2413.
38. Wu, Z.; Lin, C.; Su, Z.; Zhou, S.; Zhou, H. Multiple landscape 'source–sink' structures for the monitoring and management of non-point source organic carbon loss in a peri-urban watershed. *Catena* **2016**, *145*, 15–29. [CrossRef]
39. Yang, M.; Li, X.; Hu, Y.; He, X. Assessing effects of landscape pattern on sediment yield using sediment delivery distributed model and a landscape indicator. *Ecol. Indic.* **2012**, *22*, 38–52. [CrossRef]
40. Jin, S.; Homer, C.; Yang, L.; Danielson, P.; Dewitz, J.; Li, C.; Zhu, Z.; Xian, G.; Howard, D. Overall Methodology Design for the United States National Land Cover Database 2016 Products. *Remote Sens.* **2019**, *11*, 2971. [CrossRef]
41. Mahmoud, A.; Alam, T.; Rahman, M.Y.A.; Sanchez, A.; Guerrero, J.; Jones, K.D. Evaluation of field-scale stormwater bioretention structure flow and pollutant load reductions in a semi-arid coastal climate. *Ecol. Eng.* **2019**, *142*, 100007. [CrossRef]
42. Gooddy, D.C.; Macdonald, D.M.J.; Lapworth, D.J.; Bennett, S.A.; Griffiths, K.J. Nitrogen sources, transport and processing in peri-urban floodplains. *Sci. Total Environ.* **2014**, *494*, 28–38. [CrossRef]
43. Wagner, K.; Moench, E. Education Program for Improved Water Quality in Copano Bay Texas Water Resources Institute Technical Report. 2009. Available online: https://oaktrust.library.tamu.edu/bitstream/handle/1969.1/93181/TR-347%20Copano%20Task%202%20Report%20031109.pdf?sequence=1&isAllowed=y (accessed on 8 April 2021).
44. Schumacher, J. Surface Water Pollution from Livestock Production. 2002. Available online: http://lshs.tamu.edu/docs/lshs/end-notes/surface%20water%20pollution%20from%20livestock%20production-2500205058/surface%20water%20pollution%20from%20livestock%20production.pdf (accessed on 27 January 2021).
45. Jeong, J.; Santhi, C.; Arnold, J.G.; Srinivasan, R.; Pradhan, S.; Flynn, K. Development of Algorithms for Modeling Onsite Wastewater Systems within SWAT. *Trans. ASABE* **2011**, *54*, 1693–1704. [CrossRef]
46. Jeong, J.; Wagner, K.; Flores, J.J.; Cawthon, T.; Her, Y.; Osorio, J.; Yen, H. Linking watershed modeling and bacterial source tracking to better assess E. coli sources. *Sci. Total Environ.* **2019**, *648*, 164–175. [CrossRef] [PubMed]
47. Olmstead, S.M. Thirsty Colonias: Rate Regulation and the Provision of Water Service. *Land Econ.* **2004**, *80*, 136–150. [CrossRef]
48. TCEQ. Eight Total Maximum Daily Loads for Indicator Bacteria in Greens Bayou Above Tidal and Tributaries. 2010. Available online: https://www.tceq.texas.gov/assets/public/comm_exec/agendas/comm/backup/Agendas/2010/6-2-2010/2009-0725-TML.pdf (accessed on 25 February 2021).
49. TCEQ. Domestic Wastewater Permits. 2020. Available online: https://www.tceq.texas.gov/permitting/wastewater/municipal/WQ_Domestic_Wastewater_Permits.html (accessed on 5 February 2021).
50. Andrews, W.J.; Masoner, J.R.; Cozzarelli, I.M. Emerging Contaminants at a Closed and an Operating Landfill in Oklahoma. *Ground Water Monit. Remediat.* **2012**, *32*, 20–130. [CrossRef]
51. EPA. National Pollutant Discharge Elimination System (NPDES). Available online: https://www.epa.gov/npdes/stormwater-discharges-municipal-sources (accessed on 27 January 2021).
52. Younos, T. Environmental Issues of Desalination: Environmental Issues. *J. Contemp. Water Res. Educ.* **2009**, *132*, 11–18. [CrossRef]
53. Sugarek, S.; Freund, R. Nueces River Authority Texas Clean Rivers Program Presentation. 2019. Available online: https://rgvstormwater.org/wp-content/uploads/2020/02/CRP_SamSugarek_NRA.pdf (accessed on 10 September 2021).
54. TCEQ. Surface Water Quality Monitoring. 2019. Available online: https://www.tceq.texas.gov/assets/public/waterquality/dma/dmrg/dmrg_complete.pdf (accessed on 12 September 2021).
55. TCEQ. Surface Water Quality Web Reporting Tool. 2021. Available online: https://www80.tceq.texas.gov/SwqmisPublic/index.htm (accessed on 10 September 2021).
56. EPA. A Quick Guide to Developing Watershed Plans to Restore and Protect Our Waters. 2013. Available online: https://www.epa.gov/sites/default/files/2015-12/documents/watershed_mgmnt_quick_guide.pdf (accessed on 7 April 2021).
57. Arroyo Colorado Watershed Partnership. A Watershed Protection Plan for the Arroyo Colorado Phase I. 2007. Available online: tps://www.lrgvdc.org/downloads/water/watershedprotectionplan%202007.pdf (accessed on 28 October 2020).

58. IBWC. Hydraulic Model of the Rio Grande and Floodways within the Lower Rio Grande Flood Control Project. International Boundary and Water Commission. 2003. Available online: https://www.ibwc.gov/Files/LRGFCPHydModRpt.pdf (accessed on 28 October 2020).
59. EPA. Summaries of Water Pollution Reporting Categories 2012. Available online: https://www.epa.gov/sites/default/files/2015-08/documents/34parentattainsdescriptions.pdf (accessed on 19 July 2021).
60. Surface Water Quality Monitoring Program, Monitoring and Assessment Section, and Water Quality Planning Division. 2020 Guidance for Assessing and Reporting Surface Water Quality in Texas. 2020. Available online: https://www.tceq.texas.gov/assets/public/waterquality/swqm/assess/20txir/2020_guidance.pdf (accessed on 12 September 2021).
61. TCEQ. Colonias. 2013. Available online: https://www.tceq.texas.gov/assets/public/border/colonias-large.jpg (accessed on 19 July 2021).
62. Krempa, H.M.; Flickinger, A.K. *Temporal Changes in Nitrogen and Phosphorus Concentrations with Comparisons to Conservation Practices and Agricultural Activities in the Lower Grand River, Missouri and Iowa, and Selected Watersheds, 1969–2015*; 2017. Available online: https://pubs.usgs.gov/sir/2017/5067/sir20175067.pdf (accessed on 19 July 2021).
63. Uddameri, V.; Singaraju, S.; Hernandez, E.A. Detecting seasonal and cyclical trends in agricultural runoff water quality—hypothesis tests and block bootstrap power analysis. *Environ. Monit. Assess.* **2018**, *190*, 157. [CrossRef] [PubMed]
64. EPA. Why Is Chlorophyll a Important? 2021. Available online: https://www.epa.gov/national-aquatic-resource-surveys/indicators-chlorophyll (accessed on 19 July 2021).
65. Brownsville/RGV Forecast Office. The Great June Flood of 2018 in the RGV. 2018. Available online: https://www.weather.gov/bro/2018event_greatjuneflood (accessed on 10 September 2021).
66. Lower Rio Grande Valley Development Council. Disaster Recovery Funding. 2021. Available online: http://www.lrgvdc.org/disaster-recovery.html (accessed on 10 September 2021).

Article

Eco-Efficiency for the G18: Trends and Future Outlook

Perry Sadorsky

Schulich School of Business, York University, Toronto, ON M3J 1P3, Canada; psadorsky@schulich.yorku.ca

Abstract: Eco-efficiency is an important ecological indicator for tracking the progress of how countries' environmental-adjusted economic activity changes over time. The objective of this research is to calculate country-level eco-efficiency for a group of 18 major countries (G18) that are part of the G20. First, the data envelope analysis (DEA) method is used to calculate eco-efficiency scores. Second, the Malmquist productivity index (MPI) is used to examine how eco-efficiency changes over time. Eco-efficiency is forecast to the year 2040 using automated forecasting methods under a business-as-usual (BAU) scenario. Over the period 1997 to 2040, eco-efficiency varies widely between these countries with some countries reporting positive growth in eco-efficiency and other countries reporting negative growth. Eco-efficiency leaders over the period 1997 to 2019 and 2019 to 2040 include Australia, Brazil, France, Germany, Great Britain, Italy, Japan, Russia, and the United States. Laggards include Canada, China, India, and Indonesia. These laggard countries recorded negative growth rates in eco-efficiency over the period 1997 to 2019 and 2019 to 2040. Negative eco-efficiency growth points to a worsening of environmental sustainability. Large variations in eco-efficiency between countries make it more difficult to negotiate international agreements on energy efficiency and climate change. For the G18 countries, the average annual change in MPI over the period 1997 to 2019 was 0.5%, while the forecasted average annual change over the period 2019 to 2040 was a 0.1% decrease. For the G18 countries, there has been little change in eco-efficiency. The G18 are an important group of developed and developing countries that need to show leadership when it comes to increasing eco-efficiency.

Keywords: eco-efficiency; DEA; CO_2 emissions; forecasting; ecological indicators

Citation: Sadorsky, P. Eco-Efficiency for the G18: Trends and Future Outlook. *Sustainability* **2021**, *13*, 11196. https://doi.org/10.3390/su132011196

Academic Editor: Antonio Boggia

Received: 23 September 2021
Accepted: 8 October 2021
Published: 11 October 2021

Publisher's Note: MDPI stays neutral with regard to jurisdictional claims in published maps and institutional affiliations.

Copyright: © 2021 by the author. Licensee MDPI, Basel, Switzerland. This article is an open access article distributed under the terms and conditions of the Creative Commons Attribution (CC BY) license (https://creativecommons.org/licenses/by/4.0/).

1. Introduction

Ecological efficiency (eco-efficiency) at the country level is an important ecological indicator for tracking the progress of how countries' environmental-adjusted economic activity changes over time [1,2]. The basic idea of eco-efficiency is to produce more goods and services while using fewer material inputs and generating less waste and pollution. In 1992, the World Business Council for Sustainable Development released their landmark publication "Changing Course", which introduced the terminology of eco-efficiency [2]. In the context of climate change at the country level, the eco in eco-efficiency often refers to CO_2 emissions, and this is the definition used in this paper. CO_2 emissions is an important indicator in discussions on climate change and transitioning to a low-carbon economy [1,3–5]. A positive trend in eco-efficiency indicates that eco-efficiency is increasing over time, while a negative trend indicates that eco-efficiency is decreasing over time. Eco-efficiency can be calculated using either non-parametric techniques such as data envelope analysis (DEA) or parametric methods such as stochastic frontier analysis (SFA) [6]. As discussed below, each method has its advantages and disadvantages. Changes in eco-efficiency over time can be analyzed using a Malmquist productivity index (MPI) [1,5,7]. The existing literature on eco-efficiency MPI at the country level reveals there is much room for improving eco-efficiency [1,5,7].

While the existing literature has calculated eco-efficiency at the country level, there are still some important unanswered questions. How does eco-efficiency compare across a large group of CO_2-emitting countries? Which countries are experiencing improvements in eco-efficiency over time, and which countries are experiencing decreases? What does the future trend in eco-efficiency look like?

The purpose of this present paper is to estimate and forecast changes in eco-efficiency over time using the Malmquist productivity index (MPI) for a group of 18 large polluting countries. These 18 countries along with Saudi Arabia and the European Union form the group of countries known collectively as the G20. The G20 is an important group of countries that accounts for 85% of global economic output, two-thirds of the world's population, and 75% of international trade [8]. Comprised of important developed and developing countries that span the world, participation and leadership from the G20 is vital for international energy and climate change policy [9]. DEA is used to calculate eco-efficiency, and MPI used to calculate eco-efficiency over time. DEA is a non-parametric approach that does not specify a parametric functional form between the inputs and outputs nor does it consider noise in the data [10,11]. SFA is an alternative approach to estimating eco-efficiency and energy efficiency that requires an explicit parametric functional form and allows for noise in the data [12–15]. Many existing studies of eco-efficiency use DEA because it is a more flexible approach, and this is the method used in this paper [10]. The DEA provides efficiency values for each year. Efficiency is a level concept, and measures of efficiency can be used to compare the performance of countries at a given point in time. Efficiency changes (or productivity changes) refer to movements in the efficiency or productivity of a country over time. To see how efficiency changes across time, these efficiency values are chained together using MPI [1,5,7]. The MPI is the product of an efficiency change component and a technical change component. The efficiency change component measures how a country's efficiency changes between time periods, and the technical change component refers to the movement of the efficient frontier between time periods. The analysis is conducted for the period 1996 to 2040. Actual data are used for the period 1996 to 2019, and forecasts are used for the period 2020 to 2040. Forecasts of eco-efficiency are made under a business as usual (BAU) scenario that assumes no major changes in economic structural or policy changes.

The analysis from this paper reveals some interesting results. Over the period 1997 to 2040, eco-efficiency varies widely between these countries with some countries reporting positive growth in eco-efficiency and other countries reporting negative growth. Eco-efficiency leaders over the sub-periods (1997 to 2019 and 2019 to 2040) include Australia, Brazil, France, Germany, Great Britain, Italy, Japan, Russia, and the United States. Laggards include Canada, China, India, and Indonesia. These laggard countries recorded negative growth rates in over the period 1997 to 2019 and 2019 to 2040. Negative eco-efficiency growth is particularly troublesome because it reflects a worsening of environmental sustainability. Large variations in eco-efficiency between countries make it more difficult to negotiate international agreements on energy efficiency and climate change.

This paper is organized as follows. The following sections of the paper set out the literature review, the methods and data, results, and discussion. The last section of the paper provides the conclusions and some policy implications.

2. Literature Review

This section presents a brief review of the literature on using DEA to estimate eco-efficiency at the country level. Bianchi et al. [16] use DEA and metafrontier analysis to measure eco-efficiency in 282 European regions for the period 2006 to 2014. For inputs, they use the employment rate and domestic material consumption per capita. The output variable is GDP per capita. They find evidence of an upward trend in eco-efficiency across European regions, although there is no evidence that regions are converging to similar levels of eco-efficiency. Halkos and Tzeremes [17] use DEA to calculate environmental efficiency for 17 OECD countries over the period 1980 to 2002. The main focus of their research is to test whether a Kuznet's-like hypothesis exists between environmental efficiency and income. The capital stock and labor are used as inputs to the DEA model, GDP is the desirable output, and sulfur emissions is the undesirable output. They do not find evidence of such a relationship. Hsieh et al. [18] use DEA to estimate the energy and environmental efficiency of 29 EU countries for the period 2006 to 2013. In their DEA analysis, labor, capital, and energy consumption are inputs. GDP is the desirable output and greenhouse gas emissions and sulfur oxide emission are undesirable outputs. About half of the countries have room for environmental performance improvements. Environmental performance is higher in the latter part of the sample period. Somewhat surprising in this study is that Great Britain, Germany, France, and Italy have relatively low environmental efficiency scores due to their greenhouse gas emissions and SO_2 emissions. Iftikhar et al. [19] use slacks-based (SBM) DEA to estimate energy and CO_2 emissions efficiency for 26 major countries for the years 2013 and 2014. The inputs are capital, labor, and energy consumption, while the desirable and undesirable outputs are GDP and carbon dioxide emissions, respectively. Larger countries with raw material intense production, and weak carbon laws are the least efficient. In particular, China, India, and Russia have much room for improvement in eco-efficiency. Lacko and Hajduova [20] study environmental efficiency among 26 EU countries covering the years 2008 to 2016. CO_2 per capita, methane per capita, and nitrous oxide per capita are the inputs and the output is GDP per capita. Eastern European countries tend to have low environmental efficiency and England and Sweden have high environmental efficiency. Climate change and socioeconomic factors are important drivers of environmental efficiency. Lozowicka [7] uses SBM DEA to analyze ecological efficiency and MPI in selected EU member states for the years 2005, 2010, and 2015. The input variables include the share of non-renewable energy, the percentage of the population not connected to wastewater treatment systems, the non-forested land ratio, and the unprotected area relative to the area of the country. The output variables include biochemical oxygen demand, the balance of nutrients, index of clean energy, and population exposed to PM2.5 air pollution. Northern Europe states have the highest eco-efficiency, while Central and Eastern Europe states have the least. Marti and Puertas [21] study the efficiency of the ecological footprint and biocapacity of 45 African countries. They use a variable returns DEA model with ecological footprint and population as the inputs and GDP as the output. Countries are divided into two groups. One group has a biocapacity surplus while the other has a deficit. Among the deficit countries, Gambia, South Africa, Swaziland, Mauritius, and Nigeria are efficient. Angola, Gabon, and Guinea-Bissau are surplus countries with high efficiency. Moutinho and Madaleno [22] use DEA to study eco-efficiency for 27 European Union (EU) countries over the period 2008 to 2018. They use a two-step estimation approach where in the first step, eco-efficiency scores are estimated, and in the second step, a fractional regression is used to estimate the impact of pollutants per area on eco-efficiency. The output variable is the ratio of GDP per capita to greenhouse gas emissions per area. The input variables are capital per capita, labor per capita, energy use per area, electricity use per area, and a temperature variable. From the second step regression, increases in CO_2/area and CH_4/area decrease eco-efficiency. Moutinho et al. [4] use constant returns to scale (CRS) and variable returns to scale (VRS) DEA to study environmental efficiency for 26 European countries. The DEA input variables include labor productivity, capital productivity, and non-fossil fuel energy share. The output variable is GDP per greenhouse gas emissions. The shares of renewable energy and non-renewable energy sources are important factors explaining differences in country-level environmental efficiency. Moutinho et al. [5] use CRS and VRS DEA and MPI to study eco-efficiency in 16 Latin American countries for the time period 1994 to 2013. The input variables include energy use, population density, labor productivity, renewable energy consumption share, and capital productivity. The output variable is the ratio of GDP to CO_2 emissions. For most countries, the degree of technical efficiency is lower than the degree of technological efficiency, indicating that some of the overall inefficiency is due to producing below the production frontier. Sarkhosh-Sara et al. [23] use network DEA to measure the sustainability of three groups of countries (high, middle, and low income). In total, 97 developed and developing countries are studied for the year 2011. The first stage DEA uses labor, capital, and energy as inputs. GDP is the desirable output, and CO_2 emissions is the undesirable output. For the second stage of the network analysis, GDP and population are used as inputs and income class is used as the output variable. Countries with high and low incomes perform well in the sustainable production stage but are weak performers in the sustainable distribution stage. Middle-income countries rank low on sustainable production but are strong performance in the sustainable distribution stage. Tsai et al. [24] use DEA-based meta frontier analysis to compare environmental efficiency between 37 European and 36 Asian countries. The input variables include the labor force, energy consumption, and government expenditures. The desirable output is GDP, and the undesirable output is CO_2 emissions. Mean meta-efficiency tends to be higher in European countries. Twum et al. [3] use DEA to calculate environmental efficiency for three Asia-Pacific regions. The desirable output is GDP and the undesirable output is CO_2 emissions. The input variables are the share of renewable energy and total patent applications. They find that East Asia is highly efficient, while South East Asia is the least efficient. They find evidence of an inverted U-shaped relationship between environmental efficiency and technological innovation. Wang et al. [1] use slacks-based DEA and MPI to investigate eco-efficiency for 17 European countries for the years 2013 to 2017. The desirable output variable is GDP per capita and the undesirable output is CO_2 emissions per capita. The input variables are energy consumption per capita, labor productivity, share of renewable energy consumption, and capital formation productivity. Nine of the 17 countries were found to have an eco-efficiency score of 1. As a group, the countries lacked eco-efficiency over the period 2013 to 2017. The lack of eco-efficiency comes mostly from a lack of technological progress.

In summary, while there is literature studying eco-efficiency at the country level for various groups of countries, there is no study that explicitly focuses on G18 eco-efficiency and how G18 eco-efficiency will evolve into the future.

3. Methods and Data

3.1. The DEA Method

DEA is a popular approach for analyzing eco-efficiency [6]. In order to account for non-radial adjustments in the inputs and outputs, a DEA slack-based model (SBM) is used [25]. The output variable is production-based CO_2 productivity as measured by the ratio of output to CO_2 emissions [5,26] and the four inputs are the capital to labor ratio, the output to labor ratio, the capital to energy ratio, and the share of non-fossil fuels in energy consumption. This choice of variables is based on related work that estimates ecological efficiency at the country level [4,5].

The basic set up of the model is as follows. The four inputs and output are represented by $x \in R^m$ and $y \in R^{s1}$, respectively. For a collection of n DMUs, define the following matrices: $X = [x_1, \ldots, x_n] \in R^{m \times n}$ and $Y = [y_1, \ldots, y_n] \in R^{s \times n}$. Assume that $X > 0$ and $Y > 0$.

The production possibility set, P, is:

$$P = \{(x,y) | x \geq X\lambda, \ y \leq Y\lambda, \lambda \geq 0\}. \tag{1}$$

In Equation (1), the intensity vector is λ, and P corresponds to constant returns to scale (CRS) technology. Variable returns to scale can be obtained by adding the constraint that the sum of the elements in λ equal unity. A DMU (x_0, y_0) is efficiency if there is no vector $(x,y) \in P$ such that $x_0 \geq x$ and $y_0 \leq y$ and there is at least one strict inequality. The SBM is:

$$[SBM] \ \varepsilon = min \frac{1 - \frac{1}{m}\sum_{i=1}^{m} \frac{s_i^-}{x_{i0}}}{1 + \frac{1}{s}\sum_{i=1}^{S} \frac{s_r^+}{y_{i0}}}. \tag{2}$$

Subject to:

$$x_0 = X\lambda + s^- \tag{3}$$

$$y_0 = Y\lambda - s^+ \qquad (4)$$

$$s^- \geq 0,\ s^+ \geq 0, \lambda \geq 0. \qquad (5)$$

The vectors s^- and s^+ refer to the excess in inputs and the shortage of output, respectively. The objective function in (2) satisfies $0 < \varepsilon \leq 1$. Eco-efficiency is represented by ε with higher values indicating a higher level of eco-efficiency.

Changes in eco-efficiency over time can be estimated using the Malmquist productivity index (MPI) [27,28]. The MPI is the product of a catch-up effect and a frontier-shift effect [7]. The catch-up effect refers to how much a DMU improves or worsens its efficiency over time and is sometimes referred to as the efficiency change component (EFFCH). The frontier-shift effect is the change in the efficient frontier over time and is sometimes referred to as the technical change component (TECH).

$$MPI = (Catch - up)(Fronter - shift) \qquad (6)$$

$$Catch - up = \frac{\varepsilon\ of\ DMU_0^{t+1}\ wrt\ period\ t+1\ frontier}{\varepsilon\ of\ DMU_0^t\ wrt\ period\ t\ frontier} \qquad (7)$$

$$Frontier - shift =$$
$$= \sqrt{\frac{\varepsilon\ of\ DMU_0^t\ wrt\ period\ t\ frontier}{\varepsilon\ of\ DMU_0^t\ wrt\ period\ t+1\ frontier} \cdot \frac{\varepsilon\ of\ DMU_0^{t+1}\ wrt\ period\ t\ frontier}{\varepsilon\ of\ DMU_0^{t+1}\ wrt\ period\ t+1\ frontier}} \qquad (8)$$

In Equations (7) and (8), the combination of letters wrt denotes "with respect to". A change in catch-up greater than unity means that the efficiency of a DMU in period t + 1 is greater than the efficiency in period t. Thus, there has been a relative improvement in efficiency. A change in frontier shift greater than unity means that the efficient frontier in period t + 1 is higher than in period t. This indicates technological innovation. Total productivity change is the product of catch-up and frontier-shift. The DEA estimations in this paper were done using the R programing language [29] and the DJL package [30].

3.2. Forecasting

In order to provide forecasts of eco-efficiency to the year 2040, forecasts of the DEA inputs and output need to be made. Since the data have a relatively short time span (annual data from 1996 to 2019), methods suited to forecasting short time series data sets are used. These methods include ETS, ARIMA, TBATS, and THETA [31]. ETS, which is based on exponential smoothing, is a state-space model with error (E), trend (T), and seasonal (S) components. The tradeoff between these components is controlled by smoothing parameters, and the optimal smoothing parameters can be determined using an automatic search algorithm. ARIMA is the acronym for autoregressive integrated moving average. While ETS models describe the trend and seasonality in the data, ARIMA models describe the autocorrelations in the data. The selection of the best-fitting ARIMA model can be easily achieved through a search algorithm. ETS and ARMA models are widely used in forecasting. The TBATS refers to an exponential smoothing state space model with Box-Cox transformations, ARMA error, trend and seasonal components. TBATS is estimated using a fully automatic modeling approach. The THETA model is equivalent to simple exponential smoothing with drift. The ETS, ARIMA, TBATS, and THETA models can be considered as examples of machine learning, since for each model, a fully automated search algorithm is used to find the best-fitting model. In order to reduce the dependence on forecasts from any one model, an average forecast is computed. Averaging forecasts often works well in practice [31]. The average forecast from these methods is referred to as the business as usual (BAU) scenario. Forecasting was done using the R package fpp2 [32].

The approach taken to forecasting in this paper is similar to the approach taken by international agencies such as the International Energy Agency (IEA) in their World Energy Outlook [33] and the US Energy Information Agency (EIA) in their Annual Energy Outlook [34] where they make long-term projections (20–30 years or so) for energy demand. A reference case, base case, or business as usual (BAU) scenario is taken as the benchmark where past data trends are assumed to continue into the future, and policy assumptions are assumed to be fixed. The forecasting methods used in this paper are useful for creating forecasts under a BAU scenario.

3.3. Data

Country-level data on CO_2 emissions, GDP, labor, capital, energy consumption, and non-fossil fuel energy consumption are required for the analysis. Data on GDP (real GDP in millions of 2011 US dollars: gdpna), capital (capital stock in millions of 2011 US dollars: rnna), and labor force (number of persons employed in millions: emp) come from the Penn World Tables (PWT 9.1) [35]. Data on CO_2 emissions (millions of tonnes) from the consumption of energy, energy (fossil fuel and non-fossil fuel) consumption (Exajoules), and non-fossil fuel energy consumption (Exajoules) come from the BP Statistical Review [36]. CO_2 emissions from the consumption of energy include emissions that result from the consumption of petroleum, natural gas, and coal and from natural gas flaring. Total energy consumption includes coal, natural gas, petroleum and other liquids, nuclear, renewables, and other. The 18 countries included in this study include Argentina (ARG), Australia (AUS), Brazil (BRA), Canada (CAN), China (CHN), France (FRA), Germany (DEU), India (IND), Indonesia (IDN), Italy (ITA), Japan (JPN), South Korea (KOR), Mexico (MEX), Russia (RUS), South Africa (ZAF), Turkey (TUR), Great Britain (GBR), and the United States of America (USA). These 18 countries along with the European Union and Saudi Arabia form the group of countries known as the G20. The dataset covers the years 1996 to 2019. Saudi Arabia is not included in the analysis because the share of non-fossil fuel energy is very low (close to zero). The dataset starts in 1996 to accommodate the breakup of the Former Soviet Union in 1991 and the turmoil that followed for those countries involved.

The inputs to the DEA analysis are the capital to labor ratio (klratio), output to labor ratio (ylratio), capital to energy ratio (keratio), and non-fossil fuel share of energy (nffshare). The output variable in the DEA analysis is labeled eco and is measured by GDP/CO_2 emissions.

The time-series pattern of production-based CO_2 productivity varies considerably between countries (Figures 1–3). Actual data are recorded up to and including 2019, after which time forecasts are shown (Figures 1–3; Table 1). In order for production-based CO_2 productivity to be increasing over time, GDP must grow faster than CO_2 emissions.

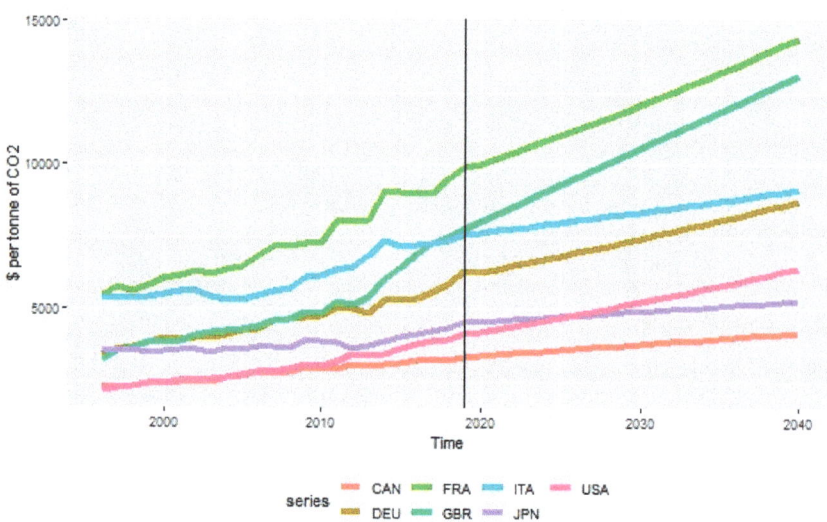

Figure 1. GDP per unit of CO_2 emissions for the G7 countries.

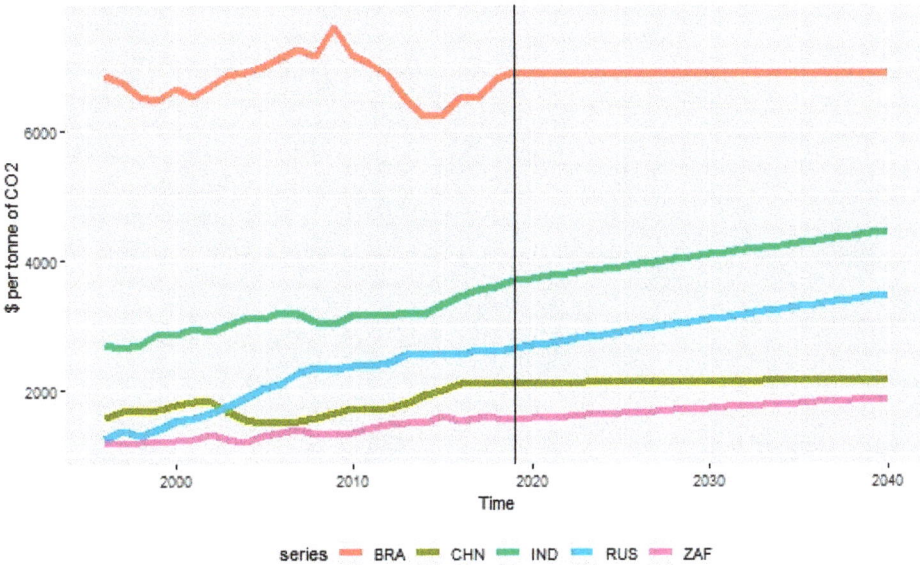

Figure 2. GDP per unit of CO_2 emissions for the BRICS countries.

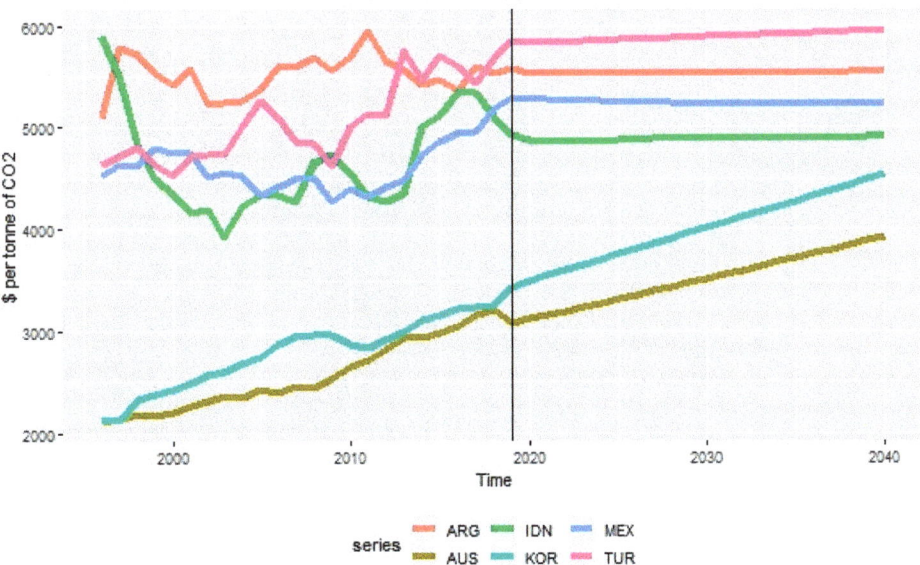

Figure 3. GDP per unit of CO_2 emissions for the other countries.

Table 1. Summary statistics for GDP/CO_2 (US dollars per tonne of CO_2 emissions).

	2000	2010	2020	2030	2040	GR1	Rank	GR2	Rank
ARG	5422.53	5694.28	5533.80	5534.30	5541.13	0.39	16	−0.03	17
AUS	2197.85	2653.32	3119.50	3513.58	3926.51	1.64	8	1.17	7
BRA	6648.00	7187.09	6889.25	6870.16	6865.03	0.03	17	−0.02	16
CAN	2445.83	2927.63	3405.59	3809.89	4213.27	1.69	7	1.06	8
CHN	1774.02	1712.71	2098.46	2123.93	2147.78	1.25	11	0.12	13
DEU	3992.10	4743.18	6286.36	7461.81	8772.57	2.66	4	1.57	4
FRA	6103.18	7316.91	10038.14	12078.57	14397.68	2.57	5	1.78	3
GBR	3875.79	4852.46	8055.22	10591.27	13127.32	3.80	1	2.48	1
IDN	4348.61	4555.83	4885.15	4893.71	4904.26	−0.78	18	−0.02	15
IND	2836.82	3143.15	3727.49	4087.08	4446.67	1.39	10	0.88	11
ITA	5508.29	6174.88	7656.65	8379.11	9152.01	1.48	9	0.89	10
JPN	3554.71	3893.36	4568.16	4932.84	5297.52	1.09	13	0.73	12
KOR	2432.16	2863.68	3495.61	4018.35	4541.09	2.11	6	1.33	5
MEX	4755.46	4394.05	5281.04	5232.37	5222.25	0.67	15	−0.06	18
RUS	1510.82	2357.20	2686.68	3091.27	3470.76	3.26	2	1.30	6
TUR	4523.68	4998.02	5826.36	5889.67	5952.98	1.02	14	0.08	14
USA	2463.67	3062.75	4225.92	5257.28	6444.34	2.76	3	2.10	2
ZAF	1223.90	1341.53	1561.66	1714.58	1867.85	1.22	12	0.95	9

GR1 and GR2 are the average annual growth rates from 1996 to 2019 and 2019 to 2040, respectively.

In 2020, the countries with the highest values of GDP per unit of CO_2 were France, Great Britain, Italy, Brazil, and Germany. The countries with the lowest values were South Africa, China, Russia, Australia, and Canada. Notice that the economics of four of these countries (South Africa, Russia, Australia, and Canada) are heavily reliant on natural resource extraction. These rankings are mostly unchanged in 2040. In 2040, the countries with the highest values of GDP per unit of CO_2 are France, Great Britain, Italy, Germany, and Brazil. As in the case of 2020, the countries with the lowest values of GDP per unit of CO_2 in 2040 are South Africa, China, Russia, Australia, and Canada. In general, production-based CO_2 productivity tends to be low in countries that have a large amount of mineral or fossil fuel resource extraction (Australia, Canada, South Africa, Russia). Canada, Australia, Russia, and South Africa are sometimes referred to as the CARS group of countries.

Great Britain, Russia, the United States, Germany, and France have recorded the highest growth rates in GDP per unit of CO_2 over the period 1996 to 2019 (Table 1). The lowest growth rates were recorded for Indonesia, Brazil, Argentina, Mexico, and Turkey. Over the period 2019 to 2040, the countries with the highest growth rates are Great Britain, United States, France, Germany, and South Korea. The countries with the lowest growth rates are Mexico, Argentina, Indonesia, Brazil, and Turkey. Four of these countries (Mexico, Argentina, Indonesia, Brazil) recorded negative growth rates, indicating that production-based CO_2 productivity is expected to decline over the period 2019 to 2040.

Each country in the G7 has experienced an increase in production-based CO_2 productivity, but the rate of increase varies considerably (Figure 1). Great Britain has the highest growth in production-based CO_2 productivity over both periods (1996 to 2009 and 2009 to 2040). France has the highest production-based CO_2 productivity and one of the highest growth rates of the countries studied. Japan has the lowest growth rate of production-based CO_2 productivity in the G7 over the period 2019 to 2040.

Among the BRICS, Brazil has the highest production-based CO_2 productivity (Figure 2). Over the period 2019 to 2040, Russia and South Africa experience the fastest growth. Brazil recorded the slowest growth in production-based CO_2 productivity.

For the remaining group of countries, Australia and South Korea have low values of production-based CO_2 productivity (Figure 3). Notice that over the period 2019 to 2040, Australia and South Korea also have the highest growth rates of production-based CO_2 productivity in this group of countries.

Summary statistics for the inputs and output to the DEA analysis are shown in Table 2. Each variable is increasing over time. Between 2000 and 2020, production-based

CO_2 productivity grew the greatest followed by the capital to energy ratio. The slowest growth was observed for the share of non-fossil fuels. In the BAU scenario, each variable grows less over the period 2020 to 2040 than it did over the 2000 to 2020 period. For each of the years shown, the coefficient of variation (CV) shows that the non-fossil fuel share has the greatest amount of variability. For most of the years shown, eco has the least variability.

Table 2. Summary statistics.

2000	klratio	ylratio	keratio	nffshare	eco
mean	277,076.531	56,563.527	964,298.382	0.148	3645.413
min	21,421.861	6647.760	371,245.827	0.034	1223.902
max	685,330.501	103,538.244	2,096,226.960	0.440	6648.001
sd	181,172.821	32,356.395	444,240.280	0.126	1633.171
CV	0.654	0.572	0.461	0.853	0.448
2010	klratio	ylratio	keratio	nffshare	eco
mean	312,698.881	63,813.004	1,083,100.190	0.155	4104.001
min	42,319.065	11,167.207	405,927.151	0.027	1341.533
max	743,960.972	119,401.134	2,532,021.912	0.456	7316.906
sd	195,609.458	32,417.909	529,437.749	0.128	1751.996
CV	0.626	0.508	0.489	0.824	0.427
2020	klratio	ylratio	keratio	nffshare	eco
mean	338,651.529	69,381.077	1,276,345.426	0.181	4963.391
min	73,993.932	19,033.970	537,705.879	0.045	1561.656
max	739,140.772	131,053.041	2,992,167.107	0.486	10,038.137
sd	190,770.768	33,649.249	647,702.338	0.126	2227.819
CV	0.563	0.485	0.507	0.697	0.449
2030	klratio	ylratio	keratio	nffshare	eco
mean	363,826.895	74,172.020	1,388,752.686	0.190	5526.655
min	105,706.833	26,265.436	558,296.433	0.044	1714.577
max	756,740.844	141,610.885	3,224,594.427	0.489	12,078.572
sd	194,533.247	34,807.152	719,988.070	0.128	2729.977
CV	0.535	0.469	0.518	0.672	0.494
BAU					
2040	klratio	ylratio	keratio	nffshare	eco
mean	392,150.585	78,910.716	1,504,329.735	0.201	6127.279
min	147,150.042	29,204.619	578,886.988	0.044	1867.851
max	774,340.915	150,934.140	3,457,021.748	0.492	14,397.679
sd	200,686.796	36,051.050	805,171.877	0.134	3364.628
CV	0.512	0.457	0.535	0.666	0.549
GR1	1.003	1.021	1.402	1.006	1.543
GR2	0.733	0.644	0.822	0.507	1.053

Klratio (US dollars per worker), ylratio (US dollars per worker), keratio (millions of US dollars per Exajoules), nffshare (a ratio between 0 and 1), and eco (US dollars per tonne of CO_2 emissions). BAU is the business-as-usual scenario. GR1 and GR2 are the average annual growth rates from 2000 to 2020 and 2020 to 2040. CV is the coefficient of variation.

4. Results

The eco-efficiency MPI for the G18 in the BAU scenario shows the highest average value in 2000 (1.020) and lowest value in 2010 (0.973) (Table 3). The drop in the average value of the MPI between 2000 and 2010 was likely due to the global financial crisis (2008–2009). The G18 mean value recovers after 2010 and records a value of 1.00 in 2040. Table 3 presents country-specific geometric mean values for the complete sample period (1997 to 2040) as well as two sub-periods. Calculations for the first sub-period (1997 to 2019) use the actual data to calculate MPI. Calculations for the second sub-period (2019 to 2040) use the forecasted values to calculate MPI. For the G18 countries, the average annual change in

MPI over the period 1997 to 2019 was 0.5%, while the forecasted average annual change over the period 2019 to 2040 was a 0.1% decrease. Over the complete sample (1997 to 2040), the average annual change in MPI was 0.2%. For the G18 countries, there has been little change in eco-efficiency.

Table 3. Eco-efficiency MPI for the BAU scenario.

	2000	2010	2020	2030	2040	Geom1	Rank	Geom2	Rank	Geom3	Rank
ARG	0.974	1.030	0.997	1.001	1.000	1.003	11	1.000	11	1.002	10
AUS	1.002	0.944	1.003	1.003	1.003	1.012	7	1.002	8	1.008	7
BRA	1.031	0.970	1.001	1.000	1.000	1.001	12	1.001	10	1.000	12
CAN	1.019	0.678	0.988	0.970	0.983	0.940	18	0.964	17	0.951	17
CHN	0.969	0.912	0.954	0.910	0.963	0.957	17	0.916	18	0.936	18
DEU	1.023	1.016	0.996	1.013	1.009	1.021	4	1.017	5	1.017	5
FRA	1.050	0.999	1.014	1.018	1.016	1.050	1	1.019	3	1.035	2
GBR	1.028	1.010	1.031	1.020	1.015	1.050	2	1.022	2	1.036	1
IDN	0.987	0.921	1.006	0.992	0.993	0.977	16	0.990	14	0.985	15
IND	0.994	0.977	1.007	0.988	0.986	0.980	15	0.988	16	0.984	16
ITA	1.044	0.992	1.014	1.029	1.005	1.014	5	1.036	1	1.024	4
JPN	1.004	1.009	0.999	1.006	1.006	1.005	9	1.005	7	1.005	8
KOR	1.016	0.999	1.015	1.003	1.004	0.998	13	1.001	9	1.000	11
MEX	1.170	0.999	1.010	0.999	1.000	1.007	8	1.000	12	1.004	9
RUS	1.098	1.049	1.041	1.012	1.007	1.031	3	1.019	4	1.026	3
TUR	0.989	1.009	1.003	0.991	0.991	1.004	10	0.990	15	0.998	13
USA	1.014	1.008	1.000	1.010	1.014	1.014	6	1.008	6	1.011	6
ZAF	0.954	0.986	1.004	1.000	1.000	0.990	14	1.000	13	0.995	14
mean	1.020	0.973	1.005	0.998	1.000	1.005		0.999		1.002	

Geometric mean computed for the periods 1997 to 2019, 2019 to 2040, and 1997 to 2040 denoted by geom1, geom2, and geom3, respectively. Rank refers to the ranking of the geomean.

Over the period 1997 to 2019, countries that recorded geometric mean values of MPI greater than unity include Argentina, Australia, Brazil, Germany, France, Great Britain, Italy, Japan, Mexico, Russia, Turkey, and the USA. France, Great Britain, and Russia record the three highest geometric mean values. Canada, China, India, Indonesia, Korea, and South Africa recorded negative average growth over this time period. Notice that the ranking of geometric mean values does not separate clearly on country income grouping. Russia, an emerging economy, has a high geometric mean value, while Canada, a developed G7 country, has a low value. The results change slightly over the second sub-period 2019 to 2040, as most countries experience lower MPI growth. One of the biggest differences is that South Korea now has a geometric mean value greater than one. For the period 1997 to 2040, Argentina, Australia, Germany, France, Great Britain, Italy, Japan, Mexico, Russia, and the United States each have improved their MPI. Over the period 1997 to 2040, the highest MPI growth is observed for Great Britain, France, and Russia, while the lowest growth is observed for Canada, China, India, Indonesia, Turkey, and South Africa. Notice that China and India, the two largest countries in the world by population, are experiencing a decline in MPI over the time period 1997 to 2040.

The G18 average catch-up value is highest in 2010 and lowest in 2040 (Table 4). The G18 experienced an increase in catch-up over the periods 1997–2019 and 1997–2040. The average catch-up effect is positive over the period 1997 to 2019 but negative over the period 2019 to 2040.

Table 4. Eco-efficiency catch-up for the BAU scenario.

	2000	2010	2020	2030	2040	Geom1	Rank	Geom2	Rank	Geom3	Rank
ARG	1.000	1.000	1.000	1.000	1.000	1.000	15	1.000	9	1.000	14
AUS	1.018	0.968	0.964	1.005	1.002	1.009	10	1.005	4	1.006	10
BRA	1.000	1.000	1.000	1.000	1.000	1.000	12	1.000	6	1.000	11
CAN	1.000	1.000	1.000	0.949	0.982	1.000	13	0.970	17	0.985	17
CHN	1.000	1.000	1.000	1.000	0.963	1.000	13	0.961	18	0.980	18
DEU	1.026	1.034	0.998	1.003	1.003	1.034	6	1.007	3	1.019	4
FRA	1.046	1.811	1.000	1.000	1.000	1.036	5	1.000	10	1.019	5
GBR	1.026	1.063	1.000	1.000	1.000	1.051	2	1.000	14	1.026	2
IDN	1.000	1.000	1.000	1.000	1.000	1.000	17	1.000	12	1.000	15
IND	1.000	1.000	1.000	1.000	1.000	1.000	16	1.000	11	1.000	13
ITA	1.000	1.000	1.000	1.000	0.997	1.048	3	0.984	16	1.017	7
JPN	1.002	1.030	0.978	1.007	1.006	1.026	8	1.007	2	1.016	8
KOR	1.017	0.983	1.012	1.004	1.003	1.015	9	1.003	5	1.010	9
MEX	1.261	1.000	1.000	1.000	1.000	1.033	7	1.000	7	1.017	6
RUS	1.092	1.054	1.084	1.000	1.000	1.061	1	1.014	1	1.038	1
TUR	1.026	1.018	1.007	0.988	0.989	0.998	18	0.986	15	0.994	16
USA	1.045	0.994	1.000	1.000	1.000	1.041	4	1.000	8	1.021	3
ZAF	1.000	1.000	1.000	1.000	1.000	1.000	11	1.000	12	1.000	12
mean	1.031	1.053	1.002	0.998	0.997	1.025		0.997		1.012	

Geometric mean computed for the periods 1997 to 2019, 2019 to 2040, and 1997 to 2040 denoted by geom1, geom2, and geom3, respectively. Rank refers to the ranking of the geomean.

Countries that have an increase in catch-up over all three sub-periods include Australia, Germany, Japan, Korea, and Russia. In other words, only five of the 18 countries studied improved their eco-efficiency catch-up over all three sub-periods.

The G18 average frontier-shift value is highest in 2020 and 2040 and lowest in 2010 (Table 5). As a group, the G18 recorded an increase in frontier-shift in the 2019 to 2040 sub-period but not in the 1997 to 2019 or 1997 to 2040 periods. Countries that showed an increase in frontier-shift growth over the period 2019 to 2040 are Brazil, Germany, France, Great Britain, Italy, Russia, Turkey, and the United States. Eight out of eighteen countries report an increase in frontier-shift over the period 2019 to 2040.

Table 5. Eco-efficiency frontier shift for the BAU scenario.

	2000	2010	2020	2030	2040	Geom1	Rank	Geom2	Rank	Geom3	Rank
ARG	0.974	1.030	0.997	1.001	1.000	1.003	4	1.000	9	1.002	6
AUS	0.985	0.976	1.040	0.997	1.001	1.004	3	0.997	14	1.002	5
BRA	1.031	0.970	1.001	1.000	1.000	1.001	5	1.001	8	1.000	7
CAN	1.019	0.678	0.988	1.022	1.000	0.940	18	0.994	15	0.965	17
CHN	0.969	0.912	0.954	0.910	1.000	0.957	17	0.953	18	0.955	18
DEU	0.997	0.982	0.999	1.000	1.007	0.987	8	1.010	4	0.998	8
FRA	1.004	0.551	1.014	1.018	1.016	1.013	1	1.019	3	1.016	1
GBR	1.002	0.950	1.031	1.020	1.015	0.999	6	1.022	2	1.009	2
IDN	0.987	0.921	1.006	0.992	0.993	0.977	12	0.990	16	0.985	15
IND	0.994	0.977	1.007	0.988	0.986	0.980	10	0.988	17	0.984	16
ITA	1.044	0.992	1.014	1.029	1.008	0.967	16	1.053	1	1.007	3
JPN	1.002	0.980	1.022	0.999	1.000	0.980	11	0.998	13	0.990	12
KOR	0.999	1.016	1.004	0.999	1.001	0.983	9	0.999	12	0.991	10
MEX	0.928	0.999	1.010	0.999	1.000	0.976	13	1.000	10	0.987	14
RUS	1.006	0.995	0.961	1.012	1.007	0.972	15	1.005	6	0.988	13
TUR	0.964	0.991	0.996	1.003	1.002	1.006	2	1.003	7	1.005	4
USA	0.970	1.014	1.000	1.010	1.014	0.974	14	1.008	5	0.990	11
ZAF	0.954	0.986	1.004	1.000	1.000	0.990	7	1.000	11	0.995	9
mean	0.990	0.940	1.003	1.000	1.003	0.988		1.002		0.995	

Geometric mean computed for the period 1997 to 2019, 2019 to 2040, and 1997 to 2040 denoted by geom1, geom2, and geom3 respectively. Rank refers to the ranking of the geometric mean.

5. Discussion

The analysis in the previous section shows that twelve out of eighteen countries recorded average annual changes in eco-efficiency MPI greater than unity over the period 1997 to 2020 (Table 3). The average eco-efficiency MPI over this period for the G18 was, at 0.5%, low. Eco-efficiency leaders over this period include France, Great Britain, Russia, Germany, Italy, and the United States. Germany, France, Great Britain, and Italy benefited from the European Union's 2020 Climate and Energy Package, which aims to reduce greenhouse gas emissions 20% from 1990 levels, target 20% of EU energy from renewables, and accomplish a 20% improvement in energy efficiency by the year 2020 [37]. Great Britain's performance is partly due to fuel switching and reduced fuel consumption. Great Britain has moved to a cleaner fuel mix in electricity generation as coal was switched for natural gas and renewables [38]. Reduced fuel consumption by business and industry also contributed to the reduction in carbon dioxide emissions. However, Great Britain's decision to exit the European Union (BREXIT) may weaken the stimulus and incentive for further eco-efficiency improvements. In addition, Germany's success comes from cross-partisan policy consistency, shared goals between political leaders and renewable energy advocates, a strong social movement for renewable energy, and decentralized energy policies [39]. These results are consistent with the results of Midova et al. [40], who study low-carbon scenarios of six northwest European countries (Netherlands, Germany, France, Denmark, the UK, and Belgium). In ranking these countries on ten criteria regarding low-carbon energy scenario design, Germany comes out on top followed by the UK. France's reliance on nuclear energy for electricity generation has helped to reduce carbon emissions but has also reduced technological innovation for other renewable energy sources. [41]. Russia's growth in eco-efficiency is related to the modernizing of the economy after the breakup of the Soviet Union. The United States benefits from economy-wide technical progress and, at times, environmentally favorable US presidency.

The eco-efficiency laggards over the period 1997 to 2019 include Canada, China, India, and Indonesia. Canada is a developed country with a large resource extraction sector. China, India, and Indonesia are populous fast-growing countries where economic growth has taken priority over environmental stewardship.

Predicting eco-efficiency into the future under a BAU scenario shows that between 2019 and 2040, the average annual rate of change in MPI, catch-up, and frontier shift is forecast at −0.1%, −0.3%, and 0.2%, respectively. A slowdown in technical efficiency is predicted to be the main reason for the decline in MPI. However, these numbers are small, indicating that even for countries where eco-efficiency MPI growth is positive, the practical impact on eco-efficiency is likely to be insignificant.

There are some limitations to this research. The forecasts for the period 2020 to 2040 were conducted under a BAU scenario, which assumes existing data trends continue into the future and there are no major changes in policy or economic structure. Small changes in the growth rate (1% or 2%) of the DEA input variables and output will have a small impact on the efficiency scores and the MPI calculations. Large changes in energy policy, the energy mix, and CO_2 emissions reductions could lead to higher eco-efficiency than those reported in the BAU scenario. Then, the question becomes, how likely is it that these large changes occur? Recent research by the IPCC indicates that climate change is widespread, rapid, and intensifying [42]. A substantial increase in eco-efficiency would require the G18 to quickly enact long-term energy policy aimed at greatly reducing fossil fuel consumption. Future research could look into conducting further scenario analysis to account for major changes in clean energy policy. Additional analysis could also be conducted on the choice of DEA model.

6. Conclusions and Policy Implications

Since the 1992 World Business Council for Sustainable Development publication "Changing Course", eco-efficiency has been an important indicator for the discussion on environmental sustainability. The focus of this research is to study how eco-efficiency has changed over time and is likely to change in the future for a group of 18 major countries (G18) that are part of the G20. DEA is used to estimate eco-efficiency, and these values are used in constructing an eco-efficiency Malmquist productivity index, which is a useful ecological indicator. Analysis is conducted over the period 1996 to 2040 with actual data being used for the period 1996 to 2019 and forecasted data for the years 2020 to 2040.

For the G18, the average annual growth in MPI over the period 1997 to 2019 was 0.5%. Over this same time period, catch-up and frontier shift average annual growth rates were 2.5% and −0.2%, respectively, indicating that efficiency change was growing positively while technical change was regressing. Over the forecast period, 2019 to 2040, the average annual rate of change in MPI, catch-up, and frontier shift is forecast at −0.1%, −0.3%, and 0.2%, respectively. These values indicate that a slowdown in efficiency change is forecast to be the main reason for the decline in MPI. However, the small magnitude of these numbers indicates that even when eco-efficiency MPI growth is positive, the practical impact on eco-efficiency is likely to be slight.

Eco-efficiency leaders over the period 1997 to 2019 and 2019 to 2040 include Australia, Brazil, France, Germany, Great Britain, Italy, Japan, Russia, and the United States. Laggards include Canada, China, India, and Indonesia. These laggard countries recorded negative growth rates in eco-efficiency over the period 1997 to 2019 and 2019 to 2040. These results are important in establishing not only what country-level eco-efficiency currently looks like but also what eco-efficiency is likely to look like in the future.

There are several policy implications stemming from this research. First, increasing eco-efficiency should be a top priority for all G18 countries. A positive trend in eco-efficiency is desirable from an environmental sustainability perspective, but it does not mean that substantial increases in eco-efficiency are being realized or that there is no room for further improvement. It could be that eco-efficiency is increasing but at such a slow rate that improvements are only marginal. This is consistent with the current values of G18 eco-efficiency and future predictions as presented in this paper. In such cases, even countries with positive eco-efficiency growth could still fall well short of meeting their nationally determined contributions (NDCs) targets, as specified under the Paris climate change agreement [43]. Countries need to prioritize increasing eco-efficiency to the forefront of economic policy making. One way to do this is to incorporate environmental sustainability into industrial policy so that future economic growth embodies environmental quality. For example, industrial policy could be focused on developing composite materials that are more lightweight and less energy intensive to construct, and there could be a greater emphasis on life-cycle analysis. The transportation sector should move away from fossil fuel-powered engines to electric motors that use electricity generated from renewable energy sources. Second, the large variations in eco-efficiency between countries make it more difficult to negotiate international agreements on energy efficiency and climate change. In general, it is easier to gain consensus on policy matters when the members share a common ground. Third, the G18 are an important group of developed and developing countries that need to show leadership when it comes to increasing eco-efficiency. The G20 countries need to establish a non-partisan environment ministry that is focused on designing and implementing aggressive goals on increasing eco-efficiency, which are consistent with the UN's SDGs. Under the current G20 structure, the chair of the G20 rotates on a yearly basis, and this offers little in the way of substantial long-term commitment to environmental policy [44]. Hopefully, the impact of COVID, record hot temperatures in 2021, and the latest IPCC research on the effects of climate change will provide the appropriate stimulus for the G20 to take environmental sustainability more seriously.

Funding: This research received no external funding.

Data Availability Statement: Publicly available datasets were analyzed in this study [35,36].

Acknowledgments: I thank the Schulich School of Business for internal funding. I thank the anonymous reviewers for their helpful comments.

Conflicts of Interest: The author declares no conflict of interest.

References

1. Wang, C.-N.; Hsu, H.-P.; Wang, Y.-H.; Nguyen, T.-T. Eco-Efficiency Assessment for Some European Countries Using Slacks-Based Measure Data Envelopment Analysis. *Appl. Sci.* **2020**, *10*, 1760. [CrossRef]
2. Huppes, G.; Ishikawa, M. (Eds.) *Quantified Eco-Efficiency: An Introduction with Applications*; Eco-Efficiency in Industry and Science; Springer: New York, NY, USA, 2007. ISBN 978-1-4020-5398-6.
3. Twum, F.A.; Long, X.; Salman, M.; Mensah, C.N.; Kankam, W.A.; Tachie, A.K. The Influence of Technological Innovation and Human Capital on Environmental Efficiency among Different Regions in Asia-Pacific. *Environ. Sci. Pollut. Res.* **2021**, *28*, 17119–17131. [CrossRef]
4. Moutinho, V.; Madaleno, M.; Robaina, M. The Economic and Environmental Efficiency Assessment in EU Cross-Country: Evidence from DEA and Quantile Regression Approach. *Ecol. Indic.* **2017**, *78*, 85–97. [CrossRef]
5. Moutinho, V.; Fuinhas, J.A.; Marques, A.C.; Santiago, R. Assessing Eco-Efficiency through the DEA Analysis and Decoupling Index in the Latin America Countries. *J. Clean. Prod.* **2018**, *205*, 512–524. [CrossRef]
6. Zhou, P.; Ang, B.W.; Poh, K.L. A Survey of Data Envelopment Analysis in Energy and Environmental Studies. *Eur. J. Oper. Res.* **2008**, *189*, 1–18. [CrossRef]
7. Łozowicka, A. Evaluation of the Efficiency of Sustainable Development Policy Implementation in Selected EU Member States Using DEA. The Ecological Dimension. *Sustainability* **2020**, *12*, 435. [CrossRef]
8. Canada, G.A.C.-A. Mondiales Canada's Participation at the 2019 G20 Summit. Available online: https://www.international.gc.ca/gac-amc/campaign-campagne/g20/index.aspx?lang=eng (accessed on 8 April 2020).
9. De Graaf, T.V.; Westphal, K. The G8 and G20 as Global Steering Committees for Energy: Opportunities and Constraints. *Glob. Policy* **2011**, *2*, 19–30. [CrossRef]
10. Zhou, P.; Ang, B.W. Linear Programming Models for Measuring Economy-Wide Energy Efficiency Performance. *Energy Policy* **2008**, *36*, 2911–2916. [CrossRef]
11. Sueyoshi, T.; Yuan, Y.; Goto, M. A Literature Study for DEA Applied to Energy and Environment. *Energy Econ.* **2017**, *62*, 104–124. [CrossRef]
12. Repkine, A.; Min, D. Foreign-Funded Enterprises and Pollution Halo Hypothesis: A Spatial Econometric Analysis of Thirty Chinese Regions. *Sustainability* **2020**, *12*, 5048. [CrossRef]
13. Chen, B. Public–Private Partnership Infrastructure Investment and Sustainable Economic Development: An Empirical Study Based on Efficiency Evaluation and Spatial Spillover in China. *Sustainability* **2021**, *13*, 8146. [CrossRef]
14. Wang, L.; Long, R.; Chen, H. Study of Urban Energy Performance Assessment and Its Influencing Factors Based on Improved Stochastic Frontier Analysis: A Case Study of Provincial Capitals in China. *Sustainability* **2017**, *9*, 1110. [CrossRef]
15. Shen, X.; Lin, B. Total Factor Energy Efficiency of China's Industrial Sector: A Stochastic Frontier Analysis. *Sustainability* **2017**, *9*, 646. [CrossRef]
16. Bianchi, M.; del Valle, I.; Tapia, C. Measuring Eco-Efficiency in European Regions: Evidence from a Territorial Perspective. *J. Clean. Prod.* **2020**, *276*, 123246. [CrossRef]
17. Halkos, G.E.; Tzeremes, N.G. Exploring the Existence of Kuznets Curve in Countries' Environmental Efficiency Using DEA Window Analysis. *Ecol. Econ.* **2009**, *68*, 2168–2176. [CrossRef]
18. Hsieh, J.; Lu, C.; Li, Y.; Chiu, Y.; Xu, Y. Environmental Assessment of European Union Countries. *Energies* **2019**, *12*, 295. [CrossRef]
19. Iftikhar, Y.; He, W.; Wang, Z. Energy and CO_2 Emissions Efficiency of Major Economies: A Non-Parametric Analysis. *J. Clean. Prod.* **2016**, *139*, 779–787. [CrossRef]
20. Lacko, R.; Hajduová, Z. Determinants of Environmental Efficiency of the EU Countries Using Two-Step DEA Approach. *Sustainability* **2018**, *10*, 3525. [CrossRef]
21. Marti, L.; Puertas, R. Analysis of the Efficiency of African Countries through Their Ecological Footprint and Biocapacity. *Sci. Total Environ.* **2020**, *722*, 137504. [CrossRef]
22. Moutinho, V.; Madaleno, M. A Two-Stage DEA Model to Evaluate the Technical Eco-Efficiency Indicator in the EU Countries. *Int. J. Environ. Res. Public Health* **2021**, *18*, 3038. [CrossRef]
23. Sarkhosh-Sara, A.; Tavassoli, M.; Heshmati, A. Assessing the Sustainability of High-, Middle-, and Low-Income Countries: A Network DEA Model in the Presence of Both Zero Data and Undesirable Outputs. *Sustain. Prod. Consum.* **2020**, *21*, 252–268. [CrossRef]
24. Tsai, W.-H.; Lee, H.-L.; Yang, C.-H.; Huang, C.-C. Input-Output Analysis for Sustainability by Using DEA Method: A Comparison Study between European and Asian Countries. *Sustainability* **2016**, *8*, 1230. [CrossRef]
25. Tone, K. A Slacks-Based Measure of Efficiency in Data Envelopment Analysis. *Eur. J. Oper. Res.* **2001**, *130*, 498–509. [CrossRef]
26. Picazo-Tadeo, A.J.; Beltrán-Esteve, M.; Gómez-Limón, J.A. Assessing Eco-Efficiency with Directional Distance Functions. *Eur. J. Oper. Res.* **2012**, *220*, 798–809. [CrossRef]
27. Caves, D.W.; Christensen, L.R.; Diewert, W.E. The Economic Theory of Index Numbers and the Measurement of Input, Output, and Productivity. *Econometrica* **1982**, *50*, 1393–1414. [CrossRef]
28. Malmquist, S. Index Numbers and Indifference Surfaces. *Trab. Estad.* **1953**, *4*, 209–242. [CrossRef]
29. R Core Team. *R: A Language and Environment for Statistical Computing*; The R Project for Statistical Computing: Vienna, Austria, 2019.

30. Lim, D.-J. *DJL: Distance Measure Based Judgment and Learning*. 2021. Available online: https://rdrr.io/cran/DJL/ (accessed on 7 October 2021).
31. Hyndman, R.; Athanasopoulos, G. *Forecasting: Principles and Practice*, 2nd ed.; OTexts.com/fpp2. 2018. Available online: https://otexts.com/fpp2/ (accessed on 7 October 2021).
32. Hyndman, R. *Fpp2: Data for "Forecasting: Principles and Practice*, 2nd ed. 2020. Available online: https://rdrr.io/cran/fpp2/ (accessed on 7 October 2021).
33. International Energy Agency. *World Energy Outlook 2016*; OECD/IEA: Paris, France, 2016.
34. US EIA Annual Energy Outlook 2021. Available online: https://www.eia.gov/outlooks/aeo/ (accessed on 1 October 2021).
35. Feenstra, R.C.; Inklaar, R.; Timmer, M.P. The Next Generation of the Penn World Table. *Am. Econ. Rev.* **2015**, *105*, 3150–3182. [CrossRef]
36. Dudley, B. *BP Statistical Review of World Energy*; BP Statistical Review: London, UK, 2019.
37. European Union. 2020 Climate & Energy Package. Available online: https://ec.europa.eu/clima/policies/strategies/2020_en (accessed on 1 June 2020).
38. CarbonBrief Analysis: Why the UK's CO_2 Emissions Have Fallen 38% Since 1990. Available online: https://www.carbonbrief.org/analysis-why-the-uks-co2-emissions-have-fallen-38-since-1990 (accessed on 12 April 2020).
39. Cheung, G.; Davies, P.J.; Bassen, A. In the Transition of Energy Systems: What Lessons Can Be Learnt from the German Achievement? *Energy Policy* **2019**, *132*, 633–646. [CrossRef]
40. Mikova, N.; Eichhammer, W.; Pfluger, B. Low-Carbon Energy Scenarios 2050 in North-West European Countries: Towards a More Harmonised Approach to Achieve the EU Targets. *Energy Policy* **2019**, *130*, 448–460. [CrossRef]
41. Millot, A.; Krook-Riekkola, A.; Maïzi, N. Guiding the Future Energy Transition to Net-Zero Emissions: Lessons from Exploring the Differences between France and Sweden. *Energy Policy* **2020**, *139*, 111358. [CrossRef]
42. IPCC Climate Change Widespread, Rapid, and Intensifying—IPCC—IPCC. Available online: https://www.ipcc.ch/2021/08/09/ar6-wg1-20210809-pr/ (accessed on 1 October 2021).
43. den Elzen, M.; Kuramochi, T.; Höhne, N.; Cantzler, J.; Esmeijer, K.; Fekete, H.; Fransen, T.; Keramidas, K.; Roelfsema, M.; Sha, F.; et al. Are the G20 Economies Making Enough Progress to Meet Their NDC Targets? *Energy Policy* **2019**, *126*, 238–250. [CrossRef]
44. Tienhaara, K. Governing the Global Green Economy. *Glob. Policy* **2016**, *7*, 481–490. [CrossRef]

Article

Model Reduction Applied to Empirical Models for Biomass Gasification in Downdraft Gasifiers

Michael Binns * and Hafiz Muhammad Uzair Ayub

Department of Chemical and Biochemical Engineering, Dongguk University-Seoul, 30 Pildong-ro 1-gil, Jung-gu, Seoul 04620, Korea; uzairayub003@gmail.com
* Correspondence: mbinns@dongguk.edu

Abstract: Various modeling approaches have been suggested for the modeling and simulation of gasification processes. These models allow for the prediction of gasifier performance at different conditions and using different feedstocks from which the system parameters can be optimized to design efficient gasifiers. Complex models require significant time and effort to develop, and they might only be accurate for use with a specific catalyst. Hence, various simpler models have also been developed, including thermodynamic equilibrium models and empirical models, which can be developed and solved more quickly, allowing such models to be used for optimization. In this study, linear and quadratic expressions in terms of the gasifier input value parameters are developed based on linear regression. To identify significant parameters and reduce the complexity of these expressions, a LASSO (least absolute shrinkage and selection operator) shrinkage method is applied together with cross validation. In this way, the significant parameters are revealed and simple models with reasonable accuracy are obtained.

Keywords: biomass gasification; machine learning; computer modeling; computer simulation; regression; model reduction; LASSO

1. Introduction

The gasification of biomass allows for the production of syngas, consisting of hydrogen and carbon monoxide, which can be used as fuel or converted to other products. This is a renewable source of energy which can take various types of biomass, including wood, straw, and various crop residues, such as shells or husks etc.

To aid the design of gasification systems, modeling can be used to avoid the cost of expensive experiments for the prediction of output composition using different feedstocks and under various operating conditions [1]. The review of Patra and Sheth mentions several categories of model biomass gasifiers including more complex models based on kinetic rate expressions or computational fluid dynamics, in addition to relatively simpler models based on thermodynamic equilibrium assumptions and empirical models based on artificial neural networks [1]. In addition, they mention the possibility of modeling inside a process simulator such as Aspen Plus, which may include kinetic or equilibrium models, for example, inside the process units or associated subroutines [1]. For example, Safarian et al. simulated a gasification process in Aspen Plus using a Gibbs reactor to calculate the equilibrium point minimizing the Gibbs free energy [2]. Marcantonio et al. also modeled gasification using a Gibbs reactor inside Aspen Plus, which they compared against a more accurate kinetic model simulated in MATLAB [3].

To avoid the complexities associated with kinetic and CFD (computational fluid dynamics) models, a large number of studies have focused on equilibrium models, artificial neural networks, and other empirical or semi-empirical models which allow for the fast simulation, sensitivity analysis, and optimization of gasification systems. However, equilibrium models are known to have some inaccuracy because the real gasifier does not necessarily reach equilibrium and can lead to an overestimation of the hydrogen and

carbon monoxide content of producer gas and an underestimation of methane content [4]. To address this inaccuracy, a number of studies have proposed adding correction factors or correlations to the equilibrium models to make the results closer to reality as detailed in the review of Ferreira et al. [5].

Despite this progress, recent studies have shown that even with corrections added, the equilibrium models still show some deviation from experimental values, leaving room for improvement [6]. Alternatively, artificial neural networks can also be utilized to predict the performance of gasifiers as shown by Baruah et al. [7]. Although they are shown to give relatively accurate predictions, this is achieved by limiting the study to woody biomass in small scale downdraft gasifiers [7]. Pandey et al. also show that an artificial neural network can achieve accurate predictions, but in that case, limited to predicting the results for gasification of municipal waste from a single lab-scale fluidized bed reactor [8]. Additionally, artificial intelligence-based machine learning has also been applied to predict the output of a downdraft gasifier in the form of least-squares support vector machines [9]. Although these and other artificial intelligence have shown high accuracy, the resulting models generally do not identify which parameters are important and their fitting requires the identification and fitting of a relatively large number of parameters (e.g., weights and bias values in the fitted equations). For example, the neural network of Baruah et al. for predicting the hydrogen content requires 25 parameters and 41 parameters for predicting the carbon monoxide content [7]. Although the sensitivity with respect to different inputs is not required for building this type of model, the relative impact of different inputs is calculated and shown in the study of Puig-Arnavat et al., for example, showing that carbon content of the feed biomass has a big effect on CO (carbon monoxide) gas yield [10].

Alternatively, simpler empirical expressions have also been considered for predicting the product gas composition as a function of the gasifier inputs and operating conditions. These have the advantage that they will typically have fewer parameters to fit, but the resulting model may be less accurate. For example, Chavan et al. compared a power-law type empirical formula against artificial neural networks for the prediction of gas production rate and heating value of gas products from coal gasification and showed that while both methods give a good fit, the artificial neural network method was slightly more accurate [11]. For the case of biomass gasification, the study of Chee looks at the experimental evaluation of a downdraft biomass gasifier and proposes various linear and non-linear correlation equations to predict outlet conditions [12]. However, these correlations are in terms of only a single inlet property and are obtained by varying only that parameter experimentally, so they cannot be used when more than one input is varied [12]. In another example, Pradhan et al. developed a number of thermodynamic models then fitted linear expressions to predict the results of the best fitting thermodynamic model [13]. They show that the linear models can adequately predict the output of the equilibrium model but do not show how well the linear expressions can predict experimental values [13]. This same procedure of developing equilibrium models then fitting linear correlations to the model outputs has also been demonstrated by Rupesh et al., who also show that linear models can fit well with the output of an equilibrium type model but do not show a comparison of experimental values against the linear correlations [14]. More recently, Pio and Tarelho have compared the prediction accuracy of equilibrium and linear models for predicting the performance of bubbling fluidized bed reactors for biomass gasification [4]. They show that the linear models can accurately be used to predict the output composition of the thermodynamic model (R squared values of 0.93 and 0.79 for hydrogen and carbon monoxide) but have limited accuracy when used to predict the experimental output composition values (R squared values of 0.04 and 0.23 for hydrogen and carbon monoxide) [4]. This could be due to the high variability of experimental composition values for bubbling fluidized bed reactors as suggested by Pio and Tarelho [4]. Alternatively, Mirmoshtaghi et al. have shown through partial least squares regression that higher prediction accuracy can be found from the resulting linear model expressions (R squared values of 0.8 and 0.53 for hydrogen and carbon monoxide) for circulating fluidized bed gasifiers [15]. Although this higher accuracy achieved by Mirmoshtaghi et al. could be explained by the fact that they use a much larger number of different input values (18 different terms in the linear expressions) [15], compared to the two input values considered in the linear relations used by Pio and Tarelho (only considering temperature and equivalence ratio) [4].

In addition to regression, Mirmoshtaghi et al. also present principal component analysis and statistical analysis of p-values from the partial least squares regression to identify significant parameters showing that the equivalence ratio is the most important parameter [15]. The study of Gil et al. also applied principal component analysis to investigate the influence of different biomass properties on the resulting producer gas for a range of different biomass feedstocks when fed to a bubbling fluidized bed reactor [16]. This showed which feedstocks lead to higher production of combustible gases CO (carbon monoxide) and CH_4 (methane) [16]. In the similar study of Dellavedova et al., they also used partial least squares regression and principal component analysis for a set of data including different types of biomass gasifiers and while they do not report R squared values, they do find that the most important parameters are equivalence ratio, steam-to-biomass ratio, higher heating value, and carbon content of the feedstock and temperature [17]. They also mention that the limited accuracy of their linear model may be due to the non-complete homogeneity (high variability) of the data set they have used [17].

While linear models are simple, they have been shown to have relatively limited accuracy for predicting the output of gasifiers and it might be assumed that quadratic expressions could achieve a better prediction accuracy, accounting for interactions between pairs of different coefficients. However, Pan and Pandey have shown that both linear and quadratic expressions give high relative errors when they try to fit them to data for fluidized bed gasifiers fed with municipal solid waste [18]. They also show that an artificial neural network and their proposed Bayesian approach using Gaussian processes can achieve a much more accurate prediction, although the main aim of their proposed method is to incorporate uncertainty [18]. However, this high error in the quadratic regression may be because they attempted to fit a very large number of parameters based on combinations of the 9 input values (potentially 45 parameters or 81 parameters if interaction pairs are counted multiple times) with a full dataset of 67 points, which could be difficult to fit [18].

In summary, a number of studies mentioned above have used simple linear empirical models fitted to the outputs of some other model (e.g., an equilibrium model) and have shown that linear empirical models can quite accurately reproduce the result of the other models [4,13,14]. However, the "other model" can contain some inaccuracies when compared to experimental values and so the fitted correlations will not necessarily reproduce experimental values well. When simple empirical models are fitted directly to experimental values, the statistical fitting appears to be worse [4] (e.g., compared to fitting an empirical model to the output of a thermodynamic model). The use of more complex methods, such as quadratic expressions or artificial neural networks, could achieve a better fit by accounting for non-linear behavior. This prediction accuracy has been demonstrated by a number of studies for artificial neural networks [7–11] but has not been demonstrated for quadratic expressions. Additionally, while dimension reducing model reduction has been successfully applied (e.g., using principal component analysis) to identify significant parameters [15–17], the use of the LASSO [19] (least absolute shrinkage and selection operator) shrinkage method, which aims to eliminate large numbers of less significant parameters, has not so far been applied for the model reduction of biomass gasification models.

In this study, both linear and quadratic expressions are fitted to a set of data from a downdraft biomass gasifier. To avoid the problem of fitting large numbers of parameters, model reduction is included using the LASSO method [19] which is implemented together with cross validation to identify significant parameters and eliminate other parameters such that reduced expressions are obtained. This can be used, for example, in cases where the number of data points is less than the total number of parameters used in the full complex expressions (since the model reduction will eliminate most of the parameters such that the number of fitted parameters in the reduced model is less than the number of data points). The resulting models are evaluated based on their ability to predict the gasifier output.

2. Development of New Empirical Models for Gasification

The empirical models are developed here relating to a number of inputs (x) to predict some output value ($\hat{y}$) as shown in Figure 1. If there are multiple outputs to be predicted, then regression models can be developed separately for each. For the case of gasification, the exact input values used depends on the gasifier design and the available data but will generally include the moisture and the elemental composition as well as the air- or steam-to-biomass ratio (or equivalence ratio). Based on these inputs, various different linear or non-linear expressions can be proposed relating to inputs with outputs which might typically include the product gas composition, gas yield/production rate etc.

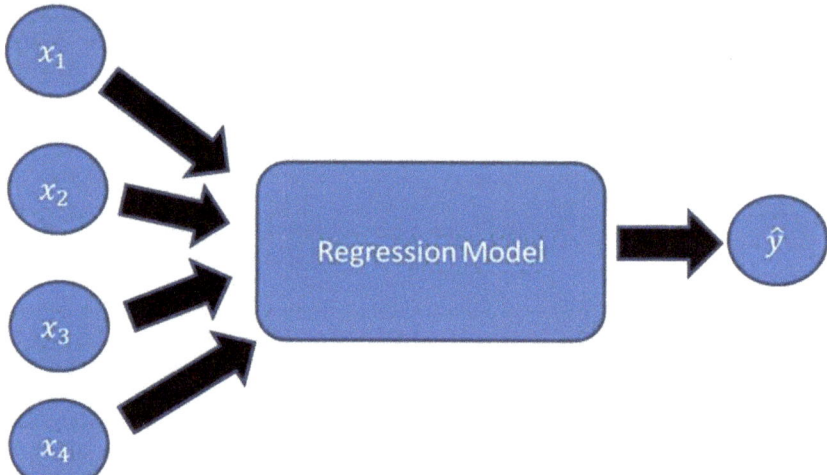

Figure 1. Simple schematic of a regression model used to take inputs (x) and calculate a predicted output value ($\hat{y}$).

2.1. Linear and Quadratic Modeling Equations

The linear model is relatively simple with a form given in Equation (1).

$$\hat{y} = \beta_0 + \sum_{i=1}^{n} \beta_i x_i \tag{1}$$

where $\hat{y}$ is the predicted value for output variable y, the x_i terms are the input values (there are n different inputs with subscripts i) and the β values are fitted parameters. Considering a quadratic expression, there will be a number of additional terms:

$$\hat{y} = \beta_0 + \sum_{i=1}^{n} \beta_i x_i + \sum_{i=1}^{n} \sum_{j=i}^{n} \beta_{ij} x_i x_j \tag{2}$$

Including the linear terms from Equation (1) in addition to pair-wise combinations of different inputs, which can lead to a large number of terms and a large number of additional parameters β_{ij}, which need to be fitted.

2.2. Model Reduction through LASSO Shrinkage

The most common method used for regression is the least squares formulation, which aims to minimize the residual sum of squares (RSS):

$$RSS = \sum_{z=1}^{N}(y_z - \hat{y}_z)^2 \qquad (3)$$

which is the sum of the differences between measured outputs and predicted outputs squared for N data points. Shrinkage methods attempt to reduce the magnitude of the predicted β values (shrinking them). This is performed by modifying Equation (3), adding an additional term, and in the case of LASSO shrinkage, this is given in Equation (4) [19]:

$$RSS = \sum_{z=1}^{N}(y_z - \hat{y}_z)^2 + \lambda \sum_{i=1}^{n}|\beta_i| \qquad (4)$$

where n is the number of input variables and λ is a tuning parameter. This is related to the linear model in Equations (1) and (2) but can also be applied to quadratic expressions as follows:

$$RSS = \sum_{z=1}^{N}(y_z - \hat{y}_z)^2 + \lambda \sum_{i=1}^{n}|\beta_i| + \lambda \sum_{i=1}^{n}\sum_{j=i}^{n}|\beta_{ij}| \qquad (5)$$

such that all the parameters in the linear and quadratic terms are included together. In either case, Equations (4) or (5) are minimized during fitting, which simultaneously reduces the error between model and measured values and reduces the magnitude the β values. This is controlled by tuning the value of λ, and increasing this value should decrease the values of fitted parameters. In this case, using the LASSO formulation with absolute values of the parameters, it can be shown that this leads to increasing numbers of parameters set to zero [19]. This in turn allows parameters set to zero to be neglected together with the associated inputs producing a simplified or reduced model [19].

2.3. Cross Validation and Model Development

For comparison, three different types of models will be developed and tested:
- Full linear model;
- Reduced linear model;
- Reduced quadratic model.

To develop these models, the procedure shown in Figure 2 was employed here for both the linear and quadratic reduced models. The available data were initially separated into separate training and testing sets. Then, only data from the training set was used in cross validation with the LASSO approach and was used to identify a λ value which minimises the cross validation MSE (mean squared error). Utilizing the LASSO method with this λ reveals which of the parameters have been set to zero and the non-zero parameters were identified to generate reduced expressions. These reduced expressions were then fitted to the full training set data giving fitted values for the identified parameters. For the full linear model, there was no cross validation and all the parameters were obtained through regression using the training set. Finally, all the fitted models were validated to see if they were able to adequately predict the results of the testing data.

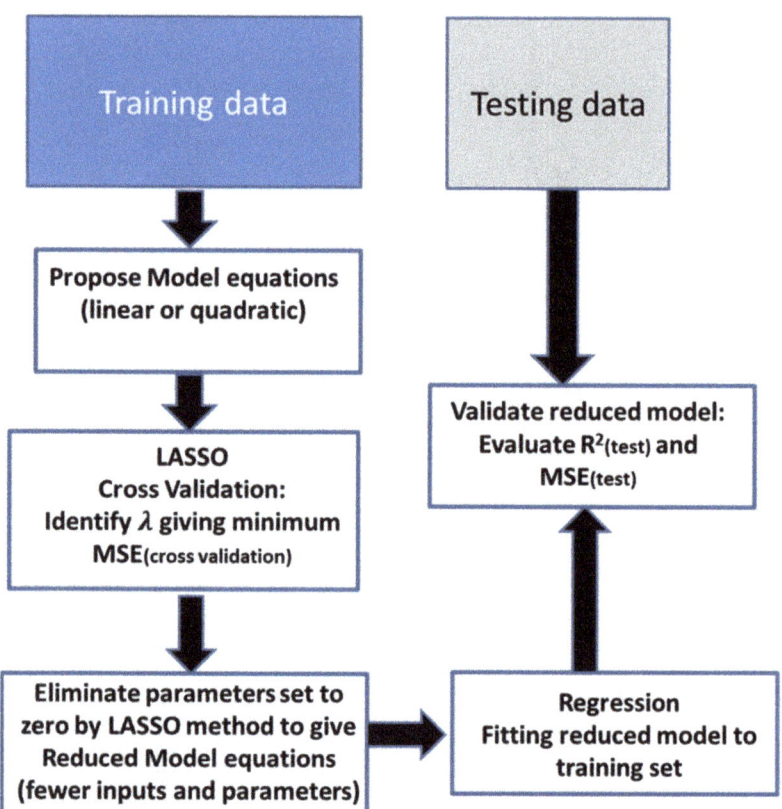

Figure 2. Procedure used to develop and validate reduced linear and quadratic models.

3. Case Study Based on a Commercial Biomass Gasifier

The measured input and output values are taken from the study of Chee, who investigated the effect of different operating conditions and different wood-based feedstocks on the performance of a commercial biomass downdraft gasifier [12]. In particular, the gasifier used by Chee had a rotating grate at the base of the fixed bed and a fan for driving the air flow and the rotation rate of these two components were investigated [12]. This data set consists of 34 data points with input values given in Table 1 [12]. Run number "201" in this study was not used here because the conditions for that run were significantly different from all the others tested (with an equivalence ratio of 0.56) [12]. From these 34 data points, 25 randomly chosen points were assigned to the training set and the remaining 9 data points were used for testing. The data values used are also given in the Supplementary data file together with additional data used for validation and all the model parameters.

Table 1. Input parameters, ranges, and average values for a commercial downdraft biomass gasifier using data from Chee [12].

Gasifier Input	Range	Average
Tgas = Gasification temperature (K)	961–1100	1039
ER = Equivalence ratio	0.1555–0.2607	0.2001
MC = Moisture content (% wet basis)	5.4–22.4	11.3
H = Hydrogen content (% dry basis)	47.88–49.44	48.53

Table 1. *Cont.*

Gasifier Input	Range	Average
O = Oxygen content (% dry basis)	5.78–6.00	5.9
C = Carbon content (% dry basis)	39.06–44.31	43.44
Ash = Ash content (% dry basis)	1.10–2.07	1.66
Gr = Grate rotation speed (rph)	2.55–20.69	5.13
Fs = Gas fan speed (rpm)	1388–2561	1750
Bulk = Wet bulk density (kg/m^3)	133–230	167.35
Void = Biomass void percent (%)	32–56	46.22

These data values are used to predict the produced gas properties:

- Hydrogen (mole %);
- Carbon monoxide (mole %);
- Carbon dioxide (mole %);
- Methane (mole %);
- Nitrogen (mole %);
- Gas/fuel ratio (kg/kg).

3.1. Cross Validation and Model Development

Cross validation and fitting with the LASSO approach was carried out here using the statistical software R and RStudio using the package "glmnet" written by Friedman et al. [20]. This software is commonly used for both linear and non-linear regression in addition to classification. To make this easier, various packages and subroutines have been written in this software including machine learning-based methods such as the LASSO. In the field of process/chemical engineering, alternative software such as Aspen Plus is a very powerful tool which can be used for both simulation and regression of parameters for both linear and non-linear expressions but as far as we know it does not include the option to include shrinkage-based model reduction (although perhaps subroutines could be written to add this functionality in the future).

An example of the output of cross validation is shown in Figure 3, which demonstrates how the mean square error (from cross validation) varies with changing the value of the tuning parameter λ. This particular graph shows the cross validation results for the prediction of hydrogen mole % in the produced gas based on a linear expression in terms of the 11 inputs. It can be seen from the number at the top edge that the number of inputs included in the model reduces as λ increases, with a minimum MSE value given with 7 out of 11 inputs.

In particular, the inputs that can be eliminated are shown from the data to be: C, H, Fs, and bulk, so the reduced linear expression can be stated as

$$H_2(\%) = \beta_0 + \beta_1 Tgas + \beta_2 ER + \beta_3 MC + \beta_4 O + \beta_5 Ash + \beta_6 Gr + \beta_7 void \qquad (6)$$

If starting from a quadratic expression, it might be expected that a larger number of inputs or combinations of inputs would result. However, the cross validation in Figure 4 shows a minimum MSE located near the point where there are only two inputs. Looking at the data, the two remaining terms after this point are TgasER, the product of gasification temperature and equivalence ratio, and MCAsh, the product of moisture content and ash content, suggesting that a very simple expression can be obtained:

$$H_2(\%) = \beta_0 + \beta_1 TgasER + \beta_2 MCAsh \qquad (7)$$

Although, at the exact minimum, a third product, ERGr (the product of equivalence ratio and grate rotation speed), and fourth, Ovoid (the product of elemental oxygen content and the void fraction), also appear.

$$H_2(\%) = \beta_0 + \beta_1 TgasER + \beta_2 MCAsh + \beta_3 ERGr + \beta_4 Ovoid \qquad (8)$$

Thus, it appears in the case of hydrogen that a quadratic expression with four terms provides a much simpler model than both the full linear model and the reduced linear model. Based on similar analysis, applying cross validation and fitting the resulting expressions to the training data, the following expressions are given in Table 2.

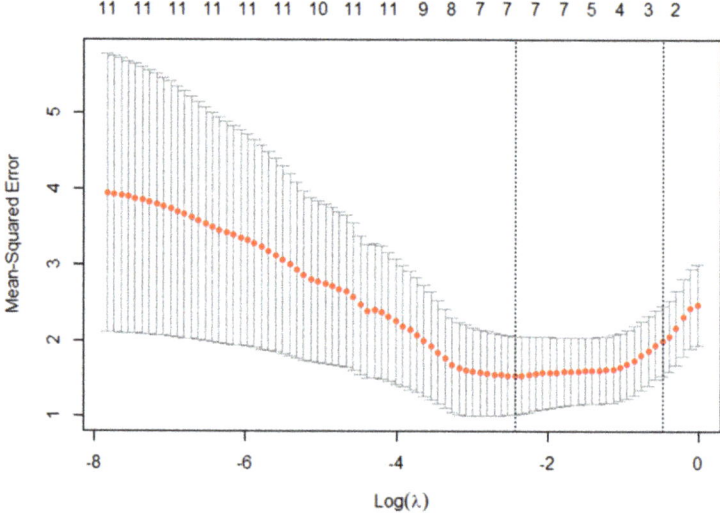

Figure 3. Plot of cross validation MSE against the log of the tuning parameter λ from Equation (4) for the prediction of hydrogen % using a linear expression. The numbers above the graph show the corresponding number of inputs with non-zero parameters.

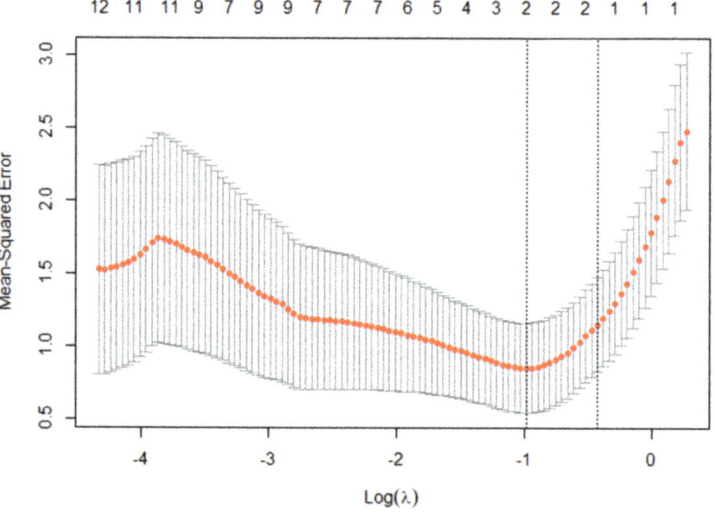

Figure 4. Plot of cross validation MSE against the log of the tuning parameter λ from Equation (5) for the prediction of hydrogen % using a quadratic expression. The numbers above the graph show the corresponding number of terms with non-zero parameters in the quadratic model.

Table 2. Reduced model expressions resulting from cross validation with the LASSO approach.

Reduced Linear Model	Reduced Quadratic Model
$H_2(\%) = \beta_0 + \beta_1 Tgas + \beta_2 ER + \beta_3 MC + \beta_4 O + \beta_5 Ash + \beta_6 Gr + \beta_7 void$	$H_2(\%) = \beta_0 + \beta_1 TgasER + \beta_2 MCAsh + \beta_3 ERGr + \beta_4 Ovoid$
$CO(\%) = \beta_0 + \beta_1 Tgas + \beta_2 ER + \beta_3 MC + \beta_4 O + \beta_5 Ash + \beta_6 Gr + \beta_7 Fs + \beta_8 bulk + \beta_9 void$	$CO(\%) = \beta_0 + \beta_1 TgasO + \beta_2 ERO + \beta_3 ERAsh + \beta_4 ERbulk + \beta_5 MCGr + \beta_6 HO + \beta_7 AshGr + \beta_8 Fsbulk$
$CO_2(\%) = \beta_0 + \beta_1 ER + \beta_2 MC + \beta_3 O + \beta_4 Ash + \beta_5 Gr + \beta_6 Fs + \beta_7 bulk + \beta_8 void$	$CO_2(\%) = \beta_0 + \beta_1 O + \beta_2 TgasER + \beta_3 TgasO + \beta_4 MCAsh + \beta_5 MCGr + \beta_6 MCbulk + \beta_7 Ovoid + \beta_8 Fsbulk + \beta_9 bulkvoid$
$CH_4(\%) = \beta_0 + \beta_1 ER + \beta_2 MC + \beta_3 C + \beta_4 H + \beta_5 Ash + \beta_6 Gr + \beta_7 Fs + \beta_8 void$	$CH_4(\%) = \beta_0 + \beta_1 TgasGr + \beta_2 ERAsh + \beta_3 ERvoid + \beta_4 MCAsh + \beta_5 MCFs + \beta_6 CC + \beta_7 Hvoid + \beta_8 Grbulk$
$N_2(\%) = \beta_0 + \beta_1 ER + \beta_2 MC + \beta_3 C + \beta_4 Gr + \beta_5 void$	$N_2(\%) = \beta_0 + \beta_1 TgasER + \beta_2 ERO + \beta_3 ERGr + \beta_4 MCAsh + \beta_5 MCvoid$
$G/F = \beta_0 + \beta_1 ER + \beta_2 C + \beta_3 H + \beta_4 O + \beta_5 Gr + \beta_6 Fs + \beta_7 void$	$G/F = \beta_0 + \beta_1 C + \beta_2 TgasO + \beta_3 ERH + \beta_4 ERFs + \beta_5 ERvoid + \beta_6 CC + \beta_7 CH + \beta_8 OO + \beta_9 Grbulk$

3.2. Model Validation

To evaluate the predictive power of the different models developed in Section 3.1, which are developed and trained using the training set (25 data points), they are also validated here through comparison with the testing set of data (9 data points). The performance of the different models was evaluated based on comparison of the mean squared error (MSE) and the R^2 values of each model with respect to the output values from the test set as shown in Table 3. It can be seen that while the full linear model can adequately predict the output for some of the predicted outputs in almost all cases, the reduced linear or quadratic models are shown to more accurately have predictions with higher R^2 and lower MSE values. An exception to this rule is the gas-to-fuel ratio, for which the full linear model has the best fit and where all the models are shown to have very high accuracy.

Table 3. Validation of models against a testing set of data showing the prediction capability of full linear and reduced linear and quadratic models.

Gasifier Input	1	H_2	CO	CO_2	CH_4	N_2	G/F
Full linear model	# terms	11	11	11	11	11	11
	MSE(test)	0.648	6.869	1.043	0.037	5.104	0.0025
	R^2	0.660	−0.009	0.649	0.753	0.440	0.953
Reduced linear model	# terms	7	9	8	8	5	7
	MSE(test)	0.146	4.850	0.800	0.010	0.502	0.0032
	R^2	0.924	0.288	0.731	0.935	0.945	0.942
Reduced quadratic model	# terms	4	8	9	8	5	9
	MSE(test)	0.777	3.317	0.830	0.011	1.232	0.0031
	R^2	0.592	0.513	0.720	0.928	0.865	0.943

It is also worth noting that the model for carbon monoxide (CO) shows a very poor prediction using the full linear model and appears to require a quadratic model to obtain a reasonable predictive power. Previous studies of Mirmoshtaghi et al. [15] and Pio and Tarelho [4] have also shown difficulty fitting empirical models to the CO output of circulating and bubbling fluidized bed reactors with R^2 values of 0.53 and 0.23, respectively. In this study, an R^2 value of 0.513 was found for the downdraft gasifier data used here.

The fitting of these models is also demonstrated in Figures 5 and 6, which show the comparison of experimental values plotted against model predictions for the test data set. This shows that all of the models appear to predict hydrogen mole percentage reasonably well, but there are some deviations for model predictions of carbon monoxide mole percentage. The reduced models are shown to give predictions closer to the experimental values for both of these outputs.

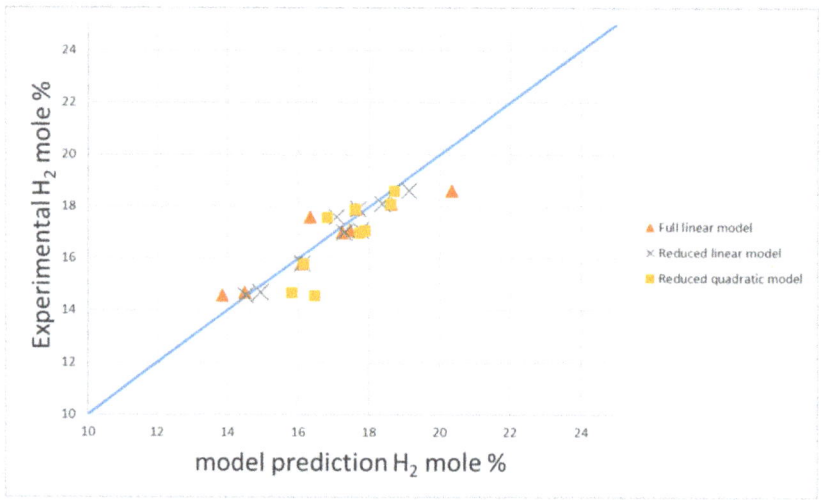

Figure 5. Parity plot of models against experimental hydrogen mole % using data from Chee [12].

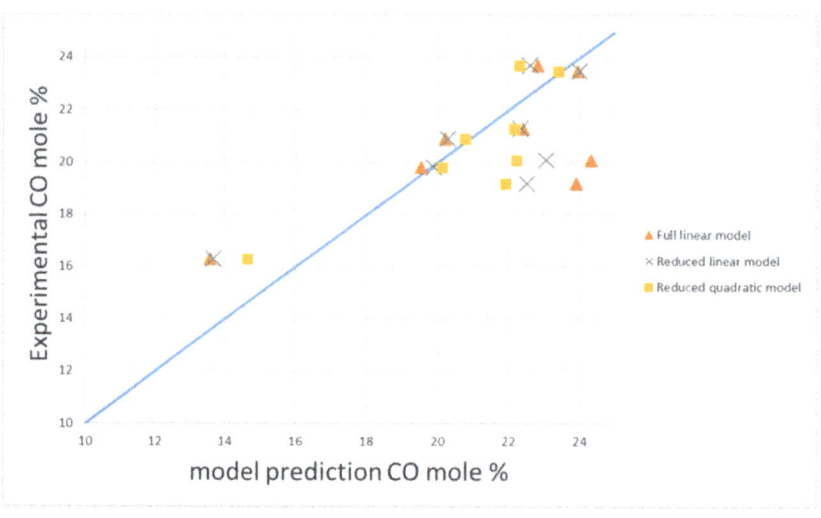

Figure 6. Parity plot of models against experimental carbon monoxide mole % using data from Chee [12].

To assess if the models generated based on fitting to the data of Chee [12] can be used for other biomass gasifiers, the best fitting models for predicting hydrogen and carbon monoxide are compared against experimental data from three other downdraft gasifier studies. In particular, this experimental data includes the gasification of rubberwood (nine data points) from the study of Jayah et al. [21], the gasification of sesame wood (four data points) from the study of Sheth and Babu [22], and the gasification of wood chips (two data points) from the study of Costa et al. [23].

Figures 7 and 8 show the parity plots of the reduced linear models against these three sets of data. It can be seen that the model gives a reasonable prediction of the data points from the study of Jayah et al. but has much lower accuracy for predicting the results of Costa et al. and Sheth and Babu.

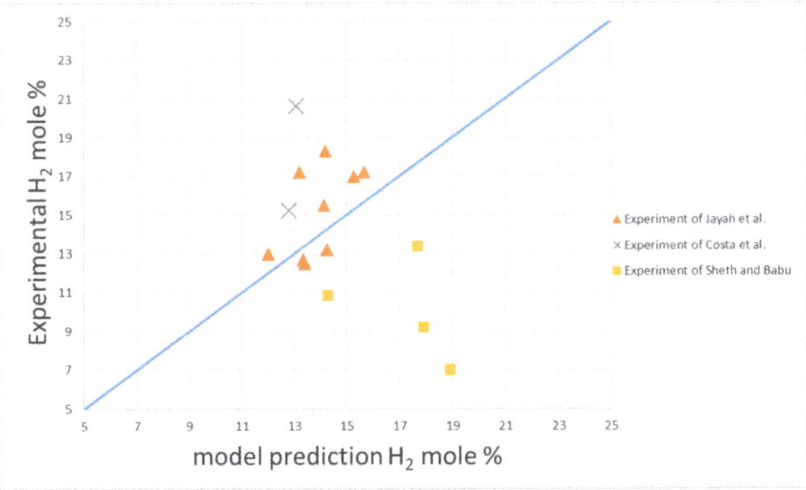

Figure 7. Parity plot of reduced linear model against experimental hydrogen mole % for data from other downdraft biomass gasifiers using experimental data from the literature [21–23].

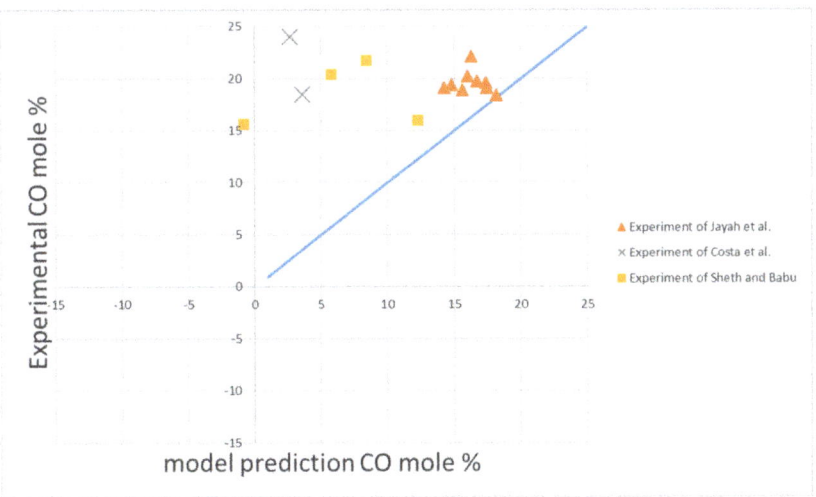

Figure 8. Parity plot of reduced linear model against experimental carbon monoxide mole % for data from other downdraft biomass gasifiers using experimental data from the literature [21–23].

Considering the reduced quadratic model, which gives the best fit to the data of Chee, when this is compared against other experimental data in Figure 9 it is shown to give poor or very poor predictions. These inaccuracies may be because of differences in the design of different downdraft gasifiers or because the conditions are outside the ranges given in Table 1. In particular, the bulk density of biomass used in all these cases are higher than those for the experiments of Chee. Additionally, these new data sources do not include grate or fan rotation speeds, so the average values from Table 1 have been assumed to utilize the reduced linear and quadratic expressions given in Table 2. Due to the second order terms in the quadratic expression, the errors associated with these assumptions lead to a much greater inaccuracy.

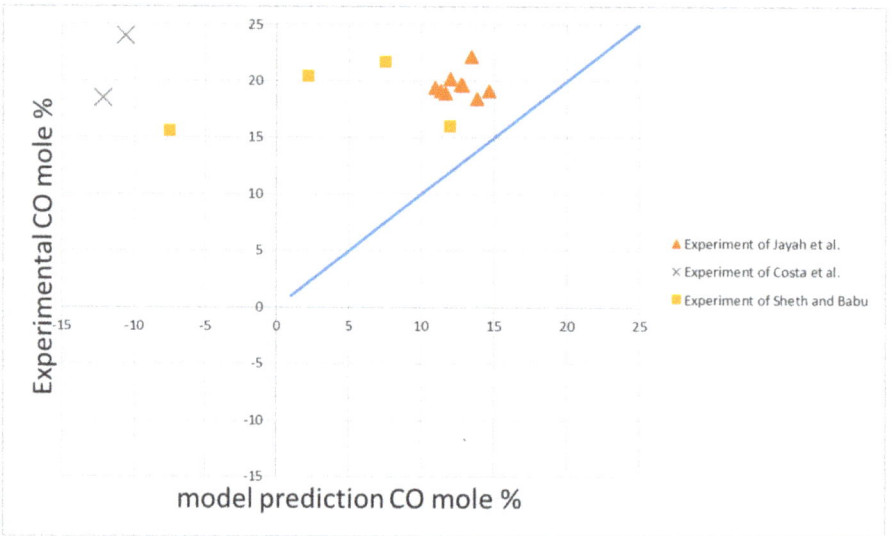

Figure 9. Parity plot of reduced quadratic model against experimental carbon monoxide mole % for data from other downdraft biomass gasifiers using experimental data from the literature [21–23].

This shows that these empirical models may only be practical for gasifiers with a similar scale and design and within the range of conditions used to build the models. This is supported by the results of Pio and Tarelho, who also found difficulty fitting empirical models to a wide range of different gasifier data sources [4], and by Baruah et al., who suggest that data must be taken from very similar scale gasifiers and with similar feedstocks [7]. However, if a large amount of data are collected from a single biomass gasifier with different conditions and feedstocks, this methodology should provide accurate models. Furthermore, due to the LASSO model reduction applied, simpler models can be obtained with much fewer parameters, which are very practical for the design of similar gasifiers.

4. Conclusions

Empirical models are proposed for the prediction of downdraft biomass gasifiers' outlet values (in particular the product gas composition). Both linear and quadratic expressions are considered, and a model reduction method is implemented based on cross validation with the LASSO method in order to select subsets of important parameters so that the resulting expressions can be simplified. This identifies significant parameters and reduces the number of parameters which must be regressed. We believe this is the first application of this LASSO model reduction method in the field of biomass gasification which is generally formulated in terms of linear models (combining Equations (1) and

(4)) [19] but can also be used for more complex quadratic equations (see Equations (2) and (5)), as demonstrated here.

This model reduction is particularly important for quadratic expressions which can contain a large number of parameters. For example, in the case study considered here, there are 11 inputs and a quadratic expression including all combinations of these 11 (as in Equation (2)) would have 78 different parameters to fit, but following the model reduction in the case study, there were 5–10 parameters needing to be identified. Considering the training data set contained only 25 data points, this means fitting the full quadratic expression with 78 parameters would not have been feasible.

In addition to reducing the complexity of fitted correlations, it is shown here that in almost all the outputs in the case study, the model reduction also leads to improved model prediction accuracy when the models were evaluated using test set data (which has not been used for training the models).

Supplementary Materials: The following are available online at https://www.mdpi.com/article/10.3390/su132112191/s1, Excel data file including "experimentaldatafull" tab containing experimental data gathered from [12,21–23], "fig5+fig6" tab containing the data used to plot Figures 5 and 6, "fig7+fig8+fig9 data" tab containing data used to plot Figures 7–9, and "fitted reduced model parameters" tab containing the fitted parameters for the models given in Table 2.

Author Contributions: Conceptualization, M.B. and H.M.U.A.; methodology, M.B.; validation, M.B.; data curation, M.B.; writing—original draft preparation, M.B.; writing—review and editing, M.B. All authors have read and agreed to the published version of the manuscript.

Funding: This research received no external funding.

Institutional Review Board Statement: Not applicable.

Informed Consent Statement: Not applicable.

Data Availability Statement: Experimental data used to build models can be found in [12], and data and models can also be found in the Supplementary file and in [21–23].

Acknowledgments: Support is acknowledged from the SRD scholarship, Dongguk University-Seoul, Seoul, South Korea.

Conflicts of Interest: The authors declare no conflict of interest.

References

1. Patra, T.K.; Sheth, P.N. Biomass gasification models for downdraft gasifier: A state-of-the-art review. *Renew. Sustain. Energy Rev.* **2015**, *50*, 583–593. [CrossRef]
2. Safarian, S.; Saryazdi, S.M.E.; Unnthorsson, R.; Richter, C. Artificial neural network integrated with thermodynamic equi-librium modeling of downdraft biomass gasification-power production plant. *Energy* **2020**, *213*, 118800. [CrossRef]
3. Marcantonio, V.; Ferrario, A.M.; Di Carlo, A.D.; Del Zotto, L.; Monarca, D.; Bocci, E. Biomass Steam Gasification: A Comparison of Syngas Composition between a 1-D Matlab Kinetic Model and a 0-D Aspen Plus Quasi-Equilibrium Model. *Comput.* **2020**, *8*, 86. [CrossRef]
4. Pio, D.T.; Tarelho, L.A.D.C. Empirical and chemical equilibrium modelling for prediction of biomass gasification products in bubbling fluidized beds. *Energy* **2020**, *202*, 117654. [CrossRef]
5. Ferreira, S.; Monteiro, E.; Brito, P.; Vilarinho, C. A Holistic Review on Biomass Gasification Modified Equilibrium Models. *Energies* **2019**, *12*, 160. [CrossRef]
6. Ayub, H.M.U.; Park, S.J.; Binns, M. Biomass to Syngas: Modified Non-Stoichiometric Thermodynamic Models for the Downdraft Biomass Gasification. *Energies* **2020**, *13*, 5668. [CrossRef]
7. Baruah, D.; Baruah, D.C.; Hazarika, M.K. Artificial neural network based modeling of biomass gasification in fixed bed downdraft gasifiers. *Biomass- Bioenergy* **2017**, *98*, 264–271. [CrossRef]
8. Pandey, D.S.; Das, S.; Pan, I.; Leahy, J.J.; Kwapinski, W. Artificial neural network based modelling approach for municipal solid waste gasification in a fluidized bed reactor. *Waste Manag.* **2016**, *58*, 202–213. [CrossRef] [PubMed]
9. Mutlu, A.Y.; Ozgun, Y. An artificial intelligence based approach to predicting syngas composition for downdraft biomass gasification. *Energy* **2018**, *165*, 895–901. [CrossRef]
10. Puig-Arnavat, M.; Hernández, J.A.; Bruno, J.C.; Coronas, A. Artificial neural network models for biomass gasification in fluidized bed gasifiers. *Biomass Bioenergy* **2013**, *49*, 279–289. [CrossRef]

11. Chavan, P.D.; Sharma, T.; Mall, B.K.; Rajurkar, B.D.; Tambe, S.S.; Sharma, B.K.; Kulkarni, B.D. Development of data-driven models for fluidized-bed coal gasification process. *Fuel* **2012**, *93*, 44–51. [CrossRef]
12. Chee, C.S. The Air Gasification of Wood Chips in a Downdraft Gasifier. Master's Thesis, Kansas State University, Manhattan, KS, USA, 1987.
13. Pradhan, P.; Arora, A.; Mahajani, S.M. A semi-empirical approach towards predicting producer gas composition in a biomass gasification. *Bioresour. Technol.* **2019**, *272*, 535–544. [CrossRef] [PubMed]
14. Rupesh, S.; Muraleedharan, C.; Arun, P.V. A comparative study on gaseous fuel generation capability of biomass materials by thermo-chemical gasification using stoichiometric quasi-steady-state model. *Int. J. Energy Environ. Eng.* **2015**, *6*, 375–384. [CrossRef]
15. Mirmoshtaghi, G.; Skvaril, J.; Campana, P.E.; Li, H.; Thorin, E.; Dahlquist, E. The influence of different parameters on bio-mass gasification in circulating fluidized bed gasifiers. *Energy Convers. Manag.* **2016**, *126*, 110–123. [CrossRef]
16. Gil, M.V.; Gonzalez-Vasquez, M.P.; Garcia, R.; Rubiera, F.; Pevida, C. Assessing the influence of biomass properties on the gasification process using multivariate data analysis. *Energy Convers. Manag.* **2019**, *184*, 649–660. [CrossRef]
17. Dellavedova, M.; Derudi, M.; Biesuz, R.; Lunghi, A.; Rota, R. On the gasification of biomass: Data analysis and regressions. *Process. Saf. Environ. Prot.* **2012**, *90*, 246–254. [CrossRef]
18. Pan, I.; Pandey, D.S. Incorporating uncertainty in data driven regression models of fluidized bed gasification: A Bayesian approach. *Fuel Process. Technol.* **2016**, *142*, 305–314. [CrossRef]
19. James, G.; Witten, D.; Hastie, T.; Tibshirani, R. *An Introduction to Statistical Learning with Applications in R*, 2nd ed.; Casella, G., Fienberg, S., Olkin, I., Eds.; Springer: New York, NY, USA, 2013; pp. 59–126.
20. Friedman, J.; Hastie, T.; Narasimhan, B.; Simon, N.; Tay, K.; Tibshirani, R. glmnet package for generalized linear models. Available online: https://glmnet.stanford.edu (accessed on 28 September 2021).
21. Jayah, T.H.; Aye, L.; Fuller, R.J.; Stewart, D.F. Computer simulation of a downdraft wood gasifier for tea drying. *Biomass-Bioenergy* **2003**, *25*, 459–469. [CrossRef]
22. Sheth, P.N.; Babu, B.V. Experimental studies on producer gas generation from wood waste in a downdraft biomass gasifier. *Bioresour. Technol.* **2009**, *100*, 3127–3133. [CrossRef] [PubMed]
23. Costa, M.; La Villetta, M.; Piazzullo, D.; Cirillo, D. A Phenomenological Model of a Downdraft Biomass Gasifier Flexible to the Feedstock Composition and the Reactor Design. *Energies* **2021**, *14*, 4226. [CrossRef]

Article

Accuracy and Predictive Power of Sell-Side Target Prices for Global Clean Energy Companies

Christoph Lohrmann * and Alena Lohrmann

School of Business & Management, LUT University, Yliopistonkatu 34, 53850 Lappeenranta, Finland; alena.lohrmann@lut.fi
* Correspondence: christoph.lohrmann@lut.fi

Abstract: Target prices are often provided as a support for stock recommendations by sell-side analysts which represent an explicit estimate of the expected future value of a company's stock. This research focuses on mean target prices for stocks contained in the Standard and Poor's Global Clean Energy Index during the time period from 2009 to 2020. The accuracy of mean target prices for these global clean energy stocks at any point during a 12-month period (Year-Highest) is 68.1% and only 46.6% after exactly 12 months (Year-End). A random forest and an SVM classification model were trained for both a Year-End and a Year-Highest target and compared to a random model. The random forest demonstrates the best results with an average accuracy of 73.24% for the Year-End target and 81.15% for the Year-Highest target. The analysis of the variables shows that for all models the mean target price is the most relevant variable, whereas the number of target prices appears to be highly relevant as well. Moreover, the results indicate that following the rare positive predictions of the random forest for the highest target return groups ("30% to 70%" and "Above 70%") may potentially represent attractive investment opportunities.

Keywords: classification; feature selection; machine learning; financial market; investing; sustainability

Citation: Lohrmann, C.; Lohrmann, A. Accuracy and Predictive Power of Sell-Side Target Prices for Global Clean Energy Companies. *Sustainability* 2021, 13, 12746. https://doi.org/10.3390/su132212746

Academic Editors: Julian Scott Yeomans and Mariia Kozlova

Received: 5 October 2021
Accepted: 10 November 2021
Published: 18 November 2021

Publisher's Note: MDPI stays neutral with regard to jurisdictional claims in published maps and institutional affiliations.

Copyright: © 2021 by the authors. Licensee MDPI, Basel, Switzerland. This article is an open access article distributed under the terms and conditions of the Creative Commons Attribution (CC BY) license (https://creativecommons.org/licenses/by/4.0/).

1. Introduction

Investors aiming to invest in the stock market to buy a company's stock face the challenge to select companies that will be successful in the future and whose stock will appreciate over time. Brokerage firms spend a considerable amount of resources, including money, on stock analysis, recommendations, and target prices, which suggests that these institutions and their clients see value in such research [1,2]. For that reason, investors and academics alike have been interested in the value of sell-side analysts' reports [3]. In this context, sell-side analyst refers to analysts employed by financial institutions such as banks, brokers, and asset management firms, which also sell securities such as stocks to their clients. These analysts provide research reports on stocks to the clients of their institution [4], which contain information about the future of these companies [5]. Their reports frequently include three elements: (1) an earnings forecast, (2) a stock recommendation, and (3) a target price for the stock [5–7], which are the result of their own evaluation of a company [6]. Stock recommendations usually come in five distinct levels ("Strong Buy", "Buy", "Hold", "Sell", "Strong Sell") [1,4,5,8], whereas the target price is provided as a support for the stock recommendation and is explicitly mentioning the expected stock value [3,6,9], usually, for the next 12 months [2,7]. Target prices often accompany stock recommendations, but previous research suggests that not all analyst reports contain target prices [5]. In particular, their inclusion in reports is more likely in case of positive recommendations (e.g., 70% for upgrades vs. 35% for downgrades [3] or 84% for "Strong Buy"/79% "Buy" vs. 27% for "Hold" [6]). However, when target prices are included in a report, it is intuitive that higher target prices for stocks are generally associated with more favorable stock recommendations [6].

Previous research has covered different aspects of stock recommendations and target prices. This includes investigating the individual analyst's ability to make recommendations and set target prices [7,10,11] as well as the performance of recommendations of different institutions [8], and the value or abnormal returns associated with stock recommendations [1,12] even when analysts face conflicts of interest [13].

It was shown that, even though analysts appear to be reluctant to make "Sell" (and "Strong Sell") and "Hold" recommendations and tend to focus on "Buy" recommendations (and "Strong Buy") [3,5,14] (e.g., "Buy" and "Strong Buy" account for 70.8% [5] or 68% [3] of all recommendations), their recommendations appear to have value. In particular, there are stock price reactions to recommendations (and recommendation revisions) [14] and investors can benefit from such recommendations [1,4] e.g., by buying highly rated stocks and by selling lowly rated ones [1].

In terms of target prices, the link between target prices and stock recommendations [6], factors affecting the accuracy of target prices [2], the impact of price targets and recommendation revisions [3–5], the impact of different valuation models on the target price [9], and the dispersion of target prices as a risk measure [15] are examples of research works found in the literature. Moreover, research has indicated that target prices and target price revisions contain new and valuable information [3,5]. However, the fact that target prices may contain relevant information for the stock market and investors does not necessarily mean that target prices are accurate [11]. Moreover, as pointed out by Bonini et al. [2], the ability to forecast future stock prices using analyst target prices is a neglected topic in the literature. The accuracy of target prices, meaning whether stock price meet target prices after or during the forecast period (e.g., a 12-month period), as well as their (absolute) forecast error, meaning how far the stock prices are away from the predicted target prices, depends on different factors. First, in terms of the institutions issuing target prices, highly reputable institutions tend to issue more accurate target prices (those target prices with positive implied return only) [11]. The evidence towards individual analysts' ability to suggest accurate target prices is limited. Bradshaw, Brown, and Huang [7] find some statistical evidence supporting a persistent differential ability of analysts in terms of accurate target price predictions, but these were shown to be trivial economically. Besides, as may be expected, analyst-specific optimism has a negative impact on the accuracy of target prices [11]. This may be linked to the fact that analysts' target prices may be used strategically [11] e.g., to create a "hype" around a stock [5] and may not always reflect the actual belief of analysts (e.g., similar for recommendations where a "Buy" recommendation is issued instead of a more suitable "Hold"/"Sell" one [13]). In terms of analyst research, the level of detail of research reports is positively affecting the target price accuracy [11] and the number of analysts providing research appears to improve the information quality [16], which may potentially also affect the target price accuracy positively. In terms of the company covered, recommendations for stocks associated with a larger price-to-book value (P/B), which can be called "glamour" stocks (e.g., technology companies) show lower forecast accuracy [11], which may be problematic given that research suggests that sell-side analysts tend to recommend such stocks more often [12]. Apart from that, setting accurate target prices appears to be especially challenging for companies that are loss-making (not earning profits) [2]. Volatility appears to impact target price accuracy as well, with lower volatility of the stock price leading to a higher accuracy [7,11]. The positive development of the stock market as a whole also affects the accuracy of target prices positively [7], which is in line with the finding that the forecast error of analysts increases during negative market environments [17]. Lastly, in terms of the target price, the accuracy and magnitude of the forecast error seem to be higher the larger the difference between the target price and current stock price (implied growth in stock price) [2,5,11].

This research work focuses on the accuracy and predictive power of target prices, specifically consensus information, meaning mean target prices. As mentioned previously, research on target price accuracy is very limited. Apart from that, the vast majority of previous research on target price accuracy has centered on individual analysts and/or individual target prices. There is some research on using consensus recommendations (e.g., the mean of recommendations) [1,12] but no research appears to have been done on using the consensus of target prices and determining the accuracy of such an aggregate estimate for the future stock price. In recent years private investors have also had easy and free access to many financial websites (e.g., Yahoo Finance, finanzen.net) that provide such mean target prices and related information [6] and make such an investigation also relevant for private investors, as well as academics and practitioners. Apart from that, no work appears to have been done using classification algorithms with target prices, which are very intuitive from an investors' perspective since they can be used for the binary decision (yes/no) whether to invest in a stock or to refrain from doing so. This study aims to address this research gap by using mean target prices and measuring the accuracy of these consensus estimates as well as using classification methods (with embedded feature selection) to build a model to predict when mean target prices will be met and when they might be missed. Moreover, the variables that are relevant for the prediction will be determined to gain further insights into potential factors that may affect the probability that a mean target price is met.

The emphasis of this work is on clean energy stocks which have attracted increased attention due to the Paris Agreement [18] and the rise of clean energy technologies as a response to the threat imposed by climate change. The road to the Paris Agreement extended multiple years, starting from around 2009 with the Copenhagen Accord [19]. The agreement was adopted by 196 Parties (almost every nation) in December 2015 to address climate change and its harmful impacts, and about 190 of those countries formally approved it [20]. The agreement sets up an ambitious target to limit the increase in mean global temperature to well below 2 °C above pre-industrial levels by reducing global greenhouse gas emissions. Among other measures, this includes ramping up efforts to accelerate the implementation of clean and sustainable energy technologies.

2. S&P Global Clean Energy Index

The Standard and Poor's Global Clean Energy Index (USD) is an equity index launched in 2007 that aims to measure the performance of companies in developed and emerging markets that have businesses linked to global clean energy [21,22]. In particular, companies contained in the index are "involved in the production of clean energy or provision of clean energy technology and equipment" [22]. Figure 1 displays the geographical location of the headquarters of the companies (as of July 2021) contained in the S&P Global Clean Energy Index. Gray color highlights the countries with headquarters in them and the marker size reflects the relative size of the company in terms of the market capitalization, as obtained from Yahoo Finance [23].

Out of the 81 companies included in this study, the headquarters of 28 companies are located in Europe (in Austria, Denmark, France, Germany, Italy, Norway, Portugal, Spain, Sweden, Switzerland, and United Kingdom). The headquarters of another 28 companies can be found in North America (in Canada and the United States). Finally, there are 15 headquarters in Northeast Asia (in China, South Korea, and Japan), 4 in South America (in Brazil and Chile), 3 in Southeast Asia (in New Zealand and Singapore), 3 in MENA (in Israel), and 1 in SAARC (in India). The largest number of companies (20) are headquartered in the United States (24.7%). In contrast to that, none of the 81 companies in the index is headquartered in Africa or the Eurasian regions. However, the authors of this study acknowledge that these companies may operate/have subsidiaries in African or Eurasian countries.

In terms of the business activity, about 52% of the companies are involved (directly or through their subsidiaries) in the power generation process, which includes the development, construction, and operation of power plants as well as the subsequent transmission and distribution of electrical energy. The second-largest group of companies (about 21% of the companies) are linked to the manufacturing of solar PV systems and their components (for instance, production of monocrystalline and polycrystalline silicon for solar PV cells, solar PV modules, inverters, storage systems, software, etc.). Apart from that, the third-largest group (10% of the companies) are developers of wind power generation systems. This group consists of companies, which, for example, design and manufacture blades and wind towers, construct wind turbines and wind farms, as well as provide various services to wind power generation companies.

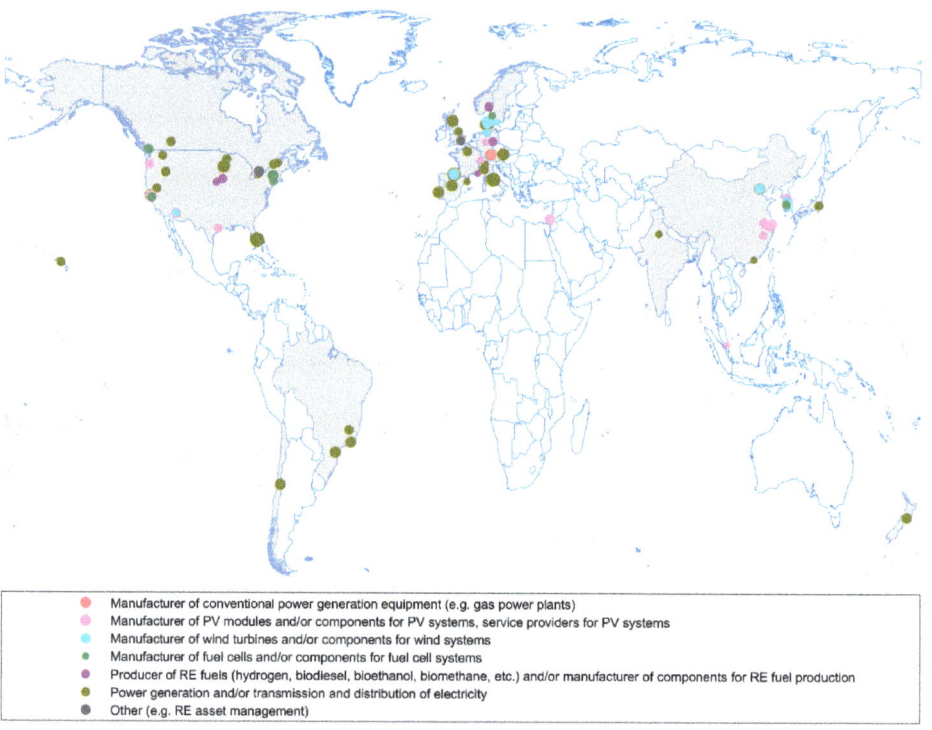

Figure 1. Location of the headquarters of the companies in the S&P global clean energy index.

Figure 2 displays the market capitalization of the companies and their corresponding Environmental, Social, and Governance (ESG) scores obtained from Thompson Reuters Datastream (see Appendix A Table A1).

The ESG score takes values from 0 to 100 and is based on self-reported (but verifiable) information of companies on their performance in terms of environmental, social, and governance indicators. In particular, the environmental score contains components such as "resource use" and "emissions", the social score elements such as "workforce" and "human rights", and the governance component for instance the "corporate social responsibility (CSR) strategy" [24]. The point labels are the Datastream symbols for the companies (shorter than the complete company names) and the levels of ESG scores (from "Low" to "Very high") were artificially created for this study for better representation of the ESG scores. The y-axis is on a logarithmic scale. In general, companies with larger market capitalization tend to be associated with higher Environmental, Social, and Governance (ESG) scores. One possible explanation for this could be that the operations of larger companies might be more in the public's attention and more exposed, which may create pressure from stakeholders such as society, civil organizations, as well as from (potential) investors. Additionally, larger companies might be able to allocate larger financial resources to reporting tools for ESG rating agencies (for instance, to provide higher quality and more comprehensive data to better fit the ESG measurement systems). Apart from that, it could be that the management enumeration of larger companies may be more tied to the accomplishment of ESG-based objectives, thus incentivizing a stronger focus on ESG-conform activities and behavior.

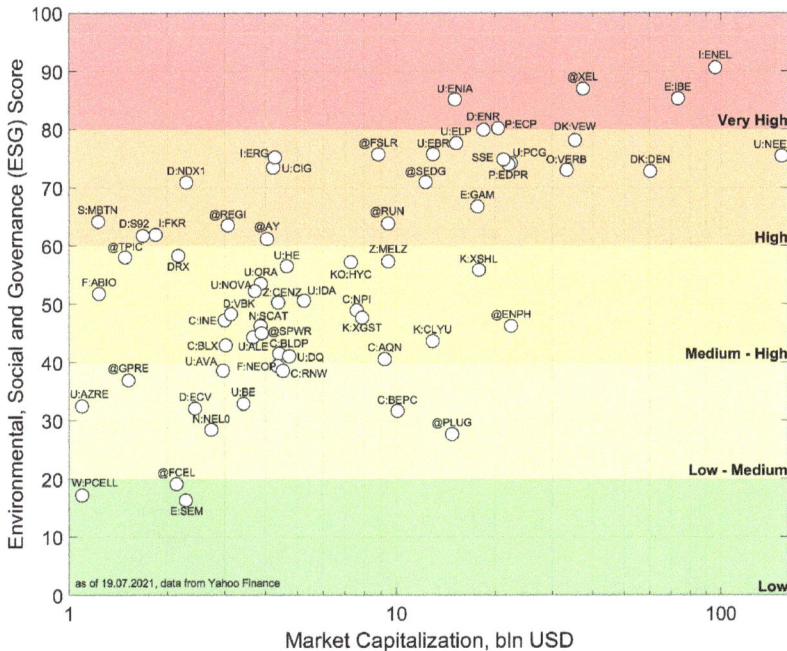

Figure 2. Market capitalization of companies in relation to the Environmental, Social, and Governance (ESG) score.

3. Data

The data for this study are from the 81 constituents of the S&P Global Clean Energy Index from 1 January 2009 until 30 June 2021. The start of the time period was selected as the year 2009 since this year marks the beginning of the steps leading up to the Paris Agreement [19]. The time-series data were obtained from the Thompson Reuters "Datastream" service with daily frequency. The variables downloaded for the companies consist of target price information (from the "Institutional Brokers Estimate System" (IBES)), company-related information such as the stock price, and the price-earnings (PE) ratio, as well as the MSCI world index, which is a broad global equity index. A complete list of the "raw" variables (incl. symbols) downloaded from Datastream can be found in Appendix A Table A1.

Target prices are most commonly set for the estimated stock price in 12 months [2,7]. Thus, taking an investor's perspective, only the information related to target prices from 1 January 2009 until 30 June 2020 were considered (a year shorter than the entire period) and compared with the actual stock prices after one year (1 January 2010 to 30 June 2021). This way, up to 2999 observations were available per company (less for those that did not have any target price information at certain points in time).

The focus of this work is on mean target prices (consensus price target) since they represent analysts' average estimated price of a stock in the future. In order to avoid including the same target prices for a company on consecutive days, the number of observations was reduced to the initial observation of a company and each observation for which the mean target price had changed compared to the previous observation—so at least a single revision/adjustment of a stock price has taken place. This decreased the number of observations to 0 to 139 per company with 5 out of 81 companies having 0 observations due to a lack of any target prices before the end of June 2020. For the (1:1) American depository receipt (ADR) of "Companhia Paranaense Denga" (Brazil), usually only a single target price was available, which was for unknown reasons consistently below the actual price (on average 80%) and, thus, was not further considered. (This issue could not be resolved by adjusting the target prices using the USD—BRL exchange rate.) For the remaining 75 companies the mean number of observations is about 77 and, overall, the data set contained 5810 observations. All target price variables (target mean price, target low price, target high price) were converted to target returns by calculating the "implied return" each of them represents compared to the corresponding current stock price. This was done in line with previous research (e.g., [7]), so that the targets of companies with target prices of different magnitude can be compared more easily. It was ensured that both the stock prices and target prices were in the same currency (usually the domestic currency) before the target returns were calculated. The list of all variables used for modeling, the corresponding pre-processing, and values are presented in Table 1.

Table 1. Variables and pre-processing.

No	Variable Name	Pre-Processing	Values
1	No Targets	None	Integer, [1, 39]
2	Mean Target Return	Converted from Target Price to Target Return	Continuous, [−92.3%, 1384%]
3	Low Target Return	Converted from Target Price to Target Return	Continuous, [−99.4%, 363.6%]
4	High Target Return	Converted from Target Price to Target Return	Continuous, [−90.5%, 2403%]
5	Std Target Ratio	Converted to Ratio by dividing by Mean Target Price	Continuous, [0, 1.07]
6	Target Up 1 Month	None	Integer, [0, 22]
7	Target Down 1 Month	None	Integer, [0, 29]
8	Low Target Above Price	Converted to binary (if Low > Current Price, then 1, else 0)	Binary, "0" (70.6%), "1" (29.4%)
9	High Target Below Price	Converted to binary (if High < Current Price, then 1, else 0)	Binary, "0" (92.4%), "1" (7.6%)
10	PE Ratio	None (Nearest known imputation)	Continuous, [0.3, 1766]
11	MSCI World Return	Converted from Index price to Index Return (previous 12 months)	Continuous, [−45.6%, 53.7%]
12	Class (Year-End)	If Price (year-end) >= Target Price, then 1, else 0	Binary, "0" (51.3%), "1" (48.7%)
13	Class (Year-Highest)	If Price (during year) >= Target Price, then 1, else 0	Binary, "0" (30.8%), "1" (69.2%)

Two additional variables were created: "Low Target Above Price" and "High Target Below Price". The first reflects that even the lowest target price of analysts exceeds the current stock price, highlighting a consensus that the stock may be undervalued and suggesting a possibly positive outlook for a company. The second reflects that even the highest target price provided by analysts is below the current stock price, indicating a potentially overvalued stock.

There are two separate targets for the classification that are based on the mean target price. The first target ("Year-End") is binary and reflects whether a stock's price after

12 months is as high or higher than the (initial) mean target price suggested ("1") or whether it did not reach the target price ("0"). The second target ("Year-Highest") is also binary, but represents whether the highest stock price accomplished during the entire 12-month interval is as high or higher than the initial mean target price ("1") or whether it was at no point during that year as high as the mean target price ("0"). In other words, the first target focuses exclusively on the year-end stock price whereas the second target emphasizes the largest stock price during the entire 12-month period. Using these two perspectives for the accuracy of target price was also taken in [2,7], whereas a focus on any point during the year—which is termed in this study "Year-Highest"—was pursued in [5,11].

4. Target Price Analysis
4.1. Analysis of Target Returns and Coverage

The average mean target return for the clean energy companies is 22.23% compared to the stock price at that time. It is unsurprising that the average low return is −8.12%, considerably lower, and the average high return is 58.20%, considerably higher than that. However, as Figure 3 illustrates, the magnitude of low, mean, and high target returns can differ considerably.

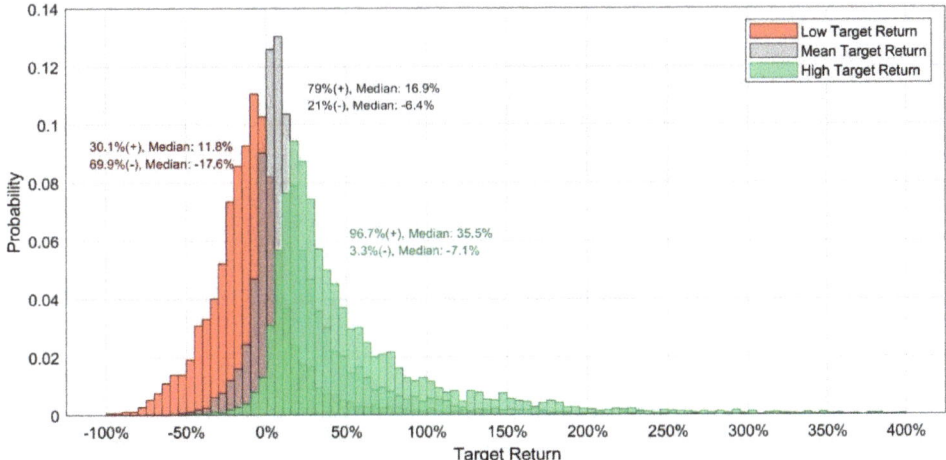

Figure 3. Distribution of low, mean, and high target returns.

It is apparent that the low target return distribution has the lowest mean and earliest peak of all distributions, followed by the mean target return and, lastly, the high target return. The first interesting observation is that low, mean, and high target returns can all be below and above the current stock price (=0% target return). For the low target prices, about 70% are below zero—implying an expected decline of the stock price over the next year. However, roughly 30% of the low target returns show the expectation of a positive return over the next year. Since the low target price reflects the lowest expectation of all analysts covering the stock, the low target price exceeding the current stock price may reflect the consensus belief of all analysts that the stock is undervalued. (It may be noted that at any point some target prices may have been provided days or weeks before the date of the observation and, thus, can potentially reflect outdated beliefs of the analysts that may be corrected in the future. Additionally, mean target prices, especially when based on numerous separate analyst target prices, may react slowly to changing market conditions or stock information since this may require many analysts to revise their target prices in a timely manner in order to affect the mean target price considerably and rapidly.) For the mean and high target prices, most implied returns are positive. About 79% of the mean target returns exceed zero and for the high price, this percentage even amounts to 96.7%. It is interesting to note that high prices tend to be highly positive but there appears to be also a small tail for target returns below zero. A high target return below zero, which is only the case for roughly 3.3% of the observations, reflects that all current analyst targets indicate that the stock is likely overvalued and will decline within the next year. It is noteworthy that all, the largest high target return (2403.5%), the largest mean target return (1835.0%), and the largest low target (363.6%) are linked to the stock of "Fuelcell Energy". In this extreme example, the target prices were lagging behind the stock price, which had declined considerably to new lows in mid-June of 2019. In general, for those 3.3% observations with a high price below the current price, the stock prices had increased or recovered from a decline and the target prices were lagging behind this surge. Similarly, the reason for some low target prices (about 4%) being 50% or higher over the current stock price was a decline in the stock price and the mean target prices' delayed correction for this decline. Moreover, both these cases—stock prices exceeding the high price considerably and low prices exceeding the stock price considerably tend both to be associated with a low number of analysts covering them (usually 1–2 analysts).

Figure 4 shows the median low, mean, and high target return as well as the median number of analysts covering a stock for each year.

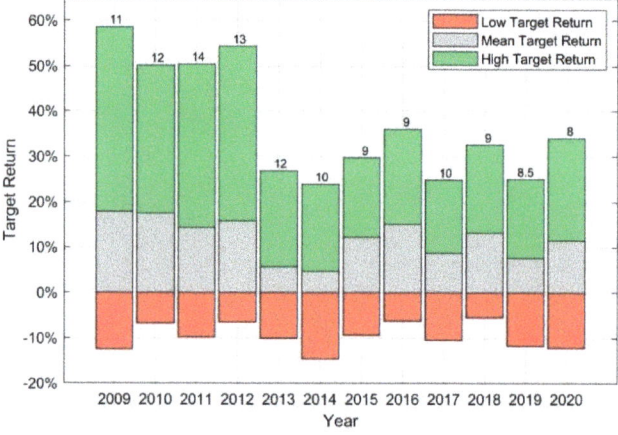

Figure 4. Median of the low, mean, and high target returns by year.

It is apparent that the target returns vary between years, with the high returns appearing most optimistic between 2009 and 2012 with medians around 50%. The low target return is with median values between −5.4% and −14.6%, consistently negative, whereas the median values for the mean and high target returns are consistently positive. The median for the mean target return ranges from 4.6% to 17.9% and for the high target return even from 24.0% to 58.7%. The median number of analysts covering a stock is between (about) 9 to 14. Overall, the median number of analyst target prices at any time is 10, the minimum 1 and the maximum number of analyst targets is 39.

4.2. Analysis of Target Price Accuracy

This research will consider two forms of accuracy (or hit rate), meaning whether the target price was met (=hit) or not (=miss)—which is a binary class label with only two outcomes. The first version, referred to as "Year-End", focuses on whether the stock price has reached the target price 12 months after a change in the mean target price (Yes/No). The second version, referred to as "Year-Highest", determines whether the stock price met the target price (Yes/No) at any point during the 12 months after a change in the mean target price. In the previous literature, the measure for achieving the target price at year-end was termed "TPMetEnd" and for accomplishing it at any point during the year "TPMetAny" [7].

For the given 75 clean energy companies and target prices over the time period from 2009 to 2020, the mean accuracy for the Year-End target is 46.6% whereas the mean accuracy for the Year-Highest setup is 68.1%. It is unsurprising that the accuracy for the Year-Highest target is higher than that of the Year-End given that it measures whether the target price is met at any time during the 12-month window (including at year-end) whereas the Year-End target only measures the accuracy at a single point in time, at the end of the 12-month period. A comparison of the implied return of target prices and the accuracies found in previous studies is displayed in Table 2 (ordered by the period). The previous studies covered different time periods and it is apparent that the average implied return is considerably higher in time periods extending from 1997 compared to all that exclude years before 2000. Only a few studies reported the accuracy of target prices and the results for the clean energy stocks covered in this study seem to be in line with these results, especially the most recent ones from Bradshaw, Brown, and Huang [7] and Kerl [11]. Since 2020 appears to have been an extraordinary year with also a very high accuracy (see Figure 5) the accuracy values excluding this year are also presented, which are even closer to the results found in the literature.

Table 2. Target price and accuracy comparison.

Authors	Companies	Target	TPMetEnd	TPMetAny	Period
Bradshaw [6]	US	36.0%	-	-	1996 to 1999
Asquith, Mikhail, and Au [5]	Global	32.9%	-	54.3%	1997 to 1999
Brav & Lehavy [3]	US	32.9% (28.0% [1])	-	-	1997 to 1999
Gleason, Johnson, and Li [9]	US	32.0%	-	-	1997 to 2003
Bonini, Bianchini, and Salvi [2]	Italy	14.9%	20.0%	33.1%	2000 to 2006
Bradshaw, Brown, and Huang [7]	US	24.0%	38.0%	64.0%	2000 to 2009
Kerl [11]	Germany	18.1%	-	56.5%	2002 to 2004
This Study	Global (Clean Energy)	22.2%	46.6% (41.5% [2])	68.1% (62.5% [3])	2009 to 2020

[1] Brav and Lehavy [3] report a one-year-ahead target price that is 28% larger than the current stock price and 32.9% higher than the preannouncement stock price (2-days prior recommendation/target price announcement). [2] Excluding the year 2020, which is exceptional due to the COVID-19 pandemic. [3] Excluding the year 2020, which is exceptional due to the COVID-19 pandemic.

It is noteworthy that Bradshaw, Brown, and Huang [7] also provide the additional inside that TPMetEnd and TPMetAny differ considerably in down and up markets with up markets resulting in accuracies of 50% and 71% whereas down markets lead to accuracies of only 17% and 49%.

In the following, the accuracy of the target prices (and, thus, of the target returns) is analyzed overall and by the magnitude of the mean target return, to determine if the predicted return appears to be linked to the accuracy of the prediction. The groups for the mean target return are (1) "Under 0%", reflecting an average estimate of no stock price increase, (2) from "0% up to 9.9%"—with the upper limit being the rounded median of the target return (11.5%), (3) from "10% to 29.9%"—representing approximately the range from the median to the third quartile (29.8%), (4) "30% to 70%"—with the upper limit being roughly the third quartile +1.5 times the interquartile range (72.2%), which is a common limit for outliers, and (5) target returns "Above 70%", which could statistically be considered outliers.

Figure 5 displays, for the Year-End target, the accuracy for each of the target return groups and for each year, and Figure 6 illustrates the average (actual) return achieved by the stocks in these target return groups. The first figure illustrates that the average accuracy of target prices can differ considerably between years (from 20.8% in 2011 to 86.3% in 2020) and generally differs considerably among target return groups. For most years, the accuracy for the "Under 0%" target return group has the highest accuracy, followed by the "0% to 9.9%" target return, which roughly represents all positive returns up to the median target return. In contrast to that, the two highest return groups, "30% to 70%" and the "Above 70%", usually are characterized by the lowest accuracy and often show 2–3 times lower accuracies than the two highest target return groups. Combining this information with the average Year-End returns for stocks in Figure 6 shows that the return group "Above 70%" has the most extreme average returns (independent of the target being hit or missed), showing in six years the highest average return and in three the lowest average return.

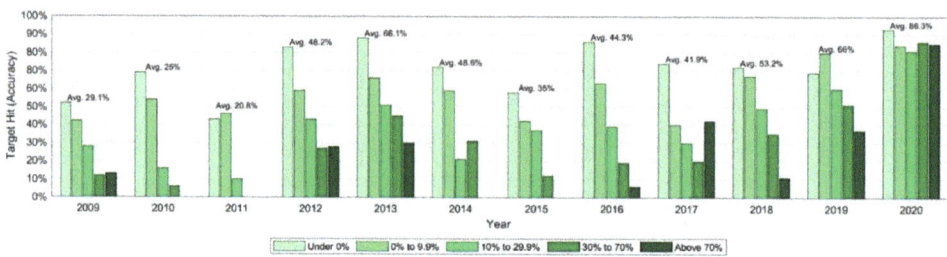

Figure 5. Accuracy of target prices by target return group and by year for Year-End class.

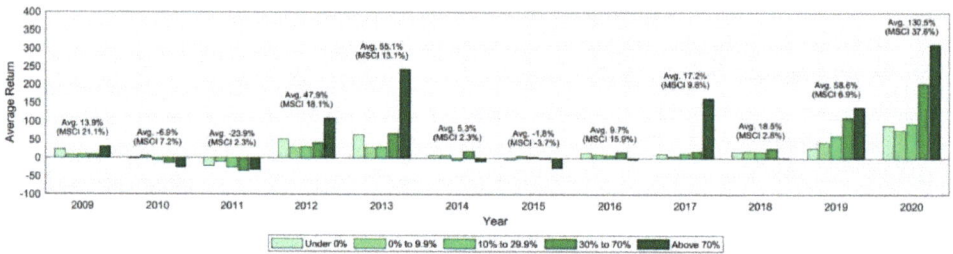

Figure 6. Average return by target return group and by year for Year-End class.

It is noteworthy that average Year-End returns are moderately positively correlated (0.77, 0.44 excl. 2020) with the average MSCI world performance during the same time period. (The MSCI world performance is not the MSCI world return during that calendar year but the average of the 1-year return of the MSCI for the 12-month time period starting at the time of each of the target prices. Thus, the performance is the average return of the MSCI world from different starting points in that year up to 12 months in the future. For instance, if the mean target price changes in March, the MSCI world return from that point in time until March of the subsequent year is recorded. This is done so that the actual return of stocks in a given timeframe can be compared with the MSCI world return in exactly the same timeframe.) In particular, in nine out of eleven years with a positive average MSCI world performance, the average return for clean energy stocks is positive as well, whereas for the one year with a negative average MSCI world performance the clean energy stocks' performance is also negative. However, as Figure 6 shows, the magnitude of positive and negative returns for clean energy stocks appears to be larger than that of the MSCI world index. The average accuracy and return for the Year-End target by target return group is displayed in Table 3.

The decrease in the average accuracy for stocks belonging to higher target return groups is in line with previous findings indicating that demonstrated that the predicted growth in the stock price is negatively impacting the forecast accuracy [2,5,11]. It is interesting to see that the average accuracy for the target prices gradually decreases with the magnitude of the implied target returns, but the same does not hold true for the average returns. The reason for that is two-fold: first, the average hit return, meaning the average return when the target price is met (=hit), tends to increase with the target return group and (2) the average miss return, meaning the average return achieved when the target price is not met, increases considerably with the target return group and, thus, is less negative. Both of these developments appear plausible. For the average hit return, the result appears plausible given that meeting higher return targets by definition means that returns below the target return group are excluded from the hit average. For instance, the average return of stocks that met their target price "Above 70%" by definition need to have achieved at least a return of 70%. In contrast, it is plausible that the average miss returns are on average negative and it appears intuitive that they increase with the target return group given that with higher return groups they may include higher returns that were still not meeting the target return. For instance, by definition, not accomplishing a return in the target return group "30% to 70%" means that returns of up to 29.9% can be contained in the miss returns. Moreover, it appears plausible that stocks with very high mean target prices tend to have higher average returns if they miss their high targets than stocks that miss considerably lower targets.

Table 3. Average accuracy and return by target return group (Year-End class).

Target Return Group	Under 0%	0% to 9.9%	10% to 29.9%	30% to 70%	Above 70%
Average Accuracy	73.1%	57.8%	37.9%	25.9%	17.1%
Average Return	26.6%	16.9%	16.8%	32.5%	55.7%
Average Hit Return	47.9%	40.2%	67.0%	156.9%	353.0%
Average Miss Return	−31.3%	−15.1%	−13.8%	−11.0%	−5.4%

Overall, it is interesting to see that the higher average hit and average miss returns tend to outweigh the decrease in the average accuracies so that even when target prices are rarely met (e.g., in the "30% to 70%" and "Above 70%" target return group), the average hit return is so high, and the average miss return is still not so low as to lead to a lower average return overall. In other words, clean energy stocks in the groups with higher mean target returns, which represent a more favorable analyst expectation than groups with lower mean target returns, also tend to be associated with higher average returns until the end of the corresponding 12-month period. This trend still holds true if target prices from the exceptional year 2020 are excluded. However, this information only provides an incomplete picture of the returns in the target return groups. It is noteworthy that while the average return tends to be higher for higher target return groups, the distribution tends to be wider, with the median showing a decreasing trend and the share of Year-End returns below zero is increasing for higher target return groups (see Figure A1 in Appendix A). The fact that the mean tends to be further from the median for higher target return groups in the most extreme case for the "Above 70%" target return the mean even exceeds the third quartile shows that there is a long tail at the higher end of the returns. Thus, higher average returns are based on a comparably small number of very high Year-End returns. This illustrates that the risk associated with stocks in higher target return groups increases but so does the potential reward, as highlighted by the average returns.

The next step is the analysis of the Year-Highest class that represents whether the target price is met at any time during the 12-month period after the mean target price changes. Figure 7 displays for the Year-Highest target the accuracy for each of the target return groups and for each year, and Figure 8 illustrates the average of the highest achievable (actual) return by the stocks in these target return groups during the 12-month period.

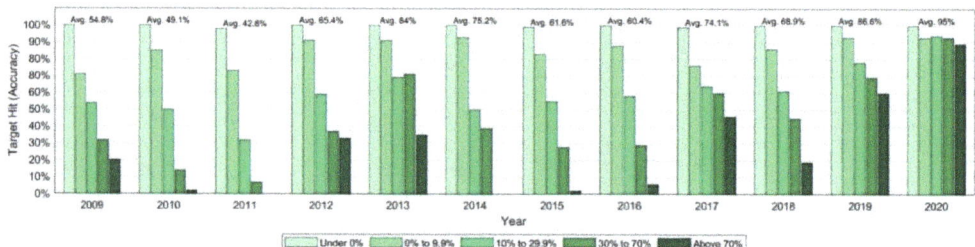

Figure 7. Accuracy of target prices by target return group and by year for Year-Highest class.

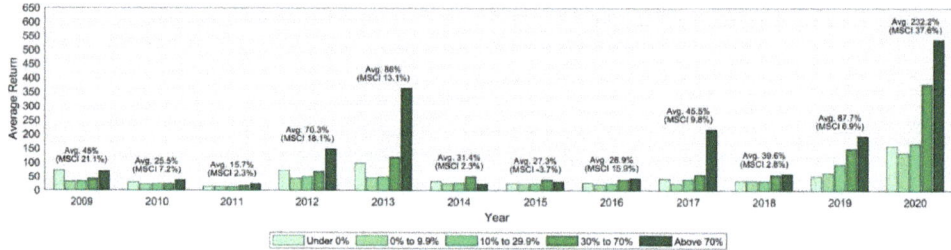

Figure 8. Average return by target return group and by year for Year-Highest class.

The average accuracies (target hit rates) are considerably less variable for the Year-Highest class than for the Year-End class and are also consistently higher in each year (see also Figure 5). The average accuracy ranges from 42.8% (2011) to 95% (in 2020) with an overall average return of 68.1%. The average accuracy for the "Under 0%" target return group is essentially 100% every year given that the stock price is already exceeding the target price at the start. The only exceptions are three observations for which the target return is only 0.2% to 5.1% below the stock price, which drops below it during the first day and never recovers from it. The tendency that lower target return groups are more likely to be met is even stronger for the Year-Highest target. It is noteworthy that the average accuracy for the "Above 70%" target return group is still often 2–3 times smaller than for the "Under 0%" and "0% to 9.9%" target return group. The average (highest) returns achievable displayed in Figure 8 follow a similar pattern to those for the average returns by Year-End in terms of the higher magnitude of average returns for the "Above 70%" target return group. The average returns for each target return group and year are positive, highlighting that, on average, stocks during the 12-month period at some point increased over their initial stock price. The correlation between the average Year-Highest returns with the MSCI world performance is still strongly to moderately positive (0.80, 0.41 excl. 2020).

The average accuracy and return for the Year-Highest target by target return group is displayed in Table 4. Similar to the Year-End average accuracies, the Year-Highest average accuracies also decline for higher target return groups. Moreover, the trend of higher average returns for higher target return groups can also be observed. Similar to the Year-End average accuracies, the Year-Highest average accuracies also decline for higher target return groups. Moreover, the trend of higher average returns for higher target return groups can also be observed.

Table 4. Average accuracy and return by target return group (Year-Highest class).

Target Return Group	Under 0%	0% to 9.9%	10% to 29.9%	30% to 70%	Above 70%
Average Accuracy	99.8%	85.1%	59.6%	39.9%	21.8%
Average Return	57.8%	36.4%	44.1%	78.1%	118.9%
Average Hit Return	57.9%	42.3%	68.4%	168.6%	420.3%
Average Miss Return	−4.1%	2.6%	8.4%	18.0%	35.1%

Similar to the Year-End average accuracies, the Year-Highest average accuracies also decline for higher target return groups. Moreover, the trend of higher average returns for higher target return groups can also be observed. The average returns for the Year-Highest class are for each target return group higher than those of the Year-End class (see Table 4), which is intuitive given that these correspond to the highest stock price during an entire year and not just those at the end of the year. The same holds true for the average hit returns and the average miss returns, which are all positive (with the single exception of the average miss return for the "Under 0%" target return group which, by definition, cannot be positive). As for the Year-End target, for the Year-Highest target the average hit and miss rates increase as the target return group increases. This highlights that clean energy stocks in the groups with higher mean target returns, which represent a more favorable analyst expectation than groups with lower mean target returns, also tend to achieve higher stock price increases over their 12-month periods. It is noteworthy that both the average as well as the median return increases with higher target return groups, highlighting that the distribution has a longer tail for the high positive returns (see Figure A1 in Appendix A). However, in contrast to the Year-End returns, the share of negative returns remains at a low, close to constant level for all target return groups.

From an investor's perspective, it is interesting to note that the Year-End returns represent the returns achieved by investing in a stock at the time where the mean target price is updated and simply holding it for the 12-month period (passive management). In contrast, the Year-Highest returns embody the highest return accomplishable during the 12-month period starting from the change of the mean target price and, thus, may require extensive monitoring and optimal market timing to be accomplished (active management). This was also pointed out by Bonini et al. [2], who stated that it is effectively not possible for investors to determine when the maximum price (or minimum price) of a stock is accomplished.

5. Feature Selection

Feature selection refers to the process of selecting features (=variables) that are relevant for a task and, thus, discarding irrelevant or redundant features from a data set [25–29]. This differentiates feature selection from another dimensionality reduction approach termed feature extraction. Feature extraction transforms the existing features into "new" ones and, subsequently, keeps only some of these new features, whereas feature selection chooses a subset of the original features to retain [30–32]. Using feature selection is generally associated with several advantages and motivations such as (1) improving (or at least not considerably decreasing) the error of the final model [33–37], (2) increasing the speed of model training, and obtaining more simple models from the data [33–36], (3) reducing computational cost and data storage requirements [33–35], and (4) obtaining more easily visualizable and interpretable data [33–35,38,39].

When feature selection is applied in the context of supervised learning, such as classification or regression, it is referred to as supervised feature selection [30,39]. Supervised feature selection can be divided into three types: filter, wrapper, and embedded methods [31,39–41]. Filter methods are part of the pre-processing of the data and only use the characteristics of features to determine their relevance, thus, they do nit involve any learning algorithm (e.g., classifier) [31,39,41,42]. Wrapper methods deploy the learning algorithm as a "blackbox" to evaluate different feature subsets (e.g., using classification accuracy) and to select the best performing one [39,43–46]. Embedded methods are as wrapper methods classifier-dependent, but unlike wrapper methods, they are part of the model training of the learning algorithm itself [25,33,47,48]. Thus, the feature subset generated by embedded methods can be seen as a byproduct of model training [47].

This research will use commonly known embedded feature selection methods, in particular random forests and support vector machines with recursive feature elimination (RFE), to train the classification models for this study. The software used for coding is Matlab version 2020a.

6. Classification Models

6.1. Random Forest

Random forests were suggested by Breiman [49] and are an ensemble of so-called decision trees [50]. A common algorithm to create decision trees is CART [51], but others exist as well [52,53]. A decision tree is a machine learning method that starts at the so-called "root" node and uses at each step the best binary split of a variable to create two child nodes [50]. This split can be considered a rule that aims to make resulting partitions of the data more "pure" in terms of the distribution of classes in each of them. This procedure is repeated until a stopping criterion is met [50], for instance, that each partition is "pure", meaning that only a single class is present. Following the resulting path of rules that are applied to each new observation leads them to a so-called "leaf" or "terminal node" which is associated with one class (either pure or majority in that partition) [52,54,55]. Thus, following the path branched out from the root node determines the class membership of an observation. This procedure of iteratively using binary splits to create "purer" partitions of the data is called "recursive partitioning" meaning that it creates regions of the instance space that belong to each of the classes in a classification problem [50,52,55].

A decision tree has multiple advantages, such as its easy interpretability due to the rules it provides for its class assignments [52,54], its ability to handle numerical and discrete variables, and that it does not require assumptions about the underlying distributions [52]. However, decision trees are sensitive to small perturbations of the data (high variance) [56] and, thus, tend to overfit.

The aim of a random forest is to overcome this weakness of decision trees by combining multiple decision trees and aggregating their class predictions [50,56]. The idea of random forests is an extension of bagging [50]. Bagging stands for "bootstrap aggregation", where "bootstrap" refers to randomly sampling observations with replacement from the training data to obtain multiple data sets of the same size as the original training data, whereas "aggregation" highlights that the results from training models on these bootstraps are averaged (=aggregated) [56]. The difference in random forests to classical bagging is that not only observations are randomly drawn from the original data but also the variables are randomly sampled (except for the target variable) [50,56]. This procedure aims to reduce the correlation between trees to obtain de-correlated trees [56]. The algorithm for a random forest [50,56] (in the context of classification) is illustrated in Algorithm 1. The algorithm illustrates that a set of decision trees are used that each cast their vote and the most common class vote is used as the class prediction for the random forest (majority voting) [56].

For this study, the number of decision trees in the random forest is set to 50. The minimum number of observations at each leaf node (minimum leaf size) is an optimized hyperparameter over the values {1, 10, 20, 50, 250, 1000, 2905}, where 2905 is the number of samples divided by two (rounded down). The Gini diversity index (GDI) is selected as the splitting criterion, the technique for variable selection (step 1.2.1. in Algorithm 1) is the interaction test [57], and the number of variables selected randomly (m) from the bootstrap sample is $\sqrt{p}$ where p is the number of all variables in the data set [50,56].

Algorithm 1 Random forest for classification

1. For $t = 1$ to T (number of decision trees in the random forest)
    1.1. Take a bootstrap sample of the training data
    1.2. Use the bootstrap sample to fit a decision tree by repeating the following steps (recursive partitioning) until a stopping criterion for the tree is met
        1.2.1. Select a subset of the variables (denoted m) of all variables (denoted p) in the bootstrap sample
        1.2.2. Determine the best binary split for any of the m variables (best splitting criterion value e.g., purity)
        1.2.3. Split the node into two child nodes using the variable and variable value for the best binary split
    End
2. Assign observations to classes by taking each tree's class prediction and using a majority vote (most common class prediction) over all decision trees (=votes) to determine the class label

6.2. Support Vector Machine—Recursive Feature Elimination

The support vector machine (SVM) originated in the work of Boser, Guyon, and Vapnik [58] and Cortes and Vapnik [59]. The general idea of an SVM is to create a decision boundary (hyperplane) that maximizes the margin between itself and the closest observations (=data points) of each of the classes [54]. The points that are closest to the boundary and, thus, are on the margin are called "support vectors" [60]. It is noteworthy that the input variables, denoted x, are often mapped into a higher-dimensional feature space using a (nonlinear) mapping that can be denoted as $\phi()$. Following the notation in [59,61], the decision function f for a data set x can be defined as

$$f(x) = w\phi(x) + b \quad (1)$$

where w are the weights for the optimal hyperplane (decision surface) that separates the classes with the largest margin, $\phi()$ is a function that transforms the input, and b is the bias value. The bias is the average over the marginal support vectors and can be calculated using the weights w [60]. The weights w for the optimal hyperplane are calculated as

$$w = \sum_i y_i \alpha_i \phi(x_i) \quad (2)$$

where x_i is a support vector, α_i is the weight for the support vector x_i, and y_i is the class label $\epsilon\{-1, 1\}$ corresponding to the support vector [59,60]. The weights of the support vectors α are the parameters of an SVM, which are optimized using convex optimization [60]. For details on the optimization problem behind an SVM, please see [56,61].

The weight vector w for the hyperplane will be used in recursive feature elimination to determine the ranking of features. Recursive feature elimination using a support vector machine (SVM-RFE) was introduced by Guyon et al. [60]. It deploys a greedy backward elimination procedure where in each step an SVM is trained and the variable with the lowest squared weight w^2 is removed from the set of the remaining variables [48,60,62,63]. Thus, w^2 can be regarded as a ranking criterion for the variables [60]. It is noteworthy that in each step one or more variables can be removed [48,60]. Thus, SVM-RFE is inherently different from random forests: the former starts with a complete variable set and iteratively removes one (or multiple) variable(s) whereas the latter functions by iteratively selecting variables. The algorithm for SVM-RFE is depicted in Algorithm 2 (similar to [48,60]).

The logic behind this procedure is that w^2 estimates the effect of each variable on the objective function (sensitivity) with larger values indicating more important variables so that the resulting variable subset leads to the best class separation with the SVM classifier [48,60]. The number of variables to retain can either be user-specified (and the number of variables to remove would, thus, be all variables minus the number of variables to retain) [62,63] or the algorithm can be run until a single variable is left and the optimal subset can be selected using cross-validation as the subset leading to the highest validation accuracy. For this study, the variables are standardized using the weighted mean and weighted standard deviation, and the optimal variable subset is determined using cross-validation.

Algorithm 2 Support vector machine—recursive feature elimination (SVM-RFE)

For $m = 1$ to M (number of features to remove)
    1. Train an SVM on the training data with the remaining features (s) (initially all features p)
    2. Determine the ranking criterion w^2 from the trained SVM
        2.1. Obtain the weights α of the support vectors from the trained SVM
        2.2. Calculate the weight vector w of the optimal hyperplane $\left(w = \sum_i \alpha_i y_i \phi(x_i)\right)$
    3. Remove the variable associated with the smallest w^2 from the set of the remaining features s
End

7. Experimental Results and Analysis

7.1. Model Performance and Feature Importance

The performance of the random forest (RF) and SVM are compared to a simple random approach using the two-class probabilities. In particular, for each observation, a random uniform number is generated and if its value is below or equal to the first class's probability, it is assigned to that class, and otherwise, it is assigned to the second class. This approach is taken to compare the random forest and SVM with a random approach but still account for the class sizes (especially for the Year-Highest class, which has a higher share of observations with the positive target class). The average classification accuracy, precision, and recall for the three models are displayed for each of the two targets ("Year-End" and "Year-Highest") in Table 5. The results are based on 20 runs of a nested cross-validation (10-fold cross-validation split for the external and also the nested cross-validation).

Table 5. Model results for the Year-End and the Year-Highest targets.

Model	Target	Accuracy ± Std [1]	Avg Precision	Avg Recall
RF	Year-End	73.24 ± 1.63 ***	72.19	69.3
SVM	Year-End	65.90 ± 1.75 ***	62.21	68.45
Random	Year-End	50.02 ± 2.09	46.34	50.02
RF	Year-Highest	81.15 ± 1.57 ***	84.51	88.55
SVM	Year-Highest	75.77 ± 1.28 ***	76.15	93.8
Random	Year-Highest	56.49 ± 1.93	68.02	56.49

The notation '***' refer to 0.1% significance level corresponding to a one-sided Welch's test of the accuracy of RF and SVM versus the accuracy of the Random model for a specific target, respectively.

The results for the Year-End target show that the random forest is, with an average accuracy of 73.24%, the most accurate model. The linear SVM model performs noticeably worse than the random forest. However, using the one-sided Welch's test, it can be demonstrated that both the random forest and the SVM are highly significantly (***) more accurate than the random model (p-value < 0.999). The average precision and recall are also the highest for the random forest model with both values being around 70%. This indicates that the model correctly predicts around 70% of the actual target price hits (recall) and that also about 70% of the positive predictions are actual hits (precision). For the Year-Highest target, the ranking of the methods is the same, with the random forest performing the best in terms of accuracy and, both the random forest and SVM show average accuracies that are highly significantly more accurate than that of the random model (p-value < 0.999). It is noteworthy that all metrics—average accuracy, average precision, and average recall are higher for all methods for the Year-Highest target than for the Year-End target. This is likely based on the fact that it is an easier classification task to determine if a certain target price is exceeded at some point during a time period than for only one point in time (year-end).

The next question investigated is that of the feature importance, meaning, which variables are relevant and used by each of the two machine learning algorithms for their models. The relevance of features (=variables) for these two models for both targets is displayed in Figure 9.

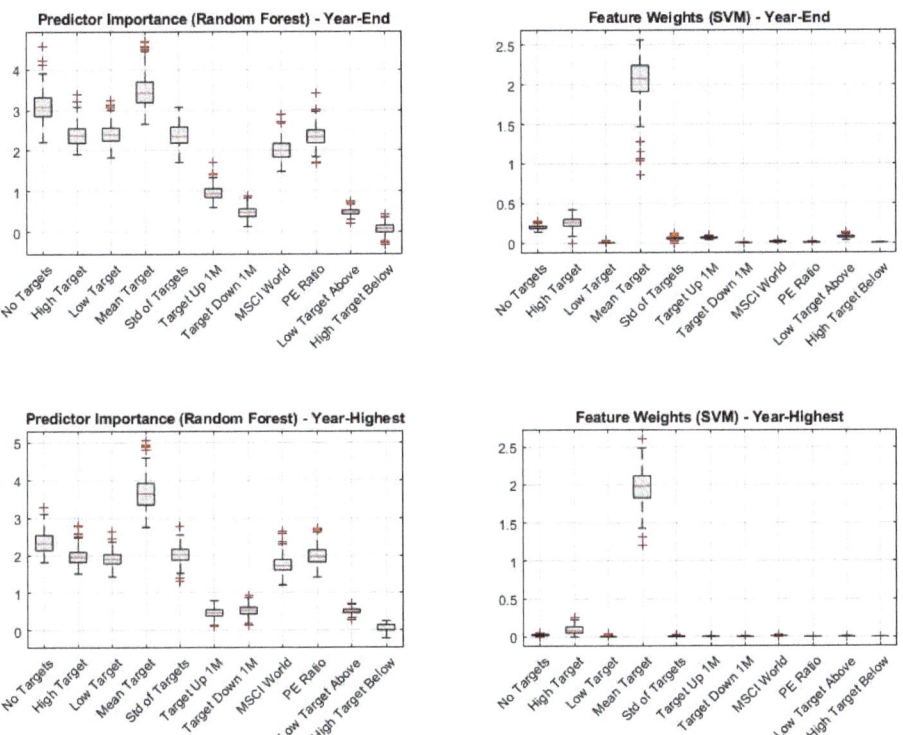

Figure 9. Feature importance by model and target.

The feature importance scores illustrate that for both the Year-End and the Year-Highest random forest and SVM models the most relevant variable is the mean target price of the stock. This may not be surprising given that (1) the mean target was the target price used to set up both of the targets and (2) it represents a consensus of analysts about the expected (average) stock price in the future. For the random forest model, the number of target prices was the second most relevant variable whereas for the SVM models it was only the third most relevant one. In order to analyze the obtained model performances in more detail and understand for which type of observations the model works particularly well, the overall accuracy accomplished is broken down by the mean target price and the number of target prices. This breakdown for the random forest and SVM model with the Year-End target is presented in Figure 10. The categories for the number of targets were created with the help of the 33rd and 67th percentile of the number of analysts covering a stock as cut-off points. Thus, the number of targets is considered "Small" when an observation is covered by 1–6 analysts, "Medium" for 7–14 analysts, and "Large" when 15 or more analysts' target prices are available.

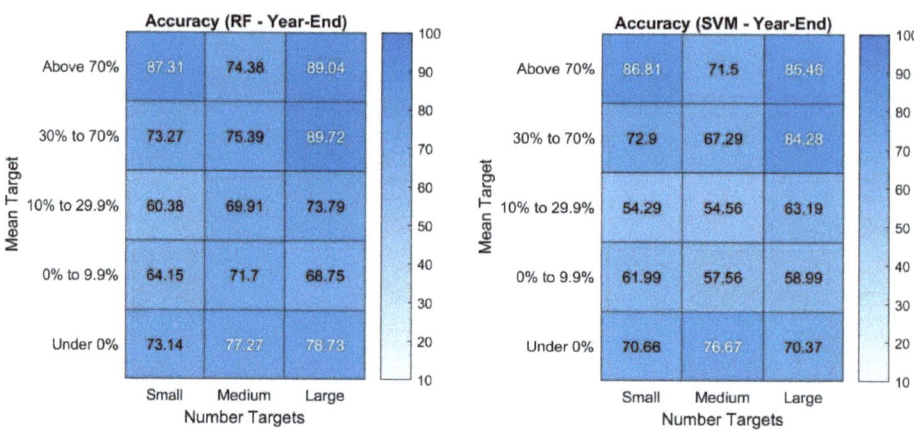

Figure 10. Model accuracy by mean target and number of targets for the Year-End target.

The results show that for both the random forest and SVM model, the average accuracies tend to be the highest for the very high mean target prices ("Above 70%" and "30% to 70%), followed by the lowest mean target prices ("Under 0%"), which imply a decrease from the current stock price. Both models rarely predict the positive class (target price met) for observations with very high and high mean target prices ("Above 70%", "30% to 70%)—but the SVM is in that case more extreme by almost never predicting a "hit" for these return groups (see in Figure A3 in Appendix A). Moreover, the precision of the random forest for these return groups tends to be rather high, indicating that when it predicts a hit (which it does not do often), then it is often correct with that prediction (see in Figure A2 in Appendix A). This holds true especially for stocks with high target returns ("30% to 70%", "Above 70%") and that are highly covered meaning that there are 15 or more (recent) analyst prices at that time available for it. These two subgroups show a precision of 84.95% and 93.06%, indicating that positive predictions are in the vast majority of cases correct. It should be pointed out that the random forest model can also be considered prudent since the recall is not high for instance 37.53% and 25.97% for these subgroups highlighting that often observations for stocks that hit their target prices are not predicted as positive. These results are very different for the SVM model for the Year-End target, which almost never predicts a positive outcome for the high return groups and even when it does, the precision is generally low. Thus, the high accuracies achieved with the SVM for the high return groups are almost exclusively based on predicting a negative outcome (which is the majority class label for these return groups). This likely makes this model less attractive for potential investors since correctly predicting hits of a target price provides usually more information than the miss. In particular, a hit states a minimum return achieved (the target return) to be an actual hit, whereas a miss does not provide other information than that the return is lower than the target return, which can still be positive or be negative (exception ("Under 0%")).

The two models are also very accurate on observations with a mean target that is below the current stock price ("Under 0%"). For these observations the model tends to predict the positive class (target price met) in 90% to 100% of the cases and, thus, unsurprisingly correctly predicts most observations that are actually positive. The observations "Under 0%" have a high share of stocks that after one year are at or above the target price, which may indicate that the mean target price is accurate or even too pessimistic. However, investors should keep in mind that the target price is below the current price, so this does not necessarily reflect an investment opportunity. However, the average actual return associated with these observations is over 26% (within 12 months) with 63.9% of observations in that group showing a positive return instead of a decline over the 12-month period.

This breakdown for the random forest and SVM model with the Year-Highest target is presented in Figure 11.

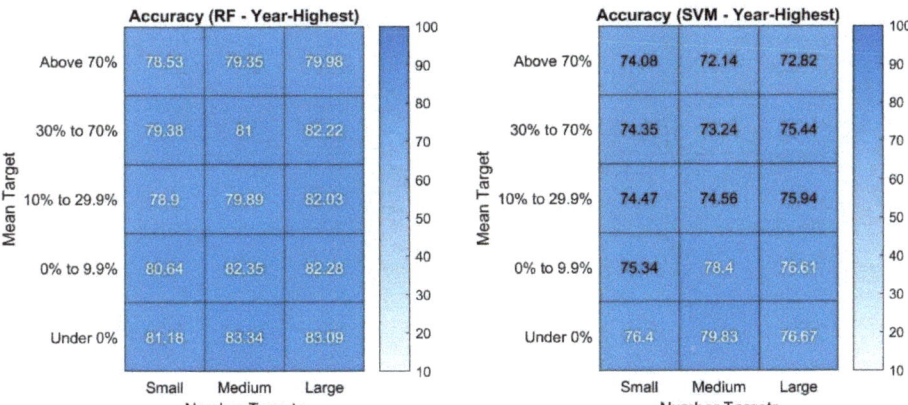

Figure 11. Model accuracy by mean target and number of targets for the Year-Highest target.

The average accuracy of both models is not just higher for the Year-Highest target than for the Year-End target (see Table 5) but there also seems to be clearly less variation among the average accuracy values for different subgroups. It is interesting to note what for both models there are more positive predictions for the high return groups, but the recall for them tends to be lower (see Figures A4 and A5 in Appendix A). However, the opposite is true for the moderate return groups such as "10% to 29.9%" or "0% to 9.9%" which tend to have the same or a larger share of positive predictions for the Year-Highest than for the Year-End target but have a higher recall. This means that for these moderate return groups the share of positive predictions that turn out to the correct is higher. The simple reason for the higher accuracy and precision on these moderate return groups is likely the fact that the magnitude of the estimated increase is not that high, and the stock price has an entire year to reach it at least at a single point in time. Since stock prices tend to fluctuate over a year, it appears plausible that especially low to moderate increases can happen at least temporarily during that entire time period. This also highlights the main problem of models using the Year-Highest target: investors do not know at which time and for how long targets may be met, thus requiring strict and continuous monitoring of the stock prices and optimal market timing to accomplish the results suggested by the Year-Highest model. However, if this is possible for an investor, then the predictions especially for the moderate target groups may be of interest due to the high precision.

7.2. Performance Comparison

From an investor's perspective, the accuracy of a classifier is only of secondary importance compared to its usefulness as a support tool for investment decisions. Figure 12 shows the Year-End and Year-Highest return distributions for positive and negative predictions conducted by the random forest and SVM model. Since the target return group "Under 0%" is assumed not to be of interest for investors since correctly predicting that a stock may reach its target price, which is lower than the current price, is likely of limited investment value, these observations are not included in the return distributions presented in Figure 12.

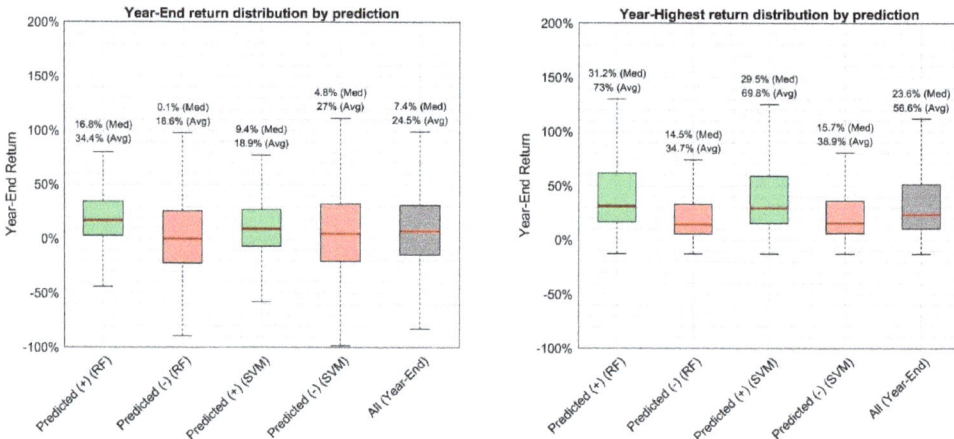

Figure 12. Actual return distribution by prediction (excl. "Under 0%" target return group).

For the Year-End, especially the random forest, which was the most accurate model for this target, showed the most interesting distributions. In particular, positive predictions of the random forest did not just have a clearly higher median and mean than all returns (in grey), the first quartile also exceeds zero (3.2%). This means that less than 25% of the stocks for which the model predicted that the target price would be reached, experienced a negative return over the subsequent year. In contrast, the negative predictions lead to a median year-end return close to zero. Thus, close to 50% of the observations were characterized with a negative return whereas overall this is only the case for about 39.4% of observations. For the SVM the average year-end return is lower than that of all observations and the third quartile for negative predictions is larger than for positive ones, indicating that the top 25% of returns for negative predictions are actually higher than for positive predictions. It is noteworthy that for both the random forest and the SVM the distribution of negative predictions is wider, reflecting that for negative predictions there is a wide variety of returns that can be obtained.

For the Year-Highest returns, the distributions look clearly different than for the Year-End returns. Both the random forest and the SVM show higher median and average returns than overall. Moreover, the positive predictions are characterized by a larger variation of the returns. Again, the random forest shows better performance in terms of the actual returns. However, it should be kept in mind that these are the Year-Highest returns, which means that the corresponding high stock prices are accomplished at some point during the year, likely not at year-end and not necessarily for a prolonged period of time. Thus, achieving such returns might be extremely challenging. In this regard, the Year-End returns might be of larger interest for investors since they only require the implementation of a buy-and-hold strategy and do not necessarily require additional monitoring.

The subsequent analysis will, thus, focus on the Year-End returns achieved using the most accurate model, the random forest. Figure 13 depicts the Year-End return by target return group accomplished with negative and positive predictions of the random forest.

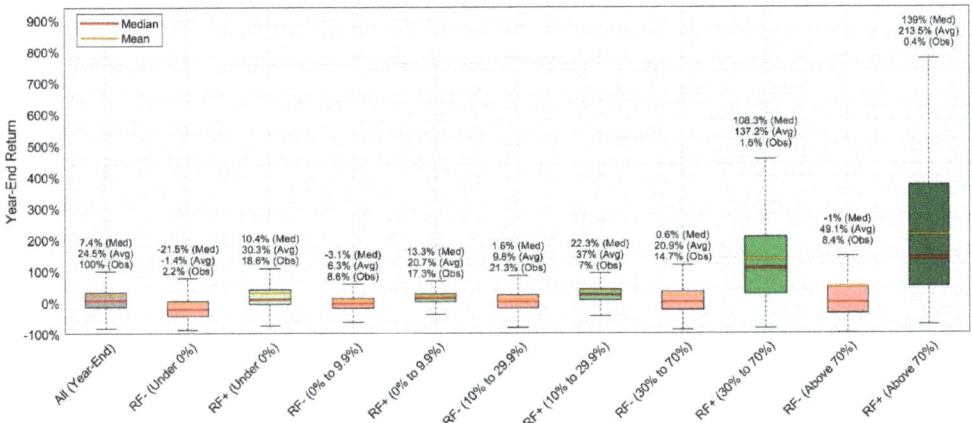

Figure 13. Year-End return distribution by random forest prediction and target return group.

It is apparent that the median and average return by year-end is considerably higher for positive predictions of the random forest for stocks with target prices between "30% to 70%" and those "Above 70%". The shares of these predictions compared to all predictions made are overall very low, 1.5% and 0.4%, respectively. However, they appear of interest as it suggests a potentially higher return for stocks with high target prices for which the random forest predicts that they will meet the target price. Positive predictions are with a share of only 4.1% even within the "Above 70%" target return low (0.4% overall). Thus, positive predictions for "Above 70%" target returns are very rare but appear to be associated with very high average and median returns.

This finding was manually verified for companies in this group (positive prediction and "Above 70%" target return), which were characterized by the highest returns (200% or higher). Of the 12 companies that were contained in this subset, these extremely high positive returns were observed during recoveries of the stock prices which were prior over 90% below their all-time highs (e.g., Vestas Wind Systems A/S in 2012, SunPower Corp. in 2012 and 2019, Enphase Energy in 2017, First Solar in 2012). Apart from that, some companies simply experienced a stock price surge to new all-time highs after 2020, which has been an exceptional year due to the COVID-19 pandemic (e.g., Enphase Energy, Sunrun Inc, Bloom Energy Corp., Sunnova Energy International). Thus, the results appear plausible, but this does not necessarily mean that they are repeatable.

Figure 14 allows a more detailed look at the positive return predictions of the random forest in terms of hits and misses.

It is unsurprising that when the model correctly predicts a target price being met (i.e., a hit), the returns achieved are higher than when a misclassification occurs (i.e., a miss). Moreover, it is intuitive that correctly predicting higher return groups leads on average to higher returns. Having said that, it is noteworthy that the magnitude of the actual returns in the "30% to 70% and the "Above 70%" target return group are very high—on average 195.2% and 296.5% respectively. However, the magnitude of the returns associated with misses appears even more interesting. The average returns are in general negative, but their magnitude decreases for higher target return groups. In other words, the higher the target return group, the smaller the consequences of misclassifications. This appears plausible given that higher average target returns reflect a higher confidence of analysts in a company's stock. Moreover, a higher target return also means that the range of positive returns a stock can accomplish while not meeting the target price is larger. The extreme case is the "Above 70%" target return group for which the average return of misclassifications is still positive with an average return of 18.6% and a median return of even 28%. The low or even positive average returns for misclassifications is one of the contributing factors for the overall high average returns of positive predictions for high return groups. Lastly, it is noteworthy that the share of hits for the positive predictions (=precision) is often around 70% and appears rather consistent throughout the return groups. This indicates that independently of the magnitude of the return group the positive predictions of the random forest model are largely correct.

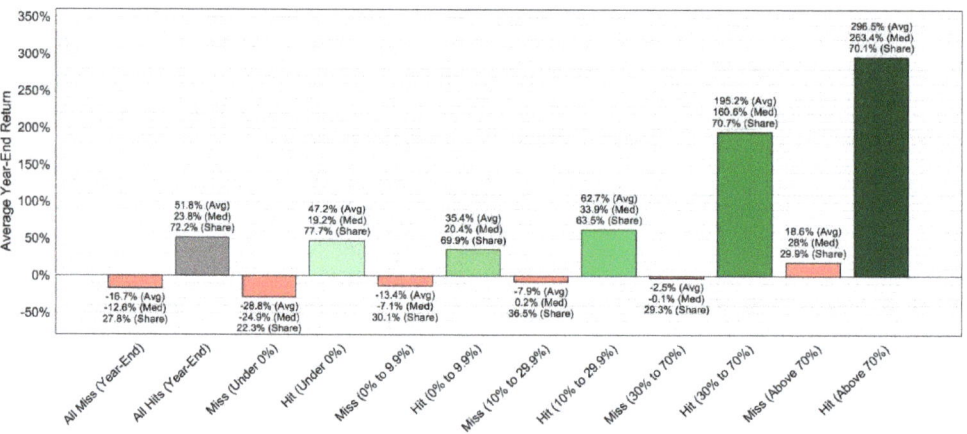

Figure 14. Average Year-End return for hits and misses of positive predictions of the random forest.

From an investors' point of view, it should be kept in mind that clean energy stocks represent a relatively new asset class that tends to be very volatile [64]. Moreover, the performance of clean energy companies is linked to the (crude) oil price where the oil price has a unidirectional short-term causality on the price of alternative energy companies [65] and the volatility of the oil price affects the profitability of these stocks [66]. Apart from that, previous research found that the volatility of the oil market (e.g., measured by OVX) impacts the volatility of clean energy companies [67] and vice versa [68] and that this spillover effect of volatility is stronger than the spillover effect of returns [69]. Moreover, during the COVID-19 pandemic, the volatility spillovers appear to have intensified [66]. Apart from the (crude) oil market, technology stocks, and investor sentiment towards renewable energy have been shown to affect the stocks of cleantech companies as well [69,70]. Finally, it is noteworthy that hedging against adverse movements of clean energy stocks can be possible using the volatility index VIX or crude oil [64] and that clean energy companies can be part of profitable hedging strategies themselves [68] as well as contributing to portfolio diversification, e.g., in times of extreme market events (e.g., a pandemic) [66].

8. Conclusions

In this paper, the accuracy and predictive power of mean target prices for the stocks of companies contained in the Standard and Poor's Global Clean Energy (USD) index were investigated. This study shows that the mean target prices for these stocks during the timeframe from 2009 to 2020 are on average 22.2% above the current stock price. This is in line with recent research works that cover time periods after 2000, whereas studies covering partially or entirely the 1990s show higher implied returns for target prices. The Year-End accuracy of 46.6% (41.5% excl. 2020) shows that only less than half of the mean target prices were met by year-end, whereas the Year-Highest accuracy of 68.1% (62.5% excl. 2020) highlights that close to two thirds of mean target prices are met at some point during the 12 months. These results are similar to those found in recent research, illustrating that the accuracy for global clean energy stocks is not considerably different than those of different cross-sections of stocks in different stock markets. In line with previous research, the average accuracy of target prices decreases as the implied target return increases, meaning that relatively higher target prices are less likely to be met.

Subsequently, a random forest and an SVM classification model were trained using both the Year-End and the Year-Highest target for the mean target prices and were compared to a random model. The random forest leads in both cases to the highest classification accuracy but both the SVM and random forest are highly significantly more accurate than the random model. Unsurprisingly, the best average accuracy of 73.24% for the Year-End target is lower than the best average accuracy of 81.15% for the Year-Highest target. This appears to reflect that meeting a target price at any point during the 12-month period is easier to predict than meeting the target price only at a single point, at the end of the 12-month period. The analysis of the variables shows that for all models the mean target price is the most relevant variable, whereas the number of target prices appears to be relevant as well. This is in line with previous research that suggested that the implied return of target prices and the number of analysts covering a stock are linked to the accuracy of target prices. A detailed analysis of the results in terms of these two variables for the Year-End target indicates for the random forest that this model is particularly accurate for the high target returns ("30% to 70%" and "Above 70%"), especially when the number of target prices is high (coverage of at least 15 analysts). For these subsets, only a few positive predictions are made but those are in the vast majority of cases correct. Thus, it is unsurprising that the actual mean and median returns for high target return groups are considerably higher than for all observations. These high actual returns are based on extremely high mean and median returns for actual hits and close to positive or even positive returns when positive predictions for high target returns are incorrect. Consequently, following the rare positive predictions of the random forest for the highest target return groups ("30% to 70%" and "Above 70%") may represent potentially attractive investment opportunities.

Some limitations apply to the results of this study. First, the results are obtained for a selection of clean energy stocks, which may not be generalizable for stocks in other sectors or even all clean energy stocks. Moreover, the results are in line with recent research but show clear differences to older research, highlighting that the implied returns and accuracies may differ in various time periods and may also be different in the future. For future research, a set of global stocks from a wider range of sectors can be investigated to confirm the findings. Moreover, additional variables linked to the company and the past stock performance can be included for the classification model, and investment strategies following the corresponding model predictions can be presented.

Author Contributions: Conceptualization, C.L. and A.L.; methodology, C.L.; software, C.L.; validation, C.L.; formal analysis, C.L.; investigation, C.L. and A.L.; data curation, C.L. and A.L.; writing—original draft preparation, C.L. and A.L.; writing—review and editing, C.L.; visualization, C.L. and A.L.; project administration, C.L. All authors have read and agreed to the published version of the manuscript.

Funding: This work was supported by the Kone Foundation, the Finnish Academy of Science and Letters, and the Finnish Strategic Research Council, grant number 313396/MFG40 Manufacturing 4.0.

Institutional Review Board Statement: Not applicable.

Informed Consent Statement: Not applicable.

Data Availability Statement: The data used in this study were obtained from the commercial Database "Datastream". The information on the location of companies' headquarters and current market capitalization are obtainable free of charge from the website finance.yahoo.com (accessed on 19 July 2021).

Conflicts of Interest: The authors declare no conflict of interest.

Appendix A

Table A1. Selected variables from Thompson Reuters Datastream.

Name	Variables	Type	Description
IBES Number of Price Targets	PTNE	Target Price	Indicates IBES Number of Price Targets.
IBES Price Target High Value	PTHI	Target Price	Indicates IBES Price Target high value.
IBES Price Target Low Value	PTLO	Target Price	Indicates IBES Price Target low value.
IBES Price Target Mean	PTMN	Target Price	Indicates IBES Price Target mean value.
IBES Price Target Standard Deviation	PTSED	Target Price	Indicates IBES Price Target Standard deviation.
Price Target Up since last monthly values	PTUP1M	Target Price	-
Price Target down since last monthly values	PTDN1M	Target Price	-
Price/Earnings Ratio (Adjusted)	PE	Other Financial	This is the price divided by the earnings rate per share at the required date.
MSCI World Price Index	MSWRLD$, PI	Other Financial	Price Index of the MSCI world stock market index.
ESG Score	TRESGS	ESG	Refinitiv's ESG Score is an overall company score based on the self-reported information in the environmental, social, and corporate governance pillars.

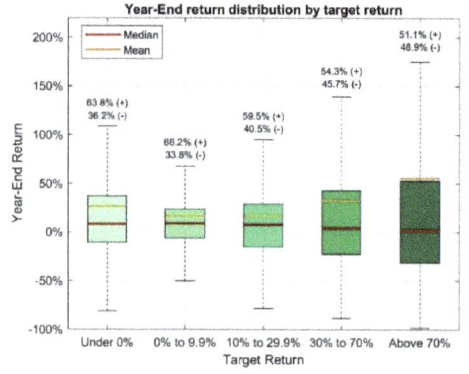
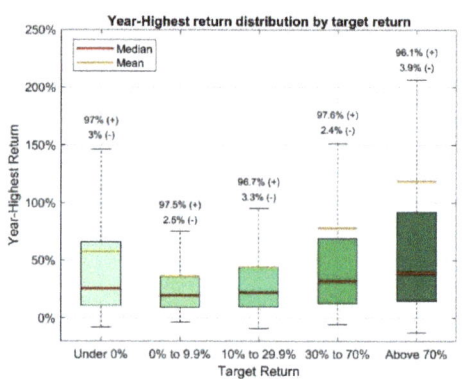

Figure A1. Year-End and Year-Highest return distribution by target return group.

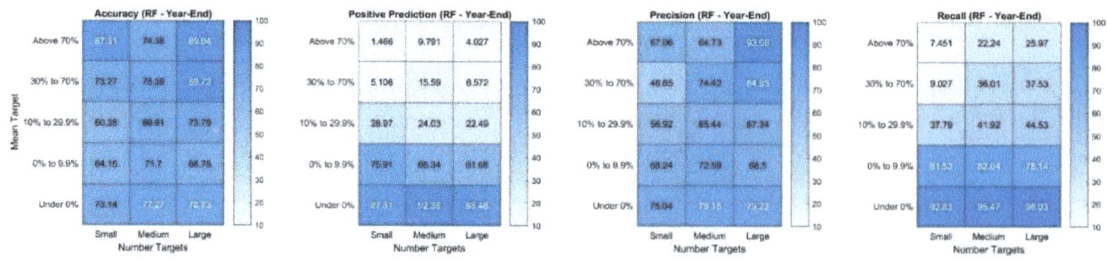

Figure A2. Accuracy, positive prediction ratio, precision, and recall for the random forest model with Year-End target.

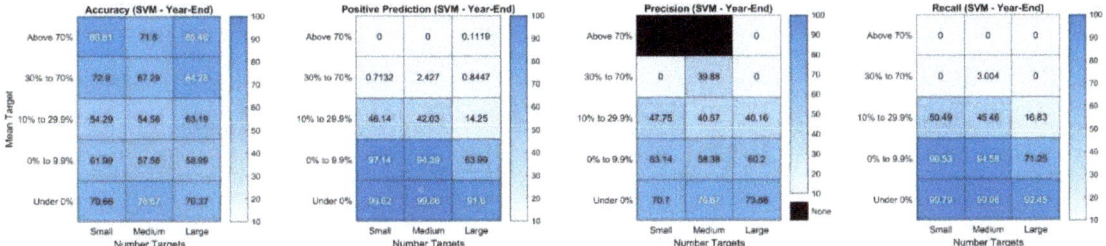

Figure A3. Accuracy, positive prediction ratio, precision, and recall for the SVM model with Year-End target.

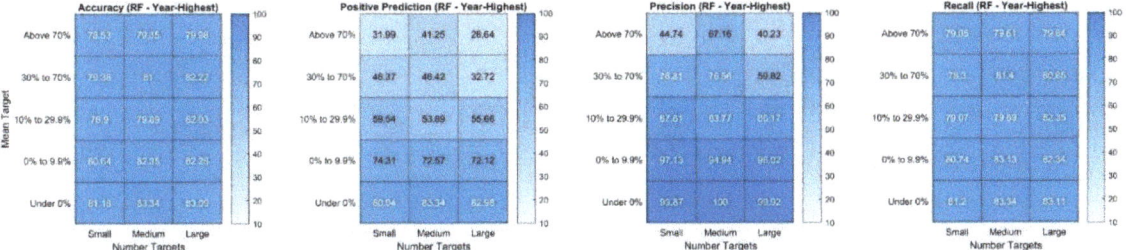

Figure A4. Accuracy, positive prediction ratio, precision, and recall for the random forest model with Year-Highest target.

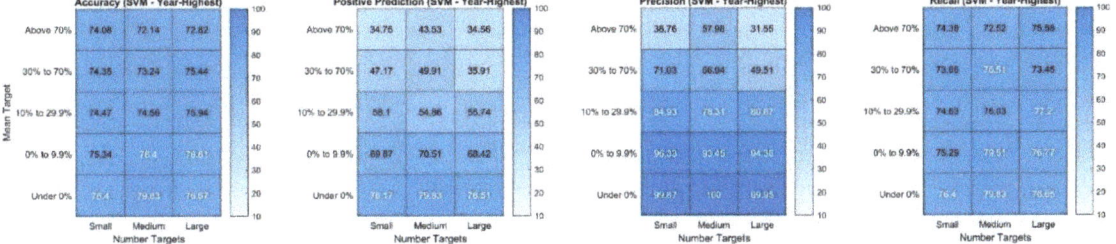

Figure A5. Accuracy, positive prediction ratio, precision, and recall for the SVM model with Year-Highest target.

References

1. Barber, B.; Lehavy, R.; McNichols, M.; Trueman, B. Can Investors Profit from the Prophets? Security Analyst Recommendations and Stock Return. *J. Financ.* **2001**, *56*, 531–563. [CrossRef]
2. Bonini, S.; Zanetti, L.; Bianchini, R.; Salvi, A. Target Price Accuracy in Equity Research. *J. Bus. Financ. Account.* **2010**, *37*, 1177–1217. [CrossRef]
3. Brav, A.; Lehavy, R. An Empirical Analysis of Analysts' Target Prices: Short-term Informativeness and Long-term Dynamics. *J. Financ.* **2003**, *58*, 1933–1967. [CrossRef]
4. Jegadeesh, N.; Kim, W. Value of analyst recommendations: International evidence. *J. Financ. Mark.* **2006**, *9*, 274–309. [CrossRef]
5. Asquith, P.; Mikhail, M.B.; Au, A.S. Information content of equity analyst reports. *J. Financ. Econ.* **2005**, *75*, 245–282. [CrossRef]
6. Bradshaw, M.T. The Use of Target Prices to Justify Sell-Side Analysts' Stock Recommendations. *Account. Horiz.* **2002**, *16*, 27–41. [CrossRef]
7. Bradshaw, M.T.; Brown, L.D.; Huang, K. Do sell-side analysts exhibit differential target price forecasting ability? *Rev. Account. Stud.* **2013**, *18*, 930–955. [CrossRef]
8. Barber, B.M.; Lehavy, R.; Trueman, B. Are all Brokerage Houses created equal? Testing for systematic Differences in the Performance of Brokerage House Stock Recommendations. *Univ. Calif. Davis Univ. Calif. Berkeley* **2000**, unpublished work.
9. Gleason, C.A.; Johnson, W.B.; Li, H. Valuation Model Use and the Price Target Performance of Sell-Side Equity Analysts. *Contemp. Account. Res.* **2012**, *30*, 80–115. [CrossRef]
10. Brown, L.D.; Mohd, E. The Predictive Value of Analyst Characteristics. *J. Account. Audit. Financ.* **2003**, *18*, 625–647. [CrossRef]
11. Kerl, A.G. Target Price Accuracy. *Bus. Res.* **2011**, *4*, 74–96. [CrossRef]
12. Jegadeesh, N.; Kim, J.; Krische, S.D.; Lee, C.M.C. Analyzing the Analysts: When Do Recommendations Add Value? *J. Financ.* **2004**, *59*, 1083–1124. [CrossRef]

13. Barber, B.M.; Lehavy, R.; McNichols, M.; Trueman, B. Buys, holds, and sells: The distribution of investment banks' stock ratings and the implications for the profitability of analysts' recommendations. *J. Account. Econ.* **2006**, *41*, 87–117. [CrossRef]
14. Womack, K.L. Do Brokerage Analysts' Recommendations Have Investment Value? *J. Financ.* **1996**, *51*, 137–167. [CrossRef]
15. Li, X.; Feng, H.; Yan, S.; Wang, H. Dispersion in analysts' target prices and stock returns. *N. Am. J. Econ. Financ.* **2021**, *56*, 101385. [CrossRef]
16. Merkley, K.; Michaely, R.; Pacelli, J. Does the Scope of the Sell-Side Analyst Industry Matter? An Examination of Bias, Accuracy, and Information Content of Analyst Reports. *J. Financ.* **2017**, *72*, 1285–1334. [CrossRef]
17. Loh, R.K.; Stulz, R.M. Is Sell-Side Research More Valuable in Bad Times? *J. Financ.* **2018**, *73*, 959–1013. [CrossRef]
18. United Nations. *Paris Agreement*; United Nations: Paris, UK, 2015; Available online: https://unfccc.int/sites/default/files/english_paris_agreement.pdf (accessed on 10 May 2021).
19. European Commission. The Road to Paris. 2015. Available online: https://ec.europa.eu/clima/policies/international/negotiations/progress_en (accessed on 10 May 2021).
20. United Nations. Status of the Paris Agreement. In *United Nations Treaty Collection*; United Nations: New York, NY, USA, 2015; Available online: https://treaties.un.org/Pages/ViewDetails.aspx?src=TREATY&mtdsg_no=XXVII-7-d&chapter=27&clang=_en (accessed on 10 May 2021).
21. S&P Global. S&P Global Clean Energy Index. 2021. Available online: https://www.spglobal.com/spdji/en/indices/esg/sp-global-clean-energy-index/#overview (accessed on 3 September 2021).
22. S&P Global. S&P Global Clean Energy Index (USD) Factsheet. 2021. Available online: https://www.spglobal.com/spdji/en/idsenhancedfactsheet/file.pdf?calcFrequency=M&force_download=true&hostIdentifier=48190c8c-42c4-46af-8d1a-0cd5db894797&indexId=5475737 (accessed on 3 September 2021).
23. Yahoo Finance. Selected Time Series. 2021. Available online: https://finance.yahoo.com (accessed on 21 July 2021).
24. Refinitiv. Refinitiv ESG Company Scores. 2021. Available online: https://www.refinitiv.com/en/sustainable-finance/esg-scores (accessed on 12 September 2021).
25. Bolón-Canedo, V.; Sánchez-Maroño, N.; Alonso-Betanzos, A. An ensemble of filters and classifiers for microarray data classification. *Pattern Recognit.* **2012**, *45*, 531–539. [CrossRef]
26. Hall, M. Correlation-based feature selection for discrete and numeric class machine learning. In Proceedings of the 17th International Conference on Machine Learning, Stanford, CA, USA, 29 June–2 July 2000; pp. 359–366.
27. Liu, H.; Setiono, R. A probabilistic approach to feature selection—A filter solution. In Proceedings of the 13th International Conference on Machine Learning, Bari, Italy, 3–6 July 1996.
28. Dash, M.; Liu, H. Feature Selection for Classification. *Intell. Data Anal.* **1997**, *1*, 131–156. [CrossRef]
29. Cai, J.; Luo, J.; Wang, S.; Yang, S. Feature selection in machine learning: A new perspective. *Neurocomputing* **2018**, *300*, 70–79. [CrossRef]
30. Ang, J.C.; Mirzal, A.; Haron, H.; Hamed, H.N.A. Supervised, Unsupervised, and Semi-Supervised Feature Selection: A Review on Gene Selection. *IEEE/ACM Trans. Comput. Biol. Bioinform.* **2015**, *13*, 971–989. [CrossRef]
31. Liu, H.; Yu, L. Toward integrating feature selection algorithms for classification and clustering. *IEEE Trans. Knowl. Data Eng.* **2005**, *17*, 491–502. [CrossRef]
32. Jain, A.K.; Zongker, D.E. Feature selection: Evaluation, application, and small sample performance. *IEEE Trans. Pattern Anal. Mach. Intell.* **1997**, *19*, 153–158. [CrossRef]
33. Guyon, I.; Elisseeff, A. An introduction to variable and feature selection. *J. Mach. Learn. Res.* **2003**, *3*, 1157–1182.
34. Sánchez-Maroño, N.; Alonso-Betanzos, A.; Tombilla-Sanoromán, M. Filter Methods for Feature Selection—A Comparative Study. In *Proceedings of the Intelligent Data Engineering and Automated Learning-IDEAL 2007*; Yin, H., Tino, P., Corchado, E., Byrne, W., Yao, X., Eds.; Springer: Berlin/Heidelberg, Germany, 2007; pp. 178–187.
35. Guyon, I.; Elisseeff, A. An Introduction to Feature Extraction. In *Feature Extraction: Foundations and Applications*; Guyon, I., Nikravesh, M., Gunn, S., Zadeh, L.A., Eds.; Springer: Berlin/Heidelberg, Germany, 2006; pp. 1–25.
36. Motoda, H.; Liu, H. Feature selection, extraction and construction. *Commun. IICM* **2002**, *5*, 67–72.
37. Dash, M.; Liu, H. Consistency-based search in feature selection. *Artif. Intell.* **2003**, *151*, 155–176. [CrossRef]
38. Das, S. Filters, wrappers and a boosting-based hybrid for feature selection. In Proceedings of the 17th International Conference on Machine Learning, Williamstown, MA, USA, 28 June–1 July 2001; pp. 74–81.
39. Li, J.; Cheng, K.; Wang, S.; Morstatter, F.; Trevino, R.P.; Tang, J.; Liu, H. Feature Selection. *ACM Comput. Surv.* **2018**, *50*, 1–45. [CrossRef]
40. Saeys, Y.; Inza, I.; Larrañaga, P. A review of feature selection techniques in bioinformatics. *Bioinformatics* **2007**, *23*, 2507–2517. [CrossRef] [PubMed]
41. Blum, A.L.; Langley, P. Selection of relevant features and examples in machine learning. *Artif. Intell.* **1997**, *97*, 245–271. [CrossRef]
42. Duch, W. Filter Methods. In *Feature Extraction: Foundations and Applications*; Guyon, I., Nikravesh, M., Gunn, S., Zadeh, L.A., Eds.; Springer: Berlin/Heidelberg, Germany, 2006; pp. 89–117.
43. Saeys, Y.; Abeel, T.; Van de Peer, Y. Robust Feature Selection Using Ensemble Feature Selection Techniques. In *Joint European Conference on Machine Learning and Knowledge Discovery in Databases*; Springer: Berlin/Heidelberg, Germany, 2008; pp. 313–325.

44. Kohavi, R.; Sommerfield, D. Feature subset selection using the wrapper method: Overfitting and dynamic search space topology. In Proceedings of the First International Conference on Knowledge Discovery and Data Mining, Montréal, QC, Canada, 20–21 August 1995.
45. Kohavi, R.; John, G.H. Wrappers for feature subset selection. *Artif. Intell.* **1997**, *97*, 273–324. [CrossRef]
46. Caruana, R.; Freitag, D. Greedy Attribute Selection. *Mach. Learn. Proc.* **1994**, *48*, 28–36. [CrossRef]
47. Huang, S.H. Supervised feature selection: A tutorial. *Artif. Intell. Res.* **2015**, *4*, 22. [CrossRef]
48. Lal, T.N.; Chapelle, O.; Weston, J.; Elisseeff, A. Embedded Methods. In *Feature Extraction: Foundations and Applications*; Guyon, I., Nikravesh, M., Gunn, S., Zadeh, L.A., Eds.; Springer: Berlin/Heidelberg, Germany, 2006; pp. 137–165.
49. Breiman, L. Random Forests. *Mach. Learn.* **2001**, *45*, 5–32. [CrossRef]
50. Cutler, A.; Cutler, D.; Stevens, J. Random Forests. *Mach. Learn.* **2011**, *45*, 157–176.
51. Breiman, L.; Friedman, J.; Stone, C.J.; Olshen, R.A. *Classification and Regression Trees*; Wadsworth Inc.: Belmont, CA, USA, 1984.
52. Maimon, O.; Rokach, L. Decision trees. In *Data Mining and Knowledge Discovery Handbook*; Springer: Boston, MA, USA, 2005; pp. 165–192.
53. Loh, W.-Y. Classification and regression trees. *Wiley Interdiscip. Rev. Data Min. Knowl. Discov.* **2011**, *1*, 14–23. [CrossRef]
54. Bishop, C.M. *Pattern Recognition and Machine Learning*; Springer: New York, NY, USA, 2006.
55. Gelfand, S.; Ravishankar, C.; Delp, E. An iterative growing and pruning algorithm for classification tree design. *IEEE Trans. Pattern Anal. Mach. Intell.* **1991**, *13*, 163–174. [CrossRef]
56. Hastie, T.; Tibshirani, R.; Friedman, J. *The Elements of Statistical Learning: Data Mining, Inference, and Prediction*; Springer: New York, NY, USA, 2009.
57. Loh, W.-Y. Regression trees with unbiased variable selection and interaction detection. *Stat. Sin.* **2002**, *12*, 361–386.
58. Boser, B.E.; Guyon, I.M.; Vapnik, V.N. A training algorithm for optimal margin classifiers. In Proceedings of the Fifth Annual Workshop on Computational Learning Theory-COLT'92, Pittsburgh, PA, USA, 27–29 July 1992; pp. 144–152. [CrossRef]
59. Cortes, C.; Vapnik, V. Support-Vector Networks. *Mach. Learn.* **1995**, *20*, 273–297. [CrossRef]
60. Guyon, I.; Weston, J.; Barnhill, S.; Vapnik, V. Gene Selection for Cancer Classification using Support Vector Machines. *Mach. Learn.* **2002**, *46*, 389–422. [CrossRef]
61. Vapnik, V.N. Methods of Pattern Recognition. In *The Nature of Statistical Learning Theory*; Springer: New York, NY, USA, 2000; pp. 123–180.
62. Gentile, C. Fast Feature Selection from Microarray Expression Data via Multiplicative Large Margin Algorithms. In *Advances in Neural Information Processing Systems*; 2004; Available online: https://proceedings.neurips.cc/paper/2003/file/ba3e9b6a519cfddc560b5d53210df1bd-Paper.pdf (accessed on 13 April 2021).
63. Rakotomamonjy, A. Variable selection using SVM based criteria. *J. Mach. Learn. Res.* **2003**, *3*, 1357–1370.
64. Ahmad, W.; Sadorsky, P.; Sharma, A. Optimal hedge ratios for clean energy equities. *Econ. Model.* **2018**, *72*, 278–295. [CrossRef]
65. Bondia, R.; Ghosh, S.; Kanjilal, K. International crude oil prices and the stock prices of clean energy and technology companies: Evidence from non-linear cointegration tests with unknown structural breaks. *Energy* **2016**, *101*, 558–565. [CrossRef]
66. Foglia, M.; Angelini, E. Volatility Connectedness between Clean Energy Firms and Crude Oil in the COVID-19 Era. *Sustainability* **2020**, *12*, 9863. [CrossRef]
67. Dutta, A. Oil price uncertainty and clean energy stock returns: New evidence from crude oil volatility index. *J. Clean. Prod.* **2017**, *164*, 1157–1166. [CrossRef]
68. Ahmad, W. On the dynamic dependence and investment performance of crude oil and clean energy stocks. *Res. Int. Bus. Financ.* **2017**, *42*, 376–389. [CrossRef]
69. Song, Y.; Ji, Q.; Du, Y.-J.; Geng, J.-B. The dynamic dependence of fossil energy, investor sentiment and renewable energy stock markets. *Energy Econ.* **2019**, *84*, 104564. [CrossRef]
70. Henriques, I.; Sadorsky, P. Oil prices and the stock prices of alternative energy companies. *Energy Econ.* **2008**, *30*, 998–1010. [CrossRef]

Article

Steering Renewable Energy Investments in Favor of Energy System Reliability: A Call for a Hybrid Model

School of Business and Management, LUT University, FI-53851 Lappeenranta, Finland; alena.lohrmann@lut.fi
* Correspondence: mariia.kozlova@lut.fi

Abstract: The global increase in electricity supply volatility due to the growing share of intermittent renewable energy sources together with recent extreme weather events draws attention to energy system reliability issues and the role of renewable energy sources within these systems. Renewable energy deployment strategies have already become a key element in debates on future global energy systems. At the same time, more extensive use of renewable energy sources implies a higher dependence on intermittent power, which puts the reliability of the electricity system at risk. Policymakers are introducing measures to increase the reliability of energy systems. Paradoxically, support for renewable energy and analyses of energy system reliability have been dealt with by two different and rarely overlapping research approaches. As a result, renewable energy promotion has often been designed without accounting for system reliability. To our knowledge, a model that captures those investment incentives and allows for tuning such financial support does not exist. This paper introduces a hybrid model that can potentially steer renewable energy investments in favor of energy system reliability. We demonstrate the idea of reliability-based support for renewable energy sources in action using a stylized case. Depending on the complementarity of different renewable energy power outputs available in the system, such reliability-based support can substantially reduce the necessity for greater backup capacity, can cut the overall costs of the energy system, and can reduce its environmental footprint.

Keywords: renewable energy support; energy modeling; sustainability; energy system design; generation profile; environmental footprint

1. Introduction

Striving to reduce their carbon footprints, governments worldwide have been introducing renewable energy policies to decarbonize power sectors. Even the COVID-19 pandemic has not slowed down the growth in the global renewable power capacity, reaching a record share of almost 30% of the global energy mix in 2020 [1]. However, such development poses challenges for energy systems. Electricity generation from many types of renewable energy sources is intermittent. However, the overall electricity supply should match the demand at every moment to avoid costly blackouts. Thus, the extensive deployment of renewable energy may threaten the reliability of energy systems. In response, various flexibility measures have been developed. They include storage technologies, such as batteries and hydrogen solutions (the latter possesses a potential for electricity transmission [2,3] and sector coupling with transportation [4]); demand-side management; smart grids; and regulatory measures to ensure reliability [5], so-called capacity mechanisms [6,7].

Recent extreme weather events have drawn the attention of policymakers and researchers towards the reliability of the power systems, with implications for widespread renewable energy adoption as well. Extreme weather events and weather variations affect both the energy demand and the reliability of energy systems. Numerous global cases of extreme weather events, such as heatwaves or severe winter storms, forced interruptions in the power generation, and even blackouts have been reported [8,9]. Perera et al. [10] estimated that future extreme weather events induced by climate change might lead to a drop in power supply reliability by up to 16%. Uncertainty in the power supply associated with weather variations may slow down the implementation of intermittent renewable energy technologies and may increase the dependence on fossil-based power generation. However, Perera et al. [10] demonstrated that further adoption of renewable energies is possible without compromising the resilience of energy supply systems if potential risks are appropriately quantified. In this regard, financial mechanisms, which promote the implementation of renewable energy while ensuring the energy system reliability, should be introduced. The idea of enabling market signals by channeling the system reliability needs in subsidies for renewable energy, advocated in the paper, was highlighted in previous studies as well [11].

Intermittent renewable energy is often mentioned as one of the causes of problems with energy system reliability in Europe [12]. Norway has the highest cost for maintaining electricity supply security in Europe partly because of their high share of small-scale intermittent hydrogeneration in the system [13]. In the academic literature, renewable energy sources are often treated as a threat to energy system reliability as well [14–16]. Such research normally inquires about what types of capacity mechanisms can better tackle the problem. For example, Bhafgwat et al. [15,16] ran simulations to determine what type of capacity mechanism would better protect against a high share of renewable energy sources. Lara-Arango et al. [14] came to the conclusion that no capacity mechanism can sufficiently tackle the issue because of the uncertainty in the electricity supply from renewable energy sources.

An emerging research direction reconsiders the adverse role of renewable energy sources for energy system reliability. Mastropietro et al. [17] demonstrated that some countries choose to include renewable energy sources into their capacity mechanisms because they do contribute to system reliability. In the same vein, Söder et al. [18] made an argument for including renewable energy power plants into capacity mechanisms. Peter and Wagner [19] showed that wind power generation in Europe is characterized by spatial and temporal heterogeneity. Thus, if wind farms are built in places better for system reliability instead of the most profitable locations, excessive amounts of backup capacity could be avoided. At the same time, existing energy models are often wired to add a fixed amount of backup capacity for every new unit of renewable energy [20], which makes it impossible to capture the complementarity effects of renewable energy sources and their subsequent benefits.

However, obtaining a model that accounts for those complementarities of renewable energy sources is insufficient. The value of renewable energy sources for system reliability needs to be translated into investment incentives. Such incentives would steer investments towards creating an optimal mix of technologies for system reliability and towards avoiding considerable costs for unnecessary backup capacity provisions. Thus, we need a different type of renewable energy support mechanism that can take system reliability into account. Such support can only be designed with the help of a model that can do both: capture the complementarity of renewable energy sources and simulate investors' behavior.

This paper aims to design a conceptual model that allows for bridging these two detached phenomena: renewable energy support and energy system reliability. With such a model, we can see whether, where, and under which conditions the support for renewable energy sources is better to be designed based on the system reliability needs. In future studies, when the model introduced here is expanded, we will be able to observe whether the capacity mechanisms steer the mix of renewable energy technologies well after their support is withdrawn, whether any modifications are required, and what the effects of the development of storage solutions are. Overall, such a model would provide in-depth insight for modern energy policymaking.

The remainder of the paper is structured as follows. First, we provide a short overview of existing energy modeling approaches for: (i) renewable energy support design and (ii) energy system reliability studies. Furthermore, we present the conceptual idea and design of the model, illustrate it in action with a stylized case, and describe the modifications required for the model to be applied to a real-world analysis. We conclude with an in-depth discussion of the model's applicability and possible policy implications.

2. Background
2.1. Modeling for Renewable Energy Support

Renewable energy support is meant to foster investments in renewable energy. In order to understand what investment incentives a policy creates, one needs to take the investor's perspective and to analyze the investment profitability and how the policy affects it. Traditionally, such an investment analysis is conducted with a cost–benefit approach and in particular real options framework [21]. The real options framework, apart from plain profitability, recognizes uncertainty connected to the project implementation and possible flexibilities that allow the benefits to be captured or the shortfalls of unfolding uncertainties to be avoided [22]. Therefore, the real options framework becomes especially useful in understanding the effects of policies since a policy aims to reduce uncertainty for investors that otherwise hinders technology diffusion.

A considerable share of renewable energy valuation studies specifically focused on the analysis of policy effects [23]. The majority of such studies recognize uncertainty coming from volatile electricity market prices, and the main type of flexibility is to postpone investment. Such a study design allows for addressing the question of whether one or another policy sufficiently shields investors from uncertainty to incentivize investments sooner rather than later. Especially beneficial for policymaking are comparative studies, where the performance of different types of support instruments is analyzed [24,25]. Methodologically, real options research encompasses both analytical and numerical methods, including standard methods such as dynamic programming, Monte Carlo simulation, and various trees and lattices [23,26]. However, the majority of studies take an individual investor's perspective.

System-level energy models rarely come down to the policy details [27]. One prominent exception is the Green-X model [28], which intentionally recognizes different types of support for renewable energy and analyzes their performance and costs on the system level. However, GREEN-X lacks modeling of realistic investment behavior. The decisions to invest are based on a plain cost–benefit analysis and investors, for example, are not given a right to postpone their investments.

Meanwhile, in the real world, professional investors and utilities behave in accordance with the real options logic [29], even if they do not use real options models for decision-making [30]. To the best of our knowledge, the only model, so far, that integrates real options logic into the energy system level is the one by Rios et al. [31]. However, it does not focus on renewable energy sources or their support policies. Instead, the aim of this model is to capture the fluctuations in investments in new power generation after electricity market liberalization. The cyclic behavior of these new capacity additions makes it possible to simulate the flexibility in postponing an investment in the model. Thus, this finer detail of investment behavior—flexibility under uncertainty—is a must-have in system-level energy models if the aim is to estimate policy effects on investments.

2.2. Modeling for System Reliability

Often in the literature, the terms *security* of electricity supply, power system *reliability*, and power system adequacy are used interchangeably. Heylen et al. [32], in their comprehensive review of reliability indicators, provided a classification where system reliability is composed of system adequacy and system security. System adequacy refers to the ability of the supply to meet the demand in regular circumstances. System security refers to the ability of the system to accommodate disturbances. Many different indicators exist in both categories and, often, they are related to each other to different extents.

Peter and Wagner [19] utilize a commonly used approach with respect to the measure of system reliability in their hybrid model. The reliability measure *expected energy unserved* (EEU) characterizes the overall system reliability. It is, essentially, the expected load level that cannot be served over a time span and is defined based on *loss of load probability* (LOLP), a common system adequacy indicator. The contribution of individual technologies to the system reliability or their *capacity value* can be defined via *equivalent firm capacity* (EFC), where the term 'firm' refers to only the amount of capacity that actually contributes to electricity generation. Thus, the capacity of an individual technology is practically a share of its overall installed capacity that contributes to the decrease in the loss of load probability and, thus, improves system reliability.

System reliability is a system-level issue and, thus, should be studied by system-level models. The reliability of electricity supply depends on all power plants, storage solutions, and demand flexibility available in the system, and all of these actors should be taken into account. Typically, long-term energy system optimization models have been used for this matter. In such models, the evolution of the power-generation technology mix can be traced, and its reliability can be assessed, usually on a year-by-year basis and sometimes while taking into account seasonal, weekly, or day/night variations in the supply and demand. However, with the increasing share of renewable energy sources, in which the power output varies from hour to hour and from day to day, a necessity for integrating more fine resolutions into those models arose [20]. Operational power system models match the supply and demand on an hourly basis and are commonly utilized by system operators to balance the system. Such models, however, do not have room for new investments and long-term technology mix evolution [33]. Thus, policymakers call for hybrid models that are able to combine short-term power variations and long-term technology development [34].

A handful of studies attempted to integrate the finer details of operational power system models into long-term energy system models [19,35]. Peter and Wagner [19] specifically focused their modeling efforts on accounting for the complementarity of renewable energy. The operational detail of the model allows for capturing the temporal and spatial heterogeneity of renewable energy power generation. When available in the region, the anti-correlation of wind speeds is translated into a reliability value for the energy system. The more nonsynchronous the power-generation profiles of wind farms, the larger their overall contribution to the energy system adequacy and the less backup capacity needed to support such a system. The authors estimate that such a wise investment approach into renewable energy would allow for avoiding 66 GW of unnecessary backup capacities at an annual cost of 3.8 billion euros by 2050 in Europe [19].

Methodologically wise, energy system models and operational power system models are often simulation-based and often embody analytical and hybrid approaches [20,36]. Critical design decisions in these models include the scope and resolution of temporal, technical, and spatial representation [20].

2.3. Summary of Models

A summary of the approaches for energy modeling is presented in Table 1. For the purposes of this research, we distinguish three conceptual levels for all energy models. The first one looks into the operational routines of power systems dealing with balancing supply and demand on an hourly (or even finer) basis. The second one reviews the development of long-term energy systems, mostly focusing on the technology mix and its implications for system reliability, environment, economics, and so forth. Both types of model take the system perspective. The third type is real options models, which take the investor's perspective to understand the effects of policies.

Table 1. Overview of different model types in energy studies and their usual design choices.

Conceptual Level	(i) Operational Power System Models	(ii) Long-Term Energy System Models	(iii) Investment Behavior, Real Options
Perspective	System perspective		Investor's perspective
Focus	Unit commitment and economic dispatch	Evolution of installed generation capacity	Investment profitability and policy effects
Time horizon	1 day–1 year	Decades	Investment lifetime
Time resolution	5 minutes–1 hour	Year	Year
Technical resolution	Unit by unit	Technology type	Single investment
Geographic scope	Power system	Countries	
Methods	Mixed-integer linear programming	Bottom-up (technology-rich) • Partial equilibrium • Optimization • Simulation • Multi-agent modeling Top-down (macroeconomic) • Input–output • Econometric • Computable general equilibrium • System dynamics	• Simulation • Differential equations • Trees and lattices • Game theory • Fuzzy logic methods
References to reviews of models	[20,33]	[20,27,33]	[23,27]
Key examples of hybrid models	x	[19]	x
		[31]	

We highlight the importance of hybrid models that combine several conceptual levels to reveal new insights and to capture new phenomena. Peter and Wagner [19] were able to note and quantify the benefits of an anti-correlation of power generation from renewable energy by integrating the fine resolution of operational power system models into a long-term energy system model. In contrast, Rios et al. [31] were able to comprehensively capture realistic investment behavior on an energy system level by embedding the real options logic into a long-term energy system model. However, for the purpose of designing a support instrument for renewable energy sources to steer their deployment in favor of system reliability, we need a model that combines all three levels: operational detail, system-level evolution and realistic investment behavior—a hybrid three-tier model.

2.4. Solutions for System Reliability

Before discussing whether and how renewable energy sources can alleviate system reliability issues, it is imperative to consider current measures and those deemed effective in the future. In this section, we draw our attention to storage, sector coupling, and regulatory solutions to support energy system reliability.

Storage solutions introduce flexibility to energy systems and allow for higher shares of renewable energy and, thus, contribute to both system reliability and decarbonization [37,38]. Pumped storage hydro (PSH) is currently dominating the global energy storage market (with a share of about 94% of the installed energy storage capacity and over 99% of the energy stored [39]), which is a commercially mature technology with 160 GW of installed capacity and 9000 GWh in energy storage capacity worldwide [37]. Other storage solutions with considerable use worldwide include thermal storage (mainly molten salt thermal storage), electro-chemical storage (batteries and electro-chemical capacitors), and mechanical storage technologies (compressed air storage and flywheel). The production of electro–chemical storage (batteries) is one of the most rapidly growing industries nowadays [38], although battery capacities accounted for only 17 GW globally in 2020 (5 GW of storage capacity was added only in 2020) [40]. Currently, the most commercially available battery storage technologies include lithium–ion iron phosphate (LFP) batteries, lithium–ion nickel manganese cobalt (NMC) batteries, lead–acid batteries, and vanadium redox flow batteries (RFBs) [41], with lithium–ion batteries being most widely used (accounting for 93% of the global battery storage capacity in 2020 [40]). Benefitting from the economic scale of lithium–ion battery production for transport applications, the cost of stationary lithium–ion batteries is expected to decrease by 54–61% by 2030 to about 145–480 USD/kWh depending on the battery chemistry, while the number of full cycles may grow by 90%, according to IRENA projections [38].

Sector coupling broadly refers to integrating different energy sectors in order to achieve more flexibility in the energy system and allows for higher shares of intermittent renewable energy sources [42]. The classical example often studied in the academic literature is deeming wide-spread electric vehicle usage as a storage capacity for solar power [43]. However, the sector coupling concept is broader and can include even information systems for better balancing and control of cross-sectoral energy flows [44].

While the technological progress offers promising prospects in the future, its current state is not sufficient to fully resolve energy system reliability issues. Therefore, governments around the world have been introducing regulatory measures to support the security of electricity supply [5]. Five countries in the world maintain strategic reserve (selected power plants that are kept away from the market and switched on in scarcity conditions), eight countries implemented capacity payments (similar to strategic reserves but power plants operate on the regular market as well), and sixteen jurisdictions operate some kind of capacity markets (arranged in parallel with electricity market and open to the majority or all of market participants) [7]. Capacity mechanisms are only 'useful' for a power capacity that can actually contribute to electricity generation. Approaches to calculating this contribution vary, and some of them are covered in Section 2.2.

With or without a capacity mechanism, we argue that a different approach to support for renewable energy sources can substantially alleviate the burden of intermittent electricity generation on energy system reliability.

3. Hybrid Three-Tier Model

In this section, we propose a hybrid three-tier model to tackle the issue of steering renewable energy in favor of energy system reliability. First, we present the conceptual design of such a model. Then, we demonstrate the model's power with an abstract and highly stylized example. Finally, we discuss what needs to be accounted for when the model is transformed from a concept to application in a real case.

3.1. Conceptual Design

The proposed hybrid three-tier model combines all three types of energy models reviewed earlier. Its concept is depicted in Figure 1. Block A is composed of an operational power system model. This block contains hourly demand load curves and power generation profiles of different technologies; projects hourly electricity prices; and comprises weather and other uncertainties with relevant diurnal, weekly, and seasonal variations in demand and supply. With hourly projections, this block is responsible for computing system reliability measures at every hour. Block A feeds its information to Block B, where investment incentives are created and investment decisions are made. Here, the support instrument for renewable energy sources is based on system reliability and can be designed and tested. If the amount of remuneration from renewable energy sources is calculated based on their contribution to system reliability, it affects the profitability of the renewable energy technology with different power generation profiles differently. Thus, the investment incentives are created and translated based on the investors' behavior. The resultant investment decisions affect the composition of the system's technology mix, which is captured using a long-term energy system model component, Block C. The technology mix, in turn, affects the hourly power generation modeled in Block A. Thus, the cycle repeats. The environmental footprint of the system is calculated within Block A based on the simulated data of the system operations.

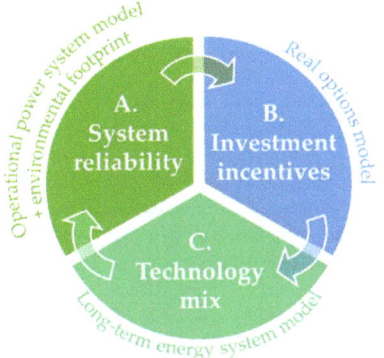

Figure 1. Concept of the hybrid three-tier model.

The model should be run for two main scenarios:

1. Conventional/existing renewable energy support (as a reference scenario);
2. Renewable energy support via the reliability-based instrument.

The difference in technology mix evolution for these two scenarios showcase the relevance of renewable energy support via a reliability-based instrument for a particular region. If a region possesses spatial and temporal complementarity of its renewable energy sources, then new investments in renewable energy sources can be optimized to favor system reliability. This, in turn, results in a reduced overall backup capacity or storage solutions needed. Overall, such a system would cover its peak demand with a smaller installed capacity and, thus, less incurred costs, compared with scenario #2, where renewable energy sources are supported in a conventional way.

Continuing the list of scenarios, the model can analyze the effects of different policy mix arrangements and technological solutions available, though not considered in this paper:

3. Only capacity market with no support for renewable energy sources at all;
4. Capacity markets with no support for renewable energy sources, and penalties for new investments that do not contribute to system reliability;
5. Infrastructure expansion (i.e., interconnectors to harvest complementarity of renewable energy sources) effects for scenarios #1–4; and
6. Storage and demand-response development effects for scenarios #1–4.

3.2. A Stylized Example

3.2.1. Assumptions

A stylized example is used to demonstrate the model's functioning on a high level of abstraction in an intuitively understandable way. We chose a region with high potentials for solar energy resources; therefore, the numbers for technology-specific estimates, such as the capacity factor and levelized cost of electricity, are taken based on California's data for 2018 [45], and as the lifetime of flexible generation, we use the estimated lifetime of gas-fired power plants [46] (Table 2).

Table 2. Technology-specific assumptions.

Technology Type	Capacity Factor	Total LCOE, USD/MWh	Lifetime, Years
Flexible generation (combined cycle)	71%	USD 114	34
Solar PV (standalone)	26%	USD 49	25
Wind (onshore)	40%	USD 54	25

In the system, 20 GW-based load facilities and 5 GW flexible generation are assumed to exist. The intraday load profile is a classic textbook example with two consumption peaks: morning and evening. It is assumed to vary between 20 and 45 GW (Figure 2a). Such demand levels correspond to a region with electricity consumption similar to California [47]. The one-day profile is assumed to be representative of the whole year. The day-ahead electricity market prices are set proportional to the demand (Figure 2a). The missing supply is deemed to be covered by renewable energy sources, solar and wind power, and extra flexible generation, if needed, is auctioned by the regulator. The solar and wind power generation profiles are sketched to resemble the most common situation, with the sun peaking during the day and winds prevailing at nighttime (Figure 2b). The power profiles are presented for 1 MWh generation per day overall for each technology.

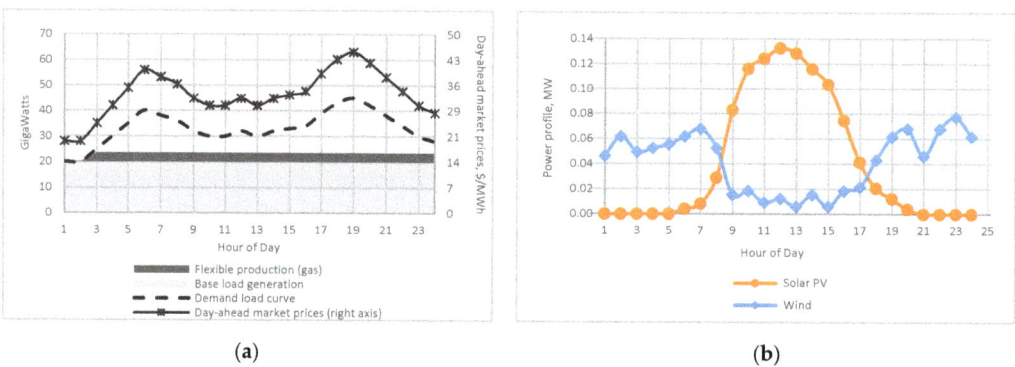

Figure 2. Initial load profile, available power, and hourly day-ahead market prices (**a**) and assumed solar and wind power profiles (**b**).

An investment decision is based on profitability by comparing the cost (LCOE) per megawatt hour and revenue per megawatt hour comparison. If the revenue exceeds the cost, the decision to invest is made. The model is entirely deterministic; therefore, there is no uncertainty and, hence, value to postpone investment. That is why profitability is defined by the deterministic net present value (benefits minus costs) rather than real options. However, industrial players behave in accordance with the real options theory [30]; therefore, it is imperative to integrate the real options framework when uncertainty is included into the model, as in the hybrid model discussed above [31]. The LCOE assumptions are presented in Table 2. The revenue is composed of the market sales (with prices depicted in Figure 2b) and a premium.

A premium is modeled in two different scenarios. The YELLOW scenario is modeled with a classic fixed premium of 20 USD/MWh on top of electricity prices. The premium remains constant and does not depend on the hour of the day or any other factors. In the GREEN scenario, we present an experimental reliability-based premium. At the core of many reliability indicators is a probability of lost load (electricity supply not meeting demand) [32]. Since our conceptual model is entirely deterministic, no probabilities. Thus, our lost load LL is calculated simply as the demand D minus the available supply S for each hour of the day h.

$$LL_h = D_h - S_h. \qquad (1)$$

Then, we set the ceiling of the premium P_{max} at 40 USD/MWh. We compute the hourly premium as a fraction of the maximum premium corresponding to the hourly lost load compared with the maximum lost load of the day.

$$P_h = P_{max} * \frac{LL_h}{LL_{max}}. \qquad (2)$$

Thus, when the need for power at a particular hour is greater, the reliability premium is higher. The hourly profile of the reliability premium, in turn, defines the profitability of technologies with different generation profiles. The need for reliability is translated into an investment incentive.

This is a simplified calculation of the reliability-based premium for the current stylized case with a fully deterministic model. In reality, many variable and stochastic factors should be taken into account, including weather, electricity demand, operating profiles of power plants, etc. With those factors taken into account, the premium should be based not on a deterministic indicator but on one of the proper indicators for a 'useful' capacity, for example, based on the loss of load probability, as discussed in Section 2.2. A detailed analysis of existing approaches to calculating the contribution of renewable energy sources to system reliability is presented in [17].

For the GREEN scenario, the auction is run in two phases. First, the reliability premium is calculated based on the current reliability situation (Figure 2a), and the most profitable technology type is selected. Then, the reliability indicator LL_h is recalculated, taking into account the generation profile of the selected technology. The reliability premium P_h is recalculated as well, taking into account the updated reliability indicator. The updated premium then may change the profitability of different technologies.

3.2.2. Results

Power System

The resultant economics per unit of generation for wind and solar power are presented in Table 3. LCOE (column 2) corresponds to the assumptions presented in Table 2. Market revenue (column 3) is calculated as the technology generation profile (Figure 2b) multiplied by the market price (Figure 2a). Wind power makes 2 USD/MWh more revenue from the market during the day, 34 USD/MWh, than solar power. However, it offsets the difference in their LCOE: 5 USD/MWh. Therefore, together with the fixed equal feed-in premium in the YELLOW scenario (column 4), solar power becomes the more profitable technology while wind power does not generate profit (column 7). Therefore, in the YELLOW scenario, only solar technology is auctioned.

Table 3. Unit economics of solar and wind in the model based on the one-day profile, USD/MWh.

Technology	LCOE	Market Revenue	Feed-In Premium (FP)	Reliability Premium (RP) Revenue		Profitability		
				Phase I	Phase II	FP	RP I	RP II
			YELLOW	GREEN		YELLOW	GREEN	
1	2	3	4	5	6	7	8	9
Solar	49	32	20	27	3	3	11	−13
Wind	54	34	20	27	24	−0	6	4

For the first round of the auction, in the GREEN scenario, the revenue from the reliability premium for solar and wind (Table 3, column 5) is the same, resulting from the average hourly reliability premium multiplied by the hourly generation. Due to the difference in costs, though, solar power is still more profitable than wind power (column 8). Thus, solar power is selected in the first phase. The reliability premium profile is recalculated after the first phase to reflect the added solar generation in the system. Now, the premium is zero during solar power peak and higher during mornings and evenings. The premium revenue is thus substantially lower for solar power and comparatively better for wind power (column 6). Overall, however, the need for power is reduced; thus, the possible revenue from the reliability premium is lower than in the first round. With this change in premium revenue, wind power becomes more profitable than solar power (column 9). Thus, wind technology is auctioned in the second phase.

The resultant generation compositions are presented in Figure 3. In the YELLOW scenario (left), the investment incentive generated by the feed-in premium favors solar power. In the absence of other market signals or regulator's intervention, only solar power is auctioned and built. Such a generation fleet leads to the peak generation exceeding demand during the day and insufficient generation during mornings and evenings, which is compensated for by the extra combined cycle generation.

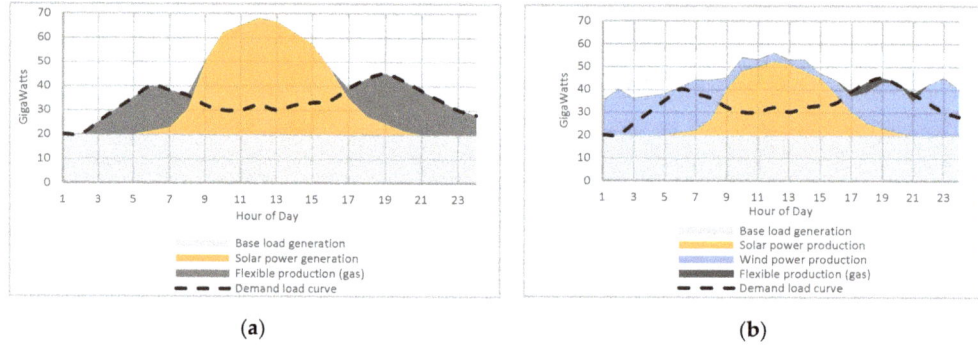

Figure 3. Resultant power generation composition under the feed-in premium in the YELLOW scenario (**a**) and under the reliability premium in the GREEN scenario (**b**).

In the GREEN scenario (Figure 3b), due to changing reliability premium, solar power is produced during the first phase and wind power is produced during the second. Together, the two resources (assumed to be complementary in this stylized case) are sufficient to meet the demand almost entirely. The existing 5 GW of flexible generation is enough to cover minor discrepancies during the evening. Such a scenario results in a very different system (Table 4).

Table 4 first shows what is already visible in Figure 3. In the YELLOW scenario, a lot of solar power needs additional flexible backup capacities to cover mornings and evenings. In the GREEN scenario, the role of flexible generation is minimized, and complementary wind and solar together contribute to a major part of the overall power generation. The striking difference between the two scenarios, however, lies in their costs. The overall investment in renewable energy sources is clearly higher in the GREEN scenario. Thus, the costs for support policies are also higher. However, the costs of extra flexible generation are a significant setback of the YELLOW scenario, which overrides the lower costs for renewable energy sources.

In total, the GREEN scenario portrays a 30% more cost-effective system (not accounting for the baseload generation costs, which are equal in both scenarios), which is a 165 billion USD difference accumulated over 25 years, which translates to 7 billion USD saved annually. Of course, this holds only for this idealistic case with a relatively high anti-correlation of renewable power generation assumed. However, the lesson learned is that, if a system possesses some complementarity of renewable energy sources, it can be harvested by channeling the needs of system reliability into investment incentives.

Table 4. Characteristics of the resultant power systems in the two scenarios.

Scenario	YELLOW		GREEN	
Support Type	Fixed Feed-In Premium		Reliability Premium	
Generation mix, GWh/year				
Base load	175,200	47%	175,200	45%
Flexible generation	65,518	18%	4015	1%
Solar PV	131,948	35%	87,965	23%
Wind	-	-	117,895	31%
Costs (25-year lifespan), billion USD				
Renewable energy fleet cost	162	24%	267	67%
New gas fleet cost	457	67%	-	0%
Support cost (premiums)	66	10%	132	33%
Total	685		398	

Environmental Footprint

The implementation of renewable energy technologies primarily aims to reduce the harmful environmental footprint of the power sector. Hence, the next step of this study was to estimate and compare the potential environmental footprint of the power systems in the two scenarios. Since the composition of the baseload in both scenarios is unknown, we compare the footprint of the flexible generation (gas power plants) and renewable technologies (solar PV and wind plants).

The environmental footprint of the two power systems was investigated from the perspective of: (i) CO_2 emissions (both direct and lifecycle) and (ii) the direct water footprint (water consumption). In this context, direct emissions refer to the emissions that appeared during the power-generation process (e.g., from burning fuel), whereas lifecycle emissions encompass the emissions from the foreground process (the power-generation process) and all background processes (extraction, processing, and transportation of fuels; construction of the power plant; etc.).

While environmental studies typically consider only CO_2 emissions, the water footprint of power-generation facilities is often overlooked [48]. For instance, thermal power generation consumes water for cooling purposes, and solar PV generation requires water for the occasional cleaning of PV modules. During the process of power generation, this water is withdrawn from the immediate water environment, which may lead to the depletion of water resources, especially in regions already characterized by high water stress [49]. According to the Water Resource Institute, two-thirds of California face high or extremely high baseline water stress [50]. Hence, an assessment of the water footprint for California's power sector is crucial.

The results of this analysis are shown in Table 5. The values were calculated for each generation type using the following formula

$$Lifecycle\ or\ direct\ emmissions\ [gCO_2eq] = Annual\ generation\ [kWh] \times emission\ factor\ \left[\frac{g}{kWh}\right] \quad (3)$$

for the annual lifecycle and direct emissions and

$$Direct\ water\ footprint\ [m^3] = Annual\ generation\ [MWh] \times water\ consumption\ factor\ \left[\frac{m^3}{MWh}\right] \quad (4)$$

for the annual water footprint.

The values presented in the table are the median estimates that were calculated using: (i) the lifecycle and direct emission factors obtained from IPCC [51]; and (ii) the water consumption factors for renewable and non-renewable technologies reported by Macknick et al. [52].

As shown in the table, the replacement of the gas capacities by solar and wind technologies in the GREEN scenario resulted in a considerable reduction in both the lifecycle and direct CO_2-eq emissions and in the direct water footprint compared with the YELLOW scenario. Assuming the same base load in both scenarios, the YELLOW scenario is associated with additional direct emissions of about 22.7 mln. tons of CO_2-eq annually compared with the GREEN scenario. To put this value into perspective, it is larger than the combined annual total CO_2 emissions of Latvia and Lithuania in 2019 [53]. The results also demonstrate that the GREEN scenario allows us to "save" approximately 30.4 mln. cubic meters of water annually. This is equivalent to 12'160 Olympic-size swimming pools. This "saved" water in the GREEN scenario can be conserved or reallocated for other purposes, for instance, food production.

Table 5. The environmental footprint of the power systems in the two scenarios.

Scenario	YELLOW		GREEN	
Support Type	Fixed Feed-In Premium		RELIABILITY PREMIUM	
Lifecycle emissions, mln. tCO$_2$-eq, median values				
Base load	NA	NA	NA	NA
Flexible generation (gas-combined cycle)	32.1	84%	2.0	26%
Solar PV	6.3	16%	4.2	56%
Wind	-	-	1.3	17%
Total	**38.4**		**7.5**	
Direct emissions, mln. tCO$_2$-eq, median values				
Base load	NA	NA	NA	NA
Flexible generation (gas-combined cycle)	24.2	100%	1.5	100%
Solar PV	0	0%	0	0%
Wind	-	-	0	0%
Total	**24.2**		**1.5**	
Direct water footprint (water consumption), mln. cubic meters, median values				
Base load	NA	NA	NA	NA
Flexible generation (gas-combined cycle and tower cooling)	32.2	99%	2.0	86%
Solar PV	0.5	1%	0.3	14%
Wind	-	-	0	0%
Total	**32.7**		**2.3**	

The intention of this simple calculation was to demonstrate the potential environmental benefits of the GREEN scenario, which aims to minimize the role of flexible (commonly fossil-based) generation in the power generation mix.

3.3. From Concept to Realization

The model presented here is highly stylized and simplified for the purposes of showing the main principle for supporting renewable energy sources in favor of system reliability. For the model to be useful in analyzing a real-world system, several developments on top of the stylized example should be envisaged. Here, we list the critical aspects to be considered when transforming the concept into a sophisticated model for a real case:

1. An existing technology mix in the power system, with its technical and economic characteristics;
2. Realistic details for load profiles with seasonal and weekly variations. The design solutions for integrating fine temporal resolution into long-term energy models are well presented and discussed in [20], and the hybrid model [19] can be used as a guiding example;
3. A unit commitment and economic dispatch model of the system used to define which power plants generate electricity;
4. Uncertainty in the demand and supply of electricity should be introduced in order to realistically estimate the needs of system reliability and electricity prices. These and other uncertainties require stochasticity and simulations envisaged in the model;
5. Available investment options and possible potential of renewable energy anti-correlation in the region;

6. Uncertainties in the system bring complexity to the investment block of the model. With these uncertainties, deferral decisions are possible, for example, investments are considered real options, and thus, the policy effects can be modeled more realistically. An example of embedding real options logic into an energy system-level model can be found in [31];
7. Existing and potential flexibilities in the power system—storage, demand response, interconnections, and import/export of electricity; and
8. Existing and available policy scenarios.

4. Discussion and Conclusions

Some models integrate hourly fluctuations in the demand and supply of electricity into long-term generation technology mix planning. These models show that renewable energy sources possess a degree of complementarity that, if captured, can reduce the needed backup capacity and can ease the requirements on system flexibility. However, a complementary renewable energy power plant might be suboptimal in terms of profitability from an investor's perspective. Thus, in order to steer renewable energy investments in favor of energy system reliability, different investment incentives need to be introduced. Such incentives need to capture the value of complementarity of a power plant to the existing power system. Numerous design choices are required to create such an incentive mechanism.

This paper introduces a conceptual model that can analyze the effects of different designs of support for reliability-based renewable energy on power system operations and development. In its simplest deterministic form, the model is applied to a stylized case, and the potential benefits in terms of power system reliability, overall technology, and policy costs and the environmental footprint are demonstrated. In contrast, currently, policymakers rely on models that are wired to calculate a fixed amount of backup capacity for every unit of newly built renewable energy source [20], hindering the very possibility to design a policy for a more efficient power system.

The hybrid model introduced in this paper allows us to redesign the support for renewable energy and to analyze whether a reliability-conditioned instrument makes sense for a particular system. The same model can be used to quantify the effects of different types of storage and demand response. With this model, one would be able to model the effects of different capacity mechanisms with or without separate support for renewable energy and to optimize the overall policy mix for the power system. The model will also be able to show the optimal limit of renewable energy adoption in a particular region. After such a limit, any more renewable energy of any type in any location would not provide any marginal contribution to the power capacity of the system. Pushing for the growth of renewable energy sources beyond this limit will become a futile attempt at decarbonization since more stable power output plants will be needed to offset the variability of renewable energy sources, which in turn would increase fossil fuel usage and jeopardize decarbonization. Instead, other sources of flexibility should be promoted in these system, such as storage, hydrogen and power-to-X solutions, and demand-response programs.

The results of such a modeling exercise would heavily depend on region-specific characteristics. They include the technology mix currently in place; the electricity demand profile; its variability and projections; the transmission capabilities in a system and its connections to neighboring areas; the system flexibility, in particular the development and deployment levels of storage and demand response solutions; the availability of renewable energy resources; and their possible complementarity. Political, economic, and social factors clearly play their roles as well; however, their effects would depend on whether they are wired to the model.

The complementarity of renewable energy sources has been shown in multiple cases, such as the temporal and spatial heterogeneity of wind power among power used on the European continent [19] and the uncaptured value of southwest-oriented solar panels in California compared with commonly built south-oriented solar panels [47]. Some studies suggest that one way to discover the complementarity of renewable energy resources is to consider them over larger geographic areas. For instance, Grams et al. [54] suggested considering continent-scale wind patterns to implement pan-European collaborations for the development of renewable energies. Of course, capturing that complementarity value requires massive network investments, of which the economic viability can be thoroughly investigated using the proposed hybrid model.

One can argue that replacing the fossil-based flexible generation with renewable energy sources is not needed since synthetic fuels will soon replace fossil fuels. However, even according to very optimistic estimations, the adoption of power-to-X technologies and the corresponding massive production of synthetic fuels as well as massive installations of storage technologies (batteries) are expected to start worldwide not earlier than in the 2030s [55]. In this light, the introduction of policies, which aim to replace the currently used fossil-based flexible generation with the optimal mix of renewable energy technologies remains relevant.

Departing from modeling-related matters, actual policy implementation has numerous issues to consider as well. The transition from support for classical renewable energy to a reliability-based instrument might not be easy due to the associated paperwork, design, and arrangement burden. Although in the recent years, a trend has switched to more market-oriented mechanisms in supporting renewable energy, that is, from fixed feed-in tariffs to premiums, auctions and certificate trading [1], they still do not have a sufficient foundation for such a change since a power system perspective and procedures for calculating reliability are missing. However, some countries have introduced capacity markets, where calculations for the contribution of renewable energy to system reliability are already a routine procedure [7]. In these cases, the transition to reliability-based support for renewable energy sources would be much smoother. Countries that have capacity mechanisms in place and, most importantly, some procedures for calculating the contribution of renewable energy sources to reliability, are displayed in Figure 4.

While the idea of reliability premium is conceptually simple, in reality, it faces multiple design choices.

- Which reliability indicator should be used? The proposed model can compare the difference in effects of various reliability indicators. However, an important factor is the existing procedures for calculating reliability for a country. Different system operators adopt different practices in that respect [17], and implementing perhaps sub-efficient but already working solutions would create much less administrative burden, better transparency, and a faster transition. The same applies to the other design choices for the calculation of reliability and system modeling.
- Should projects be exposed to a dynamically changing premium, or should it be fixed for a project's lifetime once calculated? The former has higher uncertainty and unpredictability for individual investors, computationally heavier systems, more room for administrative disorder, and more room for human mistakes. The latter allows for better order and provides more certainty for investors but might result in a less dynamic and responsive system.
- If the reliability premium is fixed, how often should it be recalculated? The recalculation can be carried out for each project, for each auction, or on an annual basis.
- If a capacity market is already in place and renewable energy sources can participate in it, how should the reliability-based premium be integrated? The two can co-exist or be merged. The former requires carefully accounting for the economic meaning of both types of support and prevents over-subsidization. In addition, a close collaboration would need to be established between the departments of system reliability and support for renewable energy sources. The latter creates a risk of distorting capacity prices and jeopardizing the effectiveness of the market by adversely affecting other categories of participants (non-renewable generation, storage, and demand response).

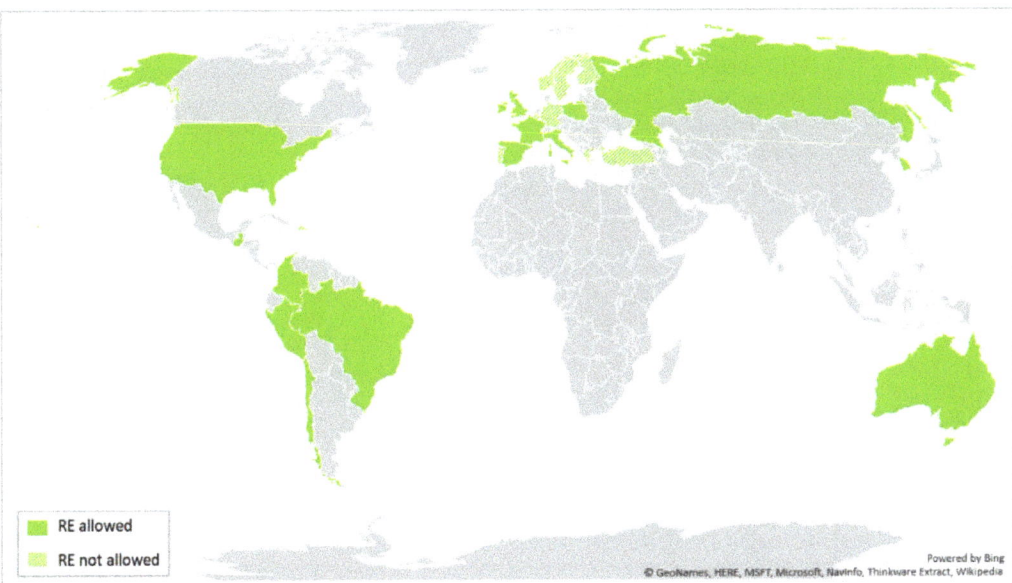

Figure 4. Geographical coverage of reliability schemes and their inclusion of renewable energy technologies, based on [7] but modified by the authors (Source: Author).

The question of which policy mix would potentially be able to steer the mix of renewable energy technologies was briefly discussed in the previous research devoted to international policy review [7]. The modeling exercise performed in this work sheds light onto and brings additional insight into this discussion. Naturally, if renewable energy sources are excluded from a capacity mechanism, the common types of renewable energy support alone would not provide investment incentives favoring system reliability. If participation in a capacity mechanism requires renewable energy sources to forgo the corresponding amount of support, the overall revenue from renewable energy sources stays the same, which again excludes incentives favoring system reliability. If, on the other hand, participation in a capacity mechanism entirely prohibits receiving other types of support, then such incentives come into the scene. The latter two points become clear with the modeling exercise performed in this paper, whereas in the previous qualitative-only analysis [7], these conjectures were made differently. Most importantly, however, is the conclusion that the incentive to steer a mix of renewable energy technologies in favor of energy system reliability can be implemented outside of a capacity mechanism and independently of its very presence.

As we can see, the introduction of such a conceptual hybrid model with the hypothetical idea of supporting renewable energy sources via a reliability-conditioned instrument leads to a variety of consequent design and implementation choices. However, the authors believe that the direction is worth perusing for the sake of more reliable, cost-efficient, and environmentally friendly energy systems.

Author Contributions: M.K.: conceptualization, data curation, methodology, writing—original draft preparation, writing—review and editing, and visualization; A.L.: conceptualization, data curation, methodology, writing—original draft preparation, and writing—review and editing. All authors have read and agreed to the published version of the manuscript.

Funding: This research was funded by the Foundation of Economic Education, grant number 200153, and by Kone Foundation, grant number 201710464.

Institutional Review Board Statement: Not applicable.

Informed Consent Statement: Not applicable.

Data Availability Statement: All used data is presented in the manuscript.

Acknowledgments: The authors deeply appreciate the extensive critical commentary from Paolo Mastropietro that allowed for improvements to be made to this paper and that inspired future research directions.

Conflicts of Interest: The authors declare no conflict of interest.

References

1. REN21 Renewables 2020 Global Status Report. Available online: http://www.ren21.net/wp-content/uploads/2018/06/17-8652_GSR2018_FullReport_web_final_.pdf (accessed on 6 August 2021).
2. Preuster, P.; Alekseev, A.; Wasserscheid, P. Hydrogen storage technologies for future energy systems. *Annu. Rev. Chem. Biomol. Eng.* **2017**, *8*, 445–471. [CrossRef]
3. Uyar, T.S.; Beşikci, D. Integration of hydrogen energy systems into renewable energy systems for better design of 100% renewable energy communities. *Int. J. Hydrogen Energy* **2017**, *42*, 2453–2456. [CrossRef]
4. Emonts, B.; Reuß, M.; Stenzel, P.; Welder, L.; Knicker, F.; Grube, T.; Görner, K.; Robinius, M.; Stolten, D. Flexible sector coupling with hydrogen: A climate-friendly fuel supply for road transport. *Int. J. Hydrogen Energy* **2019**, *44*, 12918–12930. [CrossRef]
5. Rodilla, P.; Batlle, C. Security of electricity supply at the generation level: Problem analysis. *Energy Policy* **2012**, *40*, 177–185. [CrossRef]
6. Lund, P.D.; Lindgren, J.; Mikkola, J.; Salpakari, J. Review of energy system flexibility measures to enable high levels of variable renewable electricity. *Renew. Sustain. Energy Rev.* **2015**, *45*, 785–807. [CrossRef]
7. Kozlova, M.; Overland, I. Combining capacity mechanisms and renewable energy support: A review of the international experience. *Renew. Sustain. Energy Rev.* **2021**, 111878. [CrossRef]
8. Roehrkasten, S.; Schaeuble, D.; Helgenberger, S. Secure and sustainable power generation in a water-constrained world. In Proceedings of the South African International Renewable Energy Conference (SAIREC), Cape Town, South Africa, 4–7 October 2015; Volume 23.
9. Penttinen, S. Texas Energy Crisis in 2021: Emerging Climate Risks, Extreme Weather and Key Takeaways to Increase Resilience. *Oil Gas Energy Law* **2021**, *19*. Available online: https://www.ogel.org/journal-advance-publication-article.asp?key=681 (accessed on 3 December 2021).
10. Perera, A.; Nik, V.M.; Chen, D.; Scartezzini, J.; Hong, T. Quantifying the impacts of climate change and extreme climate events on energy systems. *Nat. Energy* **2020**, *5*, 150–159. [CrossRef]
11. Rosnes, O. Subsidies for renewable energy in inflexible power markets. *J. Regul. Econ.* **2014**, *46*, 318–343. [CrossRef]
12. European Commission Press Release. State Aid: Commission Approves Six Electricity Capacity Mechanisms to Ensure Security of Supply in Belgium, France, Germany, Greece, Italy and Poland. Available online: http://europa.eu/rapid/press-release_IP-18-682_en.htm (accessed on 3 December 2021).
13. Tennbakk, B.; Capros, P.; Delkis, C.; Tasios, N.; Zabara, M.; Noreng, H.; Skånlund, A.; Jenssen, Å. *Capacity Mechanisms in Individual Markets within the IEM*; THEMA Consulting Group: Oslo, Norway, 2013.
14. Lara-Arango, D.; Arango-Aramburo, S.; Larsen, E.R. Uncertainty and the long-term adequacy of supply: Simulations of capacity mechanisms in electricity markets. *Energy Strategy Rev.* **2017**, *18*, 199–211. [CrossRef]
15. Bhagwat, P.C.; Iychettira, K.K.; Richstein, J.C.; Chappin, E.J.; De Vries, L.J. The effectiveness of capacity markets in the presence of a high portfolio share of renewable energy sources. *Util. Policy* **2017**, *48*, 76–91. [CrossRef]
16. Bhagwat, P.C.; Richstein, J.C.; Chappin, E.J.; de Vries, L.J. The effectiveness of a strategic reserve in the presence of a high portfolio share of renewable energy sources. *Util. Policy* **2016**, *39*, 13–28. [CrossRef]
17. Mastropietro, P.; Rodilla, P.; Batlle, C. De-rating of wind and solar resources in capacity mechanisms: A review of international experiences. *Renew. Sustain. Energy Rev.* **2019**, *112*, 253–262. [CrossRef]
18. Söder, L.; Tómasson, E.; Estanqueiro, A.; Flynn, D.; Hodge, B.; Kiviluoma, J.; Korpås, M.; Neau, E.; Couto, A.; Pudjianto, D. Review of wind generation within adequacy calculations and capacity markets for different power systems. *Renew. Sustain. Energy Rev.* **2020**, *119*, 109540. [CrossRef]
19. Jakob, P.; Wagner, J. Optimal Allocation of Variable Renewable Energy Considering Contributions to Security of Supply. *Energy J.* **2021**, *42*, 229–259.
20. Collins, S.; Deane, J.P.; Poncelet, K.; Panos, E.; Pietzcker, R.C.; Delarue, E.; Ó Gallachóir, B.P. Integrating short term variations of the power system into integrated energy system models: A methodological review. *Renew. Sustain. Energy Rev.* **2017**, *76*, 839–856. [CrossRef]
21. Menegaki, A. Valuation for renewable energy: A comparative review. *Renew. Sustain. Energy Rev.* **2008**, *12*, 2422–2437. [CrossRef]
22. Trigeorgis, L. *Real Options: An Overview*; Praeger: Westport, CT, USA, 1995.
23. Kozlova, M. Real option valuation in renewable energy literature: Research focus, trends and design. *Renew. Sustain. Energy Rev.* **2017**, *80*, 180–196. [CrossRef]

24. Boomsma, T.K.; Linnerud, K. Market and policy risk under different renewable electricity support schemes. *Energy* **2015**, *89*, 435–448. [CrossRef]
25. Kitzing, L.; Juul, N.; Drud, M.; Boomsma, T.K. A real options approach to analyse wind energy investments under different support schemes. *Appl. Energy* **2017**, *188*, 83–96. [CrossRef]
26. Trigeorgis, L.; Tsekrekos, A.E. Real Options in Operations Research: A Review. *Eur. J. Oper. Res.* **2018**, *270*, 1–24. [CrossRef]
27. Tsani, S.; Kozlova, M. *Energy Modelling for Sustainable Policy making: State of the Art and Future Challenges*; Sustainable Politics and Economics of Natural Resources; Elgar: Cheltenham Glos, UK, 2021.
28. Capros, P.; Paroussos, L.; Fragkos, P.; Tsani, S.; Boitier, B.; Wagner, F.; Busch, S.; Resch, G.; Blesl, M.; Bollen, J. Description of models and scenarios used to assess European decarbonisation pathways. *Energy Strategy Rev.* **2014**, *2*, 220–230. [CrossRef]
29. Linnerud, K.; Andersson, A.M.; Fleten, S. Investment timing under uncertain renewable energy policy: An empirical study of small hydropower projects. *Energy* **2014**, *78*, 154–164. [CrossRef]
30. Fleten, S.; Linnerud, K.; Molnár, P.; Nygaard, M.T. Green electricity investment timing in practice: Real options or net present value? *Energy* **2016**, *116*, 498–506. [CrossRef]
31. Rios, D.; Blanco, G.; Olsina, F. Integrating Real Options Analysis with long-term electricity market models. *Energy Econ.* **2019**, *80*, 188–205. [CrossRef]
32. Heylen, E.; Deconinck, G.; Van Hertem, D. Review and classification of reliability indicators for power systems with a high share of renewable energy sources. *Renew. Sustain. Energy Rev.* **2018**, *97*, 554–568. [CrossRef]
33. Emmanuel, M.; Doubleday, K.; Cakir, B.; Marković, M.; Hodge, B. A review of power system planning and operational models for flexibility assessment in high solar energy penetration scenarios. *Sol. Energy* **2020**, *210*, 169–180. [CrossRef]
34. Gonzalez, I.H.; Ruiz, P.; Sgobbi, A.; Nijs, W.; Quoilin, S.; Zucker, A.; Heinrichs, H.U.; Silva, V.; Koljonen, T.; Kober, T. Addressing flexibility in energy system models. *Eur. Comm. Jt. Res. Cent. Inst. Energy Transp.* **2015**, 1–80. Available online: https://www.researchgate.net/profile/Sylvain_Quoilin/publication/304525458_Addressing_flexibility_in_energy_system_models/links/5793468d08aeb0ffccdcdb93.pdf (accessed on 3 December 2021).
35. Mastropietro, P.; Herrero, I.; Rodilla, P.; Batlle, C. A model-based analysis on the impact of explicit penalty schemes in capacity mechanisms. *Appl. Energy* **2016**, *168*, 406–417. [CrossRef]
36. Zhou, P.; Jin, R.Y.; Fan, L.W. Reliability and economic evaluation of power system with renewables: A review. *Renew. Sustain. Energy Rev.* **2016**, *58*, 537–547. [CrossRef]
37. International Hydropower Association 2019 Hydropower Status Report—Sector Trends and Insights. 2019. Available online: https://www.hydropower.org/publications/status2019 (accessed on 3 December 2021).
38. Ralon, P.; Taylor, M.; Ilas, A.; Diaz-Bone, H.; Kairies, K. *Electricity Storage and Renewables: Costs and Markets to 2030*; International Renewable Energy Agency: Abu Dhabi, UAE, 2017.
39. Rogner, M.; Troja, N. *The World's Water Battery: Pumped Hydropower Storage and the Clean Energy Transition*; IHA: London, UK, 2018.
40. International Energy Association Energy Storage Report. Available online: https://www.iea.org/reports/energy-storage (accessed on 3 December 2021).
41. Mongird, K.; Viswanathan, V.; Alam, J.; Vartanian, C.; Sprenkle, V.; Baxter, R. 2020 Grid Energy Storage Technology Cost and Performance Assessment. 2020; pp. 1–117. Available online: https://in.minenergo.gov.ru/upload/iblock/550/550e0f55febe8f3ac4d4b40ab9eeca2b.pdf (accessed on 3 December 2021).
42. Ramsebner, J.; Haas, R.; Ajanovic, A.; Wietschel, M. The sector coupling concept: A critical review. *Wiley Interdiscip. Rev.: Energy Environ.* **2021**, *10*, e396. [CrossRef]
43. Brown, T.; Schlachtberger, D.; Kies, A.; Schramm, S.; Greiner, M. Synergies of sector coupling and transmission reinforcement in a cost-optimised, highly renewable European energy system. *Energy* **2018**, *160*, 720–739. [CrossRef]
44. Fridgen, G.; Keller, R.; Körner, M.; Schöpf, M. A holistic view on sector coupling. *Energy Policy* **2020**, *147*, 111913. [CrossRef]
45. California Energy Commission Estimated Cost of New Utility-Scale Generation in California: 2018 Update. Available online: https://www.energy.ca.gov/sites/default/files/2021-06/CEC-200-2019-005.pdf (accessed on 3 December 2021).
46. Fleten, S.; Näsäkkälä, E. Gas-fired power plants: Investment timing, operating flexibility and CO_2 capture. *Energy Econ.* **2010**, *32*, 805–816. [CrossRef]
47. Huntington, S.C.; Rodilla, P.; Herrero, I.; Batlle, C. Revisiting support policies for RES-E adulthood: Towards market compatible schemes. *Energy Policy* **2017**, *104*, 474–483. [CrossRef]
48. Lohrmann, A.; Child, M.; Breyer, C. Assessment of the water footprint for the European power sector during the transition towards a 100% renewable energy system. *Energy* **2021**, *233*, 121098. [CrossRef]
49. Franco, E.G. *The Global Risks Report 2020*; World Economic Forum: Cologny, Switzerland, 2020.
50. Iceland, C. California Sleepwalks into Water Crisis. 2015. Available online: https://www.wri.org/insights/california-sleepwalks-water-crisis (accessed on 3 December 2021).
51. Schlömer, S.; Bruckner, T.; Fulton, L.; Hertwich, E.; McKinnon, A.; Perczyk, D.; Roy, J.; Schaeffer, R.; Sims, R.; Smith, P.; et al. 2014: Annex III: Technology-specific cost and performance parameters. In *Climate Change 2014: Mitigation of Climate Change*; Cambridge University Press: Cambridge, UK; New York, NY, USA, 2014.
52. Macknick, J.; Newmark, R.; Heath, G.; Hallett, K.C. Operational water consumption and withdrawal factors for electricity generating technologies: A review of existing literature. *Environ. Res. Lett.* **2012**, *7*, 045802. [CrossRef]

53. Ritchie, H.; Roser, M. CO$_2$ and greenhouse gas emissions. *Our World Data* **2020**. Available online: https://ourworldindata.org/co2-and-other-greenhouse-gas-emissions (accessed on 3 December 2021).
54. Grams, C.M.; Beerli, R.; Pfenninger, S.; Staffell, I.; Wernli, H. Balancing Europe's wind-power output through spatial deployment informed by weather regimes. *Nat. Clim. Chang.* **2017**, *7*, 557–562. [CrossRef]
55. Bogdanov, D.; Gulagi, A.; Fasihi, M.; Breyer, C. Full energy sector transition towards 100% renewable energy supply: Integrating power, heat, transport and industry sectors including desalination. *Appl. Energy* **2021**, *283*, 116273. [CrossRef]

Article

Profitability Determinants of Unlisted Renewable Energy Companies in Germany—A Longitudinal Analysis of Financial Accounts

Maria-Kristiine Luts [1], Jyrki Savolainen [1,*] and Mikael Collan [1,2]

[1] School of Business and Management, LUT-University, Yliopistonkatu 34, 53850 Lappeenranta, Finland; mariak.luts@gmail.com (M.-K.L.); mikael.collan@vatt.fi (M.C.)
[2] VATT Institute for Economic Research, Arkadiankatu 7, 00101 Helsinki, Finland
* Correspondence: jyrki.savolainen@lut.fi

Citation: Luts, M.-K.; Savolainen, J.; Collan, M. Profitability Determinants of Unlisted Renewable Energy Companies in Germany—A Longitudinal Analysis of Financial Accounts. *Sustainability* **2021**, *13*, 13544. https://doi.org/10.3390/su132413544

Academic Editors: Julian Scott Yeomans and Mariia Kozlova

Received: 25 October 2021
Accepted: 25 November 2021
Published: 7 December 2021

Publisher's Note: MDPI stays neutral with regard to jurisdictional claims in published maps and institutional affiliations.

Copyright: © 2021 by the authors. Licensee MDPI, Basel, Switzerland. This article is an open access article distributed under the terms and conditions of the Creative Commons Attribution (CC BY) license (https:// creativecommons.org/licenses/by/ 4.0/).

Abstract: The fight against a climate crisis has urged nations and the global community to cut emissions and to define ambitious environmental goals. This has highlighted the importance of the renewable energy (RE) industry. Germany has been one of the most active countries in RE adoption. In this vein, the purpose of this research is to study and identify key profitability determinants of unlisted German electricity-producing RE-companies, many of which have been supported by the German Feed-in Tariff (FIT). A multi-year analysis based on panel data from 783 companies for the years 2010–2018 is used. The results show that both company- and industry-specific profitability determinants are statistically significant, but the company-specific determinants seem to be more important. The results shed new light on what drives the profitability of private German RE companies during the period of financial aid from the government and are of use to managers, regulators and investors alike, e.g., when the effects of different regulatory climates and industry environments, as well as states of business life cycle are considered. Furthermore, the implications of this study have wider environmental and economic importance as the performance of the RE companies is critical in achieving the emission targets of the energy industry and ensuring a more sustainable energy production for the future.

Keywords: renewable energy; electricity production; unlisted companies; Germany; feed-in tariff

1. Introduction

After 2010, the fight against the climate crisis intensified and supranational bodies started to act. In 2020, the EU Commission proposed a Climate Target plan of cutting carbon dioxide (CO_2) emissions by at least 55% by the year 2030 and set a goal of carbon neutrality by 2050 [1]. Germany has been one of the most active countries in turning to renewable energy (RE) as a remedy to tackle CO_2 emissions. The German RE markets are the fifth largest in the world (after China, US, Brazil, and India [2]) and are well established due to the long-lasting efforts by the German government to promote green energy with a Feed-in-Tariff (FIT) support mechanism. Transition in the RE support mechanism has already been started and new mechanisms will most likely be introduced.

This research focuses on uncovering the profitability determinants of unlisted German electricity-producing RE companies. Profitability is examined in terms of companies' yearly profit and loss statements and not from an investment or a plant operations perspective. This research falls under the umbrella of studies that concentrate on firm performance. Lebas and Euske (2007) [3] defined firm performance as a set of quantifiable financial and non-financial indicators that can be illustrated with a causal model, reflecting the future outcomes of current actions. The selected indicators of financial performance used in this study include measures of profitability such as the Return on Investment (ROI), Return on Assets (ROA), and Return on Equity (ROE) and measures of growth such as the growth of revenues and assets.

It is well known, see, e.g., [4] that the profitability indicators are prone to accounting manipulation, undervaluation of assets, and different depreciation policies, which makes comparing companies complicated. As we are looking only at German companies, the accounting regulation and the legal structures that all companies in the sample use are uniform and we expect that all companies in the sample act in a profit-maximizing way within the limits set by the law. While profitability can also be measured by using a more holistic set of indicators [5], we limit the focus to company-level profit indicators only.

The rest of this paper is constructed as follows: In the following section, the background and motivation of the study are discussed following the review of the literature and hypotheses. The second chapter introduces the data, selected variables, and the panel-data-method used in the analysis. The third chapter presents the results of the panel data analysis and the answers to the hypotheses made about the models used and the significance of different firm- and industry-specific determinants to firm profitability. The fourth chapter discusses the results in light of the previous research. Finally, the contribution of this paper is summarized and ideas for further research are discussed.

1.1. Background

This research is motivated by the lack of existing studies that focus on the profitability and the determinants of profitability of unlisted German electricity-producing RE companies. Thus, there is a research gap that the results of this research fill. In addition to understanding the profitability issues better, we wish to know what effect the German RE support mechanism, the Feed-in Tariffs, has had on company profitability. Understanding these issues is important because of the role of the energy industry in reaching the ambitious goals of carbon neutrality in Germany (see Figure 1).

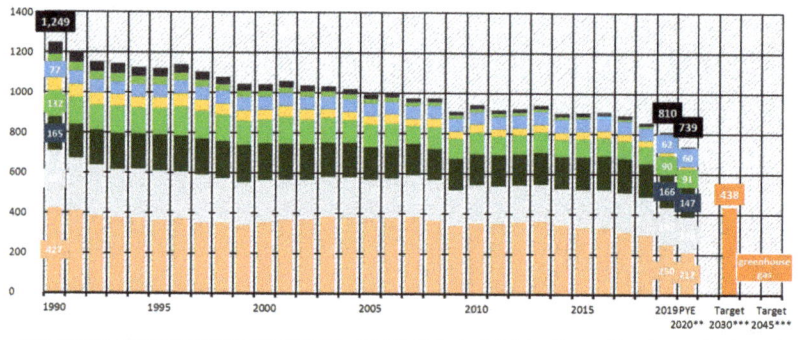

Figure 1. CO_2 emissions in Germany in millions of tons of CO_2 equivalents. (* Industry: Energy and process-related emissions from industry (1.A.2 & 2); Other emissions: Other combustion (rest of CRF 1.A.4, 1.A.5 military) & fugitive emissions from fuels (1.B) ** PYE: Previous Year-Estimate for 2020; *** Targets 2030 and 2045: according to the revision of the Federal Climate Protection Act (KSG) as of 12 May 2021) according to [6,7].

Renewable, green, or alternative energy all describe energy either in the form of heat, electricity, or fuel that is derived from constantly renewing natural sources and processes. The sources usually prescribed as renewables are solar, wind, geothermal, marine, hydro, and bioenergy. According to the European Commission (2021), in 2020, Germany's share of renewables in the gross final energy consumption was 18.6% and 45.4% in the gross power consumption. Germany has set a goal to increase the share of renewables in gross power consumption to 65% by 2030, and that by 2050 all electricity generated or consumed in Germany be greenhouse-gas neutral. (see, e.g., [8–10]). In 2020, the largest share of renewable electricity generation in Germany was by wind onshore power (42%), followed by solar (20%), and biomass (7%) [11].

Germany has been a renewable energy policy pioneer with its energy transition "Energiewende" that started as opposition to nuclear energy in the late 1970s. The long-term energy transition has included a reorientation of energy policy from the traditional fossil energy forms towards renewable energies along with the nuclear energy phase-out into concrete actions. By 2022, the last nuclear facility is set to shut down and the latest Coal Phase-Out Act mandates a gradual phase-out of coal-burning leading to all coal plants having to cease operations by 2038 [12,13].

In 1991, the Electricity Feed-in Law (EFL) was introduced in Germany. Its objective was to make sure that electricity produced from renewable energy sources had access to the grid. The electricity from renewable energy power plants was paid a premium price (Feed-in Tariff, FIT), a cost that was borne by the electricity supply utilities and their customers. As the support was highest for wind and solar plants, the law contributed to the expansion of renewable energy production, especially in the form of wind farms. [14]

According to IAE [15], the Renewable Energy Sources Act (Erneuerbare-Energien-Gesetz, EEG) replaced the EFL in 2000 and obligates grid operators, instead of the suppliers, to buy renewable energy and to effectively pay the FIT. The tariffs were determined for each sector separately and according to the actual production costs, and upon initialization, the main target was to double the share of renewable electricity by 2010 [15]. The plants initially eligible for the FIT remuneration will soon face the end of the support period as Germany is shifting out from the FIT system. As of 2021, there is also a discussion about completely ending the renewables levy (EEG surcharge) that has been paid by electricity consumers. Possible discontinuation of the renewables levy may be offset by an increase in the price of CO_2 emissions, a part of the EU Emissions Trading System, and Germany's own national emissions trading [16,17].

The 2017 amendment to the EEG introduced public tenders, the goal of which is to aid the shift from FIT to a market-oriented price mechanism. From 2017 onwards, on-shore and offshore wind, solar and biomass projects have had to bid a price in an auction to ensure contracts for 20 years [8].

1.2. Review of Literature on Profitability Determinants

The determinants that explain profitability can be examined on different levels: the firm-level, industry-level, and country-level, or, for example, on regional or temporal levels. Early research on the topic emphasized the importance of industry structure and a competitive environment on firm performance through the Structure-Conduct-Performance paradigm [18] and the Porter's famous five competitive forces model [19]. Gradually, the focal point of research has shifted from thinking of the industry as an aggregate as the main determinant of profitability towards recognizing individual company characteristics as important profitability drivers [20]. This is also the focus in this research. According to the summary in [21], several variance decomposition analyses across industries, from the 1980s until 2007, reported that firm-specific effects explain from zero to 66% of the variance in firm profitability. In particular, in the manufacturing industry, the firm-level effects explain more variance than they do in other industries [21].

Capon et al.'s (1990) [22] meta-analysis covered results from 320 published studies on financial performance between the years 1921 and 1987 across industries, with different performance measures (see, Table 1). More recent studies [23,24] have found that profitability is positively affected by company size in terms of sales and as the number of employees. Goddard et al.'s (2005) [23] study on European firms implied that the relationship between company size in terms of assets and profitability is negative. They suggest that a rapid expansion of successful firms may have a negative influence on short-term profitability, while at the same time, the positive effect of market/industry concentration implies that costly strategies may be conducted to gain a larger market share.

Adner and Helfat (2003) [25] studied 30 firms in the energy industry and concluded that firm-level effects explain the largest share of variance in profitability. Westerman et al. (2020) [26] studied publicly listed energy firms located in Western Europe over the period of 2009–2015 and reported that firm size indicated by total assets and EBIT/total sales are positively correlated with return on assets (ROA), especially with renewable firms. They also found a negative relationship between Debt-to-Assets (D/A) and ROA, and that diversification has a negative relationship with firm profitability (ROA) in the energy industry. Jaraite and Kažukauskas (2013) [27] provided evidence that the higher profitability of the electricity production is related to the higher market concentration (a percentage of a market share of the (four) largest firms).

Table 1. Selected firm- and industry-specific determinants of profitability summarized from the results of a meta-analysis by Capon et al. (1990). +: significantly more positive than negative relationship, significance level 5%, −: significantly more negative than positive relationship, significance level 5%, Ns: count of positive vs. negative relationships reported not significantly different, significance level 5% [22].

Determinant Type	Determinant Name	Significance	Nr of Studies
Firm-specific	Leverage/Debt	−	23
	Capital Investment	−	29
	Diversification	−	17
	Growth in Sales	+	22
	Market Share	+	42
	Capacity Utilization	+	15
	Variability in Return	+	11
	Size (Sales)	Ns	48
	Size (Assets)	Ns	47
	Price (relative)	Ns	18
Industry-specific	Imports	−	19
	Exports	−	10
	Growth (Sales)	+	59
	Capital Investment	+	51
	Geographic dispersion (Production; reg. vs. nat.)	+	32
	Economies of scale	+	13
	Barriers of Entry	+	16
	Industry Concentration	+	99

A study by Tsai and Tung (2017) [28] on RE firms from across the world found that the share of renewables in the overall primary energy consumption has a significant and negative effect on the ROA of renewable energy companies. They also found that a nation's energy consumption impacts ROA negatively, whereas employee growth rate has a positive effect on ROA. We observe that companies typically tend to hire more people into profitable businesses. According to [29], the degree of innovation and the development of the technology sector nationally have been found to positively affect the performance of RE firms on the country level. Shah et al. (2018) [30] found mixed evidence on the effect of macro-level shocks on the return on RE investments. In their study, oil prices have had both a positive and a negative effect on the return on RE investments, depending on the level of government subsidies: an increase in oil price boosted the profitability of RE-companies operating in a market-driven regulatory environment.

A study by Hassan (2019) [31] analyzed 420 RE-companies from the OECD countries and reported a significant positive relationship between different RE support mechanisms, including the FIT, and accounting-based measures of financial performance (Earnings per share, Return on Capital Employed = ROCE). Milanés-Montero et al. (2018) [32] specifically analyzed the effect the FIT—which is also of interest in this paper—had on the performance of photovoltaic (solar) farms in Germany, Italy, France, and Spain. They report that the FIT had a positive statistically significant influence on the profitability of the firms when measured in terms of Return on Investment (ROI). The study also confirmed that among the firm-specific determinants, total assets and leverage had a significant positive effect on the photovoltaic firms' performance; the result is contrary to the one from the meta-analysis of [22]. Neves et al. used the generalized method of moments to study Portuguese energy companies' determinants during the periods of 2010–2014 [33] and 2011–2018 [34].

In summary, the previous literature across industries recognizes the determinants "size in sales" and "size in assets" with both positive and negative effects, and the growth in sales and assets with a positive effect on profitability. Leverage has mostly been found to have a significant negative effect on profitability, with the exception of the above-mentioned study on solar power firms. Liquidity has been found to have a positive effect on firm-level profitability. Furthermore, market concentration has been found to have a significant positive effect in most of the studies and these results are supported by the studies in the RE industry as well. Lastly, the Feed-in-Tariffs have been found to have a significant positive influence on profitability.

For this paper, a panel data analysis is run to investigate the subject from the perspective of unlisted German RE companies.

1.3. Hypotheses

We formulate three hypotheses based on the previous literature on profitability determinants of renewable energy. Specifically, we are interested in how important the firm-specific and industry-specific determinants are in the case of the data of non-listed German RE producers, and which determinants explain the largest variance in the selected profitability ratios.

The previous literature across industries has suggested that firm determinants (such as the financials chosen for this analysis) explain more variance in profitability than industry determinants, but that industry determinants, especially industry growth and concentration, are also significant. Furthermore, according to more recent studies on the markets, where the FIT support has been applied, the FIT has shown to be significant in determining the profitability of renewable electricity generators.

Based on the review of literature on profitability determinants, the following hypotheses were formed:

Hypothesis 1 (H1). *The model with industry-specific determinants and the model with firm-specific determinants are both significant when a 5% significance level is adopted in the statistical testing.*

Hypothesis 2 (H2). *The explanatory power of the included firm-specific determinants is higher than that of the included industry-specific determinants.*

Hypothesis 3 (H3). *The average annual Feed in Tariff (FIT) has a significant positive effect on the RE companies' profitability.*

2. Data and Methods

The data which the results are based on were acquired from the Amadeus database (hosting the data of the 565,000 largest public and private companies in 43 European countries) with a query (Applied industry classification code "3511", "production of electricity" in NACE Rev. 2 based classification system) with the following conditions: "active and not bankrupt"; "operating in Germany"; "generating electricity in the RE industry (solar, wind, biomass, hydro, and geothermal)"; "no conventional electricity production"; "not publicly listed". The query returned data for 783 electricity-producing companies with financial accounts available for the period of 2010–2018. The sampling period was chosen based on the availability of the data and the fact that the FIT-support was active during the years of the sampling period for all RE technologies studied in this paper.

The retrieved data were sorted by name and "trade description" according to the activity of generating or transmitting renewable electricity from any RE source. The data include companies in all the above-mentioned RE sectors except for geothermal power and some of the firms are active with multiple RE technologies.

Company-specific data were combined with data on feed-in tariffs and energy statistics. Data on feed-in tariffs and the industry and energy statistics for the nine years in question were obtained from the European Commission's Eurostat statistics database [35], the World Bank database [36], and the OECD [37] databases.

Company size was used to classify the companies into two cohorts, for which analysis was performed separately; the cohorts were constructed by combining the companies in the Amadeus size categories "very large" and "large" into one cohort (n = 401) and companies in categories "medium" and "small" into another (n = 332), see Table 2 for information about these categories. The decision was made to study the possible difference between SMEs and large firms. That is, the category "Very Large" was excluded from the study, representing a minor share of the overall data when taking into account the number of companies (9/733 companies = 1.2%). Although the cohort of large companies is larger, in the analysis used, the observations of the large companies are significantly lower than with the SMEs and stay at around 100 observations due to the unbalanced panel.

Table 2. Company size categories and the resulting number of firms in the analyzed data. Size categories adopted from Amadeus.

	Very Large	Large	Medium	Small
Operating Revenue	≥100 M€	≥10 M€	≥1 M€	<1 M€
Total Assets	≥200 M€	≥20 M€	≥2 M€	<2 M€
Employees	≥1000	≥150	≥15	<15
Firms in Data	9	392	278	54

2.1. Variable Selection

Three dependent variables in the measurement of profitability were selected: Return on Equity (ROE), Return on Assets (ROA), and Return on Capital Employed (ROCE). ROE implies the average annual return generated for the equity owners, ROA is the return generated concerning the total assets in the firm and an indicator of how efficiently the company is using its assets. ROCE is a measure for comparing companies in capital-intensive industries (with a lot of debt), as it indicates how well a company is using its overall available capital. The definitions used for the three dependent variables are as follows:

$$\text{ROE} = [\text{Net Income} + \text{Taxes}]/[\text{Average Stockholders' Equity}] \qquad (1)$$

$$\text{ROA} = [\text{Net Income} + \text{Taxes}]/[\text{Average Total Assets}] \qquad (2)$$

$$\text{ROCE} = [\text{Net Income} + \text{Taxes}]/([\text{Average Total Assets}]-[\text{Current liabilities}]) \qquad (3)$$

The independent variables were selected in such a way that they include both firm-specific and industry-specific determinants. The variables were selected based on earlier choices made in the previous literature. The "net income" used as a control variable includes the effect of taxes (net of tax) in order to eliminate company-specific efforts to minimize taxes. The firm variables were retrieved from the Amadeus database and the industry variables from selected databases (see Table 3). The annual average Feed-in-Tariff rates for solar-, biomass-, geothermal-, wind-, and hydro-energy are studied for the effect on profitability for each one of the studied years.

Table 3. Selected independent variables, their specifications, and the source of data. Explanations: * Annual percentage growth rate of GDP per capita in €. GDP per capita is the gross domestic product divided by midyear population. ** Market share of the largest generator in the electricity market. *** (Share of renewable energy sources in gross power consumption).

Original Variable	Specification	Analyzed Variable	Source
Company Variables			
Net Income inc. taxes	Sales − costs general expenses and interest + taxes, in thousands €	Net Income	Amadeus
Total Assets	$LOG\_Assets = LOG(TotalAssets)$	Company Size (assets)	Amadeus
Total Assets	$Assets\_G = \frac{TotalAssets_t - TotalAssets_{t-1}}{TotalAssets_t} \times 100$	Growth in Assets	Amadeus
Sales	$Sales\_G = \frac{Sales_t - Sales_{t-1}}{Sales_t} \times 100$	Growth in Sales	Amadeus
Sales	$LOG_{Sales} = LOG(Sales)$	Company Size (sales)	Amadeus
Debt	$D\_E = \frac{Debt_t}{Shareholder\,funds_t}$	Leverage (Debt/Equity)	Amadeus
Debt	$D\_A = \frac{Debt_t}{TotalAssets_t}$	Leverage (Debt/Assets)	Amadeus
Current ratio	$CurrentRatio = \frac{Current\,Assets_t}{Current\,Liabilities_t}$	Liquidity	Amadeus
Industry Variables			
Average annual power price for households	Elecprice h (€/kWh taxes and renewable levies included)	Price level	Eurostat
Annual final electricity consumption	$ElecCons\_G = \frac{ElecCons_t - ElecCons_{t-1}}{ElecCons_{t-1}} \times 100$ (GWh)	Change of annual final electricity consumption	Eurostat
Economic growth (GDP per capita) *	$GDPG = \frac{GDPG_t - GDPG_{t-1}}{GDPG_{t-1}} \times 100$	Economic Growth	World Bank
Market concentration (annual) **	$Marketconcentration\_G = \frac{Marketconcentration_t - Marketconcentration_{t-1}}{Marketconcentration_{t-1}} \times 100$	Industry/Market concentration	Eurostat
Share of renewables ***	$Elecshare_G = \frac{Elecshare_t - Elecshare_{t-1}}{Elecshare_{t-1}} \times 100$	Industry growth	UBA Arbeitsgruppe Eneurbare Energien-Statistik (AGEE-Stat)
Average annual Feed-in-Tariff per renewable energy source	FITavg (Average annual FIT for all renewable energy sources)	Level of RE incentive	OECD Statistics OECD.stat

Two of the independent variables, [TotalAssets] and [Sales], were log-transformed to make them approximately follow the normal distribution required in the statistical analysis. From the industry-specific determinants, the "change from the previous year's share of RE in electricity consumption" was chosen as a proxy for industry growth. Market concentration was also added as a growth rate, "a percentage increase from the previous year's share of the largest electricity generator in the industry". We found it important to study the separate effects of the company's size in terms of assets and in terms of sales, as well as the growth in sales and assets, as these variables have different implications.

As it is not possible to acquire the amount of FIT-support received by individual companies from public databases, an attempt was made to include them in the quantitative analysis model and to test whether they (partially) explain the variance. The average FIT used in the analysis is an aggregate mean of the average annual FIT received by all the RE sectors.

The selected variables that had a significant correlation with some another independent variable were removed and only one variable from such a pair was kept in the analysis. For the purposes of this research, the variables with a significant correlation larger or equal to ±0.6 to another independent variable were removed from the analysis. More specifically, in the SME data, a strong and statistically significant (5% level) positive correlation of 0.89 between the leverage variables D/A and D/E was found, thus D/E was excluded from the analysis of the SMEs. A strong negative and statistically significant correlation (−0.64) between the Electricity price (Elecpriceh) and the growth rate of the Share of Renewables in Electricity consumption (Elecreshare_G) was found. Electricity price also correlates strongly with the growth rate of Electricity consumption (ElecCons_G) (−0.62) and the annual average Feed-in Tariff price (Fitavg) (−0.77); thus, the variable Electricity price was removed from the analysis in both data sets.

2.2. Method

The collected data included both a time-series dimension and a cross-sectional dimension, and were thereby transformed into panel-data form. Each firm is observed repeatedly in the vertical dimension with a length of (the number of individuals), I × (the number of periods), T, and the dependent and independent variables K are presented in the horizontal dimension. The overall size of the matrix equals I × T × K observations.

What is typical to panel data and distinguishes them from simple time-series regression is the presence of unobserved heterogeneity that is due to the cross-sectional dimension. Unobserved heterogeneity is the time persistent differences between the individual studied units also called "individual effects" that cannot be estimated with the simple pooled (OLS) regression [38]. When heterogeneity is present in the data, which is typically the case, a model able to take it into account should be used. For this reason, fixed effects and random effects -models that can handle longitudinal and heterogeneous data are used in this research. The fixed effects (FE) or "within"-estimator used has the following form:

$$Y_{it} = \beta_0 + \sum_{k=1}^{K} \beta_k \times X_{it}^k + e_{it} + a_i \qquad (4)$$

The within-estimator models the time-invariant heterogeneity in the unknown parameter a_i. The data are transformed by time demeaning all the variables, a.k.a. subtracting the variables' individual means over time from all the variables. The result is a formulation in terms of deviations from the individual means. The a_i term, as well as the constant β_0 (see, Equation (4)) that is simply the individual mean, and all the time-invariant independent variables cancel out in this calculation. This eliminates the problem of individual effects, hence it is said to be "fixed" [38].

The coefficients of the FE model can be interpreted as the effect that the unit of change from the individual mean of the respective independent variable has on the same individual's dependent variable from its mean. The main downside of the FE estimators is that one cannot include time-invariant independent variables since they would be canceled out in the model estimation. This simplifies the estimation process but fails to account for the time-invariant variables although they could potentially be significant in determining the values of the dependent variable. To deal with the possible handicaps of the FE in the context of the studied data, a random-effects (RE) model is also applied.

In the random-effects model (RE), the individual differences are allowed and the variation between the individuals is assumed to be random and uncorrelated with the independent variables. The random individual effects are modeled as the error term u_i. The RE-effects model used is defined as follows:

$$Y_{it} = \beta_0 + \sum_{k=1}^{K} \beta_k \times X_{it}^k + e_{it} + u_i \tag{5}$$

In Equation (5), the intercept corresponds to the mean of the unobserved heterogeneity and the error term u_i is the random time-invariant heterogeneity specific to the individual unit. In the random-effects model, the generalized least squares (GLS) estimator is used. The data are "quasi time-demeaned", which means that a part of the within-individual variation is taken out. For a more comprehensive introduction to the Random Effects model, see [39].

The application of fixed-effects and random-effects models was considered to be sufficient for the purposes of this research in terms of the reliability of the results. We point out that the use of more advanced methods, such as the generalized method of moments (GMM), which control for the violations of the random-effects model and the possible endogeneity problems in the data may reveal deeper and better results from the same data. The use of more advanced methods is left as a topic for future research.

3. Results

Both Fixed- and Random-Effects models are used to obtain results for both company-size cohorts. The results for both the FE and RE analysis are listed in the Appendix A (Tables A1 and A2). To find out whether the RE model provides new information in addition to the results from the FE estimation, the Hausman test, which tests the presence of individual effects by comparing the FE and RE models' coefficients, was performed. If there are no significant differences, the individual effects are random and thus either of the estimators can be used [40]. The alternate hypothesis (p-value < 0.05) is that the FE and RE coefficients are different from each other and in such a case, only the FE estimator is consistent.

Tests on heteroskedasticity and autocorrelation indicate that they were present regularly. Arellano's (1987) [41] and White's heteroskedasticity robust standard errors [42] are used in the analysis when heteroskedasticity is present (see Tables A1 and A2).

3.1. Results for the SME Cohort

The results for the SME cohort are presented in Table 4. The results from the Hausman test (at the 5% significance level) imply that individual effects are present in the data and that the FE estimator should be used.

The company determinants appear significant mostly when profitability is measured with ROA and ROCE. Net income (Netincome), controlling for the nominator in the profitability ratios, is significant and positive in all six tests, with a small effect on profitability as expected (around 0.055, see Table A1). Company size in sales (LOG_Sales) is statistically significant and positive in three out of six of the tests, with a larger effect on profitability when measured with ROA and ROCE (3.890, 8.081, 6.959) but the effect is non-significant on ROE. Size in Assets (LOG_Assets) is statistically significant only at the 10% level in one of the tests (3.658). Liquidity (CurrentRatio) is significant at the 10% level in three of the tests and positive with a small effect on ROA and ROCE (0.649, 0.580, 0.574) and Leverage (D_A) is significant at the 5% level once with a large negative effect on ROCE (−4.131). Growth in sales (Sales_G) is significant at the 10% level with a positive effect on ROA (0.013). Growth in assets (Assets_G) is not significant in any of the tests (see Table A1).

Table 4. Summary of FE model results for both the SMEs and large firms. Legend: +: positive relationship; −: negative relationship, ***: significance level 1%; **: significance level 5%, *: significance level 10%, Ns: not significant.

Determinant's Effect from Previous Studies	SMEs		Large Firms	
	Effect	Occurrence n/6 Number of Tests	Effect	Occurrence n (Number of Tests)
Net Income	+	6/6 ***	+	6/6 ***
Size (sales) +	+	3/6 **	+	6/6 **
Size (assets) +	+	1/6 *	−	6/6 **
Liquidity +	+	3/6 *	−	1/6 **
Leverage −	−	1/6 **	+	1/6 **
Growth in sales +	+	1/6 *		Not included
Growth in assets +	Ns	Ns	+	1/6 *
Change in the Electricity Consumption −	−	5/6 ***	−	3/6 **
Change in the share of RE in overall electricity consumption (industry growth) +	+	3/6 ***	+	3/6 **
Change in the Market Concentration +	+	5/6 ***	+	1/6 **
FIT average +	−	5/6 ***	−	3/6 **
GDP +	+	1/6 **	Ns	Ns
Electricity Price −		Not included		Not included

Among the industry determinants, the variables proxying for the industry growth are significant at the 5% level. These include Change in the Electricity Consumption (ElecCons_G) with a moderate (−1.343, −0.607, −0.398, −0.646, −0.486) negative effect in five out of the six tests and Change in the share of RE in the overall electricity consumption (Elecreshare_G) in three out of the six tests, with a smaller positive effect (0.316, 0.081, 0.114) on profitability. The change in the market concentration a.k.a. the market share of the largest generator in the market (Marketconcentration_G) is significant at the 5% level in five out of the six tests, with a small or moderate positive effect (0.438, 0.343, 0.122, 0.178, 0.061). The GDP growth rate (GDPG) is once significant at the 5% level with a positive (0.146) effect on ROA. The annual average Feed-in Tariffs across the RE sectors is significant at the 5% level in five out of the six tests with a very large negative effect on profitability (−162.8, −110.8, −46.6, −30.4, −52.5) (see Table A1).

This significant and large effect is explained by the unlikeliness of the one unit rise in the independent variable as the average FIT range in these data is from 0.11 to 0.19.

3.2. Results for the Large Firm Cohort

When analysis is repeated with the large firm cohort, the Hausman test again indicates that the FE estimator should be used with all the dependent variables (see Table A2). The results for the large companies are summarized in Table 4.

Of the company determinants, Net income is significant at the 5% level in all six tests, with a similar small positive effect (0.011, 0.010, 0.002, 0.003) as with the SME cohort. Company size in sales (LOG_Sales) is statistically significant at the 5% level and positive in all tests with a larger effect on profitability ratios (12.4, 14.5, 2.7, 2.6). Size in Assets (LOG_Assets) is statistically significant at the 5% level in all six tests, as well as showing a larger negative effect on profitability (−16.7, −21.3, −5.04, −4.6, −5.8, −7.1). Liquidity (CurrentRatio) is once significant at the 5% with a larger negative effect (−3.225) on ROE. Leverage measured with Debt to Assets (D_A) is significant at the 5% level once with a large positive effect on ROCE (7.113). Growth in sales (Sales_G) is not included in the analysis due to the very low observation count in the large firm cohort (n = 249) Growth in assets (Assets_G) is significant once at the 10% level with a small positive effect (0.04) on ROA (see Table A2).

Among the industry determinants, the Change in the Electricity Consumption (ElecCons_G) is significant at the 5% level in three out of the six tests, with a large or moderate (−2.6, −0.735, −0.901) negative effect. The Change in the share of RE in the overall electricity consumption (Elecreshare_G) is significant at the 5% level in three out of the six tests, with a smaller positive effect (0.457, 0.112, 0.108) on profitability. The change in the market concentration (Marketconcentration_G) is significant at the 5% level once with a moderate positive effect (0.643) on ROE. The GDP growth rate (GDPG) is not significant in any of the tests. The annual average FIT is significant at the 5% level in three out of the six tests, again with a very large negative effect (−289.3, −87.5, −91.1). The industry determinants' effects are not significant in the tests of the model where both firm and industry determinants are included (see Table A2).

3.3. Testing the Hypotheses

According to the analysis results, specifically based on the results from the Fixed Effects model, there is clear evidence to support Hypothesis 1 "*The model with industry-specific determinants and the model with firm-specific determinants are both significant when 5% significance level is adopted in the statistical testing*". In both company-size cohorts, all the models are statistically significant.

When it comes to Hypothesis 2 "*The explanatory power of the included firm-specific determinants is higher than that of the included industry-specific determinants*", the explanatory power for the models with firm-specific determinants for SMEs and Large firms respectively are 0.74/0.76 (ROE), 0.77/0.91 (ROA) and 0.72/0.88 (ROCE), while the R^2 for the industry-specific determinants are 0.149/0.23 (ROE), 0.177/0.33 (ROA), and 0.155/0.28 (ROCE). This result means that Hypothesis 2 can be accepted. The models that combine both determinants have the explanatory power of 0.762/0.78 (ROE), 0.796/0.91 (ROA), and 0.74/0.89 (ROCE) (Appendices A and B).

The analysis results of the firm-specific determinants imply that the size in terms of assets matters when a company is large and that the size in assets has a negative effect on the profitability of large firms. Net income and Log of sales appear to have a consistent and significant positive effect on profitability ratios with both firm cohorts, based on the analysis (see Table 4).

Leverage or liquidity did not appear to be consistently significant for neither size-group. When Debt to Assets (D_A) was significant, it was negative for the SMEs and positive for the large firms. Growth in Assets or Sales was not consistently, or at all, significant with either of the cohorts, indicating that the firm-specific determinants related to size and net income, as well as, the ones related to liquidity and leverage, together explain most of the variance in the profitability ratios.

In the analysis of the industry-specific determinants, the growth from the previous year in the share of renewables in electricity consumption appeared to have a significant positive effect on the profitability ratios. The change from the previous year's market concentration had a significant and positive effect on profitability more or less consistently with the SMEs. The change from the previous year's electricity consumption had a significant negative effect on profitability ratios, without exception, in both samples. However, in the sample of large firms, these effects disappeared, when both the firm-specific and industry-specific determinants were included in the FE model. This finding also supports the second hypothesis with regards to the explanatory power of the firm-specific determinants being remarkably higher than that of the industry-level determinants.

Based on the analysis, there was no support for Hypothesis 3: "*The average annual Feed in Tariff (FIT) has a significant positive effect on the RE companies' profitability*". The annual average FIT does seem to have a statistically significant effect on profitability, but the effect is opposite to what was expected. The variable had a negative effect on profitability with both firm size categories in eight tests out of the total twelve. However, the share of FIT-supported firms in the data was unknown in the analysis done in this research and the negative effect could be on the firms that were not receiving any FIT at the time of the analysis.

4. Discussion

It can be observed that the results are generally in line with the results obtained in previous studies of a similar type (see Tables 1 and 4). This study extends the research to cover the unlisted German companies that have, to the best of our knowledge so far been left "unattended" by previous research. The results presented here widen the scope of knowledge we have about the factors that affect the profitability of companies operating within the German RE industry. In this respect, the finding is that the unlisted companies do not differ from the previously studied companies listed.

Based on the results, it is clear that the firm-specific determinants outrank the industry-specific counterparts in importance, as was also suggested by the previous studies. One of the findings is that company size in terms of assets matters when the firm is large and that the size in assets has a negative effect on the profitability of large firms. The size of assets is not significant with regard to the profitability of the SMEs. This result is supported by previous research [23] that suggested that the rapid expansion of firms may have a negative influence on profitability, implying that large firms may follow costly strategies to gain a bigger share of the markets. One explanation could be that in an investment phase (which is ongoing on the German RE markets), there are profitability lags. The capital investment intensity (data which was not available for this analysis) is also proven to be a determinant of profitability and could explain the negative effect of the assets in case the effect of the capital investment intensity is significantly negative for larger firms, as was pointed out by the previous research.

The positive relationship between the liquidity and profitability of the SMEs may be an implication of the power of slack income that the firms can invest to generate profit. Then again, leveraging profit might be the chosen strategy for large firms that have the position to take more risks. Nonetheless, too many and/or far-fetching conclusions should not be drawn about the determinants that appeared significant less consistently in the analysis.

The average Feed-in-Tariff had a negative effect in most of the tests with the SMEs and in three tests with large firms. These findings are not in line with the previous results [27,31] and our expectations. The previous analyses found that the FIT has a positive effect on the profitability of electricity firms, but the data used were from the companies that in fact received support from the FIT. The share of FIT-supported firms in the data used in this study is unknown to us. Thus, the negative effect result may be caused by the effect of FIT on firms that did not receive FIT-support and were affected negatively by the support their competitors received. The authors conclude that the counter-intuitive result can also be a consequence of the aggregation method used in treating the variable and the reader is suggested to take the result as preliminary.

The change in electricity consumption had a negative effect on profitability, as suggested by previous studies (in past studies energy consumption was analyzed, instead of electricity consumption). This result may reflect the increasing competition in the industry, as the demand has only increased during the period of the analysis in terms of the final electricity consumption in the country. Furthermore, the trend of the market concentration growth rate in the data of this analysis shows that the competition is intensifying in the industry structure, and this seems to especially benefit especially the SMEs according to the analysis. Moreover, the share of renewables seemed to be beneficial for both the SMEs and large companies.

5. Conclusions

The objective of this study was to examine the profitability determinants of unlisted German renewable energy firms that produce electricity. The models with firm-specific determinants had a higher explanatory power than models with the industry-specific determinants only. The results are mostly in line with results from previous similar studies. German private RE companies during a period of active remuneration have not been studied before from the same perspective and the results should be useful in understanding what determines the profitability of these companies. The results are usable in forecasting the same also in other countries that have applied Feed-in-Tariff-based support to boost the production of renewable electricity. Furthermore, a separate analysis was conducted for the SMEs and Large companies which offers insight into the differences between these size cohorts.

The results of the study are of use to managers of the RE companies when the effects of different industry environments and states of business life cycle are considered, as the authors found that the smaller and medium sized companies in terms of returns on total assets might be more affected by market concentration. Moreover, the result implying that the larger companies are negatively affected by size, and that the effect is the opposite with smaller companies, is of interest to managers and investors alike. For German policy-makers, the results mean that within the scope of this research, no remarkable difference between listed and unlisted companies was uncovered in terms of the determinants that drive profitability. This information is important from the (rate-of-return) regulation point of view as it means the same regulation model can be used for both company types, from the point of view of this context.

One of the limitations of the analysis was the quality of data, as the number of observations was limited. This was especially true for the data on large companies. The analysis did not include the largest companies on the market as they were few in number (nine out of 733 companies). In addition, according to the names and descriptions of the companies, the data did not include any companies producing energy from geothermal sources. The sample sizes differed depending on the model, as typically is the case with unbalanced panel data.

There are certainly many other determinants—not addressed in this paper—that could explain firm profitability, such as managerial capabilities, other management-related variables, and investment intensity. As a topic of future research, the corporate-parent and dynamic effects and the more technical variates related to the capacity of the power facility, etc., could be added to the analysis if relevant data become available. The analysis conducted in this paper could not distinguish the firms that benefited or suffered from the FIT support, hence, the observed negative effect of the average FIT, calculated with the annual FIT level of all the RE sectors, is somewhat debatable. This is another topic for further research and for repetitive studies to understand the reasons behind these differences. Possible methodological additions and avenues for further study would be opened by using a correlated random effects model, which can provide an option for estimating the random effects model even if the assumptions of the random effects model do not hold (see, e.g., [40,43,44]) and by using the generalized method of moments, which would provide yet another methodological perspective to the study.

Author Contributions: Conceptualization, M.-K.L. and J.S.; methodology, M.-K.L.; validation, M.-K.L. and J.S.; formal analysis, M.-K.L.; investigation, M.-K.L.; writing—original draft preparation, J.S.; writing—review and editing, M.C.; visualization, M.-K.L.; supervision, M.C.; project administration, J.S.; funding acquisition, M.C. All authors have read and agreed to the published version of the manuscript.

Funding: This research has received support from the Finnish Strategic Research Council (SRC) at the Academy of Finland through the Manufacturing 4.0-project, grant #335980 and # 335990.

Institutional Review Board Statement: Not applicable.

Informed Consent Statement: Not applicable.

Data Availability Statement: The data presented in this study are available on request from the corresponding author.

Conflicts of Interest: The authors declare no conflict of interest.

Appendix A. Panel Data Model Results for German RE-Companies Fitted in This Study

Table A1. Panel Data Fixed Effects models for the SMEs.

	ROE			ROA			ROCE		
	(FE Firm)	(FE Ind)	(FE Both)	(FE Firm)	(FE Ind)	(FE Both)	(FE Firm)	(FE Ind)	(FE Both)
CurrentRatio	1.573 (1.647)		1.434 (1.771)	0.649 * (0.335)		0.580 * (0.301)	0.574 * (0.328)		0.500 (0.476)
Netincome	0.055 *** (0.012)		0.053 *** (0.011)	0.008 *** (0.002)		0.008 *** (0.002)	0.004 *** (0.001)		0.004 *** (0.001)
D_A	13.329 (26.528)		24.475 (27.102)	−4.752 * (2.556)		−3.137 (2.621)	−4.131 ** (2.206)		−2.528 (2.986)
LOG_Sales	8.878 (9.380)		4.909 (9.437)	3.890 ** (1.604)		2.788 (1.753)	8.081 *** (1.478)		6.959 *** (2.067)
LOG_Assets	−5.590 (8.279)		7.736 (13.782)	−0.739 (0.710)		3.658 * (2.004)	−0.882 (0.572)		3.494 (2.456)
Assets_G	0.146 (0.279)		0.037 (0.310)	0.023 (0.022)		−0.008 (0.028)	0.044 (0.028)		0.012 (0.031)
Sales_G	0.013 (0.038)		0.027 (0.046)	0.007 (0.006)		0.013 * (0.007)	0.010 (0.006)		0.015 (0.009)
Elecreshare_G		0.316 *** (0.074)	0.052 (0.072)		0.081 *** (0.016)	0.004 (0.013)		0.114 *** (0.020)	0.020 (0.012)
Marketconcentration_G		0.438 *** (0.136)	0.232 ** (0.105)		0.122 *** (0.031)	0.048 * (0.026)		0.178 *** (0.043)	0.061 ** (0.030)
GDPG		0.025 (0.443)	0.317 (0.356)		0.188 * (0.103)	0.146 ** (0.068)		0.088 (0.141)	0.144 * (0.085)
ElecCons_G		−1.343 *** (0.516)	−0.851 (0.881)		−0.607 *** (0.117)	−0.398 ** (0.191)		−0.646 *** (0.153)	−0.486 ** (0.236)
Fitavg		−162.755 *** (23.972)	−110.755 *** (50.823)		−46.639 *** (5.296)	−30.410 ** (14.077)		−54.524 *** (7.565)	−31.859 * (17.270)
Observations	222	746	222	264	936	264	261	860	261
Hausman (p)	0.0329		0.0026	0.0028		0.0026			
Heteroskedasticity (p)	1.443×10^{-12}	1.488×10^{-12}	3.559×10^{-9}	1.19×10^{-7}	$<2.2 \times 10^{-16}$	4.027×10^{-7}	8.969×10^{-6}	$<2.2 \times 10^{-16}$	1.466×10^{-6}
Autocorrelation (p)	1.435×10^{-5}	0.6913	0.0001	0.0596	0.1647	0.01	0.3852	0.6848	$<2.2 \times 10^{-16}$
R^2		1.779×10^{-5}			0.0733		5.013×10^{-13}	0.0366	0.0589
	0.742	0.149	0.762	0.777	0.177	0.796	0.720	0.155	0.740
F Statistic	55.067 *** (df = 7; 134)	17.901 *** (df = 5; 511)	34.490 *** (df = 12; 129)	83.173 *** (df = 7; 167)	28.388 *** (df = 5; 659)	52.554 *** (df = 12; 162)	60.122 *** (df = 7; 164)	21.834 *** (df = 5; 594)	37.702 *** (df = 12; 159)

Note: Robust SEs used; * $p < 0.1$; ** $p < 0.05$; *** $p < 0.01$.

Table A2. Panel Data Fixed Effects models for the Large firms.

	ROE				ROA			ROCE	
	(FE firm)	(FE Ind)	(FE Both)	(FE Firm)	(FE Ind)	(FE Both)	(FE Firm)	(FE Ind)	(FE Both)
CurrentRatio	−3.245 ** (1.513)		−2.850 (1.954)	0.012 (0.128)		−0.084 (0.159)	−0.293 * (0.175)		−0.409 (0.258)
Netincome	0.011 *** (0.003)		0.010 *** (0.003)	0.002 *** (0.0003)		0.002 *** (0.0003)	0.003 *** (0.0003)		0.002 *** (0.0004)
D_A	10.485 (21.431)		8.289 (25.071)	−0.357 (3.022)		0.137 (2.766)	7.113 ** (3.435)		3.943 (8.211)
D_E	1.700 (1.660)		1.571 (1.346)	−0.075 (0.202)		−0.098 (0.193)	−0.196 (0.204)		−0.151 (0.306)
LOG_Sales	12.386 *** (4.174)		14.502 ** (5.786)	2.677 *** (0.555)		2.584 *** (0.698)	2.458 *** (0.821)		2.864 ** (1.216)
LOG_Assets	−16.704 ** (7.425)		−21.314 ** (10.662)	−5.041 *** (0.762)		−4.576 *** (0.956)	−5.819 *** (1.100)		−7.060 ** (3.046)
Assets_G	0.191 (0.156)		0.158 (0.154)	0.040 * (0.023)		0.035 (0.024)	0.040 (0.025)		0.041 (0.030)
Elecreshare_G		0.457 *** (0.144)	0.012 (0.122)		0.112 *** (0.034)	−0.011 (0.020)		0.108 *** (0.039)	−0.009 (0.022)
Marketconcentration_G		0.643 ** (0.270)	−0.135 (0.178)		0.116 * (0.067)	−0.037 (0.030)		0.136 * (0.079)	−0.059 (0.045)
GDPG		−0.767 (0.834)	0.570 (0.710)		−0.301 (0.195)	−0.065 (0.158)		−0.190 (0.184)	−0.152 (0.148)
ElecCons_G		−2.550 *** (0.847)	0.225 (0.590)		−0.735 *** (0.210)	0.094 (0.115)		−0.901 *** (0.242)	0.283 (0.377)
Fitavg		−289.273 *** (46.056)	36.929 (43.354)		−87.543 *** (5.805)	−3.499 (5.822)		−91.133 *** (13.324)	11.606 (22.618)
Observations	115	359	115	111	391	111	118	415	118
Hausman (p)	0.0031	1.185×10^{-8}	4.26×10^{-5}	5.701×10^{-8}	1.071×10^{-6}	0.0002	6.072×10^{-6}	2.44×10^{-5}	2.235×10^{-8}
Heteroskedasticity (p)	6.186×10^{-14}	0.0401	6.286×10^{-13}	0.2226	0.0851	0.0018	0.0292	0.6794	0.4192
Autocorrelation (p)	0.0186	0.5085	0.0452	2.878×10^{-7}	0.5979	4.194×10^{-7}	7.336×10^{-7}	0.972	1.024×10^{-5}
R^2	0.758	0.232	0.775	0.912	0.326	0.918	0.882	0.275	0.893
F Statistic	25.897 *** (df = 7; 58)	14.707 *** (df = 5; 243)	15.237 *** (df = 12; 53)	84.815 *** (df = 7; 57)	26.662 *** (df = 5; 276)	48.709 *** (df = 12; 52)	63.899 *** (df = 7; 60)	21.451 *** (df = 5; 283)	38.182 *** (df = 12; 55)

Note: Robust SEs used; * $p < 0.1$; ** $p < 0.05$; *** $p < 0.01$.

Appendix B. Descriptive Statistics for Both Cohorts

Table A3. Descriptive statistics for the SMEs.

Statistic	N	Mean	St. Dev.	Min	Pctl (25)	Pctl (75)	Max
CurrentRatio	1062	1.320	0.813	0.000	0.702	1.869	3.608
Netincome	910	43.514	139.702	−290.132	−39.599	130.055	385.324
D_A	1523	0.833	0.153	0.418	0.737	0.951	1.270
D_E	1315	2.837	2.349	−3.287	1.157	4.247	8.877
LOG_Sales	694	7.004	0.652	5.445	6.639	7.442	8.556
LOG_Assets	1634	8.827	0.815	6.488	8.278	9.473	10.873
Assets_G	1092	−5.954	3.727	−14.918	−8.180	−3.608	3.256
Sales_G	488	1.780	13.179	−35.871	−8.158	11.301	40.249
Elecreshare_G	2696	10.672	6.054	0.317	6.356	15.022	20.000
Marketconcentration_G	2696	−1.391	5.278	−9.375	−5.057	1.490	6.338
GDPG	3033	2.085	1.273	0.418	1.268	2.602	4.180
ElecCons_G	2696	0.035	1.419	−2.165	−0.540	0.480	3.032
Fitavg	3033	0.154	0.029	0.115	0.126	0.176	0.193
Elecpriceh	3033	0.283	0.022	0.241	0.264	0.298	0.305
Elecpriceh_G	2696	2.832	3.728	−1.788	0.380	4.421	10.795
ROE	877	7.384	16.862	−37.857	−2.087	15.638	57.278
ROA	957	1.039	2.797	−6.129	−0.757	2.853	8.237
ROCE	879	3.948	3.433	−4.724	1.685	6.082	12.647

Table 4. Descriptive statistics for large firms.

Statistic	N	Mean	St. Dev.	Min	Pctl (25)	Pctl (75)	Max
CurrentRatio	1070	1.263	0.886	0.000	0.539	1.767	3.889
Netincome	416	536.546	870.148	−1715.000	−44091	1034.094	2780.630
D_A	1315	0.852	0.148	0.429	0.760	0.973	1.288
D_E	1136	3.051	2.938	−5.431	0.792	4.712	11.245
LOG Sales	404	8.543	0.901	6.231	8.028	9.216	10.993
LOG Assets	1215	10.381	0.440	9.246	10.135	10.663	11.521
Assets_G	878	−5.162	4.447	−16.586	−7.534	−3.282	7.458
Sales_G	249	2.116	12.840	−29.960	−6.934	11.510	36.213
Elecreshare_G	3208	10.672	6.053	0.317	6.356	15.022	20.000
Marketconcentration_G	3208	−1.391	5.278	−9.375	−5.057	1.490	6.338
GDPG	3609	2.085	1.273	0.418	1.268	2.602	4.180
ElecCons_G	3208	0.035	1.419	−2.165	−0.540	0.480	3.032
Fitavg	3609	0.154	0.029	0.115	0.126	0.176	0.193
Elecpriceh	3609	0.283	0.022	0.241	0.264	0.298	0.305
Elecpriceh_G	3208	2.832	3.728	−1.788	0.380	4.421	10.795
ROE	1048	7.704	16.897	−37.857	−1.915	16.088	57.278
ROA	394	2.259	3.507	−6.645	−0.119	4.274	11.106
ROCE	424	4.754	3.985	−5.799	1.854	7.074	15.057

References

1. Wehrmann, B. Germany's Climate Action Programme 2030. 2019. Available online: https://www.cleanenergywire.org/factsheets/germanys-climate-action-programme-2030 (accessed on 15 September 2021).
2. Irena Wind Energy. 2020. Available online: https://irena.org/wind (accessed on 2 August 2021).
3. Lebas, M.; Euske, K. *A Conceptual and Operational Delineation of Performance*; Cambridge University Press: Cambridge, UK, 2007; pp. 125–140. [CrossRef]
4. Chakravarthy, B.S. Measuring Strategic Performance. *Strateg. Manag. J.* **1986**, *7*, 437–458. [CrossRef]
5. Santos, J.B.; Brito, L.A.L. Toward a subjective measurement model for firm performance. *BAR Braz. Adm. Rev.* **2012**, *9*, 95–117. [CrossRef]
6. Wilke, S. Indicator: Greenhouse Gas Emissions. 2017. Available online: https://www.umweltbundesamt.de/en/data/environmental-indicators/indicator-greenhouse-gas-emissions (accessed on 2 August 2021).
7. German Environment Agency. *National Inventory Reports for the German Greenhouse Gas Inventory 1990 to 2019 and Previous Year Estimate for 2020*; German Environment Agency: Dessau-Roßlau, Germany, 2021.

8. IEA 2017 Amendment of the Renewable Energy Sources Act (EEG 2017). 2016. Available online: https://www.iea.org/policies/6125-2017-amendment-of-the-renewable-energy-sources-act-eeg-2017?q=EEG%202017 (accessed on 2 August 2021).
9. Wehrmann, B.; Appunn, K. Germany 2021: When Fixed Feed-In Tariffs End, How Will Renewables Fare? *Energypost.eu* 2019. Available online: https://energypost.eu/germany-2021-when-fixed-feed-in-tariffs-end-how-will-renewables-fare/ (accessed on 2 August 2021).
10. Eurostat Renewable Energy Statistics. 2021. Available online: https://ec.europa.eu/eurostat/statistics-explained/index.php?title=Renewable_energy_statistics (accessed on 1 September 2021).
11. Reuters. *Renewables Meet 46.3% of Germany's 2020 Power Consumption, up 3.8 pts*; Reuters: London, UK, 2020.
12. Gesley, J. Germany: Law on Phasing-Out Coal-Powered Energy by 2038 Enters into Force | Global Legal Monitor. 2020. Available online: https://www.loc.gov/law/foreign-news/article/germany-law-on-phasing-out-coal-powered-energy-by-2038-enters-into-force/ (accessed on 1 September 2021).
13. Appunn, K. The History Behind Germany's Nuclear Phase-Out. 2021. Available online: https://www.cleanenergywire.org/factsheets/history-behind-germanys-nuclear-phase-out (accessed on 2 September 2021).
14. IEA Electricity Feed-In Law of 1991 ("Stromeinspeisungsgesetz")—Policies. 2013. Available online: https://www.iea.org/policies/3477-electricity-feed-in-law-of-1991-stromeinspeisungsgesetz (accessed on 2 September 2021).
15. IEA Renewable Energy Sources Act (Erneuerbare-Energien-Gesetz EEG). 2014. Available online: https://www.iea.org/policies/3858-renewable-energy-sources-act-erneuerbare-energien-gesetz-eeg (accessed on 2 September 2021).
16. Wettengel, J. Germany's Carbon Pricing System for Transport and Buildings. 2019. Available online: https://www.cleanenergywire.org/factsheets/germanys-planned-carbon-pricing-system-transport-and-buildings (accessed on 2 September 2021).
17. Wettengel, J. Germany Debates Future of Renewables Support. 2021. Available online: https://www.cleanenergywire.org/news/germany-debates-future-renewables-support (accessed on 2 September 2021).
18. Bain, J.S. Relation of Profit Rate to Industry Concentration: American Manufacturing, 1936–1940. *Q. J. Econ.* **1951**, *65*, 293–324. [CrossRef]
19. Porter, M.E. Industry Structure and Competitive Strategy: Keys to Profitability. *Financ. Anal. J.* **1980**, *36*, 30–41. [CrossRef]
20. Bass, F.M.; Cattin, P.; Wittink, D.R. Firm Effects and Industry Effects in the Analysis of Market Structure and Profitability. *J. Mark. Res.* **1978**, *15*, 3–10. [CrossRef]
21. McGahan, A.M.; Porter, M.E. How Much Does Industry Matter, Really? *Strateg. Manag. J.* **1997**, *18*, 15–30. [CrossRef]
22. Capon, N.; Farley, J.U.; Hoenig, S. Determinants of Financial Performance: A Meta-Analysis. *Manage. Sci.* **1990**, *36*, 1143–1159. [CrossRef]
23. Goddard, J.; Tavakoli, M.; Wilson, J.O.S. Determinants of profitability in European manufacturing and services: Evidence from a dynamic panel model. *Appl. Financ. Econ.* **2005**, *15*, 1269–1282. [CrossRef]
24. Asimakopoulos, I.; Samitas, A.; Papadogonas, T. Firm-specific and economy wide determinants of firm profitability: Greek evidence using panel data. *Manag. Financ.* **2009**, *35*, 930–939. [CrossRef]
25. Adner, R.; Helfat, C.E. Corporate effects and dynamic managerial capabilities. *Strateg. Manag. J. Strat.* **2003**, *24*, 1011–1025. [CrossRef]
26. Westerman, W.; De Ridder, A.; Achtereekte, M. Firm performance and diversification in the energy sector. *Manag. Financ.* **2020**, *46*, 1373–1390. [CrossRef]
27. Jaraitė, J.; Kažukauskas, A. The profitability of electricity generating firms and policies promoting renewable energy. *Energy Econ.* **2013**, *40*, 858–865. [CrossRef]
28. Tsai, Y.; Tung, J. The Factors Affect Company Performance in Renewable Energy Industry. *Int. J. Innov. Educ. Res.* **2017**, *5*, 188–204. [CrossRef]
29. Gupta, K. Do economic and societal factors influence the financial performance of alternative energy firms? *Energy Econ.* **2017**, *65*, 172–182. [CrossRef]
30. Shah, I.H.; Hiles, C.; Morley, B. How do oil prices, macroeconomic factors and policies affect the market for renewable energy? *Appl. Energy* **2018**, *215*, 87–97. [CrossRef]
31. Hassan, A. Do renewable energy incentive policies improve the performance of energy firms? Evidence from OECD countries. *OPEC Energy Rev.* **2019**, *43*, 168–192. [CrossRef]
32. Milanés-Montero, P.; Arroyo-Farrona, A.; Pérez-Calderón, E. Assessment of the Influence of Feed-In Tariffs on the Profitability of European Photovoltaic Companies. *Sustainanility* **2018**, *10*, 3427. [CrossRef]
33. Neves, M.E.; Henriques, C.; Vilas, J. Financial performance assessment of electricity companies: Evidence from Portugal. *Oper. Res.* **2021**, *21*, 2809–2857. [CrossRef]
34. Neves, M.E.D.; Baptista, L.; Dias, A.G.; Lisboa, I. What factors can explain the performance of energy companies in Portugal? Panel data evidence. *Int. J. Product. Perform. Manag.* **2021**. ahead-of-print. [CrossRef]
35. Eurostat Electricity Price Statistics. 2021. Available online: https://ec.europa.eu/eurostat/statistics-explained/index.php?title=Electricity_price_statistics (accessed on 3 September 2021).
36. The World Bank. World Bank Open Data. *GDP Growth (Annual%)—Germany*. 2021. Available online: https://data.worldbank.org/indicator/NY.GDP.MKTP.KD.ZG?locations=DE (accessed on 2 October 2021).
37. ECD. OECD Data. *Renewable Energy Feed-In Tariffs*. 2021. Available online: https://stats.oecd.org/Index.aspx?DataSetCode=RE_FIT (accessed on 12 October 2021).

38. Brooks, C. *Introductory Econometrics for Finance | Finance*, 3rd ed.; Cambridge University Press: Cambridge, UK, 2014.
39. Greene, W.H. *Econometric Analysis*, 8th ed.; Stern School of Business, New York University: New York, NY, USA, 2018; ISBN 9780134811932.
40. Hausman, J.A.; Taylor, W.E. Panel Data and Unobservable Individual Effects. *Econometrica* **1981**, *49*, 1377–1398. [CrossRef]
41. Arellano, M. Practitioners' Corner: Computing Robust Standard Errors for within-groups Estimators. *Oxf. Bull. Econ. Stat.* **1987**, *49*, 431–434. [CrossRef]
42. White, H. A Heteroskedasticity-Consistent Covariance Matrix Estimator and a Direct Test for Heteroskedasticity. *Econometrica* **1980**, *48*, 817–838. [CrossRef]
43. Mundlak, Y. On the Pooling of Time Series and Cross Section Data. *Econometrica* **1978**, *46*, 69–85. [CrossRef]
44. Woolridge, J.M. *Econometric Analysis of Cross Section and Panel Data*; The MIT Press: Cambridge, MA, USA, 2010; ISBN 9780262232586.

Article

Ex-Ante Study of Biofuel Policies–Analyzing Policy-Induced Flexibility

Inka Ruponen [1], Mariia Kozlova [1,*] and Mikael Collan [1,2]

1. School of Business and Management, LUT University, Yliopistonkatu 34, 53850 Lappeenranta, Finland; inka.ruponen@student.lut.fi (I.R.); mikael.collan@lut.fi (M.C.)
2. VATT Institute for Economic Research, Arkadiankatu 7, 00101 Helsinki, Finland
* Correspondence: mariia.kozlova@lut.fi

Abstract: A variety of policy types are available to foster the transition to a low-carbon economy. In every sector, including transportation, heat and power production, policymakers face the choice of what type of policy to adopt. For this choice, it is crucial to understand how different mechanisms incentivize investments in terms of improving their profitability, shaping the flexibility available for investors, and how they are affected by the surrounding uncertainty. This paper focuses on transportation-biofuel policies, particularly on the financial incentives put on the bio-component of fuel and the combination of using penalties and tax-relief. Delivery of vital policymaking insights by using two modern simple-to-use profitability analysis methods, the pay-off method and the simulation decomposition method, is illustrated. Both methods enable the incorporation of uncertainty into the profitability analyses, and thus generate insight about the flexibilities involved, and the factors affecting the results. The results show that the combination of penalties and tax-relief is a way to steer fuel-production towards sustainability. The two methods used for analysis complement each other and provide important insights for analysis and decision-making beyond what the commonly used profitability analysis methods typically provide.

Keywords: biofuel policy; investment profitability analysis; the pay-off method; simulation decomposition

Citation: Ruponen, I.; Kozlova, M.; Collan, M. Ex-Ante Study of Biofuel Policies–Analyzing Policy-Induced Flexibility. *Sustainability* 2022, *14*, 147. https://doi.org/10.3390/su14010147

Academic Editor: Grigorios L. Kyriakopoulos

Received: 26 November 2021
Accepted: 20 December 2021
Published: 23 December 2021

Publisher's Note: MDPI stays neutral with regard to jurisdictional claims in published maps and institutional affiliations.

Copyright: © 2021 by the authors. Licensee MDPI, Basel, Switzerland. This article is an open access article distributed under the terms and conditions of the Creative Commons Attribution (CC BY) license (https://creativecommons.org/licenses/by/4.0/).

1. Introduction

In the fight against climate change, multiple environmental policies arise to guide the markets towards a sustainable future [1]. Such policies aim to steer new investments towards cleaner technology choices. Better energy efficiency, greener heat and power production, electric vehicles and biofuels in the transportation sector-are among the means to reduce emissions [2]. In this paper we concentrate on biofuel-related support policies and how the profitability effect of these policies can be analyzed ex-ante with modern analysis methods.

Green investments are still generally characterized by high costs relative to older technologies and high uncertainty is involved [3,4] (in the power sector many types of renewables are already cheaper than conventional generation [5], but extra costs arise due to their intermittency when the system reliability issues are taken into account [6–8]). For these reasons support mechanisms that are meant to incentivize green investments have been put in place. Many of the support mechanisms are based on simple policies that guarantee profitability by way of providing extra revenue to the investment [1]. Simply providing extra revenue however often leads to a too high subsidy level and consequently may cause policy changes [9,10]. As predictability and a low political-risk environment is crucial in attracting long-term investments, it is important to design policies that address investment risks and uncertainties [11,12] in a way that does not require unexpected and dramatic adjustments. Pre-analysis of the policy effects is important for succeeding in the creation of such policies, thus the issue of using proper analysis-techniques is highlighted.

The ex-ante analysis of the profitability of complex investment projects and the ex-ante analysis of the profitability effects of specific policies often includes the use of methods that allow for a comprehensive inclusion of the risks and uncertainties that surround the studied cases [13,14]. Methods that underlie modern real option analysis are such methods and real option thinking is a framework that supports the inclusion of uncertainty in the ex-ante profitability analysis context. Real options thinking recognizes and acknowledges the value of flexibility in the face of uncertainty and embraces the thinking that flexibility that is, the ability to steer/change an investment when change takes place, should be built into investments when it can be done in a cost-effective way. This observation has instigated a whole new "world" in investment design, where flexibility is pre-planned into investments in cases where the investment has a high likelihood of facing dramatic enough changes in its environment (markets). These analyses combine the study of uncertainty and flexibility simultaneously. To mention a few typical types of flexibility that allow investment managers to steer investments towards better outcomes when change takes place, we mention an option to delay investment, options related to scaling the size of investments up and down, option to temporarily shut down an investment, and options to change inputs and outputs to/from (typically production) investments [15–18]. Pre-investment planning and testing the effect of construction of flexibility into investments is something that can still be said to be "young" in terms of how widespread it is in the industry, some academic research on the topic exists, see, for example, [19].

Taking this thinking of combining the study of uncertainty and policy-induced flexibility into the world of ex-ante policy evaluation is also new and in the context of supporting policies for green investments it is very new. Some previous academic work, concentrating on renewable energy support mechanisms exists, see, e.g., [10,17,20]. In other words, the "concept" of what we are looking at here is the study of how policies and support mechanisms created to incentivize green investments may be constructed in a way that they include flexibility and thus change, when changes in the "environment in which the policy exists" take place. Furthermore, how the flexibility within the policies affects the investments which the policies are aimed at incentivizing is focal here. It seems rational to expect that similar methods that work for real option analysis (ex-ante analysis of effects of flexibility) for investments work also for ex-ante policy evaluation.

In this vein, in this paper we select two modern analysis techniques used in the analysis and the valuation of flexibility, the pay-off method [21] and (Monte Carlo) simulation based analysis, called "simulation decomposition" [22] and use them to study incentive-policies in the context of biofuels. The reason for selecting these two methods is the fit of these methods to the type of uncertainty that surrounds the context of biofuel-policies [23]. These methods have also previously been used in the analysis of environmental policies [24–26].

To the best of our knowledge this is the first time these techniques are applied in the context of biofuel-policy evaluation. The application of the methods, the analyses, and the obtained results are illustrative, yet helpful in understanding the benefits brought about by using modern analysis methods in the context of ex-ante policy evaluation.

The remainder of the paper is structured as follows. First, we provide a brief overview of the biofuel-policies to introduce the context of the case study. Then we introduce the two methods, the pay-off method and simulation decomposition. We illustrate the use of the methods in the analysis of a biofuel-policy. The discussion and conclusion section summarizes and discusses the results, looks into the comparative performance of the used methods, and outlines implications for policy analysis.

Biofuel Promotion Schemes

In the context of the transportation sector, there are two main directions in the overall policy efforts directed at the fuels used, to make the sector more environmentally conscious [1,27]. One policy-direction aims at the electrification of traffic and another pursues the substitution of fossil fuels with biofuels. As discussed above, here we concentrate on the second-mentioned policy focus.

As with the widely spread tariff-based support instruments in the power sector, some countries opt for financial incentives to promote biofuels. Thailand directly subsidizes the retail price of biofuel, while the US and Brazil chose tax-relief [1]. Nevertheless, such financial incentives remain an unpopular policy choice in the world.

One of the most common policies is the biofuel blending mandate [1]. Such a policy imposes a requirement on fuel-suppliers to supply a certain minimum share of biofuels in the fuel mix. The European Union has adopted this policy. The EU 32% renewable energy target in the overall energy consumption by 2030 has been supplemented with a sub-target for the transport sector equaling a 14% share of renewables in the supplied fuel mix [28]. Member states are free to set higher targets. Finland, for example, imposes a mandate on fuel suppliers to introduce a gradually growing share of renewable fuels in road transport, reaching 30% by 2029 [29]. Overall, 70 countries around the world have a biofuel blending mandate, however, if left without enforcement achieving the set goals may be jeopardized [1].

Many countries use penalties to enforce biofuel mandates, the list includes Germany, Finland, Italy, and Sweden [30]. In Finland, if the fuel supplier fails to ensure the required volume of biofuels on that specific year of gradual mandate increase, the fuel supplier must pay penalties for each excess liter of fossil fuel produced [29]. The Finnish Government sets the amount of penalty to be 0.04 EUR/MJ, which corresponds to 1355 EUR/liters of diesel equivalent [31]. In addition to penalties, Finland employs tax-relief for renewable fuels. Overall, the biofuel gets a 0.30 EUR/l tax discount if produced purely, and 0.26 EUR/l if in the mix with fossil fuel [32].

Considering the world experience with different policies to support biofuels, we choose to comparatively analyze direct financial incentive, and the combination of penalties and tax-relief, contrasting their policy effects with the benchmark case of no policy support in place.

2. Methods and Data

Both methods presented here are based on the fundamental concept of the time value of money and discounted cash-flows [33]. Both methods require constructing a cash-flow model of the investment project and computing its net present value (NPV). Both methods are based on constructing a distribution of possible project NPVs to present and handle the uncertainty that surrounds the investment. The fuzzy pay-off method operates partly in the possibilistic framework and builds a possibilistic NPV distribution or, put simply, a fuzzy number NPV. Simulation decomposition is based on probabilistic Monte Carlo simulation and utilizes the resulting probability distribution of NPVs further to decompose it into input-output analysis-based cohorts. The two methods are described in more detail below.

2.1. Pay-Off Method

The fuzzy pay-off method [21,34] approaches building the distribution through setting scenarios. Usually, three scenarios are defined, pessimistic, realistic, and optimistic, although more can be created if reasonable. First, managers are asked to provide estimates of input values, like costs, prices, production volumes, etc., for every scenario. The idea is to generate the estimates for the worst possible scenario (pessimistic) such that nothing worse can happen, for the best possible scenario (optimistic) such that nothing "better" can be expected to happen, and the one with the most realistic estimates (realistic or best estimate). Second, net present value is calculated for each scenario. Third, the three NPVs are used to form a triangular pay-off distribution for the project NPVs are mapped on the value (x) axis, while the y-axis depicts the membership degree within the set of possible outcomes. Full membership (equal to 1) is assigned to the "realistic" scenario value, and limit to zero membership to the pessimistic and the optimistic scenario NPVs, implying that anything worse or better correspondingly is not expected to take place. The relationship between the positive and the negative and the realistic scenario value is assumed to be linear. Thus, in the final stage, a triangle is formed that represents the possibilistic range of the project's NPVs and that is treated as a triangular fuzzy number, for details see [13,26].

Descriptive statistics can be calculated directly from the pay-off distribution and accompany the material provided for decision-making. For example, the mean value of the distribution and the variance can be calculated. Furthermore, the real option value can be computed based on the expected mean of the positive part of the distribution [34,35]. The main steps of the method are visualized in Figure 1.

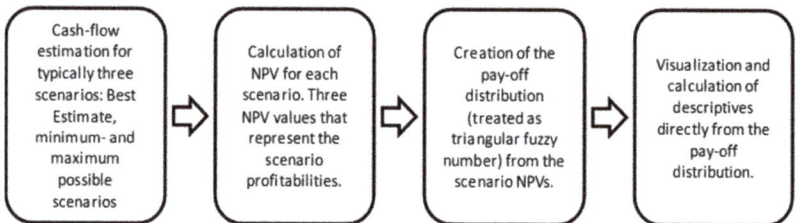

Figure 1. The fuzzy pay-off method in four steps.

The fuzzy pay-off method has been used in many application areas, including energy and oil investments [26,36–38], screening and selection of research and development projects [39,40], and management of a patent portfolios [41].

2.2. Simulation-Based Profitability Analysis and Simulation Decomposition

Simulation-based analysis is based on two parts, one part is a (computer) model that contains stylized (often much-simplified) structure of the studied system that nevertheless carries a strong resemblance with reality. The system model includes a number of inputs and outputs to and from the system that can be studied to understand what the system "does". The best system models have a high requisite variety (requisite complexity) [42] and thus offer relatively high credibility by way of fidelity with the real world. System-models may also be dynamic and change as a function of (simulation) time. The second part is simulation, which is typically arranged by means of automated software inputting a large number of input variable-combinations (vectors, input scenarios) into the system and collecting the corresponding output values. The input value-combinations are selected from input-value distributions that are pre-determined for each input (and may also be single values, crisp). The output-values are typically presented as histograms or frequency distributions and it is common to assume that the distribution is a probabilistic representation of the occurrence frequency of the outputs from the system. A Monte Carlo simulation is a simulation, where the input value selection is made randomly by the simulation software from the input-value distributions for a typically pre-set number of times [43,44].

In the context of ex-ante profitability analysis or policy-effect analysis the system underlying the simulation analysis is the profitability analysis cash-flow model of the investment that is facing the policy, and the cash-flows that are received by the investment are regulated by the policy as a function of the environment that the investment is facing, described in terms of the input-variable value-combinations. This means that the system used includes both the profitability analysis model and the policy-model. The simulation software is then used to reveal the outputs from the system under various (randomly drawn) real-world scenarios [45,46].

Simulation decomposition is based on the Monte Carlo simulation framework and thus, in contrast with the pay-off method, belongs to the probabilistic framework. Simulation Decomposition decomposes the results of the simulated output probability distribution into sub-distributions that are matched with the input variable value range combinations from which they result. The input range combinations can be understood as scenarios. This input-output matching reveals important information about cause and effect and allows decision-makers to better understand what effect the various scenarios will have on the output. The procedure is based on (i) identifying the relevant variables that can be affected by the project owner, their relevant "states", and boundaries for each state; (ii) forming "groups" or scenarios by combining the states; (iii) running the simulation, while keeping track on the input-output "inference"; (iv) visualizing the results such that the outcome resulting from each input group (scenario) is separately visualized and allows better understanding of "what leads to what". The procedure is depicted in Figure 2. The detailed description of the procedure, how the results from it are visualized, and available implementation tools can be found in [22,47].

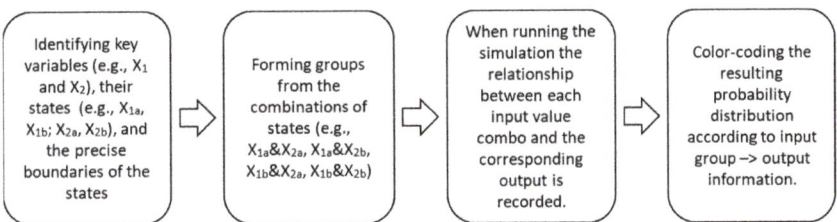

Figure 2. Schematic visualization of the simulation decomposition procedure.

If simulation decomposition is performed by using a single variable, one can see the influence of this variable on the outcome in the presence of other uncertainties. The two extremes would be zero (low) influence, if all the scenarios are "lying" on top of each other (share same output values on the x-axis), and strong influence, if the scenarios are vertically separated from each other (do not share same output values on the x-axis). If the decomposition is performed by using two or more variables, one can observe the interplay of variables and possible synergies, if any are hidden in the system. The more nonlinearities and various what-if rules the system has, the more valuable the decomposition potentially becomes.

Simulation decomposition has demonstrated its value in renewable energy policy analysis [22,48], in other environmental policy issues [25,49], and can be generally applied to any problem modeled with Monte Carlo simulation independent of the context [47].

A similar scenario decomposition can be made within the possibilistic framework, by framing an input-output system by using a fuzzy inference system (FIS), see [24]. This approach has benefits and drawbacks. Using FIS avoids simulation and thus requires less computational time, however, the necessity of manual construction of the many scenarios typically overrides the time savings. In the simulation decomposition method, scenarios are created and valued automatically, based on the user-specified partitions of the input variables.

2.3. Numerical Assumptions

This study makes numerical assumptions based on publicly available literature and following the practice presented in [50]. The economic life of a biorefinery plant typically varies between 20–25 years, and in this study, the lifetime of 20 years is used. The corporate tax-rate is assumed to be 20% and the discount is set at 10%. The numerical assumptions about the biofuel production-plant investment are estimates taken from [51]. These estimates include the investment cost of a 500 million liters per year of renewable diesel production 430 M€ and operating cost of 0.86 EUR/liter. The assumptions related to policies supporting the use of biofuels are related to the Finnish biofuel policy. Tax-rates used in this study are retrieved from the Finnish Tax Administration (2021), and the amount of penalty for not achieving the required share of biofuels is retrieved from the decisions of the Finnish Parliament (2018). All numerical assumptions made in this study are listed in Table 1.

Table 1. Numerical assumptions for the studied system.

Parameter	Value	Comment
Time horizon	20 years	Corresponds to the average lifetime of a biofuel plant, see, e.g., [52]
Corporate tax	20%	The corporate tax-rate in Finland
Discount rate	10%	Discount rate, see e.g., [52]
Price of fuel (taxes included)	1.12 €/liter	The average price of Diesel in Finland 2012–2019
Fossil fuel (diesel)		
Plant size	1166 million liters per year	Calculated to get 30% biofuel blend with 500 Ml/year biofuel plant
Operating costs	0.37 €/liter	Estimated operating costs, [51]
Biofuel (renewable diesel)		
Plant size	500 million liters per year	Estimates from [53]
Operating costs	0.86 €/liter	
Investment cost	430 M€	
Assumptions related to policies		
Tax-relief	0.26 €/ liter	Based on the Finnish biofuel policy, [32]
Penalties	1.36 €/ liter	Based on the Finnish biofuel policy, [31]
Financial incentive	0.26 €/ liter	The same as tax-relief to provide the exact profitability for the 30% blend scenario

3. Results

To analyze the effects of different policies, we take an investor's perspective. We assume a fuel producer already has facilities for producing fossil fuel. The producer has a choice to invest in biodiesel production to produce fuel blend, or to leave the business as is. The profitability of the operations with and without biofuel investment is analyzed under different policy types. In particular, we consider the cases with (i) no support (benchmark), (ii) a financial incentive, and (iii) a biofuel mandate reinforced by tax-relief and penalties.

3.1. The Pay-Off Method Based Analysis

For the pay-off method case, instead of assuming variations in many input parameters of the investment, we elect to let only the biofuel blend vary. This means that we calculate, ceteris paribus, the net present value of an investment with three different biofuel blend scenarios.

We assign the "30% biofuel blend" as be the base case scenario and consider two extreme scenarios, "standalone conventional fuel production", and "pure biofuel production". This way, we isolate the effect of different policies on the decision with respect to the fuel blend only. The resulting fuzzy NPV distribution demonstrates the effect of different fuel blends on the NPV. In the case of no policy support, Figure 3, only fossil fuel production is profitable. Investment in biofuel facilities deteriorates the profitability compared to only fossil fuel production. Already 30% share of biofuel makes the operations unprofitable, whereas pure biofuel production is in deeply negative territory.

Paying a financial subsidy for every liter of biofuel produced shifts the profitability of the 30% blend scenario and the biofuel only scenario, Figure 4. The 30% blend scenario becomes profitable. Pure biofuel production lags behind and still remains unprofitable, due to the heavier cost structure. Profitability of the fossil fuel production remains unchanged and remains the most profitable option.

The combination of tax-relief for biofuel and penalties for not reaching the blending target creates a very different picture, Figure 5. The tax-relief has a similar effect on the 30% blend scenario and the biofuel only scenario, as financial incentives. The 30% blend scenario is profitable, while the biofuel-only production remains in the negative profitability zone. In contrast to financial benefits, the fossil fuel only scenario becomes deeply unprofitable due to the penalties. Only penalties create this effect since in the previous policy situations (Figures 3 and 4) the fossil fuel production is profitable. Thus, the combination of penalties and tax-relief generates a two-fold effect, making biofuel blend production attractive to the investors, while discouraging fossil fuel only production.

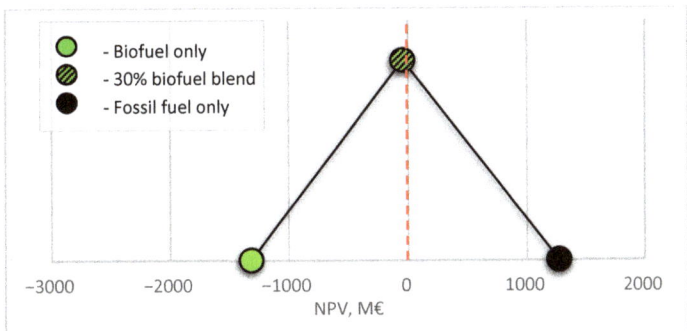

Figure 3. Pay-off net present value (NPV) distribution of fuel production with different fuel blends under no support.

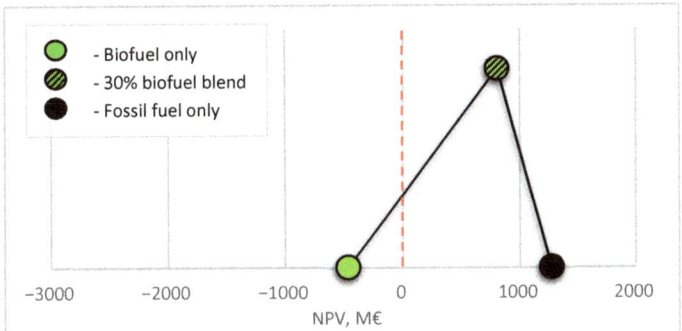

Figure 4. Pay-off net present value (NPV) distribution of fuel production with different fuel blends under financial incentive.

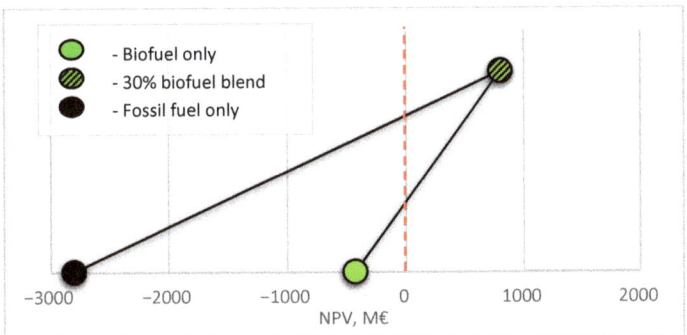

Figure 5. Pay-off net present value (NPV) distribution of fuel production with different fuel blends under a combination of penalties and tax-relief.

Overall, use of the fuzzy pay-off method, when only the change in the critical parameter is analyzed, enables a clear demonstration of the effects of different policies.

However, the system studied is surrounded by uncertainties, and the critical one is the fuel-price uncertainty that, according to [50], has a major influence on the profitability of the operations compared to all other factors. Therefore, to further analyze the policy effects, we should have a method that is able to capture the interplay of several sources of uncertainty simultaneously, for this we turn to Monte Carlo simulation and the simulation decomposition method.

3.2. Simulation Decomposition Based Analysis

Simulation decomposition is based on the Monte Carlo simulation. The same underlying assumptions and NPV cash-flow model that is used for the pay-off method-based analysis is utilized for the simulation. The variation of input variables is allowed for multiple variables simultaneously.

The fossil fuel production is assumed to be preexistent, and its size is now considered fixed, while the size of the biofuel production is relaxed and ranges from 0 to 1000 million liters per year that corresponds to the variation of the share of the biofuel in the fuel blend from 0 to 46%. For simplicity, the investment cost is assumed to be a linear function of the production quantity. Thus, we are not looking at a separate pure biofuel production anymore, but at the fossil fuel production supplemented with biofuel.

The second source of uncertainty is the price of the final product. We assume it to be independent of the fuel-mix sold and to vary in the upper range from the current level from 1.0 to 1.5 EUR/liter. Clearly, the biofuel blends are expected to be sold at a premium compared to fully fossil fuel, however, a natural fuel-price variation exists among countries [54] and fuel-producers might be willing to consider different price-levels independently of their production-blend. Both sources of uncertainty are modeled with a uniform distribution. The uniform distribution, compared to, e.g., a normal distribution, places more weight on the extreme values and thus, creates a more detailed picture of the extent of policy effects.

For the decomposition, we break down the biofuel production-size into two ranges–below the 30% share blend (0–500 million liters per year) and to equal or above 30% (500–1000 million liters per year). The price-range is divided into three equally "wide" pieces, see Table 2. The overall number of all possible combinations of these two variables' states or scenarios is six.

Table 2. Assumptions for Monte Carlo simulation and simulation decomposition.

Parameter	Range	States	
Biodiesel production size, million liters per year	0–1000	<30%	[0, 500)
		≥30%	[500, 1000]
Price of fuel, €/liter	1.00–1.50	low	[1.00, 1.17)
		medium	[1.17, 1.34)
		high	[1.34, 1.50]

In the absence of support (Figure 6) fossil fuel production with less than 30% of biofuel (sc1–3) is profitable in the high price region and partially profitable in the medium price region. Producing higher shares of biofuel in the blend becomes unprofitable in the low-price region (sc4) and only slightly less profitable in the medium and high price regions (sc5,6). This happens, because at these high prices the standalone biofuel production becomes less unprofitable and therefore adding more production facilities does not harm the profitability of the current fossil-fuel production that much.

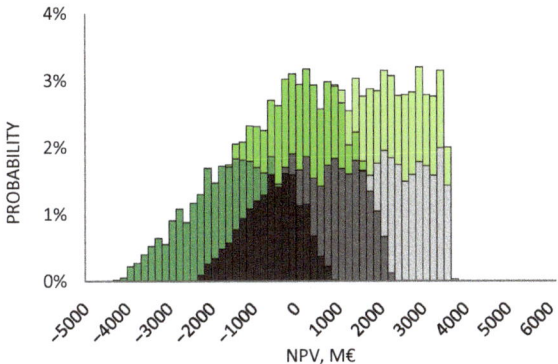

Figure 6. Simulation decomposition for fuel production net present value (NPV) with different fuel blends and price uncertainty under no support.

Under the financial incentive, we can see a shift of the higher-share biofuel production (sc4–6) into a more profitable range, while the less share biofuel production (sc1–3) remains relatively unchanged (Figure 7), a similar phenomenon to what was seen with the fuzzy pay-off method (Figure 2) is revealed. This happens, because the financial incentive is paid per liter of biofuel produced in the blend and affects more the higher-share operations. Nevertheless, the overall picture has not changed much. The price variation dilutes the effect of the subsidy. Scenarios with high prices (sc3,6) are profitable in both, the no-support situation and with the financial subsidy, which translates into a deteriorated incentive to increase the share of biofuel production, when the future price development is uncertain.

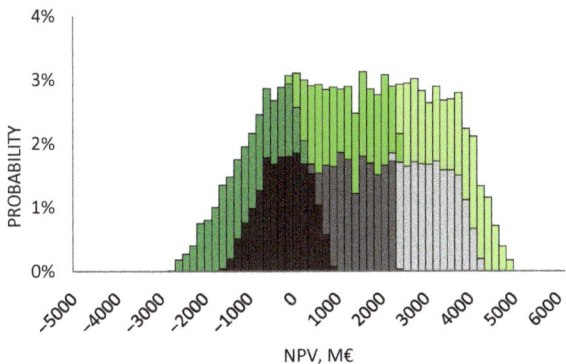

Figure 7. Simulation decomposition for fuel production net present value (NPV) with different fuel blends and price uncertainty under financial incentive.

Figure 8 demonstrates how different the profitability of fuel-blend production looks like under the combination of penalties and tax-relief. The lower bounds of low-share biofuel production (sc1–3), which represent the standalone conventional fuel production, are all pushed into the negative profitability zone. of the cases within these scenarios that are closer to the 30% biofuel requirement still stay in the positive profitability zone. The high biofuel share operations are almost entirely found to be in the positive profitability range due to the tax-relief and the absence of penalties. The difference remains sharp even under the vast price uncertainty. This contrast between the green (sc4–6) and the fossil scenarios (sc1–3) is an embodiment of the incentive to switch to the production of a high share of biofuel blend.

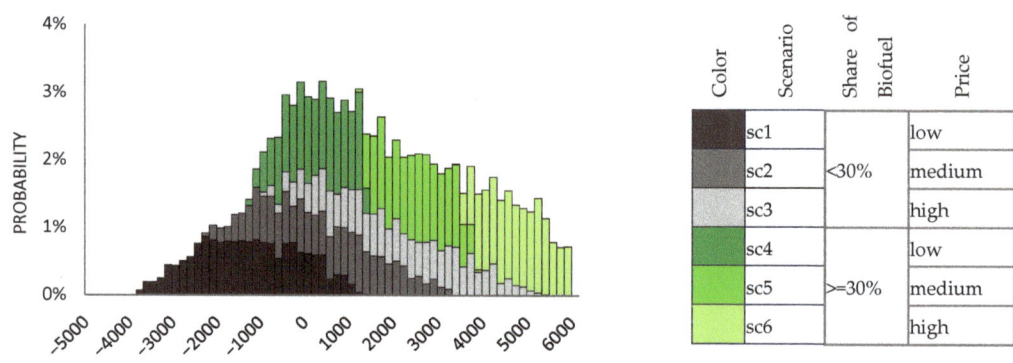

Figure 8. Simulation decomposition for fuel production net present value (NPV) with different fuel blends and price uncertainty under a combination of penalties and tax-relief.

The above-described differences between the effects the different policies become even more evident, if the graphs are presented together, see Table 3.

Table 3. Summary of the results.

	Pay-Off Method	**Simulation Decomposition**
	Fuel mix variation only	*Fixed fossil fuel production + variable size of biofuel production + price uncertainty*
No support	A	D
Financial incentive	B	E
Penalties & tax-relief	C	F

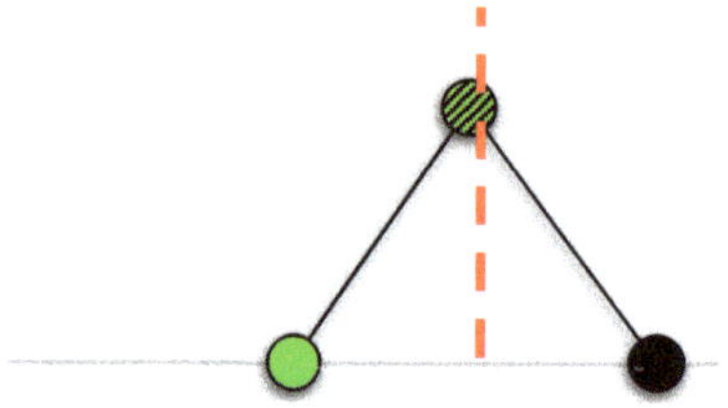

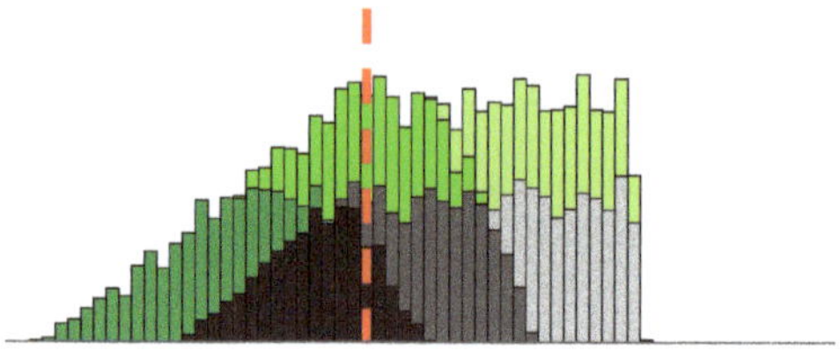

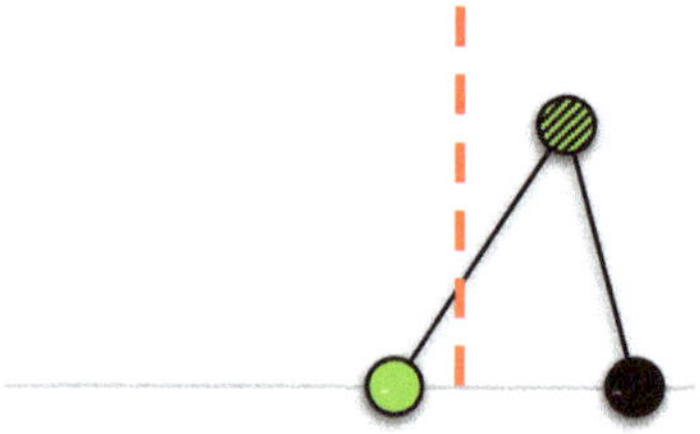

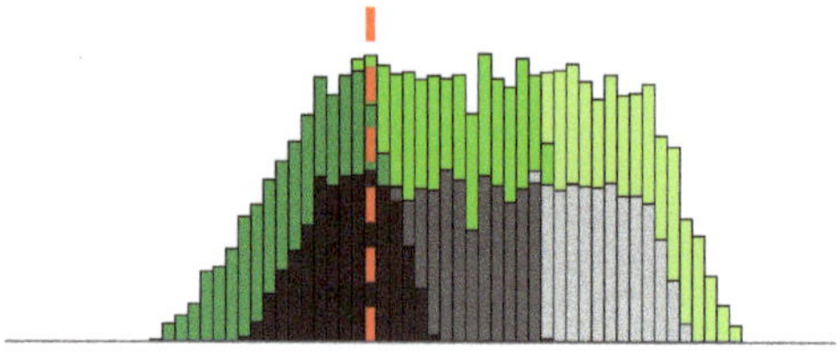

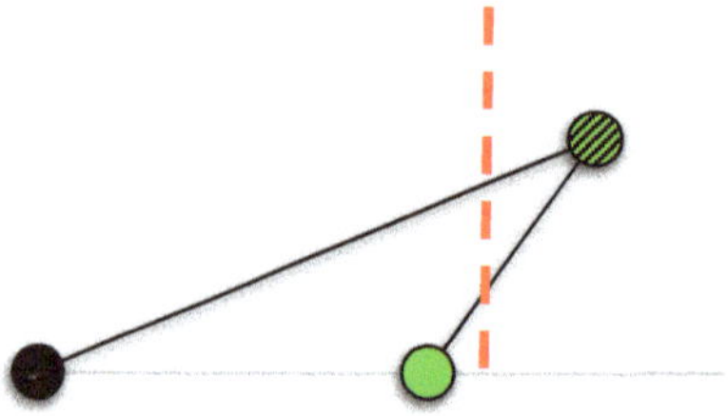

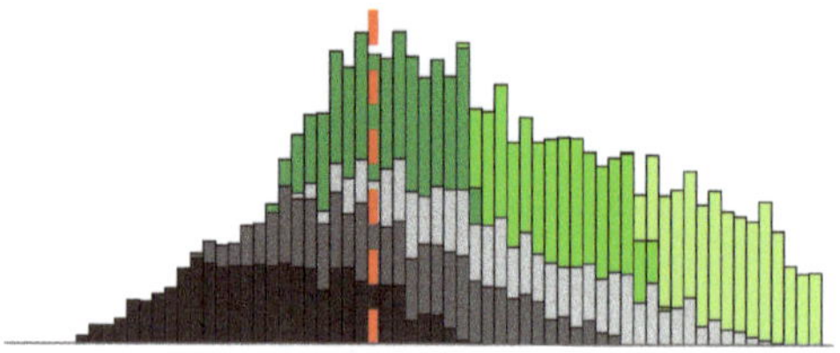

Table 3. Cont.

Legend	Pay-Off Method		Simulation Decomposition			
			Color	Scenario	Share of Biofuel	Price
	● - Biofuel only		■ (dark)	sc1	<30%	low
	◐ - 30% biofuel blend		■ (gray)	sc2		medium
	● - Fossil fuel only		■ (light)	sc3		high
			■ (dark green)	sc4	>=30%	low
			■ (green)	sc5		medium
			■ (light green)	sc6		high

4. Discussion

All obtained graphical results are demonstrated side by side in Table 3. The pay-off method (column 2) shows the distributions with only fuel mix variations between the extremes of standalone fossil fuel and pure biofuel production scenarios. The simulation decomposition technique (column 3) is applied to a case with fixed fossil fuel production size, variable biofuel addition, and price uncertainty. The important difference is that the pay-off distribution is constructed out of discreet scenarios, whereas probability distributions display the continuous change of the size of the biofuel production. For the simplicity of representation, the graphs are stripped from axes and titles, however, the scale is kept consistent within the columns and the zero profitability is marked with the red dashed line and aligned within each column. Different policy types are shown in rows, and the final row presents the legends for the graphs for convenience.

The general pattern that can be observed is that no matter which analysis technique we are using, the first two rows in Table 3 look similar. Financial incentive (B) improves the profitability of the biofuel blends production, but does not change the entire picture especially, when considering different price levels (E). It can be concluded that this policy-type introduces more flexibility for investors by enabling other profitable options in addition to the conventional ones. Tax-relief alone would have the same effect as the financial incentive. One can observe that biofuel only and 30% biofuel blend scenarios have the same NPV with the pay-off method under the financial incentive (B) and the combination of penalties and tax-relief (C). The price-variation accounted for in the simulation decomposition method, pushes the profitability of high-share of biofuel scenarios (sc4–6) upwards in the "penalties & tax-relief" policy (F) in comparison to the financial incentive only policy (E). In addition, the penalties change the profitability outlook for fossil fuel as well. Both methods show that fossil fuel production becomes deeply unprofitable when penalized (C, F). Such an effect translates into shrinking flexibility for investors. Under this policy type the only profitable choice is the biofuel blend.

Biofuel production is more costly than conventional fuel production, and therefore, requires subsidies. Production of biofuel alone seems to be too expensive under any policy. However, co-production becomes profitable in the case of the combined penalties and tax-relief policy and the financial incentive. Financial incentives alone do not discourage offering 100% fossil fuel, whereas the combined policy does by means of penalties. A policy that is a mix of penalties and incentives may help the industry navigate efficiently towards a desired outcome. These conclusions are shown to be "obtainable" with the pay-off method and the simulation decomposition method. This is in line with the previous use of the pay-off method in comparing different projects [40,55] or scenarios of the same project [56]. Here the use of the method was not exactly what has been seen before as the variation was in terms of policies, which makes this research novel in that respect also from the methodological point of view.

To complement the analysis with the pay-off method, we have used the simulation decomposition method. As a standalone technique, simulation decomposition has often been used for policy analysis [25,57]. In this research we have combined market, fuel price, and investment factors. Such a combination has allowed us to observe possible preferences of investors that depend on market development. The results allow us to see the effect of both uncertainty and the joint effect of these factors simultaneously.

While the pay-off method exposes the policy effects on a key decision of how much biofuel to introduce to the blend, simulation decomposition complements the analysis by incorporating market uncertainty into the investment profitability profile.

Previous academic literature has pointed out the possibility of adopting complex and sophisticated methods for the ex-ante study of policy effects and a quasi-unanimous conclusion found in the literature is that ex-ante policy decision-making support is crucial also in the shift towards more renewable fuels. Araujo Enciso et al. [58] arrive at this conclusion by using a sophisticated stochastic recursive-dynamic multi-commodity model. Moncada et al. [59] employ a complex multi-agent model to show that a combination of penalties for fossil fuel with incentives for biofuel provides the best biofuel adoption results. In this paper, we demonstrate that novel, but simple-to-implement and understand methods are able to keep up with more complex techniques in terms of analytical richness both in the inclusion of multiple variables and especially in the provision of visual and in-depth insights for decision-making.

Based on what has been seen here we are ready to recommend the combined use of the fuzzy pay-off method and the simulation decomposition for ex-ante policy analysis and more generally for gaining better understanding of profitability analysis problems with several key factors the interplay of which have an effect on the end result.

5. Conclusions

This paper showcases the use of the two modern profitability analysis techniques, the fuzzy pay-off method, and simulation decomposition, in the environmental policy analysis. Both methods are able to depict uncertainty, and when used in conjunction, provide important insights for ex-ante analysis of policy effects. Both methods are relatively easy to implement, and their results are easy to visualize and interpret, which, coupled with their analytical power, make them appealing candidates for tools used for policy analysis. We analyzed policies to incentivize investments in biofuel production in the transportation sector. The illustrative conclusion reached is that a combination of penalties and tax-relief is a realistic policy alternative for sustainability transition.

Our conclusions are based on a stylized investment case and numerical assumptions available for Finland. If the analysis is performed for another country, the numerical assumptions need to be modified. However, we are employing methods that can handle uncertainty, data variation and imprecision. Wide ranges of input factors are considered. Therefore, we believe that our conclusions hold under a variety of circumstances and are generalizable.

Extending the range of applications and exploring complementarity of the considered techniques with other approaches are possible directions for future research.

Author Contributions: I.R.: conceptualization, data curation, methodology, writing—original draft preparation, and visualization; M.K.: conceptualization, data curation, methodology, writing—original draft preparation, writing—review and editing, and visualization; M.C.: conceptualization, methodology, and writing—review and editing. All authors have read and agreed to the published version of the manuscript.

Funding: The authors acknowledge funding received from the Foundation of Economic Education, grant number 200153, and the support from the Finnish Strategic Research Council (SRC) at the Academy of Finland through the Manufacturing 4.0-project, grant number 335980 and grant number 335990.

Institutional Review Board Statement: Not applicable.

Informed Consent Statement: Not applicable.

Data Availability Statement: All used data is presented in the manuscript.

Conflicts of Interest: The authors declare no conflict of interest.

References

1. REN21 Renewables 2020 Global Status Report. 2020. Available online: http://www.ren21.net/wp-content/uploads/2018/06/17-8652_GSR2018_FullReport_web_final_.pdf (accessed on 13 December 2021).
2. European Environmental Agency Urban Sustainability: How Can Cities Become Sustainable? Available online: https://www.eea.europa.eu/themes/sustainability-transitions/urban-environment (accessed on 13 December 2021).
3. IEA Global EV Outlook 2021. Available online: https://www.iea.org/reports/global-ev-outlook-2021 (accessed on 13 December 2021).
4. IEA Transport Biofuels. Available online: https://www.iea.org/reports/transport-biofuels (accessed on 13 December 2021).
5. IEA Projected Costs of Generating Electricity 2020. Available online: https://www.iea.org/reports/projected-costs-of-generating-electricity-2020 (accessed on 13 December 2021).
6. Kozlova, M.; Lohrmann, A. Steering Renewable Energy Investments in Favor of Energy System Reliability: A Call for a Hybrid Model. *Sustainability* **2021**, *13*, 13510. [CrossRef]
7. Kozlova, M.; Overland, I. Combining capacity mechanisms and renewable energy support: A review of the international experience. *Renew. Sustain. Energy Rev.* 2021; 111878, in press. [CrossRef]
8. Jakob, P.; Wagner, J. Optimal Allocation of Variable Renewable Energy Considering Contributions to Security of Supply. *Energy J.* **2021**, *42*, 1–35.
9. Sendstad, L.H.; Hagspiel, V.; Mikkelsen, W.J.; Ravndal, R.; Tveitstøl, M. The impact of subsidy retraction on European renewable energy investments. *Energy Policy* **2022**, *160*, 112675. [CrossRef]
10. Boomsma, T.K.; Linnerud, K. Market and policy risk under different renewable electricity support schemes. *Energy* **2015**, *89*, 435–448. [CrossRef]
11. Kitzing, L.; Fitch-Roy, O.; Islam, M.; Mitchell, C. An evolving risk perspective for policy instrument choice in sustainability transitions. *Environ. Innov. Soc. Transit.* **2020**, *35*, 369–382. [CrossRef]
12. Habermacher, F.; Lehmann, P. Commitment Versus Discretion in Climate and Energy Policy. *Environ. Resour. Econ.* **2020**, *76*, 39–67. [CrossRef]
13. Trigeorgis, L.; Tsekrekos, A.E. Real Options in Operations Research: A Review. *Eur. J. Oper. Res.* **2018**, *270*, 1–24. [CrossRef]
14. Kozlova, M. Real option valuation in renewable energy literature: Research focus, trends and design. *Renew. Sustain. Energy Rev.* **2017**, *80*, 180–196. [CrossRef]
15. Savolainen, J.; Collan, M.; Luukka, P. Analyzing operational real options in metal mining investments with a system dynamic model. *Eng. Econ.* **2016**, *62*, 54–72. [CrossRef]
16. De Oliveira, D.L.; Brandao, L.E.; Igrejas, R.; Gomes, L.L. Switching outputs in a bioenergy cogeneration project: A real options approach. *Renew. Sustain. Energy Rev.* **2014**, *36*, 74–82. [CrossRef]
17. Kozlova, M.; Fleten, S.; Hagspiel, V. Investment timing and capacity choice under rate-of-return regulation for renewable energy support. *Energy* **2019**, *174*, 591–601. [CrossRef]
18. Fleten, S.; Fram, B.; Ledsaak, M.; Mehl, S.; Røstum, O.E.; Ullrich, C.J. The Effect of Capacity Payments on Peaking Generator Availability in PJM; Local Energy, Global Markets. In Proceedings of the 42nd IAEE International Conference, Montreal, QC, Canada, 29 May–1 June 2019.
19. Savolainen, J.; Pedretti, D.; Collan, M. Incorporating Hydrologic Uncertainty in Industrial Economic Models: Implications of Extreme Rainfall Variability on Metal Mining Investments. *Mine Water Environ.* **2019**, *38*, 447–462. [CrossRef]
20. Kitzing, L.; Juul, N.; Drud, M.; Boomsma, T.K. A real options approach to analyse wind energy investments under different support schemes. *Appl. Energy* **2017**, *188*, 83–96. [CrossRef]
21. Collan, M. *The Pay-off Method: Re-Inventing Investment Analysis*; CreateSpace Inc.: Charleston, NC, USA, 2012.
22. Kozlova, M.; Collan, M.; Luukka, P. Simulation decomposition: New approach for better simulation analysis of multi-variable investment projects. *Fuzzy Econ. Rev.* **2016**, *21*, 3. [CrossRef]
23. Collan, M.; Haahtela, T.; Kyläheiko, K. On the usability of real option valuation model types under different types of uncertainty. *Int. J. Bus. Innov. Res.* **2016**, *11*, 18–37. [CrossRef]
24. Kozlova, M.; Collan, M.; Luukka, P. New investment decision-making tool that combines a fuzzy inference system with real option analysis. *Fuzzy Econ. Rev.* **2018**, *23*, 63–92. [CrossRef]
25. Kozlova, M.; Yeomans, J.S. Multi-Variable Simulation Decomposition in Environmental Planning: An Application to Carbon Capture and Storage. *J. Environ. Inform. Lett.* **2019**, *1*, 20–26. [CrossRef]

26. Hietanen, L.; Kozlova, M.; Collan, M. Analyzing Renewable Energy Policies–Using the Pay-off Method to Study the Finnish Auction-Based Renewable Energy Policy. *J. Environ. Inform. Lett.* **2020**, *4*, 50–56. [CrossRef]
27. European Commission European Green Deal. Available online: https://ec.europa.eu/info/strategy/priorities-2019-2024/european-green-deal_en (accessed on 15 June 2021).
28. European Commission Renewable Energy—Recast to 2030 (RED II). Available online: https://ec.europa.eu/jrc/en/jec/renewable-energy-recast-2030-red-ii (accessed on 15 June 2021).
29. Finnish Parliament Act on the Use of Biofuels in Transport 2007/446 [in Finnish]. 2007. Available online: https://finlex.fi/fi/laki/ajantasa/2007/20070446 (accessed on 19 December 2021).
30. International Council on Clean Transportation Advanced Biofuel Policies in Select EU Member States. 2018. Available online: https://theicct.org/sites/default/files/publications/Advanced_biofuel_policy_eu_update_20181130.pdf (accessed on 19 December 2021).
31. Finnish Parliament Government Proposal HE 199 /2018 to the Parliament for Laws to Promote the Use of Biofuel [in Finnish]. 2018. Available online: https://www.eduskunta.fi/FI/vaski/HallituksenEsitys/Sivut/HE_199+2018.aspx (accessed on 19 December 2021).
32. Finnish Tax Administration Tax Rates on Liquid Fuels. Available online: https://www.vero.fi/yritykset-ja-yhteisot/verot-ja-maksut/valmisteverotus/nestemaiset-polttoaineet/verotaulukot/ (accessed on 15 June 2021).
33. Fisher, I. *The Rate of Interest: Its Nature, Determination and Relation to Economic Phenomena*; Macmillan: New York, NY, USA, 1907.
34. Collan, M.; Fullér, R.; Mezei, J. A fuzzy pay-off method for real option valuation. *J. Appl. Math. Decis. Sci.* **2009**, *2009*, 165–169. [CrossRef]
35. Stoklasa, J.; Luukka, P.; Collan, M. Possibilistic fuzzy pay-off method for real option valuation with application to research and development investment analysis. *Fuzzy Sets Syst.* **2021**, *409*, 153–169. [CrossRef]
36. Bednyagin, D.; Gnansounou, E. Real options valuation of fusion energy R&D programme. *Energy Policy* **2011**, *39*, 116–130.
37. Borges, R.E.P.; Dias, M.A.G.; Neto, A.D.D.; Meier, A. Fuzzy pay-off method for real options: The center of gravity approach with application in oilfield abandonment. *Fuzzy Sets Syst.* **2018**, *353*, 111–123. [CrossRef]
38. Kozlova, M.; Collan, M.; Luukka, P. Comparison of the Datar-Mathews Method and the Fuzzy Pay-Off Method through Numerical Results. *Adv. Decis. Sci.* **2016**, *2016*, 7836784. [CrossRef]
39. Hassanzadeh, F.; Collan, M.; Modarres, M. A practical approach to R&D portfolio selection using the fuzzy pay-off method. *Fuzzy Syst. IEEE Trans.* **2012**, *20*, 615–622.
40. Collan, M.; Luukka, P. Evaluating R&D projects as investments by using an overall ranking from four new fuzzy similarity measure-based TOPSIS variants. *Fuzzy Syst. IEEE Trans.* **2014**, *22*, 505–515.
41. Collan, M.; Kyläheiko, K. Forward-looking valuation of strategic patent portfolios under structural uncertainty. *J. Intellect. Prop. Rights* **2013**, *18*, 230–241.
42. Ashby, W.R. Requisite variety and its implications for the control of complex systems. In *Facets of Systems Science*; Springer: Berlin/Heidelberg, Germany, 1991; pp. 405–417.
43. Mooney, C.Z. *Monte Carlo Simulation*; Sage Publications: New York, NY, USA, 1997; Volume 116.
44. Rubinstein, R.Y.; Kroese, D.P. *Simulation and the Monte Carlo Method*; John Wiley & Sons: Hoboken, NJ, USA, 2016; Volume 10.
45. Platon, V.; Constantinescu, A. Monte Carlo Method in risk analysis for investment projects. *Procedia Econ. Financ.* **2014**, *15*, 393–400. [CrossRef]
46. Kwak, Y.H.; Ingall, L. Exploring Monte Carlo simulation applications for project management. *Risk Manag.* **2007**, *9*, 44–57. [CrossRef]
47. Kozlova, M.; Yeomans, J.S. Monte Carlo Enhancement via Simulation Decomposition: A "Must-Have" Inclusion for Many Disciplines. In *INFORMS Transactions on Education*; Institute for Operations Research and the Management Sciences (INFORMS): Catonsville, MD, USA, 2020. [CrossRef]
48. Hietanen, L. *Comparative Analysis of Renewable Energy Policy Schemes of Finland*; LUT University: Lappeenranta, Finland, 2020.
49. Deviatkin, I.; Kozlova, M.; Yeomans, J.S. Simulation decomposition for environmental sustainability: Enhanced decision-making in carbon footprint analysis. *Socioecon. Plann. Sci.* **2021**, *75*, 100837. [CrossRef]
50. Ruponen, I. *Profitability Analysis of Biofuels and the Impact of Biofuel Policies in Finland*; LUT University: Lappeenranta, Finland, 2021.
51. Festel, G.; Würmseher, M.; Rammer, C.; Boles, E.; Bellof, M. Modelling production cost scenarios for biofuels and fossil fuels in Europe. *J. Clean. Prod.* **2014**, *66*, 242–253. [CrossRef]
52. Brown, T.R.; Thilakaratne, R.; Brown, R.C.; Hu, G. Regional differences in the economic feasibility of advanced biorefineries: Fast pyrolysis and hydroprocessing. *Energy Policy* **2013**, *57*, 234–243. [CrossRef]
53. Landälv, I.; Waldheim, L.; van den Heuvel, E.; Kalligeros, S. *Building Up the Future Cost of Biofuel*; European Commission, Sub Group on Advanced Biofuels: Brussels, Belgium, 2017.
54. IEA Fuel Price Distribution. Available online: https://www.iea.org/data-and-statistics/charts/fuel-price-distribution-2019 (accessed on 19 December 2021).
55. Collan, M.; Fedrizzi, M.; Luukka, P. A multi-expert system for ranking patents: An approach based on fuzzy pay-off distributions and a TOPSIS–AHP framework. *Expert Syst. Appl.* **2013**, *40*, 4749–4759. [CrossRef]
56. Kozlova, M.; Collan, M.; Luukka, P. Renewable Energy in Emerging Economies: Shortly Analyzing the Russian Incentive Mechanisms for Renewable Energy Investments. In Proceedings of the International Research Conference "GSOM Emerging Markets Conference-2015: Business and Government Perspectives", New York, NY, USA, 15–17 October 2015.

57. Kozlova, M.; Yeomans, J. Visual Analytics in Environmental Decision-Making: A Comparison of Overlay Charts versus Simulation Decomposition. *J. Environ. Inform. Lett.* **2021**, *4*, 93–100. [CrossRef]
58. Enciso, S.R.A.; Fellmann, T.; Dominguez, I.P.; Santini, F. Abolishing biofuel policies: Possible impacts on agricultural price levels, price variability and global food security. *Food Policy* **2016**, *61*, 9–26. [CrossRef]
59. Moncada, J.A.; Verstegen, J.A.; Posada, J.A.; Junginger, M.; Lukszo, Z.; Faaij, A.; Weijnen, M. Exploring policy options to spur the expansion of ethanol production and consumption in Brazil: An agent-based modeling approach. *Energy Policy* **2018**, *123*, 619–641. [CrossRef]

Article

Why Do Companies Need Operational Flexibility to Reduce Waste at Source?

Yara Kayyali Elalem [1], Isik Bicer [2,*] and Ralf W. Seifert [1,3]

[1] College of Management of Technology (CDM), École Polytechnique Fédérale de Lausanne, CH-1015 Lausanne, Switzerland; yara.kayyalielalem@epfl.ch (Y.K.E.); ralf.seifert@epfl.ch (R.W.S.)
[2] Schulich School of Business, York University, 111 Ian MacDonald Blvd, Toronto, ON M3J 1P3, Canada
[3] IMD—International Institute for Management Development, Chemin de Bellerive 23, P.O. Box 915, CH-1001 Lausanne, Switzerland
* Correspondence: bicer@schulich.yorku.ca

Abstract: We analyze the environmental benefits of operational flexibility that emerge in the form of less product waste during the sourcing process by reducing overproduction. We consider three different options for operational flexibility: (1) lead-time reduction, (2) quantity-flexibility contracts, and (3) multiple sourcing. We use a multiplicative demand process to model the evolutionary dynamics of demand uncertainty. We then quantify the impact of key modeling parameters for each operational-flexibility strategy on the waste ratio, which is measured as the ratio of excess inventory when a certain operational-flexibility strategy is employed to the amount when an offshore supplier is utilized without any operational flexibility. We find that the lead-time reduction strategy has the maximum capability to reduce waste in the sourcing process of buyers, followed by the quantity-flexibility and multiple-sourcing strategies, respectively. Thus, our results indicate that operational-flexibility strategies that rely on the localization of production are key to reducing waste and improving environmental sustainability at source.

Keywords: sustainability; sourcing; operational flexibility

Citation: Elalem, Y.K.; Bicer, I.; Seifert, R.W. Why Do Companies Need Operational Flexibility to Reduce Waste at Source? *Sustainability* **2022**, *14*, 367. https://doi.org/10.3390/su14010367

Academic Editor: Ming-Lang Tseng

Received: 30 November 2021
Accepted: 23 December 2021
Published: 30 December 2021

Publisher's Note: MDPI stays neutral with regard to jurisdictional claims in published maps and institutional affiliations.

Copyright: © 2021 by the authors. Licensee MDPI, Basel, Switzerland. This article is an open access article distributed under the terms and conditions of the Creative Commons Attribution (CC BY) license (https://creativecommons.org/licenses/by/4.0/).

1. Introduction

Improving sustainability on the production and consumption sides of product life cycles has proven to be critical in reducing the carbon footprint and combating global warming [1]. For this reason, one of the United Nations Sustainable Development Goals (i.e., Goal #12) explicitly addresses the problems associated with unsustainable production and consumption (https://www.un.org/sustainabledevelopment/sustainable-development-goals/ (accessed on 22 December 2021). Many manufacturers shift production to low-cost and distant countries to benefit from low production costs, but the long production and shipping lead times between production and the market bases contribute to significant amounts of excess inventory [2] that risk going to waste in retail stores without ever reaching consumers. The cost of excess inventory in the retail industry was estimated to be USD 471 billion in 2014 [3]. In other words, the Earth's resources to a value of USD 471 billion are wasted in producing goods that are never sold, and hence never used, by any consumer.

Let us consider the apparel industry, which is responsible for 8–10% of global carbon emissions [4]. The industry is dominated by strong brands that outsource production to contract manufacturers in offshore countries that rely on coal-fueled power plants. These contract manufacturers sometimes even outsource production to yet other countries to further reduce production costs and increase their capacity to fulfill increasing global demand [5]. These offshoring waves have severe effects on the environment. The industry is reported to be responsible for around 35% of oceanic microplastic pollution, 20% of industrial water pollution, and more than 8% of global carbon emissions [4]. Despite this environmental destruction, for 30–40% of clothes produced, there is no customer demand [6], resulting in a loss of profit for the apparel brands. Therefore, 30–40% of the environmental disaster could be eliminated by avoiding holding excess inventory, which is also appealing for retailers because it helps them increase their profits.

Operational flexibility has been proposed by scholars as an effective method for minimizing mismatches between supply and demand under demand uncertainty [2]. If demand exceeds supply, companies incur the opportunity cost of losing the demand. If demand falls short of supply, companies end up with excess inventory and incur inventory holding costs. In addition to the negative impact on profits, excess inventory has a catastrophic impact on the environment due to the carbon emissions and pollution that arise during the production and logistics operations for goods that are not even demanded by customers. It is therefore important to conduct a comprehensive study of operational and environmental trade-offs arising from the interaction between different supply chain processes such as procurement and inventory management [7]. In the extant literature, the merits of operational flexibility are quantified from the perspective of its impact on profits [2,8–11]. However, its benefits for environmental sustainability have not been addressed yet. In this research, we aim to fill this gap in the literature by addressing the following two questions:

- What is the environmental value of operational flexibility measured in the form of waste reduction?
- What types of operational-flexibility strategies are highly effective in increasing profits while improving environmental sustainability?

We consider three different operational-flexibility strategies. The first is lead-time reduction, which can be achieved by localizing production near the market bases. Lead-time reduction allows a buyer to postpone ordering decisions until credible information from the market about the final demand has been collected. Therefore, decision makers base their decisions on accurate demand forecasts and hence are able to reduce supply–demand mismatches [2]. Second, we analyze quantity flexibility whereby an offshore supplier offers the buyer flexibility to update the initial order quantity, within some limits, after the buyer has improved its demand forecasts [10]. Compared with lead-time reduction, quantity flexibility does not require the localization of production near the market bases. Finally, we consider multiple sourcing, in which a buyer employs a domestic supplier and an offshore supplier to exploit the market responsiveness of the domestic supplier and the cost efficiency of the offshore supplier at the same time [9]. Although it has been well established in the extant literature that these three strategies are highly effective in reducing supply–demand mismatches, their impact on reducing waste is not well known. We assume a profit-oriented buyer who aims to maximize profit and employs operational-flexibility strategies just to reduce mismatch costs. Based on the profit-maximizing decisions of the buyer, we quantify the secondary positive impacts of the operational-flexibility strategies on environmental sustainability.

Following [12], we use a multiplicative demand process to model the evolutionary dynamics of demand uncertainty. Then, we quantify the impact of key modeling parameters for each operational-flexibility strategy on the waste ratio, which is measured as the ratio of excess inventory when a certain operational-flexibility strategy is employed to the amount when an offshore supplier is utilized without any operational flexibility. Suppose, for example, the expected excess inventory is 100 units if a buyer sources products from an offshore supplier. Then, the supplier offers the buyer quantity flexibility, helping the buyer reduce the expected excess inventory to 60 units. For the quantity-flexibility strategy employed, the waste ratio obtained is $60/100 = 60\%$. Our results show that the lead-time reduction strategy has the maximum capability to reduce waste in the sourcing process of buyers, followed by the quantity-flexibility and multiple-sourcing strategies, in order. Therefore, operational-flexibility strategies that rely on the localization of production are key to reducing waste and improving environmental sustainability at source.

We organize the remainder of the paper as follows. In Section 2, we position our research by reviewing the extant literature on circular operations management and operational flexibility. We present the model preliminaries in Section 3. Then, we analyze each operational strategy and present some numerical examples in Section 4, where we also discuss the environmental implications further in Section 5. Finally, we provide concluding remarks and envision future research directions in Section 6.

2. Literature Review

Our research is connected to two streams of the operations management literature: (1) circular operations management and (2) operational flexibility. One of the fundamental problems in the circular operations management literature is how to transform the linear "take-make-dispose" operational model to a circular structure, so that products can stay in the market after their lifetime to minimize waste on the consumption side [13,14]. The phenomenon of circular operations management is also known as closed-loop supply chain management (CLSC). There are three different layers of CLSC, which aim to minimize product waste on the consumption side. We depict these layers in Figure 1.

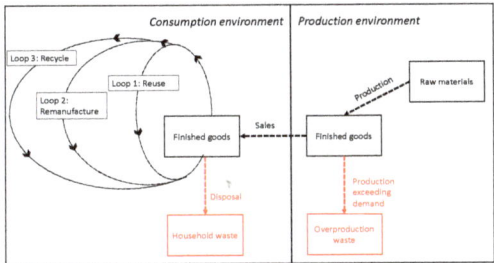

Figure 1. Closing the loop in supply chains.

The first layer of the CLSC is *reusing*, which focuses on strategies to extend the consumption length of products [14–16]. If a product is damaged or loses its functionality, it must be repaired to increase the length of the consumption period. When a customer loses interest in using a product, it must be sold in the secondary market or shared with other people. Therefore, the ease of repairing, resharing, and selling in secondary markets are key elements of the first layer [14,16]. One of the successful applications of reuse is the online marketplace of Patagonia, an outdoor apparel firm, where customers can exchange their clothes when they lose interest in them [17]. Another example is the product ownership program of Xerox whereby the printing company retains ownership of the printers and leases them to customers [14]. When a customer terminates its contract, Xerox leases the product to a new customer, so the company's products are shared over their lifetime.

The second layer of the CLSC is *remanufacturing*, whereby a set of refurbished and new components are used to manufacture products [18–20]. There are two main challenges regarding the implementation of remanufacturing. The first is uncertainty about the flow of used components, which will later be refurbished for use in the manufacturing process. The second challenge is the cannibalization of the original items because introducing the remanufactured products to the market would result in lower sales of the original ones, leading to lower profits. Ref. [19] address the first challenge by developing a queuing-theory model that dynamically estimates the flow of used products and then applying an aggregate base-stock policy to optimize the inventory policy. To address the second challenge, [20] develop a diffusion model and categorize products depending on their market diffusion and purchase frequency. The authors outline a decision typology that shows the product categories with the maximum potential for remanufacturing.

The last layer of the CLSC is *recycling*, whereby products at the end of their life go through a series of operations to manufacture new items. Well-known examples of recycling are paper and plastic recycling, which are observed in the recycling centers of municipalities of big cities. Yet, the most important challenge of recycling remains the collection of products from households. Ref. [14] give the example of Norway, where the recycling rate for plastic bottles is impressively high—97%. Norwegians achieve this by providing government funds to support retail stores in collecting plastics via reverse vending machines (the same system can be observed in other western European countries such as the Netherlands). Another approach to increasing the recycling rate is to mandate manufacturers to develop collection and recycling mechanisms for their products, which is popularly known as extended producers responsibility (EPR) [21]. EPR has been popularized in the electronics industry, with an example being the Minnesota Electronics Recycling Act [22]. According to this act, the state of Minnesota imposes strict collection and recycling targets on producers as a percentage of their total sales volume [22].

Studies in the extant literature successfully address the most important problems related to improving sustainability on the consumer side. Once a product reaches the market, keeping it in the loop of the CLSC has certain environmental benefits. However, the extant literature does not quantify the environmental impact of overproduction nor develop remedies for that problem. We contribute to the literature by filling this gap.

Our research is also related to a second stream of literature that prices the value of operational flexibility. Companies establish operational flexibility in different ways, such as lead-time reduction [2,8], quantity-flexibility contracts [10], and multiple sourcing [9,23]. These operational-flexibility strategies make it possible for buyers to determine order quantities after the partial or full resolution of demand uncertainty, helping them to better match supply with uncertain demand. One of the challenges in the extant literature is related to demand modeling because the demand model should involve the time element in order to quantify the benefits of delaying the ordering decision. In practice, manufacturers often employ demand planning teams that collect credible information from customers and update demand forecasts over time. Thus, demand forecasts are improved over time as a result of such efforts. For this reason, the modeling approaches used in the operational-flexibility literature incorporate the evolutionary dynamics of demand forecasts in order to price the value of operational flexibility. Ref. [8] use a multiplicative demand process to price the value of lead-time reduction. Ref. [2] later extend the multiplicative demand model by incorporating sudden changes in the demand forecasts and show that the value of lead-time reduction increases with positive jumps in the demand forecasts. Ref. [10] use a multiplicative demand model to price the value of quantity flexibility and show that the value is jointly affected by the order-adjustment flexibility and the time when the order adjustments are made. Ref. [23] develop a tailored capacity model, which is analogous to the multiple-sourcing model that we consider in this research. In their model, a buyer utilizes a speculative capacity under demand uncertainty, but also reserves a reactive capacity that can be utilized once the demand is known. Ref. [9] extends [23] by using the extreme-value theory, so the tailored capacity model can be applied to a wider selection of product categories.

Our contribution to the operational-flexibility literature is that we quantify the environmental benefits of operational flexibility that appear in the form of reduced product waste during the sourcing process. The studies in the extant literature are based on a profit-oriented view of the firm such that a reduction in the supply–demand mismatch costs determines the value of operational flexibility. We hopefully expect that companies will be less concerned about increasing their profits in the future, focusing rather on understanding the environmental impact of their operations. Our research aims to fill this gap in the literature by showing how operational flexibility can help minimize product waste during the sourcing process.

3. Model Preliminaries

To quantify the impact of operational flexibility on excess inventory, we model the evolutionary dynamics of demand forecasts. There are two types of demand models that can be used for such a purpose: (1) the additive demand model and (2) the multiplicative demand model [12,24]. The *difference* between the successive demand forecasts follows a normal distribution in the additive demand model, whereas the *ratio* of the successive demand forecasts follows a normal distribution in the multiplicative demand model. It has been well established in the literature that the additive demand model fits the empirical data well when the forecast horizon is short and the demand uncertainty is low. However, the multiplicative demand model fits the empirical data well when the forecast horizon is long and the demand uncertainty is high [24]. In this paper, we consider the multiplicative demand model because the lead times are expected to be long when companies source from offshore suppliers. Additionally, we focus on products with high demand uncertainty because the magnitude of excess inventory is more pronounced for products with high demand uncertainty than for those with low demand uncertainty.

We use D_i to denote the demand forecast at time t_i, such that $t_0 \leq t_i \leq t_n$. The forecast-updating process starts at time t_0 and ends at t_n. We fix t_n to the time when the actual demand is realized, so the final demand is fully known at t_n. Therefore, the length of the forecast horizon is $t_n - t_0$. The demand forecasts are updated at each time epoch t_i for $i \in \{0, 1, \cdots, n\}$. According to the multiplicative demand model, the demand forecast D_i is formulated as follows:

$$D_i = D_0 e^{(\nu(t_i - t_0) + \varepsilon_1 + \varepsilon_2 + \cdots + \varepsilon_i)}. \quad (1)$$

The ν term denotes the drift rate, and the ε terms are the forecast adjustments that follow a normal distribution:

$$\varepsilon_i \sim \mathcal{N}(-\varsigma^2/2, \varsigma), \quad \forall i \in \{1, \ldots, n\}, \quad (2)$$

where ς is the volatility parameter.

The drift rate can take non-zero values depending on the forecast-updating process. Ref. [12] gives an example of a forecast-updating process such that demand planners use only the advance demand information to update the demand forecasts, which is modeled by a multiplicative demand model with a positive drift rate. When the forecasts are updated based on an unbiased judgmental demand process, the drift rate should be set equal to zero [12]. The multiplicative demand model, given by Equation (1), yields a lognormal distribution for the end demand, which is conditional on the demand forecast at t_i:

$$\ln(D_n)|D_i \sim \mathcal{N}(\ln(D_i) + (\nu - \varsigma^2/2)(t_n - t_i), \varsigma\sqrt{t_n - t_i}), \quad \forall i \in \{0, \ldots, n-1\}. \quad (3)$$

The location parameter of the lognormal distribution is $\ln(D_i) + (\nu - \varsigma^2/2)(t_n - t_i)$, and the scale parameter is $\varsigma\sqrt{t_n - t_i}$.

In Figure 2, we present an example of the multiplicative demand model with a drift rate of zero and a volatility parameter of one. We normalize the initial demand forecast to one and scale the length of the forecast horizon to one. Thus, $D_0 = 1$, $t_0 = 0$, and $t_1 = 1$. We simulate a random path of the evolution of demand forecasts and calculate the 95% confidence interval over the forecast horizon. The black curve represents the demand forecasts, and the pink area shows the 95% confidence interval. For example, the demand forecast at $t = 0$ is equal to one, and the actual demand is expected to be between zero and four at $t = 0$ given by the limits of the pink area. As shown in the figure, the distance between the limits of the confidence interval decreases over time. This observation indicates that the accuracy of the demand forecasts improves over time as the time for the realization of the final demand approaches, which is consistent with practice. Therefore, the multiplicative model is very effective in capturing the dynamics of demand-updating mechanisms in practice [12,24].

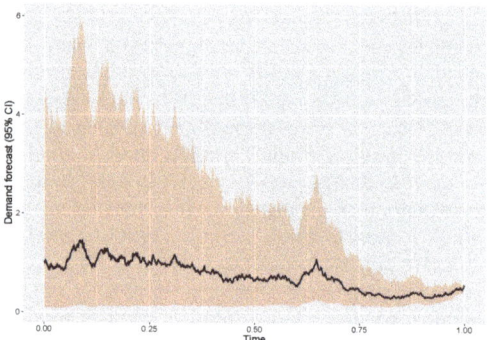

Figure 2. Evolution of demand forecasts for the multiplicative process with $D_0 = 1$, $\nu = 0$, and $\varsigma = 1$.

We now apply the multiplicative demand model given by Equation (3) to develop the expected profit, optimal order quantity, and expected excess inventory derivations. We consider the classical newsvendor model such that a buyer sells the products in a market with uncertain demand. We use p to denote the selling price of a product per unit. The buyer incurs a purchasing cost of c per unit. Unsold inventory is salvaged at a salvage value of s per unit. The salvage value can be negative in some industries where companies pay to throw away the excess inventory. In the pharmaceutical industry, for example, unsold drugs must be destroyed after their shelf life because of strict regulations, making the salvage value negative for pharmaceutical companies. The critical-fractile solution was developed to determine the optimal order quantity in the classic paper of Arrow et al. [25]:

$$\beta = \frac{p-c}{p-s}, \qquad (4)$$

where β is known as the critical fractile or the critical ratio. When the demand follows the lognormal distribution given by Equation (3), the optimal order quantity is found by:

$$Q^* = e^{\ln(D_i) + (\nu - \varsigma^2/2)(t_n - t_i) + \Phi^{-1}(\beta)\varsigma\sqrt{t_n - t_i}}, \qquad (5)$$

where $\Phi^{-1}(\cdot)$ is the inverse of the standard normal distribution function $\Phi(\cdot)$.

To find the expected profit, we first need to derive the standardized order quantity. When the buyer orders Q units, the standardized order quantity becomes:

$$z_Q = \frac{\ln(Q/D_i) - (\nu - \varsigma^2/2)(t_n - t_i)}{\varsigma\sqrt{t_n - t_i}}. \qquad (6)$$

Then, the expected profit for an order quantity of Q units is given by Bicer and Hagspiel [10]:

$$E(\Pi(Q)|D_i) = (p-c)Q - (p-s)\left[Q\Phi(z_Q) - D_i e^{\nu(t_n - t_i)}\Phi(z_Q - \varsigma\sqrt{t_n - t_i})\right]. \qquad (7)$$

The first term on the right-hand side of Equation (7) gives the total profit when all the units ordered are sold in the market at the selling price. However, the demand is uncertain, and it can be less than Q units. The second term on the right-hand side of the expression can be considered as the cost of an insurance policy that fully hedges the excess inventory risk. The term in brackets is the expected excess inventory:

$$E(\text{Excess Inventory} \mid Q, D_i) = Q\Phi(z_Q) - D_i e^{\nu(t_n - t_i)}\Phi(z_Q - \varsigma\sqrt{t_n - t_i}). \qquad (8)$$

The last expression indicates that the excess inventory (hence the waste) can be reduced using two different approaches. First, postponing the ordering decision leads to a reduction in the time window $t_n - t_i$, which in turn helps decrease the expected excess inventory. Second, reducing the order quantity results in a decrease in the expected excess inventory.

These results provide useful insights regarding the use of operational flexibility to improve sustainability by reducing waste in the sourcing process. The lead-time reduction and quantity-flexibility practices make it possible for the buyer to postpone their ordering decision. Therefore, these two operational-flexibility strategies help decrease excess inventory. Utilizing multiple sources (one offshore supplier and one domestic supplier), the buyer can reduce the quantity ordered from an offshore supplier. Thus, multiple sourcing also helps reduce the excess inventory.

4. Analysis of the Impact of Operational Flexibility on Excess Inventory

We now look at the impact of the three operational-flexibility strategies (i.e., lead-time reduction, quantity flexibility, and multiple sourcing) on the excess inventory in order to quantify the environmental benefits of operational flexibility. The analytical derivations of the optimal policies for these strategies are given in detail in de Treville et al. [8] for lead-time reduction, Bicer and Hagspiel [10] for quantity-flexibility contracts, and Biçer [9] for multiple sourcing. The following subsections first discuss the analytical derivations of the optimal policies for these strategies and then quantify the impact of operational flexibility on excess inventory.

4.1. Lead-Time Reduction

Suppose that a buyer purchases products from an offshore supplier and sells them in a market with uncertain demand. The buyer places the purchase order at time t_l, and the products are delivered at time t_n such that $t_0 \leq t_l \leq t_n$. The buyer sells the products in the market at time t_n. This setting applies to fashion apparel brands that use contract manufacturers to make their clothes and sell them to retail stores at the beginning of each selling season. The length of $t_n - t_l$ is the decision lead time, which is the time elapsed between when the ordering decision is made and when the actual demand is observed. The demand is highly uncertain at time t_l, which in turn exposes the buyer to excess inventory risk.

We assume that the selling price is \$$p$ per unit, and the salvage value is \$$s$ per unit. We use c_l to denote the cost of ordering from the offshore supplier per unit. Then, the optimal order quantity can be found by Equation (5). When the buyer places the optimal order quantity, its expected profit and expected excess inventory can be found by Equations (7) and (8) conditional on the optimal order quantity.

We now consider the case that the buyer aims to reduce the lead time by switching to a local responsive supplier. This makes it possible for the buyer to place the order at time t_s such that $t_s \geq t_l$. However, the buyer incurs a higher purchasing cost when buying products from the local supplier. We use c_s to denote the cost per unit of ordering from the local supplier such that $c_s \geq c_l$. Therefore, the buyer is exposed to a trade-off between postponing the ordering decision and incurring a higher ordering cost. This trade-off has a significant impact on the buyer's profits and the excess inventory.

In Figure 3, we present an example of a buyer who would like to decide whether to purchase products from an offshore or a domestic supplier. The selling price of the product is USD 300 per unit; the cost of purchasing from the offshore supplier is USD 40 per unit; the cost of purchasing from the domestic supplier is USD 50 per unit. Unsold inventory is thrown away, so the salvage value is set equal to zero. We normalize the initial demand forecast to one ($D_0 = 1$) and change the demand parameters accordingly. The drift rate of the multiplicative demand model is set equal to zero, and the volatility is equal to one. We also normalize the long lead time (i.e., when an order is placed with the offshore supplier) to one such that $t_n - t_l = 1$ by setting $t_n = 1$ and $t_l = 0$.

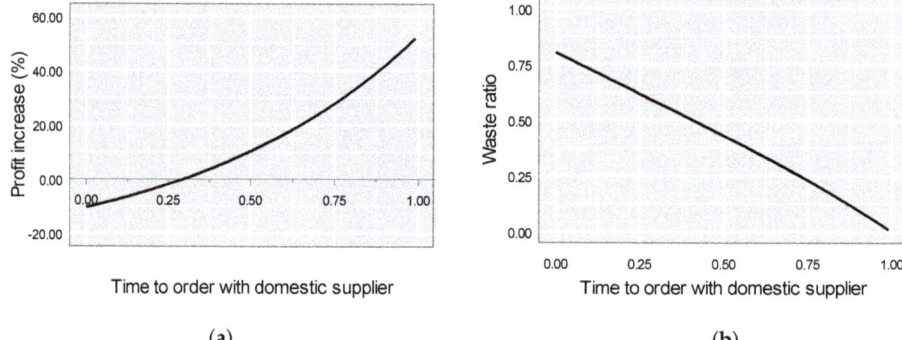

Figure 3. Analysis of lead-time reduction: (**a**) Impact of lead-time reduction on profit increase; (**b**) Impact of lead-time reduction on waste ratio.

We present the percentage change in profit in Figure 3a when the buyer switches from the offshore supplier to the domestic supplier. The x-axis represents the time of ordering with the domestic supplier (i.e., t_s), and the y-axis represents the percentage increase in profits. When the domestic supplier is not responsive enough, the benefits of local sourcing disappear, resulting in a loss of profit. As shown in the figure, the profit increase is negative when $t_s < 0.29$. In this case, it is not advantageous for the buyer to order from the domestic supplier, so a buyer aiming to maximize profit would continue to source from the offshore supplier. If the domestic supplier is responsive enough to let the buyer postpone the ordering decision to later than $t = 0.29$—that is, $t_s > 0.29$—the buyer would increase their profit by switching from the offshore supplier to the domestic supplier. If the lead time is reduced by half (i.e., $t_s = 0.5$), Figure 3a shows that ordering from the domestic supplier leads to a profit increase of around 10%. If the lead time is reduced by 90% so that $t_s = 0.9$, the buyer can increase their profit by around 40%.

In addition to these economic benefits, the lead-time reduction helps the buyer reduce waste, thus having a positive environmental impact on the sourcing process. Figure 3b shows the waste ratio, which is the ratio of excess inventory when the buyer orders from the domestic supplier to the excess inventory when they order from the offshore supplier. The x-axis represents the t_s value, and the y-axis represents the waste ratio. When $t_s = 0$, the lead time for ordering from the offshore supplier is the same as the lead time for ordering from the domestic supplier. Even if the lead times are the same for both sourcing alternatives, the waste ratio is lower than one for $t_s = 0$, meaning that local sourcing helps reduce waste even in the absence of a lead-time reduction. The waste ratio of 0.8 for $t_s = 0$ is a result of the difference in ordering costs between the domestic and offshore suppliers. The cost of ordering from the domestic supplier is more than ordering from the offshore supplier ($c_s > c_l$). This leads to lower ordering levels when the domestic supplier is used rather than the offshore supplier. Therefore, the 20% reduction in waste for $t_s = 0$ can only be attributed to the lower ordering levels, which is independent of the benefits of a lead-time reduction. However, this improvement is not attainable because Figure 3a shows that the buyer prefers the offshore supplier over the domestic one when $t_s = 0$.

When the t_s value increases, Figure 3b shows that the waste ratio decreases. Therefore, the buyer can reduce waste during the sourcing process by cutting the lead time with the domestic supplier. When sourcing from the domestic supplier makes it possible to reduce the lead time substantially, the buyer reaches alignment between the economic and environmental incentives of local sourcing. On the one hand, the buyer can increase their profit due to better matching between supply and demand. On the other hand, they can also reduce the waste at source by minimizing the excess inventory. Apart from these direct benefits, promoting local production may also help improve the extent of remanufacturing and recycling because it increases product know-how in local markets.

4.2. Quantity-Flexibility Contracts

When the buyer does not have the possibility of implementing local sourcing, a quantity-flexibility contract can be used to increase profits and reduce excess inventory. Under a quantity-flexibility agreement, the buyer determines the initial order quantity at time t_l and the flexibility percentage. We use Q_l to denote the initial order quantity and following the terminology in [10] we use α to denote the flexibility percentage. Then, the buyer determines the final order quantity Q_f at time $t_s > t_l$ within some limits:

$$(1-\alpha)Q_l \leq Q_f \leq (1+\alpha)Q_l. \tag{9}$$

If the demand forecasts are updated upward from t_l to t_s, the buyer would increase the order quantity up to $(1+\alpha)Q_l$ units. Otherwise, the buyer would decrease the order quantity down to $(1-\alpha)Q_l$ units. Thus, the final order quantity depends on the demand forecast at time t_s, the initial order quantity, and the flexibility percentage. It is given by [10]:

$$Q_f = \begin{cases} Q_l(1-\alpha) & \text{if } D_s < D_{s1}, \\ Q_f^* = D_s e^{(\nu-\varsigma^2/2)(t_n-t_s)+\Phi^{-1}(\beta)\varsigma\sqrt{t_n-t_s}} & \text{if } D_{s1} \leq D_s \leq D_{s2}, \\ Q_l(1+\alpha) & \text{if } D_{s2} < D_s, \end{cases} \tag{10}$$

where:

$$D_{s1} = Q_l(1-\alpha)e^{-(\nu-\varsigma^2/2)(t_n-t_s)-\Phi^{-1}(\beta)\varsigma\sqrt{t_n-t_s}}, \tag{11}$$

$$D_{s2} = Q_l(1+\alpha)e^{-(\nu-\varsigma^2/2)(t_n-t_s)-\Phi^{-1}(\beta)\varsigma\sqrt{t_n-t_s}}. \tag{12}$$

The D_{s1} and D_{s2} terms can be interpreted as the lower and upper critical values for the demand forecast at time t_s. If the demand forecast D_s turns out to be higher than D_{s2}, the buyer should order the maximum allowable quantity based on the quantity-flexibility contract, which is equal to $Q_l(1+\alpha)$ units. If the demand forecast D_s turns out to be lower than D_{s1}, the buyer should reduce the order quantity to the minimum allowable level, which is equal to $Q_l(1-\alpha)$ units. If the demand forecast D_s is between these limits, the buyer should set the order quantity to the profit-maximizing level. Based on the final order quantity, the expected profit and the expected excess inventory can be calculated by Equations (7) and (8), respectively.

In Figure 4, we present an example of a buyer who orders products from an offshore supplier and has the flexibility to update the initial order quantity based on a quantity-flexibility contract. The cost parameters are the same as above: The selling price is USD 300 per unit, the cost of purchasing from the offshore supplier is USD 40 per unit, and there is no salvage value for unsold inventory. Likewise, the demand parameters are the same as above. The demand forecast at t_0 is normalized to one. The drift rate and the volatility are equal to zero and one, respectively. The initial order quantity is determined at the very beginning such that $t_l = 0$. The final order quantity is determined at t_s within the quantity-flexibility limits.

Figure 4a shows the impact of flexibility on the percentage profit increase. The x-axis represents the flexibility percentage α, and the y-axis represents the percentage increase in profits as a result of the order-adjustment flexibility. To calculate the values of the profit increase, we generate 100,000 random demand paths for each α value. We compare the demand realization at t_s along each sample path with D_{s1} and D_{s2} limits to determine the final order quantity. Then, the expected profit is calculated using Equation (7). Figure 4a demonstrates that the percentage change in profit increases with a decreasing rate as the flexibility increases. When $\alpha = 0.4$, the buyer can achieve around 20% profit increase compared with the no-flexibility case.

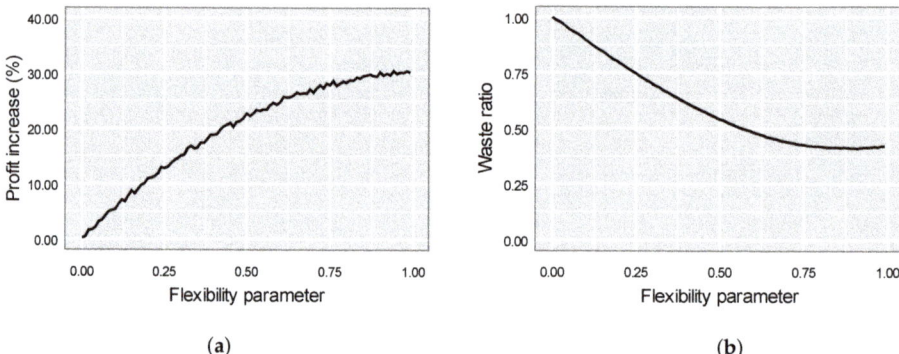

Figure 4. Analysis of quantity flexibility: (**a**) Impact of the flexibility parameter on profit increase; (**b**) Impact of the flexibility parameter on waste ratio.

Figure 4b depicts the waste ratio as a function of the flexibility parameter. We calculate the waste ratio as the ratio of the expected excess inventory when the buyer has the flexibility to update the initial order quantity to the expected excess inventory when the buyer has no flexibility. Therefore, the waste ratio is close to one when the flexibility percentage is near zero. As the flexibility percentage increases, the waste ratio decreases with a decreasing rate. The curve becomes flatter for high α values such that the waste ratio cannot be reduced below 40%. These results indicate that quantity flexibility has positive economic and environmental impacts on the sourcing process of the buyer. However, its environmental impact is more limited than what can be achieved with lead-time reduction.

4.3. Multiple Sourcing

In the lead-time reduction and quantity-flexibility practices, the buyer can source products from only one supplier. In the former case, the buyer can source products from either an offshore supplier or a domestic supplier but not from both at the same time. In the latter case, the buyer can only order from an offshore supplier that provides the flexibility to adjust the initial order quantity in a later time epoch. We now consider an alternative strategy, whereby the buyer can source products from two different suppliers at the same time: One is the offshore supplier and the other the domestic.

The multiple sourcing strategy is very effective in mitigating the risk of supply–demand mismatches [9]. By utilizing an offshore supplier, the buyer benefits from the cost advantages of offshore production. If the buyer orders lower quantities from the offshore supplier, the excess inventory risk can also be minimized. If the demand turns out to be unexpectedly high, the buyer then utilizes the domestic supplier to meet the surplus demand. Therefore, a multiple-sourcing strategy allows the buyer to benefit from the cost advantages of the offshore supplier and the responsiveness of the domestic supplier at the same time. However, one of the implementation challenges of this strategy is that the domestic supplier may not always be utilized at a high level. If the demand turns out to be low, the quantity ordered from the domestic supplier would not be high enough to fully utilize its available capacity. Therefore, domestic suppliers are exposed to the risk of capacity underutilization when a multiple-sourcing strategy is employed. To compensate for this risk, domestic suppliers often charge their buyers a capacity reservation fee.

To capture these dynamics, we consider a multiple-sourcing setting with one buyer, one offshore supplier, and one domestic supplier. The buyer determines the order quantity of Q_l units from the offshore supplier and reserves a capacity of K units with the domestic supplier at time t_l. We use c_l and c_k to denote the cost of ordering from the offshore supplier and the capacity reservation cost at the domestic supplier per unit, respectively. At time $t_n > t_l$, the buyer observes the final demand and determines the final order quantity of Q_s

units from the domestic supplier such that $Q_s \leq K$. The domestic supplier is additionally paid c_s per each unit ordered. The formulation of Q_s is given by Biçer [9]:

$$Q_s = \max(\min(D_n, Q_l + K), Q_l) - Q_l, \qquad (13)$$

where D_n is the final demand for the product, which is observed at time t_n. Following up from Biçer [9], we first define two ratios to derive the optimal values of Q_l and K. They are:

$$\beta_1 = \frac{c_s + c_k - c_l}{c_s - s}, \qquad (14)$$

$$\beta_2 = \frac{p - c_s - c_k}{p - c_s}. \qquad (15)$$

Then, the optimal values are given by Biçer [9]:

$$Q_l^* = D_l e^{(\nu - \varsigma^2/2)(t_n - t_l) + \Phi^{-1}(\beta_1)\varsigma\sqrt{t_n - t_l}}, \qquad (16)$$

$$K^* = D_l e^{(\nu - \varsigma^2/2)(t_n - t_l)} \left[e^{\Phi^{-1}(\beta_2)\varsigma\sqrt{t_n - t_l}} - e^{\Phi^{-1}(\beta_1)\varsigma\sqrt{t_n - t_l}} \right]. \qquad (17)$$

Then, the profit in the multiple-sourcing setting is formulated as follows:

$$\Pi(Q_l, K, Q_s) = p \min(D_n, Q_l + K) + s \max(Q_l - D_n, 0) - c_l Q_l - c_k K - c_s Q_s. \qquad (18)$$

Using this formula and simulating the demand paths, the expected inventory for the optimal Q_l and K levels can be found. The expected excess inventory can also be calculated by plugging Q_l into Equation (8).

We now present an example to demonstrate the impact of multiple sourcing on the buyer's profits and excess inventory. We assume the same demand parameters as the examples given above. The cost of purchasing from the offshore supplier is USD 40 per unit, and the cost of purchasing from the domestic supplier is USD 50 per unit. The domestic supplier also charges USD 15 for each unit of capacity reserved. Unlike the lead-time reduction and quantity-flexibility examples, we cannot vary the key decision parameter that determines the magnitude of operational flexibility in the multiple-sourcing setting. In the multiple-sourcing setting, operational flexibility is directly influenced by the reactive capacity K. However, the reactive capacity is not a control variable. It is a decision variable that has to be optimized depending on the cost and demand parameters. For that reason, we vary the selling price between USD 150 and USD 300 in our analysis because Equation (17) indicates that the optimal capacity level increases with the selling price. In other words, we can observe the impact of responsiveness on profits and the waste ratio by varying the selling price because the selling price is directly correlated with the capacity level.

Figure 5a shows the impact of the selling price on the percentage profit increase such that the profit increases with the selling price. Doubling the selling price from USD 150 to USD 300 increases the profit by almost 190%. Figure 5b demonstrates that the waste ratio does not change depending on the selling price. This is because the optimal order quantity from the offshore supplier does not depend on the selling price but only on the cost parameters. For this reason, there is no environmental benefit to improving operational flexibility with the multiple-sourcing strategy. Both the profit increase and waste ratios in Figure 5a,b are calculated with respect to the resulting profit and waste when the selling price is set at USD 150.

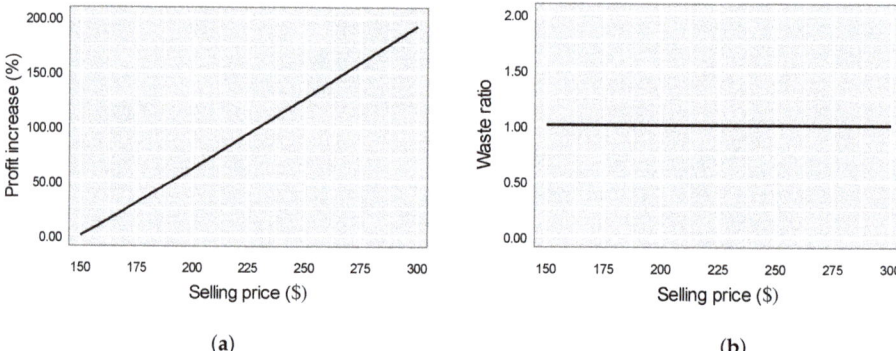

Figure 5. Analysis of multiple sourcing: (**a**) Expected profit depending on the selling price with multiple sourcing; (**b**) Waste ratio depending on the selling price with multiple sourcing.

We summarize the results of the three operational-flexibility strategies in Table 1 below. For each strategy, the profit increase and waste ratio reported are calculated by setting the parameter of the strategy in the table to the maximum value in comparison to setting the parameter to the minimum value within the given range. The results show that lead-time reduction has the highest potential in reducing waste while improving the profits of companies. In Section 5, we further elaborate on and discuss the results of the three strategies.

Table 1. Summary of results of the operational-flexibility strategies.

Strategy	Control Variable	Control Variable Range	Profit Increase	Waste Ratio
Lead-time reduction	Lead time with domestic supplier (t_s)	$t_s \in [0, 0.99]$	51.94%	0.01
Quantity-flexibility contracts	Flexibility parameter (α)	$\alpha \in [0, 0.99]$	29.98 %	0.42
Multiple sourcing	Selling price (p)	$p \in [150, 300]$	191.98%	1.00

5. Discussion

So far, we have shown the effect on the change in profit and the waste ratio of three supply chain flexibility strategies: (1) lead-time reduction, (2) quantity-flexibility contracts, and (3) multiple sourcing. The numerical analysis of lead-time reduction shows that when a firm reduces its lead-time by utilizing an onshore supplier instead of an offshore supplier, the firm can achieve both profit increase and waste reduction due to the decrease in demand uncertainty at the order time. When t_s is greater than 0.29, the firm starts experiencing a positive change in profit, which exceeds 50% as t_s increases to 1. As for the waste, even if $t_s = t_l = 0$, the firm still experiences waste reduction of 20% due to the increased cost, which lowers the newsvendor order quantity. The waste ratio decreases to zero as t_s increases to one, since the actual demand is known at this point and the firm does not operate under demand uncertainty anymore.

If firms cannot order from an onshore supplier, they can still benefit from the flexibility of an offshore supplier with a quantity flexibility contract where, up to time t_s, the firm can still adjust its order quantities by a factor of α. For a fixed t_s, our analysis shows that firms can achieve a 30% increase in profit, and waste reduction can reach more than 50% as the flexibility parameter increases to 1.

For multiple sourcing, the numerical analysis is performed based on the selling price of the product. It shows that doubling the selling price from USD 150 to USD 300 results in a profit increase of almost 190%. The waste, however, does not change with different pricing as it is calculated based on the offshore order quantity, which is independent of price.

The selection of a given flexibility strategy is also dependent on the risk associated with it. On the one hand, although single sourcing with lead-time reduction has the highest effect in reducing waste while still increasing a firm's profits, it can amplify the exposure to risk in the presence of uncertainty. On the other hand, multiple sourcing can present higher costs, and this is not accounted for as a result of having to manage several suppliers [26]. It is therefore critical for firms to assess all the benefits and risks arising from choosing a specific strategy in pursuit of improved sustainability and profits.

6. Conclusions

Improving sustainability in every aspect of our lives is vital to safeguard a durable future for the next generation. Manufacturers ought to pay special attention to sustainability because what they produce, how they produce, and where they produce has a substantial impact on the carbon footprint. The extant literature on sustainable operations management mainly focuses on the consumption side of product life cycles, with an intention to extend the product lifetime and reduce household waste. However, significant inefficiencies exist on the production side of product life cycles, whereby manufacturers overutilize the Earth's limited resources and generate carbon emissions when producing products in excessive amounts. A significant number of these products may never reach consumers. Prominent examples reported in the media include Amazon destroying thousands of unsold TVs and laptops in one of its warehouses [27].

In this research, we aim to fill the gap in the literature by demonstrating how operational flexibility can help organizations achieve sustainability at source. We focus on three different operational-flexibility strategies: (1) lead-time reduction, (2) quantity-flexibility contracts, and (3) multiple sourcing. Our results indicate that lead-time reduction has the highest potential to reduce waste while improving the profits of companies. Therefore, operational-flexibility strategies that promote local production are key to reducing waste and improving sustainability.

In particular, in our numerical analysis, where ordering time varies between 0 (start of planning horizon) and 1 (beginning of sales season), we show that lead-time reduction can result in a profit increase when orders are placed with onshore suppliers at a time t_s greater than 0.29, compared with being placed with an offshore supplier at time $t_l = 0$. The profit increase can go up to around 40% when orders are placed at $t_s = 0.9$, even if ordering costs are higher. Waste in terms of excess unsold inventory also decreases, even when $t_s = t_l = 0$ when the onshore supplier is used, and results in a 20% waste reduction compared with ordering from an offshore supplier as a result of the higher ordering costs, which result in lower order quantities. The waste decreases as t_s increases and finally approaches zero when orders can be placed during the selling season, when $t_s = 1$.

The results of our research offer some useful insights regarding the development of effective environmental policies. Because lead-time reduction is the most effective strategy, environmental policies should target cutting lead times, not only for inbound but also for outbound logistics. Increasing the import and export tariffs and imposing trade barriers would force countries to promote local production, which in turn leads to shorter lead times and lower waste. Although such policies conflict with the free trade and economic development ideas, we envision that environmental concerns would be highly dominant in the near future and governments would incrementally pass some regulations to reduce the volume of imports and exports. One of the side benefits of local production would be to establish a close connection between local manufacturers and local authorities such that recycling and remanufacturing can be easily implemented near the market bases. Therefore, local production may also help increase the product life cycle along the stages of the closed loop supply chains (Figure 1).

One of the limitations of our research is that we mainly focus on the dynamics on the production side of the product life cycle without connecting it with the consumption side. We mainly consider a newsvendor setting such that the buyer sells the products in the market at a certain price. The classical utility theory [28] suggests that the life cycle of a product is positively associated with the price paid for it. We believe that there is a need for empirical research that investigates the relationship between price and the length of a product's lifetime in the retail industry for different categories. We envision that this would be an interesting avenue for further research.

Another direction for future research is how digital transformation could contribute to lead-time reduction. Recent research focuses on lean manufacturing in the Industry 4.0 era [29]. Studies on lean manufacturing show that lead-time reduction is an important factor that enhances reliability and flexibility while decreasing inventory carrying costs and that integrating lean management and collaboration in the supply chain has important social, environmental, and economic benefits [30]. Therefore, we foresee that studies of the effect of Industry 4.0 on decreasing waste and increasing profit through lead-time reduction are a potential field for future work.

Author Contributions: Conceptualization, I.B.; methodology, Y.K.E. and I.B.; software, Y.K.E. and I.B.; validation, Y.K.E. and I.B.; formal analysis, Y.K.E. and I.B.; investigation, Y.K.E. and I.B.; resources, I.B.; writing—original draft preparation, Y.K.E. and I.B.; writing—review and editing, Y.K.E., I.B. and R.W.S.; visualization, Y.K.E. and I.B.; supervision, I.B. and R.W.S.; project administration, I.B. and R.W.S. All authors have read and agreed to the published version of the manuscript.

Funding: This research received no external funding.

Institutional Review Board Statement: Not applicable.

Informed Consent Statement: Not applicable.

Conflicts of Interest: The authors declare no conflict of interest.

References

1. Martí, J.M.C.; Seifert, R.W. Assessing the comprehensiveness of supply chain environmental strategies. *Bus. Strategy Environ.* **2013**, *22*, 339–356. [CrossRef]
2. Biçer, I.; Hagspiel, V.; de Treville, S. Valuing supply-chain responsiveness under demand jumps. *J. Oper. Manag.* **2018**, *61*, 46–67. [CrossRef]
3. Gustafson, K. Retailers Are Losing $1.75 Trillion over This. CNBC. 2015. Available online: https://www.cnbc.com/2015/11/30/retailers-are-losing-nearly-2-trillion-over-this.html (accessed on 22 December 2021).
4. Niinimäki, K.; Peters, G.; Dahlbo, H.; Perry, P.; Rissanen, T.; Gwilt, A. The environmental price of fast fashion. *Nat. Rev. Earth Environ.* **2020**, *1*, 189–200. [CrossRef]
5. Donahue, B. China Is Turning Ethiopia Into a Giant Fast-Fashion Factory. Bloomberg BusinessWeek. 2018. Available online: https://www.bloomberg.com/news/features/2018-03-02/china-is-turning-ethiopia-into-a-giant-fast-fashion-factory (accessed on 22 December 2021).
6. Hausman, W.H.; Thorbeck, J.S. Fast fashion: Quantifying the Benefits. In *Innovative Quick Response Programs in Logistics and Supply Chain Management*; International Handbooks on Information Systems; Cheng, T., Choi, T.M., Eds.; Springer: Berlin/Heidelberg, Germany, 2010; pp. 315–329. [CrossRef]
7. Martí, J.M.C.; Tancrez, J.S.; Seifert, R.W. Carbon footprint and responsiveness trade-offs in supply chain network design. *Int. J. Prod. Econ.* **2015**, *166*, 129–142. [CrossRef]
8. De Treville, S.; Bicer, I.; Chavez-Demoulin, V.; Hagspiel, V.; Schürhoff, N.; Tasserit, C.; Wager, S. Valuing lead time. *J. Oper. Manag.* **2014**, *32*, 337–346. [CrossRef]
9. Biçer, I. Dual sourcing under heavy-tailed demand: an extreme value theory approach. *Int. J. Prod. Res.* **2015**, *53*, 4979–4992. [CrossRef]
10. Bicer, I.; Hagspiel, V. Valuing quantity flexibility under supply chain disintermediation risk. *Int. J. Prod. Econ.* **2016**, *180*, 1–15. [CrossRef]
11. Biçer, I.; Seifert, R.W. Optimal Dynamic Order Scheduling under Capacity Constraints Given Demand-Forecast Evolution. *Prod. Oper. Manag.* **2017**, *26*, 2266–2286. [CrossRef]
12. Biçer, I.; Lücker, F.; Boyacı, T. Beyond Retail Stores: Managing Product Proliferation along the Supply Chain. *Prod. Oper. Manag.* **2021**, doi:10.1111/poms.13598. [CrossRef]
13. Abbey, J.D.; Guide, V.D.R., Jr. Closed-Loop Supply Chains: A Strategic Overview. In *Sustainable Supply Chains*; Springer Series in Supply Chain Management; Bouchery, Y., Corbett, C., Fransoo, J., Tan, T., Eds.; Springer: Cham, Switzerland, 2017; Volume 4, pp. 375–393. [CrossRef]
14. Atasu, A.; Dumas, C.; Van Wassenhove, L.N. The Circular Business Model. Harvard Business Review. 2021. Available online: https://hbr.org/2021/07/the-circular-business-model (accessed on 22 December 2021).
15. Bras, B. Sustainability and product life cycle management—Issues and challenges. *Int. J. Prod. Lifecycle Manag.* **2009**, *4*, 23–48. [CrossRef]

16. Agrawal, V.V.; Atasu, A.; Van Wassenhove, L.N. OM Forum—New Opportunities for Operations Management Research in Sustainability. *Manuf. Serv. Oper. Manag.* **2018**, *21*, 1–12. [CrossRef]
17. Casadesus-Masanell, R.; Kim, H.; Reinhardt, F.L. Patagonia. Harvard Business School Case#: 711-020. 2010. Available online: https://www.hbs.edu/faculty/Pages/item.aspx?num=39312 (accessed on 22 December 2021).
18. Guide, V.D.R., Jr.; Van Wassenhove, L.N. The Evolution of Closed-Loop Supply Chain Research. *Oper. Res.* **2009**, *57*, 10–18. [CrossRef]
19. Toktay, L.B.; Wein, L.M.; Zenios, S.A. Inventory Management of Remanufacturable Products. *Manag. Sci.* **2000**, *46*, 1412–1426. [CrossRef]
20. Debo, L.G.; Toktay, L.B.; Van Wassenhove, L.N. Joint Life-Cycle Dynamics of New and Remanufactured Products. *Prod. Oper. Manag.* **2006**, *15*, 498–513. [CrossRef]
21. Alev, I.; Agrawal, V.V.; Atasu, A. Extended Producer Responsibility for Durable Products. *Manuf. Serv. Oper. Manag.* **2019**, *22*, 364–382. [CrossRef]
22. Alev, I.; Huang, X.N.; Atasu, A.; Toktay, L.B. A Case Discussion on Market-Based Extended Producer Responsibility: The Minnesota Electronics Recycling Act. *J. Ind. Ecol.* **2018**, *23*, 208–221. [CrossRef]
23. Cattani, K.D.; Dahan, E.; Schmidt, G.M. Tailored capacity: Speculative and reactive fabrication of fashion goods. *Int. J. Prod. Econ.* **2008**, *114*, 416–430. [CrossRef]
24. Oh, S.; Özer, Ö. Mechanism design for capacity planning under dynamic evolutions of asymmetric demand forecasts. *Manag. Sci.* **2013**, *59*, 987–1007. [CrossRef]
25. Arrow, K.J.; Harris, T.; Marschak, J. Optimal inventory policy. *Econom. J. Econom. Soc.* **1951**, *19*, 250–272. [CrossRef]
26. Costantino, N.; Pellegrino, R. Choosing between single and multiple sourcing based on supplier default risk: A real options approach. *J. Purch. Supply Manag.* **2010**, *16*, 27–40. [CrossRef]
27. Wood, Z. Amazon Faces MPs' Scrutiny after Destroying Laptops, Tablets and Books. The Guardian. 2021. Available online: https://www.theguardian.com/technology/2021/jun/22/amazon-faces-mps-scrutiny-after-destroying-laptops-tablets-and-books (accessed on 22 December 2021).
28. Lancaster, K.J. A New Approach to Consumer Theory. *J. Political Econ.* **1966**, *74*, 132–157. [CrossRef]
29. Tseng, M.L.; Tran, T.P.T.; Ha, H.M.; Bui, T.D.; Lim, M.K. Sustainable industrial and operation engineering trends and challenges Toward Industry 4.0: A data driven analysis. *J. Ind. Prod. Eng.* **2021**, *38*, 581–598. [CrossRef]
30. Tseng, M.L.; Tran, T.P.T.; Wu, K.J.; Tan, R.R.; Bui, T.D. Exploring sustainable seafood supply chain management based on linguistic preferences: Collaboration in the supply chain and lean management drive economic benefits. *Int. J. Logist. Res. Appl.* **2020**. [CrossRef]

Article

Effects of Weather on Iowa Nitrogen Export Estimated by Simulation-Based Decomposition

Vishal Raul [1], Yen-Chen Liu [1], Leifur Leifsson [2,*] and Amy Kaleita [3]

[1] Department of Aerospace Eng., Iowa State University, Ames, IA 50011, USA; vvsraul@iastate.edu (V.R.); clarkliu@iastate.edu (Y.-C.L.)
[2] School of Aeronautics and Astronautics, Purdue University, West Lafayette, IN 47907, USA
[3] Department of Agricultural and Biosystems Eng., Iowa State University, Ames, IA 50011, USA; kaleita@iastate.edu
* Correspondence: leifur@purdue.edu

Abstract: The state of Iowa is known for its high-yield agriculture, supporting rising demands for food and fuel production. But this productivity is also a significant contributor of nitrogen loading to the Mississippi River basin causing the hypoxic zone in the Gulf of Mexico. The delivery of nutrients, especially nitrogen, from the upper Mississippi River basin, is a function, not only of agricultural activity, but also of hydrology. Thus, it is important to consider extreme weather conditions, such as drought and flooding, and understand the effects of weather variability on Iowa's food-energy-water (IFEW) system and nitrogen loading to the Mississippi River from Iowa. In this work, the simulation decomposition approach is implemented using the extended IFEW model with a crop-weather model to better understand the cause-and-effect relationships of weather parameters on the nitrogen export from the state of Iowa. July temperature and precipitation are used as varying input weather parameters with normal and log normal distributions, respectively, and subdivided to generate regular and dry weather conditions. It is observed that most variation in the soil nitrogen surplus lies in the regular condition, while the dry condition produces the highest soil nitrogen surplus for the state of Iowa.

Keywords: Iowa food-energy-water nexus; nitrogen export; system modeling; weather modeling; simulation decomposition

1. Introduction

Nutrients, such as nitrogen (N), are necessary in farming for raising crop and forage productivity, but they can also bring potential harm to the socioeconomic system. A hypoxic zone is a phenomenon where low dissolved oxygen (hypoxia) occurs in aquatic environments, which is primarily caused by excess nutrients running off or leaching from the contributing watershed. Over 400 hypoxic zones have been found in the world and the problem of hypoxia is worsening [1]. In the US, the environment and socioeconomic system of the Gulf of Mexico are impacted by hypoxia which has one of the largest hypoxic zones in the world [2]. Nitrogen (N) is one of the major contributors to the creation of the hypoxic zone of the Gulf of Mexico through the nitrates (NO_3) lost from watersheds within the Mississippi River Basin, which moves downstream to the Gulf of Mexico [3]. Studies show that the state of Iowa, one of the major producers of corn, soybean, ethanol, and animal products, contributes a considerable amount of nitrogen loads to the Mississippi River basin [4,5]. As the largest producer of corn in the US, nearly 57% of Iowa's corn is used for ethanol production [6]. The manure produced by animal agriculture is also rich in nitrogen [7]. The current research aims at creating strategies and policies to mitigate the excess nitrogen originating from the Iowa food-energy-water (IFEW) system.

Climate variability has major effects on FEW systems. For example, extreme events, such as floods or droughts, can reduce water availability and quality. In southern East

Africa, infrastructure design is challenging due to multi-year drought [8]. Furthermore, changes in the weather impact energy usage and demands of human activities. Moreover, in the food system, the needs for livestock watering and crop fertilizer can be severely impacted due to climates changes. Though Iowa uses primarily rain-fed agricultural production, in other areas irrigation water for crops is also significantly impacted (both in supply and in requirements) by weather and climate. Arizona is a predominantly irrigated agriculture state and supplies food to at least six major cities. It is especially vulnerable to climate changes [9]. Therefore, it is important to investigate the effects of weather variability on the sustainable management of FEW systems.

It is important to capture the complex interactions of the different domains to determine the exported nitrogen of the system. In this work, weather, water, agriculture, animal agriculture, and energy are considered in modeling the IFEW system. The macro-level simulation-based IFEW model introduced in [10] to determine the surplus nitrogen in the state of Iowa is extended to include a crop-weather model using linear regression of historical weather parameters, which is based on a prior study [11]. Simulation decomposition (SD) [12,13] is used to visualize the effects of weather variability on the IFEW nitrogen export. Furthermore, SD analysis is used to distinguish the influences of different weather scenarios affecting the surplus nitrogen.

The next section gives the details of the IFEW system model and the SD analysis technique. The following section presents the numerical results of SD applied to the proposed IFEW simulation model for several weather scenarios. The last section summarizes the work and discusses potential future work.

2. Methods

This section gives a high-level description of the IFEW system model interdependencies. The macro-level simulation-based model of the IFEW system and the SD technique are described.

2.1. IFEW System Model Interdependencies

The IFEW system model has five distinct macro-level domains, namely, weather, water, agriculture, animal agriculture, and energy (Figure 1). The weather discipline provides environmental factors, such as vapor pressure, temperature, rainfall, and solar radiation. Rainfall and snowfall supply surface water and groundwater components for the water discipline. The amount of crop production in the agriculture discipline is strongly related to precipitation and temperature [11]. The water discipline supplies water for drinking and service usage for the animal agriculture discipline, and the production and ethanol and fertilizer for the energy system. Dry distillers' grain soluble (DDGS) that is produced during the ethanol production process and commercial fertilizers provide protein to animals and fertility to soil in the animal agriculture and agricultural domains, respectively. Demand for food protein by society is satisfied by the animal agriculture discipline. Corn yield in the agricultural discipline is used for ethanol production in the energy discipline and the satisfaction of socioeconomic demand. Other socioeconomic demands are satisfied by the corresponding domains except the weather discipline. The excess nitrogen from animal lands and crop fields is carried by water flow in the form of nitrates draining into the Mississippi River basin and further into the Gulf of Mexico.

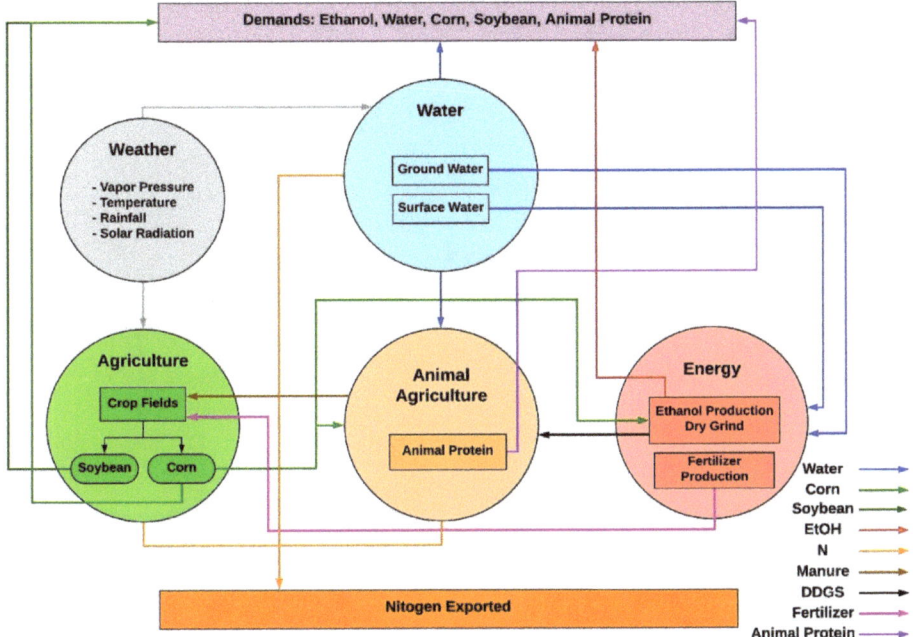

Figure 1. A model of the interdependencies of the Iowa food-energy-water (IFEW) system.

2.2. IFEW Macro-Level Simulation Model

In this work, an extended simulation-based model of the IFEW system introduced in [10] is proposed to calculate the surplus nitrogen (N_s) considering only the weather, agriculture, and animal agriculture domains in Figure 1. Figure 2 shows the flow of components and the process of calculation via an extended design structure matrix (XDSM) diagram [14]. The input parameters are the weather model parameters (w_{1-5}), May crop planting progress (cw_1), rate of commercial nitrogen for corn (x_3), rate of commercial nitrogen for soybean (x_4), the total hog/pig population (x_5), number of beef cows (x_6), number of milk cows (x_7), and number of other cattle (x_8) including the population of steers, heifers, and slaughter cattle. Other intermediate response parameters are corn yield (x_1), soybean yield (x_2), the application of commercial nitrogen (CN), nitrogen generated from manure (MN), nitrogen fixed by soybean crop (FN), and the nitrogen present in harvested grain (GN). The model estimates the nitrogen surplus (N_s) based on output quantities yielded by each discipline.

This simulation model is an extension from the authors' previous work with the addition of the crop-weather model [10]. Westcott and Jewison [11] discovered that the amount of corn yield is linear to mid-May planting progress, July temperature, and June precipitation short fall, but is nonlinear to July precipitation. Meanwhile, the productivity of soybean is linear to the average value of July and August temperatures, and June precipitation short fall, but is nonlinear to the average value of July and August precipitations. The crop-weather model of the work is developed based on [11] given a set of temperature and precipitation data of certain months over a 10-year period (2009–2019) from [15]: July temperature (w_1), July precipitation (w_2), June precipitation (w_3), July-August average temperature (w_4), and July-August average precipitation (w_5). The corn yield (x_1) is estimated by a regression model with May planting progress (cw_1), July temperature (w_1), July precipitation (w_2), and June precipitation (w_3). Similar to the corn model, the model for soybean yield (x_2) is created using June precipitation (w_3), July-August average temperature (w_4), and July-August average precipitation (w_5). For simplicity, July and August average values are represented by July values in this work.

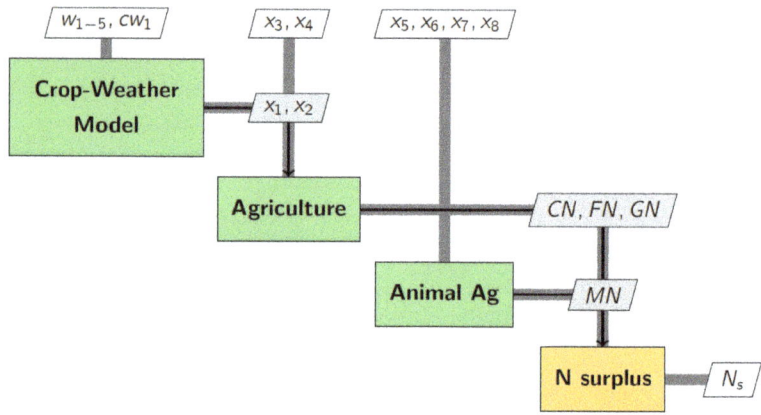

Figure 2. An extended design structure matrix diagram of the proposed Iowa nitrogen export model.

The nitrogen present in harvested grain (*GN*) is calculated using two input parameters, namely, the corn yield (x_1) and soybean yield (x_2) as

$$GN = \left(x_1 \left(\frac{1.18}{100} \right) A_{corn} + x_2 \left(\frac{6.4}{100} \right) A_{soy} \right) / A, \quad (1)$$

where A_{corn} and A_{soy} represent the Iowa corn and the soybean acreage, whereas A represents the total area under corn and soybean crop. It is assumed that 6.4% and 1.18% of nitrogen are in the soybean seed and the corn seed while harvesting, respectively [16]. The biological nitrogen fixation from the soybean crop (*FN*) is estimated as [17].

$$FN = (81.1 x_2 - 98.5) A_{soy} / A. \quad (2)$$

The commercial nitrogen (*CN*) is estimated using the rate of commercial nitrogen for corn (x_3) and the rate of commercial nitrogen for soybean (x_4) as

$$CN = (x_3 A_{corn} + x_4 A_{soy}) / A. \quad (3)$$

The values of the corn and soybean acreages are obtained from the USDA [18]. The annual manure nitrogen contribution of each animal type is estimated [19]

$$MN_{animal} = P\, A_{MN}\, LF, \quad (4)$$

where P, A_{MN}, and LF are the livestock group population, nitrogen in animal manure, and life cycle of animal, respectively. P is substituted by the corresponding parameters with respect to different animal alternatives: the total hog/pig population (x_5), number of beef cows (x_6), number of milk cows (x_7), and number of other cattle (x_8). The total nitrogen generated from manure (*MN*) can be determined by the normalized sum of *MN* for each livestock group with total area A as

$$MN = \left(MN_{Hog/pigs} + MN_{Beef-cattle} + MN_{Milk-cow} + MN_{other-cattle} \right) / A. \quad (5)$$

Table 1 gives the nitrogen content in manure and life cycle for livestock groups used in (5). Lastly, the rough agronomic annual nitrogen budget of Iowa [16,20] provides the function calculated for the nitrogen surplus (N_s) given as

$$N_s = CN + MN + FN - GN. \tag{6}$$

Table 1. Nitrogen content in manure and life cycle for livestock groups used in manure N calculation [19].

Livestock Group	Nitrogen in Manure (A_{MN}) (kg per Animal per Day)	Life Cycle (*LF*) (Days per Year)
Hog/pigs	0.027	365
Beef cattle	0.15	365
Milk cows	0.204	365
Heifer/steers (0.5 × other cattle)	0.1455	365
Slaughter cattle (0.5 × other cattle)	0.104	170

2.3. Simulation Decomposition

The simulation decomposition (SD) [12] approach is an extension to the Monte Carlo simulation [21] that enhances the explanatory capability of the simulation results by exploiting the inherent cause-and-effect relationship between the input and output parameters [13].

SD has recently been developed and successfully used on problems involved in different domains such as geology, business, and environmental science [22]. It has been shown to provide a deeper understanding of the interaction between different sources of uncertainties and its impact on output uncertainty and its distribution to stakeholders. The current section provides a brief description of SD from an application point of view. A detailed description of SD can be found in [12].

In this section, the fundamental steps of implementing SD are described using an analytical model problem. Consider a simple analytical function given as

$$y = v_1 + v_2^2, \tag{7}$$

where v_1 and v_2 are the real numbered input parameters and y the real number output parameter. The SD process has the following steps [12]:

1. Identify the input parameters (v_1, v_2) and their corresponding distribution ranges in which these parameters are expected to vary. Table 2 provide input parameters and their corresponding distributions. For this example, a uniform distribution is assumed for each parameter.
2. Next, for each parameter the states are identified. The states of each input parameter represent a category of outcomes (e.g., low, or high). Based on the state for each parameter, a value range is determined as seen in Table 2 for the example problem.
3. Generate every possible combination of the parameter states. Each combination of states represents a unique scenario (Sc_i) of the to-be-decomposed simulation of the output. The number of scenarios depends on the number of states of each parameter. For the example problem, the number of scenarios is four, as shown in Table 3.
4. Run the Monte Carlo simulations by randomly sampling the parameters, identifying parameter states, and evaluating output. Register output of each simulated iteration for producing full output distribution and simultaneously group the output based on the scenarios for producing decomposed sub-distribution for each scenario.
5. Finally, construct appropriate output graphs or tables to better understand the cause-and-effect relationship between input and output parameters. In particular, the stacked histogram is an informative graph that displays the full output distribution and the decomposed output superimposed on full distribution. Figure 3 shows the full and decomposed distribution of the simulated output.

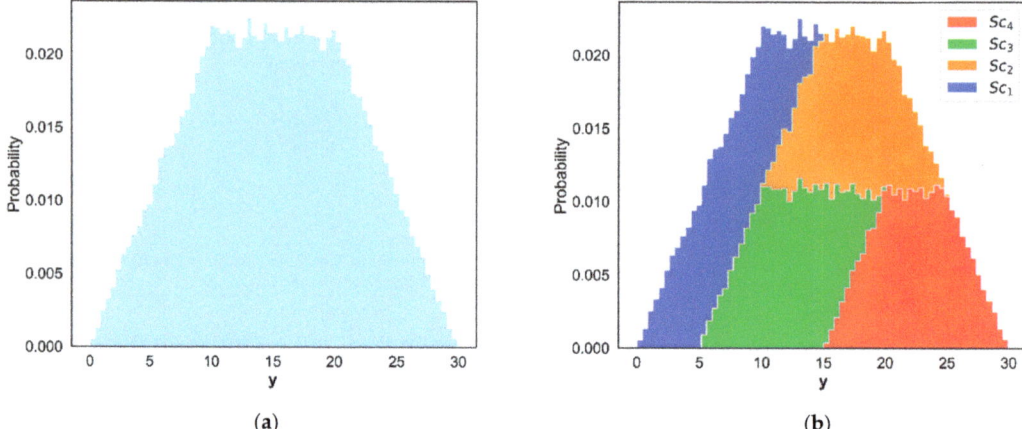

Figure 3. Probability distribution of simulation output for example problem: (**a**) output full distribution, and (**b**) decomposed distribution based on scenarios.

Table 2. Input parameter details.

Parameter	Distribution/Range	State	Boundary
v_1	U [0, 10]	Low High	[0–5] (5–10]
v_2	U [0, 10]	Low High	[0–5] (5–10]

Table 3. Generating scenarios from parameter states.

Scenario	Combination of States
Sc_1	v_1: Low, v_2: Low
Sc_2	v_1: Low, v_2: High
Sc_3	v_1: High, v_2: Low
Sc_4	v_1: High, v_2: Low

3. Results

This section presents the results of applying SD to the proposed extended nitrogen export model which includes a weather model. In particular, the current work focuses on understanding the effects of weather parameters on the nitrogen surplus in different scenarios.

For this study, the weather parameters temperature (T) and precipitation (PPT) for July are taken as input parameters, whereas soil nitrogen surplus is considered as an output parameter computed from the IFEW simulation model. Furthermore, the July temperature is assumed to be normally distributed with a mean of 74 °F and a standard deviation of 2 °F, whereas the July precipitation is assumed to have a lognormal distribution with a standard deviation of 0.4 in., a shape parameter of 0, and median at 4 as shown in Table 4. All other parameters considered in the IFEW simulation model are kept constant.

Table 4. Input parameter details for performing simulation decomposition with IFEW simulation model.

Parameter	Distribution/Range	State	Boundary
July temperature (w_1)	N [2, 74]	Regular	$\leq$76 °F
		High	>76 °F
July precipitation (w_2)	LogN [0.4, 0, 4]	Regular	$\geq$2.5 in
		Low	<2.5 in

In the crop-weather model, May plantation progress and June precipitation is assumed to be 80% and 5.5 in., respectively. The parameters used in the animal agriculture model (x_{5-8}) are based on the 2012 Iowa animal population data [19]. The commercial nitrogen application rate for corn (x_3) and soybean (x_4) agriculture are considered to be constant and set as 185 kg/ha and 17 kg/ha based on the Iowa State University extension guidelines for the nitrogen application rate for corn [23] and on the fertilizer use and price data [24].

After setting up the IFEW model, Monte Carlo simulations are performed using Latin hypercube sampling (LHS) [25]. The LHS sampling method ensures that the input parameter ranges are represented appropriately. The input parameter states and boundary details are presented in Table 4. For July temperature, any temperature above 76 °F is considered to be under state high where all other temperature values are considered to be under state regular. Similarly, for July precipitation, any precipitation value below 2.5 in. is labeled under state low precipitation and all other values are under state regular. Table 5 presents the scenarios based on a combination of states. The parameter states are selected to produce some of the extreme condition scenarios (e.g., Table 5 dry condition).

Table 5. Scenarios for simulation decomposition approach with IFEW model.

Scenario	Combination of States	Description
Sc_1	w_1: Regular, w_2: Low	Regular-T Low-PPT
Sc_2	w_1: Regular, w_2: Regular	Regular condition
Sc_3	w_1: High, w_2: Low	Dry condition
Sc_4	w_1: High, w_2: Regular	High-T Regular-PPT

A total 10^5 samples of input weather parameters (w_1 and w_2) are generated using LHS and SD approach is implemented using the IFEW simulation model. Figure 4 shows the distribution of sampled weather parameters in two states and four scenarios as mentioned in Tables 4 and 5. Most of the generated samples are observed under regular condition (Sc_2) whereas the least number of samples are observed in dry condition (Sc_3).

The input weather parameters are supplied to a crop-weather module which computes corn yield (x_1) and soybean yield (x_2). The computed crop yield values are then passed to an agriculture module where CN, FN, and GN values are computed as mentioned in Section 2.2. Here, the contribution of CN will be constant for every IFEW model evaluation due to the assumption of a constant commercial nitrogen application rate for corn (x_3) and soybean (x_4).

Figure 5 shows the decomposed distribution of corn and soybean yield along with the variation in FN and GN values. The effect of different scenarios due to combinations of weather parameters can be clearly seen in crop yield distribution. It is interesting to note that in dry condition (Sc_3) corn yield drops compared to the yield in regular condition, whereas higher soybean yield is observed in dry condition compared to the regular condition. The computation of GN is influenced by both corn and soybean yield values (Figure 5c). The computation of FN is only influenced by soybean yield values (Section 2.2); thus, the FN distribution is observed to be similar to soybean yield distribution.

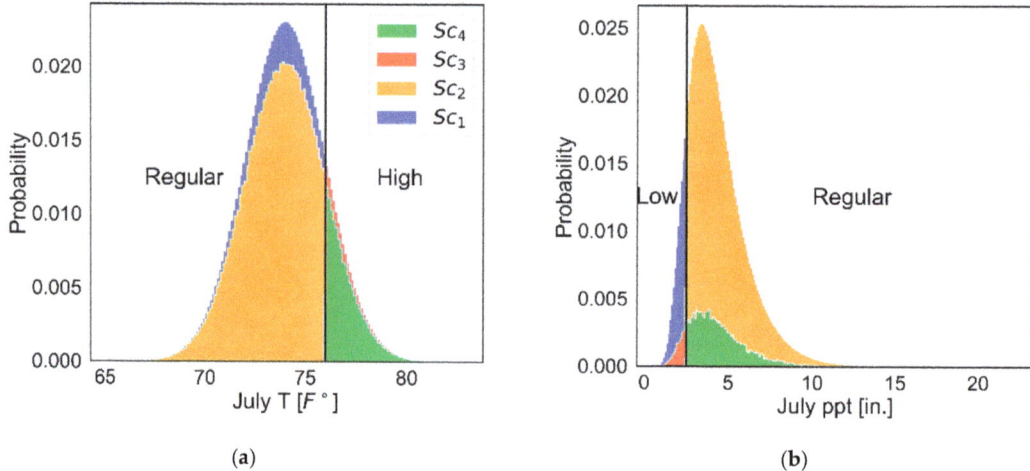

Figure 4. Decomposed distribution of input parameters from simulation decomposition: (**a**) July temperature (w_1), and (**b**) July precipitation (w_2).

Figure 6 shows the decomposed distribution of nitrogen surplus (N_s), the final output of the IFEW simulation model. The soil nitrogen surplus is usually affected by *CN*, *MN*, *GN*, and *FN* magnitudes. However, in this study, only *GN* and *FN* influence the variation in nitrogen surplus. This is mainly because the parameters affecting *CN* and *MN* are kept constant. The variation in nitrogen surplus shown in this work is purely due to uncertainty in weather parameters. From Figure 6, it is observed that most of the variation in nitrogen surplus lies in regular condition (Sc_2), varying approximately between 0 and 20 kg/ha. The scenarios with high July temperatures (Sc_3 and Sc_4) are observed to produce mid to high nitrogen surplus values. Similarly, scenario Sc_1, with very low July precipitation and regular July temperature, tends to produce higher nitrogen surplus than in regular conditions. The dry condition with high July temperature and low July precipitation produces the highest soil nitrogen surplus, varying between 20 and 30 kg/ha. The accumulated nitrogen in the soil is highly water-soluble and could get exported at a high rate to the Mississippi River through melting snow or rainfall before the next growing season. Figure 6 provides the expected magnitude of nitrogen load from state of Iowa to the Mississippi River in different weather scenarios.

The SD in this work uses the Monte Carlo sampling approach which could be used to provide approximate probability of a scenario occurring in any given year considering the assumptions made earlier are true. Based on the data available in the current study, probabilities of scenarios Sc_1, Sc_2, Sc_3, and Sc_4 occurring are 0.1, 0.74, 0.02, and 0.12, respectively. The probability of dry condition (Sc_3) occurring is lowest whereas regular condition (Sc_2) has the highest probability of occurring (Figure 6).

The SD approach implemented in the current study provides valuable results to gauge the impact of weather parameters on soil nitrogen surplus along with crop yields and nitrogen transfer in agriculture systems. However, the particular distributions used for the weather parameters are not data based, and the two input weather parameters are assumed to be independent of each during the Monte Carlo sampling process. Temperature and precipitation are correlated. Thus, there is a possibility that some combination of scenarios may not entirely occur. For example, high precipitation and high temperature may not occur at the same time because with high precipitation, the average temperature drops. Further, the probability distributions of the weather parameters are challenging to estimate as they typically do not have continuous distributions. Thus, it is advisable to use weather generators which have been trained on historical datasets to predict weather parameters rather than using continuous probability distributions. In future studies, weather generators will be included in the IFEW simulation model to predict weather data for more realistic predictions of soil nitrogen surplus.

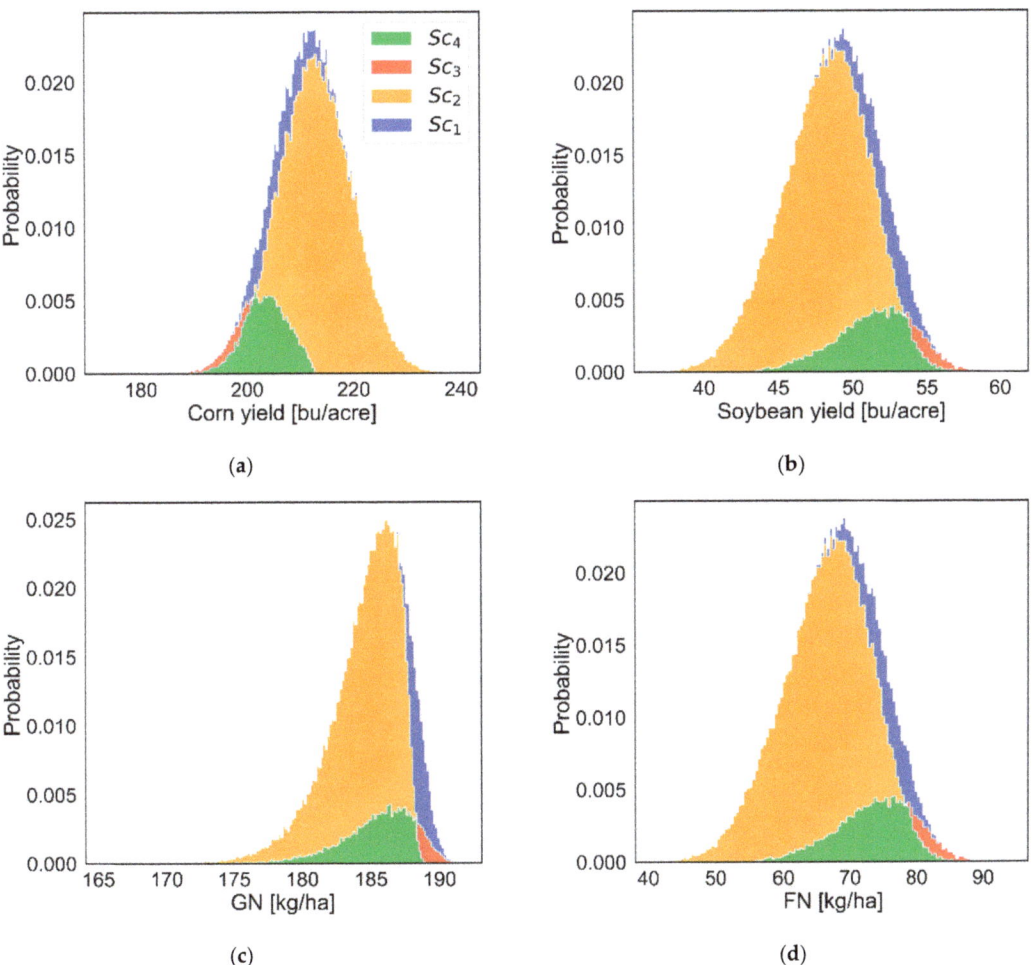

Figure 5. Decomposed distribution of intermittent IFEW model parameters from simulation decomposition: (**a**) corn yield (x_1), (**b**) soybean yield (x_2), (**c**) *GN*, and (**d**) *FN*.

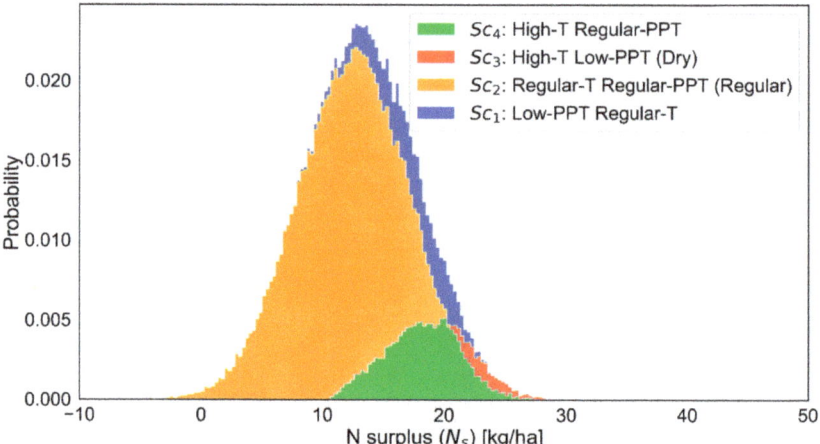

Figure 6. Distribution of IFEW simulation model output: nitrogen surplus (N_s).

4. Conclusions

In this work, the simulation decomposition (SD) approach is implemented with the Iowa food-energy-water (IFEW) system simulation model to better understand the impact of weather behavior on nitrogen export from Iowa. In particular, the previously developed nitrogen export model, which computes the soil nitrogen surplus, is extended with a crop weather model to include the dependence of weather in the IFEW system. The updated IFEW simulation model with SD is used to provide decomposed soil nitrogen surplus distribution in different weather scenarios.

It is observed that July temperature and precipitation directly impact corn and soybean yields. Interestingly, it is observed that in the dry condition, corn yield reduces, whereas soybean yield increases compared to the yield values in regular conditions. The variation in crop yields affects nitrogen transfer in the agriculture system through fixation nitrogen (FN) and grain nitrogen (GN), affecting the soil nitrogen surplus. The SD approach provides the distribution of nitrogen surplus in various scenarios. It is observed that the regular condition covers most variation in the full distribution. Scenarios with high July temperature and low precipitation tend to produce mid to high range of nitrogen surplus values. The dry condition scenario produces the highest nitrogen surplus. Overall, the SD approach provides a deeper understanding of the cause-and-effect relationship between weather parameters and soil nitrogen surplus.

Furthermore, the current study identified that continuous distribution on weather parameters could generate unrealistic scenarios. Thus, in future studies, highly validated weather generators will be used for estimating weather parameters, providing a more realistic distribution of soil nitrogen surplus based on weather. Additionally, the IFEW simulation model will be extended to report nitrogen loads for Iowa's nine crop reporting districts, providing spatially resolved information from the state of Iowa.

Author Contributions: Conceptualization, L.L. and A.K.; methodology, V.R.; software, V.R.; validation, V.R. and Y.-C.L.; writing—original draft preparation, V.R. and Y.-C.L.; writing—review and editing, V.R., Y.-C.L., L.L. and A.K.; visualization, V.R. and Y.-C.L.; supervision, L.L. and A.K. All authors have read and agreed to the published version of the manuscript.

Funding: The United States National Science Foundation under grant No. 1739551.

Institutional Review Board Statement: Not applicable.

Informed Consent Statement: Not applicable.

Data Availability Statement: Not applicable.

Acknowledgments: This material is based upon work supported by the United States National Science Foundation under grant No. 1739551.

Conflicts of Interest: The authors declare no conflict of interest.

References

1. Diaz, R.J.; Rosenberg, R. Spreading Dead Zones and Consequences for Marine Ecosystems. *Science* **2008**, *321*, 926–929. [CrossRef] [PubMed]
2. EPA. Northern Gulf of Mexico Hypoxic Zone. Available online: https://www.epa.gov/ms-htf/northern-gulf-mexico-hypoxic-zone (accessed on 2 December 2021).
3. Burkart, M.R.; James, D.E. Agricultural-Nitrogen Contributions to Hypoxia in the Gulf of Mexico. *J. Environ. Qual.* **1999**, *28*, 850–859. [CrossRef]
4. Jones, C.S.; Schilling, K.E. Iowa Statewide Stream Nitrate Loading: 2017–2018 Update. *J. Iowa Acad. Sci.* **2019**, *126*, 6–12. [CrossRef]
5. NDEE. Ethanol Facilities' Capacity by State. Available online: https://neo.ne.gov/programs/stats/inf/121.htm (accessed on 5 December 2021).
6. Urbanchuk, J.M. Contribution of the Renewable Fuels Industry to the Economy of Iowa. Agricultural and Biofuels Consulting. Available online: https://iowarfa.org/wp-content/uploads/2020/03/2019-Iowa-Economic-Impact-Final-2.pdf (accessed on 4 December 2021).
7. Bakhsh, A.; Kanwar, R.; Karlen, D. Effects of liquid swine manure applications on NO3–N leaching losses to subsurface drainage water from loamy soils in Iowa. *Agric. Ecosyst. Environ.* **2005**, *109*, 118–128. [CrossRef]
8. Siderius, C.; Kolusu, S.R.; Todd, M.C.; Bhave, A.; Dougill, A.J.; Reason, C.J.; Mkwambisi, D.D.; Kashaigili, J.J.; Pardoe, J.; Harou, J.J.; et al. Climate variability affects water-energy-food infrastructure performance in East Africa. *One Earth* **2021**, *4*, 397–410. [CrossRef]
9. Berardy, A.; Chester, M.V. Climate change vulnerability in the food, energy, and water nexus: Concerns for agricultural production in Arizona and its urban export supply. *Environ. Res. Lett.* **2017**, *12*, 035004. [CrossRef]
10. Raul, V.; Leifsson, L.; Kaleita, A. System Modeling and Sensitivity Analysis of the Iowa Food-Water-Energy Nexus. *J. Environ. Inform. Lett.* **2020**, *4*, 73–79. Available online: http://www.jeiletters.org/index.php?journal=mys&page=article&op=view&path%5B%5D=202000044 (accessed on 1 August 2021). [CrossRef]
11. Westcott, P.C.; Jewison, M. *Weather Effects on Expected Corn and Soybean Yields*; Feed Outlook No. (FDS-13G-01); USDA Economic Research Service: Washington, DC, USA, 2013. Available online: https://www.ers.usda.gov/publications/pub-details/?pubid=36652 (accessed on 23 November 2021).
12. Kozlova, M.; Collan, M.; Luukka, P. Simulation decomposition: New approach for better simulation analysis of multi-variable investment projects. *Fuzzy Econ. Rev.* **2016**, *21*, 3–18. [CrossRef]
13. Kozlova, M.; Yeomans, J.S. Multi-Variable Simulation Decomposition in Environmental Planning: An Application to Carbon Capture and Storage. *J. Environ. Inform. Lett.* **2019**, *1*, 20–26. [CrossRef]
14. Lambe, A.B.; Martins, J.R.R.A. Extensions to the design structure matrix for the description of multidisciplinary design, analysis, and optimization processes. *Struct. Multidiscip. Optim.* **2012**, *46*, 273–284. [CrossRef]
15. USDA. Crop Production 2019 Summary. Crop Production 2019 Summary 01/10/2020 (usda.gov) 2020. Available online: https://www.nass.usda.gov/Publications/Todays_Reports/reports/cropan20.pdf (accessed on 4 December 2021).
16. Blesh, J.; Drinkwater, L.E. The impact of nitrogen source and crop rotation on nitrogen mass balances in the Mississippi River Basin. *Ecol. Appl.* **2013**, *23*, 1017–1035. [CrossRef] [PubMed]
17. Barry, D.A.J.; Goorahoo, D.; Goss, M.J. Estimation of Nitrate Concentrations in Groundwater Using a Whole Farm Nitrogen Budget. *J. Environ. Qual.* **1993**, *22*, 767–775. [CrossRef]
18. USDA. National Agricultural Statistics Service Quick Stats. Available online: https://quickstats.nass.usda.gov/ (accessed on 24 November 2021).
19. Gronberg, J.M.; Arnold, T.L. *County-Level Estimates of Nitrogen and Phosphorus from Animal Manure for the Conterminous United States, 2007 and 2012* (No. 2017-1021); US Geological Survey: Reston, VA, USA, 2017. [CrossRef]
20. Jones, C.S.; Drake, C.W.; Hruby, C.E.; Schilling, K.E.; Wolter, C.F. Livestock manure driving stream nitrate. *Ambio* **2019**, *48*, 1143–1153. [CrossRef] [PubMed]
21. Kroese, D.P.; Brereton, T.; Taimre, T.; Botev, Z.I. Why the Monte Carlo method is so important today. *WIREs Comput. Stat.* **2014**, *6*, 386–392. [CrossRef]
22. Kozlova, M.; Yeomans, J.S. Monte Carlo Enhancement via Simulation Decomposition: A "Must-Have" Inclusion for Many Disciplines. *INFORMS Trans. Educ.* **2020**. [CrossRef]
23. Sawyer, J.E. *Nitrogen Use in Iowa Corn Production*; Crop 3073; Iowa State University Extention and Outreach: Ames, IA, USA. Available online: https://store.extension.iastate.edu/Product/Nitrogen-Use-in-Iowa-Corn-Production (accessed on 20 November 2021).

24. USDA. Fertilizer Use and Price. Available online: https://www.ers.usda.gov/data-products/fertilizer-use-and-price/ (accessed on 29 November 2021).
25. McKay, M.D.; Beckman, R.J.; Conover, W. A comparison of three methods for selecting values of input variables in the analysis of output from a computer code. *Technometrics* **2000**, *42*, 55–61. [CrossRef]

Article

Technical Advances in Aviation Electrification: Enhancing Strategic R&D Investment Analysis through Simulation Decomposition

Mariia Kozlova [1],*, Timo Nykänen [2] and Julian Scott Yeomans [3]

[1] School of Business and Management, LUT University, FI-53851 Lappeenranta, Finland
[2] School of Energy Systems, LUT University, FI-53851 Lappeenranta, Finland
[3] Operations Management and Information Systems Area, Schulich School of Business, York University, Toronto, ON M3J 1P3, Canada
* Correspondence: mariia.kozlova@lut.fi

Abstract: Computational decision-making in "real world" environmental and sustainability contexts frequently requires the need to contrast numerous uncertain factors and difficult-to-capture dimensions. Monte Carlo simulation modelling has frequently been employed to integrate the uncertain inputs and to construct probability distributions of the resulting outputs. Visual analytics and data visualization can be used to support the processing, analyzing, and communicating of the influence of multi-variable uncertainties on the decision-making process. In this paper, the novel Simulation Decomposition (SimDec) analytical technique is used to quantitatively examine carbon emission impacts resulting from a transformation of the aviation industry toward a state of greater airline electrification. SimDec is used to decompose a Monte Carlo model of the flying range of all-electric aircraft based upon improvements to batteries and motor efficiencies. Since SimDec can be run concurrently with any Monte Carlo model with only negligible additional overhead, it can easily be extended into the analysis of any environmental application that employs simulation. This generalizability in conjunction with its straightforward visualizations of complex stochastic uncertainties makes the practical contributions of SimDec very powerful in environmental decision-making.

Keywords: business aviation; turboprop; electric motor; specific power; Monte Carlo simulation

Citation: Kozlova, M.; Nykänen, T.; Yeomans, J.S. Technical Advances in Aviation Electrification: Enhancing Strategic R&D Investment Analysis through Simulation Decomposition. *Sustainability* 2022, 14, 414. https://doi.org/10.3390/su14010414

Academic Editor: Lynnette Dray

Received: 8 December 2021
Accepted: 29 December 2021
Published: 31 December 2021

Publisher's Note: MDPI stays neutral with regard to jurisdictional claims in published maps and institutional affiliations.

Copyright: © 2021 by the authors. Licensee MDPI, Basel, Switzerland. This article is an open access article distributed under the terms and conditions of the Creative Commons Attribution (CC BY) license (https://creativecommons.org/licenses/by/4.0/).

1. Introduction

Environmental sustainability problems frequently require the need for practical, "real world" decision-making to compute solutions to situations possessing numerous uncertain factors and unquantified dimensions [1]. This study applies a novel analytical technique to quantitatively examine the carbon emission impacts resulting from a transformation of the aviation industry toward a state of greater airline electrification.

The link between carbon emissions from the aviation industry to climate change was firmly established in the 1992 report of the United Nations Framework Convention on Climate Change (UNFCC) [2]. Today, it is estimated that aviation emissions annually contribute between 2–5% of all global emissions [3–5] with some estimates forecasting that with the current growth trajectory, 25% of all emissions could be attributed to flying by 2050 [5,6]. In fact, while many industry sectors have actively been reducing their carbon footprints, the emissions from the aviation industry have increased by more than 75% from their 1990 levels [5,7]. The biggest culprits in aviation emissions are the long-distance, commercial flights, and this long-haul aviation segment is the hardest to decarbonize, by far [4].

At the recent UNFCC Conference of the Parties meeting (COP26) in Glasgow—in which, ironically, the vast majority of the 26,000 delegates arrived via air—there were strong calls for immediate action to be taken to reduce airline emissions [8]. Consequently, decreasing the overall carbon contributions from the aviation industry has become one of the primary initiatives within the current global climate policy formulation and represents a significant component of the overall strategy for achieving climate neutrality by 2050 [2,6,9]. Clearly, technological progress can serve as the most significant, enabling factor for accelerating the pace of air traffic decarbonization. While biofuels have generally been viewed as the primary remedy for emissions from long-haul aviation [10], electrification is now considered the more viable option for regional, short-haul flights [8,11].

In comparison to combustion engines, electric aircraft are less expensive to operate as there is no need to acquire expensive kerosene, and the maintenance of an electric powertrain is far less complicated and cheaper. According to some estimates, the cost per hour from operating an electric aircraft is less than one-third that of an otherwise similarlysized, fueled aircraft. Economically, lower costs translate into lower overall prices, thereby enabling higher traffic volumes. Some experts envision the possibility of completely disruptive innovation in regional traffic flows, where all-electric turboprops provide a substitute for train-, bus-, and car-travel [12]. For example, one interesting development is Airbus' concept of urban air mobility that employs its all-electric, vertical-takeoff, remotely piloted, four-seater CityAirbus. Some airlines that only engage in short distance flights have experimented with switching to an all-electric fleet (e.g., see [13]).

Short-haul flights form a separate business community. So-called business aviation is comprised of charter flights, corporate aviation, and air taxis, though the explicit definition and composition differs depending on the source organization [14]. Short-haul business aviation creates many benefits for businesses, the environment, and economies, in general. These benefits can be expected to intensify in conjunction with an increased electrification of aircraft fleets in combination with consequent price decreases. Improved business aviation can connect many currently isolated communities in rural and remote locations, contributing a significant boost to their economic growth and investments. On-demand scheduling substantially increases efficiencies for business by saving time spent engaging in large airport procedures and avoiding unnecessary waiting time at stopovers [15].

In aviation electrification research, prior R&D investment studies have generally analyzed only selected scenarios that tend to be focused primarily on battery technology. For example, Brdnik et al. [16] focused on the existing specific energy levels of batteries and their impacts on the resulting flying ranges of three different aircraft sizes. Schäfer et al. [17] estimated the economic and environmental consequences of high-level, specific energy batteries. Unfortunately, due to the weight of the batteries, electrification is practicable only for the 20% of commercial flights under a distance of 1500 km [5]. Hence, for commercial aviation implementation purposes, an appropriately realistic balance must be struck between electrification for short-haul flights and combustion engine aircraft for longer distances. Achieving this satisfactory balance between short- and long-haul flight strategies in aviation is analogous to computing a solution to the environmental equilibrium requirements specified in the range limited routing problem of electrical- versus combustion-engine transportation methods in urban logistics planning [18–23].

Consequently, this paper aims to portray a more holistically sustainable aviation electrification picture by concurrently integrating environmental impacts from the ongoing technological developments of electric motors for short-haul flights into the R&D investment analysis. This is achieved by employing a Monte Carlo study in combination with a novel computational ancillary analysis technique to model the flying range of an all-electric aircraft based upon improvements to its batteries together with its electric motor. Monte Carlo simulation has been applied to a wide spectrum of environmental planning problems to incorporate disparate uncertain inputs with their corresponding outputs frequently portrayed visually as probability distributions.

In order to progress beyond a selected scenario approach, the Monte Carlo study undertaken will be extended using the recently introduced, innovative approach called simulation decomposition (SimDec) [24]. The SimDec method has been created to expand the analytical capacity of simulation by significantly broadening its cause-and-effect explanatory powers [24–27]. SimDec provides a very powerful, straightforward approach for visually analyzing the impacts of combinations of variables on output measures [24,26]. It is a generally usable method that is not context-dependent [25]. In SimDec, selected uncertain input variable combinations are used to "decompose" output distributions into a number of state-influenced sub-distributions [24]. These sub-distributions are superimposed onto an output distribution, thereby permitting an explicit visualization of the cause-and-effect impacts of the decomposed multi-variable groups of input combinations and/or their various interactions [24]. The practical contributions from the decomposed visualization facilitates subsequent decision-maker insights with respect to the underlying simulation model. SimDec supplies both sensitivity and scenario contributions that are frequently employed by decision-makers in conjunction with "real world" quantitative analyses [24–27]. At the strategic level, SimDec enables a visual analytic display in continuous numerical space of the simultaneous interaction between multiple different factors that affect the flying range of electrical aircraft, thereby more fully portraying the financial and environmental benefits of aviation electrification to the decision-makers.

The remainder of the paper is structured in the following way: Section 2 provides a general description of the SimDec method; Section 3 summarizes the key aspects associated with aviation electrification; Section 4 describes the computational and Monte Carlo model used for capturing the environmental impacts from electrification; Section 5 provides the results from the Monte Carlo and discusses the environmental impacts discovered in the decomposition of the output; and Section 6 concludes the outcome of the SimDec analysis for evaluating the environmental contributions of aircraft electrification to aviation decarbonization.

2. The Simulation-Decomposition Approach

SimDec is an analytical approach that was recently introduced to expand the explanatory capabilities of Monte Carlo by exploring inherent cause–effect links between combinations of input variable groupings and their resulting impacts on output variables [24]. While this section reviews the key steps for the decomposition of a simulation, more extensive descriptions can be found in [24–27].

The SimDec procedure constructs sub-distributions of the entire simulation output distribution by partitioning certain input variables into pre-determined states, constructing various multi-variable combinations of these states, and then clustering the simulated outputs using these partition combinations [25,27]. This process enables the construction of both an "overall" output distribution and the simultaneous projection of the decomposed multi-variable input combinations onto this figure [26]. In decomposing an overall output distribution, SimDec simultaneously highlights multi-variable combination impacts using only a single simulation run, which, thereby, circumvents the need to perform individual simulation runs to test each input combination separately. Therefore, SimDec explicitly can be considered an explicit variance reduction approach for evaluating simulated outputs [25]. The visualization from SimDec is subsequently obtained by color-coding each portion of the overall distribution represented by each of the multi-variable partitions [24,26]. Because the projected effect of each subdivided partition can be clearly visualized on the output distribution, SimDec can visually expose previously unrecognized relationships between the multi-variable input partitions and their resulting fundamental consequences on the outputs [26].

The specific algorithmic steps in SimDec are as follows [25,27]:

Step (1) From the complete set of input variables that are to be simulated in the Monte Carlo model, choose a subset of variables that are of interest for more explicit scrutiny.

Step (2) Create relevant states that correspond to different outcomes for each of the variables identified in Step 1 (e.g., good-bad, optimistic-expected-pessimistic, etc.).

Step (3) For each state of each of the variables, construct suitable numerical boundaries that correspond to that variable's possible value ranges. These boundary ranges must be mutually exclusive and collectively exhaustive for the set of states of each variable.

Step (4) Construct a listing of every possible combination of the different variable state partitions. Each combination represents a multi-variable partition of the inputs in the future decomposition.

Step (5) Perform a Monte Carlo simulation. On each simulated iteration, map the randomly generated values of each selected input variable into its corresponding partition state, then map the specific combination of all individual states for the iteration onto the corresponding multi-variable partition combination. Allocate the result of each simulated iteration to the output distribution corresponding to the "complete" simulation, while simultaneously keeping track of the decomposed state combination that produced it.

Step (6) Construct output graphs and/or tables of the simulation outputs. These graphs/tables will portray both the overall summaries of the outputs together with the state decompositions superimposed on top of the global figures.

In summary, the SimDec procedure can be used to break down the regions of the simulation's overall output distribution into a set of distinct partitions [24]. The corresponding stratification enables an effective visualization and assessment of any inherent cause–effect relationships within the simulation results [26]. The determination of which input combinations to use in any given decomposition is at the discretion of the decision-maker. SimDec can be added to any Monte Carlo study with essentially negligible additional computational overhead and can be incorporated independently of the simulation context [25]. In the subsequent sections, SimDec will be employed to analyze the impacts from a simulation model of aviation electrification.

3. Electrification of Aviation

In essence, there are two main types of aircraft—turbo-propeller aircraft (or turboprops) and jets. The turboprops were the first aircraft type to be electrified due to the technical simplicity of such a modification: directly substituting an electric motor for the engine and batteries for the fuel tank [28]. Regional aviation, where electrification provides a feasible option, operates mostly in the realm of "business aviation", as opposed to the major airlines' scheduled business models. In Europe, turboprops constitute 34% of the business aviation fleet and are responsible for 26% of the flights [29], see Table 1.

Table 1. Characteristics of aircraft segments in European business aviation.

Segment	Number of Movements (Arrivals and Departures)		Fleet		Average Distance, km	Average Speed, km/h
Turboprop	242,003	26%	1085	34%	483	378
Light Jet	371,514	40%	994	31%	760	590
Midsize jet	114,428	12%	334	10%	1108	680
Heavy jet	189,585	21%	805	25%	2099	754
Total	917,530	100%	3218	100%		

The European turboprop fleet of over 1000 aircraft is represented by ten main brands of airplane from seven manufacturers in the US and Europe, Table 2.

The specific energy of batteries, defined as how much energy a battery contains per its mass, is currently considered to be the main constraining factor for electrical aviation [30]. In a nutshell, batteries are simply too heavy. The existing specific energy levels for batteries range between 0.1 to 0.25 kWh/kg, which is ten times lower than the energy density of kerosene in combination with the specific power of combustion engine [16]. Nevertheless, by extrapolating along major historic technology improvement trends, the airline industry forecasts storage solutions to easily increase to 0.8 kWh/kg within the coming decades [17].

A second major factor frequently under-explored in current aviation research is the actual specific power of an electric motor [31]. Table 3 highlights the specific power progression of Siemens motors over since 2015 [32], which clearly demonstrates the recent rapid technological progression of electric motors.

Table 2. Major characteristics of business aviation turboprops operating in the EU in 2020, based on [29], with data added for seats and maximum takeoff weight from each aircraft description.

Aircraft Brand	Manufacturer	Country	Seats	Maximum Takeoff Weight, kg	Number of Movements (Arrivals and Departures)	Fleet	Average Distance, km	Average Speed, km/h
King Air 200	Hawker Beechcraft	US	13	5700	86,379	185	337	374
Pilatus PC-12	Pilatus	Switzerland	9	4100	67,461	215	515	381
Piaggio P180 Avanti	Piaggio Aerospace	Italy	9	5488	20,510	93	560	480
Piper Malibu Meridian	Piper Aircraft	US	6	2310	15,457	159	474	365
Socata TBM 700	Daher-Socata	France	6	2984	15,421	56	442	384
King Air 90	Hawker Beechcraft	US	5	4378	10,837	108	384	329
King Air 350	Hawker Beechcraft	US	8	6800	10,035	66	525	346
Socata TBM 850	Daher-Socata	France	6	3354	5773	43	578	423
Socata TBM 900 series	Daher-Socata	France	4	3354	5574	36	594	440
Cessna 208 Caravan	Cessna	US	9	3629	4556	124	420	260

Table 3. Characteristics of Siemens electric motors developed for aviation, based on [32].

Motor	Development Timeline	Continuous Power, kW	Rotational Speed, rpm	Mass, kg	Specific Power, kW/kg
SP45D	2015	45	2500	28	1.6
SP55D	2016	55	3000	27	2.0
SP70D	2018	70	2600	26	2.7
SP200D	2017	204	1300	49	4.2
SP2000D	Under development	2000	6500	261	7.7

Since the power of the motor is a function of its torque and rotational speed, high-speed solutions can substantially increase specific power as illustrated in the last motor in Table 3. Unfortunately, such high-speed motors subsequently require the addition of a gearbox that is connected to the propeller (all the other motors from Table 3 operate via direct drive) [32]. Consequently, any additional gearbox mass must be accounted for when comparing the specific power of different electric motors. For example, when accounting for (say) a standard 50 kg aircraft gearbox, the overall specific power of the powertrain of the Siemens SP2000D would be reduced to 6.4 kWh/kg.

4. Model

4.1. Computational Logic

The computational model aims to estimate the flying range of an all-electric aircraft based upon improvements to its powertrain arising from the specific energy of batteries (kWh/kg) and the specific power of the electric motors (kW/kg). For simplicity, the overall mass of the aircraft is fixed, so that any improvement in the powertrain directly translates into additional "space" for more batteries that are subsequently used to replenish the aircraft's total mass back up to its fixed amount. In reality, of course, any improvement in the powertrain could invoke numerous alternative aircraft design possibilities. However, for the purposes of systematically tracing the effect of technological improvements on the aircraft flying range, we assume the design and the mass of the aircraft to be fixed. To compute the flying range, we employ the aircraft electrification flight equations derived in [16].

The mass, m, of an all-electric aircraft consists of (i) the mass of the empty aircraft, m_e, (ii) the mass of the passengers and the crew, together with their luggage, m_p, and (iii) the mass of the batteries, m_b.

$$m = m_e + m_p + m_b \qquad (1)$$

In aviation modelling, the mass of passengers is normally approximated as the number of seats multiplied by 100 kg. The ratio m_e/m is observed to be independent of the aircraft model and is equal to 0.62 for turboprops.

The energy consumption of an aircraft is defined as:

$$E = \frac{mgs}{(L/D)_{max} \mu_p \mu_e} \tag{2}$$

where g is gravitational acceleration equal to 9.81 m/s^2; s is flying range; $(L/D)_{max}$ is the maximal lift-to-drag ratio, currently 20 is achievable; μ_p and μ_e are efficiencies of the propeller and the powertrain, respectively, typically both equal to 0.8. With given numerical assumptions,

$$E/ms = w_s = 0.22 \text{ kWh/ km t} \tag{3}$$

where w_s is energy consumption and t stands for tonnes.

The mass of batteries can be defined as:

$$\frac{m_b}{m} = \frac{gs}{(L/D)_{max} \mu_p \mu_e \rho_E} \tag{4}$$

where ρ_E is the specific energy of batteries.

The flying range can be defined from (4) and (1) as:

$$s = \frac{\rho_E}{1.6 w_s}\left(0.61 - \frac{m_p}{m_e}\right) \tag{5}$$

The required power, P, is calculated based upon cruise speed v_c and rate of climb $v_{r.o.c}$ requirements as:

$$P = \frac{mg}{\mu_p \mu_e}\left(\frac{v_c}{(L/D)_{max}} - v_{r.o.c}\right) \tag{6}$$

Combining this computational logic and the assumptions derived from existing turboprops (Table 2), we arrive at the following numerical estimations for the model aircraft, Table 4.

Table 4. Basic numeric parameters of the aircraft considered.

Parameter	Value	Comments
Number of seats	8	Average of existing turboprops, Table 2
Payload, kg	800	Computed, fixed
Mass of an empty aircraft, kg	1904	Computed, fixed
Mass of batteries, kg	365	Computed
Total mass, kg	3069	Computed (1), fixed
Specific energy of batteries, kWh/kg	0.25	To be varied during the simulation
Flying range, km	135	Computed (4), output variable
Cruise speed, km/h	380	Average of speeds, Table 2
Rate of climb, m/s	8	Average climb rate for a turboprop [16]
Power required, kW	719	Computed (5), fixed
Specific power of electric motor, kW/kg	varied	The last two variables will be varied during the simulation to estimate their
Specific energy of batteries, kWh/kg	varied	effects. Their numeric assumptions are described in the next section.

The computational logic is validated by the calculation of the flying range for the specified assumptions for current levels of specific energy of batteries 0.25 kWh/kg. Batteries at current technological development (LiFePo4, specific power of 2 kW/kg, specific energy of 0.12 kWh/kg) would constitute 7.5–15% of the total mass of a hybrid electric aircraft [16]. In our calculations batteries in this base case constitute 12% of the mass of the aircraft and the flying range is 135 km, the number of the same magnitude comparing to estimated ranges for different aircraft sizes in [16].

In the constructed model, the two input variables, (i) specific energy of batteries and (ii) specific power of electric motor, will be varied in order to determine their effects on the output variable, flying range. If only the specific energy of batteries is changed, the aircraft is assumed to be able to fly longer from the same mass of batteries on the board. If the specific power of the motor is changed, the same required power for a given aircraft can be achieved with a lighter motor. Any freed mass is assumed to be refilled by more batteries of the same specific energy to maintain a constant total mass of the airplane. More batteries onboard enable longer flight ranges. Thus, with such a model design, we are able to directly ascertain the effect of powertrain technological improvements on the flying range of an aircraft in a continuous numeric space.

4.2. Simulation

In this section, a Monte Carlo simulation model is set up and the SimDec method is employed on it to analyze the sensitivity of the output to the selected input factors, as well as for assessing the impact from any underlying interactions [24]. The SimDec approach falls under the general auspices of variance-based sensitivity analyses techniques [33] commonly used in engineering evaluation [34]. However, instead of relying solely on calculated numerical indices, SimDec provides powerful visualization analytics that can uncover previously hidden interactions in a much more intuitive format for most decision-makers [24].

Firstly, the key input factors, specific energy of batteries and specific power of electric motor, are modeled as random values generated from a uniform distribution. The model is recalculated 10,000 times and the resulting values of the output, flying range, as well as the corresponding input factor values are recorded. Secondly, the key input factors are broken down into meaningful ranges based on their ongoing technological progress. The specific energy of the batteries is segmented into three states, the existing level [0.1, 0.25] kWh/kg, the near-term possible level (0.25, 0.5] kWh/kg, and the "on the horizon" level (0.5, 0.8] kWh/kg. The existing level simply reflects the real specific energy of existing batteries [16]. Some prototypes of lithium-sulfur batteries already achieved 0.4 kWh/kg specific energy, and more are expected in the near future [35]. Therefore, we chose 0.5 kWh/kg as the upper threshold for the near-term possible level. Finally, 0.8 kWh/kg specific energy is deemed achievable by the mid-century by some experts [17], and, thus, chosen as an upper limit for the on the horizon level.

The ranges of the specific power of the electric motor are comprised of the existing level [1.5, 4.0] kW/kg, an under-development level (4.0, 8.0] kW/kg, and a futuristic level (8.0, 20.0] kW/kg. The upper boundaries of the existing and under-development levels reflect the development of Siemens electric motors and correspond to the data presented in Table 3. The upper limit for the futuristic level reflects existing targets in state-of-the-art R&D projects [36].

Taken together, all the states generate nine scenarios, found in Table 5. It is important to note that the correctness of the numerical thresholds between states is not critical, since we are not interested in the precise boundaries of the resulting scenarios (which will be different for different aircrafts, anyway), but in the behavior of causalities between input and output factors, for which the precise position of the thresholds is not relevant.

Having recorded the simulation output data and the attributions of the input variables to their identified scenario partitions, each individual output value can be mapped onto its scenario index. Furthermore, a color-coding of this mapping is then applied onto the overall frequency histogram of the simulation (namely, the probability distribution of the flying range). Consequently, the resulting distribution of flying ranges, combined with the descriptive statistics of each scenario, enable a direct visualization of the individual effects of the input factors together with their interactions on the flying range output.

Table 5. Three states of the key input variables each form nine scenarios for decomposition.

Scenarios for Simulation Decomposition			Specific Power of Electric Motor, kW/kg		
			Existing [1.5, 4.0]	Under Development (4.0, 8.0]	Futuristic (8.0, 20.0]
Specific energy of batteries, kWh/kg	Existing	[0.1, 0.25]	sc1	sc2	sc3
	Near-term possible	(0.25, 0.5]	sc4	sc5	sc6
	On the horizon	(0.5, 0.8]	sc7	sc8	sc9

The computation logic described in Section 4.1 is transformed into a model. The actual Monte Carlo simulation and SimDec analysis are performed using already existing macros previously implemented as an Excel tool introduced in [24] (where it can be downloaded for free).

5. Results and Discussion

From the Monte Carlo simulation, the decomposed distribution of the possible flying range based upon the specific energy of batteries and the specific power of an electric motor is illustrated in Figure 1. In addition, the figure also provides numeric details from each scenario.

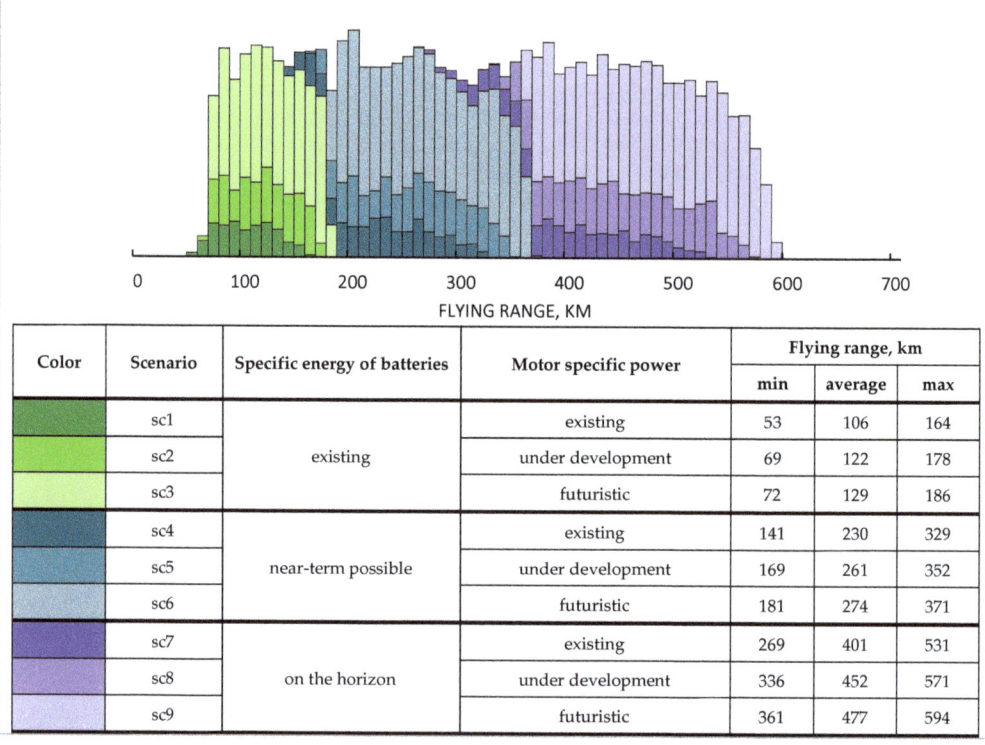

Color	Scenario	Specific energy of batteries	Motor specific power	Flying range, km		
				min	average	max
	sc1	existing	existing	53	106	164
	sc2		under development	69	122	178
	sc3		futuristic	72	129	186
	sc4	near-term possible	existing	141	230	329
	sc5		under development	169	261	352
	sc6		futuristic	181	274	371
	sc7	on the horizon	existing	269	401	531
	sc8		under development	336	452	571
	sc9		futuristic	361	477	594

Figure 1. Decomposed distribution of flying range for an eight-seat turboprop with varying technological improvements of the powertrain.

The three different color groupings denote the three levels of specific energy of batteries. The gradations of the colors within each group are indicative of the distinct levels of motor specific power. The numerical descriptives in the legend can be directly derived from the probability distribution figure. For example, the minimum value for sc1, 53, is the leftmost edge of the whole distribution.

The first takeaway that one can be derived from the decomposition is that the specific energy of batteries is, indeed, a critical factor. Namely, any improvement in the specific energy produces a substantial gain in the number of extra kilometers flown. With only minor overlap, the three groups (of colors) appear distinctively partitioned on the graph, thereby suggesting a strong influence from the underlying factor.

Secondly, the effect of the increasing motor specific power is also substantial, but nonlinear. With the existing levels of battery specific energy, improving the motor provides only incremental benefits. However, with a higher specific energy of batteries, the effect of improving the motor becomes more and more pronounced. For example, one can readily observe the difference between the right edge of sc1 and sc2 (178 − 164 = 13) and sc7 and sc8 (571 − 531 = 40)—a veritable two-fold increased improvement in flight range. This occurs because the weight saved from using a motor with higher specific power provides more of a benefit if batteries also have higher specific energy. The consequences of this observation lead to an important implication. Although with the existing levels of battery specific energy, investing in electric-motor R&D might not look particularly beneficial, it will lead to significant, tangible, positive differences when conducted in simultaneous conjunction with the development of battery technology.

However, the impact from improving the electric motor, alone, is also nonlinear. Specifically, within the same level of battery specific energy (e.g., the on the horizon), the difference between the right edges of existing and under development motor specific power, sc7 and sc8 (571 − 531 = 40) is higher than the difference between under development and futuristic, sc8 and sc9 (594 − 571 = 24). Indeed, increasing the electric motor specific power from 5 to 10 kW/kg generates a 100% yield in specific power, and thus, the output flight range, while from 15 to 20 kW/kg, there is only a 33% increase. Although this linear function of relative specific power yield might be obvious for engineers, financial decision-makers involved in investment planning may consider absolute values (km, €, etc.)—thus, the relation becomes nonlinear. Irrespective of the starting point, a five kW/kg increase in specific power may well imply similar levels of R&D investment costs. However, the benefit—and thus the pay-off of such an investment—will differ dramatically, depending on the specific power of the motor that has already been achieved. Consequently, the value of every "next step" in electric motor development should be weighed against its cost.

The three main conclusions from the SimDec decomposition can be summarized as:

1. Increasing the specific energy of batteries extends the flight range.
2. Increasing motor specific power has an incremental effect for the current level of battery specific energy, but this impact will increase significantly with better batteries.
3. The marginal benefit from electric-motor improvement, alone, decreases.

Although our analysis focuses on the flying range, the derived distances directly translate into economic and environmental benefits. Any extended flying ranges directly correspond to an increased number of possible routes or pairs of towns that can be connected. In Europe, fewer than a hundred airports connect towns within a distance of 50 km between each other. However, if the inter-town distance is expanded to 500 km, nearly a thousand airports could be connected. Apart from the increased flying distance, the improved powertrain technology enables electrifying larger planes that can transport more passengers or larger loads per flight. Furthermore, fully electrified aircraft fleets would entirely eliminate the emissions from fuel combustion. The corresponding environmental impact would, therefore, be dependent upon which electricity is used to charge the batteries or, more specifically, from the specific combination of each respective country's actual power mix. Even so, there are still other life cycle emissions aspects that are associated with specific aircraft design and operations. More detailed life-cycle estimates of the environmental impacts of such air-traffic electrification are presented in [17].

6. Conclusions

Decision-making in multifaceted environmental arenas requires complex computational modelling and, thus, clever analytics and visualization solutions that are able to capture multiple dimensions, simultaneously. Monte Carlo simulation modelling has frequently been employed to integrate the uncertain inputs and to construct probability distributions of the resulting outputs. Visual analytics and data visualization can be used to support the processing, analyzing, and communicating of the influence of multi-variable uncertainties on the decision-making process. SimDec enables one to observe the output distribution of the variables of interest and simultaneously trace which components of the output distribution are attributable to specific combinations of the input variables.

In this study, SimDec was used to decompose a Monte Carlo model of the flying range of all-electric aircraft based upon improvements to batteries and electric motors. While the analysis focused upon the flying range for electrified aircraft, the distance findings extend directly into corresponding environmental and economic benefits. The decomposed results show that: (i) increased battery specific energy leads to increased flight distance; (ii) increased motor specific power has a significant effect when the batteries' specific energy is high; and, (iii) there is a decrease in the marginal benefits from motor improvement, alone. While the first observation cannot be considered surprising because there is a linear relationship between flight range and battery specific energy (Equation (5)), the latter two findings would not be inherently obvious to decision-makers without specialized aeronautical engineering backgrounds, and the SimDec analysis provides a perfect means to effectively demonstrate and communicate them.

The aviation electrification problem has illustrated how SimDec enables the simultaneous projection from combinations of multi-variable input uncertainties directly onto an output distribution. It demonstrated how SimDec stratified two sources of electrification uncertainty into distinct, coloured partitions that enabled a visualization of previously unidentified cause-and-effect influences of input variable combinations onto the flight distance output in the R&D investment analysis of aviation electrification. Since SimDec computations can be run concurrently with any Monte Carlo model with only negligible additional overhead, SimDec could easily be extended into the analysis of any environmental application that uses simulation—not just aircraft electrification. This generalizability, in conjunction with its straightforward visualizations of complex stochastic uncertainties, makes the practical contributions of SimDec very powerful in environmental decision-making. The efficacy for extending SimDec into more diverse environmental and sustainability applications beyond aviation electrification will be considered in future research.

Author Contributions: Conceptualization, M.K. and J.S.Y.; data curation, M.K. and T.N.; formal analysis, M.K.; methodology and validation, T.N.; writing—original draft preparation, M.K. and J.S.Y.; visualization, M.K.; writing—review and editing, J.S.Y. All authors have read and agreed to the published version of the manuscript.

Funding: This research was funded by the Natural Sciences and Engineering Research Council grant number OGP0155871, and by Finnish Foundation for Economic Foundation grant number 200153.

Institutional Review Board Statement: Not applicable.

Informed Consent Statement: Not applicable.

Acknowledgments: The inspiration for this work was kindly provided by the eMAD team, including Juha Pyrhönen, Ilya Petrov, and Alexander Matrosov. The authors appreciate the fruitful and inspiring discussions with Nisse Nurmi on the state of the aviation industry.

Conflicts of Interest: The authors declare no conflict of interest.

References

1. Yeomans, J.S. Computational Analytics for Supporting Environmental Decision-Making and Analysis: An Introduction. *J. Environ. Informatics Lett.* **2020**, *4*, 48–49. [CrossRef]
2. UNFCCC. United Nations Framework Convention on Climate Change. 1992. Available online: https://unfccc.int/resource/docs/convkp/conveng.pdf (accessed on 7 August 2021).
3. United Nations Framework Convention on Climate Change (UNFCC). Methodological Issues under the Convention: Emissions from Fuel Used for International Aviation and Maritime Transport. Available online: https://www.icao.int/environmental-protection/Documents/SBSTA51%20ICAO%20submission_Final.pdf (accessed on 7 December 2021).
4. Van Evra, J. Green Air Travel Is Still Decades Away. Here's Why. Available online: https://www.cbc.ca/radio/whatonearth/green-air-travel-is-still-decades-away-here-s-why-1.5939159 (accessed on 7 December 2021).
5. David Suzuki Foundation Air Travel and Climate Change. Available online: https://davidsuzuki.org/what-you-can-do/air-travel-climate-change/ (accessed on 7 December 2021).
6. Government of Canada Joint Statement by Transport Canada and the U.S. Department of Transportation on the Nexus between Transportation and Climate Change. Available online: https://www.canada.ca/en/transport-canada/news/2021/02/joint-statement-by-transport-canada-and-the-us-department-of-transportation-on-the-nexus-between-transportation-and-climate-change.html (accessed on 7 December 2021).
7. Government of Canada Canada's Action Plan to Reduce Greenhouse Gas Emissions from Aviation. Available online: https://tc.canada.ca/sites/default/files/migrated/aviationghgactionpan_eng.pdf (accessed on 7 December 2021).
8. Stroh, P. As More Travellers Return to the Skies, Aviation's Environmental Impact Fuels Concern. Available online: https://www.cbc.ca/news/business/the-national-emissions-aviation-1.6109874 (accessed on 7 December 2021).
9. European Commission Climate Action: 2050 Long-Term Strategy. Available online: https://ec.europa.eu/clima/eu-action/climate-strategies-targets/2050-long-term-strategy_en (accessed on 7 December 2021).
10. Schäfer, A. The Prospects for Biofuels in Aviation. In *Biofuels for Aviation*; Academic Press: Cambridge, MA, USA, 2016; pp. 3–16. [CrossRef]
11. Ribeiro, R.F.; Trapp, L.G.; Lacava, P. Economical Aspects of Aircraft Propulsion Electrification. In Proceedings of the AIAA Propulsion and Energy 2021 Forum, Virtual Event, Reston, VA, USA, 9–11 August 2021; p. 3329. [CrossRef]
12. Johnson, S. $25 Flights and Zero Emissions: How Electric Planes Could Change Air Travel. Available online: https://www.freethink.com/series/make-it-count/electric-planes (accessed on 20 October 2021).
13. Pawson, C. Vancouver Seaplane Company to Resume Test Flights with Electric Commercial Airplane. Available online: https://www.cbc.ca/news/canada/british-columbia/vancouver-electric-seaplane-test-flights-1.5884479 (accessed on 7 December 2021).
14. Hiltunen, J. Business Model for Operations of a Single Engine Aircraft in Europe. Master's Thesis, Aalto University, Espoo, Finland, 2017; p. 95.
15. European Business Aviation Association (EBAA) European Busienss Aviation: Economic Value & Business Benefits. Available online: https://www.ebaa.org/app/uploads/2018/01/EBAA-Economic-report-2017_compressed.pdf (accessed on 20 October 2021).
16. Brdnik, A.P.; Kamnik, R.; Marksel, M.; Božičnik, S. Beginning Steps of the Electrification of Commercial Passenger Aircraft Transport; In European Transport Conference 2019, Association for European Transport (AET); 2019. Available online: https://trid.trb.org/view/1729185 (accessed on 28 December 2021).
17. Schäfer, A.W.; Barrett, S.R.H.; Doyme, K.; Dray, L.; Gnadt, A.R.; Self, R.; O'Sullivan, A.; Synodinos, A.; Torija, A.J. Technological, economic and environmental prospects of all-electric aircraft. *Nat. Energy* **2018**, *4*, 160–166. [CrossRef]
18. Gunalay, Y.; Yeomans, J.S. An Algorithm for Computing Solutions to the Range Limited Routing Problem Using Electrical Trucks. *WSEAS Trans. Comput.* **2020**, *19*, 47–53. [CrossRef]
19. Gunalay, Y.; Yeomans, J.S. An Innovative Modelling and Decision-Support Approach for Evaluating Urban Transshipment Problems Using Electrical Trucks. *Int. J. Smart Veh. Smart Transp.* **2020**, *3*, 19–37. [CrossRef]
20. Winkelhaus, S.; Grosse, E.H. Logistics 4.0: A systematic review towards a new logistics system. *Int. J. Prod. Res.* **2019**, *58*, 18–43. [CrossRef]
21. Hernandez, M.; Messagie, M.; Hegazy, O.; Marengo, L.; Winter, O.; Van Mierlo, J. Environmental impact of traction electric motors for electric vehicles applications. *Int. J. Life Cycle Assess.* **2015**, *22*, 54–65. [CrossRef]
22. Weiss, M.; Patel, M.K.; Junginger, M.; Perujo, A.; Bonnel, P.; van Grootveld, G. On the electrification of road transport-Learning rates and price forecasts for hybrid-electric and battery-electric vehicles. *Energy Policy* **2012**, *48*, 374–393. [CrossRef]
23. European Environmental Agency New Registrations of Electric Vehicles in Europe. Available online: https://www.eea.europa.eu/ims/new-registrations-of-electric-vehicles (accessed on 7 December 2021).
24. Kozlova, M.; Yeomans, J.S. Monte Carlo Enhancement via Simulation Decomposition: A "Must-Have" Inclusion for Many Disciplines. *INFORMS Trans. Educ.* **2020**. [CrossRef]
25. Deviatkin, I.; Kozlova, M.; Yeomans, J.S. Simulation decomposition for environmental sustainability: Enhanced decision-making in carbon footprint analysis. *Socio-Economic Plan. Sci.* **2020**, *75*, 100837. [CrossRef]
26. Kozlova, M.; Yeomans, J.S. Visual Analytics in Environmental Decision-Making: A Comparison of Overlay Charts versus Simulation Decomposition. *J. Environ. Informatics Lett.* **2020**, *4*, 93–100. [CrossRef]

27. Kozlova, M.; Yeomans, J.S. Multi-Variable Simulation Decomposition in Environmental Planning: An Application to Carbon Capture and Storage. *J. Environ. Informatics Lett.* **2019**, *1*, 20–26. [CrossRef]
28. Domone, J. *The Challenges and Benefits of the Electrification of Aircraft*; SNC Lavalin: Montreal, QC, Canada, 2018. Available online: https://www.researchgate.net/publication/344248637_The_Challenges_and_Benefits_of_the_Electrification_of_Aircraft (accessed on 28 December 2021).
29. European Business Aviation Association (EBAA) Yearbook. Top 50 Aircraft. Available online: https://yearbook.ebaa.org/public-aircraft-list. (accessed on 7 December 2021).
30. Rezende, R.N. General Aviation Electrification: Challenges on the Transition to New Technologies. *AIAA Propulsion and Energy 2021 Forum.* 2021, p. 3330. Available online: https://arc.aiaa.org/doi/10.2514/6.2021-3330 (accessed on 28 December 2021).
31. Marinus, B.G.; Quodbach, L. Data and Design Models for Civil Turbopropeller Aircraft. *J. Aircr.* **2020**, *57*, 1252–1267. [CrossRef]
32. Anton, F. eAircraft: Hybrid-elektrische Antriebe für Luftfahrzeuge. Available online: https://www.bbaa.de/fileadmin/user_upload/02-preis/02-02-preistraeger/newsletter-2019/02-2019-09/02_Siemens_Anton.pdf (accessed on 20 October 2021).
33. Owen, A.B. Variance Components and Generalized Sobol' Indices. *SIAM/ASA J. Uncertain. Quantif.* **2013**, *1*, 19–41. Available online: https://epubs.siam.org/doi/abs/10.1137/120876782?mobileUi=0 (accessed on 28 December 2021). [CrossRef]
34. Kucherenko, S.; Klymenko, O.; Shah, N. Sobol' indices for problems defined in non-rectangular domains. *Reliab. Eng. Syst. Saf.* **2017**, *167*, 218–231. [CrossRef]
35. Cerdas, F.; Titscher, P.; Bognar, N.; Schmuch, R.; Winter, M.; Kwade, A.; Herrmann, C. Exploring the Effect of Increased Energy Density on the Environmental Impacts of Traction Batteries: A Comparison of Energy Optimized Lithium-Ion and Lithium-Sulfur Batteries for Mobility Applications. *Energies* **2018**, *11*, 150. [CrossRef]
36. LUT University. Ultra-High-Power and High-Torque-Density Compact Electrical Machines. 2021. Available online: https://www.lut.fi/school-of-energy-systems/ultra-high-power-and-high-torque-density-compact-electrical-machines (accessed on 27 December 2021).

Article

A Fuzzy-Interval Dynamic Optimization Model for Regional Water Resources Allocation under Uncertainty

Meiqin Suo [1,2,*], Feng Xia [1,2] and Yurui Fan [3]

1. School of Water and Hydroelectric Power, Hebei University of Engineering, Handan 056038, China; 18834321643@163.com
2. Hebei Key Laboratory of Intelligent Water Conservancy, Hebei University of Engineering, Handan 056038, China
3. Department of Civil and Environmental Engineering, Brunel University London, London UB8 3PH, UK; yurui.fan@brunel.ac.uk
* Correspondence: suomeiqin@hebeu.edu.cn

Abstract: In this study, a fuzzy-interval dynamic programming (FIDP) model is proposed for regional water management under uncertainty by combining fuzzy-interval linear programming (FILP) and dynamic programming (DP). This model can not only tackle uncertainties presented as intervals, but also consider the dynamic characteristics in the allocation process for water resources. Meanwhile, the overall satisfaction from users is considered in the objective function to solve the conflict caused by uneven distribution of resources. The FIDP model is then applied to the case study in terms of water resources allocation under uncertainty and dynamics for the City of Handan in Hebei Province, China. The obtained solutions can provide detailed allocation schemes and water shortage rates at different stages. The calculated comprehensive benefits of economy, water users' satisfaction and pollutant discharge (i.e., COD) are [2264.72, 2989.33] $\times 10^8$ yuan, [87.50, 96.50] % and [1.23, 1.65] $\times 10^8$ kg respectively with a plausibility degree (i.e., $\lambda_{opt}^{\pm}$) ranging within [0.985, 0.993]. Moreover, the benefit from FIDP model under consideration of dynamic features is more specific and accurate than that of FILP model, whilst the water shortage rate from FIDP is [5.10, 9.10] % lower than that of FILP model.

Keywords: optimal allocation; interval; fuzzy; dynamic programming; water resources

1. Introduction

Due to population growth, economic development and consumption upgrade, global water consumption has increased by six times, and it has been continuing to grow steadily at an annual rate of about 1% during the past 100 years [1]. All of these would lead to the water shortage problem that is already pessimistically even severer, and seriously hinders the sustainable development of social economy. Managing water resources is an effective way to deal with the above challenges. However, in the process of management, experts and governors have encountered a lot of problems [2–6], such as dynamic variability and uncertainty, which are thorny and inevitable. Besides, in areas with water shortage, when the available water cannot meet the needs, unreasonable water allocation will lead to conflicts among users [7]. Therefore, it is definitely necessary to put forward a comprehensive model to deal with dynamic variabilities and uncertainties in water resources system as well as the contradiction between different users, so as to improve the management efficiency and the users' satisfaction.

The water resources system is of great complexities involving many uncertain factors, such as water use efficiency, water demand, pollutant discharge, water supply capacity and so on, and these uncertain factors could affect the structure for the optimal allocation model of water resources and resulting solutions [8–11]. Previously, scholars in related fields have got fruitful achievements in dealing with uncertainties in water resources management. For the optimization under uncertainties, mathematical methods that are commonly used include stochastic programming [12], fuzzy programming [13], interval programming [14], and various coupling programming methods [15]. Among them, fuzzy programming can deal with the conflicts among multi-objective functions well, making it a new flexible planning problem [16], while the interval programming can reflect the uncertain coefficients in the form of intervals, and convert the uncertain planning problems into deterministic planning problems [17]. Both of them are helpful to solve uncertain planning problems. Based on these models, a large number of integrated models have been developed to optimize the allocation of water resources, such as uncertain two-stage stochastic water resources optimal allocation model [18], improved interval linear optimal allocation model [19], chance constrained water resources optimal allocation model [20], multi-objective interval linear water resources optimal allocation model [21], and so on [22–24]. Li et al. [25] proposed a multi-objective water resources optimal allocation model under uncertainties by integrating constrained programming, semi-infinite programming, integer programming and interval linear programming. Suo et al. [26] presented an approach for interval multi-objective planning by coupling fuzzy programming and improved two-step method, and then proved the objectivity and stability of this method by comparing it with the weighted sum method. Li et al. [27] formulated a new two-stage random interval parameter fuzzy planning strategy model by considering various uncertainties in planning and management of water resources and water environment systems, which was then applied to reveal the relationship between local economic goals and environmental goals. The above-mentioned models can well deal with the uncertainty in data acquisition in the system. However, they are insufficient to handle the dynamic features in the allocation process of water resources.

In the process of water resources optimization, it is essential to give a full consideration to dynamic characteristics, and thus provide the best scheme for water distribution at different stages of the planning period [28]. Dynamic programming cannot only solve the optimization problem of multi-stage decision process in water resources allocation [29], but also obtain the optimal strategy of the whole process and the optimal sub-strategy of each stage [30–34]. Peng [35] established a multi-objective dynamic water resources allocation model to achieve a dynamic balance for the optimal water resources allocation by using a modified simplex method with the addition of a time variable. Feng [36] set up a multi-objective dynamic water resources optimization configuration model and introduced the satisfaction function to realize the dynamic balance of optimal allocation of water resources on the time scale. Ramírez et al. [37] used stochastic dynamic programming to provide release decisions for each stage, and combined genetic algorithm and reservoir operation simulation program to obtain the annual release curve. These models proposed above are able to solve the multi-stage decision-making problem and get satisfactory allocation results. However, they took less consideration for uncertainties in water resources system.

Therefore, in order to comprehensively consider uncertainties and dynamic variability in the water resources system, a fuzzy-interval dynamic (FIDP) optimal allocation model is proposed in this study by integrating fuzzy-interval linear programming (FILP) and dynamic programming (DP) into a general framework. In addition, in order to realize the fairness of water resources allocation, the satisfaction function is added as one objective function to reduce the contradictions among users. The main innovative points of this study can be summarized as: (i) By introducing FILP into the FIDP model, the uncertainty coefficients and constraints, such as water use efficiency and water demand in water resources system, can be reflected in the form of interval numbers, which would make the results more accurate and reasonable. (ii) By introducing DP into FIDP model, not only the annual optimization scheme, but also the detailed water distribution scheme of each stage in planning year can be obtained. (iii) For FIDP model, the principle of fairness for water users is added to the objective function, which can reduce the contradictions between government and water users, as well as among different water users. This model is then applied to Handan City, Hebei Province, China, where water volume is small and uneven, to pursue the maximization for social benefits, overall satisfaction of water users, and environmental benefits. Finally, the FIDP model is compared with the traditional FILP model, to prove the dynamic superiority of the proposed model with stage changes. It is expected that this model would be helpful to optimize the allocation of regional water resources under uncertainties and dynamics to reduce water shortage and conflict, and promote sustainable development of local society and economy.

This paper is composed of the following parts. Section 2 expounds the generation process of the general FIDP method. Section 3 puts forward a specific FIDP model suitable for Handan city. Section 4 presents the result analysis, which briefly expounds the water consumption characteristics of users at different stages of the planning year, and then compares the proposed FIDP model with FILP model. Section 5 is the summary of this study.

2. Methodology

2.1. Fuzzy-Interval Linear Programming (FILP)

On account of parameter uncertainties and objective inconsistency in multi-objective programming [38–40], the FILP model can well handle the uncertainty parameters denoted by interval numbers, and also coordinate the conflicts among different objective functions by introducing membership function λ, which makes the resulting solutions more scientific and reliable. The model is summarized as follows [26]:

$$Max \lambda^{\pm} \tag{1a}$$

Subject to:

$$C_g^{\pm} X^{\pm} \geq f_g^- + \lambda^{\pm}(f_g^+ - f_g^-) \quad g = 1, 2, \ldots, m \tag{1b}$$

$$C_h^{\pm} X^{\pm} \leq f_h^+ - \lambda^{\pm}(f_h^+ - f_h^-) \quad h = m+1, \ldots, n \tag{1c}$$

$$A_i^{\pm} X^{\pm} \leq B_i^{\pm} \quad i = 1, 2, \ldots, k \tag{1d}$$

$$X^{\pm} \geq 0 \tag{1e}$$

$$0 \leq \lambda^{\pm} \leq 1 \tag{1f}$$

It is worth noting that:

$$C_g^{\pm} X^{\pm} = Max \, f_g^{\pm} \quad g = 1, 2, \ldots, m \tag{2a}$$

$$C_h^{\pm} X^{\pm} = Min \, f_h^{\pm} \quad h = m+1, \cdots, n \tag{2b}$$

where $C_g^{\pm} \in \{R_1^{\pm}\}^{1 \times t}$, $C_h^{\pm} \in \{R_2^{\pm}\}^{1 \times t}$, $A_i^{\pm} \in \{R_3^{\pm}\}^{1 \times t}$, $X^{\pm} \in \{R_4^{\pm}\}^{t \times 1}$, and $R_e^{\pm}$ means a set of interval numbers ($e \in [1, 2, 3, 4]$), g and h are core markers for maximizing and minimizing the objective functions individually, and i is the index of the constraints. f^-, f^+ are the lower and upper bounds of $f^{\pm}$, and $\lambda^{\pm}$ is the membership function in fuzzy decision-making. The larger the $\lambda^{\pm}$ is, the more credible the calculation result would be; on the contrary, the smaller $\lambda^{\pm}$ would lead to less credible results.

2.2. Dynamic Programming (DP)

The basic idea of dynamic programming is that it not only separates the current stage from the future stages, but also considers the current benefit and the future benefit together. Therefore, the optimal decision selection of each stage is from the overall consideration, which is generally different from the optimal choice of this stage [41]. Concretely, for a multi-stage decision-making problem, dynamic programming can divide it into several stages according to time or other characteristics, and each stage has several states and decision strategies [42]. The system transfers from one stage to the next according to a certain rule, and the purpose is to obtain the optimal strategy combining each stage [43]. The following Equation (3) is the state transition formula of dynamic programming, and it is also the most important part of dynamic programming.

$$S_j = T(S_{j-1}, x_{j-1}) \quad j = 1, 2, \ldots, l \tag{3}$$

where S_j stands for the state variable at stage j, with l stages in total. x_{j-1} represents the decision variable at stage $j-1$, and $T(S_{j-1}, x_{j-1})$ is the state transition function [44].

2.3. Fuzzy-Interval Dynamic Programming (FIDP)

It is noted that multiple uncertainties and dynamic variability exist in the water resources system, which seriously affect effective planning and management of water resources. Although FILP and DP can efficiently address interval uncertainty, coordinate conflicts among different objective functions and characterize systems' dynamics individually, they are unable to deal with those problems at the same time. Therefore, this paper aims to propose a FIDP model by incorporating FILP and DP into one framework to comprehensively reflect both uncertainties and dynamic features in the water resources system. In addition, the function of the users' satisfaction is considered to solve the contradiction caused by uneven distribution of resources. The developed model is shown as follows.

$$Max\lambda^{\pm} \tag{4a}$$

Subject to:

$$C_g^{\pm} X^{\pm} \geq f_g^- + \lambda^{\pm}(f_g^+ - f_g^-) \quad g = 1, 2, \ldots, m \tag{4b}$$

$$\frac{X^{\pm}}{G^{\pm}}\alpha \geq f_p^- + \lambda^{\pm}(f_p^+ - f_p^-) \quad p = m+1, m+2, \ldots, r \tag{4c}$$

$$C_h^{\pm} X^{\pm} \leq f_h^+ - \lambda^{\pm}(f_h^+ - f_h^-) \quad h = r+1, r+2, \ldots, n \tag{4d}$$

$$A_i^{\pm} X^{\pm} \leq B_i^{\pm} \quad i = 1, 2, \ldots, k \tag{4e}$$

$$S_j^{\pm} = T(S_{j-1}^{\pm}, x_{j-1}^{\pm}) \quad j = 1, 2, \ldots, l \tag{4f}$$

$$A_j^{\pm} X^{\pm} \leq S_j^{\pm} \quad j = 0, 1, \ldots, l \tag{4g}$$

$$0 \leq X^{\pm} \leq G^{\pm} \tag{4h}$$

$$S_0^{\pm} = 0 \tag{4i}$$

$$0 \leq \lambda^{\pm} \leq 1 \tag{4j}$$

where the symbol $G^{\pm}$ means the user's ideal demand for resources, and α is the weight coefficient of different users. And Equation (4c) can reflect the fairness for different users, Equation (4f) realizes the dynamic transition, and the state constraint after phase transition is achieved by Equation (4g).

The steps of solving the FIDP model can be summarized as: (i) Establish FIDP model. (ii) Divide the model into two submodels through an improved two-step method [45]. In order to maximize $\lambda^{\pm}$, the upper bound submodel should be formulated firstly. (iii) Solve the upper bound submodel and obtain x_{opt}^+ and λ_{opt}^+. (iv) Formulate the lower bound submodel for the FIDP model. (v) Solve the lower bound and obtain x_{opt}^- and λ_{opt}^-. (vi) According to the results of the above two models, the objective function values are calculated by formulate (2). (vii) Combining these two submodels, the optimal solution can be expressed as $f_{g\ opt}^{\pm} = [f_{g\ opt}^-, f_{g\ opt}^+]$ ($g = 1, 2, \ldots, m$), $f_{p\ opt}^{\pm} = [f_{p\ opt}^-, f_{p\ opt}^+]$ ($p = m+1, m+2, \ldots, r$), $f_{h\ opt}^{\pm} = [f_{h\ opt}^-, f_{h\ opt}^+]$ ($h = r+1, r+2, \ldots, n$), $\lambda_{opt}^{\pm} = [\lambda_{opt}^-, \lambda_{opt}^+]$, $X_{opt}^{\pm} = [X_{opt}^-, X_{opt}^+]$.

In general, the presented model can be applicable for the following problems: (i) For those problems with uncertain factors, this method can reflect them in model establishment, solution process and results in the form of interval numbers. (ii) For multi-stage decision-making problems, this model can provide specific schemes for every stage and global optimal solutions for the whole process. (iii) For multi-objective and multi-user problems, this model can coordinate the conflicts among different objective functions by maximizing satisfaction of the objective functions, and reduce the contradictions among users by considering the principle of fairness.

3. Case Study
3.1. Overview of Handan City

The city of Handan is located in the southernmost part of Hebei Province, China, at the eastern foot of Taihang Mountain, bordering Shandong in the east, Henan in the south, Shanxi Province in the west and Xingtai City in the north. Its jurisdiction covers 6 districts, 1 county-level city and 11 counties. Its geographical location ranges 36°04′~37°01′ N and, 113°28′~115°28′ E with warm temperate semi-humid and semi-arid continental monsoon climate. The location of the area is shown in Figure 1.

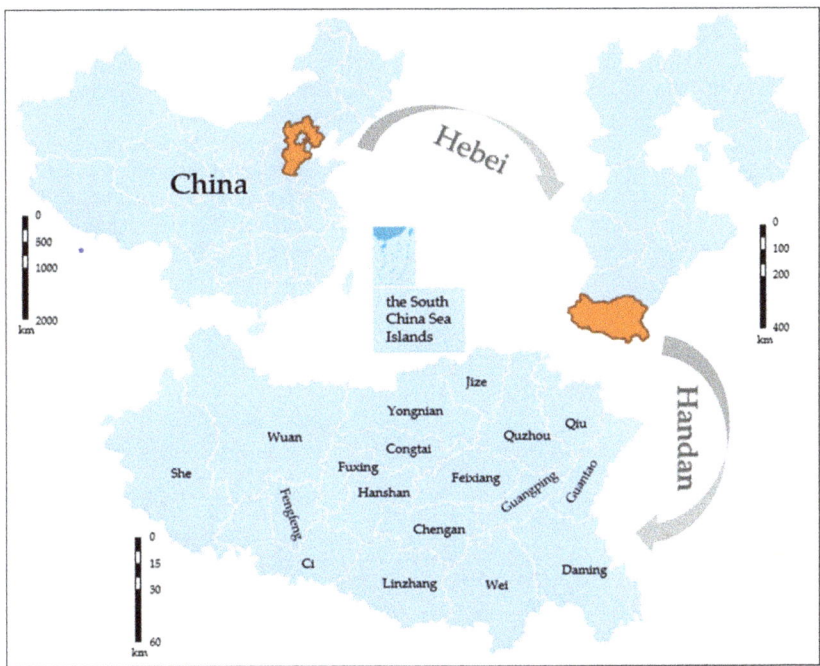

Figure 1. Location of Handan city.

At present, water resource managers in Handan are facing with many water resource problems, such as water resource shortage, uneven distribution of precipitation, and serious water pollution. For example, according to the Water Resources Bulletin [46], the per capita water consumption of the city in 2019 is 2.02×10^2 m^3 with a population of 9.55 million. However, the water supply in 2019 is only 1927.84×10^6 m^3, and the water shortage is 1.26×10^6 m^3. In addition, 61.30%~76.50% of the annual precipitation falls between June and September, which is extremely inconsistent with the needs from various water users. Actually, each user's water demand, especially the agricultural water demand, is different with the season changes. The growing period of crops in Handan mainly ranges from March to August, with the largest water demand occurring at the second stage which would account for about 50% of the annual water consumption. It is noted that the development of agricultural cultivation is paid the most attention in Handan City, and its water consumption accounts for about 55% of the total water consumption. So how to provide periodic water allocation for each user is a challenge for managers. Moreover, due to the uncertainties existing in water supply and the temporal variations of the planning horizon, the water resources system also has a number of uncertain factors, such as the water inflows at different stages, water efficiency, water demand, and pollutant discharge, which should be fully considered. Therefore, how to allocate water resources reasonably to ensure the sustainable development of this region is an urgent problem for managers to solve under condition of discordant water supply and demand, as well as various uncertain factors.

3.2. Application of FIDP Model

In order to primely solve the problems mentioned above, FIDP is applied to optimize the allocation of water resources in Handan city. In detail, the established FIDP model would not only considers multiple objectives, such as the maximum economic benefit, the maximum overall satisfaction of water users, and the maximum environmental benefit, but also take the satisfaction of each water users into account. Meanwhile, the constraints would refer to the water supply capacity, the minimum guaranteed water demand, the ideal water demand, the water delivery capacity, and the COD emission limit. In addition, the uncertain factors involved in this model (e.g., water use benefit coefficient, ideal water demand, minimum guaranteed water demand, weight coefficient, COD discharge coefficient, maximum COD discharge, available water supply, water inflow at different stages, and water delivery capacity) can be expressed as interval parameters. Moreover, the dynamic factors in the process of water resources optimization, such as the water users' ideal water demand, guaranteed water demand, available water supply and water allocation changing with the stage, would be reflected by dynamic programming. The frame diagram of constructed FIDP model can be seen in Figure 2. In order to facilitate managers to make decisions, each stage is divided equally by the planning year, in which, January-March is the first stage, April-June is the second stage, the third stage is from July to September, and the fourth stage is from October to December. Its formulation would be expressed in the following form:

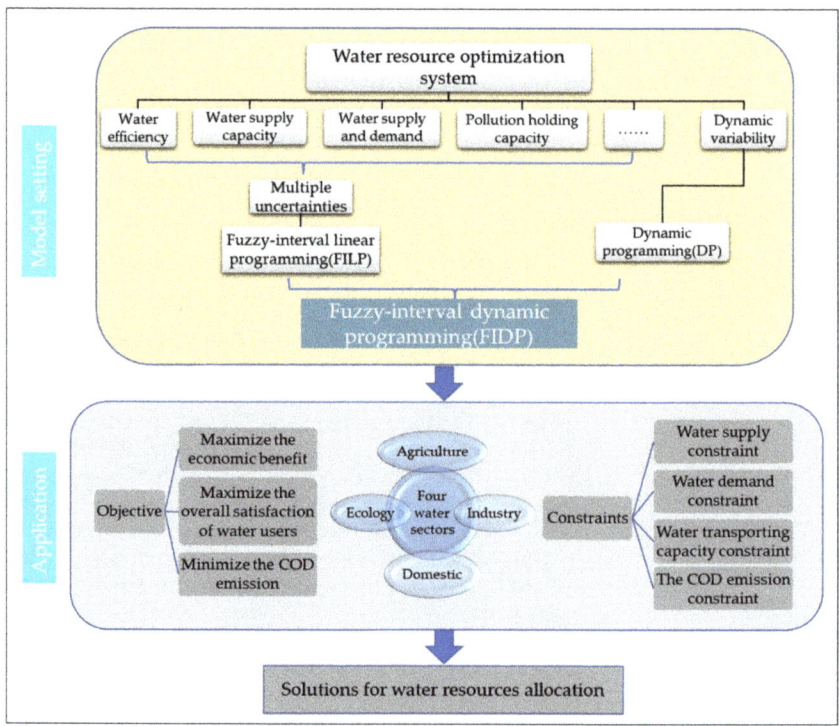

Figure 2. Framework of the fuzzy-interval dynamic programming (FIDP) model.

3.2.1. Objective Functions

The goal of this model is to maximize its membership function:

$$Max \lambda^{\pm} \tag{5a}$$

3.2.2. Constraints

Economic benefit constraint (maximize the economic benefit):

$$\sum_{t=1}^{4}\sum_{i=1}^{4}\sum_{j=1}^{16}\sum_{k=1}^{4} e_{tijk}^{\pm} a_{tijk} x_{tijk}^{\pm} \geq f_1^{-} + \lambda^{\pm}(f_1^{+} - f_1^{-}) \tag{5b}$$

where t denotes stage of the planning year ($t = 1, 2, 3, 4$), i is water source ($i = 1, 2, 3, 4$, representing surface water, underground water, diverted water and recycled water), j means region ($j = 1, 2, 3, \ldots, 16$, representing Urban, Wuan, Jize, Qiu, Quzhou, Guantao, She, Guangping, Chengan, Wei, Ci, Linzhang, Daming, Fengfeng, Yongnian and Feixiang), k stands for water user ($k = 1, 2, 3, 4$, representing agricultural, industrial, domestic and ecological), $e_{tijk}^{\pm}$ is net efficiency coefficient of water used by user k in region j in the t stage of planning year (yuan/m^3), a_{tijk} denotes water relationship provided by water source i to user k in region j in stage t of planning year (water distribution is 1, unmatched water is 0), $x_{tijk}^{\pm}$ means water allocation from water source i to user k in region j in the stage t of planning year (m^3).

Social benefit constraint (maximize the overall satisfaction of water users):

Considering the principle of fairness and justice, the weight coefficient α is introduced to balance the water satisfaction among water users and reduce the contradictions between water users and water supply departments.

$$\sum_{t=1}^{4}\sum_{j=1}^{16}\sum_{k=1}^{4} \frac{\sum_{i=1}^{4} a_{tijk} x_{tijk}^{\pm}}{G_{tjk}^{\pm}} \alpha_{tjk}^{\pm} \geq f_2^{-} + \lambda^{\pm}(f_2^{+} - f_2^{-}) \tag{5c}$$

where $G_{tjk}^{\pm}$ is the ideal water demand of user k in region j in stage t (m^3); $\alpha_{tjk}^{\pm}$ means the weight coefficient of user k in the region j of the t stage.

Environmental constraint (minimize the chemical oxygen demand (COD) discharge of major pollutants in the region):

While achieving the economic development, the pollution in the water utilization process should be comprehensively considered. The objective function should be established to measure the COD of the main pollutants in the region, so as to realize the balanced development of environment and economy.

$$\sum_{t=1}^{4}\sum_{i=1}^{4}\sum_{j=1}^{16}\sum_{k=1}^{4} d_{tjk}^{\pm} x_{tijk}^{\pm} \leq f_3^{+} - \lambda^{\pm}(f_3^{+} - f_3^{-}) \tag{5d}$$

where $d_{tjk}^{\pm}$ denotes the unit oxygen consumption generated by user k per unit water consumption in region j in stage t (kg/m^3).

Water supply constraint:

In the tth stage, the sum of water supply from water source i to all water users is less than the maximum water supply of water source i.

$$\sum_{j=1}^{16}\sum_{k=1}^{4} x_{tijk}^{\pm} \leq S_{ti}^{\pm} \tag{5e}$$

where $S_{ti}^{\pm}$ stands for the maximum available water supply of water source i in stage t (m^3).

Water demand constraint:

The amount of water supplied to water users should be greater than or equal to the minimum guaranteed water demand of the user and less than or equal to the ideal water storage capacity of the user.

$$D_{tjk}^{\pm} \leq \sum_{i=1}^{4} a_{tijk} x_{tijk}^{\pm} \leq G_{tjk}^{\pm} \tag{5f}$$

where $D_{tjk}^{\pm}$ means the minimum water demand of user k in region j in stage t (m³).

State transition equation:

The maximum available water supply from different water sources in each stage is taken as the state variable, and the dynamic configuration of the model is realized through the water balance equation.

$$S_{ti}^{\pm} = S_{(t-1)i}^{\pm} + C_{ti}^{\pm} - \sum_{j=1}^{16} \sum_{k=1}^{4} a_{(t-1)ijk} x_{(t-1)ijk}^{\pm} \tag{5g}$$

where $C_{ti}^{\pm}$ is the inflow of water source i in stage t (m³).

Water transporting capacity constraint:

The total amount of water used in each region would be limited by the water transporting capacity in the region.

$$\sum_{k=1}^{4} x_{tijk}^{\pm} \leq Q_{tij}^{\pm} \tag{5h}$$

where $Q_{tij}^{\pm}$ denotes the maximum capacity of water source i transporting to the region j in stage t (m³).

The COD emission constraint:

Due to serious damages of human activities to the ecological environment in recent years, more and more managers begin to pay attention to the impact of ecological environment with the development of economy. Accordingly, each region has formulated the discharge capacity of pollutant COD to control environmental pollution. Therefore, the optimal allocation of water resources should meet this requirement.

$$\sum_{t=1}^{4} \sum_{i=1}^{4} \sum_{k=1}^{4} d_{tjk}^{\pm} x_{tijk}^{\pm} \leq F_j^{\pm} \tag{5i}$$

where $F_j^{\pm}$ is the rated of COD emission in region j (kg).

Nonnegative constrains:

$$x_{tijk}^{\pm} \geq 0 \tag{5j}$$

$$S_{0i}^{\pm} = 0 \tag{5k}$$

$$1 \geq \lambda^{\pm} \geq 0 \tag{5l}$$

3.3. Data Collection and Analysis

This article takes Handan City as the research region and selects 2030 as the planning year. Due to the administrative adjustment of the city in recent years, this paper merged the Fuxing district, the Congtai district and the Hanshan district into the urban district to facilitate data compilation and calculation. The data needed in this model are related to economy, society, environment and water resources. All of these data are collected from related literature, field surveys, local statistical yearbooks and website information. Specifically, the water distribution relationship between water sources and users is obtained from the water resources bulletin [46]. The weight coefficient α is calculated based on the proportion of the added value of different users in each region in the recent two years' yearbooks [47]. The planned annual water transport capacity is obtained by combining the water conveyance capacity over the years and the pipeline network construction in recent years (https://www.h2o-china.com/news/295843.html, accessed on 14 June 2021). The unit oxygen consumption d and regional COD emissions are derived from related papers [48,49]. The benefit coefficient of agricultural water and industrial water is determined by the method of net output value allocation [48], and the benefit coefficient of domestic and ecological water use is obtained from relevant literatures [50,51]. According to the priority principle of domestic and ecological water use, the benefit coefficient was adjusted appropriately in this pater to rationalize the results, which are shown in Table 1.

Table 1. Net benefit coefficient of water use (yuan/m^3).

Districts	Agricultural	Industrial	Domestic	Ecological
Urban	[14.10, 17.70]	[247.28, 265.63]	[336.50, 412.50]	[342.50, 420.50]
Wuan	[69.70, 85.60]	[247.28, 265.63]	[336.50, 412.50]	[342.50, 420.50]
Jize	[13.50, 17.00]	[247.28, 265.63]	[336.50, 412.50]	[342.50, 420.50]
Qiu	[20.90, 26.00]	[247.28, 265.63]	[336.50, 412.50]	[342.50, 420.50]
Quzhou	[6.80, 8.80]	[247.28, 265.63]	[336.50, 412.50]	[342.50, 420.50]
Guantao	[4.70, 6.20]	[247.28, 265.63]	[336.50, 412.50]	[342.50, 420.50]
She	[24.70, 30.70]	[247.28, 265.63]	[336.50, 412.50]	[342.50, 420.50]
Guangping	[29.10, 36.10]	[247.28, 265.63]	[336.50, 412.50]	[342.50, 420.50]
Chengan	[6.80, 8.80]	[247.28, 265.63]	[336.50, 412.50]	[342.50, 420.50]
Wei	[21.70, 27.00]	[247.28, 265.63]	[336.50, 412.50]	[342.50, 420.50]
Ci	[1.50, 2.30]	[247.28, 265.63]	[336.50, 412.50]	[342.50, 420.50]
Linzhang	[4.40, 5.80]	[247.28, 265.63]	[336.50, 412.50]	[342.50, 420.50]
Daming	[10.30, 13.00]	[247.28, 265.63]	[336.50, 412.50]	[342.50, 420.50]
Fengfeng	[8.50, 10.80]	[247.28, 265.63]	[336.50, 412.50]	[342.50, 420.50]
Yongnian	[30.30, 37.40]	[247.28, 265.63]	[336.50, 412.50]	[342.50, 420.50]
Feixiang	[8.40, 10.70]	[247.28, 265.63]	[336.50, 412.50]	[342.50, 420.50]

The available water supply of surface water, groundwater and diverted water in the planning year were predicted by the trend analysis method. The amount of recycled water was obtained according to the predicted regeneration rate of water consumption in the planning year. By comparing the predicted results with the water situations in recent years, it can be seen that there is similar water inflow situation in 2019. Thus, the water inflow situation of each stage in the planning year can be obtained based on the analysis of water supply proportion in 2019. 110% and 90% of the inflow were taken as the upper and lower bounds individually, and the results are shown in Figure 3.

It is necessary to calculate the planned annual water demand for optimal allocation of water resources. In this paper, the quota method was employed to forecast the water demand for agricultural, domestic and ecological use, whilst the equidimensional complementary residuals-residual modified GM (1, 1) model [52] was adopted to forecast the industrial water demand. Then, the water consumption situation in 2019 was analyzed to derive the water demand of every user at different stages of the planning year. Among them, the proportion of water demand at different stages of agriculture in the planning year is 15.80%, 49.80%, 23.40% and 11.00% respectively. The proportion of industrial water demand is 23.50%, 24.00%, 26.60% and 25.90%. The proportion of domestic water demand is 23.00%, 29.00%, 23.00% and 24.00%. The proportion of ecological water demand is 23.40%, 28.20%, 25.00% and 23.40%. In the planning year, 110% and 90% of the predicted water demand of different users in each region are taken as the upper and lower bounds of their water demand, respectively. The predicted results are shown in Table 2.

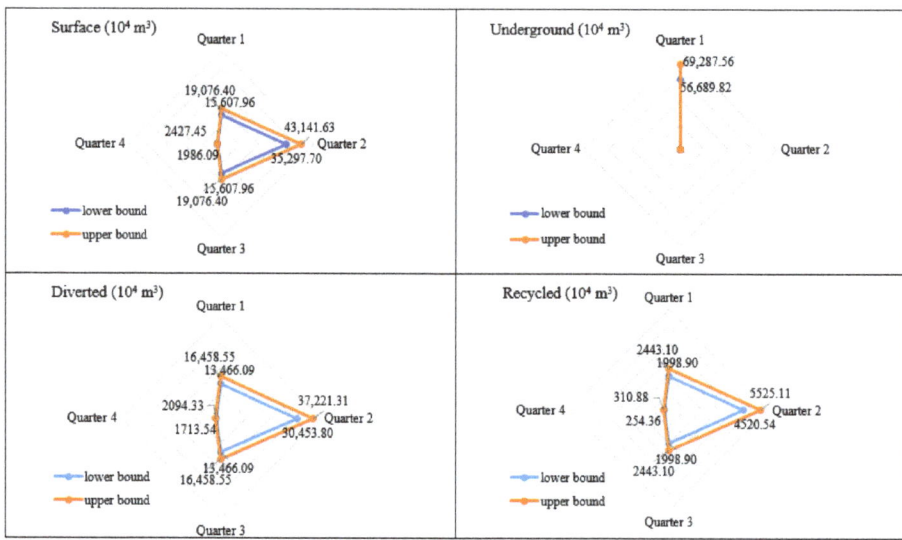

Figure 3. The amount of different water sources in the planning year (10^4 m^3).

Table 2. Water demand (10^4 m^3).

Districts	Agricultural	Industrial	Domestic	Ecological
Urban	[20,648.43, 25,236.97]	[13,030.43, 15,926.09]	[11,141.42, 13,617.29]	[3959.13, 4838.93]
Wuan	[2859.84, 3495.36]	[17,817.97, 21,777.51]	[2641.36, 3228.32]	[143.24, 175.07]
Jize	[5495.04, 6716.16]	[815.64, 996.90]	[910.23, 1112.51]	[0.00, 0.00]
Qiu	[1834.11, 2241.69]	[11.93, 14.58]	[1027.04, 1255.27]	[214.86, 262.60]
Quzhou	[2713.14, 3316.06]	[851.19, 1040.35]	[1945.83, 2378.23]	[19.10, 23.34]
Guantao	[5127.48, 6266.92]	[10.67, 13.05]	[853.80, 1043.54]	[190.99, 233.43]
She	[11,532.15, 14,094.85]	[2262.35, 2765.09]	[2552.62, 3119.86]	[582.51, 711.95]
Guangping	[2309.04, 2822.16]	[0.00, 0.00]	[764.05, 933.83]	[895.73, 1094.78]
Chengan	[6932.34, 8472.86]	[29.06, 35.52]	[968.93, 1184.25]	[236.83, 289.45]
Wei	[17,979.03, 21,974.37]	[654.69, 800.17]	[1832.58, 2239.82]	[477.47, 583.57]
Ci	[1717.47, 2099.13]	[574.94, 702.70]	[1674.10, 2046.12]	[582.51, 711.95]
Linzhang	[6200.46, 7578.34]	[208.99, 255.43]	[1712.83, 2093.45]	[248.28, 303.46]
Daming	[13,722.21, 16,771.59]	[1379.86, 1686.50]	[2352.65, 2875.46]	[2669.02, 3262.14]
Fengfeng	[1714.23, 2095.17]	[6448.68, 7881.72]	[1772.83, 2166.79]	[0.00, 0.00]
Yongnian	[13,051.17, 15,951.43]	[883.64, 1080.00]	[3772.67, 4611.04]	[173.80, 212.42]
Feixiang	[2107.44, 2575.76]	[282.57, 345.37]	[1166.81, 1426.11]	[1145.92, 1400.56]

4. Results and Discussion

4.1. Results Analysis

In this study, the FIDP model suitable for Handan's water management was established to obtain the objective function values and water resources allocation schemes, which can be seen in Table 3. The λ^+, λ^- represent the maximum subordinate degree and the minimum subordinate degree respectively. In detail, by solving the model, the value of λ^+_{opt} is 0.993, the corresponding economic benefit is 2989.33 $\times$ 10^8 yuan, the satisfaction of users is 96.50%, and the social benefit is 1.23 $\times$ 10^8 kg. On the contrary, the value of λ^-_{opt}

is 0.985, whilst the corresponding economic benefits, satisfaction and social benefits are 2264.72 × 10^8 yuan, 87.50% and 1.65 × 10^8 kg, respectively.

Table 3. Solutions of objective functions (FIDP).

λ^+ = 0.993			λ^- = 0.985			
Economic Benefit (10^8 yuan)	Satisfaction	COD Emission (10^8 kg)	Economic Benefits (10^8 yuan)	Satisfaction	COD Emission (10^8 kg)	
2989.33	96.50%	1.23	2264.72	87.50%	1.65	

Table 4 shows the total amount of water allocated to different users in different regions of Handan City in the planning year, while Table 5 shows the total amount of water allocated from different water sources to different regions. It can be seen that the total amount of allocated water in Handan City in 2030 will be [175,412.60, 219,210.86] × 10^4 m^3, and the total water shortage will reach [34,051.91, 36,800.32] × 10^4 m^3 according to the water demand forecasting results. As the minimum water demand in the planning year will reach [167,571.50, 204,809.62] × 10^4 m^3, which is less than the allocated water, the water allocation in the planning year can meet its minimum guaranteed water demand on the whole.

Table 4. Water allocations of different users in each region in the planning year (10^4 m^3).

Districts	Agricultural	Industrial	Domestic	Ecological
Urban	[16,518.74, 20,189.58]	[10,424.35, 12,740.87]	[9218.52, 10,784.89]	[3959.13, 4373.08]
Wuan	[2287.87, 3147.22]	[14,254.37, 17,422.01]	[2614.94, 3196.04]	[143.24, 175.07]
Jize	[4396.03, 6047.23]	[652.51, 996.90]	[901.13, 1101.38]	[0.00, 0.00]
Qiu	[1467.29, 2171.44]	[9.54, 14.58]	[1016.76, 1242.71]	[214.86, 262.60]
Quzhou	[2170.51, 2985.78]	[680.95, 1040.35]	[1926.37, 2354.45]	[19.10, 23.34]
Guantao	[4101.98, 5349.44]	[9.48, 13.05]	[845.26, 1033.10]	[190.99, 233.43]
She	[9225.72, 11,275.88]	[1809.88, 2765.09]	[2527.09, 3088.67]	[582.51, 711.95]
Guangping	[1847.23, 2822.16]	[0.00, 0.00]	[756.41, 924.50]	[895.73, 1094.78]
Chengan	[5545.87, 6964.69]	[23.25, 35.52]	[959.24, 1172.41]	[236.83, 289.45]
Wei	[14,383.22, 17,579.50]	[523.75, 800.17]	[1814.25, 2217.42]	[477.47, 583.57]
Ci	[1373.98, 2099.13]	[459.95, 702.70]	[1657.36, 2025.66]	[582.51, 711.95]
Linzhang	[4960.37, 6229.40]	[167.19, 255.43]	[1695.70, 2072.52]	[248.28, 303.46]
Daming	[10,977.77, 13,417.27]	[1103.89, 1686.50]	[2329.12, 2846.70]	[2669.02, 3262.14]
Fengfeng	[1371.38, 2095.17]	[5158.94, 6305.38]	[1755.10, 2145.12]	[0.00, 0.00]
Yongnian	[10,440.94, 12,761.14]	[706.91, 1080.00]	[3734.94, 4297.48]	[173.80, 212.42]
Feixiang	[1685.95, 2319.21]	[226.06, 345.37]	[1155.15, 1411.84]	[1145.92, 1400.56]

In 2030, the agricultural water consumption in Handan City will account for [52.90, 53.60] % of the total water distribution with the detailed allocation being [92,754.97, 117,454.65] × 10^4 m^3. Since the agricultural water demand is affected by the season and climate, the water demand also changes at different stages of the planning year. In detail, the second stage is the main growth period of crops, and the agricultural water demand in this stage also increases correspondingly, accounting for [48.80, 49.80] % of the annual water demand. On the contrary, the amount of water distribution in the fourth stage accounts for the least proportion, which is only [11.10, 11.50] % of the total agricultural water distribution. The difference between these two stages is [35,988.55, 43,789.37] × 10^4 m^3. The calculation results show that the satisfaction of the agricultural is [80.00, 82.90] % in 2030, and it reaches 80% in each stage, meeting its minimum water demand. Supported by the soil characteristics of each region, the leading agricultural industries in Urban, Weixian, Daming, and Yongnian have been developing rapidly, and the agricultural water consumption in these four regions would account for [54.40, 56.40] % of the total agricultural water consumption in the city. The agricultural water distribution in the planning year is shown in Figure 4.

Table 5. Water allocations of different water sources in each region in the planning year (10^4 m^3).

Districts	Surface Water	Groundwater	Diverted Water	Recycled Water
Urban	[7535.90, 21,990.98]	[6028.35, 26,097.44]	[0.00, 26,556.50]	[0.00, 0.00]
Wuan	[9076.72, 15,847.51]	[3943.55, 7350.32]	[0.00, 6246.64]	[33.52, 742.51]
Jize	[0.00, 3912.47]	[652.56, 996.90]	[1384.64, 6047.23]	[0.00, 1101.38]
Qiu	[14.58, 730.71]	[364.03, 852.45]	[1021.3, 2434.04]	[103.99, 878.69]
Quzhou	[306.46, 1086.30]	[1341.67, 2403.00]	[1068.88, 3009.12]	[238.76, 1746.66]
Guantao	[6.60, 3056.51]	[6.44, 1146.23]	[850.03, 5582.87]	[94.95, 1033.10]
She	[3913.91, 12,987.32]	[1950.42, 4550.79]	[0.00, 7365.07]	[303.47, 915.80]
Guangping	[0.00, 1352.17]	[0.00, 1320.49]	[534.83, 3916.94]	[291.86, 924.50]
Chengan	[27.17, 2761.84]	[351.78, 3361.19]	[525.30, 7254.14]	[116.86, 828.97]
Wei	[1968.76, 8824.34]	[399.29, 3747.87]	[1623.22, 18,163.07]	[649.55, 3003.27]
Ci	[894.02, 2402.74]	[537.57, 1705.73]	[1474.05, 2599.13]	[0.00, 0.00]
Linzhang	[1157.12, 3693.06]	[1170.83, 1810.47]	[1408.51, 6532.85]	[0.00, 159.50]
Daming	[9860.84, 15,954.89]	[1646.85, 3072.37]	[0.00, 5572.11]	[0.00, 2185.35]
Fengfeng	[5309.80, 5726.69]	[963.06, 4818.98]	[0.00, 1329.62]	[0.00, 682.95]
Yongnian	[4577.21, 6491.13]	[800.28, 5482]	[1263.73, 12,973.57]	[0.00, 1819.72]
Feixiang	[0.00, 753.86]	[675.35, 2026.42]	[875.11, 3719.78]	[328.00, 1311.54]

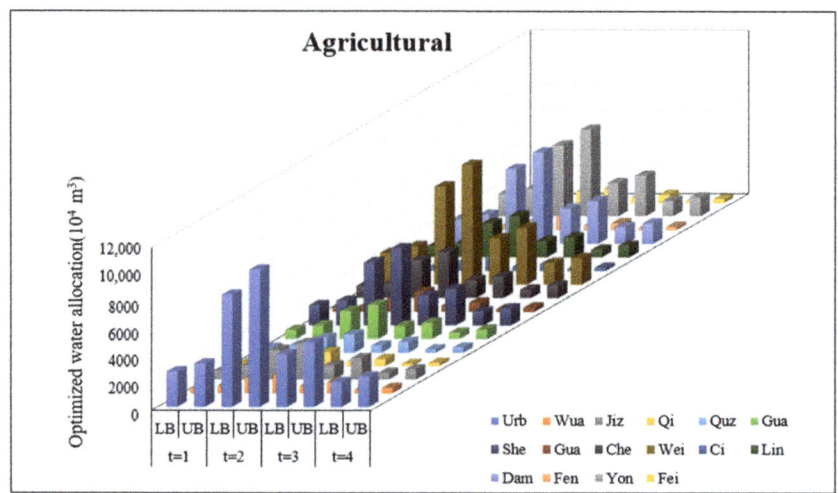

Figure 4. Water allocations for agricultural use in the planning year.

By solving the model, the industrial water distribution of Handan City in 2030 will be [36,210.94, 46,203.93] × 10^4 m^3, accounting for [20.60, 21.10] % of the total water distribution. The satisfaction of industrial water consumption is [80.00, 83.50] % in the whole year, and such satisfaction is higher than 80.00% in each stage, meeting its minimum water demand. According to the solution results as shown in Figure 5, the third stage has the largest industrial water distribution, which is [9631.84, 12,290.27] × 10^4 m^3, whereas the water distribution in the first stage is least with the allocation amount of [8509.83, 10,859.91] × 10^4 m^3, and the difference between the two stages is [1122.11, 1432.34] × 10^4 m^3. Among them, Urban, Wu'an and Fengfeng are the major industrial water users, making a contribution of [78.90, 82.40] % for the whole city's industrial water consumption.

In 2030, the domestic water distribution in Handan City will be [34,907.31, 41,915.24] × 10^4 m^3, accounting for [19.10, 19.90] % of the total water distribution. The satisfaction of domestic water use in the whole year is [93.40, 95.10] %, and it is higher than 92.00% in each stage indicating a high degree for guaranteed domestic water. With the change of temperature, the domestic water consumption at different stages also changes slightly to some extent. Specifically, the proportion of domestic water in the four stages of the planning year is [23.01, 23.44] %, [28.80, 29.00] %, [23.40, 24.10] % and [24.00, 24.40] % respectively. Obviously, the second stage consumes the most domestic water, whereas the first stage consumes the least proportion. During the planning year, the population in Urban and Yongnian will reach 3.40×10^6, and the water allocated to these two areas will be $[12,953.41, 15,082.32] \times 10^4$ m^3 correspondingly, accounting for [36.00, 37.10] % of the domestic water distribution to the whole city. The annual domestic water distribution in the planning year is shown in Figure 6.

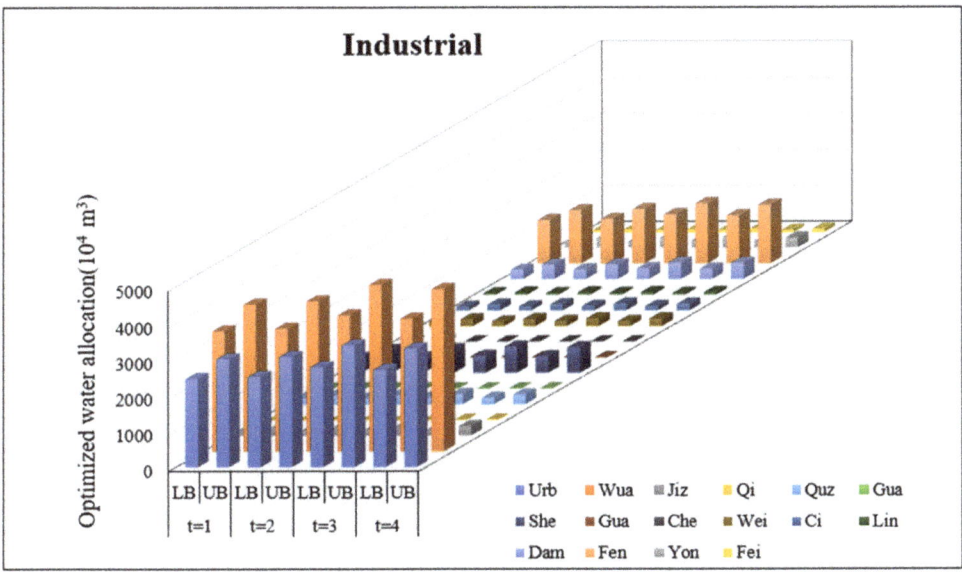

Figure 5. Water allocations for industrial use in the planning year.

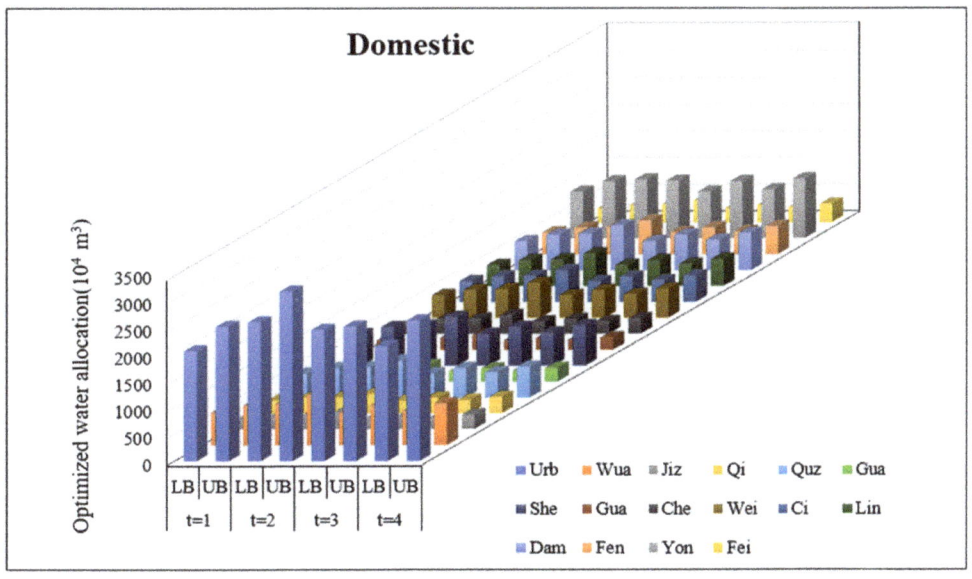

Figure 6. Water allocations for domestic use in the planning year.

To a certain extent, the development degree of ecological environment reflects the sustainability level of the region. In 2030, the ecological water distribution in Handan will be [11,539.41, 13,638.02] × 10^4 m^3, with a contribution of [6.20, 6.60] % for the total water distribution. The satisfaction of ecological water use is [96.70, 100.00] % in the whole year with the satisfaction degree over 93.00% in each stage, which reflects the priority in ecological development. It can be seen from Figure 7 that the distribution of ecological water reaches the annual maximum amount of [3254.21, 3704.50] × 10^4 m^3 in the second stage, which is [404.34, 554.02] × 10^4 m^3 more than the least water distribution in the first stage. The ecological water consumption in the third and fourth stage is [2884.81, 3333.10] × 10^4 m^3 and [2700.24, 3300.23] × 10^4 m^3 respectively, accounting for [24.40, 25.00] % and [23.40, 24.20] % of the ecological water consumption in the whole year. Among them, the ecological water consumption in the urban area and Daming county is relatively huge, contribution [32.10, 34.30] % and [23.10, 23.90] % to the total ecological water consumption respectively. This indicates that these two regions pay close attention to ecological environment construction.

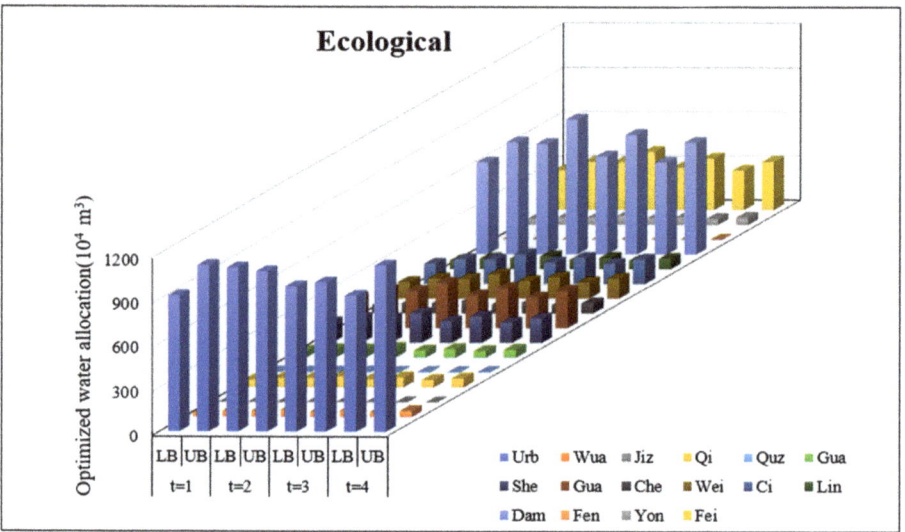

Figure 7. Water allocations for ecological use in the planning year.

Based on the analysis above, it can be known that FIDP model can provide global optimal solutions for the planned annual water distribution scheme, as well as specific water distribution schemes at different stages of the year under dynamics and uncertainties. In the planning year, the second stage has the largest water distribution of [68,246.70, 84,190.91] × 10^4 m^3, while the fourth stage has the smallest water distribution of [30,648.40, 39,012.42] × 10^4 m^3. The water distribution difference between the two stages is [37,598.12, 45,178.58] × 10^4 m^3, and the difference accounts for [20.60, 21.40] % of the annual water distribution.

4.2. Model Comparison

In order to verify the effectiveness of the proposed FIDP model, the application of FILP model to the case study is provided for comparison, which is shown in Appendix A. The difference between FILP model and FIDP model is that it deletes dynamic programming and parameter t, but their objective functions, constraints, decision variables and solution methods remain the same. Because the FIDP model takes into account the dynamic factors in different stages of water resources system, the solution results cannot only conform to the case study, but also achieve global optimization under the local optimal conditions of each stage. However, the FILP model only aims at optimality over the whole planning year without considering the dynamic variability of regional water resources system, which would imply that the water use efficiency, water consumption, water demand, water supply and other factors in the FILP model cannot be adjusted correspondingly with the seasonal changes. Therefore, the FIDP model has better optimal solutions and stronger applicability than FILP. The detailed analysis is as follows.

Based on the FILP model, the membership function $\lambda^\pm$ = [0.952, 0.992], $f_1^\pm$ = [2171.42, 3124.16] × 10^8 yuan, $f_2^\pm$ = [75.00, 84.00] %, $f_3^\pm$ = [1.17, 1.85] × 10^8 kg, and the comparison result of two models is shown in Figure 8. It can be seen that, compared with the FILP model, the ranges of the solution results of the FIDP model are reduced in different degrees, making the results more specific and accurate. In detail, the $\lambda^\pm$ of the FIDP model is not only reduced in scope, but also presents increases in its overall value, with its upper bound and lower bounds increased by 0.10% and 3.30% respectively. For $f_1^\pm$ and $f_3^\pm$, not only the ranges of their value are reduced by 23.90% and 38.20%, but also their lower bounds are increased by 93.30 × 10^8 yuan and 0.06 × 10^8 kg respectively, which are more accurate. The value of $f_2^\pm$ in FIDP model is improved by 12.50%, which will alleviate the conflicts between local government and users, and among different users more effectively. Consequently, it can be concluded that FIDP model proposed in this paper performs better and is more suitable for the optimization of water resources allocation in this area.

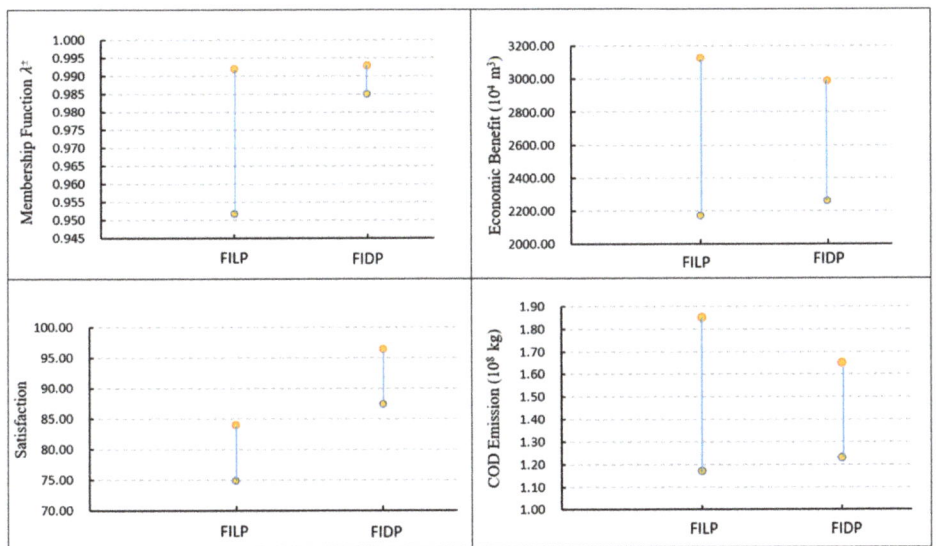

Figure 8. Comparison of the objective functions between FILP and FIDP.

The water distribution scheme of FILP model is shown in Table 6, and the water shortage rate of the two models is compared in Figure 9. As presented in Table 6, the total water distribution of the FILP model is [167,643.11, 205,259.94] × 10^4 m^3, which is reduced by [7769.43, 13,951.80] × 10^4 m^3 compared with the FIDP model. As the water distribution decreases, the corresponding water shortage rate will be [19.70, 20.00] %, with an increase of [5.10, 9.10] % compared with [10.60, 14.90] % from the FIDP model. Compared with FILP, the water shortage rate from FIDP has declined in all regions, especially in Qiu, Quzhou, Guangping, Ci and Feixiang, with a decrease of [7.90, 16.70] %, [7.00, 15.00] %, [8.30, 20.00] %, [9.90, 20.00] %, and [9.80, 14.30] % respectively. Therefore, the model has good applicability to water resources allocation in water-scarce areas.

Table 6. Water allocation of different users in different regions in the planning year (10^4 m^3).

	Agricultural	Industrial	Domestic	Ecological
Urban	[16,518.74, 20,189.58]	[10,424.35, 12,740.87]	[8824.00, 10,784.89]	[3167.30, 3871.15]
Wuan	[2287.87, 2796.29]	[14,254.37, 17,422.01]	[2091.95, 2556.83]	[143.23, 175.07]
Jize	[4396.03, 5372.93]	[652.51, 797.52]	[720.90, 881.11]	[0.00, 0.00]
Qiu	[1467.29, 1793.35]	[11.92, 14.58]	[813.41, 994.17]	[171.89, 262.60]
Quzhou	[2170.51, 2652.85]	[680.95, 832.28]	[1541.09, 1883.56]	[19.10, 23.34]
Guantao	[4101.98, 5013.54]	[10.67, 13.05]	[676.21, 826.48]	[152.79, 233.43]
She	[9225.72, 11,275.88]	[1809.88, 2212.07]	[2021.67, 2470.93]	[466.01, 569.56]
Guangping	[1847.23, 2257.73]	[0.00, 0.00]	[605.12, 739.60]	[716.58, 875.82]
Chengan	[5545.87, 6778.29]	[29.06, 35.52]	[767.39, 937.93]	[189.46, 289.45]
Wei	[14,383.22, 17,579.50]	[523.75, 640.14]	[1451.40, 1773.94]	[381.97, 484.41]
Ci	[1373.98, 1679.30]	[459.95, 562.16]	[1325.89, 1620.53]	[466.01, 569.56]
Linzhang	[4960.37, 6062.67]	[167.19, 255.43]	[1356.56, 1658.02]	[198.63, 303.46]
Daming	[10,977.77, 13,417.27]	[1103.89, 1349.20]	[1863.29, 2277.36]	[2135.22, 2609.71]
Fengfeng	[1371.38, 1676.14]	[5158.94, 6305.38]	[1404.08, 1716.10]	[0.00, 0.00]
Yongnian	[10,440.94, 12,761.14]	[706.91, 864]	[2987.95, 3651.94]	[167.60, 212.42]
Feixiang	[1685.95, 2060.61]	[226.06, 345.37]	[924.12, 1129.48]	[916.73, 1120.45]

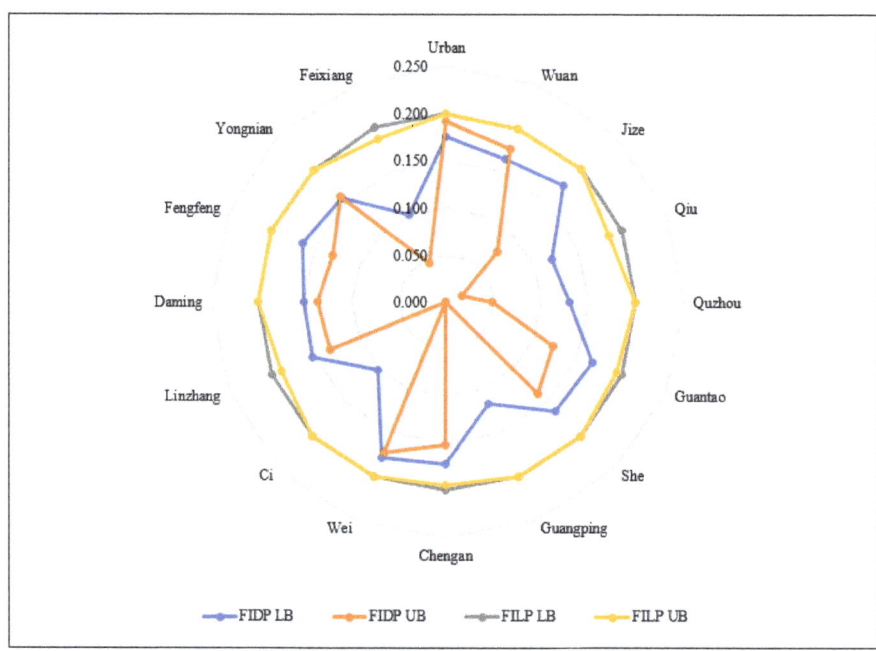

Figure 9. Comparison of water shortage rates between FILP and FIDP.

In summary, the FIDP model has the following advantages over the FILP model: (i) The obtained target value intervals are more specific and accurate. (ii) This model can improve the overall satisfaction of the water users and alleviate the water contradiction among them. (iii) The water shortage rate of FIDP model is lower than that of FILP, which effectively alleviates the contradiction between water supply and demand. (iv) Last but not least, FIDP model can get the allocation schemes of each stage in the planning year, and provide theoretical basis for water distribution decision-making in more detail way. Therefore, the model has a good performance in dealing with the dynamic changes of water resources system, and has advantages in optimizing the target value and reducing the water shortage rate.

5. Conclusions

This study combines fuzzy-interval linear programming and dynamic programming to establish a fuzzy-interval dynamic programming (FIDP) method. The system uncertainty is expressed in the form of interval numbers in the model establishment and results presentation. In order to solve the conflicts among users caused by uneven distribution of resources, the FIDP model incorporates the overall satisfaction of users into the objective function in order to reflect fairness in the solution results. As for the dynamic variability, the FIDP model introduces dynamic programming to obtain the specific allocation schemes at different stages of the planning year. Therefore, the model is able to handle the problem of uneven resources allocation under uncertainty and dynamics.

In this paper, the water resources allocation under uncertainty and dynamics in Handan City is studied to verify the feasibility of the model. The solutions cannot only get the optimized target value in this area, but also get the specific water allocations and water shortages for each water user at different stages in the form of intervals, so that the government and users can adjust their strategies to deal with the crisis in time. In addition to the economic and environmental goals, the obtained solution also provides the satisfaction of water users by introducing a weight coefficient, which effectively alleviates the contradictions among users. Through model comparison, the FIDP is proved to be superior to FILP model in this area. Consequently, the developed FIDP model would be more rational and applicable for regional water allocation under uncertainty and dynamics, which is of great help to the sustainable development of the region.

Author Contributions: Conceptualization, M.S. and F.X.; methodology, M.S. and F.X.; writing—original draft preparation, M.S. and F.X.; writing—review and editing, M.S. and Y.F.; funding acquisition, M.S. All authors have read and agreed to the published version of the manuscript.

Funding: This research was supported by Nation Natural Science Foundation of China (61873084), and Natural Science Foundation of Hebei, in China (D2019402235).

Institutional Review Board Statement: Not applicable.

Informed Consent Statement: Not applicable.

Data Availability Statement: The data that support the findings of this study are available from the corresponding author upon reasonable request.

Acknowledgments: The authors are grateful to the editors and the anonymous reviewers for their unique and profound comments and suggestions.

Conflicts of Interest: The authors declare no conflict of interest.

Appendix A

When applied to the case study, the FILP model can be formulated as follows:
Objective functions
Maximize its membership function:

$$Max \lambda^{\pm} \tag{A1}$$

Constraints

Maximize the economic benefit:

$$\sum_{i=1}^{4}\sum_{j=1}^{16}\sum_{k=1}^{4} e_{jk}^{\pm} a_{ijk} x_{ijk}^{\pm} \geq f_1^- + \lambda^{\pm}(f_1^+ - f_1^-) \tag{A2}$$

Maximize the overall satisfaction of water users:

$$\sum_{j=1}^{16}\sum_{k=1}^{4} \frac{\sum_{i=1}^{4} a_{ijk} x_{ijk}^{\pm}}{G_{jk}^{\pm}} \alpha_{jk}^{\pm} \geq f_2^- + \lambda^{\pm}(f_2^+ - f_2^-) \tag{A3}$$

Minimize the chemical oxygen demand (COD) discharge of major pollutants in the region:

$$\sum_{i=1}^{4}\sum_{j=1}^{16}\sum_{k=1}^{4} d_{jk}^{\pm} x_{ijk}^{\pm} \leq f_3^+ - \lambda^{\pm}(f_3^+ - f_3^-) \tag{A4}$$

Water supply constraint:

$$\sum_{j=1}^{16}\sum_{k=1}^{4} x_{ijk}^{\pm} \leq S_i^{\pm} \tag{A5}$$

Water demand constraint:

$$D_{jk}^{\pm} \leq \sum_{i=1}^{4} a_{ijk} x_{ijk}^{\pm} \leq G_{jk}^{\pm} \tag{A6}$$

Water transporting capacity constraint:

$$\sum_{k=1}^{4} x_{ijk}^{\pm} \leq Q_{ij}^{\pm} \tag{A7}$$

The COD emission constraint:

$$\sum_{i=1}^{4}\sum_{k=1}^{4} d_{jk}^{\pm} x_{ijk}^{\pm} \leq F_j^{\pm} \tag{A8}$$

Nonnegative constrains:

$$x_{ijk}^{\pm} \geq 0 \tag{A9}$$

$$1 \geq \lambda^{\pm} \geq 0 \tag{A10}$$

References

1. UN Water. *The United Nations World Water Development Report 2020: Water and Climate Change*; UNESCO: Paris, France, 2020.
2. Kang, A.; Li, J.; Lei, X.; Ye, M. Optimal allocation of water resources considering water quality and the absorbing pollution capacity of water. *Water Resour.* **2020**, *47*, 336–347. [CrossRef]
3. Xiao, Y.; Fang, L.; Hipel, K.W. Conservation-targeted hydrologic-economic models for water demand management. *J. Environ. Inform.* **2019**, *37*, 49–61. [CrossRef]
4. Wang, L.; Huang, Y.; Zhao, Y.; Li, H.; He, F.; Zhai, J.; Zhu, Y.; Wang, Q.; Jiang, S. Research on optimal water allocation based on water rights trade under the principle of water demand management: A case study in Bayannur City, China. *Water* **2018**, *10*, 863. [CrossRef]
5. Sun, J.; Li, Y.P.; Suo, C.; Liu, J. Development of an uncertain water-food-energy nexus model for pursuing sustainable agricultural and electric productions. *Agr. Water Manag.* **2020**, *241*, 106–384. [CrossRef]
6. Zhang, Y.F.; Li, Y.P.; Sun, J.; Huang, G.H. Optimizing water resources allocation and soil salinity control for supporting agricultural and environmental sustainable development in Central Asia. *Sci. Total Environ.* **2019**, *704*, 135281. [CrossRef] [PubMed]
7. Sun, Y.G.; Gu, S.H.; He, J.K. Game Analysis for Conflicts in Water Resource Allocation. *Syst. Eng.-Theory Pract.* **2022**, *1*, 16–25.
8. Ren, C.H.; Guo, P.; Li, M.; Gu, J.J. Optimization of industrial structure considering the uncertainty of water resources. *Water Resour. Manag.* **2013**, *27*, 3885–3989. [CrossRef]

9. Yang, G.Q.; Li, M.; Guo, P. Monte Carlo-Based Agricultural Water Management under Uncertainty: A Case Study of Shijin Irrigation District, China. *J. Environ. Inform.* **2020**. [CrossRef]
10. Sun, J.; Li, Y.; Suo, C.; Liu, Y. Impacts of irrigation efficiency on agricultural water-land nexus system management under multiple uncertainties—A case study in Amu Darya River basin, Central Asia. *Agr. Water Manag.* **2019**, *216*, 76–88. [CrossRef]
11. Fan, Y.; Huang, W.; Li, Y.; Huang, G.; Huang, K. A coupled ensemble filtering and probabilistic collocation approach for uncertainty quantification of hydrological models. *J. Hydrol.* **2015**, *530*, 255–272. [CrossRef]
12. Bravo, M.; Gonzalez, I. Applying stochastic goal programming: A case study on water use planning. *Eur. J. Oper. Res.* **2009**, *196*, 1123–1129. [CrossRef]
13. Kumar, S.S.; Prasad, Y.S. Modeling and optimization of multi object non-linear programming problem in intuitionistic fuzzy environment. *Appl. Math. Model.* **2015**, *39*, 4617–4629.
14. Fan, Y.R.; Huang, G.H.; Li, Y.P. Robust interval linear programming for environmental decision making under uncertainty. *Eng. Optimi.* **2012**, *44*, 1321–1336. [CrossRef]
15. Zou, R.; Liu, Y.; Liu, L.; Guo, H. REILP Approach for uncertainty-based decision making in civil engineering. *J. Comput. Civ. Eng.* **2010**, *24*, 357–364. [CrossRef]
16. Zeng, X.; Chen, C.; Sheng, Y.; An, C.; Kong, X.; Zhao, S.; Huang, G. Planning Water Resources in an agroforest ecosystem for improvement of regional ecological function under uncertainties. *Water* **2018**, *10*, 415. [CrossRef]
17. Zhang, J.; Huang, G.H.; Liu, Y.; Kai, A.N. Dispatch model for combined water supply of multiple sources under the conditions of uncertainty. *J. Hydraul. Eng.* **2009**, *40*, 160–165.
18. Huang, G.H.; Loucks, D.P. An inexact two-stage stochastic programming model for water resources management under uncertain. *Civ. Eng. Environ. Syst.* **2000**, *17*, 95–118. [CrossRef]
19. Zhou, F.; Huang, G.; Chen, G.-X.; Guo, H.-C. Enhanced-interval linear programming. *Eur. J. Oper. Res.* **2009**, *199*, 323–333. [CrossRef]
20. Liu, Y.; Guo, H.; Zhou, F.; Qin, X.; Huang, K.; Yu, Y. Inexact chance-constrained linear programming model for optimal water pollution management at the watershed scale. *J. Water Res. Plan. Manag.* **2008**, *134*, 347–356. [CrossRef]
21. Gu, J.J.; Huang, G.H.; Guo, P.; Shen, N. Interval multistage joint-probabilistic integer programming approach for water resources allocation and management. *J. Environ. Inform.* **2013**, *128*, 615–624. [CrossRef] [PubMed]
22. Guo, P.; Chen, X.H.; Li, M.; Li, J.B. Fuzzy chance-constrained linear fractional programming approach for optimal water allocation. *Stoch. Environ. Res. Risk Assess.* **2014**, *28*, 1601–1612. [CrossRef]
23. Wang, H.; Zhang, C.; Ping, G. An interval quadratic fuzzy dependent-chance programming model for optimal irrigation water allocation under uncertainty. *Water* **2018**, *10*, 684. [CrossRef]
24. Han, Y.; Huang, Y.-F.; Wang, G.-Q.; Maqsood, I. A multi-objective linear programming model with interval parameters for water resources allocation in Dalian city. *Water Resour. Manag.* **2011**, *25*, 449–463. [CrossRef]
25. Li, M.; Guo, P. A Multi-objective optimal allocation model for irrigation water resources under multiple uncertainties. *Appl. Math. Model.* **2014**, *38*, 4897–4911. [CrossRef]
26. Suo, M.Q.; Wu, P.F.; Zhou, B. An Integrated Method for Interval Multi-Objective Planning of a Water Resource System in the Eastern Part of Handan. *Water* **2017**, *9*, 528. [CrossRef]
27. Li, J.; Qiao, Y.; Lei, X.; Kang, A.; Wang, M.; Liao, W.; Wang, H.; Ma, Y. A two-stage water allocation strategy for developing regional economic-environment sustainability. *J. Environ. Inform.* **2019**, *244*, 189–198. [CrossRef] [PubMed]
28. Burt, O.R. On optimization methods for branching multistage water resource systems. *Water Resour. Res.* **2010**, *6*, 345–346. [CrossRef]
29. Liu, H.Q.; Zhao, Y.; Li, H.H. Optimal water resources allocation based on interval two-stage stochastic programming in Beijing. *South-North Water Transf. Water Sci. Technol.* **2020**, *18*, 34–41.
30. Trzaskalik, T. Multi-objective dynamic programming in bipolar multistage method. *Ann. Oper. Res.* **2021**, *4*, 1–21.
31. Agliardi, R. Optimal hedging through limit orders. *Stoch. Models* **2016**, *32*, 593–605. [CrossRef]
32. Huang, K.C.; Lu, H. A Linear Programming-based Method for the Network Revenue Management Problem of Air Cargo. *Transp. Res. Procedia* **2015**, *7*, 459–473. [CrossRef]
33. Elvan, G. Fertilizer application management under uncertainty using approximate dynamic programming. *Comput. Ind. Eng.* **2021**, *161*, 107624.
34. Liu, H.; Wang, Y.; Liu, S.; Liu, Q.; Xie, Y.; Ma, X. Research on multi-objective optimal scheduling strategy of photovoltaic and energy storage based on dynamic programming. *IOP Conf. Ser. Earth Environ. Sci.* **2021**, *781*, 42011. [CrossRef]
35. Peng, J.; Yuan, X.; Qi, L.; Li, Q. A study of multi-objective dynamic water resources allocation modeling of Huai River. *Water Sci. Tech-Water Sup.* **2015**, *15*, 817. [CrossRef]
36. Feng, J.H. Optimal allocation of regional water resources based on multi-objective dynamic equilibrium strategy. *Appl. Math. Model.* **2021**, *90*, 1183–1203. [CrossRef]
37. Ramírez, R.M.; Juárez, M.L.A.; Mora, R.D.; Morales, L.D.P.; Mariles, Ó.A.F.; Reséndiz, A.M.; Elizondo, E.C.; Paredes, R.B.C. Operation Policies through Dynamic Programming and Genetic Algorithms, for a Reservoir with Irrigation and Water Supply Uses. *Water Resour. Manag.* **2021**, *35*, 1573–1586. [CrossRef]
38. Fan, Y.R.; Huang, G.H.; Veawab, A. A generalized fuzzy linear programming approach for environmental management problem under uncertainty. *J. Air Waste Manag. Assoc.* **2012**, *62*, 72–86. [CrossRef] [PubMed]

39. Fan, Y.R.; Huang, G.H.; Huang, K.; Baetz, B.W. Planning water resources allocation under multiple uncertainties through a generalized fuzzy two-stage stochastic programming method. *IEEE Trans. Fuzzy Syst.* **2015**, *23*, 1488–1504. [CrossRef]
40. Nie, S.; Huang, C.Z.; Huang, W.W.; Liu, J. A Non-Deterministic Integrated Optimization Model with Risk Measure for Identifying Water Resources Management Strategy. *J. Environ. Inform.* **2021**, *38*, 41–55. [CrossRef]
41. Deng, Y.; Xu, Z.; Zhou, L.; Liu, H.; Huang, A. Study on adaptive chord allocation algorithm based on dynamic programming. *J. Fudan Univ. (Nat. Sci.)* **2019**, *58*, 393–400.
42. Bellman, R.E.; Kalaba, R.E.; Teichmann, T. Dynamic programing. *Phys. Today* **1966**, *19*, 99–105.
43. Ye, X. *Practical Operations Research*; China Renmin University Press: Beijing, China, 2013.
44. Guo, Y.X. *Operations Research*; South China University of Technology Press: Guangzhou, China, 2012.
45. Wang, X.; Huang, G.H. Violation analysis on two-step method for interval linear programming. *Inform. Sci.* **2014**, *281*, 85–96. [CrossRef]
46. Handan Water Conservancy Bureau. *Handan Water Resources Bulletin*; Handan City General Management Office: Handan, China, 2019.
47. Handan Bureau of Statistics. *Handan Statistical Yearbook*; China Statistics Press: Beijing, China, 2017.
48. Wang, M.J. *Multiobjective Planning of Water Resources in Wuhu City*; Hefei University of Technology: Hefei, China, 2018.
49. Wang, Y.J. *Study on Optimal Allocation of Water Resources in Sixian County based on Multi Objective Programming*; Hebei University of Engineering: Handan, China, 2020.
50. Liu, M.Y. *Research on Security Evaluation and Optimal Allocation of Water Resources in Haixing County*; Hebei University of Engineering: Handan, China, 2019.
51. Li, S.; Liu, B. Application of improved artificial fish swarm algorithm in optimal allocation water resources in Handan. *Water Resour. Power* **2016**, *34*, 10–14.
52. Liu, Y.L.; Cao, W.J.; Li, F. Application of metabolic GM(1, 1) power model in predicting the incidence of viral hepatitis. *Chin. J. Health Stat.* **2019**, *36*, 854–856.

MDPI
St. Alban-Anlage 66
4052 Basel
Switzerland
Tel. +41 61 683 77 34
Fax +41 61 302 89 18
www.mdpi.com

Sustainability Editorial Office
E-mail: sustainability@mdpi.com
www.mdpi.com/journal/sustainability

www.ingramcontent.com/pod-product-compliance
Lightning Source LLC
LaVergne TN
LVHW070506100526
838202LV00014B/1797